Accounting for business

THIRD EDITION
ACCOUNTING FOR BUSINESS

PETER SCOTT

OXFORD
UNIVERSITY PRESS

OXFORD
UNIVERSITY PRESS

Great Clarendon Street, Oxford, OX2 6DP,
United Kingdom

Oxford University Press is a department of the University of Oxford.
It furthers the University's objective of excellence in research, scholarship,
and education by publishing worldwide. Oxford is a registered trade mark of
Oxford University Press in the UK and in certain other countries

First edition 2012
Second edition 2016

Impression: 4

Published in the United States of America by Oxford University Press
198 Madison Avenue, New York, NY 10016, United States of America

British Library Cataloguing in Publication Data
Data available

Library of Congress Control Number: 2018949230

ISBN 978-0-19-880779-7

Printed in Great Britain by
Bell & Bain Ltd., Glasgow

Brief table of contents

Full table of contents

Part 2 Cost and Management Accounting

Acknowledgements

Thanks are due to many individuals. Firstly, to all the staff at Oxford University Press who have been involved with this project: to Amber Stone-Galilee, Commissioning Editor, who has overseen production of the third edition of the book; to Development Editor Kat Rylance, who has awaited with great patience my revision of each chapter; and to Fiona Burbage, who was responsible for updating the online resource material. Secondly, a big thank-you to all the reviewers for their positive and constructive comments and their input into the revision process. Thirdly, thanks must go to the innumerable students who have, over the years, been the guinea pigs for much of the material presented here; their ability to grasp concepts, ideas and techniques presented in various different ways has helped guide me in the formulation of my ideas on the most effective ways in which to present introductory material to the target audience. Fourthly, thanks go to all my former colleagues at De Montfort University for their continued encouragement and enthusiasm for the project and their very positive response to the first and second editions. Finally, the deepest debt of gratitude must go to my family and above all to my wife, Christine, for their forbearance, patience and encouragement during the time it took to revise and improve this book.

Peter Scott, May 2018

The author and publisher would like to sincerely thank all those people who gave their time and expertise to review draft chapters throughout the writing process. Your help was invaluable.

- Mahmoud Al-Sayed, University of Southampton
- Tracy Clewlow, Staffordshire University
- Rachel Holmes, Edinburgh Napier University
- Octavian Ionescu, University of East Anglia
- Henk Jager, Hanzehogeschool, Groningen
- Martin Kelly, Queen's University Belfast
- David McAree, Ulster University
- Rennie Tjerkstra, University of Kent at Canterbury
- Androniki Triantafylli, Queen Mary University of London

- Andy Turton, University of Sunderland
- Ahmad Alshehabi, Canterbury Christ Church University
- Samuel Hinds, University of Surrey
- Gayle Waddell, University of Liverpool
- Chandana G Alawattage, University of Aberdeen
- Adriana van Cruysen, Zuyd University of Applied Sciences

Thanks are also extended to those who wished to remain anonymous.

Preface

Why is accounting relevant to me?

Welcome to your accounting studies. You are probably wondering why you are required to study accounting when you have come to university to study marketing, economics, strategy or human resource management. Your first reaction might well be to say that you are not interested in accounting, so why is this subject a compulsory part of your course of study? In both the book and the online workbook, we will be showing you why a knowledge of accounting and its integral role in all organizations are of vital importance to you in your career in business.

This package is designed to be used as an introduction to the practice and techniques of accounting in the business world. It is aimed specifically at you as a non-specialist studying an introductory accounting module as part of your degree in a business related subject. The book thus aims to provide ongoing and constant illustration of the value of accounting as part of a wider business qualification. Throughout both the book and the online workbook, you are invited to engage actively in the study of accounting as one of the foundations for your role as a business professional. In your aspirations for your future career, you will find that a working knowledge of accounting terminology and techniques and an ability to interpret financial information will be essential in your day-to-day working life and in your career progression.

The approach to the subject adopted in this package is unashamedly practical: accounting is a 'doing' subject and the best way to learn how it works and what it does is to practice the various techniques and approaches as frequently as possible. You are provided with careful step-by-step guides showing you how to construct and evaluate various accounting statements. You are then given numerous further opportunities to apply what you have learnt with a view to enhancing your understanding and ability to produce and interpret accounting information.

How this package works

Alongside this textbook, you will have received access to your free online workbook (for details on how to access this, please refer to the 'Guided tour of the online workbook').

The aim of this integrated provision is to provide the supportive learning environment necessary to assist you as a non-specialist in the reinforcement of your learning and understanding of the subject.

The online workbook

You are offered numerous opportunities to revisit, reinforce and revise your understanding through the provision in the online workbook of exercises and examples that are fully integrated with the material in each chapter. You are thus able to strengthen your understanding of the material covered as approaches and techniques are regularly reviewed and recapped through the use of running examples across both the financial and management accounting sections.

The textbook

The first part of the textbook focuses on financial accounting. You are initially introduced to the three key financial accounting statements (the statement of profit or loss, the statement of financial position and the statement of cash flows) and shown how these are constructed from first principles. You are then provided with an in-depth and detailed guide to interpreting these statements to show what information these statements provide about an entity's profitability and performance and its ability to survive into the future.

The second part of the book deals with cost and management accounting and the ways in which accounting can be used in decision making and in controlling a business's future development through planning and forecasting. The key techniques of costing, budgeting and capital investment appraisal are covered in the requisite depth and detail to provide you with a ready guide to the production of meaningful information for use both in the running of a business and in the evaluation of its performance.

A note on terminology

Business is increasingly international in its focus. As a result, the accounting terminology adopted throughout this book is that of international accounting standards rather than that of UK standards or legislation. Where different terms for the same statements are in common usage, these are noted throughout the book as they arise. The opportunity has been taken in this current edition to update all the relevant terminology as a result of the issue of the International Accounting Standards Board's revised Conceptual Framework in March 2018.

Guided tour of the book

Identifying and defining

Learning outcomes

Clear, concise learning outcomes begin each chapter and help to contextualize the chapter's main objectives. This feature can help you plan your revision to ensure you identify and cover all the key concepts.

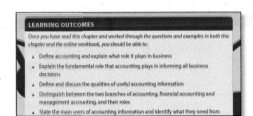

Key terms and glossary

Key terms are highlighted where they first appear in the chapter and are also collated into a glossary at the end of the book. This provides an easy and practical way for you to revise and check your understanding of definitions.

Understanding accounting principles

Illustrations

The illustrations display accounting statements and documents, and serve to set out the numbers discussed in the text in an easily readable format. This enables you to follow closely the explanations and to become familiar with the layout of such documents.

In-text examples

Regular examples are presented throughout each chapter and illustrate how accounting material is used in a variety of different contexts from the world of business. The diversity in cases demonstrates how accounting information can be interpreted in different ways to achieve different ends according to business needs.

Accounting in practice

'Give me an example' boxes

Topical examples taken from the *Financial Times*, BBC, and other news outlets will help your understanding of how the theory being discussed in the chapter relates to a real-world case. There are also numerous references to financial statements from real companies which highlight how the accounting theory discussed plays out in business practice.

> **GIVE ME AN EXAMPLE 2.1   Intangible assets**
>
> Premier Foods plc is the owner of some of the best known grocery brands in the UK, with Mr Kipling, Sharwoods and Oxo among them. On its statement of financial position at 1 April 2017 the company records an amount of £464.0 million under the heading 'Other intangible assets.' The reader of the report and accounts is then referred to Note 13 in the notes to the financial
>
> statements for further information. Note 13 shows that the intangible assets recognized are Software and Licences at £37.4 million, Brands, Trademarks and Licences at £422.5 million and Assets under Construction at £4.1 million.
>
> Source: *Premier Foods annual report and accounts for the financial period ended 1 April 2017* www.premierfoods.co.uk

'Why is this relevant to me?' boxes

These short and frequent explanations demonstrate exactly how the accounting material under discussion will be relevant to business professionals and decision makers, not just to those aiming for a career in accounting. They are an important reminder of how integral accounting knowledge is to successful business professionals.

> **WHY IS THIS RELEVANT TO ME?   Accounting definition**
>
> To enable you as a business professional and user of accounting information to:
> - Understand what accounting is
> - Appreciate that the production of accounting information is not an end in itself but is a tool to enable you to understand, direct and control business or other activities

Testing and applying understanding

End-of-chapter questions

There is a set of questions at the end of every chapter designed to test your knowledge of the key concepts that have been discussed. They are divided into two tiers according to difficulty allowing you to track your progress. Use them during your course to ensure you fully understand the accounting principles before moving on, or for revision to make sure you can confidently tackle the more difficult questions. The answers can be found in the back of the book.

> **END-OF-CHAPTER QUESTIONS**
>
> Solutions to these questions can be found at the back of the book from page 428.
>
> ❯ **DEVELOP YOUR UNDERSTANDING**
>
> ❯ **Question 1.1**
>
> What accounting and other information would the managers of the following organizations require in order to assess their performance and financial position?
> - A charity
> - A secondary school
> - A university
> - A manufacturing business
>
> ❯ **Question 1.2**
>
> A premier league football club has received an offer for its star striker from Real Madrid. The star striker is eager to leave and join the Spanish team and the board of directors has reluctantly agreed to let him go for the transfer fee offered. The team now needs a new striker and the manager has been put in charge of identifying potential new centre forwards that the club could bid for. You have been asked by the manager to draw up a chart listing the numerical information about potential targets that the manager should take into account when evaluating possible replacements.

Chapter summary

Each chapter concludes with a bulleted list linking to the learning outcomes, outlining the key points you should take away from the chapter.

> **CHAPTER SUMMARY**
>
> You should now have learnt that:
> - Accounting summarizes numerical data relating to past events and presents this data as information to managers and other interested parties as a basis for both decision making and control purposes
> - Accounting information is the bedrock upon which all business decisions are based
> - Financial information should possess the two fundamental characteristics of relevance and

Guided tour of Dashboard

Simple. Informative. Mobile.

Dashboard is a cloud-based online assessment and revision tool. It comes pre-loaded with all of the online resources included on the book's accompanying website, as well as additional questions to use for assessment, and functionality to check your students' progress.

Visit www.oxfordtextbooks.co.uk/dashboard for more information.

Simple: With a highly intuitive design, it will take you less than 15 minutes to learn and master the system.

Informative: Assignment and assessment results are automatically graded, giving you a clear view of the class's understanding of the course content.

Mobile: You can access Dashboard from every major platform and device connected to the internet, whether that's a computer, tablet or smartphone.

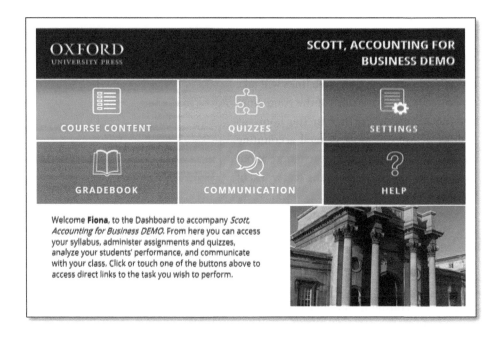

Gradebook

Dashboard's Gradebook functionality automatically marks the assignments that you set for your students. The Gradebook also provides heat maps for you to view your students' progress, and identify quickly areas of the course where your students may need more practice or support, as well as the areas in which they are most confident. This feature helps you focus your teaching time on the areas that matter.

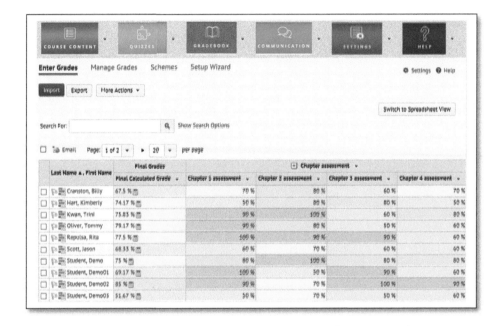

Part 1

Financial accounting

Introduction to accounting

LEARNING OUTCOMES

Once you have read this chapter and worked through the questions and examples in both this chapter and the online workbook, you should be able to:

- Define accounting and explain what role it plays in business
- Explain the fundamental role that accounting plays in informing all business decisions
- Define and discuss the qualities of useful accounting information
- Distinguish between the two branches of accounting, financial accounting and management accounting, and their roles
- State the main users of accounting information and identify what they need from accounting information
- Explain what accounting does not do and the limitations of accounting information
- Understand why a knowledge of accounting is important to you

Introduction

Welcome to your accounting studies. You are probably wondering why you are required to study accounting when you have come to university to study business, marketing, strategy or human resource management. Thus your first reaction might be to say that you are not interested in accounting, so why is this a compulsory part of your course of study? In this book we will show you why a knowledge of accounting and its integral role in all organizations are of vital importance to you in your career in business. We will take a good look at the three key accounting statements you will encounter on a regular basis to provide you with a working knowledge of how these are put together and how you can interpret the information they present. We will also consider how accounting is a valuable tool in planning for the future and in evaluating outcomes and the ways in which these techniques can help you become a much more rounded, much more valuable part of your organization.

What skills do I need?

Many students find the thought of accounting worrying as they do not feel they have the necessary mathematical ability to be able to understand or apply the subject in practice. However, do be assured that accounting needs no particular mathematical strengths, just some basic applications of arithmetic and an ability to reason. As long as you can add up, subtract, multiply and divide figures you have all the arithmetical skills you will need to undertake the calculations and apply this subject. The ability to reason is a skill that you will need in every subject of study and it will be fundamental to the success of any career, not just to your accounting studies.

Once you have learnt how to apply the basic techniques, accounting is much more about understanding what the figures are telling you and about interpreting the data in front of you—this requires you to think in a logical fashion and to investigate the meaning beneath the surface. Therefore, it is far more accurate to say that accounting requires the ability to communicate and express your ideas in words rather than being dependent upon mathematical skills. As we shall see in this chapter, no matter what particular specialist area of business you are studying and no matter what your career aims are, a working knowledge of accounting will be essential to your success in both your studies and in business life.

WHY IS THIS RELEVANT TO ME?   Skills needed to study accounting

- To reassure you that the study of accounting requires no further special skills than those you already possess
- To enable you to appreciate that the study of accounting will further develop the skills you have already acquired in reaching your current level of education

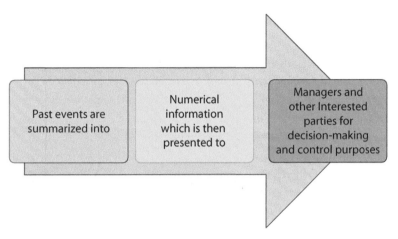

Figure 1.1 What is accounting?

What is accounting?

Let's start with a definition.

Accounting summarizes numerical data relating to past events and presents this data as information to managers and other interested parties as a basis for both decision-making and control purposes, as presented in Figure 1.1.

This is quite a lot to take in, so let's unpick the various strands of this definition.

1. Numerical data: accounting information is mostly but not always presented in money terms. It could just as easily be a league table of football teams with details of games won, games lost and games drawn, goals for and goals against and points gained, all of which is numerical information. Or it could be a list of schools in a particular area with percentages of pupils gaining five GCSEs grades 1–9 and average A level points at each school. In a business, it could be the number of units of product produced rather than just their cost or the number of units sold in a given period of time. The critical point here is that accounting data is presented in the form of numbers.

2. Relating to past events: accounting systems gather data and then summarize these data to present details of what has happened. A league table is a summary of past results. Similarly, a total of sales for the month will be a summary of all the individual sales made on each day of that month and relating to that past period of time.

3. Information presented to managers: managers have the power and authority to use accounting information to take action now to maintain or improve future outcomes. In the same way, if a team is in the middle of the league table but aspires to a higher position, the team manager can take steps to hire better coaches, buy in the contracts of players with higher skill levels and sell the contractual rights of underperforming players. If a school wants to improve their

1

examination results, they will take steps to determine what is preventing better performance and try to correct these deficiencies.

4. As a basis for decision making: accounting information is used to determine what went well and which events did not turn out quite as anticipated. For example, demand for a business's product over the past month might not have reached the levels expected. If this is the case, managers can take steps to determine whether the selling price is too high and should be reduced, whether there are defects in the products that require rectification or whether the product is just out of date and no longer valued by consumers. On the other hand, if demand for a product is outstripping supply, then managers can take the decision to divert business resources to increase production to meet that higher demand.

5. Control purposes: businesses, as we shall see in Chapter 11, prepare budgets prior to the start of an accounting period (usually 12 months) which set out what they aim to achieve in terms of sales, **profits** and cash flows. A comparison of actual outcomes with the budget will enable managers to decide where the budget was met, where the budget was exceeded and where the budget failed to reach expectations. Then the causes of the last two outcomes can be investigated and action taken to address the reasons behind the underperformance or to take advantage of better than expected results. The future is uncertain, but businesses will still plan by predicting to the best of their ability what they expect to occur in the following months and then compare actual outcomes with what they expected to happen as a means of controlling operations.

WHY IS THIS RELEVANT TO ME?   Accounting definition

To enable you as a business professional and user of accounting information to:

- Understand what accounting is
- Appreciate that the production of accounting information is not an end in itself but is a tool to enable you to understand, direct and control business or other activities

---

SUMMARY OF KEY CONCEPTS   How well have you remembered the definition of accounting given above? Revise this definition with Summary of key concepts 1.1.

GO BACK OVER THIS AGAIN!   If this all still seems very complicated and not relevant to you, visit the **online workbook** Exercises 1.1 and 1.2 to enable you to appreciate that you are already working with accounting data on a daily basis.

GO BACK OVER THIS AGAIN!   Quite certain you can define accounting? Go to the **online workbook** Exercises 1.3 to make sure you can say what accounting is and what role it performs in a business context.

Control, accounting and accountability

The function of accounting information as a mechanism through which to control outcomes and activities can be illustrated further. Representatives are accountable for their actions to those people who have placed them in positions of power or trust. Accounting information is thus provided so that individuals and organizations can render an account of what they have done with the resources placed in their care. Example 1.1 provides an everyday illustration of these ideas.

EXAMPLE 1.1

Your employer pays your salary into your bank account while various payments are made out of your account to pay your bills and other outgoings. Your bank then provides you with a statement (either online or in paper copy) on a regular basis so that you can check whether they have accounted for your money correctly or not.

In the same way, company **directors** present financial statements (accounts) to **shareholders** and other interested parties on an annual basis to present an account of how they have looked after the money and other resources entrusted to them and how they have used that money to invest and generate income for shareholders. Local and national governments regularly publish information on the taxes collected and how those taxes have been spent. This information enables politicians to render an account of how taxes collected have been used to provide goods and services to citizens.

Where power and resources are entrusted to others, it is important that they are accountable for what they have done with that power and those resources. If your bank makes mistakes in the management of your account or charges you too much for managing your account, then you can change banks. If shareholders are unhappy with their directors' performance, they will not reappoint them as directors of their company. Instead, they will elect other directors to replace them in the expectation that these new directors will manage their investment much more carefully and profitably. Alternatively, they can sell their shares and invest their money in companies that do provide them with higher profits and higher **dividends**. If voters are unhappy with how their local and national politicians have taxed them or how they have spent their taxes, they will vote for different representatives with different policies more to their liking.

Persons entrusted by others with resources are in the position of stewards, looking after those resources for the benefit of other parties. Providing an account of their **stewardship** of those resources helps those other parties control the actions of their stewards. At the same time, accounts enable these other parties to make decisions on whether to continue with their current stewards or to replace them with others who

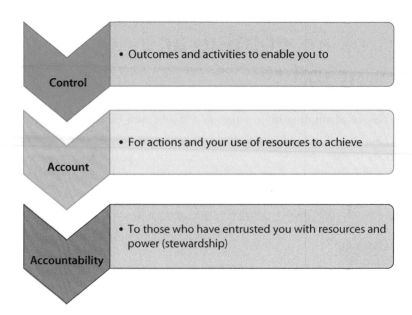

Control • Outcomes and activities to enable you to

Account • For actions and your use of resources to achieve

Accountability • To those who have entrusted you with resources and power (stewardship)

Figure 1.2 Control, accounting and accountability

will perform more effectively and provide them with a more efficient and profitable service. These relationships are summarized in Figure 1.2.

WHY IS THIS RELEVANT TO ME?   Control, accounting and accountability

To enable you as a business professional and user of accounting information to:

• Appreciate that accounting functions as a control on the actions of others

• Understand how you will be entrusted with a business's resources and that you will be accountable for your stewardship of those resources

GO BACK OVER THIS AGAIN!   Do you really understand how accounting helps with control and accountability? Go to the **online workbook** Exercises 1.4 to make sure you understand the links between accounting, accountability and control.

The role of accounting information in business decision making

Businesses are run to make a profit. Businesses that do not make a profit fail and are closed down. In order to achieve this profit aim, businesses need to make and implement decisions on a daily basis. Such decisions might comprise, among others, some or all of the following:

- What products should we produce?
- What services should we provide?
- How much do our products cost to make?
- How much do our services cost to provide?
- What price should we charge for our products or services?
- Should we be taking on more employees?
- How much will the additional employees cost?
- Will the cost of the new employees be lower than the income they will generate?
- Should we be expanding into bigger premises?
- Will the costs of the bigger premises be outweighed by the increase in income?
- How will we finance our expansion?
- Should we take out a bank loan or ask the shareholders to buy more shares?

All of these decisions will require accounting input:

- The marketing department can use reports from sales personnel and consumer evaluations to tell us what the demand for a product is, but it will be up to the accounting staff to tell us what the product costs to make and what the selling price should be in order to generate a profit on each sale.

- The personnel department can tell us about hiring new staff and the legal obligations incurred in doing so, the training required and the market rates for such workers, but it will be the accounting staff who can tell us what level of productivity the new employees will have to achieve in order to generate additional profit for the business.

- The strategy department can tell us what sort of premises we should be looking for, how these new premises should be designed and what image they should present, but it will be the accounting staff who can tell us how many products we will have to make and sell for the new premises to cover their additional costs and the best way in which to finance this expansion.

Accounting is thus at the heart of every decision and every activity that a business undertakes, as shown in Figure 1.3.

At this early stage of your studies, it is easy to think of each department in a business as just sticking to its own specialist field of expertise, operating in isolation from all the others, concentrating on their own aims and goals. You might reply that you would never think of a business as just a loose grouping of separate departments all doing

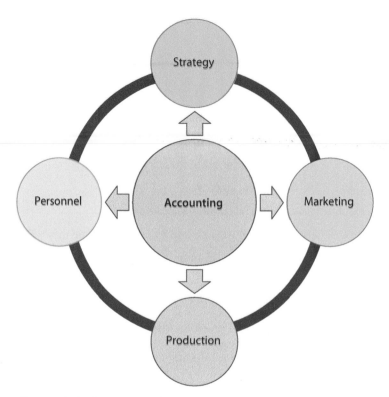

Figure 1.3 The central role of accounting in business activity and business decision making

their own thing with no thought for the bigger picture. But pause for a moment and ask yourself whether you treat all your current year study modules as interlinked or as totally separate subjects? You should see them as fully interlinked and look to see how all the subjects interact, but it is too easy to adopt a blinkered approach and compartmentalize each different aspect of your studies.

As the previous decisions and discussion illustrate, all business decisions require input from different departments and information from one department has to be integrated with information from other departments before an overall coordinated plan of action can be put into operation. Businesses operate as cohesive entities, with all departments pulling in the same direction rather than each following their own individual pathway. Management make decisions and implement strategies, but underpinning all these decisions and strategies is accounting information.

This central role for accountants and accounting information puts accounting staff under pressure to perform their roles effectively and efficiently. After all, if the information presented by the accounting staff is defective in any way, the wrong decision could be made and losses rather than profits might result. Therefore, accountants have to ensure that the information they provide is as accurate and as up to date as possible to enable management to make the most effective decisions. Ideally, accounting staff will always be striving to improve the information they provide to management as better information will result in more informed and more effective decisions.

To illustrate the importance of the accounting function, take a moment to think what would happen if we did not have accounting information. Businesses would be lost without the vital information provided by accounting. If accounting did not exist, there would be no information relating to costs, no indication of what had been achieved in the past as a point of comparison for what is being achieved now, no figures on which to base taxation assessments, no proof that results are as companies claim they are. In short, if accounting did not exist, someone would have to invent it.

WHY IS THIS RELEVANT TO ME?   The role of accounting information in business decision making

To enable you as a business professional to:

- Appreciate that business decisions depend upon input from different departments and that decisions are not made in isolation by one department acting on its own
- Appreciate the importance of accounting information in business decision making
- Persuade you that you should see your studies as an integrated, coherent whole rather than as a collection of disparate, unrelated subjects

MULTIPLE CHOICE QUESTIONS   Convinced that you understand what role accounting plays in business decision making? Go to the **online workbook** Multiple choice questions 1.1 to make sure you can suggest how accounting and accounting information would be used in the context of a business decision.

What qualities should accounting information possess?

Given the pivotal role of accounting information in business decision making, what sort of qualities should such information possess for it to be useful in making these decisions? Helpfully, the International Accounting Standards Board (IASB) in its *Conceptual Framework for Financial Reporting* provides guidance in this area. The IASB states that financial information should possess the following two fundamental qualitative characteristics:

- Relevance
- Faithful representation

1

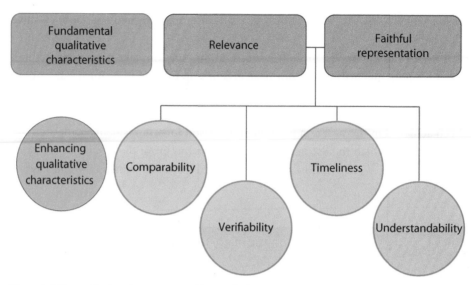

Figure 1.4 The qualitative characteristics of financial information

In addition, the IASB's *Conceptual Framework* identifies the following qualitative characteristics that enhance the usefulness of information that is relevant and faithfully represented:

- Comparability
- Verifiability
- Timeliness
- Understandability

This hierarchy of qualitative characteristics is shown in Figure 1.4.

What does each of the above qualitative characteristics represent? Table 1.1 considers the characteristics of each of the two fundamental and four enhancing qualities of financial information.

Table 1.1 The qualities of accounting information

Qualitative characteristic	Considerations
Relevance	• Relevant information must be capable of making a difference in the decisions made by users. • Relevant information may be predictive and assist users in making predictions about the future or it may be confirmatory by assisting users to assess the accuracy of past predictions. • Relevant information can be both predictive and confirmatory.

Table 1.1 (*continued*)

Qualitative characteristic	Considerations
Faithful representation	• Financial information must not only represent relevant economic phenomena (transactions and events), but it must also faithfully represent the substance of the phenomena that it purports to represent. • Perfectly faithful representation of economic phenomena in words and numbers requires that the information presented must have three characteristics: it must be complete, neutral and free from error. • Do note that free from error does not mean that information must be perfectly accurate. Much accounting information relies on best estimates or the most likely outcomes. The IASB *Conceptual Framework* makes it clear that 'free from error means there are no errors or omissions in the description of the phenomenon, and the process used to produce the reported information has been selected and applied with no errors in the process. In this context, free from error does not mean perfectly accurate in all respects'. (IASB *Conceptual Framework for Financial Reporting*, paragraph 2.18)
Comparability	• Information should be comparable over time. • The usefulness of information is enhanced if it can be compared with similar information about other entities for the same reporting period and with similar information about the same entity for other reporting periods. • Where information is comparable, similarities and differences are readily apparent. • Comparability does not mean consistency. However, consistency of presentation and measurement of the same items in the same way from year to year will help to achieve comparability. • Similarly, comparability does not mean that economic phenomena must be presented uniformly. Information about the same phenomena will be presented in similar but not in the same ways by different entities. The differences in the presentation of such phenomena will not be so great as to prevent comparability.
Verifiability	• Verifiability provides users with assurance that information is faithfully presented and reports the economic phenomena it purports to represent. • To ensure verifiability, it should be possible to prove the information presented is accurate in all major respects. • The accuracy of information can be verified by observation or recalculation. • Financial information will often be subject to independent audit and the independent auditors will use various techniques and approaches to verify the financial information presented.

→

1

Table 1.1 (*continued*)

Qualitative characteristic	Considerations
Timeliness	• The decision usefulness of information is enhanced if it is available to users in time for it to be capable of influencing their decisions. • The decision usefulness of information generally declines with time although information used in identifying trends continues to be timely in the future.
Understandability	• This characteristic should not be confused with simplicity. • Accounting can involve very complex calculations, details and disclosures. Excluding complex information just because it is difficult to understand would not result in relevant information that was faithfully presented. Reports that excluded such information would be incomplete and would thus mislead users. • Readers of financial reports are assumed to have a reasonable knowledge of business and economic activities in order to make sense of what they are presented with. If they are unable to understand the information presented, then the IASB recommends using an adviser. • To help users understand information presented, that information should be classified, characterized and presented clearly.

EXAMPLE 1.2

Let's think about how the qualities considered above apply to accounting information. Taking the bank statement example considered under Control, accounting and accountability earlier in this chapter, our thoughts might be as shown in Table 1.2.

Table 1.2 How your bank statement fulfils the qualities of financial information

Relevant?	• Your bank statement is capable of making a difference to the decisions you make. Depending on your current level of cash, you are able to decide to spend less, increase the income into your bank account or decide to invest surplus funds in high interest accounts. • Looking at your current income and expenditure, you can predict what is likely to happen in the future in your bank account. Where you have made predictions about what cash you would have left at the end of each month, you can then confirm how accurate or inaccurate those predictions were and make future predictions about how much you will have left at the end of the next month to decide what you should do with these surplus funds. • Accurate predictions in the past will enable you to be confident that your future predictions will be accurate too.

Table 1.2 (*continued*)

Faithfully represented?	• Your bank statement is presented by your bank, so this should be a faithful representation of your income and expenditure (economic phenomena, transactions and events) over a given period of time. • It is in your bank's interest to ensure that the information presented in your bank statement is complete, neutral (the statement just presents the facts of your income and expenditure) and free from error. Any errors you do pick up can be notified to your bank for correction.
Comparable?	• Presentation of your bank statement does not differ over time and is presented in the same format every month so this information is comparable over different periods of time. • This consistency of presentation and measurement of income and expenditure in the same way from month to month and year to year will help to achieve the required comparability.
Verifiable?	• The accuracy of your statement can be verified by reference to your list of standing orders, direct debits, debit card transactions, cheques written and income from payslips and other sources. • You can add up your bank statement to make sure the balance at the end of each month is correct (recalculation). • You are thus the auditor of your own bank account, checking and verifying that the information presented is accurate and free from error to ensure that your statement is faithfully presented and reports the substance of the economic phenomena it purports to represent.
Timely?	• Your bank statement is received each month (or you can access it instantly online), so it is presented in time for it to be capable of influencing your decisions. If your bank statement were to be sent annually, this would be much less relevant information as it would be seriously out of date by the time you received it and much less capable of making a difference to the decisions you make. • However, past bank statements are still timely when comparing trends of income and expenditure across different periods of time.
Understandable?	• You can certainly understand your bank statement as it shows you the money going into and out of your account. • You have a reasonable knowledge of your finances so you can make sense of what your bank statement presents you with. If you are unable to understand the information presented, then you can always contact your bank for advice. • To help you understand the information presented, transactions are classified, characterized and presented clearly in your bank statement.

1

GO BACK OVER THIS AGAIN! Certain you can define relevance, faithful representation, comparability, verifiability, timeliness and understandability? Go to the **online workbook** Exercises 1.5 to make sure you can define these qualities of financial information accurately.

SUMMARY OF KEY CONCEPTS Can you state and define the two fundamental and four enhancing qualities of financial information? Check your grasp of these qualities with Summary of key concepts 1.2–1.7.

Materiality

A further requirement of financial information for decision making purposes is that it should not be overloaded with unnecessary detail. This brings us to the concept of materiality. The IASB defines materiality as follows:

> Information is material if omitting it or misstating it could influence decisions that . . . users . . . make on the basis of . . . financial information about a specific reporting entity. In other words, materiality is an entity-specific aspect of relevance based on the nature or magnitude, or both, of the items to which the information relates in the context of an individual entity's financial report.
>
> Source: IASB *Conceptual Framework for Financial Reporting*, paragraph 2.11

How is materiality applied in practice? Example 1.3 provides instances of the circumstances in which an item might be defined as material.

EXAMPLE 1.3

An item could be material by size (magnitude in the above definition). If a shop makes £2 million of sales a year, then the sale of a 50p carton of milk missed out of those sales will not be material. However, in a steel fabrication business making £2 million of sales a year, the omission of a £250,000 sale of a steel frame for a building would be material as it makes up 12.5% of the sales for the year.

As well as size, items can be material by nature. The theft of £5 from the till by a member of staff would be unlikely to be material. However, the theft of £5 from the till by the managing director would be: if you are an investor in the business, this tells you that your investment might not be very safe if the managing director is willing to steal from the business.

MULTIPLE CHOICE QUESTIONS Totally confident you can decide whether a piece of information is material or not? Go to the **online workbook** Multiple choice questions 1.2 to make sure you can determine whether information is material or not.

SUMMARY OF KEY CONCEPTS Can you recall the definition of materiality? Check your grasp of this definition in Summary of key concepts 1.8.

Cost v. benefit

The IASB recognizes that there is a cost in collecting, processing, verifying and disseminating financial information (IASB *Conceptual Framework for Financial Reporting*, paragraphs 2.39–2.43). Therefore, information should only be presented if the benefits of providing that information outweigh the costs of obtaining it. Example 1.4 suggests how you might weigh up the costs and benefits in a practical but non-accounting situation.

EXAMPLE 1.4

You know that there is a wonderful quote in a book that you have read that would really enhance your essay and provide you with a brilliant conclusion. However, you have forgotten where to find this quote and you have not written down the name of the book or the page reference. Your essay must be handed in by 4.00 pm today and it is already 3.40 pm. You still have to print off your essay before handing it in. If your essay is handed in after 4.00 pm you will be awarded a mark of 0% and so fail the assignment.

The costs of searching for the quote outweigh the benefits of finding it as you will not receive any marks if your essay is late so you print off your essay and hand it in on time and, when it is returned, you have scored 65% and gained a pass on this piece of coursework.

WHY IS THIS RELEVANT TO ME?   The qualities of accounting information

To enable you as a business professional and user of accounting information to:

- Understand what qualities useful accounting information should possess
- Appreciate the constraints imposed upon the provision of useful accounting information by the materiality concept and the cost/benefit consideration

GO BACK OVER THIS AGAIN!   Quite sure you understand how cost v. benefit works? Visit the **online workbook** Exercises 1.6 to reinforce your understanding.

SUMMARY OF KEY CONCEPTS   Can you define cost v. benefit? Check your grasp of this definition in Summary of key concepts 1.9.

The users of accounting information

As we have seen, accounting is all about providing information to interested parties so that they can make decisions on the basis of that information. But who are the users of this accounting information and what decisions do they make as a result of receiving that information?

There are two branches of accounting which we will consider in this book and which you will meet in your studies and in your career in business. One of these branches provides information to external users and the other provides information to internal users. The information needs of both these user groups differ in important ways, as we shall see.

Accounting branch 1: financial accounting

Financial accounting is the reporting of past information to users outside the organization. This information is presented in the annual report and accounts that all companies are obliged to produce by law, publish on their websites and lodge with the Registrar of Companies at Companies House. Directors of companies produce these annual reports and accounts for issue to shareholders to provide an account of how they have used the resources entrusted to them to generate profits, dividends and value for those shareholders. Even if a **business entity** is not a company and there is no legal obligation to produce accounts, it will still produce financial statements to provide evidence of what it has achieved over the past year. These accounts will also be used as a basis for enabling the business's managers or owners and its lenders and advisers to make decisions based upon them as well as being used by the taxation authorities to determine the tax due on the profits for the year.

What is the aim of these financial accounts and reports and what do they provide? The IASB states that the objective of financial reporting (not just financial statements) is as follows:

> The objective of general purpose financial reporting is to provide financial information about the reporting entity that is useful to existing and potential investors, lenders and other creditors in making decisions relating to providing resources to the entity. Those decisions involve decisions about:
>
> (a) buying, selling or holding equity and debt instruments;
>
> (b) providing or settling loans and other forms of credit; or
>
> (c) exercising rights to vote on, or otherwise influence, management's actions that affect the use of the entity's **economic resources**.
>
> Source: IASB *Conceptual Framework for Financial Reporting*, paragraph 1.2

While the IASB focuses on the financial information needs of existing and potential investors, lenders and other creditors, it does envisage that other users might find general purpose financial reports useful:

> Other parties, such as regulators and members of the public other than investors, lenders and other creditors, may also find general purpose financial reports useful. However, those reports are not primarily directed to these other groups.
>
> Source: IASB *Conceptual Framework for Financial Reporting*, paragraph 1.10

Financial information is reported to users external to the organization through three key statements: the statement of financial position, the statement of profit or loss and

WHY IS THIS RELEVANT TO ME? Knowledge of accounting

- To enable you as a business professional to appreciate the all-pervading role that account-ing plays in the workings of business
- To encourage you to get to grips with accounting now so that you can use this knowledge to your benefit later on in your studies and in your career

CHAPTER SUMMARY

You should now have learnt that:

- Accounting summarizes numerical data relating to past events and presents this data as information to managers and other interested parties as a basis for both decision making and control purposes
- Accounting information is the bedrock upon which all business decisions are based
- Financial information should possess the two fundamental characteristics of relevance and faithful representation
- The qualitative characteristics of comparability, verifiability, timeliness and understandabil-ity will enhance the usefulness of information that is relevant and faithfully represented
- Financial accounting generates reports for users external to the business
- Financial accounting information is primarily aimed at existing and potential investors, lenders and other creditors who will find this information useful in making decisions about providing resources to the reporting entity
- Other user groups such as employees, customers, governments and the public may also find financial reporting information useful in making decisions and evaluating the perform-ance of organizations
- Management accounting is prepared for internal users in a business to help them manage the business's activities
- Accounting does not measure, among other things, quality, pollution, social and environ-mental damage, human resources and the skills and knowledge base of organizations
- A knowledge of accounting is essential to the success of any career in business

QUICK REVISION   Test your knowledge with the online flashcards in Summary of key con-cepts and attempt the Multiple choice questions in the **online workbook**. www.oup.com/uk/scott_business3e/

1

END-OF-CHAPTER QUESTIONS

Solutions to these questions can be found at the back of the book from page 428.

❯ DEVELOP YOUR UNDERSTANDING

❭ Question 1.1

What accounting and other information would the managers of the following organizations require in order to assess their performance and financial position?

- A charity
- A secondary school
- A university
- A manufacturing business

❭ Question 1.2

A premier league football club has received an offer for its star striker from Real Madrid. The star striker is eager to leave and join the Spanish team and the board of directors has reluctantly agreed to let him go for the transfer fee offered. The team now needs a new striker and the manager has been put in charge of identifying potential new centre forwards that the club could bid for. You have been asked by the manager to draw up a chart listing the numerical information about potential targets that the manager should take into account when evaluating possible replacements.

The statement of financial position

LEARNING OUTCOMES

Once you have read this chapter and worked through the questions and examples in both this chapter and the online workbook, you should be able to:

- Define assets and liabilities
- Determine whether an entity should or should not recognize specific resources and obligations on its statement of financial position
- Distinguish between non-current and current assets and liabilities
- State the accounting equation
- Draw up a statement of financial position for organizations in compliance with the International Accounting Standards Board (IASB)'s requirements
- Explain how assets and liabilities are measured in monetary amounts at the statement of financial position date
- State what the statement of financial position does and does not show
- Understand how transactions affect two or more accounts on the statement of financial position (the duality principle)
- Record correctly the effect of transactions on the assets, liabilities and equity in the statement of financial position

Introduction

Figure 2.1 summarizes the elements that make up the statement of financial position. All financial statements present a **statement of financial position**. This is a summary, in money terms, of the **assets** an organization controls and the **liabilities** an organization owes to outside parties. To enable you to see how this statement is presented in full before we look at the detail, Illustration 2.1 shows the statement of financial position of Bunns the Bakers plc, a regional baker with a bakery and 20 shops in the East Midlands. At first glance, this might look complicated as there are all kinds of seemingly complex words and jargon. However, don't worry as, after working your way through this chapter and the materials in the online workbook, you will soon have a much clearer idea of what the words and jargon mean.

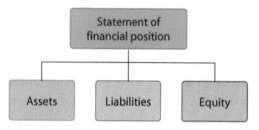

Figure 2.1 The statement of financial position

Notice that there are various headings provided and that these headings contain the words 'assets', 'liabilities' and 'equity'. In this chapter we will be looking at what constitutes an asset and a liability and how equity is calculated. We shall also review the criteria for recognizing assets and liabilities and how those assets and liabilities are classified as **current** or **non-current**. Just as assets and liabilities can be recognized in an organization's statement of financial position so, once assets have been used up or liabilities discharged, they are derecognized. This just means that they are removed from the statement of financial position as they are no longer controlled or owed by the entity.

Once the definitions are clear, we shall move on to constructing simple statements of financial position from given data. We shall then consider what the statement of financial position shows us and, equally importantly, what it does not show us. There are many misconceptions about what a statement of financial position represents. This chapter will dispel these misconceptions and provide you with a very precise idea of what the statement of financial position provides by way of information and what it does not.

Finally, at the end of the chapter, we will have a quick look at how new transactions affect the statement of financial position. Double entry bookkeeping is not dealt with in any depth or detail in this book, but a quick appreciation of how this works will give you an insight into the logic of accounting and how new transactions have a two-fold effect on figures in the financial statements of an organization.

Terminology: statement of financial position/ balance sheet

International Financial Reporting Standards use the term statement of financial position for what has traditionally been called the **balance sheet**. In keeping with the international focus of this book, the term statement of financial position will be used throughout. However, you will find the two terms used interchangeably in your wider reading, so you should understand that the terms balance sheet and statement of financial position refer to the same summary statement of assets, liabilities and equity.

Illustration 2.1 Bunns the Bakers plc: statement of financial position at 31 March 2019

	2019	2018
	£000	£000
Assets		
Non-current assets		
Intangible assets	50	55
Property, plant and equipment	11,750	11,241
Investments	65	59
	11,865	11,355
Current assets		
Inventories	60	55
Trade and other receivables	62	75
Cash and cash equivalents	212	189
	334	319
Total assets	12,199	11,674
Liabilities		
Current liabilities		
Current portion of long-term borrowings	300	300
Trade and other **payables**	390	281
Current tax liabilities	150	126
	840	707
Non-current liabilities		
Long-term borrowings	2,700	3,000
Long-term provisions	200	200
	2,900	3,200
Total liabilities	3,740	3,907
Net assets	8,459	7,767
Equity		
Called up share capital (£1 ordinary shares)	2,500	2,400
Share premium	1,315	1,180
Retained earnings	4,644	4,187
Total equity	8,459	7,767

GO BACK OVER THIS AGAIN!   A copy of this statement of financial position is available in the **online workbook**: you might like to keep this on screen or print off a copy for easy reference while you work your way through the material in this chapter. There is also an annotated copy of this statement of financial position in the **online workbook** to go over the relevant points again to reinforce your knowledge and learning.

Assets

Assets: definition

Illustration 2.1 shows you the statement of financial position for Bunns the Bakers plc. As noted in the introduction, the first part of this statement of financial position shows you the assets that an entity controls. However, the first questions to ask are: 'What is an asset?' and 'What does an asset represent?'

The IASB's *Conceptual Framework for Financial Reporting* provides the following definition of an asset:

> A present economic resource controlled by the entity as a result of past events.
>
> An economic resource is a right that has the potential to produce economic benefits.
>
> Source: IASB *The Conceptual Framework for Financial Reporting*, paragraphs 4.3 and 4.4

This sounds complicated. However, once we consider the words carefully and analyse what they mean, we will find that this definition is actually very simple and presents a very clear set of criteria to determine whether an asset exists or not. So what does this definition tell us? Let's look at the key points:

- Control: 'an entity controls an economic resource if it has the present ability to direct the use of the economic resource and obtain the economic benefits that flow from it' (IASB *Conceptual Framework*, paragraph 4.20). A resource is controlled if it is owned or leased (rented) by an organization which can enforce its legal rights over that resource. Control is therefore established if an entity can legally prevent anyone else from using that resource and obtaining the economic benefits from it.

- As a result of past events: to gain control of a resource it is likely that a contract has been signed transferring or granting the right to use that resource to the current owner and money has been paid to other parties in exchange for the transfer or rights to use that resource. Contractual rights gained over the resource mean that an entity can enforce its legal rights over that resource.

- Present: firstly, the economic resource must be under the control of an entity at the statement of financial position date. Any economic resource that is not under the control of the entity at the statement of financial position date cannot be included in the entity's statement of financial position. Secondly, the economic resource must have the potential to produce economic benefits at the statement of financial position date. If the economic resource does not have this potential then it cannot be recognized as an asset on the statement of financial position.

- Economic benefits: the economic resource will be used within an organization to generate cash and profit from the sale of goods or services to other persons.

From this definition it follows that an asset represents a store of potential economic benefits, the ability to use the asset within an organization to generate cash and profit. Example 2.1 presents a practical example of how this definition can be applied in a real-world situation.

EXAMPLE 2.1

Let us take the example of Bunns the Bakers. The company bought a city centre shop from a property developer ten years ago for £500,000, with both the seller and the buyer of the shop signing a contract transferring legal title in the shop to Bunns the Bakers. The shop sells bread, cakes, hot and cold snacks, drinks and sandwiches. Does this constitute an asset of the business? Applying our criteria:

- Do Bunns the Bakers *control* the shop (the resource)? Yes: the company *owns* the shop and, by virtue of the contract signed at the time the shop was purchased from the property developer, Bunns the Bakers can go to court to assert their legal rights to the shop and to prevent anyone else from using that shop for their own purposes. The company thus has the ability at the statement of financial position date (the present ability) to direct the use of this economic resource (the shop) and to obtain the economic benefits that flow from it.

- Is there *a past event*? Yes: Bunns the Bakers' representatives signed the contract and paid £500,000 to acquire the shop, so this is the *past event* giving rise to control of the economic resource.

- Does the economic resource (the shop) have the potential to produce economic benefits? Yes: Bunns the Bakers is using the shop to sell goods produced by the company and bought in from suppliers to customers in order to generate cash and profits from those sales. You can also view the shop as a store of potential economic benefits for Bunns the Bakers. The company can continue to use the shop to make sales, profits and cash into the future. Alternatively, that store of potential economic benefits could be realized by selling the shop to another company. This would still generate economic benefits as the sale of the shop would release the cash (= the economic benefits) tied up in that shop. Even if Bunns the Bakers did not sell the shop but chose to rent it out to another party, this would still represent potential economic benefits as monthly rental payments would be received in cash from the person or organization renting the shop.

Thus, the shop represents an asset to the business as it meets the IASB criteria for recognition of an asset.

Assets: faithful representation

Our definition of what constitutes an asset now seems very clear. However, there is one further test to satisfy before an asset (or liability) can be recognized in the statement of financial position. As we saw in Chapter 1 (What qualities should accounting information possess?), the IASB requires financial information to be relevant and faithfully represented. Faithful representation requires the presentation of information that is complete, neutral and free from error. Since the elements (assets, liabilities and equity) that make up the statement of financial position must be quantified in money terms (IASB, *Conceptual Framework*, paragraph 6.1), these items must be measured at a monetary value before they can be recognized. While an accurate value for many assets and liabilities can be determined easily from the accounting records of an entity, there will be times when estimates have to be used. When values are estimated, they are subject to measurement uncertainty. In cases where the level of measurement uncertainty is so high that the faithful representation of an asset or liability is in doubt, no asset or liability is recognized (IASB, *Conceptual Framework*, paragraphs 5.19–5.22). Thus, when the possible range of values for an asset or liability is very wide or when measurement is based on very subjective measures, then the completeness, neutrality and freedom from error required for a faithful representation cannot be achieved and no asset or liability is recognized in the statement of financial position. Can the cost of the shop be quantified in monetary terms in such a way that it is faithfully represented in the statement of financial position? Yes, as the cost of the shop was £500,000 this is a complete, neutral and error free measurement and so the shop can be recognized in Bunns the Bakers' statement of financial position as an asset.

Asset recognition: summary of the steps to follow

Diagrammatically, the steps to follow to determine whether an asset can be recognized on the statement of financial position are shown in Figure 2.2.

WHY IS THIS RELEVANT TO ME? Definitions: assets

To enable you as a business professional and user of accounting information to:

- Understand what assets on the statement of financial position actually represent
- Understand the strict criteria that must be met before an asset can be recognized on the statement of financial position
- Be equipped with the necessary tools to determine whether an asset should be recognized on the statement of financial position or not

2

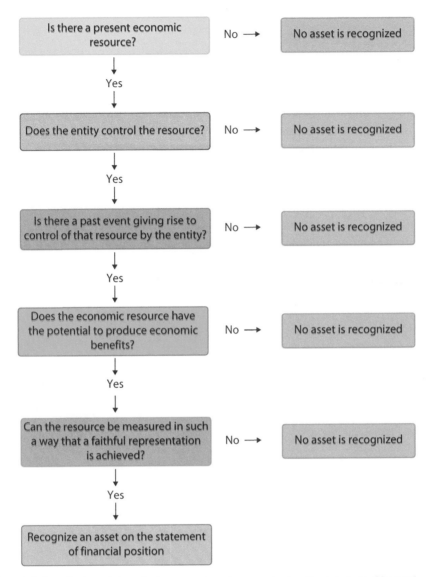

Figure 2.2 Steps in determining whether an asset can be recognized on the statement of financial position or not in accordance with the IASB *Conceptual Framework for Financial Reporting*

SUMMARY OF KEY CONCEPTS   Convinced that you can define an asset? Revise this definition with Summary of key concepts 2.1 to reinforce your knowledge.

GO BACK OVER THIS AGAIN!   Sure that you have grasped the asset recognition criteria? Go to the **online workbook** Exercises 2.1 to make sure you understand how the asset recognition criteria are applied in practice.

2

Assets in the statement of financial position

Now we have found out what assets are and the criteria for their recognition, let's look again at the statement of financial position of Bunns the Bakers plc to see what sort of assets a company might own and recognize.

Illustration 2.1 shows that Bunns the Bakers has two types of assets, non-current assets and current assets. Non-current assets are split into intangible assets, property, plant and equipment and investments. Current assets are split into inventories, trade and other receivables and cash and cash equivalents. Total assets are calculated by adding together non-current and current assets as shown in Figure 2.3. What is the distinction between current and non-current assets? Let us look in more detail at these two types of assets and then the categorization of assets as non-current or current will readily become apparent.

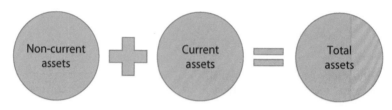

Figure 2.3   The composition of total assets

Non-current assets

Non-current assets are those assets that are:

- Not purchased for resale in the normal course of business: this means that the assets are retained within the business for periods of more than one year and are not acquired with the intention of reselling them immediately or in the near future.
- Held for long-term use in the business to produce goods or services.

An example of a non-current asset would be the shop we considered in Example 2.1. This shop was not purchased with the intention of reselling it, but is held within the business for the long-term purpose of selling bakery goods to customers over many years.

SUMMARY OF KEY CONCEPTS Totally confident that you can define non-current assets? Revise this definition with Summary of key concepts 2.2 to check your understanding.

Intangible assets are those assets that have no material substance (you cannot touch them). Examples of such assets would be purchased goodwill, patents, trademarks and intellectual property rights. Tangible assets are those assets that do have a material substance (you can touch them) and examples of these would be land and buildings, machinery, vehicles and fixtures and fittings.

Intangible assets are represented on Bunns the Bakers' statement of financial position in Illustration 2.1 and these probably relate to trademarks for the company's products. You would, however, need to consult the notes to the accounts to find out precisely what assets were represented by these figures, as shown in Give me an example 2.1.

GIVE ME AN EXAMPLE 2.1   Intangible assets

Premier Foods plc is the owner of some of the best known grocery brands in the UK, with Mr Kipling, Sharwoods and Oxo among them. On its statement of financial position at 1 April 2017 the company records an amount of £464.0 million under the heading 'Other intangible assets'. The reader of the report and accounts is then referred to Note 13 in the notes to the financial statements for further information. Note 13 shows that the intangible assets recognized are Software and Licences at £37.4 million, Brands, Trademarks and Licences at £422.5 million and Assets under Construction at £4.1 million.

Source: *Premier Foods annual report and accounts for the financial period ended 1 April 2017* www.premier-foods.co.uk

---

The property, plant and equipment heading represents the tangible assets of the business. As this is a bakery retail business, these tangible assets will consist of shops, bakeries, delivery vans, counters, tills and display cabinets in the shops and any other non-current, long-term assets that the company requires to conduct its business.

Investments are just that, holdings of shares or other financial assets (such as loans to other entities) in other companies. These investments represent long-term investments in other companies or operations that are held in order to realize a long-term capital gain when they are eventually sold.

GO BACK OVER THIS AGAIN! Do you think you can distinguish between intangible non-current assets, property, plant and equipment and investments? Go to the **online workbook** and complete Exercises 2.2 to make sure you can make these distinctions.

GIVE ME AN EXAMPLE 2.2 Non-current assets

We have thought about intangible non-current assets, property, plant and equipment and investments, but what other categories of non-current assets do companies present in their financial statements? The consolidated balance sheet (= statement of financial position) at 31 December 2017 for Taylor Wimpey plc, a large UK residential housing developer, shows the following non-current assets.

	31 December	
	2017	2016
Non-current assets	£m	£m
Intangible assets	3.9	3.5
Property, plant and equipment	22.8	21.0
Interests in joint ventures	50.9	50.3
Trade and other receivables	60.1	87.2
Deferred tax assets	29.3	57.4
	167.0	219.4

Source: *Taylor Wimpey plc annual report and accounts 2017* www.taylorwimpey.co.uk

Intangible assets are made up of software development costs, while property, plant and equipment consists of land and buildings, plant, equipment and leasehold improvements. Joint ventures are entered into with other companies and Taylor Wimpey's statement of financial position records the share of the joint ventures' net assets attributable to the company. The other companies involved in the joint ventures will record their share of the net assets of the joint ventures in their statements of financial position. It may seem odd to see trade receivables recorded as a non-current asset when Bunns the Bakers shows this as a current asset. However, Taylor Wimpey has provided mortgages to customers to assist them with the purchase of their homes. Mortgages are long term assets which will be repayable more than 12 months after the statement of financial position date so these mortgages are recorded as non-current trade and other receivables. Deferred tax is a very complex subject and it can be either an asset (leading to a reduction in future tax payments) or a liability (leading to an increase in future tax payments).

Current assets

Current assets, by contrast, are short-term assets that are constantly changing. On Bunns the Bakers' statement of financial position the following items are found:

- **Inventory**: inventory is another word for stock of goods. Inventory represents goods held for production or sale. As Bunns the Bakers is a baker, inventories held for production will consist of raw materials such as flour, sugar, eggs and other bakery ingredients. As such raw materials deteriorate rapidly, these inventories will be used and replaced on a regular basis as bakery activity takes place, goods are produced, delivered to the shops and sold to the public. Inventory goods for sale might be bread and cakes produced today and held in cool storage ready for next day delivery to the shops. All inventories thus represent potential cash that will be generated from the production and sales of goods.

- Trade and other **receivables**: where organizations make their sales on credit terms to customers, customers are given time in which to pay so that the money due from these customers is recognized as money receivable. A moment's thought will convince you that, as Bunns the Bakers sells food products to the public for cash, there will be very few **trade receivables**. Any trade receivables that there are might arise from a business-to-business contract to supply large quantities of goods to another retailer such as a supermarket chain. As well as small amounts of trade receivables from such contracts, the company will also have other amounts receivable such as tax refunds or amounts paid in advance for services that have yet to be provided (these are called prepayments—see Chapter 3, Prepayments and accruals for a detailed discussion of prepayments). While trade and other receivables represent the right to cash in the future, they are not cash yet and so are recognized in this separate category of current assets. You will find some sets of accounts that refer to trade and other receivables as **debtors**.

- Cash and cash equivalents: this category of current assets comprises amounts of cash held in the tills at the end of the year, cash held in the company's current account at the bank and cash held in short-term deposit accounts with banks and other financial institutions (for more detail on the components of cash and cash equivalents, see Chapter 4, Cash and cash equivalents).

MULTIPLE CHOICE QUESTIONS   Reckon that you can distinguish between different types of current assets? Go to the **online workbook** and have a go at Multiple choice questions 2.1 to make sure you can make these distinctions.

GIVE ME AN EXAMPLE 2.3   Current assets

When looking at the published financial statements of companies, you will find the same categories of current assets presented on the statement of financial position. The statement of financial position of Nichols plc, an international soft drinks producer, at 31 December 2017 shows the same current assets as Bunns the Bakers.

	Years ended 31 December	
	2017	**2016**
Current assets	£000	£000
Inventories	4,815	6,717
Trade and other receivables	34,740	31,508
Cash and cash equivalents	36,058	39,754
Total current assets	75,613	77,979

Source: *Nichols plc financial statements 2017* www.nicholsplc.co.uk

The distinction between non-current and current assets

The distinction between non-current and current assets comes down to one of time. As we have seen, non-current assets are held by businesses to provide benefits in accounting periods exceeding one year. On the other hand, current assets are held only for a short time in order to produce goods to be sold to convert into cash which can then be used to buy in more raw materials to produce more goods to convert into more cash in a short but constantly repeating trading cycle.

However, to decide whether a resource is a non-current or current asset it is also important to determine the business in which an entity is engaged. For example, you might think that a car would be a non-current asset in any business, an asset to be used for the long term. But if that car is parked on the premises of a motor trader, is this car an item of inventory, held in stock for resale, a car owned by the motor trading business for long-term use in the business or the property of a member of staff who drives to work each day (and so not a business asset at all)? Further enquiries would have to be made to determine whether the car is a business asset and, if it is, the exact statement of financial position classification of this vehicle.

WHY IS THIS RELEVANT TO ME?   Non-current and current assets

To enable you as a business professional and user of accounting information to:

- Develop a clear understanding of the different types of assets entities recognize on their statement of financial position
- Distinguish effectively between the two types of assets
- Understand how the different types of assets can be used in evaluating entities' efficiency and working capital management (discussed in detail in Chapters 6 and 7)

GO BACK OVER THIS AGAIN!   How easily can you distinguish between current and non-current assets? Go to the **online workbook** Exercises 2.3 to make sure you can make this distinction.

Liabilities

Liabilities: definition

As shown in Illustration 2.1, liabilities appear lower down the statement of financial position and represent amounts that are owed to parties outside the business. As with assets, the first questions to ask are: 'What is a liability?' and 'What does a liability represent?'

The IASB's *Conceptual Framework for Financial Reporting* provides the following definition of a liability:

A present obligation of the entity to transfer an economic resource as a result of past events.

Source: IASB *The Conceptual Framework for Financial Reporting*, paragraph 4.26

While this definition again might seem complex, your experience gained in unravelling the meaning of the definition of assets will certainly help you in understanding the various terms employed here. To put it simply, liabilities are the contractual or legal claims of outside parties against an entity. These contractual or legal claims may be short term (current liabilities) or long term (non-current liabilities). Again, let's break down this definition into its constituent parts in order to enable us to apply it in determining whether an entity has a liability or not:

- Present obligation: the obligation must exist at the statement of financial position date in order for any liability arising under that obligation to be recognized in the statement of financial position. Therefore, entities cannot recognize just any liability that they think they might incur at any time in the future. The event giving rise to the obligation must have taken place by the statement of financial position date to enable the entity to recognize that liability.

- As a result of past events: to give rise to an obligation, it is likely that a contract has been signed agreeing to pay for goods delivered but not yet paid for from a supplier or to take out a loan or an overdraft at the bank that will have to be repaid at some point in the future.

- Economic resource: the obligation will result in the entity transferring cash to an outside party in order to settle the liability or, possibly, transferring other assets by way of settlement. The term economic resource has exactly the same definition as that provided under Assets: definition (this chapter).

Importantly, the obligation must be unavoidable: if the entity can avoid transferring cash or other economic resources then there is no obligation and no liability exists.

The IASB *Conceptual Framework* also requires that liabilities measured and presented in the statement of financial position must also meet the same standards of faithful representation as required for assets (this chapter, Assets: faithful representation). Where these standards of faithful representation are not met, no liability is recognized in the statement of financial position. Example 2.2 shows how application of this definition works in practice.

EXAMPLE 2.2

Let us take the example of Bunns the Bakers in Example 2.1. When the company bought the city centre shop from the property developer ten years ago, the purchase was financed by a loan from the bank of £500,000. This loan is currently repayable in full in 8 years' time. Does this loan constitute a liability of the business? Applying our criteria above:

- Does Bunns the Bakers have a present obligation at the statement of financial position date? Yes: the loan exists and is outstanding at the current year end. The obligating event (taking out the loan) had taken place by the statement of financial position date.

- Is the obligation to repay the loan unavoidable? Yes: the bank will hold signed documentation from the company agreeing that the loan was taken out and there will be entries in the relevant account at the bank and in bank statements to show the loan being received by the company. Should the company try to avoid repaying the loan, the bank will be able to enforce its legal rights against the company for repayment of the loan.
- Does the obligation arise as a result of past events? Yes: a loan agreement was signed by Bunns the Bakers at the time the loan was taken out and the money transferred to the company with which to buy the shop.
- Will Bunns the Bakers transfer an economic resource? Yes: the company will have to transfer cash to settle the obligation. If the company is unable to meet the obligation in cash, the bank will accept the shop as a suitable substitute for repayment of the loan. The shop embodies the potential to produce economic benefits as we saw in Example 2.1, so taking the shop instead of repayment will still be a transfer of an economic resource.
- Does the measurement of the liability result in a faithful representation? Yes: the loan is measured at £500,000 as a result of the cash transferred. This measurement is complete, neutral and free from error and so is a faithful representation of the amount of the obligation due to the bank.

Thus, the loan represents a liability of the business as it meets the IASB criteria for recognition of a liability.

Liability recognition: summary of the steps to follow

Diagrammatically, the steps to follow to determine whether a liability should be recognized on the statement of financial position are shown in Figure 2.4.

WHY IS THIS RELEVANT TO ME?   Liabilities

To enable you as a business professional and user of accounting information to:

- Understand what liabilities on the statement of financial position actually represent
- Understand the strict criteria that must be met before a liability can be recognized on the statement of financial position
- Be equipped with the necessary tools to determine whether a liability should be recognized on the statement of financial position or not

SUMMARY OF KEY CONCEPTS   Certain you can define a liability? Revise this definition with Summary of key concepts 2.3 to reinforce your knowledge.

GO BACK OVER THIS AGAIN!   How well have you grasped the liability recognition criteria? Go to the **online workbook** Exercises 2.4 to make sure you understand how the liability recognition criteria are used in practice.

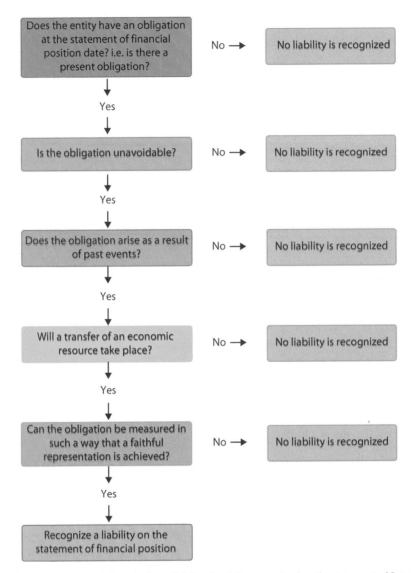

Figure 2.4 Steps in determining whether a liability should be recognized on the statement of financial position or not in accordance with the IASB *Conceptual Framework for Financial Reporting*

Liabilities in the statement of financial position

Now that we have considered what the term 'liabilities' means and the criteria for liability recognition in the statement of financial position, let us look again at the statement of financial position of Bunns the Bakers plc in Illustration 2.1 to consider what sorts of liabilities a company might recognize.

Liabilities, just as in the case of assets, are split into non-current and current. Total liabilities are calculated by adding current and non-current liabilities together, as shown in Figure 2.5.

Non-current liabilities are long-term liabilities that the entity will only have to meet in more than one year's time while current liabilities will have to be paid within the course of the next year. Current liabilities are not due on the day immediately after the statement of financial position date but they will be due for settlement over the course of the next 12 months.

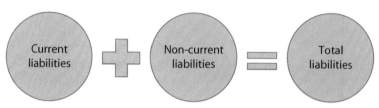

Figure 2.5 The composition of total liabilities

Current liabilities

Just as with current assets, current liabilities are short-term liabilities that are constantly changing. Looking at Bunns the Bakers' statement of financial position the following liabilities are shown:

- Current portion of long-term borrowings: these are the loan instalments due to be repaid to lenders within the next 12 months.

- Trade and other payables: any organization that is involved in business will trade on credit with their suppliers, both consuming services and ordering goods that are delivered but not paid for immediately. Customers then either use the goods received to produce more goods to sell to the public and businesses or just resell those goods. Suppliers are paid from the proceeds of the sales of goods produced or resold. Normal trading terms are that suppliers are (usually) paid within 30 days of receipt of goods by the customer. Clearly, suppliers will not wait a long time for payment for goods delivered as they have their own suppliers and employees to pay. Therefore, suppliers will expect their cash to be returned to them quickly so trade and other payables are short-term, current liabilities. In the case of Bunns the Bakers, trade payables will consist of amounts of money owed to suppliers for flour, eggs, sugar, salt and other bakery ingredients as well as services provided by, for example, their legal advisers or their accountants.

- Current tax liabilities: Bunns the Bakers plc has made a profit over the course of the year. This profit is subject to tax and the tax liability on this year's profit is recognized as an obligation on the statement of financial position. The government will want the tax due reasonably quickly so that it can meet its own obligations to provide services to the public and contribute to the running of government departments so this, too, is a short-term, current liability.

Non-current liabilities

On Bunns the Bakers' statement of financial position, the following non-current liabilities are represented:

- Long-term borrowings: these are loans and other finance provided by lenders to finance the long-term non-current assets of the business. In the case of Bunns the Bakers, these could be loans used to finance the acquisition of shops (as in Example 2.2), the building of a new state of the art bakery or the purchase of new plant and equipment with which to produce goods. Other companies may take out loans to finance the acquisition of other companies. Long-term borrowings are repayable in accounting periods beyond the next 12 months.

- Long-term provisions: these are liabilities that the entity knows it must meet but which will not be due in the next accounting period but in accounting periods beyond the next 12 months. An example of such a long-term provision would be deferred taxation, but this is a very technical subject that is beyond the scope of this book.

GIVE ME AN EXAMPLE 2.4   Non-current and current liabilities

What categories of non-current and current liabilities do companies present in their financial statements? The statement of financial position at 31 December 2017 of Nichols plc shows the following current and non-current liabilities.

	31 December	
	2017	**2016**
Current liabilities	£000	£000
Trade and other payables	21,031	21,456
Current tax liabilities	2,536	2,355
Total current liabilities	23,567	23,811
Non-current liabilities	£000	£000
Pension obligations and employee benefits	2,921	6,395
Deferred tax liabilities	1,586	1,101
Total non-current liabilities	4,507	7,496
Total liabilities	28,074	31,307

Source: *Nichols Plc Annual report and financial statements 2017* www.nicholsplc.co.uk

As in the case of Bunns the Bakers, Nichol's current liabilities present trade and other payables and current tax liabilities. Nichols plc has no borrowings so this is not a category of either current or non-current liabilities on the statement of financial position. Non-current liabilities are made up of deferred tax and pension liabilities, both long-term obligations for the business.

WHY IS THIS RELEVANT TO ME? Current and non-current liabilities

To enable you as a business professional and user of accounting information to:

- Appreciate the different types of liabilities an entity recognizes on its statement of financial position
- Distinguish between the two types of liabilities
- Use the different types of liabilities in assessing an entity's financial position, short-term liquidity and long-term financial stability (discussed in detail in Chapter 7)

GO BACK OVER THIS AGAIN! Quite convinced that you can distinguish between current and non-current liabilities? Go to the **online workbook** Exercises 2.5 to make sure you can make this distinction.

The accounting equation

Before we think about the third element on Bunns the Bakers' statement of financial position, equity, we need to think about the **accounting equation**. Looking at the statement of financial position, we notice that the net assets (total assets – total liabilities) and the total equity are the same figure. What does this tell us about the relationship between the assets, liabilities and equity in an entity? From this observation, we can draw up the following equations that express the link between the three elements in the statement of financial position:

Either:

Total assets = total liabilities + equity

Or:

Total assets – total liabilities = equity

Equity is thus the difference between the total assets (the sum of the current and non-current assets) and the total liabilities (the sum of the current and non-current liabilities). As the two equations add to the same figure, the statement of financial position is said to balance.

WHY IS THIS RELEVANT TO ME? The accounting equation

To enable you as a business professional and user of accounting information to:

- Appreciate how the two halves of the statement of financial position balance
- Balance your own statements of financial position when you draw these up in the future

---

SUMMARY OF KEY CONCEPTS   Can you state the accounting equation? Revise this equation with Summary of key concepts 2.4.

Equity

2

The IASB defines equity as follows:

> The residual interest in the assets of the entity after deducting all its liabilities.
>
> Source: IASB *The Conceptual Framework for Financial Reporting*, paragraph 4.63

This is exactly the same as the accounting equation that says assets – liabilities = equity. In theory, equity represents the amount that owners of the entity should receive if the assets were all sold and the liabilities were all settled at their statement of financial position amounts. The cash received from these asset sales less payments made to discharge liabilities would belong to the owners and they would receive this cash on the winding up of the business. As well as the term equity, you will often find the term capital being used to describe this difference between assets and liabilities.

The components of equity

Different forms of business entity present the equity part of the statement of financial position in different ways. We shall discuss the characteristics of different types of business entity in much more detail in Chapter 5. The two ways in which to present the equity section of the statement of financial position that we shall consider at this point are firstly the equity of limited companies and public limited companies (both incorporated businesses) and secondly the equity of sole traders and other unincorporated businesses.

1. The equity section of the statement of financial position: limited companies and public limited companies (plcs)

Bunns the Bakers' equity is made up of the following elements:

(a) Called up **share capital**: this is the number of shares issued multiplied by the **par value** (face value or nominal value) of each share (Chapter 5, Share capital: share issues at par value).

(b) **Share premium**: where each share is issued for an amount greater than its par value, then any amount received in excess of par value is entered into the share premium account (Chapter 5, Share capital: shares issued at a premium).

(c) Retained earnings: these are profits that the business has earned in past accounting periods that have not yet been distributed to shareholders as dividends.

You will see many company statements of financial position in practice that have many different accounts (other reserves) under the equity heading (see Give me an example 2.5). Many of these accounts arise from statutory requirements governing transactions entered into by the company and, due to their specialized nature, consideration of these accounts does not form part of this book. However, when you come across these accounts at later stages of your studies and during your career in business, you should just be aware that these accounts exist and form part of equity. The basic calculation of equity for limited companies and plcs is shown in Figure 2.6.

GIVE ME AN EXAMPLE 2.5   Equity

The consolidated balance sheet (= statement of financial position) of First Group plc at 31 March 2017 provides an illustration of the many different accounts that can make up equity. As in the case of Bunns the Bakers, First Group plc reports figures for share capital, share premium and retained earnings but also presents various other reserves that are included within its total equity figure.

	31 March	
	2017	2016
Equity	£m	£m
Share capital	60.4	60.2
Share premium	678.9	676.4
Hedging reserve	(17.9)	(68.6)
Other reserves	4.6	4.6
Own shares	(1.2)	(1.4)
Translation reserve	708.4	352.2
Retained earnings	621.9	585.4
	2,055.1	1,608.8

Source: *First Group plc annual report and accounts for the year ended 31 March 2017* www.firstgroupplc.com

---

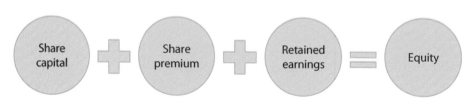

Figure 2.6 Limited companies and plcs: the components of equity

2. Sole traders and unincorporated entities

   Not all businesses are incorporated as limited companies. Such businesses do not, therefore, have issued share capital, but they still have an equity section. For sole traders and unincorporated entities, this is called the **capital account**. This comprises the following headings:

   (a) Capital at the start of the year: this is the capital account balance at the end of the previous accounting period. At the beginning of the first accounting period, the first year in which the unincorporated entity starts trading, the balance at the start of the year is £nil.

   (b) Capital introduced: this is the owner's own money that has been introduced into the business during the current accounting period.

   (c) Retained profits for the year: any profit retained in the business during the year is added to the capital account as this profit belongs to the business's owner. Should the business make a loss during the year, then this loss is deducted from the capital account.

   (d) Capital withdrawn: the business's owner will draw money out of the business to meet personal rather than business expenses during the year. This is treated as a repayment of part of the capital of the business to the owner. These withdrawals of capital are called **drawings** and are a deduction from the capital account. This is an application of the **business entity convention** (Chapter 3, Drawings and the business entity assumption) that states that the business and its owner(s) are totally separate individuals. Only business transactions are included in the financial statements of the business with any non-business, personal transactions excluded.

Just as in the case of limited companies and plcs, the amount in the capital account is the amount that would, in theory, be paid out to the owner(s) of the business if all the assets of the business were sold at the amounts recorded in the statement of financial position and all the liabilities of the business were settled at their statement of financial position amounts. The components and calculation of the capital account (equity) balance for sole traders and unincorporated entities is shown in Figure 2.7.

WHY IS THIS RELEVANT TO ME?   Equity and the components of equity

To enable you as a business professional and user of accounting information to:

- Understand that equity is the difference between an entity's total assets and total liabilities
- Appreciate the different components of equity in incorporated and unincorporated businesses
- Distinguish elements of equity from assets and liabilities

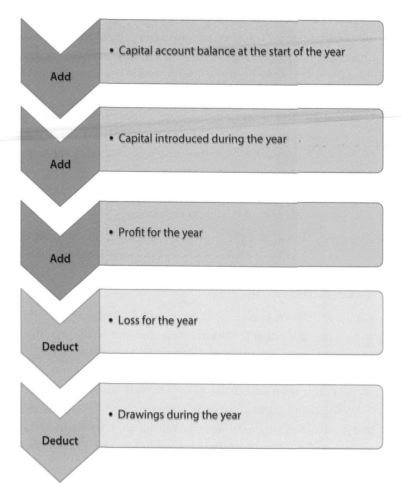

Figure 2.7 Sole traders and unincorporated entities: the components of equity (the capital account)

MULTIPLE CHOICE QUESTIONS   Confident that you could calculate the equity of a business from a given set of information? Go to the **online workbook** and have a go at Multiple choice questions 2.2 to make sure you can make these calculations.

SUMMARY OF KEY CONCEPTS   Sure you can state the components of equity? Revise these components with Summary of key concepts 2.5 and 2.6.

Drawing up the statement of financial position

We now know what assets and liabilities are and how they relate to equity, but what steps should we follow in drawing up the statement of financial position? This section provides a step-by-step approach using Example 2.3 to preparing the statement of financial position from the account balances at the end of the financial year.

EXAMPLE 2.3

The following is a list of balances for Misfits Limited at 31 December 2019. You are required to draw up the statement of financial position from this list of balances.

Illustration 2.2 Misfits Limited: account balances at 31 December 2019

	£000
Trade receivables	2,000
Trade payables	1,500
Bank loan repayable in six years' time	10,000
Bank overdraft	200
Land and buildings	15,000
Trademarks	1,000
Fixtures and fittings	2,500
Share capital	1,800
Retained earnings	7,500
Share premium	2,300
Inventories	2,750
Cash in the tills	50

Guidelines on the approach to adopt in drawing up the statement of financial position are as follows:

1. First, decide whether each of the balances is an asset, a liability or an element of equity.

2. Once you have categorized the balances, think about whether the assets and liabilities are current or non-current.

3. Some of the balances might need adding together to produce one figure in the statement of financial position. For example, there might be cash in hand or in the safe, cash in the bank current account and cash on deposit in a short-term investment account at the bank. All of these balances would be added together and shown as one figure for cash and cash equivalents.

4. Once you have made all your decisions, slot the figures into the relevant headings (use the headings in Illustration 2.1, adding any additional headings you might need and removing headings you do not need), add it all up and it should balance.

Illustration 2.3 Misfits Limited: statement of financial position at 31 December 2019

	£000	Note
Assets		
Non-current assets		
Intangible assets	1,000	1
Property, plant and equipment	17,500	2
	18,500	3
Current assets		
Inventories	2,750	4
Trade receivables	2,000	4
Cash and cash equivalents	50	4
	4,800	5
Total assets	23,300	6
Liabilities		
Current liabilities		
Bank overdraft (you could call this short-term borrowings)	200	7
Trade payables	1,500	7
	1,700	8
Non-current liabilities		
Bank loan (you could call this long-term borrowings)	10,000	7
Total liabilities	11,700	9
Net assets (total assets – total liabilities)	11,600	10
Equity		
Called up share capital	1,800	11
Share premium	2,300	11
Retained earnings	7,500	11
Total equity	11,600	12

Notes to the above statement of financial position for Misfits Limited:

1. Trademarks are intangible assets, as we noted previously (this chapter, Non-current assets).

2. Land and buildings and fixtures and fittings are both classified under the heading 'Property, plant and equipment'. The land and buildings are property and the fixtures and fittings are plant and equipment. £15,000,000 for the land and buildings + £2,500,000 for the fixtures and fittings give the total figure of £17,500,000 for Property, plant and equipment.

3. This is the total of the two non-current asset headings £1,000,000 + £17,500,000 = £18,500,000.

4. These figures are as given in the list of balances.

5. £4,800,000 is the total of all the current assets added together.

6. £23,300,000 is the total non-current assets of £18,500,000 added to the total current assets of £4,800,000 to give the figure for total assets.

7. These figures are as given in the list of balances. If you were in any doubt that the loan is a non-current liability, look at the timing of repayment: the loan is due for repayment in six years' time so this liability is repayable more than 12 months after the statement of financial position date. Remember that current liabilities include all obligations payable within 12 months of the year end date so that any liability payable after this is a non-current liability.

8. £1,700,000 is the total of the bank overdraft of £200,000 and of the trade payables of £1,500,000.

9. £11,700,000 is the total of the current liabilities of £1,700,000 and of the non-current liabilities of £10,000,000.

10. The figure for net assets is given by deducting the total liabilities figure of £11,700,000 from the total assets figure of £23,300,000 to give you net assets (total assets – total liabilities) of £11,600,000.

11. Called up share capital, Share premium and Retained earnings are all as given in the list of balances.

12. This is the total of the three elements of equity added together.

WHY IS THIS RELEVANT TO ME? Drawing up the statement of financial position

To enable you as a business professional and user of accounting information to:

- Understand how the statement of financial position is put together from the balances at the year end date
- Draw up and present your own statements of financial position

---

SHOW ME HOW TO DO IT   Did you understand how Misfits Limited's statement of financial position was drawn up? View Video presentation 2.1 in the **online workbook** to see a practical demonstration of how this statement of financial position was put together.

NUMERICAL EXERCISES   Are you sure that you could draw up a statement of financial position from a list of year end balances? Go to the **online workbook** Numerical exercises 2.1 to practise this technique.

How are assets and liabilities valued?

Historic cost v. fair value

How should we value assets and liabilities for inclusion in the statement of financial position? At their cost price? Selling price? Market value? Or some other amount?

Accounting has traditionally dictated that the value of all assets and liabilities recognized in the statement of financial position should be based on their original cost: this is called the **historic cost** convention. Thus, for example, inventory is valued at its cost to the business, not its selling price or current market value, while trade payables are valued at their invoice amount and loans are valued at the amount borrowed less any repayments made.

However, this accounting convention has been relaxed over the past 50 years and entities can now choose to value different classes of assets either at their historic cost or at their **fair value**. Fair value is equivalent to market value, the amount at which an asset could be sold or a liability settled in the open market. However, although the cost or fair value option exists, organizations rarely choose the fair value alternative. The only class of assets that entities might wish to present at their fair value is land and buildings as these assets tend to rise in value over time. For all other assets and liabilities historic cost is preferred.

But there is one exception to this option. The IASB has made market valuations mandatory for all investments held by organizations. This is often called the 'mark to market' approach to valuation of these assets.

A mixture of original cost and fair value: problems

So, users can be presented with a mixture of assets at cost and at fair value. Does this failure to present all assets and liabilities consistently at fair/market values cause any problems for users of the statement of financial position?

Historic cost is seen as objective as it is verifiable by reference to a transaction at a fixed point in time. It is thus a reliable measure as it was determined by the market at the date of the transaction. With short-term current assets and liabilities this is not a problem as these assets and liabilities are, as we have seen, always changing and being replaced by new current assets at more recent, up-to-date values. However, when long-term, non-current assets and liabilities are measured at historic cost these costs gradually become more and more out of date as time moves on. As a result, these costs become less and less relevant in decision making as the market moves forward and asset and loan values rise and fall in real terms with the onward march of the economy.

We will not consider this problem any further in this text, but it is a difficulty of which you should be aware. The cost v. fair/market value debate has been raging for well over a century and an acceptable solution is no nearer than it was when the problem was first pointed out. It is therefore going to be a continuing shortcoming of the statement of financial position for the indefinite future and a limitation that you will need to take into account whenever you are looking at these statements in your career in business.

WHY IS THIS RELEVANT TO ME?   Historic cost and fair/market values

To enable you as a business professional and user of accounting information to:

- Understand the basis upon which the figures in the statement of financial position are determined
- Appreciate the limitations of continuing to value non-current assets and liabilities at historic cost
- Appreciate that there are alternative valuation bases for non-current assets and liabilities, but that companies rarely make use of these alternatives

---

What does the statement of financial position show?

This leads us neatly on to a discussion of what the statement of financial position shows and what it does not show.

Put simply, the statement of financial position shows the financial situation of an entity on the last day of its accounting year. However, it is important to remember that the statement of financial position just shows the financial situation on that one day in the year and it is thus a snapshot of the entity at this one point in time. A totally different view would be shown if the picture were taken on any other day in the year. It is true to say that, at this one point in time, the statement of financial position does show the financially measurable resources (assets) and financially measurable obligations (liabilities) of the business in money terms, but this might seem to present a rather limited view.

In order to gain a better understanding of what the statement of financial position represents, it is useful to consider what the statement of financial position does not show.

2

What the statement of financial position does not show

The statement of financial position does not show:

- All the assets of the organization. The statement of financial position does not include or value the most valuable assets of an organization. These are made up of the skills and knowledge of the employees, goodwill, brands, traditions and all the other intangible but extremely difficult to value assets that make an organization what it is. All entities are so much more than the sum of their financial assets and liabilities. Any attempted valuation of these assets would present values that were so uncertain and subjective that the information presented would lack the relevance and faithful representation required by the IASB in its *Conceptual Framework* (this chapter, Assets: faithful representation).

- All the liabilities of a business. There might be liabilities for damage caused to the environment or to consumers as a result of product liability legislation, claims for damages or breaches of contract, none of which has come to light by the year end date: as a result, these additional liabilities will not be reflected in the statement of financial position at the accounting year end.

- The market value of an entity. This is a common misconception about the statement of financial position. The monetary value of any entity is determined by the amount a third party would be willing to pay not only for all the known assets and liabilities but also for the unrecognized assets of the organization noted above. However, the amount an outside party would be willing to pay will change on a daily basis as more information comes to light about hidden liabilities or the true value of assets or as the economy moves from a boom to a recession or vice versa.

The IASB recognizes these limitations of financial statements in full:

> General purpose financial reports are not designed to show the value of a reporting entity; but they provide information to help existing and potential investors, lenders and other creditors to estimate the value of the reporting entity . . . The *Conceptual Framework* does not allow the recognition in the statement of financial position of items that do not meet the definition of an asset, a liability or equity. Only items that meet the definition of an asset, a liability or equity are recognized in the statement of financial position.

> Source: IASB *Conceptual Framework for Financial Reporting*, paragraphs 1.7, 5.5 and 5.6

You should therefore remember that what the statement of financial position does not recognize is just as or even more important than what it does include.

EXAMPLE 2.4

A moment's thought will show you that this is equally true of your own circumstances. You might know the monetary value of the cash you hold in various bank and savings accounts and you might have a collection of various assets such as a tablet, a mobile phone, digital music and clothing, all of which you could value in money terms. But these assets are not the sum total of what represents you. There are your friends, family, memories and achievements, none of which can be valued or quantified, but which is just as or even more important to you than those tangible items that can be given a monetary value. Give me an example 2.6 demonstrates this further.

GIVE ME AN EXAMPLE 2.6 The statement of financial position does not show the true value of an entity

The published report and accounts for the year ended 31 December 2016 of Ablynx, the Belgian biotech group, showed a net assets (total assets less total liabilities) figure of €103m. In January 2018, Sanofi agreed to pay €3,900m to acquire Ablynx. Sanofi was bidding not for Ablynx's net assets but for its nanobody technology, its drugs in development, patented medicines and research, all of which represent value over and above the value of the net assets in the statement of financial position.

Sources: *Ablynx annual report for the year ended 31 December 2016* www.ablynx.com; *The Financial Times 30 January 2018* and Hargreaves Lansdown http://www.hl.co.uk/shares/stock-market-news/company--news/sanofi-to-buy-belgian-biotech-group-ablynx-for-3.9bn

WHY IS THIS RELEVANT TO ME? What the statement of financial position shows and does not show

To enable you as a business professional and user of accounting information to:

• Appreciate the limitations of the monetary information presented in the statement of financial position

• Have the necessary awareness of what the statement of financial position includes and does not include

• Be aware that the statement of financial position will not provide all the answers needed to evaluate an entity's financial and economic position

• Think outside the parameters of the statement of financial position when assessing an entity's standing in the business world

---

GO BACK OVER THIS AGAIN! Do you think that you can say clearly what the statement of financial position does and does not show? Go to the **online workbook** Exercises 2.6 to test your knowledge of this area.

2

The dual aspect concept

The statement of financial position for Misfits Limited was drawn up from a list of balances at a given point in time. But businesses are not static and new transactions will change the figures on the statement of financial position as they occur. These transactions have an effect on two or more accounts and may cause the balances on those accounts to rise or fall as new assets or liabilities are created or as assets are used up or liabilities settled. Accountants describe this dual aspect as double entry and the entries to the accounts affected by transactions as debits and credits. You might prefer to think of these transactions as pluses and minuses or increases and decreases in the various accounts in the following examples and in the online workbook. We are not going to look at double entry in any great depth in this book and you will not need a detailed knowledge of double entry bookkeeping for your career in business. However, an awareness of accountants' terminology and what this means in practice will be useful to you.

As an example, think about how you would record the receipt of goods from a supplier that are to be paid for in 30 days' time. This receipt of goods will increase the inventory that is held by the business, but also increase the amounts owed to trade payables. If the goods were bought for cash, this would still increase the inventory but reduce the cash held in the bank account (if the company has a positive balance in their account). In both of these examples, two accounts were affected, inventory and trade payables or cash.

Examples 2.5 and 2.6 will show you how the dual aspect concept works and how the statement of financial position will still balance after each transaction is completed.

EXAMPLE 2.5

Misfits Limited's statement of financial position at 31 December 2019 is reproduced in Illustration 2.4 in the left hand column. On 2 January 2020 the company receives a £50,000 payment from one of its trade receivables. This payment is paid into the bank account. How would this transaction be recorded in the statement of financial position? Trade receivables go down by £50,000 as this receivable has paid what was owed. The money has been paid into the bank so the bank overdraft (money owed to the bank) also goes down as less money is now owed to the bank. Recording the transactions as follows gives us the new statement of financial position at 2 January 2020:

Illustration 2.4 Misfits Limited: the effect on the statement of financial position of cash received from a trade receivable

Misfits Limited	Statement of financial position at 31 December 2019	Increase (plus)	Decrease (minus)	Statement of financial position at 2 January 2020
Non-current assets	£000	£000	£000	£000
Intangible assets	1,000			1,000
Property, plant and equipment	17,500			17,500
	18,500			18,500
Current assets				
Inventories	2,750			2,750
Trade receivables	2,000		– 50	1,950
Cash and cash equivalents	50			50
	4,800			4,750
Total assets	23,300			23,250
Current liabilities				
Bank overdraft	200		– 50	150
Trade payables	1,500			1,500
	1,700			1,650
Non-current liabilities				
Bank loan	10,000			10,000
Total liabilities	11,700			11,650
Net assets	11,600			11,600
Equity				
Called up share capital	1,800			1,800
Share premium	2,300			2,300
Retained earnings	7,500			7,500
	11,600			11,600

Current assets have been reduced by £50,000 and current liabilities have been reduced by £50,000 so the statement of financial position still balances.

EXAMPLE 2.6

Let's try another example. On 3 January 2020, the company receives £100,000 of inventory from a supplier, the invoice to be paid in 30 days' time, and acquires a new piece of property, plant and equipment for £75,000 paid for from the bank. How will these transactions change the figures in the statement of financial position? Illustration 2.5 shows the account headings affected.

Illustration 2.5 Misfits Limited: the effect on the statement of financial position of cash paid to buy new plant and equipment and inventory acquired on credit

Misfits Limited	Statement of financial position at 2 January 2020	Increase (plus)	Decrease (minus)	Statement of financial position at 3 January 2020
	£000	£000	£000	£000
Non-current assets				
Intangible assets	1,000			1,000
Property, plant and equipment	17,500	+ 75		17,575
	18,500			18,575
Current assets				
Inventories	2,750	+ 100		2,850
Trade receivables	1,950			1,950
Cash and cash equivalents	50			50
	4,750			4,850
Total assets	23,250			23,425
Current liabilities				
Bank overdraft	150	+ 75		225
Trade payables	1,500	+ 100		1,600
	1,650			1,825
Non-current liabilities				
Bank loan	10,000			10,000
Total liabilities	11,650			11,825
Net assets	11,600			11,600
Equity				
Called up share capital	1,800			1,800
Share premium	2,300			2,300
Retained earnings	7,500			7,500
	11,600			11,600

Non-current assets increase by £75,000 and the overdraft also increases by £75,000 as a result of the acquisition of the new piece of equipment paid for from the bank: assets have risen, but more money is now owed to the bank as more has been paid out so the bank overdraft goes up. Similarly, inventory has increased by £100,000, but more is now owed to trade payables so this figure has also risen by £100,000.

2

GO BACK OVER THIS AGAIN!   Do you understand how the dual aspect concept applies to new transactions? Go to the **online workbook** Exercises 2.7 to look at further examples of the dual aspect and the effect of new transactions on the statement of financial position.

NUMERICAL EXERCISES   Are you quite convinced that you could record new transactions accurately in the statement of financial position? Go to the **online workbook** Numerical exercises 2.2 to test out your abilities in this area.

MULTIPLE CHOICE QUESTIONS   Are you confident that you could state the correct entries to record a new transaction in the statement of financial position? Go to the **online workbook** and have a go at Multiple choice questions 2.3 to test your knowledge in this area.

This is probably the first time you have come across the duality principle, so if you are finding this confusing this should not surprise you. Further practice at more examples will help to reduce this confusion and you will gradually appreciate how the duality principle works and how transactions affect two or more accounts on the statement of financial position. However, do remember that you do not need to understand double entry to be able to evaluate sets of accounts, so do not give up at this early stage of your accounting studies.

CHAPTER SUMMARY

You should now have learnt that:

- An asset is a present economic resource controlled by the entity as a result of past events

- An economic resource is a right that has the potential to produce economic benefits

- A liability is a present obligation of the entity to transfer an economic resource as a result of past events

- Assets and liabilities are only recognized in the statement of financial position if their monetary values can be faithfully represented

- Non-current assets are resources not purchased for resale in the normal course of business and are held for long-term use in the business to produce goods or services

- Current assets consist of inventory, trade and other receivables and cash and cash equivalents whose economic benefits will be used up within 12 months of the statement of financial position date

- Current liabilities are obligations that will be settled within 12 months of the statement of financial position date, while non-current liabilities are obligations that will be settled in accounting periods beyond the next 12 months

- The accounting equation states that total assets – total liabilities = equity (capital)

- Some assets in the statement of financial position may be shown at historic cost, while some may be shown at fair (market) value

- The statement of financial position only presents figures for monetary resources (assets) whose economic benefits have not yet been consumed and figures for monetary obligations that have not yet been settled

- The statement of financial position does not show all the assets and liabilities of an entity nor does it give a market value for an entity

- Under the dual aspect concept (the duality principle), new accounting transactions affect two or more statement of financial position account headings

QUICK REVISION Test your knowledge with the online flashcards in Summary of key concepts and attempt the Multiple choice questions, all in the **online workbook**. www.oup.com/uk/scott_business3e/

END-OF-CHAPTER QUESTIONS

Solutions to these questions can be found at the back of the book from page 431.

❯ DEVELOP YOUR UNDERSTANDING

> Question 2.1

Using the criteria outlined in the summary in Figure 2.2, explain why the following items are assets that entities recognize on the statement of financial position:

(a) Motor vehicles purchased by an entity.

(b) Inventory received from suppliers.

(c) Cash and cash equivalents.

Using the criteria outlined in the summary in Figure 2.2, explain why the following items are *not* assets and why they are not recognized on entities' statements of financial position:

(a) Redundant plant and machinery that has been replaced by faster, more technologically advanced machinery. This redundant plant and machinery is no longer used in the business or industry and has no resale or scrap value.

(b) A trade receivable from a customer who is bankrupt and from whom no payment is expected.

(c) A highly skilled workforce.

> Question 2.2

The directors of Oxford Academicals Football Club Limited are discussing whether player registrations can be recognized as assets on the club's statement of financial position. There are two groups of players. The first group consists of those players whose contracts have been bought by the club from other teams through the transfer market. The second group is made up of players who have come up through the youth scheme and who have been playing at various levels for the club since the age of 12. The accounts department has informed the directors that the transfer fees for the bought in contracts amount to £25 million. The directors, however, cannot agree on a valuation for the players that have been developed by the club. The managing director thinks these players should be valued at £30 million, while the finance director thinks this is far too high a figure and would value these players at £15 million. Various offers have been received from other clubs to sign the players developed by the club and the combined values of these offers have ranged from £10 million to £25 million. Advise the directors on whether any of the players' registrations can be recognized in the statement of financial position and, if they can be recognized, the category of assets that these registrations would appear under and the value that can be recorded.

> Question 2.3

The following balances have been extracted from the books of the limited companies Alma, Bella, Carla, Deborah and Eloise at 30 April 2019. Using the statement of financial position format presented in this chapter, draw up the statement of financial positions for the five companies at 30 April 2019.

	Alma £000	Bella £000	Carla £000	Deborah £000	Eloise £000
Share capital	1,000	5,000	2,500	3,000	4,500
Cash at bank	—	800	—	550	200
Goodwill	—	—	400	250	500
Inventory	1,000	700	800	750	900
Trade payables	1,450	4,000	1,750	5,600	5,800
Plant and machinery	2,000	9,500	3,750	4,250	5,000
Trade receivables	1,750	3,000	2,750	2,950	3,100
Bank overdraft	800	—	1,250	—	—
Loans due on 30 April 2026	1,000	10,000	1,500	—	—
Loans due by 30 April 2020	200	400	300	—	—
Land and buildings	4,500	17,100	10,200	8,750	15,000
Taxation payable	540	1,100	800	—	—
Cash in hand	10	25	15	8	12
Trademarks	—	—	200	100	450
Motor vehicles	—	1,500	1,950	1,250	1,600
Tax repayment due	—	—	—	250	800
Retained earnings	2,770	4,625	7,465	5,508	8,262
Share premium	1,500	7,500	4,500	5,000	9,000

> **Question 2.4**

Maria runs a small corner shop. Her statement of financial position at 31 October 2019 is shown below.

	£
Non-current assets	
Property, plant and equipment	15,000
Current assets	
Inventory	20,000
Other receivables	3,000
Cash and cash equivalents	500
	23,500
Total assets	38,500
Current liabilities	
Bank overdraft	7,000
Trade and other payables	8,000
Taxation	3,000
Total liabilities	18,000
Net assets	20,500
Capital account	
Balance at 31 October 2019	20,500

The following transactions took place in the first week of November 2019:

- Trade payables of £3,500 were paid from the bank account.
- Maria paid £10,000 of her own money into the bank account.
- Inventory of £1,200 was sold for £2,000 cash, a profit of £800 for the week.
- New inventory of £2,500 was purchased on credit from her suppliers (trade payables).
- Maria withdrew £300 from cash for her own personal expenses.

Required

Show how the above transactions would increase or decrease the various balances on the statement of financial position and draw up and balance the new statement of financial position at 7 November 2019.

▶▶ TAKE IT FURTHER

» **Question 2.5**

Andy Limited's statement of financial position at 30 June 2019 is shown. The following transactions took place in the first week of July 2019:

- 1 July 2019: paid a trade payable with a bank transfer of £2,500 and received cash of £3,000 by bank transfer from a trade receivable.

- 2 July 2019: took out a bank loan (full repayment is due on 30 June 2022) with which to buy a new vehicle costing £20,000. The vehicle purchase agreement was signed on 2 July 2019.

- 4 July 2019: sold goods which had cost Andy £7,500 to a customer on credit terms, the customer agreeing to pay for those goods on 3 August 2019. The goods were sold for a selling price of £10,000.

- 5 July 2019: sold goods which had cost Andy £2,500 to a customer for £3,250. The customer paid cash for the goods.

- 6 July 2019: received new inventory from a supplier. The new inventory cost £15,000 and Andy Limited has agreed to pay for the inventory on 5 August 2019.

- 7 July 2019: paid tax of £3,000 and a trade payable of £7,000 by transfers from the bank account.

Required

Show how the above transactions would increase or decrease the various balances on Andy's statement of financial position and draw up and balance the new statement of financial position at 7 July 2019.

Andy Limited	
Statement of financial position at 30 June 2019	
ASSETS	**£**
Non-current assets	
Property, plant and equipment	320,000
Current assets	
Inventories	50,000
Trade receivables	75,000
Cash and cash equivalents	20,000
	145,000
Total assets	465,000
LIABILITIES	
Current liabilities	
Trade payables	80,000
Taxation	20,000
	100,000
Non-current liabilities	
Bank loan (long-term borrowings)	250,000
Total liabilities	350,000
Net assets	115,000
EQUITY	
Called up share capital	20,000
Retained earnings	95,000
Total equity	115,000

» Question 2.6

(a) The following figures have been extracted from the books of account of Frankie Limited at 31 December 2019.

	£000
Cash at bank	600
Land and buildings	15,500
Loans due for repayment by 31 December 2020	850
Share premium	4,000
Loans due for repayment on 31 December 2028	8,500
Cash in hand	5
Share capital	2,000
Goodwill	1,000
Taxation payable	1,380
Fixtures and fittings	1,670
Trade receivables	4,910
Plant and machinery	10,630
Trade payables	6,720
Retained earnings	13,365
Inventory	2,500

Required

Using the statement of financial position format presented in this chapter, draw up the statement of financial position for Frankie Limited at 31 December 2019.

(b) During January 2020, the following transactions took place:

- Bought £12,200,000 of inventory on credit from suppliers.
- Made sales on credit to customers of £15,500,000. The inventory cost of the sales made was £11,450,000.
- Took out a loan of £2,500,000 with which to purchase new plant and machinery for £2,500,000. The new loan is due for repayment on 31 December 2024.
- Held a share issue, which raised cash of £1,500,000. £500,000 of the total amount raised represents share capital while the remaining £1,000,000 represents share premium.

- Made a tax payment from the bank account of £690,000.
- Received £6,450,000 from trade receivables.
- Paid trade payables £8,210,000.
- Sold a surplus piece of land that had cost £2,000,000 for £2,500,000.
- Made a short-term loan repayment of £200,000.

Required

Using the statement of financial position for Frankie Limited drawn up at 31 December 2019, show how the above transactions would increase or decrease the various balances on the statement of financial position and draw up and balance the new statement of financial position at the end of January 2020.

3 The statement of profit or loss

LEARNING OUTCOMES

Once you have read this chapter and worked through the questions and examples in both this chapter and the online workbook, you should be able to:

- Define income and expenses

- Understand the different expense categories and profit figures that are presented in published financial statements

- Understand that revenue and costs in the statement of profit or loss represent income earned and expenditure incurred in an accounting period not just the cash received and cash paid in that period

- Apply the accruals basis of accounting in determining income earned and expenditure incurred in an accounting period

- Calculate prepayments and accruals at the end of an accounting period

- Define and calculate depreciation using both the straight line and reducing balance methods

- Make accounting adjustments to the statement of profit or loss to reflect the effect of irrecoverable debts, the allowance for receivables, sales returns, purchase returns, discounts allowed and discounts received

- Prepare a statement of profit or loss for an accounting period together with the statement of financial position at the end of that accounting period from a given set of information

Introduction

In the last chapter we looked at the statement of financial position. We noted that this statement just presents an entity's financial position on one day in the year, the financial year-end date. However, many users of financial information turn first of all not to the statement of financial position but to the main source of information about an entity's financial performance during an accounting period, **the statement of profit or loss**. This statement shows the income and expenditure of the entity for the year. The difference between income and expenditure represents the profit or loss that the entity has made during that financial year. It is this profit or loss figure that initially tends to be of most interest to financial statement users. A quick skim through the financial press on any day of the week will show you that profit or loss is one of the most discussed numbers in any set of financial statements. It is this figure, in many people's (and shareholders' and the stock market's) view, that determines whether a company has had a successful or unsuccessful year as shown by the two examples in Give me an example 3.1.

GIVE ME AN EXAMPLE 3.1   The importance of profits for businesses

Compare the stock market's reactions to these announcements from two different companies in late January and early February 2018.

On 31 January 2018, Capita plc, the outsourcing group, announced that profit before tax for the year to 31 December 2018 would be in the region of £270m–£300m. The market had been expecting a forecast profit for the 2018 calendar year of £400m. In the same announcement, the company said that it was suspending the dividend and looking to raise £700m through an issue of new shares. This news saw the share price fall to 182.50 pence from a closing price on 30 January 2018 of 347.80 pence. On 1 February 2018, the share price of the company fell further to 158.60 pence, a twenty year low.

Source: http://investors.capita.com

On 8 February, Compass Group, the worldwide food services group, announced revenue growth in the three months to 31 December 2017 of 5.9%. Based on this sales growth and other information in the trading update, analysts predicted a rise in profit before tax of over 5% for the year to 30 September 2018. Compass Group's shares rose 76.50 pence to 1,513.50 pence on the day, a rise of 5.32%.

Sources: https://www.compass-group.com and https://uk.webfg.com/news/news-and-announcements/compass-points-towards-north-end-of-growth-targets--3123305.html

---

Illustration 3.1 presents the statement of profit or loss for Bunns the Bakers plc for the years ended 31 March 2019 and 31 March 2018. This statement begins with income (**revenue**) and then deducts various categories of expenditure to reach the profit for the year. However, income and expenditure are not just simply money received and money spent during the year. There are various accounting conventions that have to be applied in the determination of income and costs for a period. How these conventions are applied to individual items of revenue and expenditure will determine the profit for each accounting period. The application of these conventions will form a large part of this chapter. Careful study of these applications will enable you to understand how income and expenditure are calculated and how, in turn, the profit or loss for a period is determined.

3

Terminology: statement of profit or loss/income statement/statement of financial performance/profit and loss account

The statement of profit or loss is also known as the income statement or the profit and loss account. In keeping with the International Financial Reporting Standards approach adopted in this book, the term 'statement of profit or loss' is used throughout, but you will still find entities presenting an 'income statement' or a 'profit and loss account'. Under the new IASB *Conceptual Framework for Financial Reporting*, the statement of profit or loss is just one component of the statement of financial performance. This statement of financial performance includes both the statement of profit or loss and a statement of other comprehensive income which presents details of other gains and losses arising in an accounting period from, for example, the revaluation of assets or changes in the valuation of pension liabilities. Consideration of the statement of other comprehensive income is beyond the scope of the present book. Our concern in this and subsequent chapters is with the income earned and expenditure incurred in the course of everyday trading operations of businesses that form the basis for the figures presented in the statement of profit or loss.

Note: in Illustration 3.1 income and profit figures are shown without brackets while items of expenditure are shown in brackets. This is to help you understand which items are subtracted and which items are added to determine the result (profit or loss) for the year. Taking revenue (= sales) and finance income as positive figures, subtract the expenses to ensure you understand the relationships between the figures and to make sure that:

- Revenue – cost of sales = gross profit
- Gross profit – distribution and selling costs – administration expenses = operating profit
- Operating profit + finance income – finance expense = profit before tax and
- Profit before tax – income tax = profit for the year.

Illustration 3.1 Bunns the Bakers plc: statement of profit or loss for the years ended 31 March 2019 and 31 March 2018

	2019	2018	
	£000	£000	
Revenue	10,078	9,575	
Cost of sales	(4,535)	(4,596)	
Gross profit	5,543	4,979	The trading part of the statement of profit or loss
Distribution and selling costs	(3,398)	(3,057)	
Administration expenses	(1,250)	(1,155)	
Operating profit	895	767	
Finance income	15	12	The financing part of the statement of profit or loss
Finance expense	(150)	(165)	
Profit before tax	760	614	
Income tax	(213)	(172)	
Profit for the year	547	442	

GO BACK OVER THIS AGAIN! A copy of this statement of profit or loss is available in the **online workbook:** you might like to keep this on screen or print off a copy for easy reference while you work your way through the material in this chapter. There is also an annotated copy of this statement of profit or loss in the **online workbook** to go over the relevant points again to reinforce your knowledge and learning.

Definitions

Illustration 3.1 shows the statement of profit or loss for Bunns the Bakers plc. As noted in the introduction, the statement of profit or loss contains items of revenue (income) and expenditure (costs incurred in making goods and selling them and in running and financing the company). Before we look at these different items of income and expenditure in more detail, let's start with some definitions.

Income

The International Accounting Standards Board (IASB) defines income as 'increases in assets, or decreases in liabilities, that result in increases in equity, other than those re-lating to contributions from holders of equity claims' (IASB *Conceptual Framework for*

Financial Reporting, paragraph 4.68). Let's break this definition down to understand what it means.

When you make a sale for cash, you have increased your cash asset. At the same time, this sales transaction also increases the equity of the business. The £s of assets are now higher as a result of the cash generated by the sale made while the £s of liabilities have remained the same (remember that assets – liabilities = equity, Chapter 2, Equity). Similarly, making a sale on credit to a customer who will pay at some later date increases the trade receivables asset while having no effect on liabilities so this increase in assets also increases the equity of the business. Likewise, a reduction in the £s of liabilities while the £s of assets remain the same will also increase equity.

However, not every increase in assets or decrease in liabilities will result in an increase in equity. Taking out a loan increases the cash asset but the borrowings liability rises by an equal and opposite amount so that there is no change in the assets – liabilities figure and, consequently, no increase in equity. Simply paying a trade payable what is owed reduces liabilities but the cash asset also falls by an equal and opposite amount so, again, there is no increase in the equity of the business. To recognize income there must always be an increase in the £s of equity when the £s of liabilities are deducted from the £s of assets.

The IASB definition of income also refers to 'increases in equity, other than those relating to contributions from holders of equity claims'. What does this mean? When business owners pay money into their businesses or shareholders subscribe for new shares in companies, these transactions increase both the cash asset and equity (Chapter 2, The components of equity). Assets have increased but these receipts are not income as they are money received from business owners or investors, both holders of equity claims: these amounts are now owed to the business's owners and shareholders and thus do not meet the definition of income.

Expenses

As you might have expected, given the definition of income, the IASB defines expenses as 'decreases in assets, or increases in liabilities, that result in decreases in equity, other than those relating to distributions to holders of equity claims' (IASB *Conceptual Framework for Financial Reporting*, paragraph 4.69). Again, let's break this definition down to understand what it means.

When a business pays cash to meet an expense, the cash asset decreases. At the same time, this transaction also decreases the equity of the business. The £s of assets are now lower as a result of the cash paid while the £s of liabilities have remained the same (assets – liabilities = equity, Chapter 2, Equity). Similarly, buying goods or services on credit will increase the trade payables liability while having no effect on the assets of the business so this increase in liabilities also decreases the equity of the business.

However, not every increase in liabilities or decrease in assets will result in a decrease in equity. Taking out a loan increases the borrowings liability but the cash asset rises by an equal and opposite amount so that there is no change in the equity (assets – liabilities) figure in the statement of financial position and, consequently, no decrease in equity. Likewise, paying cash to settle what is owed to a trade payable reduces the cash asset but it also reduces the trade payables liability by an equal and opposite amount so, again, there is no decrease in the equity of the business. To recognize an expense there must always be a decrease in the £s of equity when the £s of liabilities are deducted from the £s of assets.

The IASB definition of expenses also refers to 'decreases in equity, other than those relating to distributions to holders of equity claims'. What does this mean? When business owners take money out of their businesses or shareholders are paid a dividend, these transactions decrease both the cash asset and equity (Chapter 2, The components of equity). Assets have decreased but these payments are not an expense as they are cash paid out to business owners and shareholders, both holders of equity claims: these amounts have been paid out to the business's owners and shareholders in their capacity as holders of equity claims and thus do not meet the definition of expenses.

WHY IS THIS RELEVANT TO ME?   Definitions: income and expenses

To enable you as a business professional and user of accounting information to:

- Understand what income and expenditure in the statement of profit or loss represent
- Appreciate how entities meet the definitions by generating income and incurring expenses

---

SUMMARY OF KEY CONCEPTS   Can you remember the income and expenses definitions? Revise these definitions with Summary of key concepts 3.1 to reinforce your knowledge.

Income in the statement of profit or loss

The first line in Illustration 3.1 refers to Revenue. Revenue represents sales income earned in an accounting period (usually one year) and may be referred to in some sets of accounts as **sales** or **turnover** as well as by the term revenue. These three terms all refer to the same type of income, income from trading goods or providing services.

Revenue appears as the first item in the statement of profit or loss and arises from sales made by an entity in the ordinary (everyday) course of business. For Bunns the Bakers plc this will mean selling bread, sandwiches, cakes, hot snacks, drinks and other products associated with their primary (everyday) activity, selling bakery and related goods. Were Bunns the Bakers to sell one of their shops, this would not be a transaction in the ordinary course of business and would not be recorded as part of revenue: selling shops is not what a bakery company would be expected to do on a regular basis. Instead, the profit or loss on the sale of the shop would be recorded in a separate line for exceptional income in the statement of profit or loss below operating profit. The way in which entities record exceptional income in their financial statements is illustrated in Give me an example 3.2.

GIVE ME AN EXAMPLE 3.2   Recording exceptional income in the statement of profit or loss

The following extract from the consolidated income statement (= statement of profit or loss) of Rolls-Royce Holdings plc for the year ended 31 December 2013 shows exceptional income recorded below the operating profit line. Note that such exceptional income is not included in Revenue.

	£m
Operating profit	1,535
Profit on transfer of joint ventures to subsidiaries	119
Profit on disposal of businesses	216
Profit before financing and taxation	1,870

Source: *Rolls-Royce Holdings annual report 2013* www.rolls-royce.com

The first six lines in the statement of profit or loss (from Revenue down to Operating profit) thus consist of items relating to the everyday trading activity of the organization. Therefore, items of income and expense that do not relate to trading are excluded from the revenue, cost of sales, distribution and selling costs and administration expenses categories in the statement of profit or loss.

Not all income will arise from an entity's regular or trading activities. The other element of income shown in Bunns the Bakers plc's statement of profit or loss is Finance income. This will consist of interest income received and receivable from the company's bank on deposits of surplus cash held in Bunns' account(s) or dividends received and receivable from the company's investments. As Bunns the Bakers is not a bank, earning interest is not part of its everyday trading activities in the ordinary course of business, so any interest earned in the period is disclosed on a separate line. This income is disclosed outside the trading part of the statement of profit or loss in its own separate section. Figure 3.1 summarizes the three different types of income in the statement of profit or loss.

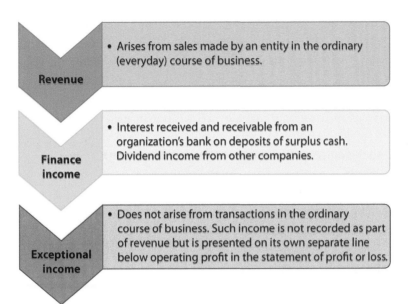

Figure 3.1 The different types of income in the statement of profit or loss

WHY IS THIS RELEVANT TO ME?   Income categorized under different headings

To enable you as a business professional and user of accounting information to:

- Read a published statement of profit or loss and to understand what each category of income represents
- Appreciate that not all income arises from sales made in the ordinary course of business

GO BACK OVER THIS AGAIN!   Are you confident that you understand how revenue in the statement of profit or loss is split into income from sales made in the ordinary course of business, finance income and exceptional income? Go to the **online workbook** and complete Exercises 3.1 to make sure you can distinguish between these different types of income.

Expenditure in the statement of profit or loss

Expenditure in Bunns the Bakers' statement of profit or loss falls under various headings. Let's look at each of these in turn.

Cost of sales

This heading comprises those costs incurred directly in the making or buying in of products. In the case of Bunns the Bakers, there will be the cost of the raw materials such as flour, fat, salt, cream, sugar and all the other ingredients that go into the bread, cakes, hot snacks and sandwiches, as well as goods bought in ready made from other manufacturers such as soft drinks and chocolate bars. In addition, the wages of the bakers, the electricity or gas used in heating the ovens and all the other associated costs of making or buying in the products will be included in cost of sales.

Determining the cost of making the products is important. The cost of the product is usually the starting point for setting a selling price at which customers will buy and to cover all the other costs of the operation so that a profit is made (see Chapter 8). In smaller entities, as we shall see shortly (Chapter 3, Statement of profit or loss by nature), cost of sales is usually calculated as: opening inventory of goods at the start of the accounting period + purchases during the accounting period − closing inventory of goods at the end of the accounting period.

Distribution and selling costs

These costs will comprise all those costs incurred in the distribution and selling of the products. For Bunns the Bakers, advertising would fall under this heading, as would the transport of bakery goods produced from the main bakery to each of the individual shops. The wages of shop staff would be part of selling costs, too, as would the costs of running the shops, including shop expenditure on goods and services such as cleaning, repairs, electricity, maintenance, rent, rates and water.

Administration expenses

This category covers all the costs of running the trading operation that do not fall under any other heading. Examples of such costs for Bunns the Bakers (and many other entities) would be legal expenses, accountancy and audit costs, directors' salaries, accounting department costs, bank charges and human resources department expenditure. Such costs are essential in running the business, but they cannot be allocated to the costs of making and producing or distributing and selling the goods sold by the organization. Figure 3.2 summarizes the different types of trading expenditure incurred in running a business.

GO BACK OVER THIS AGAIN!   Are you convinced that you can distinguish between expenses that belong in the cost of sales, selling and distribution and administration sections of the statement of profit or loss? Go to the **online workbook** and complete Exercises 3.2 to make sure you can make these distinctions.

Finance expense

As with finance income, this expense is not incurred as part of the trading activities of the business. Finance expense is made up of interest paid on the borrowings used to finance the business. Look back at Illustration 2.1: Bunns the Bakers' statement

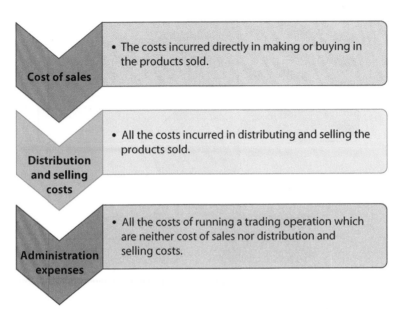

Cost of sales
- The costs incurred directly in making or buying in the products sold.

Distribution and selling costs
- All the costs incurred in distributing and selling the products sold.

Administration expenses
- All the costs of running a trading operation which are neither cost of sales nor distribution and selling costs.

Figure 3.2 The different types of trading expenditure incurred in running a business

of financial position shows that the company has borrowings under current and non-current liabilities. The finance expense will be the interest charged on these borrowings.

Income tax

The final expense to be deducted in Bunns the Bakers' statement of profit or loss is income tax. All commercial entities have to pay tax on their profits according to the tax law of the country in which they are resident and in which they operate. UK companies pay corporation tax on their profits but the IASB presentation format requires the heading income tax for all taxes paid on company profits. This income tax charge is based on the profits of the entity for the accounting period and the entity would expect to pay this tax at some point in the coming financial year. Figure 3.3 represents the five different categories of costs that are found in the statement of profit or loss.

WHY IS THIS RELEVANT TO ME?   Expenditure categorized under different headings

To enable you as a business professional and user of accounting information to:

- Appreciate that expenses are categorized according to different types of expenditure
- Read a published statement of profit or loss and understand what each category of expenditure represents

Figure 3.3 The different categories of costs (expenditure) in a typical statement of profit or loss

---

MULTIPLE CHOICE QUESTIONS   Are you certain that you can distinguish between items that belong in the various categories of income and expenditure in the statement of profit or loss? Go to the **online workbook** and complete Multiple choice questions 3.1 to make sure you can make these distinctions.

Different categories of profit

Bunns the Bakers' statement of profit or loss presents several different lines describing various different numbers as 'profit'. Why are there so many different figures for profit and what does each of them tell us about the profits of the company? The following observations can be made:

- **Gross profit** = revenue – cost of sales: this is the profit that arises when all the direct costs of production of the goods sold are deducted from the sales revenue earned in the accounting period.

- **Operating profit** = gross profit – distribution and selling costs – administration expenses: the profit that remains when all the other operating costs not directly associated with the production or buying in of goods are deducted from the gross profit. Alternatively, this is the profit after all the costs of trading, direct (cost of sales) and indirect (distribution and selling costs and administration expenses), are deducted from sales revenue.

- **Profit before tax** = operating profit + finance income – finance expense: the profit that remains once the costs of financing operations have been deducted and any finance or other income has been added onto operating profit.

- **Profit for the year** = profit before tax – income tax (also called the **profit after tax** or the **net profit**): this is the profit that is left once the tax on the profits for the

Figure 3.4 The different categories of profit in a typical company statement of profit or loss

accounting period has been deducted from the profit before tax. Alternatively, this is the profit that remains once all the expenses have been deducted from the sales revenue and any other income for the accounting period added on. This profit is now available to the company to distribute to the shareholders as a dividend or to retain within the business to finance future expansion. Figure 3.4 presents the different categories of profit.

WHY IS THIS RELEVANT TO ME?   Different categories of profit

To enable you as a business professional and user of accounting information to:

- Understand the accounting terminology describing the various categories of profit
- Understand how trading and financing activities have contributed to the results for the accounting period

GO BACK OVER THIS AGAIN!   Quite sure that you can remember how each different profit figure is calculated and what it means? Go to the **online workbook** and complete Exercises 3.3 to reinforce your learning.

SUMMARY OF KEY CONCEPTS   Can you state the different profit figure calculations? Revise these calculations with Summary of key concepts 3.2 to check your understanding.

Statement of profit or loss by nature

The statement of profit or loss for Bunns the Bakers plc (Illustration 3.1) is presented in the format that you will find in published financial statements for limited and public limited companies which requires the classification of expenses by function (cost of sales, distribution and selling costs, administration expenses, finance expense). How-ever, the rest of this chapter will use examples and exercises based on the statement of profit or loss format in Illustration 3.2 , the format that is used every day by traders and companies as a simple way to present income and expenditure to determine whether a profit or loss has been made. Study this format now along with the notes below.

Illustration 3.2 A trader: statement of profit or loss by nature for the year ended 31 March 2019

	£	£
Sales		347,250
Opening inventory	13,600	
Purchases	158,320	
Closing inventory	(17,500)	
Cost of sales (opening inventory + purchases – closing inventory)		154,420
Gross profit (sales – cost of sales)		192,830
Expenses (can be listed in any order required)		
Heat and light	9,500	
Motor expenses	12,250	
Rent and rates	25,685	
Wages and salaries	48,345	
Administration expenses	10,050	
Accountancy	2,000	
Legal expenses	1,950	
Bank interest	6,000	
Depreciation of non-current assets	24,000	
Insurance	7,500	
Miscellaneous	1,890	
Total expenses (all expenses items added together)		149,170
Bank interest received		950
Net profit (gross profit – total expenses + bank interest received)		44,610

GO BACK OVER THIS AGAIN! How would the income and expenditure in Illustration 3.2 be presented in the published financial statements format which presents expenses by func-tion? Go to the **online workbook** Exercises 3.4 to see how the above information would be summarized ready for publication.

Notes to the statement of profit or loss in Illustration 3.2:

- The statement of profit or loss by nature consists of three sections: sales, cost of sales and expenses.

- Just as in the case of published statements of profit or loss, sales are made up of all the revenue derived from the ordinary activities of the business.

- Cost of sales is the opening inventory of unsold goods at the start of the year, plus purchases of goods during the year, less the closing inventory of unsold goods at the end of the year.

- Expenses are listed in any order: there is no set order in which expenses have to be presented.

- Expenses would include finance expense if an entity has incurred any interest costs relating to money borrowed to finance the business (Bank interest in Illustration 3.2) while finance income (interest receivable) is shown on a separate line below total expenses (Bank interest received in Illustration 3.2).

- Note the format of the statement: the component parts of Cost of sales and Expenses are listed in the left hand column and then the figures for Cost of sales and Expenses are totalled in the right hand column and deducted from Sales and Gross profit respectively.

- As in Bunns the Bakers' statement of profit or loss, sales – cost of sales = gross profit and gross profit – total expenses = net profit (profit for the year) for the accounting period.

WHY IS THIS RELEVANT TO ME?   Statement of profit or loss by nature

To enable you as a business professional and user of accounting information to understand:

- That statements of profit or loss for internal use within businesses adopt a different format to that presented in published statements of profit or loss

- How to draw up statements of profit or loss by nature for presentation to interested parties

- What the income and two categories of expenditure represent

---

NUMERICAL EXERCISES   Do you think that you could prepare statements of profit or loss by nature from a given set of information? Go to the **online workbook** and complete Numerical exercises 3.1 to test out your ability to prepare these statements.

SUMMARY OF KEY CONCEPTS   Reckon that you can state how cost of sales is calculated? Revise this calculation with Summary of key concepts 3.3 to check your knowledge.

Now that we have looked at the presentation of the statement of profit or loss and what it contains, it is time to find out how income and expense are determined in an accounting period.

Determining the amount of income or expense

At the start of this chapter we noted that income and expenditure are not just simply money received and money spent, though cash received and cash paid are the starting point when preparing any set of financial statements. Revenue for an accounting period consists of all the sales made during that period, whether the cash from those sales has been received or not. Where a sale has been made but payment has not been received the entity recognizes both a sale and a trade receivable at the end of the accounting period. This trade receivable is money due to the entity from a customer to whom the entity has made a valid sale. Thus, the entity recognizes this sale in the statement of profit or loss as part of sales for the period and as a trade receivable in the statement of financial position. Where a sale has been made and the cash received, the entity recognizes the sale in the statement of profit or loss and the increase in cash in the statement of financial position.

Diagrammatically, the above transactions can be represented as shown in Table 3.1.

Table 3.1 Cash and credit sales: statement of profit or loss and statement of financial position effects

	Statement of profit or loss effect	Cash received?	Statement of financial position effect
Sale made for cash	Increase revenue	Yes	Increase cash
Sale made on credit, payment due in 30 days	Increase revenue	No	Increase trade receivables
Cash received from trade receivable	No effect: no new revenue	Yes	Increase cash, decrease trade receivables

Give me an example 3.3 illustrates Nestlé's revenue recognition policy, which matches exactly the approach outlined in Table 3.1. As soon as goods are sent to a customer, Nestlé recognizes the sale whether the cash has been received from the customer or not.

GIVE ME AN EXAMPLE 3.3   At what point in time do commercial organizations recognize revenue in their financial statements?

The following accounting policy regarding the timing of revenue recognition is taken from Nestlé's financial statements for the year ended 31 December 2017:

Revenue

Sales represent amounts received and receivable from third parties for goods supplied to the customers and for services rendered. Revenue from the sales of

→

goods is recognized in the income statement [= statement of profit or loss] at the moment when the significant risks and rewards of ownership of the goods have been transferred to the buyer, which is mainly upon shipment.

Source: *Nestlé financial statements 2017* www. nestle.com, p. 71

Note that revenue comprises both cash received ('amounts received') and cash receivable ('amounts receivable'). Revenue is thus not just the cash received in an accounting period, it represents all the revenue that an entity has earned during an accounting period whether the cash has been received or not.

Similarly, expenses are not just the money paid during an accounting period for goods and services received but *all* the expenses incurred in that period whether they have been paid for or not. Where an entity has incurred an expense during an accounting period but not paid this amount by the statement of financial position date, then the entity records the expense along with a trade payable. This trade payable represents an obligation owed by the entity at the end of the accounting period for an expense validly incurred during that accounting period. If the expense has been paid then the expense is recognized along with a reduction in cash.

Diagrammatically, these transactions can be represented as shown in Table 3.2.

Table 3.2 Cash and credit expenses: statement of profit or loss and statement of financial position effects

	Statement of profit or loss effect	Cash paid?	Statement of financial position effect
Expense paid for with cash	Increase expenses	Yes	Decrease cash
Expense incurred on credit, payment due in 30 days	Increase expenses	No	Increase trade payables
Cash paid to trade payable	No effect: no new expense	Yes	Decrease cash, decrease trade payables

Give me an example 3.4 illustrates Nestlé's expenses recognition policy, which matches exactly the approach outlined in Table 3.2. As soon as goods or service are received, Nestlé recognizes the expense whether the cash has been paid by the company or not.

GIVE ME AN EXAMPLE 3.4 At what point in time do commercial organizations recognize costs and expenses in their financial statements?

The following accounting policy regarding the timing of expense recognition is taken from

Nestlé's financial statements for the year ended 31 December 2017:

Expenses

Cost of goods sold is determined on the basis of the cost of production or of pur-

chase, adjusted for the variation of inventories. All other expenses, including

→

those in respect of advertising and promotions, are recognized when the Group receives the risks and rewards of ownership of the goods or when it receives the services.

Source: *Nestlé financial statements 2017* www. nestle.com, p. 72

Note that expenses are recognized not when cash is paid but when goods and services are received and when the company has an obligation to pay for those goods and services (the point at which the risks and rewards of ownership are received, that is, when the goods or services are delivered to the company).

GO BACK OVER THIS AGAIN!   Totally convinced that you understand how to determine the correct amount of income or expense for a given period? Go to the **online workbook** and complete Exercises 3.5 to reinforce your learning.

The accruals basis of accounting

The principle that all income earned and expenditure incurred in an accounting period is recognized in that accounting period is referred to as the **accruals basis of accounting**. Under this basis, the timing of cash payments and receipts is irrelevant as transactions are matched (allocated) to the time period in which they occur not to the time periods in which they are paid for or in which cash is received.

Why is the accruals basis of accounting applied to financial statements? If the accruals basis of accounting did not exist, entities could time their cash receipts and payments to manipulate their cash-based statement of profit or loss to show the picture they wanted to show rather than the portrait of the income actually earned and the expenses actually incurred during an accounting period. Thus, some accounting periods would show high sales receipts, low expense payments and high profits, while other accounting periods would show low sales receipts, high expense payments and low profits or even losses. Results would depend upon money received and money paid out rather than reflecting all the business activity that had actually taken place within a given period of time.

An ability to manipulate the accounts in this way would lead to a lack of comparability between different accounting periods and between different organizations. We saw in Chapter 1 that comparability is an enhancing qualitative characteristic of accounting information. Lack of comparability would make it very difficult for users to gain an understanding of how the entity is making (or failing to make) progress in terms of profits earned or increases in sales made due to the fluctuating nature of cash inflows and outflows. The IASB recognizes the importance of accruals accounting and how this approach to accounting for transactions provides much more useful information relating to an entity's financial performance and financial position to users:

Accrual accounting depicts the effects of transactions and other events and circumstances on a reporting entity's economic resources and claims in the periods in which those effects occur, even if the resulting cash receipts and payments occur in a different period. This is important because information about a reporting entity's economic resources and claims and changes in its economic resources and claims during a period provides a better basis for assessing the entity's past and future performance than information solely about cash receipts and payments during that period.

Source: IASB *Conceptual Framework for Financial Reporting*, paragraph 1.17

WHY IS THIS RELEVANT TO ME? The accruals basis of accounting

To enable you as a business professional and user of accounting information to appreciate that:

- The timing of cash received and cash paid is irrelevant in the preparation of financial statements

- Transactions are reflected in financial statements on the basis of when they took place not on the basis of when cash was received or paid

---

SUMMARY OF KEY CONCEPTS Can you say what the accruals basis of accounting means? Revise this definition with Summary of key concepts 3.4 to check your learning.

The accruals basis of accounting looks like a difficult concept to grasp, but with practice you will soon be able to apply this concept readily to accounting problems. Let's look at how the principles are applied in Examples 3.1 and 3.2 to show the ways in which the accruals basis of accounting works in practice. Think about the outcomes you would expect and compare your expectations to the actual answers. Remember that income and expenditure is allocated to an accounting period on the basis of income earned and expenditure incurred in that accounting period not on the timing of cash receipts and payments.

EXAMPLE 3.1

The Traditional Toy Company has an accounting year end of 30 June. On 1 January 2018, the company paid its annual insurance premium of £1,000, giving the company and its activities cover up to 31 December 2018. On 1 January 2019, the company paid its annual insurance premium of £1,200, which covers the company and its activities up to 31 December 2019. What expense should the Traditional Toy Company recognize for insurance for its accounting year 1 July 2018 to 30 June 2019?

The answer is £1,100. How did we arrive at this figure?

The premium paid on 1 January 2018 relates to the 12 months to 31 December 2018. Six of the months for the accounting period 1 July 2018 to 30 June 2019 are covered by this insurance premium, namely July, August, September, October, November and December 2018. Therefore 6/12 of the £1,000 belong in the accounting year to 30 June 2019, the other 6/12 of this payment (January to June 2018) belong in the accounting year 1 July 2017 to 30 June 2018.

Similarly, the premium paid on 1 January 2019 covers the whole calendar year to 31 December 2019. However, as the Traditional Toy Company's accounting year ends on 30 June 2019, only six months of this insurance premium belong in the financial year ended on that date, namely January, February, March, April, May and June 2019. Therefore 6/12 of £1,200 belong in the accounting year to 30 June 2019, the other 6/12 of this payment (July to December 2019) belong in the accounting year 1 July 2019 to 30 June 2020.

The total insurance expense recognized in the statement of profit or loss for the accounting year to 30 June 2019 is thus:

$$£1,000 \times 6/12 + £1,200 \times 6/12 = £1,100$$

While £1,200 was paid for insurance in the accounting year 1 July 2018 to 30 June 2019, the accruals basis of accounting requires that an expense of £1,100 for insurance is recognized in this financial year as this was the actual cost of insurance during this time period. Figure 3.5 will help you understand how the amounts paid in the above example have been allocated to the different accounting periods.

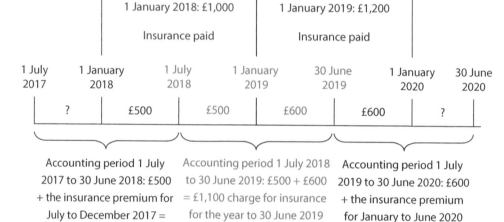

Figure 3.5 The accruals basis of accounting: insurance expense recognized in the Traditional Toy Company's accounting year 1 July 2018 to 30 June 2019

EXAMPLE 3.2 Hand Made Mirrors Limited has an accounting year end of 30 September. On 1 July 2018, the company paid its annual rates bill of £3,000 covering the period 1 July 2018 to 30 June 2019. On 1 July 2019, Hand Made Mirrors Limited received its annual rates bill for £3,600 covering the year to 30 June 2020 but did not pay this bill until 30 November 2019. What expense should the company recognize for rates for its accounting year 1 October 2018 to 30 September 2019?

The answer is £3,150. How did we arrive at this figure?

The rates paid on 1 July 2018 relate to the 12 months to 30 June 2019. Nine of the months for the accounting period 1 October 2018 to 30 September 2019 are covered by this rates bill, namely October, November and December of 2018 and January, February, March, April, May and June of 2019. Therefore 9/12 of this £3,000 belong in the accounting year to 30 September 2019.

Similarly, the rates paid on 30 November 2019 cover the whole year from 1 July 2019 to 30 June 2020. However, as Hand Made Mirrors Limited's accounting year ends on 30 September

2019, only three months of this rates bill belong in the accounting year ended on that date, namely July, August and September 2019. Therefore 3/12 of £3,600 belong in the accounting year to 30 September 2019.

The total rates expense recognized in the statement of profit or loss for the year to 30 September 2019 is thus:

$$£3,000 \times 9/12 + £3,600 \times 3/12 = £3,150$$

No rates have been paid in the financial year 1 October 2018 to 30 September 2019. However, the accruals basis of accounting requires a cost of £3,150 to be recognized as this is the expense incurred in the financial year ended 30 September 2019. Again, a diagram as shown in Figure 3.6 will help you understand how the amounts paid in the above example have been allocated to the different accounting periods.

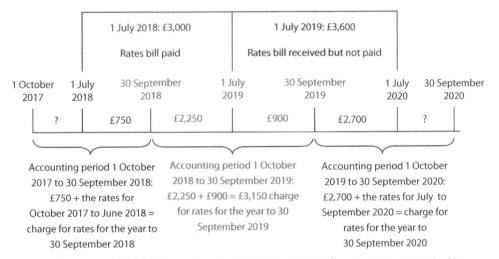

Figure 3.6 The accruals basis of accounting: Hand Made Mirrors Limited's rates expense recognized in the accounting year 1 October 2018 to 30 September 2019

MULTIPLE CHOICE QUESTIONS Do you think you can allocate costs to accounting periods on an expense incurred basis under the accruals basis of accounting? Go to the **online workbook** and have a go at Multiple choice questions 3.2 to make sure you can make these allocations.

Prepayments and accruals

The previous two scenarios provide us with one example of a **prepayment** and one example of an **accrual** at the end of an accounting period.

Prepayments

A prepayment is an expense paid in advance of the accounting period to which it relates. As this expense has been paid in advance, it is an asset of the entity.

3

At 30 June 2019, in the case of the Traditional Toy Company, there is a prepaid insurance premium of £1,200 × 6/12 = £600. This prepayment is an asset as it is a present economic resource controlled by the entity as a result of past events (the payment of the insurance premium) and confers on the company a right that has the potential to produce economic benefits (the right to enjoy the protection pro- vided by payment of the insurance premium in the next six months). While recog- nizing the insurance expense of £1,100 for the accounting year to 30 June 2019, the entity also recognizes a prepayment of £600 at the statement of financial position date of 30 June 2019.

At the end of the previous accounting period, at 30 June 2018, the Traditional Toy Company also had an insurance prepayment amounting to £1,000 × 6/12 = £500 (covering the months of July to December 2018 and paid in advance at 30 June 2018) so the insurance expense charge for the year is the £500 prepayment at the end of last year plus the £1,200 paid in the year less the prepayment at the end of the year of £600, thus:

£500 (prepayment at the end of last year) + £1,200 (payment in the year) − £600 (prepayment at the end of this year) = £1,100 insurance expense charge for the year

When attempting the multiple choice questions and exercises in the online workbook (and in real-life situations), you can apply the rule presented in Figure 3.7 when you have an expense prepayment at the start and at the end of the financial year.

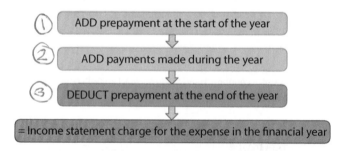

Figure 3.7 Calculating the statement of profit or loss expense for the financial year when there is a prepayment at the start and at the end of the accounting period

Accruals

An accrual is an expense owing at the end of the financial year for goods and services received but not yet paid for. As this expense is owed at the end of the year it represents a liability. At 30 September 2019, Hand Made Mirrors Limited has a liability for unpaid rates of £3,600 × 3/12 = £900. This is a liability of the company at 30 September 2019 as it is a present obligation of the entity to transfer an economic resource (in the form of a cash payment to the local council on 30 November 2019) as a result of past events (the consumption of services). While recognizing the total expense of £3,150 in the statement of profit or loss, Hand Made Mirrors Limited also recognizes a £900 liability under trade and other payables in its statement of financial position at 30 September 2019. Remember that this is an expense incurred but not yet paid, so you should increase the expense and increase the trade payables.

There was no accrual at the end of the previous accounting year. Had there been such an accrual this would have been treated as a deduction in arriving at the expense charge for the current accounting year. This is because an accrual at the end of the previous accounting period is a liability for a cost that was incurred in the previous accounting period but which will be paid in the current accounting period. The payment to discharge this liability has no bearing on the current accounting period's charge for this expense, so it is a deduction from the total payments made in the current accounting period.

When attempting the multiple choice questions and exercises in the online workbook (and in real-life situations), you can apply the rule presented in Figure 3.8 when you have an expense accrual at the start and at the end of the financial year to find the amount you should recognize in the statement of profit or loss for that particular expense in the current financial year.

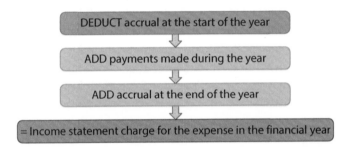

Figure 3.8 Calculating the statement of profit or loss expense for the financial year when there is an accrual at the start and at the end of the accounting period

---

WHY IS THIS RELEVANT TO ME?   Prepayments and accruals

To enable you as a business professional and user of accounting information to understand how:

- Costs are allocated to the accounting periods in which they are incurred
- To calculate accruals and prepayments at the end of an accounting period
- Assets and liabilities arise as a result of prepaid and accrued expenses

---

MULTIPLE CHOICE QUESTIONS   Are you totally convinced that you can calculate statement of profit or loss expenses when there are prepayments and accruals at the start and end of the financial year? Go to the **online workbook** and have a go at Multiple choice questions 3.3 to test your ability to make these calculations.

Depreciation

When we looked at the statement of financial position in Chapter 2, we noted that there are various types of non-current assets such as property, plant and equipment, patents and copyrights among others. These assets are purchased by business organizations with a view to their long term employment within the business to generate revenue, profits and cash. Businesses pay money for these assets when they buy them and then place these assets initially on the statement of financial position at their cost to the business.

A problem then arises. How should the cost of these non-current assets be allocated against income generated from those assets? The total cost of these assets is not allocated immediately against the income and profits made from those assets. Instead, the total cost is posted to the statement of financial position when the non-current asset is first acquired. Should we then allocate the cost of the asset to the statement of profit or loss at the end of the asset's life when the asset is worn out and of no further use to the business? Again, this will not happen. Setting the total cost of the asset against profit at the start or at the end of the asset's life would result in a very large one-off expense against profit in the year in which the asset is either bought or scrapped, so there has to be a better way to allocate the cost of non-current assets to accounting periods benefiting from their use. This is where **depreciation** comes in. Depreciation allocates the cost of a non-current asset to all the accounting periods benefiting from its use, as illustrated in Example 3.3.

EXAMPLE 3.3 Pento Printing Press buys a printing machine for £100,000 and expects this non-current asset to be used within the business for the next five years. By simply dividing the asset's cost by the number of years over which the asset will be used in the business, this will give us an annual allocation of the cost of this asset of £100,000 ÷ 5 years = £20,000 per annum. This means that there will be a charge in Pento's statement of profit or loss in year 1 of £20,000 for use of the asset in the business, a charge in the statement of profit or loss of £20,000 in year 2 for use of the asset and so on until the end of the five years when the asset is scrapped and a replacement asset is purchased.

The allocation of depreciation in this way has a dual effect: part of the cost of the asset is charged as an expense to the statement of profit or loss each year and at the same time the unallocated cost of the asset on the statement of financial position reduces each year. Table 3.3 shows how the annual depreciation is allocated to each accounting period benefiting from the printing machine's use and the effect that this will have on Pento's statement of financial position figure for this asset at the end of each financial year. In accounting terminology, this is expressed as follows: the original cost of the asset – the depreciation charged to the statement of profit or loss each year = the **carrying amount** of the asset shown on the statement of financial position at the end of each financial year.

The £20,000 depreciation on the asset is charged as an expense in the statement of profit or loss of each annual accounting period in which the asset is used within the business.

The accumulated depreciation charged rises each year as the printing machine ages. At the end of the first year, the accumulated depreciation is the same as the annual depreciation charge. By the end of the second year the accumulated depreciation of £40,000 is made up of the first year's charge of £20,000 plus the second year's charge of £20,000. Then, by the end of year 3, the accumulated depreciation of £60,000 is made up of three years' charges of £20,000 each year and so on until the end of the printing machine's useful life. At the end of year 5, the accumulated depreciation of £100,000 is the same as the original cost of £100,000. As each year progresses, the carrying amount of the printing machine (cost – the accumulated depreciation) gradually falls. Thus, the carrying amount reduces as more of the original cost is allocated against profit each year.

Table 3.3 Straight line depreciation on Pento Printing Press' printing machine costing £100,000 with £nil value at the end of five years

Year	Statement of profit or loss: annual charge for depreciation on printing machine	Accumulated depreciation	Statement of financial position: carrying amount of printing machine at the end of each financial year
	£	£	£
1	20,000	20,000	80,000
2	20,000	40,000	60,000
3	20,000	60,000	40,000
4	20,000	80,000	20,000
5	20,000	100,000	Nil

WHY IS THIS RELEVANT TO ME?   Depreciation

To enable you as a business professional and user of accounting information to understand how:

- The use of non-current assets within a business results in an annual depreciation expense in the statement of profit or loss
- The cost of non-current assets is allocated to the statement of profit or loss each year
- The carrying amount of non-current assets is calculated at the end of each financial year

MULTIPLE CHOICE QUESTIONS   How well do you understand the calculation of accumulated depreciation and carrying amount? Go to the **online workbook** and have a go at Multiple choice questions 3.4 to test your understanding of how to make these calculations.

Residual value and the annual depreciation charge

In Example 3.3 we assumed that all of the cost of the printing machine would be consumed over the five-year period and that it would have no value at the end of its projected five-year life. This might be a realistic scenario in the case of assets such as computers, which will be completely superseded by advancing technology and so have no value at the end of their useful lives within a business. However, it is just as likely that assets could be sold on to another buyer when the business wishes to dispose of them. A car, for example, will usually have some resale value when a company comes to dispose of it and, in the same way, second-hand machinery will find willing buyers.

It is thus normal practice, at the time of acquisition, to estimate a residual value for each non-current asset. Residual value is the amount that the original purchaser thinks that the asset could be sold for when the time comes to dispose of it. When calculating the annual depreciation charge, the residual value is deducted from the original cost so that the asset is depreciated down to this value. If the residual value is estimated at £nil, then the full cost of the asset is depreciated over its useful life. Example 3.4 illustrates the effect an estimated residual value has on the annual depreciation charge.

> **EXAMPLE 3.4** The directors of Pento Printing Press now decide that their new printing machine will have an estimated residual value of £10,000 at the end of its five-year life. The annual depreciation charge will now fall to (£100,000 original cost − £10,000 residual value)/5 years = £18,000. Charging £18,000 depreciation each year will depreciate the asset down to its residual value as shown in Table 3.4.

Table 3.4 Pento Printing Press: straight line depreciation of a printing machine costing £100,000 with a £10,000 residual value

Year	Statement of profit or loss: annual charge for depreciation on printing machine	Accumulated depreciation	Statement of financial position: carrying amount of printing machine at the end of each financial year
	£	£	£
1	18,000	18,000	82,000
2	18,000	36,000	64,000
3	18,000	54,000	46,000
4	18,000	72,000	28,000
5	18,000	90,000	10,000

WHY IS THIS RELEVANT TO ME?   Residual value

To enable you as a business professional and user of accounting information to understand that:

• The estimated residual value of an asset at the end of its useful life reduces the annual depreciation charge

• Residual value is just an estimate of expected resale value at the end of a non-current asset's useful life

Profits and losses on disposal of non-current assets

You might now wonder what will happen if Pento Printing Press does not sell the asset at the end of the five years for £10,000. If the asset were to be sold for £8,000, £2,000 less than its carrying amount at the end of year 5, then Pento Printing Press would just record a loss (an additional expense) of £2,000 on the disposal of the printing machine in the statement of profit or loss. Profits would be reduced by that additional expense of £2,000. If, on the other hand, the asset were to be sold for £11,000, £1,000 more than the carrying amount at the end of the five years, Pento Printing Press would recognize a profit (a surplus) on the disposal of that asset in the statement of profit or loss. Small profits on the disposal of non-current assets are recorded as a deduction from expenses. Where the gain or loss on the disposal of a non-current asset is a material amount, this gain or loss would be disclosed separately on the face of the statement of profit or loss as an exceptional item (this chapter, Income in the statement of profit or loss). Do note that the sale proceeds on the disposal of non-current assets are not recorded as revenue in the statement of profit or loss as such disposals are not an ordinary, everyday source of revenue.

There would be no need for Pento Printing Press to go back and recalculate the depreciation for each of the five years in either of these cases as companies accept that the estimation of residual value is just that, a best guess at the time of acquisition of the asset of what the asset might be sold for at the end of its useful life within the business. It is quite normal for companies to recognize small gains and losses on the disposal of assets when they are sold on or scrapped either at the end of their useful lives or during the time in which they are being used within the business.

WHY IS THIS RELEVANT TO ME?   Profits and losses on disposal of non-current assets

To enable you as a business professional and user of accounting information to understand that:

- Profits on the disposal of non-current assets are recognized as income (a reduction in expenses) in the statement of profit or loss in the year of the asset's disposal
- Losses on the disposal of non-current assets are recognized as an expense in the statement of profit or loss in the year of the asset's disposal
- The profit or loss on disposal is calculated as the difference between the sale proceeds and the carrying amount of the asset at the date of disposal

MULTIPLE CHOICE QUESTIONS   Can you calculate profits and losses arising on the disposal of non-current assets? Go to the **online workbook** and have a go at Multiple choice questions 3.5 to test your ability to make these calculations.

Methods of depreciation: straight line and reducing balance

The approach used in the Pento Printing Press examples (Examples 3.3 and 3.4) to calculate depreciation resulted in the same depreciation charge for each year of the printing machine's useful life. This is the **straight line** basis of depreciation as it allocates an equal amount of depreciation to each year that the asset is used within the business.

An alternative method of depreciation that is also used is the **reducing balance** basis. This approach uses a fixed percentage of the cost in year 1 and the same fixed percentage of the carrying amount in subsequent years to calculate the annual depreciation charge. When using the reducing balance basis, residual value is ignored as the percentage used will depreciate the original cost down to residual value over the number of years in which the asset is used within the business. Example 3.5 shows how depreciating non-current assets on the reducing balance basis works.

EXAMPLE 3.5 Continuing with the Pento Printing Press example, a suitable percentage at which to depreciate the new printing machine on a reducing balance basis would be 36.90%. Let's see how this will work in Table 3.5.

The annual depreciation figures were calculated as follows:

- In year 1, depreciation is calculated on cost. This gives a figure of £100,000 × 36.90% = £36,900. This depreciation is then deducted from the original cost of £100,000 to leave a carrying amount at the end of year 1 of £100,000 − £36,900 = £63,100.

- In years 2 and onwards, depreciation is calculated on the carrying amount at the end of the preceding financial year. Carrying amount at the end of year 1 is £63,100, so depreciation for year 2 is £63,100 × 36.90% = £23,284 (rounding to the nearest £). This then gives a carrying amount at the end of year 2 of £63,100 − £23,284 (or £100,000 − £36,900 − £23,284) = £39,816.

- In year 3, depreciation is calculated on the carrying amount at the end of year 2. This gives an annual depreciation charge of £39,816 × 36.90% = £14,692 and a carrying amount at the end of year 3 of £39,816 − £14,692 = £25,124.

Work through the figures for years 4 and 5 to make sure that you understand how reducing balance depreciation works and to reinforce your learning.

Figure 3.9 visually represents the annual depreciation charge under both the reducing balance (the blue line) and the straight line (the red line) methods. The straight line method of depreciation charges exactly the same depreciation each year, £18,000 (Table 3.4), so this is a straight line drawn across the graph through the £18,000 mark on the y-axis. Reducing balance depreciation charges a high level of depreciation in the first year of the asset's life and this then gradually reduces each year, thereby producing the curved blue line on the graph.

Table 3.5 Pento Printing Press: reducing balance depreciation of a printing machine costing £100,000 with a £10,000 residual value

Year	Statement of profit or loss: annual charge for depreciation on printing machine	Accumulated depreciation	Statement of financial position: carrying amount of printing machine at the end of each financial year
	£	£	£
1	36,900	36,900	63,100
2	23,284	60,184	39,816
3	14,692	74,876	25,124
4	9,271	84,147	15,853
5	5,850	89,997	10,003

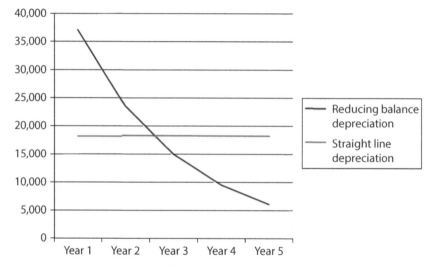

Figure 3.9 Graph representing the annual depreciation charges under both the reducing balance and straight line methods of depreciation for Pento Printing Press' printing machine costing £100,000 with a residual value of £10,000

Which depreciation method is most appropriate in practice?

When selecting a method of depreciation, entities should always ask themselves how the economic benefits of each asset will be consumed. If most of the economic benefits that the asset represents will be used up in the early years of an asset's life, then reducing balance depreciation would be the most suitable method to use. Reducing balance would charge a higher proportion of the cost to the early years of the asset's life, thereby reflecting the higher proportion of economic benefits used up in these early years. Where benefits from the asset's use will be used up evenly over the asset's life, then straight line depreciation is the most appropriate method to use.

WHY IS THIS RELEVANT TO ME?   Methods of depreciation: straight line and reducing balance

To enable you as a business professional and user of accounting information to understand:

- The two main methods of depreciation that are applied in practice
- How to undertake depreciation calculations to assess the impact of depreciation upon profits in the statement of profit or loss and upon the carrying amounts of assets in the statement of financial position
- The criteria to be used in the selection of the most appropriate depreciation method for non-current assets

To illustrate how depreciation is applied by organizations in practice, Give me an example 3.5 presents the depreciation policy of Finsbury Food Group.

GIVE ME AN EXAMPLE 3.5   Depreciation

What sort of depreciation rates and methods do companies use in practice? The following extract from the accounting policies detailed in the report and accounts of Finsbury Food Group plc for the 52 weeks ended 1 July 2017 gives different depreciation rates for different classes of property, plant and equipment assets. Can you decide whether Finsbury Food Group uses the straight line or the reducing balance basis to calculate the annual depreciation charge?

Depreciation

Depreciation is provided to write off the cost, less estimated residual value, of the property, plant and equipment by equal instalments over their estimated useful economic lives to the Consolidated Statement of Profit and Loss. When parts of an item of property, plant and equipment have different useful lives, they are accounted for as separate items

(major components) of property, plant and equipment.

The depreciation rates used are as follows:

Freehold buildings 2%–20%	Plant and equipment 10%–33%
Leasehold property Up to the remaining life of the lease	Assets under construction Nil
Fixtures and fittings 10%–33%	Motor vehicles 25%–33%

Did you notice the words 'equal instalments' in the extract? Equal instalments means that Finsbury Food Group uses the straight line basis of depreciation when allocating the cost of non-current assets to the consolidated statement of profit and loss. Equal instalments = the same charge each year, i.e. the straight line basis.

Source: *Finsbury Food Group plc annual report and accounts 2017* http://www.finsburyfoods.co.uk

MULTIPLE CHOICE QUESTIONS Are you totally confident you can calculate depreciation charges on both the straight line and the reducing balance bases? Go to the **online workbook** and have a go at Multiple choice questions 3.6 to test your ability to make these calculations.

What depreciation is and what depreciation is not

There are many misconceptions about what depreciation is and what it represents. The following notes will help you distinguish between what depreciation is and what it is not:

- Depreciation is a deduction from the cost of a non-current asset that is charged as an expense in the statement of profit or loss each year.

- This depreciation charge represents an allocation of the cost of each non-current asset to the accounting periods expected to benefit from that asset's use by an organization.

- Depreciation is another application of the accruals basis of accounting. Just as the accruals basis of accounting matches income and expenditure to the periods in which they occurred, so depreciation matches the cost of non-current assets to the periods benefiting from their use.

- Depreciation is NOT a method of saving up for a replacement asset.

- Depreciation does NOT represent a loss in value of a non-current asset (see Example 3.6).

- Depreciation does NOT represent an attempt to provide a current value for non-current assets at each statement of financial position date (see Example 3.6).

EXAMPLE 3.6 Think about these last two points. Suppose you were to buy a car today for £15,000 and expect to use that car for five years before buying a replacement. The resale value of that car the next day would not be £15,000 less one day's depreciation, the original cost less a very small charge for the asset's economic benefits used up by one day's travelling. The showroom that sold you the car the day before would probably offer you half of the original cost of £15,000. The car is now second-hand and so worth much less on the open market than you paid for it the day before even if it only has five miles on the clock and is still in immaculate condition. Thus, the carrying amount of non-current assets on a company's statement of financial position is just the original cost of those assets less the depreciation charged to date. This carrying amount represents the store of potential economic benefits that will be consumed by the entity over the remaining useful lives of those assets rather than presenting the current market value of those non-current assets.

3

Further adjustments to the statement of profit or loss

We have now looked at how the statement of profit or loss reflects the actual income and expenditure incurred in an accounting period rather than just the receipts and payments of cash during that accounting period together with the subject of depreciation. There are some further adjustments that are made to figures in the statement of profit or loss and statement of financial position that you should be aware of before we work through a comprehensive example.

Irrecoverable debts

Where entities trade with their customers on credit, providing customers with goods now and allowing them a period of time in which to pay, there will inevitably be times when some customers are unable or refuse to pay for whatever reason. When this situation arises, an administrative expense is recognized for the amount of the trade receivable that cannot be collected and trade receivables are reduced by the same amount. Note that these irrecoverable debts are not deducted from sales (revenue) but are treated as an expense of the business.

Irrecoverable debts are recognized as an expense and a deduction from trade receivables when there is objective proof that the customer will not pay. Usually, this objective proof is in the form of a letter from the customer's administrator advising the company that no further cash will be forthcoming to settle the trade receivable owed.

The allowance for receivables

As well as known irrecoverable debts, organizations will also calculate an allowance for receivables, trade receivables that may not be collected rather than irrecoverable debts, receivables that will definitely not pay. An allowance for receivables is an application of the **prudence** principle, being cautious and avoiding over optimistic expectations, making an allowance for a potential loss just in case. An allowance for receivables thus builds up a cushion against future irrecoverable debts, charging an expense now rather than in the future.

The allowance for receivables is calculated as a percentage of trade receivables after deducting known irrecoverable debts. The allowance for receivables is deducted in its entirety from trade receivables in the statement of financial position while only the increase or decrease in the allowance over the year is charged or credited to administrative expenses (not sales) in the statement of profit or loss. Example 3.7 will help you understand how an allowance for receivables is calculated and the accounting entries required.

EXAMPLE 3.7 Gemma runs a recruitment agency. She has year-end trade receivables at 30 September 2019 of £300,000. She knows that one trade receivable owing £6,000 will not pay as that company is now in liquidation. Gemma's experience tells her that 5% of the remaining trade receivables will not pay. Her allowance for receivables at 30 September 2018 was £12,000. What is the total amount that she should recognize in her statement of profit or loss for the year to 30 September 2019 for irrecoverable debts and the allowance for receivables? What figure for net trade receivables will appear in her statement of financial position at that date?

Irrecoverable debts and allowance for receivables charge in the statement of profit or loss

	£	£
Irrecoverable debts charged directly to the statement of profit or loss		6,000
Movement in the allowance for receivables:		
Year-end trade receivables (total)	300,000	
Less: known irrecoverable debts charged directly to the statement of profit or loss	(6,000)	
Net trade receivables on which allowance is to be based	294,000	
Allowance for receivables on £294,000 at 5%	14,700	
Less: allowance for receivables at 30 September 2018	(12,000)	
Increase in the allowance charged to this year's statement of profit or loss		2,700
Total statement of profit or loss charge for irrecoverable debts and the allowance for receivables for the year ended 30 September 2019		8,700
Trade receivables in the statement of financial position		

	£
Total trade receivables at 30 September 2019	300,000
Less: known irrecoverable debts charged directly to the statement of profit or loss	(6,000)
	294,000
Less: allowance for receivables at the start of the year	(12,000)
Less: increase in the allowance for receivables during the year	(2,700)
Net trade receivables at 30 September 2019	279,300

The total allowance for receivables is made up of the allowance at the end of last year and the increase (or decrease) during the current year. The total allowance of £14,700 is deducted from trade receivables at the end of the year. The allowance for receivables charge (or credit) for the year in the statement of profit or loss, however, is just the increase (or decrease) during the year.

MULTIPLE CHOICE QUESTIONS   Do you reckon that you can calculate allowances for receivables and the amounts to charge or credit to the statement of profit or loss? Go to the **online workbook** and have a go at Multiple choice questions 3.7 to test your ability to make these calculations.

Discounts allowed (early settlement discounts)

To encourage trade receivables to pay what they owe early, companies will offer a discount. As an example, a trade receivable is allowed 30 days in which to pay for goods supplied. However, the seller might offer a discount of, say, 2% if payment is made within 10 days of receipt of the goods. The seller of the goods does not know whether the trade receivable will take up this discount or not. Therefore, the invoice for the goods supplied will present two prices: the first price is after allowing for the early settlement discount, the second is the price if the early settlement discount is not taken up. Thus, if a customer is sold goods with a selling price of £3,000 but offered a 2.5% discount for payment within 10 days, the seller of the goods records a sale and a trade receivable of £3,000 × (100% − 2.5%) = £2,925. If the customer pays within ten days then the seller's cash increases by £2,925 and trade receivables decrease by £2,925. However, should the customer not take up the early settlement discount but pay £3,000 after 30 days, then cash will increase by £3,000, trade receivables will decrease by £2,925 and the additional £75 will be added to sales revenue. Discounts allowed are thus not treated as an expense but are deducted from the initial selling price and then added to sales if the discounts are not taken up.

Discounts received (bulk discounts)

Suppliers will reward their customers with discounts for buying goods in bulk. These bulk discounts are a source of income in the statement of profit or loss and are deducted from cost of sales and from trade payables.

Sales returns

Sometimes, goods are just not suitable, are not of the requisite quality or they are faulty. In this case, customers will return these goods to the supplier. These returns are treated as a deduction from sales, as the return of goods amounts to the cancellation of a sale and a deduction from trade receivables.

Purchase returns

Similarly, when entities return goods to their suppliers, suppliers will reduce the amount that is owed to them by the issue of a credit note. As this is the cancellation of a purchase, the purchases part of cost of goods sold and trade payables are reduced.

Closing inventory

At the end of the financial year, entities count up the goods in stock and value them at cost to the business. To value closing inventory at selling price would be to anticipate profit. This would contravene the realization principle of accounting which says that profits should not be anticipated until they have been earned through a sale. The cost of these goods is carried forward to the next accounting period by deducting the cost of this inventory from purchases in the statement of profit or loss and recognizing an asset in the statement of financial position. This is a further application of the accruals basis of accounting, carrying forward the cost of unsold goods to a future accounting period to match that cost against sales of those goods when these arise.

3

WHY IS THIS RELEVANT TO ME?   Further adjustments to the statement of profit or loss

To provide you as a business professional and user of accounting information with:

- Knowledge of additional transactions resulting in figures that affect both income and expenditure and the statement of financial position
- Details of how these adjustments are treated in practice
- An ability to apply these adjustments in business situations

---

We will look at how these adjustments are applied in practice in our comprehensive example (Example 3.8) and in Numerical exercises 3.2 in the online workbook.

Preparing the statement of profit or loss

We have now considered all the building blocks for the statement of profit or loss. It is time to look at a comprehensive example to see how the statement of profit or loss is put together from the accounting records and how it relates to the statement of financial position. You will need to work through this comprehensive example several times to understand fully how all the figures are derived, but this is quite normal. Even those at the top of the accountancy profession today would have struggled with this type of problem when they first started out on their accounting studies. It is just a case of practice and familiarizing yourself with the techniques involved in putting a set of accounts together.

The following list of points is a quick summary of how to prepare a statement of profit or loss and the statement of financial position, starting with a simple list of receipts and payments presented by a business:

- First, summarize the receipts into and payments out of the entity's bank account: this will give you the basic sales receipts and expenses as well as any non-current assets that the entity may have purchased.

- Once you have completed the bank account you will have a difference between the receipts and payments in the period: if receipts are greater than payments, you have a positive cash balance in the bank account, a current asset. If the payments are greater than the receipts, you have a negative cash balance in the bank account, an overdraft, and this will be recorded as a current liability.

- Using the cash received and paid you should then adjust income and expenditure for the accruals basis of accounting. Add to sales any income earned in the accounting period for which cash has not yet been received and recognize a trade receivable for the outstanding balance due. For expenses, determine what the expense should be based on, the time period involved and then add additional expenditure where a particular cost is too low (and add to current liabilities as an accrual, an obligation incurred but not yet paid) and deduct expenditure where a particular cost is too high (and add to current assets as a prepayment of future expenditure that relates to a later accounting period).

- Remember to depreciate any non-current assets at the rates given, provide for any irrecoverable debts that might have arisen, make an adjustment for the increase or decrease in the allowance for receivables, adjust sales and purchases for returns and deduct discounts received from purchases.

Example 3.8 will now demonstrate these stages in the process of preparing the statement of profit or loss and the statement of financial position.

EXAMPLE 3.8 Your friend Julia started a business on 1 April 2019 buying and selling sports equipment from a shop on the high street. It is now 30 June 2019 and Julia is curious to know how well or badly she is doing in her first three months of trading. She has no idea about accounts and presents you with the following list of amounts received and paid out of her bank account.

Illustration 3.3 Julia's bank account receipts and payments summary

Date		Receipts	Payments
		£	£
1 April 2019	Cash introduced by Julia	30,000	
1 April 2019	Three months' rent paid on shop to 30 June 2019		5,000
1 April 2019	Cash register paid for		1,000
1 April 2019	Shelving and shop fittings paid for		12,000
30 April 2019	Receipts from sales in April 2019	20,000	
5 May 2019	Sports equipment supplied in April paid for		15,000
12 May 2019	Rates for period 1 April 2019 to 30 September 2019 paid		800
19 May 2019	Cash withdrawn for Julia's own expenses		2,000
30 May 2019	Receipts from sales in May 2019	25,000	
5 June 2019	Sports equipment supplied in May paid for		20,000
10 June 2019	Shop water rates for the year 1 April 2019 to 31 March 2020 paid		400
30 June 2019	Receipts from sales in June 2019	30,000	
30 June 2019	Balance in bank at 30 June 2019		48,800
		105,000	105,000

Julia is very pleased with her first three months' trading and regards the additional £18,800 cash in the bank as her profit for the three months. Is she right? Has she really made £18,800 profit in the three months since she started trading? Her argument is that she started with £30,000 and now has £48,800 so she must have made a profit of £18,800, the difference between her opening and closing cash figures. Let us have a look and see how her business has really performed in its first three months of operations.

Our first job is to split the receipts and payments down into trading receipts and payments and statement of financial position (capital) receipts and payments. Have a go at this on your own before you look at the answer. You will need to add up the receipts for sales and payments for purchases and other expenses: make a list of these individual totals.

You should now have the following statements:

Illustration 3.4 Julia's receipts and payments account for the three months ended 30 June 2019

	£	£
Sales £20,000 (April) + £25,000 (May) + £30,000 (June)		75,000
Purchases £15,000 (May) + £20,000 (June)		35,000
Gross surplus (sales – purchases)		40,000
Expenses		
Rent £5,000 (April)	5,000	
Rates £800 (May)	800	
Water rates £400 (June)	400	
Total expenses		6,200
Net surplus for the three months		33,800

Illustration 3.5 Julia's statement of financial position based on her receipts and payments for her first three months of trading at 30 June 2019

	£
Non-current assets	
Cash register	1,000
Shelving and shop fittings	12,000
	13,000
Bank balance at 30 June 2019	48,800
Total assets	61,800
Equity	
Capital introduced by Julia	30,000
Drawings (cash withdrawn from the business for personal expenses)	(2,000)
Surplus for the three months	33,800
	61,800

All we have done here is restated the figures from Julia's bank account, splitting them into statement of profit or loss and statement of financial position items on a purely receipts and payments basis. Sales and expenses have been entered into the statement of profit or loss, while non-current assets (the cash register and the shelving and shop fittings: those assets that are used long term in the business) have been entered into the statement of financial position. The statement of financial position also shows the cash asset in the bank at the end of the financial period, along with the capital introduced by Julia less her drawings in the three-month period plus the surplus the business has made during that period.

Are you completely happy with the way in which Julia's bank receipts and payments were allocated to the receipts and payments account and the related statement of financial position? View Video presentation 3.1 in the **online workbook** to see a practical demonstration of how these allocations were made.

However, there is a problem with receipts and payments accounts. As we have seen in the earlier part of this chapter, what we need to do now is adjust these receipts and payments for the accruals basis of accounting, matching all the income and expenses to the three months in which they were earned and incurred rather than just allocating them to the three-month period on the basis of when cash was received or paid. By doing this we can then determine the actual sales made during the period and what it actually cost Julia to make those sales. This will give her a much clearer idea of the profits she has actually earned in her first three months of trading.

You mention this problem to Julia, who provides you with the following additional information:

- She counted up and valued the inventory at the close of business on 30 June 2019: the cost of this inventory at that date was £10,000.

- At 30 June 2019, Julia owed £25,000 for sports equipment she had purchased from her suppliers on credit in June. She paid this £25,000 on 5 July 2019.

- While her main business is selling sports equipment for cash, Julia has also made sales to two local tennis clubs in June on credit. At 30 June 2019, the two clubs owed £2,500, although one club disputes £50 of the amount outstanding, saying that the goods were never delivered. Julia has no proof that these goods were ever received by the club and has reluctantly agreed that she will never receive this £50.

- During the month of June, Julia employed a part time sales assistant who was owed £300 in wages at the end of June 2019. These wages were paid on 8 July 2019.

- On 5 July 2019, Julia received a telephone bill for £250 covering the three months 1 April 2019 to 30 June 2019 together with an electricity bill for £200 covering the same period.

- Julia expects the cash register and shelving and shop fittings to last for five years before they need replacement. The level of usage of these assets will be the same in each of the next five years. She also expects that the assets will have no residual value at the end of their useful lives and that they will just be scrapped rather than being sold on.

- The cash register contained £500 in cash at 30 June 2019 representing sales receipts that had not yet been banked.

- On 29 June 2019, one of the tennis clubs she trades with on credit returned goods with a sales value of £400. These goods were faulty. Julia returned these goods to her supplier: the goods had originally cost Julia £250.

Taking into account the additional information, together with the transactions through the bank account and our receipts and payments account, Julia's statement of profit or loss and statement of financial position are presented in full in Illustrations 3.6 and 3.7.

Illustration 3.6 Julia's statement of profit or loss for the three months ended 30 June 2019

	£	£	Note
Sales £75,000 (cash received) + £2,500 (sales invoiced but cash not yet received) − £400 (goods returned: no sale or trade receivable recognized) + £500 (cash in till representing unrecorded sales)		77,600	1
Purchases £35,000 (cash paid) + £25,000 (goods received not yet paid for) − £250 (faulty goods returned to supplier: no cost or liability recognized)	59,750		2
Less: closing inventory (inventory of goods not yet sold at 30 June 2019)	(10,000)		3
Cost of sales (purchases − closing inventory)		49,750	4
Gross profit (sales − cost of sales)		27,850	5
Expenses			
Rent	5,000		6
Rates £800 − (£800 × 3/6) (payment is for a six-month period, therefore three months out of six are prepaid)	400		7
Water rates £400 − (£400 × 9/12) (12-month period, so nine months are prepaid)	100		8
Irrecoverable debt £50 (sale made but no cash will be received)	50		9
Wages £300 (work performed for wages in June but paid in July)	300		10
Telephone £250 (service received but paid in July)	250		11
Electricity £200 (electricity received but paid in July)	200		12
Cash register depreciation (£1,000/5 years × 3/12 months)	50		13
Shelving and fittings depreciation (£12,000/5 years × 3 /12 months)	600		14
Total expenses		6,950	15
Net profit for the three months		20,900	16

3

Illustration 3.7 Julia's statement of financial position at 30 June 2019

	£	Notes
Non-current assets		
Cash register £1,000 – (£1,000/5 years × 3/12 months)	950	13
Shelving and shop fittings £12,000 – (£12,000/5 years × 3/12 months)	11,400	14
	12,350	
Current assets		
Inventory (inventory of goods not yet sold at 30 June 2019)	10,000	3
Trade receivables £2,500 (sales invoiced but cash not yet received) – £50 (sale made but no cash will be received) – £400 (goods returned: no sale or trade receivable recognized)	2,050	1,9
Rates prepayment £800 × 3/6 (6 month period, therefore 3/6 prepaid)	400	7
Water rates prepayment £400 × 9/12 (12 month period, 9 months prepaid)	300	8
Bank balance at 30 June 2019	48,800	
Cash in cash register at 30 June 2019 (£500 cash in till representing unrecorded sales, increase sales and increase cash)	500	1
	62,050	
Total assets (£12,350 non-current assets + £62,050 current assets)	74,400	
Current liabilities		
Trade payables £25,000 (goods received not yet paid for) – £250 (goods returned to supplier: no cost or liability recognized)	24,750	2
Wages accrual	300	10
Telephone accrual	250	11
Electricity accrual	200	12
Total liabilities	25,500	
Net assets (total assets (£74,400) – total liabilities (£25,500))	48,900	
Equity (capital account)		
Capital introduced by Julia	30,000	
Drawings (cash paid from the business for personal expenses)	(2,000)	
Net profit for the three months	20,900	
Capital account at 30 June 2019	48,900	

Notes to Julia's statement of profit or loss and statement of financial position:

1. This figure consists of the sales represented by cash banked (£75,000) + the additional sales made on credit of £2,500 + the unrecorded cash of £500 representing sales made on 30 June 2019. The £2,500 credit sales are recognized now as they are sales that occurred in the three-month period to 30 June 2019 and so are matched to this accounting period even though the cash from these sales will not be received until after the end of the three-month period. Similarly, the £400 goods returned are recognized as a deduction from the sales total as this

sale was cancelled during the three-month period. Money owed by trade receivables is £2,100 (£2,500 credit sales made – £400 selling price of goods returned) while cash rises by £500 as these sales had already been realized in cash. Note that the irrecoverable debt of £50 is not deducted from sales but is disclosed as a separate expense in the statement of profit or loss.

2. Goods purchased on credit in the period and not paid for are likewise matched to the period in which the transaction occurred. Failure to recognize this expense in the period would incorrectly increase the profit for the period and give a completely false picture of how well the business is performing. The receipts and payments account initially showed purchases of £35,000. Once we have added in the additional purchases in the period and deducted the £250 of faulty goods returned to the supplier, the purchases figure has risen to £59,750, a significant increase on the original figure, but one that is required by the accruals basis of accounting. Just as the purchases expense has risen by £24,750 (£25,000 – £250), trade payables have risen by the same amount to reflect the amount owed by the business at 30 June 2019.

3. Closing inventory of goods is treated as a deduction in the statement of profit or loss as the cost of these unsold goods is carried forward to match against future sales of these goods. While cost of sales is thus reduced by £10,000, the statement of financial position reflects the same amount as an asset, an economic resource the business owns which it can sell in future periods to generate economic benefits for the organization.

4. Cost of sales, as we noted earlier in the chapter, is calculated as opening inventory (= last year's closing inventory) + purchases during the period – closing inventory. In Julia's case, there is no opening inventory as this is her first trading period, so opening inventory is £nil.

5. Gross profit is calculated as: sales – cost of sales, income earned less the costs incurred in generating that income. Gross profit is an important figure in assessing the performance of an entity as we shall see in Chapter 6.

6. Rent is one figure that does not need adjusting. As stated in the bank receipts and payments, the rent paid is for the months of April, May and June 2019 and is paid right up to 30 June, so there is no prepayment (money paid in advance for services still to be received) or accrual (unpaid amount for services already received) of rent at the end of the three-month accounting period.

7. The rates are for the half year from 1 April 2019 to 30 September 2019. The whole amount due for the six months has been paid during the period. At 30 June 2019, the payment for July, August and September 2019 has been made in advance so half the £800 is a prepayment at 30 June 2019. The true cost of rates for the three months to 30 June 2019 is 3/6 of £800, so that only £400 is matched as an expense for the quarter.

8. Similarly, the water rates are paid for the whole year from 1 April 2019 to 31 March 2020, so that only three of the twelve months represented by this payment have been used up by 30 June 2019 (April, May and June 2019) leaving the nine months 1 July 2019 to 31 March 2020 prepaid. Again, the water rates expense for the period is only 3/12 of the total paid and this is the expense to match to the three-month period to the end of June 2019. The remainder of this expense is carried forward at the end of the three-month period to match against water usage in future accounting periods.

9. The irrecoverable debt is recognized as an expense and not as a deduction from sales. As well as being charged as an expense in the period to which it relates, it is also deducted from trade receivables. As this £50 will not be received, it no longer represents an asset with the potential to generate economic benefits so it is deducted from trade receivables in the statement of financial position and charged as an expense in the statement of profit or loss.

10. The £300 wages cost has been incurred by 30 June 2019 and, while this amount is not paid until after the end of the three-month period, it is matched with the income that those wages helped to generate during June 2019. Expenses increase by £300 and, as this amount has not been paid by the period end, it is recognized as a liability.

11. Similarly, the telephone service has been received over the three-month accounting period so there is a liability at the end of the period together with an expense of £300 matched to the period in which it was incurred.

12. Again, the electricity has been consumed during the three-month period to 30 June 2019, so that a liability exists at the period end for this amount and this, too, is recognized as an expense matched to the accounting period in which it was incurred.

13. As we saw earlier in this chapter, depreciation is charged on non-current assets to reflect the economic benefits of those assets consumed during each accounting period. Julia expects the same level of usage each year from the cash register and the shelving and shop fittings, so this implies the straight line basis of depreciation, an equal amount charged to the periods benefiting from their use. As there is no residual value, the total cost is used to calculate the depreciation charge for the three-month period. In the case of the cash register, £1,000 divided by five years gives an annual depreciation charge of £200. However, as the accounting period is less than one year, the depreciation charge is spread out over the relevant months to give an expense of £200 × 3/12 = £50.

14. In the same way, the straight line basis of depreciation gives an annual charge of £12,000/5 = £2,400 on the shelving and shop fittings. As the accounting period is only three months long, only 3/12 of this annual depreciation is matched to

the current accounting period, so that £2,400 × 3/12 = £600 charged to reflect the economic benefit of these assets used up in the accounting period.

15. Total expenses are the sum of all the expenses from rent down to shelving and fittings depreciation.

16. Net profit for the period is given by the gross profit – total expenses.

Drawings and the business entity assumption

Julia's drawings for her personal expenditure have been deducted from equity. Why are these costs not treated as part of the business's expenditure? Firstly, the business's affairs and the owner's affairs must be kept entirely separate as the business and the owner are treated as two separate entities. Where the owner takes money out of the business for non-business, personal expenditure, any such personal expenditure is deducted from the owner's interest in the business as it is not expenditure incurred on behalf of the business. Secondly, in accordance with the IASB *Conceptual Framework*, while the payment of cash to Julia represents a decrease in assets and a decrease in equity, this is not an expense but a decrease in equity resulting from a distribution to holders of equity claims (this chapter, Expenses). The owner's interest in the business is represented by the amounts in the capital account, as we saw in Chapter 2 (The components of equity). Any amounts for personal expenditure withdrawn from the business's bank account are treated as repayments of the capital owed to the owner and are not charged as an expense of the business.

SHOW ME HOW TO DO IT   Are you certain you understand how Julia's statement of profit or loss and statement of financial position were put together? View Video presentation 3.2 in the **online workbook** to see a practical demonstration of how these two statements were drawn up.

WHY IS THIS RELEVANT TO ME?   Comprehensive example: statement of profit or loss and statement of financial position

To enable you as a business professional and user of accounting information to appreciate:

- How the statement of profit or loss and statement of financial position are drawn up from the receipts and payments for an accounting period together with the application of the accruals basis of accounting

- How you should approach statement of profit or loss and statement of financial position preparation problems

NUMERICAL EXERCISES   Are you totally confident that you could prepare statements of profit or loss and statements of financial position from a given set of information? Go to the **online workbook** and complete Numerical exercises 3.2 to test out your ability to prepare these two statements.

CHAPTER SUMMARY

3

You should now have learnt that:

- Statements of profit or loss and statements of financial position are drawn up on the accruals basis of accounting

- Statement of profit or loss income and expenditure represent income earned and expenditure incurred during an accounting period

- Statement of profit or loss income and expenditure do not just represent cash received and cash paid during an accounting period

- Accruals are expenses incurred in an accounting period but not yet paid

- Accruals give rise to additional expenditure in the statement of profit or loss and a current liability in the statement of financial position

- Prepayments are expenses paid in advance of the accounting period to which they relate

- Prepayments reduce current period expenditure and represent a current asset on the statement of financial position

- Depreciation is the allocation of the cost of non-current assets to the accounting periods benefiting from their use

- Depreciation does not represent a loss in value of non-current assets

- Depreciation is not a way of presenting non-current assets at market values

QUICK REVISION   Test your knowledge with the online flashcards in Summary of key concepts and attempt the Multiple choice questions, all in the **online workbook**. www.oup.com/uk/scott_business3e/

END-OF-CHAPTER QUESTIONS

Solutions to these questions can be found at the back of the book from page 447.

❱ DEVELOP YOUR UNDERSTANDING

❭ **Question 3.1**

Abi runs a market stall selling fashion clothing for cash. Her business bank account balance at 1 September 2018, the start of her most recent trading year, was £7,342. She also had inventory of £2,382 and trade payables of £3,445 on that date. She rents her market stall at an annual cost of £6,000 payable quarterly in advance from 1 September each trading year. Abi paid all the rent that was due during the year to 31 August 2019. Her cash receipts from sales to customers for the year to 31 August 2019 totalled up to £157,689, but she also gave refunds to customers for returned goods of £3,789. She paid the outstanding trade payables at 1 September 2018 on 5 September 2018. Her purchases for the year totalled up to £120,465, of which she paid £116,328 during the year to 31 August 2019. At 31 August 2019 Abi valued her inventory of clothing at a cost of £4,638. From 1 September 2018 she employed a part time assistant, Kate, agreeing to pay her £100 a week for the year. At the end of August 2019, while Abi had paid Kate all the amounts due for the first 50 weeks of the year, she still owed her £200 for the last two weeks of August 2019. To improve the presentation of her fashion clothing ranges, Abi paid £600 to buy some display stands on 1 September 2018. Abi reckons that these display stands will last her for three years and that they will have a scrap value of £30. On 31 August 2019, Abi had £650 in cash representing sales that had not yet been banked. Abi withdrew £1,500 a month for her own personal expenses from the business bank account.

Required

(a) Calculate Abi's opening capital account (equity) balance (remember the accounting equation) at 1 September 2018.

(b) Draw up Abi's bank account for the year to 31 August 2019.

(c) Prepare Abi's statement of profit or loss by nature for the year ended 31 August 2019 together with a statement of financial position at that date.

❭ **Question 3.2**

Alison runs an online gift shop, trading for cash with individual customers and offering trading on credit terms to businesses. She presents you with the following figures from her accounting records for the year ended 31 December 2019:

	£
Purchases of goods for resale	225,368
Accumulated depreciation on racks, shelving and office furniture at 31 December 2019	14,650
Trade receivables	27,400
Administration expenses	15,265

→

	£
Racks, shelving and office furniture at cost	33,600
Telephone expenses	5,622
Capital account at 1 January 2019	52,710
Sales	437,990
Accumulated depreciation on computers at 31 December 2019	13,850
Inventory at 1 January 2019	27,647
Purchase returns (already deducted from trade payables)	5,724
Bank balance (asset)	52,315
Trade payables	24,962
Rent on warehouse and office unit	15,000
Business rates	9,325
Computer equipment at cost	20,775
Discounts received (already deducted from trade payables)	2,324
Delivery costs	36,970
Electricity and gas	8,736
Insurance	3,250
Drawings	40,000
Depreciation charge for the year on non-current assets	13,255
Sales returns (already deducted from trade receivables)	17,682

Alison provides you with the following additional information.

• Alison valued the inventory at 31 December 2019 at a cost of £22,600.

• All depreciation charges on non-current assets for the year to 31 December 2019 are included in the depreciation figures above.

• Rent on the trading unit prepaid at 31 December 2019 amounted to £3,000.

• Rates prepaid at 31 December 2019 amounted to £1,865.

• Accountancy costs of £1,250 had not been paid by the year end and are not included in the figures above.

• There were no other prepaid or accrued expenses at the year end.

• Alison would like to include an allowance for receivables of 10% of year-end trade receivables. There was no allowance for receivables at 31 December 2018.

Required

Using the list of balances and the additional information prepare Alison's statement of profit or loss by nature for the year ended 31 December 2019 together with a statement of financial position at that date.

> **Question 3.3**

The following figures have been extracted from the accounting records of Volumes Limited, a book binder, at 30 September 2019:

	Assets and expenses £000	Income, liabilities and equity £000
Plant and machinery: cost	2,000	
Plant and machinery: accumulated depreciation at 30 September 2019		800
Sales		4,750
Trade receivables	430	
Administration expenses	300	
Selling and distribution costs	200	
Production costs	2,600	
Finance expense	100	
Cash at bank	175	
Loan (due 30 September 2028)		500
Trade payables		300
Finance income		25
Called up share capital		250
Share premium		125
Retained earnings at 30 September 2018		155
Inventory at 1 October 2018	100	
Production wages	1,000	
	6,905	6,905

Additional information

- Inventory at 30 September 2019 was valued at a cost of £150,000.
- Taxation on the profit for the year has been estimated to be £250,000.
- All depreciation charges for the year to 30 September 2019 have been calculated in the balances above.

Required

Using the list of balances and the additional information prepare the statement of profit or loss and statement of financial position for Volumes Limited in a form suitable for publication. You will need to produce a working to calculate cost of sales.

You may find that consulting Illustrations 2.1 and 3.1 will assist you in the preparation of the statement of profit or loss and statement of financial position.

⟫ TAKE IT FURTHER

⟫ Question 3.4

The following figures have been extracted from the accounting records of Textiles Limited, a cloth manufacturer and wholesaler, at 30 June 2019:

	Assets and expenses £000	Income, liabilities and equity £000
Plant and machinery: cost	3,000	
Plant and machinery: accumulated depreciation at 30 June 2018		1,200
Motor vehicles: cost	800	
Motor vehicles: accumulated depreciation at 30 June 2018		400
Trade receivables	1,050	
Cost of sales	4,550	
Sales returns (already deducted from trade receivables)	150	
Issued share capital		200
Trade payables		300
Finance expense	110	
Purchase returns (already deducted from trade payables)		80
Administration expenses	700	
Bank overdraft		200
Selling and distribution costs	1,000	
Sales		7,550
Discounts received (already deducted from trade payables)		125
Loan (due for repayment on 30 June 2027)		1,000
Retained earnings at 30 June 2018		545
Inventory at 30 June 2019	300	
Allowance for receivables at 30 June 2018		60
	11,660	11,660

Additional information

- Audit and accountancy fees (to be charged to administration expenses) of £10,000 have not been taken into account at 30 June 2019.

- Administration expenses include payments for insurance premiums of £30,000 for the 12 months to 31 December 2019.

- Since the year end, a customer of Textiles Limited has gone into liquidation owing £50,000. Textiles Limited does not expect to receive any cash from this trade receivable.

- The allowance for receivables is to be adjusted to 4% of trade receivables after deducting known irrecoverable debts. All irrecoverable debts and the movement in the allowance for receivables are to be charged to administration expenses.

- Depreciation for the year to 30 June 2019 still has to be calculated. Plant and machinery is to be depreciated at 20% straight line and motor vehicles are to be depreciated at 25% reducing balance. Plant and machinery depreciation should be charged to cost of sales and motor vehicle depreciation should be charged to distribution and selling expenses.

- Taxation on the profit for the year is to be calculated as 25% of the profit before tax.

Required

Prepare the statement of profit or loss for the year ended 30 June 2019 and the statement of financial position at that date in a form suitable for publication in accordance with International Financial Reporting Standards.

» Question 3.5

Laura was made redundant on 1 July 2018 and received £50,000 in redundancy pay. With this money, she opened a business bank account and set up a small building company undertaking household and small industrial construction work. She started trading on 1 September 2018 and she has now reached her year end of 31 August 2019. She has produced a summary of payments and receipts into her business bank account along with additional information that she thinks will be useful in preparing her statement of profit or loss and statement of financial position for her first year of trading. The details she has presented you with are as follows:

1. Laura's customers usually pay cash at the end of each job. Cash received and banked from these sales totals up to £112,000. However, her small industrial clients keep her waiting for payment. Her invoices to her small industrial customers add up to a total of £48,000 for work carried out during the year, but she had only collected £36,000 of this amount by 31 August 2019.

2. Laura buys her construction materials on credit from a local wholesaler. Her total spending on materials this year has been £45,000 of which she had paid £38,000 by 31 August 2019. Her annual trading summary from the wholesaler received on 5 September 2019 tells her that she has qualified for a bulk purchase discount of £1,000 on all her purchases up to 31 August 2019. She will deduct this amount from her next payment to her supplier in September 2019.

3. Since 31 August 2019, a small industrial customer has gone into liquidation, owing Laura £2,500. The liquidator has told Laura that no payment towards settling this trade receivable will be made. The liquidation of this customer has made Laura think about the solvency of her other trade receivables. She decides that she would like to create an allowance for receivables of 10% of her remaining trade receivables.

4. Laura bought a second-hand van for £6,000 on 1 September 2018. She reckons this van will last for three years before she has to replace it. She anticipates that the trade-in value

of this van will be £600 in three years' time. Laura expects the van to travel 5,000 miles each year on journeys for business purposes.

5. Van running expenses and insurance for the year amounted to £4,000. All of these expenses were paid from the business bank account. No van running expenses were outstanding or prepaid at 31 August 2019.

6. On 1 September 2018, Laura paid £5,000 for various items of second-hand construction equipment. These assets should last four years and fetch £60 as scrap when they are replaced. Laura expects to make the same use of these assets in each of the four years of their expected useful life.

7. Two part-time helpers were employed for 13 weeks during June, July and August 2019. By 31 August 2019, Laura had paid both these helpers 12 weeks of their wages amounting to £9,600 out of the business bank account.

8. Comprehensive business insurance was taken out and paid for on 1 September 2018. As a new business customer, Laura took advantage of the insurance company's discount scheme to pay £1,800 for 18 months cover.

9. Laura counted up and valued her inventory of building materials at 31 August 2019. She valued all these items at a cost to the business of £4,500.

10. Bank charges of £400 were deducted from Laura's business bank account during the year. The bank manager has told her that accrued charges to the end of August 2019 amount to an additional £75. These charges will be deducted from her business bank account during September 2019.

11. Laura's bank account was overdrawn in the early part of her first year of trading. The bank charged her £200 interest on this overdraft. Since then, her bank account has shown a positive balance and she has earned £250 in interest up to 31 July 2019. The bank manager has told her that in August 2019 her interest receivable is a further £50 and this will be added to her account in October 2019.

12. Laura withdrew £2,500 each month from her business bank account for her personal expenses. As she had so much cash in the bank in August 2019, on 31 August 2019 she used £90,000 from her business bank account to repay half of the mortgage on her house.

Required

(a) Prepare Laura's bank account for the year ended 31 August 2019.

(b) Prepare a statement of profit or loss by nature for Laura's business for the year to 31 August 2019 and a statement of financial position at that date.

4 The statement of cash flows

LEARNING OUTCOMES

Once you have read this chapter and worked through the questions and examples in both this chapter and the online workbook, you should be able to:

- Understand that profit does not equal cash

- Appreciate that without a steady cash inflow from operations an entity will not be able to survive

- Describe the make-up of operating, investing and financing cash flows

- Prepare simple statements of cash flows using both the direct and indirect methods

- Explain the importance of statements of cash flows as the third key accounting statement alongside the statement of profit or loss and statement of financial position

- Understand why statements of cash flows on their own would be insufficient to present a clear picture of an entity's performance and financial position

- Summarize and describe the conventions upon which accounting is based

Introduction

The last two chapters have considered two of the three main accounting statements that entities publish relating to each accounting period. The statement of financial position gives us a snapshot of an entity's assets and liabilities at the end of each accounting period, while the statement of profit or loss shows us the profit or loss based on the income generated and expenditure incurred within each accounting period. This chapter will consider the third key accounting statement, the statement of cash flows, which presents users of financial information with details of cash inflows and outflows for an accounting period. As we shall see, the statement of cash flows links together the statement of profit or loss and the statement of financial position to demonstrate changes in an entity's financial position over each accounting period arising from operating, investing and financing activities.

4

Without a steady inflow of cash, businesses cannot survive. Thus, if cash is not generated from sales, there will be no money with which to pay liabilities owed, to pay wages to employees to produce or sell goods, to pay rent on facilities hired, to pay returns to investors or to finance growth and expansion. Over time, cash inflows must exceed cash outflows in order for an entity to remain a **going concern**, a business that will continue into the foreseeable future. The ability of a business to generate cash is thus critical to its survival as, without a steady inflow of cash, the business cannot carry on, no matter how profitable. It is hugely important to appreciate that profit does not represent cash. To illustrate this fact, Give me an example 4.1 presents the case of Salesforce.com which generates a modest profit while enjoying very strong cash inflows from its daily operations.

GIVE ME AN EXAMPLE 4.1   Salesforce.com

In the financial year to 31 January 2018, Salesforce.com, the customer relationship management software business, reported a net profit of $127.5m. However, cash generated from operations amounted to $2,738.0m, a difference of $2,610.5m. How does this difference arise? Many if not all customers pay in full for the services they buy when they sign the contract.

However, the sales income and profit from each contract are recognized over the life of that contract which may extend for several months or even years. Cash is thus received far in advance of the point in time at which services are provided.

Source: http://investor.salesforce.com

> **WHY IS THIS RELEVANT TO ME?**   The importance of cash
>
> To enable you as a business professional and user of financial information to understand that:
>
> - Profit is not equivalent to cash
> - Turning profits into cash is a most important task for businesses
> - Without cash, businesses will not be able to meet their commitments or fund their expansion plans and will fail

---

GO BACK OVER THIS AGAIN!   Do you really appreciate how important cash and cash inflow are? Go to the **online workbook** Exercises 4.1 to make sure you have grasped this critical lesson.

4

Statement of cash flows: format

What format does the statement of cash flows take? Illustration 4.1 shows the statement of cash flows for Bunns the Bakers plc for the years ended 31 March 2019 and 31 March 2018 in the format required by International Financial Reporting Standards. As with the statement of financial position and the statement of profit or loss, we shall present the complete statement before we consider the detail of how each part of the statement is constructed and what the terminology means.

Note: cash inflows (money coming in) are shown without brackets while cash outflows (money going out) are shown in brackets. Work through the statement of cash flows, adding the figures without brackets and deducting the figures in brackets to help you understand how the cash inflows and outflows add up to the subtotals presented.

The net increase in cash and cash equivalents for the year ended 31 March 2019 of £23,000 is calculated by adding the net cash inflow from operating activities (+ £1,219,000) and then subtracting the net cash outflow from investing activities (−£891,000) and subtracting the net cash outflow from financing activities (−£305,000). Check back to the statement of financial position for Bunns the Bakers plc (Chapter 2, Illustration 2.1) to make sure that the figure given for cash and cash equivalents at 31 March 2019 is £212,000. Repeat the calculations for 2018 to make sure you understand how the figures in the statement of cash flows are derived.

SUMMARY OF KEY CONCEPTS   Do you think that you know how to calculate the net increase (decrease) in cash and cash equivalents? Check your knowledge with Summary of key concepts 4.1.

GO BACK OVER THIS AGAIN!   A copy of this statement of cash flows (Illustration 4.1) is available in the **online workbook**. You might like to keep this on screen or print off a copy for easy reference while you work your way through the material in this chapter. There is also an annotated copy of this statement of cash flows in the **online workbook** to go over the relevant points again to reinforce your knowledge and learning.

Illustration 4.1 Bunns the Bakers plc statement of cash flows for the years ended 31 March 2019 and 31 March 2018

	2019	2018
	£000	£000
Cash flows from operating activities		
Profit for the year	547	442
Income tax expense	213	172
Finance expense	150	165
Finance income	(15)	(12)
(Increase)/decrease in inventories	(5)	8
Decrease in trade and other receivables	13	9
Increase/(decrease) in trade and other payables	109	(15)
Amortization of intangible non-current assets	5	7
Depreciation of property, plant and equipment	394	362
(Profit)/loss on the disposal of property, plant and equipment	(3)	4
Cash generated from operations	1,408	1,142
Taxation paid	(189)	(154)
Net cash inflow from operating activities	1,219	988
Cash flows from investing activities		
Acquisition of property, plant and equipment	(910)	(600)
Acquisition of investments	(6)	(11)
Proceeds from the sale of property, plant and equipment	10	47
Interest received	15	12
Net cash outflow from investing activities	(891)	(552)
Cash flows from financing activities		
Proceeds from the issue of ordinary share capital	235	148
Dividends paid	(90)	(72)
Repayment of the current portion of long-term borrowings	(300)	(300)
Interest paid	(150)	(165)
Net cash outflow from financing activities	(305)	(389)
Net increase in cash and cash equivalents	23	47
Cash and cash equivalents at the start of the year	189	142
Cash and cash equivalents at the end of the year	212	189

4

Constructing the statement of cash flows

Illustration 4.1 shows that Bunns the Bakers' statement of cash flows consists of three sections:

- Cash flows from operating activities
- Cash flows from investing activities
- Cash flows from financing activities

These three sections represent the inflows and outflows of cash for all entities. Let us look at each of these categories in turn.

Cash flows from operating activities

All entities operate with a view to generating cash with which to finance their day-to-day operations, their operating activities, and with the intention and expectation of generating surplus cash for future investment and expansion. This cash generated will consist of the cash from sales less the cash spent in both generating those sales and in running the organization.

As we have already seen, Bunns the Bakers produces bakery goods and buys in other goods for resale in the shops. Operating cash inflows will thus consist of money received from sales in the shops while operating cash outflows will be made up of the money spent on:

- Producing the goods
- Buying goods in for resale
- Distributing the goods to shops
- Selling those goods in the shops
- Administration expenses incurred in the running of the business

The difference between the trading and operating cash flowing into the business and the trading and operating cash flowing out of the business will give the net operating cash inflows or outflows for each accounting period, the cash generated from operations. Any taxation paid by the entity will also be deducted from operating cash flows, as shown in Illustration 4.1. Tax arises as a consequence of profits made from operating activities, so any tax paid in an accounting period will be deducted from the cash generated from operations.

Bunns the Bakers' statement of cash flows is an example of the **indirect method** of cash flow preparation. This approach requires that the profits for the year be subjected to certain adjustments: these adjustments are given in the cash flows from operating activities calculation in the first part of Illustration 4.1. These adjustments to the profit for the year firstly add back the income tax expense, finance expense and finance income to arrive at the operating profit line in the statement of profit or loss. Further adjustments then represent the effect of non-cash income and expenses in the statement of profit or loss alongside movements in working capital (changes in inventory, trade and other receivables and trade and other payables over the course of the accounting period) and are made in order to work back to the actual cash generated from operating activities. These adjustments and how they are derived are explained in more detail later in this chapter (The indirect method). Give me an example 4.2 presents the cash flows from operating activities for Greggs plc to illustrate many of the adjustments made to the profit for the year to determine the cash flows from operating activities that you will come across in practical situations.

4

GIVE ME AN EXAMPLE 4.2   Cash flows from operating activities

What sort of cash flows from operating activities do companies present in their annual reports and accounts? The following extract is taken from the statements of cash flows of Greggs plc for the 52 weeks ended 30 December 2017 and the 52 weeks ended 31 December 2016.

Cash flow statement—cash generated from operations

	2017	2016
	£000	£000
Profit for the financial year	56,906	57,993
Amortization	3,435	2,100
Depreciation	50,044	43,453
(Reversal of impairment)/impairment	(415)	488
Loss on sale of property, plant and equipment	2,719	2,476
Release of government grants	(472)	(472)
Share-based payment expenses	1,835	1,994
Finance expense	368	26
Income tax expense	15,039	17,149
Increase in inventories	(2,754)	(490)
Increase in receivables	(2,652)	(3,066)
Increase in payables	4,497	11,845
Increase in provisions	5,920	277
Cash from operating activities	134,470	133,773

Source: *Greggs plc annual report and accounts 2017* https://corporate.greggs.co.uk/investors/results-centre

→

Just as in the case of Bunns the Bakers, Greggs plc presents the movements in working capital (changes in inventory, receivables and trade payables as well as provisions), adds back amortization and depreciation charged on non-current assets together with losses on the sale of non-current assets and adds back the income tax and finance expenses deducted from operating profit in calculating the profit for the year. In addition, Greggs makes an entry for the impairment of non-current assets: this is a loss in the carrying value of non-current assets over and above the regular charge for depreciation that is added to the statement of profit or loss as an expense as soon as it is known: charges for (or reversals of) impairment are an expense (income) in the statement of profit or loss but do not involve any cash inflow or outflow. Companies that receive government grants record the cash received in the year of receipt as a cash inflow from financing activities but release a portion of each grant to the statement of profit or loss each year: as this allocation to the statement of profit or loss is not a cash flow, the income is deducted from operating profit to arrive at cash flows from operating activities. Payments in shares are an expense but do not involve cash as shares are used to make the payments, so these share-based payment expenses are also added back to profit for the year in calculating cash flows from operating activities.

GO BACK OVER THIS AGAIN!   Are you totally convinced that you can distinguish between cash inflows and cash outflows from operating activities? Go to the **online workbook** and complete Exercises 4.2 to make sure you can make these distinctions.

Cash flows from investing activities

In order to expand a business, entities must invest in new capacity in the form of non-current assets. Any cash paid out to buy new property, plant and equipment or intangible assets such as trademarks will appear under this heading as this represents investment of cash into new long-term assets with which to generate new income by expanding, improving and updating the business. Where an entity has surplus funds that cannot currently be used to invest in such assets, it will place those funds in long-term investments to generate interest or dividend income that will increase the profits of the organization. Thus, any investment in non-current asset investments will also appear under this heading. Note that both of these uses of cash represent outflows of cash as cash is leaving the business in exchange for new property, plant and equipment or new long-term investments.

In addition to these outflows of cash, investing activities also give rise to inflows of cash. When buying new property, plant and equipment, it is quite likely that some other non-current assets will be sold or scrapped at the same time, as these are now worn out or surplus to requirements. Selling or scrapping these assets will result in a cash inflow and any cash raised in this way will be classified under investing activities. Likewise, any interest or dividends received from investing surplus funds in current or non-current asset investments are also cash inflows under investing activities: the investments were made with a view to generating investment income, so such cash inflows are logically included under this heading. Cash inflows and outflows from investing activities are summarized in Figure 4.1, while Give me an example 4.3 presents the cash flows from investing activities for Greggs plc to provide a real-life illustration of these cash inflows and outflows.

GIVE ME AN EXAMPLE 4.3   Cash flows from investing activities

What sort of cash flows from investing activities do companies present in their annual reports and accounts? The following extract is taken from the statements of cash flows of Greggs plc for the 52 weeks ended 30 December 2017 and the 52 weeks ended 31 December 2016. All the entries will be familiar to you from the statement of cash flows of Bunns the Bakers.

Investing activities	2017	2016
	£000	£000
Acquisition of property, plant and equipment	(68,646)	(74,016)
Acquisition of intangible assets	(3,918)	(6,106)
Proceeds from sale of property, plant and equipment	2,171	4,698
Interest received	249	124
Net cash outflow from investing activities	(70,144)	(75,300)

Source: *Greggs plc annual report and accounts 2017* https://corporate.greggs.co.uk/investors/results-centre

---

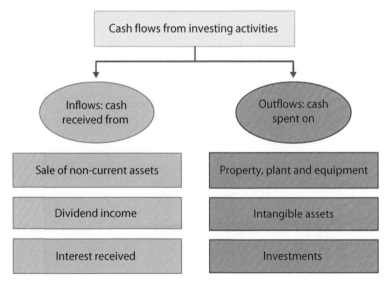

Figure 4.1 Cash inflows and outflows from investing activities

GO BACK OVER THIS AGAIN!   Quite sure that you could say whether a transaction is a cash inflow or cash outflow from investing activities? Go to the **online workbook** and complete Exercises 4.3 to make sure you can make these decisions correctly.

Cash flows from financing activities

There are three main sources of finance for a business. The first of these is cash generated from operations. This source of cash has already been dealt with earlier (this chapter, Cash flows from operating activities).

The second source of finance for business is from the issue of share capital. Bunns the Bakers have issued shares during the year for cash and so this is recorded as a cash inflow to the business: money has been paid into the company in return for new shares. Shareholders expect a return on their investment in the company: the cash outflows related to share capital are the dividends paid out to shareholders (Chapter 5, Dividends). The payment of dividends is an outflow of cash and is recorded under financing activities as it relates to the cost of financing the business through share capital.

The third source of finance is provided by lenders, money borrowed from banks or the money markets to finance expansion and the acquisition of new non-current assets. As the expansion/new non-current assets generate cash from their operation, these cash inflows are used to repay the borrowings over the following years, much as a taxi driver might borrow money to buy a taxi and then repay that loan from monthly fares earned. This is the case for Bunns the Bakers this year. While no new borrowings have been taken out (this would be an inflow of cash) part of the money previously borrowed has now been repaid from cash generated from operations in the current year. Repayments of borrowings are an outflow of cash. Any interest paid that arises from borrowing money is recorded as an outflow of cash under financing activities. Just as dividends are paid as a result of financing operations or expansion through the issue of share capital, interest is paid when financing operations or expansion through borrowing and so is matched to the financing activities section of the statement of cash flows. Figure 4.2 summarizes the cash inflows and outflows from financing activities while Give me an example 4.4 presents the cash flows from financing activities for Greggs plc to provide a real-life example of these cash inflows and outflows.

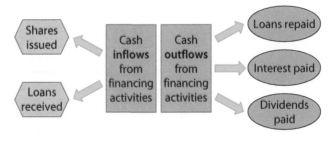

Figure 4.2 Cash inflows and cash outflows from financing activities

GIVE ME AN EXAMPLE 4.4 Cash flows from financing activities

What sort of cash flows from financing activities do companies present in their annual reports and accounts? The following extract is taken from the statements of cash flows of Greggs plc for the 52 weeks ended 30 December 2017 and the 52 weeks ended 31 December 2016.

Financing activities

	2017	2016
	£000	£000
Sale of own shares	5,358	4,063
Purchase of own shares	(11,352)	(12,398)
Dividends paid	(32,187)	(30,936)
Net cash outflow from financing activities	(38,181)	(39,271)

Source: *Greggs plc annual report and accounts 2017* https://corporate.greggs.co.uk/investors/results-centre

Just as in the case of Bunns the Bakers, cash from the sale of shares is an inflow of cash to the business while dividends paid are an outflow. Why would Greggs buy its own shares? As noted under Give me an example 4.2, Cash flows from operating activities, Greggs incurs share-based payment expenses. The company buys shares in the stock market and then uses these shares to make the share-based payments. Give me an example 4.2 made the point that share-based payments do not involve a cash outflow. Instead, the cash outflow occurs when the company buys its shares with which to meet the share-based payments.

GO BACK OVER THIS AGAIN! How easily can you distinguish between cash inflows and cash outflows from financing activities? Go to the **online workbook** and complete Exercises 4.4 to make sure you can make these distinctions.

Cash and cash equivalents

The sum of all three cash flow sections will equal the movement in cash and cash equivalents during the accounting period. The meaning of cash is quite clear, but you might be puzzled by the phrase cash equivalents. Is there really an equivalent to cash?

What this means is anything that is close to cash, a source of cash that could be called upon immediately if required. Such a source might be a bank deposit account rather than money held in the current account for immediate use. Where money held in bank deposit accounts is readily convertible into cash then this is a cash equivalent. Thus, cash held in a deposit account requiring 30 days' notice would be a cash equivalent as the cash can easily be converted into a fixed sum of cash in a maximum of

30 days. However, cash currently held in a bond with a maturity date in two years' time would not be a cash equivalent as it cannot be converted easily to cash now or in the very near future. The International Accounting Standards Board allows any deposit of cash with a notice term of 90 days or less to be classified as a cash equivalent alongside money held in current accounts and held as cash on the business premises.

4

> **WHY IS THIS RELEVANT TO ME?** Cash flows from operating activities, investing activities and financing activities
>
> To enable you as a business professional and user of financial information to:
> - Understand the different sources from which cash flows into and out of an entity
> - Read statements of cash flows and understand what the various cash inflows and outflows of an organization represent, along with the transactions behind them

MULTIPLE CHOICE QUESTIONS Do you think that you can say to which category of cash flows a cash inflow or outflow belongs? Go to the **online workbook** and complete Multiple choice questions 4.1 to make sure you can identify these accurately.

GO BACK OVER THIS AGAIN! Reckon you can categorize cash inflows and outflows correctly? Go to the **online workbook** and complete Exercises 4.5 to check your understanding.

SUMMARY OF KEY CONCEPTS Are you quite sure that you can say what makes up cash flows from operating activities, investing activities and financing activities? Revise these categories with Summary of key concepts 4.2–4.4.

Profit ≠ cash

We have already touched upon the idea both in the Julia example in Chapter 3 (Preparing the statement of profit or loss) and at the start of this chapter that profit does not equal cash. It is now time to show how true this statement is in Example 4.1.

EXAMPLE 4.1

Start Up begins a wholesale trading business on 1 January and makes sales of £20,000 in January, £30,000 in February and £40,000 in March. The cost of purchases is £15,000 in January, £22,500 in February and £30,000 in March. All goods purchased each month are sold in that month so that cost of sales equals cost of purchases.

The statement of profit or loss for Start Up for each month and in total for the three months will be as follows:

	January	February	March	Total
	£	£	£	£
Sales	20,000	30,000	40,000	90,000
Cost of sales	15,000	22,500	30,000	67,500
Gross profit	5,000	7,500	10,000	22,500

Start Up makes a profit each month. Profit is rising so the owners of Start Up will be pleased. However, to show that profit is not cash, let's look at two alternative scenarios for the way in which Start Up collects its cash from customers and pays cash to its suppliers.

4

Start Up cash flow: scenario 1

Start Up is unable to gain credit from its suppliers and so pays for goods in the month of purchase. In order to build up trade with its customers, Start Up offers generous credit terms and allows its customers to pay for goods delivered two months after sales are made. There is no cash in the bank on 1 January and each month that the company is overdrawn a charge of 1% of the closing overdraft is incurred on the first day of the following month. Each month that the company is in credit (has a surplus in its account) the bank pays interest of 0.5% on the credit balance at the end of the month on the first day of the following month. The cash flow for the three months ended 31 March will be as follows:

	January	February	March	Total
	£	£	£	£
Opening cash balance	—	(15,000)	(37,650)	—
Cash receipts from sales	—	—	20,000	20,000
Cash paid to suppliers	(15,000)	(22,500)	(30,000)	(67,500)
Interest received	—	—	—	—
Overdraft charges (1%)	—	(150)	*(377)	(527)
Closing cash balance	(15,000)	(37,650)	(48,027)	(48,027)

* Rounded to the nearest whole £.

Despite the profit made according to the statement of profit or loss, look how poorly trading has turned out from a cash flow point of view. All the purchases have been paid for in the month in which they were made, but the company is still owed £70,000 by customers (£30,000 for February + £40,000 for March: might any of these trade receivables become irrecoverable debts?) at the end of March. In addition, Start Up has incurred overdraft charges of £527 in February and March with the prospect of another £480 to pay in April (£48,027 × 1%).

Clearly, the £22,500 gross profit for the three months has not translated into surplus cash at the end of the three-month period. Start Up's bank manager might begin to worry about the increasing overdraft and put pressure on the company to reduce this. But, with cash being paid out up front to suppliers while customers enjoy a two-month credit period in which to pay, a reduction in the overdraft in the near future looks highly unlikely. Many small businesses when they start up offer generous credit terms to customers while being forced to pay quickly by their suppliers, so it should come as no surprise that many small businesses collapse within a year of starting to trade as their cash flow dries up and banks close them down to recover what they are owed.

Start Up cash flow: scenario 2

Facts are as in scenario 1, except that this time Start Up pays for its supplies one month after the month of purchase and collects cash from its customers in the month in which sales are made. The three-month cash flow will now be as shown in the table below.

	January £	February £	March £	Total £
Opening cash balance	—	20,000	35,100	—
Cash receipts from sales	20,000	30,000	40,000	90,000
Cash paid to suppliers	—	(15,000)	(22,500)	(37,500)
Interest received	—	100	*176	276
Overdraft charges	—	—	—	—
Closing cash balance	20,000	35,100	52,776	52,776

*Rounded to the nearest whole £.

What a difference a change in the terms of trade makes. By requiring customers to pay immediately for goods received and deferring payments to suppliers for a month, the cash flow has remained positive throughout the three months and additional interest income has been received from the bank by keeping cash balances positive. Suppliers are still owed £30,000, but there is more than enough cash in the bank to meet this liability and still have money available with which to keep trading.

Notably, the cash in the bank again bears no relationship to the gross profit of £22,500, so, once again, this example illustrates the key point that profit does not equal cash. The lesson to learn here is clear: if you can make sure that your customers pay before cash has to be paid to suppliers, the business will survive. In situations in which customers pay what is owed after suppliers have been paid, then the business will struggle to maintain cash inflows and be in danger of being closed down by the banks to which the business owes money.

WHY IS THIS RELEVANT TO ME?   Profit ≠ cash

To enable you as a business professional and user of financial information to:

- Appreciate that profit does not equal cash in an accounting period
- Realize that the timing of cash inflows and cash outflows has to be finely balanced to ensure that positive cash inflows are achieved
- Understand that positive cash inflows are critical to a business's ability to survive

---

NUMERICAL EXERCISES   Are you quite convinced that you could calculate cash flows from given terms of trade? Go to the **online workbook** Numerical exercises 4.1 to test out your abilities in this area.

4

Cash is cash is cash: the value of statements of cash flows

The statement of profit or loss and the two cash flows for Start Up in Example 4.1 also illustrate the advantages and the true value of the statement of cash flows when making comparisons between entities. If two companies presented exactly the same statement of profit or loss figures, it would be very difficult, if not impossible, to choose between the two and to say which company enjoyed the more stable, cash generative financial position. However, by looking at the statements of cash flows, we could say instantly that the company that presented the cash flow shown in scenario 2 was in a much better position financially compared to the company presenting the cash flow in scenario 1. Without the statement of cash flows we would not see that one company is doing very well from a cash management point of view while the other is doing very poorly. Hence the value of the statement of cash flows in enabling users to determine the financial position of an entity, information that is not available from just the statement of profit or loss.

However, the two statements of cash flows illustrate further advantages of this statement. As we saw in Chapter 3 (The accruals basis of accounting and Preparing the statement of profit or loss), the statement of profit or loss is drawn up on the accruals basis of accounting, which requires income and expenditure to be recognized in the period in which it was earned and incurred. The statement of cash flows just presents the cash inflows and outflows relating to that period. As we have seen, profit, the difference between income earned and expenditure incurred, does not equate to cash. Therefore, the provision of a statement of cash flows enables users to see much more clearly how quickly profit is turned into cash: in scenario 2 cash is clearly being generated very effectively whereas in scenario 1 the company looks as though it is about to collapse. While the accrual of expenses and income into an accounting period can produce the impression of an excellent result from a profit point of view, since cash is cash is cash it does not suffer from any distortion that might arise in the timing of income and expenditure recognition.

WHY IS THIS RELEVANT TO ME?   The value of statements of cash flows

To enable you as a business professional and user of financial information to appreciate how statements of cash flows:

- Enable users to discriminate between different entities with the same levels of profit

- Are not distorted by the effect of the accrual of income and expenditure into different accounting periods

---

GO BACK OVER THIS AGAIN!   Quite sure that you appreciate why statements of cash flows are so valuable? Go to the **online workbook** Exercises 4.6 to test your grasp of their value.

Is the statement of cash flows enough on its own?

If statements of cash flows are so useful, why do entities have to present the statement of profit or loss and the statement of financial position as well? Why not just require all organizations to produce the statement of cash flows only? This is a valid question and it leads us into thinking about why the statement of cash flows in isolation does not actually tell us very much beyond the cash generated and the cash spent during an accounting period. Let's think first about how useful the statement of financial position and the statement of profit or loss are.

In Chapter 2, we saw that the statement of financial position provides us with details of:

- Liabilities to be paid
- Assets employed within the organization

Users of financial statements can look at an entity's assets and make an assessment of whether they will be able to generate the cash necessary to meet the liabilities as they fall due. If only a statement of cash flows were to be presented, then there would be no details of either assets or liabilities and so no assessment of an entity's cash generating potential would be possible.

In Chapter 3, we saw that the statement of profit or loss presents details of:

- Income earned
- Expenditure incurred

Users of financial statements can then assess how profitable an organization is and, in conjunction with the statement of cash flows, how effectively it can turn profits into cash with which to meet operating expenses and liabilities as they fall due. Without a statement of profit or loss, the statement of cash flows cannot tell us how profitable an organization is and so how quickly those profits are being turned into cash.

A statement of cash flows on its own could be subject to manipulation. Entity owners or directors could time their cash inflows and outflows to present the most flattering picture of their organization (Chapter 3, The accruals basis of accounting). Therefore, just as a statement of profit or loss or statement of financial position in isolation does not tell us very much, so a statement of cash flows presented as the sole portrait of an entity's financial performance would also be much less informative without its fellow financial statements.

The International Accounting Standards Board (IASB) in its *Conceptual Framework for Financial Reporting* recognizes that all three statements are essential in providing information to users about the cash generating potential of businesses and that a statement of cash flows on its own is insufficient:

> Accrual accounting [in the statement of profit or loss and statement of financial position] depicts the effects of transactions and other events and circumstances on a reporting entity's economic resources and claims in the periods in which those effects occur, even if the resulting cash receipts and payments occur in a different period. This is important because information about a reporting entity's economic resources and claims [the statement of financial position] and changes in its economic resources and claims during a period [the statement of profit or loss] provides a better basis for assessing the entity's past and future performance than information solely about cash receipts and payments during that period. Information about a reporting entity's financial performance during a period [the statement of profit or loss], reflected by changes in its economic resources and claims . . . is useful in assessing the entity's past and future ability to generate net cash inflows. That information indicates the extent to which the reporting entity has increased its available economic resources, and thus its capacity for generating net cash inflows through its operations . . . Information about a reporting entity's cash flows during a period also helps users to assess the entity's ability to generate future net cash inflows . . . It [the statement of cash flows] indicates how the reporting entity obtains and spends cash, including information about its borrowing and repayment of debt, cash dividends or other cash distributions to investors and other factors that may affect the entity's liquidity or solvency. Information about cash flows helps users understand a reporting entity's operations, evaluate its financing and investing activities, assess its liquidity or solvency and interpret other information about financial performance.

> Source: IASB *Conceptual Framework for Financial Reporting*, paragraphs 1.17, 1.18 and 1.20

Thus, any one (and indeed any two) of the three financial statements on their own will not provide all the information that users will need to make the necessary evaluations. Figure 4.3 summarizes the interactions between and the interconnected nature of the three main financial statements.

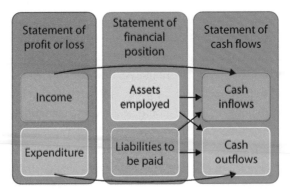

Figure 4.3 The three main financial statements and the ways in which they interact

WHY IS THIS RELEVANT TO ME?   Is the statement of cash flows enough on its own?

To enable you as a business professional and user of financial information to appreciate how:

- Statements of cash flows would not on their own provide sufficient useful information about an entity's financial position and performance

- The three main financial statements work together to provide useful information to users

GO BACK OVER THIS AGAIN!   Are you convinced that you understand how statements of cash flows work in conjunction with the other two financial statements? Go to the **online workbook** Exercises 4.7 to test your grasp of the value of statements of cash flows.

GO BACK OVER THIS AGAIN!   Can you see how the statement of cash flows explains the changes in the financial position of an entity? Go to the **online workbook** Exercises 4.8 to see how the one statement explains the changes in the other.

Preparing the statement of cash flows

There are two approaches to preparing the statement of cash flows, the direct and indirect methods. We will use the example of Julia from Chapter 3 (Preparing the statement of profit or loss) to illustrate both methods.

The direct method

Julia's bank summary for the three months ended 30 June 2019 from Chapter 3 (Example 3.8, Illustration 3.3) is reproduced in Illustration 4.2.

Illustration 4.2 Julia's bank account receipts and payments summary

Date		Receipts £	Payments £
1 April 2019	Cash introduced by Julia	30,000	
1 April 2019	Three months' rent paid on shop to 30 June 2019		5,000
1 April 2019	Cash register paid for		1,000
1 April 2019	Shelving and shop fittings paid for		12,000
30 April 2019	Receipts from sales in April 2019	20,000	
5 May 2019	Sports equipment supplied in April paid for		15,000
12 May 2019	Rates for period 1 April 2019 to 30 September 2019 paid		800
19 May 2019	Cash withdrawn for Julia's own expenses		2,000
30 May 2019	Receipts from sales in May 2019	25,000	
5 June 2019	Sports equipment supplied in May paid for		20,000
10 June 2019	Shop water rates for the year 1 April 2019 to 31 March 2020 paid		400
30 June 2019	Receipts from sales in June 2019	30,000	
30 June 2019	Balance in bank at 30 June 2019		48,800
		105,000	105,000

While Illustration 4.2 is already almost a complete statement of cash flows, showing cash received and cash paid out, all these transactions (together with the cash not yet banked from sales on 30 June 2019) would be presented in the required format as shown in Illustration 4.3.

Illustration 4.3 Julia: statement of cash flows for the three months ended 30 June 2019 using the direct method

	£	£
Cash flows from operating activities		
Receipts from sales banked 20,000 + 25,000 + 30,000	75,000	
Cash sales not yet banked	500	
Payments to trade payables for sports equipment 15,000 + 20,000	(35,000)	
Payments for expenses 5,000 (rent) + 800 (rates) + 400 (water)	(6,200)	
Net cash inflow from operating activities		34,300
Cash flows from investing activities		
Payments to acquire shop fittings and shelving	(12,000)	
Payments to acquire cash register	(1,000)	
Net cash outflow from investing activities		(13,000)
Cash flows from financing activities		
Cash introduced by Julia	30,000	
Cash withdrawn by Julia	(2,000)	
Net cash inflow from financing activities		28,000
Net increase in cash and cash equivalents		49,300
Cash and cash equivalents at the start of the period		—
Cash and cash equivalents at the end of the period		49,300

The figure for cash and cash equivalents at the end of the period is exactly the same as the bank balance plus the cash in the till at 30 June 2019 as shown in Julia's statement of financial position in Chapter 3, Illustration 3.7.

NUMERICAL EXERCISES Are you certain that you could prepare statements of cash flows using the direct method? Go to the **online workbook** Numerical exercises 4.2 to test out your ability to prepare these statements.

The indirect method

The statement of cash flows for Julia in Illustration 4.3 represents an example of the **direct method** of cash flow preparation: this takes all the cash inflows and outflows from operations and summarizes them to produce the net cash inflow from operating activities. Thus, receipts from sales are totalled up to give the cash inflow from sales and payments to suppliers and payments for expenses are totalled up to give a figure for payments to trade payables and other suppliers of services in the period. The difference between the inflows of cash from sales and the outflows of cash for expenses represents the operating cash inflows for the three months.

However, as we noted in this chapter in the Cash flows from operating activities section, the example of Bunns the Bakers' statement of cash flows in Illustration 4.1 represents an example of the indirect method of cash flow preparation. Under this method, the total inflows and outflows from operations are ignored and the operating profit for a period is adjusted for increases or decreases in inventory, receivables, prepayments, payables and accruals and for the effect of non-cash items such as depreciation. As we saw in Chapter 3 (Depreciation), depreciation is an accounting adjustment that allocates the cost of non-current assets to the accounting periods benefiting from their use. Therefore, depreciation is NOT a cash flow. The actual cash flows associated with non-current assets are the cash paid to acquire the assets in the first place and the cash received on disposal of those assets when they are sold or scrapped at the end of their useful lives. Illustration 4.4 presents Julia's statement of cash flows for the three months ended 30 June 2019 using the indirect method.

Illustration 4.4 Julia: statement of cash flows for the three months ended 30 June 2019 using the indirect method

	£	£
Cash flows from operating activities		
Net profit for the 3 months to 30 June 2019 (Illustration 3.6)		20,900
Add: depreciation on shelving and fittings (Illustration 3.6)		600
Add: depreciation on the cash register (Illustration 3.6)		50
Deduct: increase in inventory		(10,000)
Deduct: increase in receivables		(2,050)
Deduct: increase in prepayments		(700)
Add: increase in payables		24,750
Add: increase in accruals		750
Net cash inflow from operating activities (= Illustration 4.3)		34,300
Cash flows from investing activities		
Payments to acquire shop fittings and shelving	(12,000)	
Payments to acquire cash register	(1,000)	
Net cash outflow from investing activities (= Illustration 4.3)		(13,000)
Cash flows from financing activities		
Cash introduced by Julia	30,000	
Cash withdrawn by Julia	(2,000)	
Net cash inflow from financing activities (= Illustration 4.3)		28,000
Net increase in cash and cash equivalents		49,300
Cash and cash equivalents at the start of the period		—
Cash and cash equivalents at the end of the period		49,300

Let's look at how using the indirect method would affect the preparation of Julia's statement of cash flows. While the direct method of cash flow preparation is very easy to understand and put together from summaries of cash receipts and payments, most entities use the indirect method.

Not surprisingly, both the direct and the indirect method give the same answer for net cash inflow for the three months, £49,300. The only differences between the two cash flows are in the calculation of the cash flow from operating activities.

In the cash flow from operating activities section, depreciation on the shelving and fittings and on the cash register is exactly the same as the depreciation charged in the statement of profit or loss for the three months ended 30 June 2019 (Chapter 3, Illustration 3.6). The changes in the amounts for inventory, receivables, prepayments, payables and accruals are usually the difference between the current period end's figures and the figures at the end of the previous accounting period. As this is Julia's first trading period, the figures for the changes in these amounts are exactly the same as the figures from her statement of financial position (Chapter 3, Illustration 3.7). The figures at the start of the business were all £nil. Thus, for example, in the case of inventory £10,000 − £nil = an increase of £10,000.

SHOW ME HOW TO DO IT   Are you certain that you understand how Julia's statement of cash flows using the indirect method was put together? View Video presentation 4.1 in the **online workbook** to see a practical demonstration of how this statement of cash flows was drawn up.

NUMERICAL EXERCISES   Do you reckon that you could prepare statements of cash flows using the indirect method? Go to the **online workbook** Numerical exercises 4.3 to test out your ability to prepare these statements.

The indirect method: cash flows from operating activities

Why are the cash flows associated with Julia's inventory, receivables and prepayments treated as outflows of cash (appearing in brackets) while the cash flows associated with payables and accruals are all inflows of cash (appearing without brackets)? The answer lies in the fact that the statement of profit or loss is prepared on the accruals basis of accounting, recognizing income and expenses in the period in which they are earned or incurred rather than in the periods in which cash is received or paid. Some income has thus been recognized in the statement of profit or loss that has not yet resulted in a cash inflow. Similarly, some expenses have been recognized in the statement of profit or loss without the corresponding cash outflow. Therefore, adjustments for these 'non-cash' figures have to be made to operating profit to determine the actual cash flows from operating activities under the indirect method. Let's look at each of these adjustments in turn.

Inventory

An increase in inventory is an increase in an asset. This represents an outflow of cash as more money will have been spent on acquiring this additional inventory. Hence the deduction from operating profit. On the other hand, if the inventory figure decreases over the year, this would mean that more inventory had been sold, resulting in larger cash inflows. Such a fall in inventory would result in an inflow of cash and be added to operating profit.

Receivables

An increase in receivables means additional sales have been recognized in the statement of profit or loss, but that cash has not yet been received from this additional income. As no cash inflow relating to these additional sales has occurred, the increase in receivables is treated as a deduction from operating profit to reflect this lack of cash inflow. As in the case of inventory, if the amount of receivables falls, this means more money has been generated from receivables so this is treated as an increase in cash inflows and is added to cash flows from operating activities.

Trade payables

On the other hand, if trade payables have increased, less money has been spent on paying suppliers. An increase in trade payables means that cash has not flowed out of the business, so this reduction in payments is added to operating profit. Where trade payables have decreased, this means more cash has been spent on reducing these liabilities, so this is treated as a decrease in cash and a deduction is made from operating profit to reflect this outflow of cash.

Prepayments and accruals

Prepayments represent expenses paid in advance so an increase in prepayments means that more cash has flowed out of the business due to an increase in payments made in the current year. This increase is deducted from operating profit. An increase in accruals on the other hand, as with the increase in payables, means that while an expense has been recognized no cash has yet been paid out so this increase is added to operating profit. Where prepayments fall, this is treated as an increase in operating cash flows as less cash has been spent on paying expenses in advance, while a decrease in accruals would represent increased cash outflows as more money would have been spent on reducing these liabilities.

Initially these rules will seem confusing, but practice will enable you to become familiar with them and to apply them confidently in preparing statements of cash flows using the indirect method. To assist you in applying these rules, Table 4.1 shows which adjustments should be added and which adjustments should be deducted from operating profit in arriving at the cash flows from operating activities when applying the indirect method. Keep this table handy when you are working through the online examples and the questions at the end of this chapter.

Table 4.1 Figures to add to and figures to deduct from operating profit to determine the cash flow from operating activities when preparing statements of cash flows using the indirect method

Starting point: operating profit in the statement of profit or loss (= profit for the year + income tax + finance expense − finance income)	
Add	Deduct
Depreciation of non-current assets	
Amortization of intangible non-current assets	
Loss on disposal of non-current assets	Profit on disposal of non-current assets
Decrease in inventory	Increase in inventory
Decrease in receivables	Increase in receivables
Decrease in prepayments	Increase in prepayments
Increase in payables	Decrease in payables
Increase in accruals	Decrease in accruals
Increase in provisions	Decrease in provisions

GO BACK OVER THIS AGAIN! How well can you remember Table 4.1? Go to the **online workbook** and complete Exercises 4.9 to check your recollection.

The only items in Table 4.1 that we have not dealt with in our cash flow studies to date are the profits and losses on the disposal of non-current assets. The actual cash flow associated with the disposal of non-current assets is the actual cash received. Just as depreciation, which was treated as an expense in arriving at operating profit, is added back to operating profit to determine the cash flows from operating activities, so losses on disposal are added as they, too, have been treated as an additional expense in arriving at operating profit. Profits on disposal, on the other hand, have been treated as income in determining operating profit and so have to be deducted in arriving at the cash flows from operating activities.

WHY IS THIS RELEVANT TO ME? The indirect method: cash flows from operating activities

To enable you as a business professional and user of financial information to understand how:

- Adjustments under the indirect method of preparing the statement of cash flows have been calculated

- Movements in the working capital (inventory, receivables and payables) impact upon the cash flows from operating activities

MULTIPLE CHOICE QUESTIONS Could you calculate profits and losses on the disposal of non-current assets? Say what the cash inflow or outflow was on a non-current asset disposal? Go to the **online workbook** and complete Multiple choice questions 4.2 to make sure you can make these calculations correctly.

Accounting principles and conventions

We have now worked through the three key accounting statements: the statement of profit or loss, the statement of financial position and the statement of cash flows. On our journey this far, we have noted various accounting principles and conventions that apply in the preparation of these three financial statements. These principles and conventions are summarized below:

- **Accruals (also known as matching)**

The accruals basis of accounting was covered in Chapter 3 (The accruals basis of accounting). This principle states that all income and expenditure incurred in an accounting period is recognized in that period irrespective of when cash is received or paid.

- **Business entity**

Under the business entity principle, the affairs of the business and the affairs of the owner are kept entirely separate. The business and the owner are thus treated as two separate entities. This principle requires that personal and business transactions are not mixed together so that the financial statements of the business present just the results and financial position of the business (Chapter 3, Drawings and the business entity assumption).

- Consistency   , + calculation of financial items

Presentation and measurement in the financial statements of the same items in the same way from year to year will assist users in understanding the information presented and in making comparisons between different accounting periods and between different business entities. Consistent presentation and measurement will help achieve comparability (Chapter 1, What qualities should accounting information possess?).

- **Dual aspect (the duality principle)**

This principle states that every transaction has a dual effect on the financial statements. As assets are created, this gives rise to an increase in liabilities, income or capital. Similarly, as liabilities are assumed this causes assets or expenditure to increase. An increase in one asset can cause a reduction in another asset or both assets and liabilities can decrease (Chapter 2, The dual aspect concept).

- **Going concern**

The financial statements of an entity are drawn up on the basis that the entity will continue in existence for the foreseeable future. In preparing the financial statements for publication, it is assumed that an entity does not intend to cease trading and that it will not be entering into liquidation. If an organization does intend to cease trading or enter into liquidation, it is not a going concern and the financial statements will be drawn up on an entirely different basis.

- **Historic cost**

The historic cost convention dictates that the assets and liabilities of a business should be valued at their original (historic) cost to the organization. This convention has been relaxed over the years and the IASB now allows (and sometimes requires) the recognition of assets and liabilities at their fair value to the organization (Chapter 2, How are assets and liabilities valued?).

- **Materiality**

Information is material if its omission or misstatement could influence the decisions of users based on the financial information provided by an entity. Information can be material by virtue of its size, its nature or both its size and nature (Chapter 1, Materiality).

- **Money measurement**

Money is the unit of measurement in financial statements. Figures presented in the statement of profit or loss, statement of financial position and statement of cash flows must be measured in money terms.

- **Periodicity**

Entities report their financial performance and their financial position at regular intervals. The usual reporting period for business organizations is at yearly intervals to allow users to assess how well the organization is performing and to enable the tax authorities to tax each entity on the basis of its financial performance.

- **Prudence**

'Prudence is the exercise of caution when making judgements under conditions of uncertainty' (IASB *Conceptual Framework for Financial Reporting*, paragraph 2.16). This means that preparers of financial statements should take care to ensure that assets, expenses, liabilities and income are neither overstated nor understated. The exercise of excessive prudence in the valuation of items in financial statements should be avoided as this will introduce bias into financial reporting and mean that the financial information presented is no longer neutral. Note that prudence only applies to judgements made under conditions of uncertainty: when there is no uncertainty, there is no requirement to exercise prudence.

- **Realization**

Profits should not be anticipated until they have been earned through a sale (Chapter 3, Closing inventory). Until a sale has been completed through the delivery of goods to and the acceptance of those goods by a customer no sale or profit should be recognized as the customer can change their mind up until that point. Once goods have been delivered to and accepted by a customer then the sale and the associated profit can be recognized by an entity.

WHY IS THIS RELEVANT TO ME?   Accounting principles and conventions

To enable you as a business professional and user of financial information to understand the principles and conventions:

- Upon which financial statements are based
- Which you will have to apply if you are ever required to produce your own financial statements

4

GO BACK OVER THIS AGAIN!   How well have you remembered what these principles and conventions state and how they are applied? Go to the **online workbook** and complete Exercises 4.10 to check your recollection.

MULTIPLE CHOICE QUESTIONS   Do you think that you can distinguish between different accounting principles and conventions? Go to the **online workbook** and complete Multiple choice questions 4.3 to test your ability to make these distinctions.

CHAPTER SUMMARY

You should now have learnt that:

- Organizations' cash flows are made up of cash flows from operating activities, cash flows from investing activities and cash flows from financing activities
- Cash generated during an accounting period is not the same as profit
- Cash flow is critical to the survival of an organization
- Statements of cash flows can be prepared using both the direct and indirect methods
- A statement of cash flows is not sufficient on its own to provide users of financial statements with all the information they will need to assess an entity's financial position, performance and changes in financial position
- Various accounting principles and conventions apply to the preparation of financial statements

---

QUICK REVISION   Test your knowledge with the online flashcards in Summary of key concepts and attempt the Multiple choice questions, all in the **online workbook**. www.oup.com/uk/scott_business3e/

END-OF-CHAPTER QUESTIONS

Solutions to these questions can be found at the back of the book from page 464.

❯ DEVELOP YOUR UNDERSTANDING

❯ Question 4.1

Look up the answer to End-of-chapter question 3.1. Using details of Abi's assets and liabilities at the start of the trading year, her statement of profit or loss, her statement of financial position and her bank account summary for the year, present Abi's statement of cash flows using both the direct and the indirect method for the year ended 31 August 2019.

❯ Question 4.2

Alison runs an online gift shop, trading for cash with individual customers and offering trading on credit terms to businesses. Alison provides you with the following list of statement of financial position balances at 31 December 2018:

	£
Non-current assets	
Computer equipment at cost	12,775
Less: accumulated depreciation on computer equipment at 31 December 2018	(7,245)
Racks, shelving and office furniture at cost	24,000
Less: accumulated depreciation on racks, shelving and office furniture at 31 December 2018	(8,000)
	21,530
Current assets	
Inventory	27,647
Trade receivables	27,200
Rent prepayment	2,500
Rates prepayment	1,965
Cash and cash equivalents	3,682
	62,994
Total assets	84,524
Current liabilities	
Trade payables	30,314
Telephone, electricity and gas accruals	1,500
Total liabilities	31,814
Net assets	52,710
Capital account	52,710

Alison provides you with the following additional information:

- During the year to 31 December 2019, Alison spent £8,000 on buying new computer equipment and £9,600 on new racks, shelving and office equipment as her business expanded.
- There were no disposals of non-current assets during the year.

Required

Using the statement of financial position at 31 December 2018 and the additional information provided, together with the answer to Question 3.2, prepare Alison's statement of cash flows for the year ended 31 December 2019 using the indirect method.

> Question 4.3

Look up the answer to End-of-chapter questions 3.5. Using the statement of profit or loss and the statement of financial position, present the statement of cash flows for Laura for the year ended 31 August 2019 using the indirect method.

≫ TAKE IT FURTHER

>> Question 4.4

The statements of financial position for Potters Limited, together with relevant notes, are given below. Potters Limited produces crockery for sale to shops and through its site on the internet.

Potters Limited: statements of financial position at 30 June 2019 and 30 June 2018

	2019	2018
	£000	£000
Assets		
Non-current assets		
Intangible assets: trademarks	100	120
Property, plant and equipment	10,200	8,600
	10,300	8,720
Current assets		
Inventories	1,000	1,100
Trade and other receivables	1,800	1,550
Cash and cash equivalents	200	310
	3,000	2,960
Total assets	13,300	11,680
Liabilities		
Current liabilities		
Trade and other payables	1,200	1,000
Current tax liabilities	300	250
	1,500	1,250
Non-current liabilities		
Long-term borrowings	3,200	2,600
Total liabilities	4,700	3,850
Net assets	8,600	7,830

4

	2019	2018
	£000	£000
Equity		
Called up share capital (£1 ordinary shares)	1,000	800
Share premium	2,500	2,150
Retained earnings	5,100	4,880
Total equity	8,600	7,830

During the year to 30 June 2019:

- Potters Limited paid £2,500,000 to acquire new property, plant and equipment
- Depreciation of £800,000 was charged on property, plant and equipment
- Plant and equipment with a carrying amount of £100,000 was sold for £150,000
- £20,000 amortization was charged on the trademarks
- Dividends of £100,000 were paid
- Taxation of £275,000 was paid
- £200,000 interest was paid on the long-term borrowings
- Operating profit for the year was £845,000
- 200,000 new ordinary shares were issued for cash at a price of £2.75 each
- Potters Limited received no interest during the year to 30 June 2019

Required

Prepare the statement of cash flows for Potters Limited for the year ended 30 June 2019 using the indirect method.

>> Question 4.5

Statements of financial position for Metal Bashers plc, together with extracts from the statement of profit or loss and relevant notes, are given below. Metal Bashers plc produces machine tools for industrial use.

Metal Bashers plc: statements of financial position at 30 September 2019 and 30 September 2018

	2019	2018
	£000	£000
Assets		
Non-current assets		
Intangible assets: patents	200	150
Property, plant and equipment	21,800	18,850
	22,000	19,000

	2019 £000	2018 £000
Current assets		
Inventories	1,400	1,200
Trade and other receivables	2,350	2,400
Cash and cash equivalents	750	400
	4,500	4,000
Total assets	26,500	23,000
Liabilities		
Current liabilities		
Current portion of long-term borrowings	500	500
Trade and other payables	2,000	2,300
Current tax liabilities	400	350
	2,900	3,150
Non-current liabilities		
Long-term borrowings	6,500	7,000
Total liabilities	9,400	10,150
Net assets	17,100	12,850
Equity		
Called up share capital (£1 ordinary shares)	3,600	2,000
Share premium	5,600	2,400
Retained earnings	7,900	8,450
Total equity	17,100	12,850

Metal Bashers plc: statement of profit or loss (extract) for the years ended 30 September 2019 and 30 September 2018

	2019	2018
Operating profit	1,725	1,500
Finance income	100	25
Finance expense	870	950
Profit before taxation	955	575
Income tax	425	275
Profit for the year	530	300

During the year to 30 September 2019:

- Metal Bashers plc paid total dividends of £1,080,000
- New patents costing £70,000 were acquired
- Amortization charged on patents was £20,000
- 1.6 million new shares were issued during the year for cash at a price of £3 each
- Finance income and finance expense represent the actual cash received and paid during the year
- Income tax of £375,000 was paid during the year
- New property, plant and equipment costing £5,000,000 was purchased during the year for cash
- Redundant property, plant and equipment with a carrying amount of £250,000 was sold for £175,000
- Depreciation of £1,800,000 was charged on property, plant and equipment during the year

Required

(a) Prepare the statement of cash flows for Metal Bashers plc for the year ended 30 June 2019 using the indirect method.

(b) If total cash received from sales amounted to £9,550,000, total cash paid to trade payables for raw materials and expenses was £5,100,000 and total cash paid to employees was £1,280,000, show how the cash flow from operating activities would be presented under the direct method for preparing the statement of cash flows.

Business organizations and the financing of business

5

LEARNING OUTCOMES

Once you have read this chapter and worked through the questions and examples in both this chapter and the online workbook, you should be able to:

- Understand the different forms of business organization and the advantages and disadvantages of each format

- Describe the various sources of finance available to the different forms of business organization

- Discuss the returns to each source of finance

- Describe the features of ordinary and preference share capital

- Understand how cash is raised from an issue of shares

- Understand how bonus issues and rights issues work

- Understand how limited companies make dividend distributions and whether they have the capacity to make such distributions

Introduction

So far we have studied various examples of accounting statements produced by a variety of different organizations. While the financial statements of these organizations seem to adopt basically the same formats, we have not yet formally considered the different types of business entity and the ways in which they differ one from another. Bunns the Bakers is a public limited company, while Julia set up her sports equipment shop and started trading as a sole trader. What are the distinctions between these two business formats? Are there any other business formats that are commonly adopted in practice? Why is one format preferable to another and why do all businesses not follow the same format? Quite commonly, what starts off as a small business trading as a sole trader becomes a limited company later on in that business's life. This chapter will deal with the different features of each type of business organization and the advantages and disadvantages of each format.

At the same time, the two business formats we have looked at seem to adopt different methods through which to finance their operations. Julia introduced her own money into her sports equipment retailing business and was allocated all the profit from that activity at the end of the accounting year. Bunns the Bakers is financed by share capital, but how is the profit from that business allocated to its investors? In this chapter we will also be looking at how different businesses finance their operations and the requirements that each different financing method imposes upon each different business format.

> **WHY IS THIS RELEVANT TO ME?**   Types of business organization and organizational finance
>
> To enable you as a business professional and user of financial information to understand:
> - The various different types of business organization you will be dealing with in practice
> - The ways in which different types of business organization are set up and the powers that each type enjoys
> - The different types of finance that are available to different types of business organization and how each type of organization raises finance to fund their operations

Types of business organization

Let's start with a review of each of the three main types of business organization. These comprise sole traders, partnerships and limited companies.

Sole traders

Simple businesses require a simple format. As the name implies, sole traders run their businesses on their own. Sole traders set their businesses up and, while they might employ other people to assist them in the day-to-day running of operations, they take all the decisions themselves and assume total responsibility for the success or failure of their businesses. Sole traders have unlimited liability for the debts incurred by their businesses and they could lose everything in the event of business failure. These losses would extend not only to business assets but also to personal assets such as houses, cars, investments, in fact anything that those sole traders own.

The sole trader format for organizing a business is most effective where operations are straightforward and where there are no complexities that could be more efficiently dealt with by adopting a different structure. Examples of sole traders would be Julia, our stand alone retailer in Chapters 3 and 4, childminders, hairdressers, market traders, taxi drivers, sports coaches, barristers and accountants working as sole practitioners. All these people operate their businesses on their own and plough a lone furrow as they make their way in the world. There are no special requirements for setting up in business as a sole trader: just start trading. The features of the sole trader business format are summarized in Figure 5.1.

Figure 5.1 The features of the sole trader business format

GO BACK OVER THIS AGAIN!   Think you understand how sole traders operate? Go to the **online workbook** and have a go at Exercises 5.1 to reinforce your understanding of sole traders and how they operate.

Partnerships

Where two or more individuals own and run a business together, then a partnership structure will be adopted for that business. Partnerships are more complex undertakings than sole traders and reflect the fact that one person cannot know everything or be talented in every activity. Thus, in a building firm partnership, one partner might be skilled as a brick layer and plasterer, one as a plumber and heating engineer, one as an electrician. Similarly, in an accounting partnership, one partner might be knowledgeable in accounts preparation and audit, one in tax and one in insolvency.

The principle in a partnership is that all the partners take part in running the business and either enjoy a share of the profits or suffer a share of the losses from that business. You might say that a partnership is two or more sole traders coming together to make a bigger business, with each partner enjoying a share of management and reward from that enlarged business. The problem in a partnership is that the partners have to be certain that they will all be able to work together effectively and that no personality clashes or disputes will cause disruption to the business. Sole traders, of course, do not have this problem. Partnerships, like sole traders, can be set up informally and just start trading. However, given the possibility that there will be disagreements between the partners, it is usual to set out the key terms of the partnership in a written agreement signed by all the partners at the start of the partnership. As was the case with sole traders, partnerships have unlimited liability for the debts incurred by the partnership. This unlimited liability is joint and several, which means that each partner is liable collectively for the partnership debts incurred not just by themselves but by their fellow partners as well. Limited liability partnerships (LLPs) can now be set up in the UK as a result of the Limited Liability Partnerships Act 2000. Under this Act, partners in an LLP can place limits on their liability for partnership debts. Further consideration of LLPs is beyond the scope of the current book. The features of the partnership business format are summarized in Figure 5.2.

GO BACK OVER THIS AGAIN!   Confident you know how partnerships work? Go to the **online workbook** and have a go at Exercises 5.2 to reinforce your understanding of partnerships and how they operate.

Limited companies

Limited companies are much more complex organizations and are subject to much greater regulation and oversight. Given this complexity, let's look at the distinguishing features of limited liability companies (summarized in Figure 5.3) one by one, comparing and contrasting limited companies with sole traders and partnerships.

Separate legal identity

Limited companies are regarded as separate legal entities with their own name and a perpetual life. Businesses that operate as sole traders or partnerships are considered to be an extension of those individuals and the businesses and their owners are not regarded as distinct legal beings. This separate legal identity means that limited companies can sue and be sued, sign undertakings and enter into contractual obligations in their own name. Sole trader and partnership businesses tend to cease when the owners retire or die, but limited companies carry on indefinitely no matter how many of their directors or shareholders leave the company.

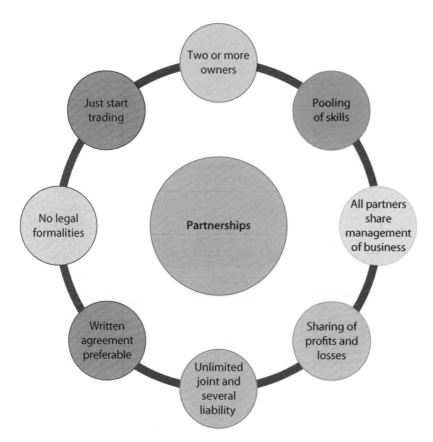

Figure 5.2 The features of the partnership business format

Share capital

Businesses can incorporate themselves as limited companies. Incorporation requires a detailed formal process (this chapter, Formation documents). On incorporation of a business, shareholders subscribe for shares in the limited company. When individuals subscribe for shares, this gives limited companies a source of finance. While sole traders and partners provide the financing for their businesses and record this in their statements of financial position as capital introduced, shareholders pay money into the company's bank account and receive shares in proportion to the capital they have invested. This share capital is recorded as issued share capital in the limited company's statement of financial position.

Limited liability

The great advantage of limited companies over sole traders and partnerships is that the liability of the shareholders to meet the debts of the limited company is restricted to the amount they have subscribed for their shares. If a limited company were to fail and go out of business, then shareholders will not have to provide any more money towards

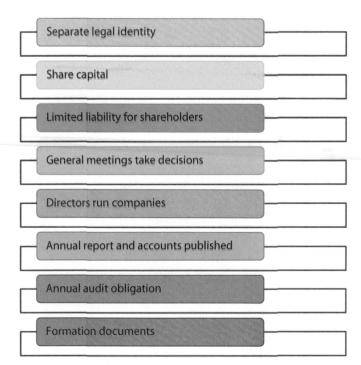

Figure 5.3 The features of the limited liability company business format

clearing the debts of the company than they have already paid for their shares. Share-holders lose the money they have already paid to acquire their shares, but they have no further liability beyond this. Thus, if a shareholder agreed to purchase one hundred £1 shares on the formation of a company, then, once the £100 has been paid to the company, the shareholder has to make no further contribution to the company should it fail. As we have seen, the situation is very different for sole traders and partnerships who have unlimited liability for the debts of their businesses with the potential to lose both business and personal assets in a business failure.

General meetings

Sole traders and partners own their businesses and answer only to themselves. Sole traders and partners thus make all the major decisions about their organizations throughout the year as and when the need arises. Limited companies, on the other hand, are accountable to their shareholders. Every year each and every limited company must hold an **annual general meeting (AGM)** at which the shareholders come together to consider and vote on various significant but standardized resolutions affecting the company. When companies undertake other business transactions which require the agreement of shareholders at other times of the year, the directors will call an **extraordinary general meeting (EGM)**. An EGM is any other company meeting other than the AGM. For example, the directors may call an EGM to ask shareholders to approve the takeover of another company. Shareholders have voting rights at the AGM and at EGMs. The size of these voting rights and the power of each shareholder depend upon the number of shares held. For each share held, a shareholder has one vote. The more shares that a shareholder owns, the more power that shareholder can exercise when voting on company resolutions.

Appointment of directors

One of the resolutions voted on at the AGM concerns the appointment of directors of the company. Limited companies, although answerable to their shareholders, are managed and run by directors appointed by the shareholders at the AGM. Directors are elected by the shareholders to run the company on their behalf. If shareholders are not happy with the performance of the current directors, they have the power to vote them out of office at the AGM and appoint different directors in their place. Directors are employees of limited companies placed in a position of trust by the shareholders. Ownership (by shareholders) and management (by directors) are thus separated, a situation that does not apply in the case of sole traders and partnerships. Of course, both directors and other employees can buy shares in their companies and thereby influence the direction and decisions of the companies which employ them. When sole traders and partnerships incorporate their businesses (transfer their business undertakings to limited companies set up for this purpose), the new companies issue shares to these former owners as payment for the assets transferred and to enable the original owners to retain control of their businesses.

Annual accounts

Because of this separation of ownership and management, the directors of limited companies have a statutory obligation under the Companies Act 2006 to present annual accounts to the shareholders at the AGM. These accounts are a financial record of how the directors have managed the monies and other resources entrusted to them by the shareholders and how they have used that money and those resources to generate profits for shareholders during the past year. As we noted in Chapter 1 (Control, accounting and accountability), the directors present this account of their stewardship of the resources entrusted to them to enable shareholders to exert control over the directors' actions and to prevent them from exceeding their powers. All limited company accounts are filed at Companies House and are available for public consultation.

Auditors and annual accounts

As shareholders do not take part in the day-to-day running of the company, they do not know whether the accounts presented by the directors are a true and fair summary of the financial achievements during the year or not. Therefore, shareholders appoint independent auditors to check the annual report and accounts for inaccuracies, omissions and misrepresentations. These auditors then report to the shareholders on whether the annual report and accounts present a true and fair view of the company's profit or loss and cash flow for the year and of the state of the company's affairs (the statement of financial position) at the year-end date. The audit report will also state whether the financial statements have been properly prepared in accordance with the relevant financial reporting standards and with the requirements of the Companies Act 2006. Shareholders are empowered by the Companies Act 2006 to choose the auditors they want to conduct the annual audit rather than the auditors that the directors would like to appoint. Auditors of limited companies enjoy various protections against removal by the directors and this enables them to perform their audits efficiently and effectively without fear or favour to the shareholders' benefit. Not every company is required to have an audit. Those companies which must have an audit and those companies for which an audit is optional are specified in the Companies Act 2006.

Sole traders and partnerships prepare annual accounts, but these are to determine any tax that is due on profits and to present to banks to support applications for loans and other borrowing facilities. There is no obligation upon sole traders or partnerships to publish their accounts publicly so that the financial affairs of sole traders and partnerships remain private and confidential. The annual accounts for sole traders and partnerships are not audited.

Formation documents

When limited companies are formed, they are registered with the Registrar of Companies. This registration comprises the name of the company and the names of the first directors (the names of the company and the directors can be changed at any time by the submission of the appropriate documentation to Companies House). In addition, two important documents are filed when a company is registered. The first is the **Memorandum of Association**. This document covers the limited company's objectives and its powers and governs the relationship of the company with the outside world. The second document is the **Articles of Association**, which covers the internal regulations of the company and governs the shareholders' relationships with each other.

WHY IS THIS RELEVANT TO ME?   Types of business organization

To enable you as a business professional and user of financial information to:

- Appreciate the different types of business organization that you will be dealing with during your career in business
- Understand how the different types of business organization operating in the economy today are set up and run
- Compare and contrast the different types of business organization you will be dealing with

Public limited and private limited companies

The Companies Act 2006 regulates all limited liability companies. However, there are two types of limited company covered in the Act: private limited companies and public limited companies. The distinctive characteristics of public limited companies are summarized in Figure 5.4. Private limited companies are prohibited from selling their shares to the public and usually have very few shareholders. Public limited companies can issue shares to the public and have many shareholders. The shares of public limited companies (but not those of limited companies which can only be traded privately) are traded on recognized stock exchanges such as those of London, New York, Paris, Hong Kong and Tokyo. Many of the businesses or websites you visit each day are run by public limited companies and these include your bank and the shops in which you buy your food. Private limited companies have the word limited or Ltd after their names while the names of public limited companies are followed by the letters plc. Look out for these company designations as you browse the web or go out into town.

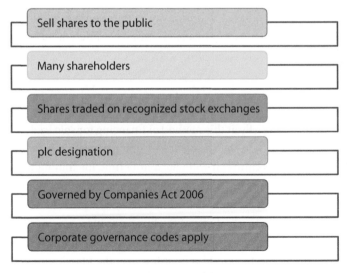

Sell shares to the public

Many shareholders

Shares traded on recognized stock exchanges

plc designation

Governed by Companies Act 2006

Corporate governance codes apply

Figure 5.4 The characteristics of public limited companies (plcs)

Public and private limited companies are subject to exactly the same rules in the Companies Act 2006. Both types of limited company produce annual reports and accounts (these are also referred to by the term financial statements). Public limited companies are also subject to stock exchange rules and regulations. A more complex financial reporting regime applies to public limited companies in that they also have to comply with various corporate governance codes, which seek to improve their ethics and accountability. Consideration of these codes is, however, outside the scope of this book.

WHY IS THIS RELEVANT TO ME?   Public and private limited companies

To enable you as a business professional and user of financial information to:

• Gain an awareness of the distinctive characteristics of the two types of limited company

• Appreciate the differences between public and private limited companies

---

GO BACK OVER THIS AGAIN!   Are you completely certain that you can distinguish between private and public limited companies? Go to the **online workbook** and have a go at Exercises 5.4 to make sure you understand the differences between private and public limited companies.

SUMMARY OF KEY CONCEPTS   Are you totally happy that you can describe the main features of private and public limited companies? Revise these main features with Summary of key concepts 5.4.

Financing business

All businesses have to raise finance at the start of their lives and at regular intervals as they expand. Providers of finance to businesses require some form of reward for providing that finance. So what sort of finance is raised by different businesses and what are the payments made to each type of finance?

Capital introduced: sole traders and partnerships

We have already looked briefly at this method of financing for sole traders in Chapter 2 (The components of equity). When a sole trader or a partnership is set up, the owners pay money into the new venture. It will take a little time for trading income to begin to flow into the business so this start-up capital is needed to buy non-current assets with which to set up the operations of the business and to provide cash to ensure the continuity of trading in the early stages of the business's life.

As an example, look back to Chapter 3, Illustration 3.3. Julia paid £30,000 into her business bank account and then used this cash to pay the initial rent of £5,000 and to buy the cash register and the shelves and fittings for her shop for £13,000 on the same day. No trading had taken place at this point so Julia had made no cash profits from which to pay for these non-current assets. Without her initial payment into the business, Julia would not have had the cash with which to make these necessary investments with which to run her retail operation. Many businesses start up in the same way with the owners paying in cash to buy assets and meet initial expenses from their own resources.

Sole traders and partners do not charge their businesses interest on this capital introduced. Instead, they draw on this capital and the profits made by the business as their source of income from which to meet their personal expenses and to finance their lifestyles. Chapter 2 (The components of equity) noted that the term for these withdrawals is 'drawings', money taken out of the business by the owner(s) for their own personal use.

As sole traders and partners are considered to be an extension of their businesses, withdrawing money in this way from their businesses is perfectly acceptable. However, it is not possible for shareholders in limited companies to withdraw money from their companies in the same way as limited companies have a separate legal identity and are regarded as completely distinct from their investors.

5

WHY IS THIS RELEVANT TO ME?   Capital introduced: sole traders and partnerships

To enable you as a business professional and user of financial information to:

- Revise capital introduced from earlier chapters
- Understand how sole traders and partnerships finance their start-up capital
- Remind yourself how the owner's capital account for sole traders and partnerships works

GO BACK OVER THIS AGAIN!   Are you sure that you understand capital introduced? Go to the **online workbook** and have a go at Exercises 5.5 to make sure you can describe capital introduced.

Bank finance: all businesses

Banks provide short- and medium-term finance to businesses in the form of overdrafts and loans. In Chapter 2 we noted that such overdrafts and loans are described as borrowings under current and non-current liabilities in the statement of financial position. The cost of both these sources of finance is interest that the bank charges on the amounts borrowed.

Bank overdrafts have the following features (summarized in Figure 5.5):

- Overdrafts are short-term finance.
- The overdraft amount varies each month depending on cash inflows and outflows during each month. The more cash received and the lower the amounts of cash paid out, the lower the overdraft will be and vice versa.

Figure 5.5 Features of bank overdrafts

- There is usually a limit on the amount of the overdraft allowed by the bank. When customers reach or exceed this overdraft limit, the bank is entitled to refuse any further credit on that account.

- Overdrafts are subject to an annual review by the bank to determine whether the overdraft limit should remain the same, increase or decrease.

- Overdrafts are not contractual arrangements and banks can ask for overdrafts to be repaid immediately.

Give me an example 5.1 presents details of bank overdrafts offered to businesses by Santander.

GIVE ME AN EXAMPLE 5.1 Bank overdrafts

Details of overdrafts offered by Santander on 8 February 2018:

Business overdraft

When you need a bit of extra cash for a short time only, a business overdraft can be an effective way to borrow:

- Business overdrafts from £500 to £25,000
- Only pay interest on the amount you borrow on the days you're overdrawn

- Easy to apply
- Quick, short-term financing
- There are fees associated with your overdraft

Interest rate

The arranged overdraft interest rate is 5.5% (variable), which is the Bank of England rate plus 5%.

Source: https://www.santander.co.uk/uk/business/borrowing-finance/business-overdrafts

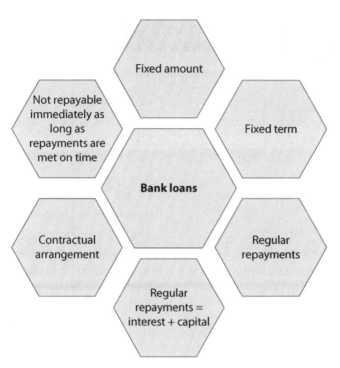

Figure 5.6 The features of bank loans

Bank loans operate as follows (the features of bank loans are summarized in Figure 5.6):

- A fixed amount is borrowed for a fixed term, usually a period of 5–10 years.
- Repayments are made on a regular basis, either monthly or quarterly.
- Each monthly repayment consists of an interest element and a repayment of part of the sum originally borrowed.
- Loans are contractual arrangements. Banks can only demand immediate repayment of loans when the borrower has failed to meet a contractual repayment or payment of interest by the due date.

Give me an example 5.2 presents details of bank loans offered to businesses by Lloyds Bank.

WHY IS THIS RELEVANT TO ME?   Bank finance

To enable you as a business professional and user of financial information to:

- Understand the difference between bank overdrafts and bank loans
- Appreciate the key features of overdraft and loan finance

GIVE ME AN EXAMPLE 5.2 Bank loans

Table 5.1 Details of business loans offered by Lloyds Bank on 8 February 2018

Base Rate Loan	Fixed Rate Loan
• Borrow from £1,000 to £50,000 over 1 to 10 years	• Borrow from £1,000 to £50,000 over 1 to 10 years
• Interest rate varies with Bank of England Bank Rate	• Fixed monthly repayments
• No arrangement fees on loans up to £25,000	• No arrangement fees on loans up to £25,000
• No early repayment costs	• No early repayment costs
• 9.0% APR Representative	• 9.3% APR Representative
Representative example: 9.0% APR based on an assumed unsecured loan amount of £8,000 with 60 monthly repayments of £164.71 at an annual interest rate of 8.65% (variable). Total amount payable £9,882.60	Representative example: 9.3% APR based on an assumed unsecured loan amount of £8,000 with 60 monthly repayments of £165.68 at an annual interest rate of 8.90% (fixed). Total amount payable £9,940.80

Commercial Fixed Rate Loan

• Borrow from £50,001 to £500,000 over 1 to 25 years

• Fixed monthly repayments

• An arrangement fee will apply and is related to the amount you borrow

• Capital repayment holidays

• Interest rate can be fixed from 1 year to the full term of the loan

Break costs may apply upon full/partial early repayment of the loan. These will be calculated based upon the loan rate compared to market rates at the time of repayment. These may be substantial.

Source: https://www.lloydsbank.com/business/retail-business/business-loans.asp

Notes to Table 5.1 (terms with which you may not be familiar):

• Bank of England Bank Rate: the Bank of England sets the interest rate (the base rate) it will pay to the commercial banks on the cash they deposit with the Bank of England. If the Bank lowers this base rate then interest rates charged by banks on loans to customers will fall. If the Bank raises this rate, then interest rates charged by banks on loans to customers will rise.

• Capital repayment holidays: the amount borrowed is called the capital element of the loan. The capital element is distinct from the interest element of the loan. For example, if a borrower borrows £25,000 at an interest rate of 5%, the capital amount of the loan is £25,000 and the annual interest on the loan is £25,000 × 5% = £1,250. Each loan instalment repaid by a borrower consists of a repayment of part of the capital of the loan and a payment of interest. Should borrowers find that cash inflows are temporarily insufficient to repay both the capital and the interest elements in each instalment on a loan, then they can stop repaying the capital part of the instalments for a set period of time, just paying the interest element. This period is called a capital repayment holiday, a break from repaying the capital element of the loan. The outstanding capital balance of what is still owed does not fall, but it does not rise either. Once the capital repayment holiday finishes, then the borrower recommences payments of both the capital and the interest elements of the loan.

• APR: annual percentage rate, the effective rate of interest charged on borrowings on an annual basis.

• Unsecured: when banks lend money to their customers, they want to be sure that they will receive the money back in the future. Banks can ask for security for loans taken out. Borrowers offer security in the form of assets such as land and buildings or other assets of the business: if the borrower is unable to repay the amounts borrowed, then the assets pledged as security to the bank will be taken by the bank and sold. The borrowings taken out are repaid from the sale proceeds generated by the sale of the assets. However, when banks allow businesses to borrow money without pledging assets on which to secure the borrowings, the lending is said to be unsecured.

GO BACK OVER THIS AGAIN!   Do you reckon that you can distinguish between overdraft and loan finance? Go to the **online workbook** and have a go at Exercises 5.6 to make sure you do understand the differences.

SUMMARY OF KEY CONCEPTS   Are you confident that you can describe the main features of overdraft and loan finance? Revise these main features with Summary of key concepts 5.5.

Other types of long-term finance: public limited companies

Public limited companies can issue **debentures**, **bonds** or **loan notes** to the public. Debentures, bonds and loan notes are long-term loans with a fixed rate of interest and a fixed repayment date. Thus a plc might issue a £500 million loan note with an interest rate of 5.25% and a repayment date of 31 January 2028. Lenders would then receive an interest payment of £26.25 million (£500m × 5.25%) every year on the anniversary of the loan note's issue and full repayment of the £500 million plus any interest outstanding up to the date of repayment on 31 January 2028.

Debentures, bonds and loan notes are traded on stock exchanges around the world so lenders can sell their holdings in these long-term loans without waiting for the repayment date.

WHY IS THIS RELEVANT TO ME?   Bond, loan note and debenture finance

To provide you as a business professional and user of financial information with:

• An awareness of bonds, loan notes and debentures as a means of raising finance for large companies

• A brief overview of the features of bonds, loan notes and debentures

GIVE ME AN EXAMPLE 5.3 Bonds

Next plc records the following corporate bond liabilities together with their associated interest rates and maturity dates in note 17 to the annual report and accounts for the financial year ended 27 January 2018.

Corporate bonds

	Balance sheet value	
	2018	2017
	£m	£m
Corporate bond 5.375% repayable 2021	328.4	329.5
Corporate bond 4.375% repayable 2026	280.1	284.0
Corporate bond 3.625% repayable 2028	300.0	300.0
	908.5	913.5

Source: http://www.nextplc.co.uk

GO BACK OVER THIS AGAIN! Are you totally convinced that you understand bonds, loan notes and debentures? Go to the **online workbook** and have a go at Exercises 5.7 to make sure you can describe these sources of finance.

SUMMARY OF KEY CONCEPTS Do you think that you can describe the main features of bond, loan note and debenture financing? Revise these main features with Summary of key concepts 5.6.

Share capital: limited companies

All limited companies, whether public or private, issue share capital. Share capital is a source of very long-term finance for a company. Shares subscribed by shareholders will be in issue for as long as the company exists. Share capital financing is not available to sole traders or partnerships unless they choose to transfer their operations to a limited company set up for this purpose. As well as issues of ordinary share capital, some companies also issue preference share capital.

Companies distribute dividends to their shareholders. Dividends are a share of the profit earned in a financial period (usually one year) paid out to the shareholders. Whereas interest on loans and overdrafts has to be paid no matter what the circumstances of the business are, companies do not have to distribute a dividend if the directors decide that it is not in the company's best interests to do so. For example, if the company were about to make a large investment in new non-current assets, it would make more sense for the company to hold onto its cash to make this investment rather than paying a dividend.

Before we consider dividends further and how these are calculated, let's look at the two types of share capital that companies issue.

Preference share capital

Preference shares are so called because holders of preference shares receive preferential treatment from the issuing company in the following ways:

- Preference shareholders must receive their dividends from the company before any distribution of profit is made to ordinary shareholders.

- Thus, if there are no profits left over for distribution after the preference dividends have been paid then the ordinary shareholders receive no dividend for that year.

- On the winding up/liquidation of a company, once all the claims of a company's creditors have been settled, any money left over and available to shareholders is repaid to preference shareholders before any payment is made to ordinary shareholders.

However, preference shareholders also suffer various restrictions as a result of this preferential treatment:

- The rate of dividend on preference shares is fixed. Thus, preference shareholders are not entitled to any further share of the profits available for distribution once their fixed rate of dividend has been paid.

- Preference shareholders have no right to vote in general meetings.

Preference shareholders' rights are restricted in the above ways as they take on a lower level of risk when compared to ordinary shareholders. Although the companies in which preference shareholders invest might still fail or not earn much profit, the fact that they are paid their dividends first and receive their money back in a liquidation before the ordinary shareholders means that they are taking less risk than ordinary shareholders who stand to lose everything. The advantages and limitations of preference shares are summarized in Figure 5.7.

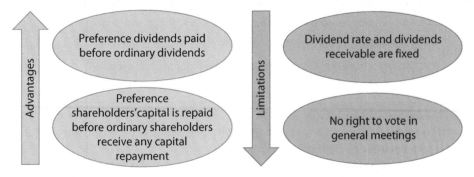

Figure 5.7 The characteristics of preference shares

Ordinary share capital

Ordinary share capital is the name given to the most common form of share capital issued by companies. You will often see ordinary share capital referred to as **equity share** capital. Ordinary shareholders take on the highest risks when they buy shares in a company. Investors in ordinary shares might receive all of a company's profits as dividends and see the value of their shares rise many times above what they originally paid for them or they could receive no dividends and nothing when the company goes into liquidation, losing all of their investment. All limited companies must issue ordinary share capital. Ordinary shares are the only shares that carry voting rights at company meetings. The positive and negative aspects of ordinary shares are summarized in Figure 5.8.

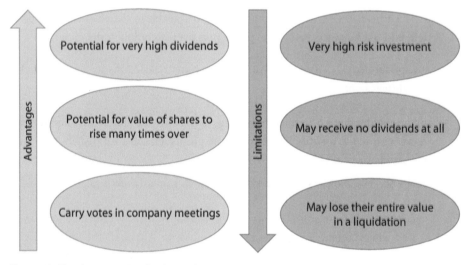

Figure 5.8 The characteristics of ordinary shares

WHY IS THIS RELEVANT TO ME?   Share capital: preference shares and ordinary shares

To enable you as a business professional and user of financial information to:

• Develop a clear awareness of the different types of share capital that companies can and do issue

• Understand the characteristics of the two different types of share capital

---

GO BACK OVER THIS AGAIN!   Are you really certain how ordinary and preference shares differ? Go to the **online workbook** and have a go at Exercises 5.8 to make sure you can distinguish between these two types of share capital.

SUMMARY OF KEY CONCEPTS   Do you reckon that you could describe the main features of ordinary and preference shares? Revise these main features with Summary of key concepts 5.7.

Share capital: share issues at par value

Under the Companies Act 2006, every company can issue as many shares as it wishes. Share capital is increased simply by issuing more shares. Example 5.1 considers share issues and par value.

EXAMPLE 5.1

Printers Limited has share capital made up of ordinary shares of £1 each and preference shares of 50 pence each. Printers can issue any number of shares it wishes. However, companies only issue shares as and when they need to raise funds rather than raising all the cash they can from shareholders immediately.

In this example, the ordinary shares have a par value of £1. The par value is the face value or nominal value of each share. Par values can be of any amount. As well as the ordinary shares with a par value of £1 each, Printers also has preference shares with a par value of 50 pence each. However, par values could be 1 penny or 12½ pence or 25 pence or any other amount that the founders of the company decide, as illustrated in Give me an example 5.4. The par value of a company's shares is stated in the Memorandum and Articles of Association.

GIVE ME AN EXAMPLE 5.4   The par value of shares

As an example of the par values of share capital, Balfour Beatty plc has ordinary shares with a par value of 50 pence each and preference shares with a par value of 1 penny each.

Source: *Balfour Beatty annual report and accounts 2017* www.balfourbeatty.com

At the start of a limited company's life, shares are issued at their par value. Thus, Printers' directors might decide to raise £20,000 on its first day to provide the company with sufficient capital to start operating. The directors decide to issue just ordinary shares. The ordinary shares have a par value of £1, so 20,000 £1 shares will need to be issued to raise the £20,000 required. Investors are said to subscribe for their shares and they pay cash to make this investment. After the share issue, the company will now have £20,000 cash in the bank and £20,000 in issued share capital.

MULTIPLE CHOICE QUESTIONS   Confident that you could calculate the sums raised from a share issue? Go to the **online workbook** and have a go at Multiple choice questions 5.1 to make sure you can calculate these amounts.

Share capital: shares issued at a premium

As companies grow, their shares increase in value. Therefore, when companies want to issue shares at a later stage of their lives, these new shares are issued at par value plus a premium to reflect this increase in value, as illustrated in Example 5.2.

EXAMPLE 5.2

Printers' directors decide to issue a further 30,000 £1 ordinary shares after one year of trading, but they now set the issue price for these additional shares at £1.25. The issue price for each share is made up of the £1 par value and a 25 pence premium. How much cash will be raised and how will this be recorded in Printers' financial statements?

The cash raised is calculated by multiplying the 30,000 shares by the £1.25 issue price for each share. This gives total cash raised of 30,000 × £1.25 = £37,500. This £37,500 comprises £30,000 of ordinary share capital (the par value of £1 × 30,000 shares) and a share premium of £7,500 (30,000 shares issued × 25 pence). The £30,000 is added to share capital and the £7,500 is added to the share premium account in the statement of financial position with the whole £37,500 raised being added to cash in the bank.

Example 5.2 tells us that the share premium is any amount raised from an issue of shares over and above the par value of the shares issued. Give me an example 5.5 presents an example of shares issued at a premium to their par value by a public company.

GIVE ME AN EXAMPLE 5.5 Shares issued at a premium to their par value

As an example of shares issued at a premium, note 22 in the Thrive Renewables 2016 annual report and financial statements presents the following information: 'In June 2016, the Company issued 433,001 new shares of £0.50 each at a premium of £1.77 each, raising new capital of £982,912.'

Source: *Thrive Renewables annual report 2016* www.thriverenewables.co.uk

WHY IS THIS RELEVANT TO ME? Share issues at par value and share issues at a premium

To enable you as a business professional and user of financial information to understand:

- How limited companies raise cash from share issues
- The financial effect of issuing shares at a premium

MULTIPLE CHOICE QUESTIONS Could you calculate the sums raised from a share issue when shares are issued at a premium? Go to the **online workbook** and have a go at Multiple choice questions 5.2 to see if you can make these calculations correctly.

SUMMARY OF KEY CONCEPTS Can you define share premium? Revise this definition with Summary of key concepts 5.8.

Share capital: bonus issues

As well as issuing shares for cash, limited companies also make what are called **bonus issues** of shares. Bonus issues are made when a company has a large surplus on its retained earnings on the statement of financial position. These retained earnings have not yet been distributed to shareholders as dividends and the company wants to keep these earnings within the business as share capital. This process is known as capitalizing reserves, turning distributable retained earnings into new non-distributable share capital. No cash is raised in a bonus issue, but the number of shares in issue increases while the retained earnings reduce by a corresponding amount. Bonus issues are only made to existing ordinary shareholders and the amount capitalized as share capital is the par value of the shares issued.

A bonus issue is always expressed as a certain number of bonus shares for a certain number of shares already held by ordinary shareholders. Thus, a one-for-four bonus issue means that one new bonus share is issued to ordinary shareholders for every four shares they already hold. A two-for-five bonus issue means that two bonus shares are issued for every five shares currently held. Let's see how a bonus issue works in Example 5.3.

EXAMPLE 5.3

James plc currently has 12 million ordinary shares of £1 each in issue. The balance on retained earnings is currently £25 million. The directors propose a four-for-three bonus issue.

In this example, four bonus shares are issued for every three shares currently held. This means that 12m × 4 new shares ÷ 3 shares currently in issue = 16m new shares of £1 each are issued to ordinary shareholders. This transaction would be presented as shown in Illustration 5.1: £16 million is added to ordinary share capital and £16 million is deducted from retained earnings.

Illustration 5.1 James plc: bonus issue of four £1 shares for every three £1 shares already held by ordinary shareholders

	Before bonus issue	+ £	− £	After bonus issue
	£			£
Equity				
Ordinary share capital	12,000,000	16,000,000		28,000,000
Retained earnings	25,000,000		16,000,000	9,000,000
	37,000,000			37,000,000

James plc now has 28 million ordinary £1 shares in issue compared to the original 12 million before the bonus issue. These newly issued bonus shares will receive dividends in the future just as the ordinary shares in issue currently do. Issuing bonus shares is a good way of increasing the number of shares in issue and strengthening the fixed capital base of a company. Once the bonus shares have been issued the retained earnings balance falls and this means that those retained earnings cannot be paid out in future as dividends.

Share capital: rights issues

From time to time, limited companies make new issues of shares to raise funds. However, companies cannot just issue new shares to anyone they want. The Companies Act 2006 prevents companies from issuing new shares to outside parties until those new shares have first been offered to current shareholders. Only when existing shareholders have turned down the opportunity to buy these new shares can the shares be offered to investors who are not currently shareholders of the company. These rights to subscribe for new issues of shares are known as **pre-emption rights**, the right to be offered first refusal on any new issue of shares.

Why does the Companies Act 2006 protect shareholders' rights in this way? Pre-emption rights prevent the dilution of existing shareholders' interests in a company. What this means and how pre-emption rights protect existing shareholders are illustrated in Example 5.4.

EXAMPLE 5.4

Joe and Bill each hold 50,000 ordinary shares in Painters Limited. Painters Limited has a total of 100,000 ordinary shares in issue, so Joe and Bill each own a 50% interest in the company. The directors decide that Painters needs to issue another 100,000 shares. If the directors were able to offer the shares to external investors, then Joe's and Bill's interest in Painters would fall to 25% each (50,000 shares ÷ (100,000 shares currently in issue + 100,000 new shares being issued)). They would thus suffer a 50% reduction in their interest in the company as a result of new shareholders being brought in. Whereas before they each controlled 50% of Painters, they now control only 25% each as a result of this new issue of shares to new investors. The Companies Act 2006 thus requires the directors to offer the new shares to Joe and Bill first so that they can take up the new shares in proportion to their current holdings and each maintain their 50% holding in the company. Only when Joe and Bill have declined the right to buy these new shares can the shares be offered to outside parties.

Rights issues: pricing

Rights issues are priced at a discount to the current market price to encourage shareholders to take up the issue. The way in which rights issues are conducted is illustrated in Example 5.5.

EXAMPLE 5.5

If the current market value of one James plc £1 ordinary share is £3, then the directors will price the rights issue at, for example, £2.20 to encourage shareholders to take up their rights. £2.20 is a discount to the current market price of 80 pence (£3.00 − £2.20). The number of shares will rise when the rights issue is complete. As you will know from studying economics, when supply increases, price goes down. Since there will be more James plc shares in issue after the rights issue the market price will fall. The discount to the current market price of the ordinary shares thus compensates James plc's shareholders for this anticipated fall in the market value of their shares.

Do note that the pricing of a rights issue at a discount to the market price is not the same as issuing shares at a discount. Issuing shares at a discount is illegal under the Companies Act 2006 and would involve, for example, selling shares with a par value of £1 for 99 pence or less. This is not allowed under company law.

How does a rights issue work? James plc's directors decide to make a rights issue of £1 ordinary shares, one for every four currently held. There are 28 million shares in issue after the bonus issue and the rights issue price is set at £2.20.

Your first task is to determine how many new shares will be issued. One new ordinary share is being issued for every four in issue, so this will give us 28,000,000 ÷ 4 = 7,000,000 new ordinary shares to issue.

How much money will this raise? Each share is being issued at £2.20, so an issue of seven million shares will raise 7,000,000 × £2.20 = £15,400,000.

You know from our previous discussions (this chapter, Share capital: shares issued at a premium) that, with the par value of the shares being £1, there is a share premium to account for as well as the new addition to share capital. How much is this premium? Issuing £1 par value shares at £2.20 means that the premium on each share issued is £2.20 − £1.00 = £1.20. The total premium on the issue of seven million shares is then 7,000,000 × £1.20 = £8,400,000. Cash thus increases by the £15,400,000 raised from the issue, ordinary share capital increases by £7,000,000, while the share premium account rises by £8,400,000.

Give me an example 5.6 presents details of a recent rights issue by Laird plc.

GIVE ME AN EXAMPLE 5.6   Rights issues of shares

On 28 February 2017, Laird plc, the electronics and technology group, announced a 4 for 5 rights issue of 217 million new shares at 85 pence per share. The company's shares were trading at 174.75 pence on the day before the rights issue was announced. The par value of each ordinary share is 28.125 pence, so the rights issue price of 85 pence per share was a large discount to the current market price but not a discount to the par value of the shares. The directors stated that the net proceeds from the rights issue of £175m would be used to reduce borrowings with the aim of strengthening the group's financial position and allowing continued investment in an operational improvement programme and in opportunities for growth in the future. Following the EGM on 16 March 2017 to approve the terms of the rights issue, the share price of Laird plc fell from 176.00 pence on 16 March to 142.50 pence on 17 March as the increase in the number of shares in issue resulted in a reduction in the share price.

Source: http://www.laird-plc.com

WHY IS THIS RELEVANT TO ME?   Bonus and rights issues

To enable you as a business professional and user of financial information to understand:

- How bonus and rights issues work
- The financial effect of bonus and rights issues

Dividends

We have already discussed the subject of dividends. It is now time to see how dividends for the year are calculated.

Dividends are distributions of profit to shareholders. They are not an expense of the distributing company in the way that wages, rent or electricity are expenses (Chapter 3, Expenses). Dividends are deducted directly from retained earnings in the statement of financial position and do not appear at all in the statement of profit or loss.

When a company decides to pay a dividend to the shareholders, a figure of pence per share is quoted. Dividends are always paid on the number of shares in issue. How does a dividend distribution work? Let's find out in Examples 5.6 and 5.7.

EXAMPLE 5.6

James plc declares a dividend of 12 pence per ordinary share. How much dividend will be paid out? There are 35 million shares in issue after the rights issue (Example 5.5). This means that holders of the 35 million £1 ordinary shares will receive 12 pence for each share that they hold. The total dividend payment will thus be 35,000,000 × £0.12 = £4,200,000. When this dividend is paid, cash at the bank will fall by £4,200,000 and retained earnings will be reduced by £4,200,000.

EXAMPLE 5.7

When calculating preference dividends, the par value of the preference shares is simply multiplied by the dividend rate. Remember that preference dividends are paid at a fixed rate and preference shareholders receive nothing more than their contractually agreed preference dividend. James plc also has 10,000,000, 50 pence, 5% preference shares in issue. This tells us that every 50 pence preference share receives a dividend of 2.5 pence (£0.50 × 5%). The total preference dividend for the year will thus be £250,000 (10,000,000 shares × £0.025). When this preference dividend is paid, cash at the bank will fall by £250,000 and retained earnings will be reduced by £250,000.

Public limited companies paying dividends usually make two distributions in each financial year. These are known as the interim dividend, paid part way through the financial year, and a final dividend based on the profits for the financial year.

Distributable and non-distributable reserves

Dividends are paid from **distributable reserves** only. Ordinary share capital, preference share capital, share premium and revaluation reserves are all capital reserves and the funds in these capital reserves are not distributable to shareholders. To make a dividend distribution from any of these reserves would be illegal under the Companies Act 2006.

For our purposes, the only distributable reserve, the one that represents realized profits of the company, is retained earnings. Retained earnings are a revenue reserve and this is the reserve from which dividends can be paid. However, if a company has retained losses and a negative balance on retained earnings, no dividends, either ordinary or preference, can be paid. Only when a company has a positive balance showing that the company has made profits can a distribution be made from the retained earnings reserve.

WHY IS THIS RELEVANT TO ME? Dividends

To enable you as a business professional and user of financial information to:

- Understand how dividends are calculated
- Distinguish between capital reserves and revenue reserves

MULTIPLE CHOICE QUESTIONS Are you confident that you could calculate dividends correctly? Go to the **online workbook** and have a go at Multiple choice questions 5.4 to make sure you can calculate dividend distributions accurately.

CHAPTER SUMMARY

You should now have learnt that:

- Very small businesses organize themselves as sole traders or partnerships that take on un-limited liability for the debts of their businesses

- Larger businesses organize themselves as limited liability companies whose investors (shareholders) have no obligation to meet the debts of their company beyond their investment in their company's share capital

- Sole traders and partnerships raise money to finance their operations from their own capital resources, from the profits of their businesses, from bank loans and from bank overdrafts

- Limited liability companies raise money to finance their operations from the issue of ordinary and preference share capital and by borrowing from banks in the form of loans or overdrafts and by issuing bonds and debentures

- The par value of a share is the face value or nominal value of that share

- A bonus issue involves the reduction of retained earnings and an increase in the issued share capital

- A rights issue is the issue of shares to shareholders at a discount to the current market price
- Dividends can only be distributed from retained earnings

QUICK REVISION   Test your knowledge with the online flashcards in Summary of key concepts and attempt the Multiple choice questions, all in the **online workbook**. www.oup.com/uk/scott_business3e/

END-OF-CHAPTER QUESTIONS

Solutions to these questions can be found at the back of the book from page 471.

❯ DEVELOP YOUR UNDERSTANDING

❯ Question 5.1

Which business format would be most suitable for the following businesses? Can you say why your chosen format would be most suited to each business?

- An oil exploration company
- A taxi driver
- A family run knitwear manufacturing business
- Two friends setting up a dance school

❯ Question 5.2

An investor has £200,000 to invest and has to choose between three different investments:

- An investment in a £200,000 bond paying 5% interest per annum
- An investment in a new issue of preference shares with a par value issue price of 50 pence paying an annual dividend of 3 pence per share
- An investment in a new issue of ordinary shares with a par value issue price of 25 pence paying an annual dividend of 2 pence per share.

How much will each investment return to the investor? Which investment would be preferable on the assumption that the investor wishes to maximize income from investing the £200,000?

❯ Question 5.3

A printing company wishes to raise £3,000,000 to finance its expansion. It can do this in one of three ways: borrowing from the bank at an annual interest rate of 5; issuing ordinary shares at their par value of 40 pence, which will require an annual dividend payment of 1.9 pence per share; or issuing preference shares with a par value of 60 pence, which requires a fixed dividend of 3.15 pence per share. Which financing option will require the lowest cash outlay for the printing company?

▶▶ TAKE IT FURTHER

» Question 5.4

Plants Limited runs a garden centre business selling garden plants and products to the public from its busy edge of town site. In the year to 31 October 2019, Plants Limited's issued share capital consists of 100,000 ordinary shares of 50 pence each and 100,000 preference shares of £1 each. The preference share dividend rate is 6%. Preference dividends are payable on 31 October each year. An interim dividend of 10 pence per share was paid on the ordinary share capital on 15 May 2019 and the directors paid a final ordinary dividend of 20 pence per ordinary share on 15 October 2019.

Required

(a) Calculate the preference dividend that Plants Limited will pay for the year ended 31 October 2019.

(b) Calculate the total ordinary dividend for the year ended 31 October 2019.

(c) If retained earnings at 1 November 2018 were £45,000 and profit for the year to 31 October 2019 was £50,000, what is the balance on retained earnings after all the dividends for the year have been paid at 31 October 2019?

» Question 5.5

Plants Limited is looking to expand its operations in the year to 31 October 2020, but needs to raise additional finance to do so. The company proposes raising £500,000 by issuing 200,000 ordinary shares on 1 May 2020. Profits for the year to 31 October 2020 are expected to be £90,000. An interim ordinary dividend of 15 pence per share will be paid on 15 April 2020 and a final ordinary dividend of 25 pence per share will be paid on 15 October 2020.

Required

Using the information above, the information from Question 5.4 and the answer to Question 5.4:

(a) Calculate the amounts to be added to ordinary share capital and share premium in the equity section of the statement of financial position in respect of the new issue of ordinary shares on 1 May 2020.

(b) Calculate the total dividends, both ordinary and preference, to be paid in the year to 31 October 2020.

(c) Calculate the expected balance on retained earnings at 31 October 2020 after dividends for the year have been paid.

» Question 5.6

At 1 July 2019 Halyson plc had 500,000 ordinary shares of 25 pence each in issue together with 300,000 7.5% preference shares of £1 each. The balance on Halyson's retained earnings at 1 July 2019 is £5,200,000.

Halyson plc is proposing a bonus issue of seven new ordinary shares for every two ordinary shares currently held. Once this bonus issue is complete, a rights issue will be made of five new ordinary shares for every three ordinary shares held at a price of £0.95. These transactions will take place on 1 April 2020.

On 28 June 2020, Halyson plc will pay the preference dividend for the year and a total ordinary dividend for the year of 30 pence per share. The loss for the year to 30 June 2020 is expected to be £1,500,000.

Required

Calculate for Halyson plc:

(a) The number of bonus shares to be issued

(b) The par value of the bonus shares to be added to ordinary share capital

(c) The number of ordinary shares to be issued in the rights issue

(d) The amount to be added to ordinary share capital and share premium as a result of the rights issue

(e) The preference dividend for the year to 30 June 2020

(f) The ordinary dividend for the year to 30 June 2020

(g) The balance on the ordinary share capital account on 30 June 2020

(h) The expected balance on retained earnings at 30 June 2020

Ratio analysis 1: profitability, efficiency and performance

6

LEARNING OUTCOMES

Once you have read this chapter and worked through the questions and examples in both this chapter and the online workbook, you should be able to:

- Understand the importance and advantages of using ratios to evaluate the profitability, efficiency, performance, liquidity and long-term financial stability of entities

- Understand how the financial statements and ratios interact in the interpretation of the profitability, efficiency, performance, liquidity and long-term financial stability of organizations

- Calculate profitability ratios for gross profit percentage, operating profit percentage, profit before tax percentage and profit after tax percentage

- Suggest economic reasons for the changes in profitability ratios year on year

- Calculate efficiency ratios for non-current asset turnover, revenue per employee and profit per employee

- Show how efficiency ratios help to explain changes in the profitability ratios

- Understand how increasing the revenue from each unit of fixed resource employed in the business will increase an entity's profits

- Calculate performance ratios for earnings per share, the price/earnings ratio, dividends per share, dividend yield and dividend cover

- Explain what the performance ratios you have calculated mean from a shareholder's point of view

- Compare an entity's profitability, efficiency and performance ratios with the profitability, efficiency and performance ratios of other companies as a way of benchmarking an entity's financial outcomes

Introduction

In Chapters 2, 3 and 4 we looked at the three major accounting statements, how they are put together, how they integrate with each other and what they tell us individually about the profits and cash generated in each accounting period and the financial position of the entity at the end of each accounting period. However, the real skill in accounting lies not in an ability to produce these statements but in analysing and interpreting the information they contain. Such analysis and interpretation enable users to draw conclusions about how well an entity is performing and the strength of its financial position. Financial information as presented in the three major statements has to be analysed to determine the **profitability** of an entity, how efficiently its assets are being used, how well an organization is performing to meet the expectations of its investors and how secure its future cash flows and financial stability are. These aspects are analysed under the headings of profitability, efficiency, performance, **liquidity** and long-term financial stability and we will consider each of these measures in turn in this and the next chapter.

When reading the business and financial pages, the importance of these indicators will readily become apparent as we see in Give me an example 6.1.

6

GIVE ME AN EXAMPLE 6.1   A selection of terms linked to the analysis of companies' results and position

- Profitability
- Earnings
- Dividend cover
- Dividend yield
- **Dividend per share**
- Revenue growth
- Solvency
- Efficiency

- Total return
- Liquidity
- Earnings per share
- Profit margins
- Price earnings
- Dividend stream

Source: taken from a quick skim read of the *Financial Times* Companies and Markets section on 10 February 2018.

What these terms mean and how they are used in evaluating entities' profitability, efficiency, performance, liquidity and long-term financial stability will become clear as you work through this chapter and the next. To appreciate how common the above terms are and how relevant they continue to be in assessing companies' performance and financial position, quickly read through the Companies and Markets section in today's *Financial Times* and see how many of the above terms, among others, continue to appear.

Evaluating financial statements: ratio analysis

How do users evaluate and assess financial statements? The technique most commonly used is ratio analysis. A ratio in its simplest form expresses the relationship between two different figures. The calculation of the same ratio over several different time periods enables comparisons to be made between those different time periods to determine whether that ratio is rising, falling or staying the same. In this way, the performance and position of entities can be evaluated by analysing the trends that emerge over time. Ratio analysis, however, is not just confined to financial information but can be applied to any sets of numbers where relationships can be established, as illustrated in Example 6.1.

EXAMPLE 6.1

When grocery shopping, you might be evaluating two different sizes of a particular product: one costs £1.50 for 100g and the other costs £4.00 for 250g: which one offers the better value? By calculating the per gram price, the ratio of cost for one unit of weight, you can determine that the 100g product costs 1.50 pence per gram, while the 250g product costs 1.60 pence per gram. Therefore, the smaller sized product offers better value. Bigger is not always cheaper!

GO BACK OVER THIS AGAIN! Are you quite sure that you understand how ratios can be used to simplify the relationship between two figures to enable comparisons to be made? Go to the **online workbook** and look at Exercises 6.1 to see how ratios can be used in this way.

WHY IS THIS RELEVANT TO ME? Evaluating financial statements: ratio analysis

To enable you as a business professional and user of accounting information to:

- Understand how ratios simplify the relationships between two figures to enable meaningful comparisons to be made
- Appreciate the role of ratios in evaluating information used for making economic decisions

Why is ratio analysis needed?

Example 6.1 shows the value of ratios, expressing one figure in relation to another to highlight information critical to making an economic decision. However, why is ratio analysis needed in the interpretation and evaluation of financial statements? Again, a simple example will help to explain why ratios are such a useful tool in analysing financial performance and position. Think about the value of ratio analysis in the scenario outlined in Example 6.2.

EXAMPLE 6.2

A pottery company has sales of £110,376 in the year to 31 December 2018 and sales of £150,826 in the year to 31 December 2019. The company owners will see the year to 31 December 2019 as a great success in terms of the increase in sales achieved. Profit for the year to 31 December 2018 was £27,594 and £34,690 for the year to 31 December 2019. Again, you might say that the company has been successful in the most recent financial year as it has generated more profit than it did in the previous year. While it is true that profit has risen, the figures alone do not tell us whether the company is now more *profitable*. The figures for sales and profits have both increased, but is each sale in the year to 31 December 2019 generating as much, less or more profit as each sale in the year to 31 December 2018? A simple comparison, shown in Table 6.1, of the profit to the sales in each year will tell us the answer to this question.

Table 6.1 Comparison of profit to sales in each year

	2019 Calculation	Ratio	2018 Calculation	Ratio
$\dfrac{\text{Profit}}{\text{Sales}} \times 100\%$	$\dfrac{£34,690}{£150,826} \times 100\%$	23%	$\dfrac{£27,594}{£110,376} \times 100\%$	25%

Calculating these two profitability ratios shows us that despite the rise in both sales and profits in 2019, each sale has generated less profit than sales in 2018. For every £1 of sales, 23 pence is profit in 2019 compared to 25 pence of profit per £1 of sales in 2018. Ratios thus provide a *relative* measure from which to determine simple relationships between the financial figures. Calculating the ratio for the two time periods has enabled us to highlight a variance in profitability that was not at all apparent from the raw figures as presented in the accounts.

GO BACK OVER THIS AGAIN!   Convinced you could calculate ratios from a given set of data and draw valid conclusions? Go to the **online workbook** and have a go at Exercises 6.2 to check your understanding.

WHY IS THIS RELEVANT TO ME?   Why is ratio analysis needed?

To enable you as a business professional and user of accounting information to appreciate:

• That larger numbers do not necessarily indicate greater success or an improvement in relative terms
• How ratios can be used to determine changes relative to other figures

Now that we have this information showing reduced profitability in 2019 we can ask questions to determine why the pottery company's profitability has fallen this year. If the company had sold exactly the same goods at exactly the same prices to exactly the same customers in both years, then the profitability percentage, the pence of profit from each £1 of sales, should have been exactly the same. As the profitability percentage has fallen, financial statement users will want to know the reasons for the change and will ask questions with a view to identifying these reasons. Questions asked will focus on changes in the business and the economic climate with a view to explaining this fall. Examples of such questions (among others) might be as follows:

- Has the pottery business reduced selling prices to increase sales in an attempt to increase the company's share of the local pottery sales market?

- Has there been an increase in the price of clay used to make the pottery or has there been a rise in the potters' wages which the owner has chosen not to pass on to customers?

- Has the pottery business offered discounted prices to bulk buyers of its goods?

- Has a rival business opened in the area forcing selling prices down through increased competition?

- Is an economic recession forcing the owner to reduce prices to attract customers?

6

GO BACK OVER THIS AGAIN! Are you sure that you understand how profitability would fall in the circumstances outlined in the questions above? Visit the **online workbook** Exercises 6.3 to see how profitability would fall as a result of the reasons suggested.

Ratios are thus a starting point in the interpretation and evaluation of financial information. Calculating the ratios gives us information about which relationships have changed. We can then seek out explanations for these changes to assist us in understanding the business and how it operates and then use this information in making decisions about the future prospects of the business.

WHY IS THIS RELEVANT TO ME? Why is ratio analysis needed?

As a business professional and user of accounting information, you will be expected to:

- Calculate ratios for the business and compare these ratios to ratios from earlier accounting periods

- Use ratios to evaluate the performance of different parts of your organization

- Use ratios to determine aspects of the business in which improvements could be made

Ratios, figures or both?

Given that ratios are so useful in interpreting an organization's results, should we just ignore the financial statement figures once we have calculated the ratios? While ratios are an excellent interpretative tool, it is important to realize that the interpretation of financial statements relies on the figures presented in the statement of profit or loss, the statement of financial position and the statement of cash flows *and* the ratios derived from these figures. Just taking the figures or the ratios on their own would be insufficient to enable users to form a full understanding of what the financial statements are telling them about the profitability, performance, efficiency and liquidity of an entity. Thus, an evaluation of an entity should look at both the figures presented in the financial statements and the ratios derived from those numbers. To understand why both the figures and the ratios are used together, consider the two situations presented in Examples 6.3 and 6.4.

6

EXAMPLE 6.3

An entity has a profitability percentage of 20% compared to its competitor with a profitability percentage of 10%. Logically, based on just this ratio, users will prefer the company with a profitability percentage of 20% as this is higher. However, the entity with the 20% profitability has a profit of £50,000 and sales of £250,000 while its competitor has a profit of £10,000,000 and sales of £100,000,000. Which is the more preferable company now? Clearly the company with sales of £100 million and profit of £10 million will attract greater attention. This is a much larger company, probably very well established and with higher profits (if not higher profitability) from which to pay regular dividends to shareholders and with a longer, more stable and more firmly grounded trading record. Hence, it is vital to look at the financial statement figures as well as the ratios when evaluating an organization's financial performance and position.

EXAMPLE 6.4

A profit of £1 million sounds impressive. However, the £1 million figure has no context. If the profit of £1 million was generated from sales of £10 million, this would give a profitability percentage of 10% (£1m/£10m × 100%). Yet if the £1 million profit was generated from sales of £100 million this would give a profitability percentage of just 1% (£1m/£100m × 100%). Profitability of 10% is preferable to 1% profitability. Hence, it is vital to look at the ratios as well as the financial statement figures when evaluating an organization's financial performance and position.

Even more useful would be information comparing the profitability percentage achieved in prior years: if the entity generating 10% profitability this year had achieved 20% profitability in each of the previous five years, the 10% profitability in the current year would be seen as a very poor performance, but might be understandable if those profits had been generated during a period of contraction in the economy. However, if the profitability percentage in the previous five years had been 5%, then doubling the profitability percentage to 10% would be seen as a very worthwhile achievement indeed.

WHY IS THIS RELEVANT TO ME? Ratios, figures or both?

As a business professional and user of accounting information, you should appreciate:

- That the figures and the ratios based on them are both equally valuable in analysing and interpreting financial statements

- The interlinking nature of both ratios and figures in the analysis and interpretation of financial results

- The different perspectives that both ratios and financial statement figures bring to the analysis and interpretation of financial results

---

GO BACK OVER THIS AGAIN! Do you fully understand how ratios and financial statement figures interact? Go to the **online workbook** and have a go at Exercises 6.4 to check your understanding.

The advantages of ratios: summary

The preceding pages have presented a lot of arguments and ideas, so let's just pause for a moment to summarize how ratios and ratio analysis are advantageous in the evaluation of financial statements:

- Ratios are easy to calculate and to understand.

- Ratios highlight trends and variances by simplifying data into key indicators.

- Ratios help to express relationships between different figures in the financial statements.

- Calculating ratios across different time periods helps us to build up a picture of the trend in a particular indicator.

- Because ratios are a proportion calculated on a consistent basis across different time periods, this helps to overcome the problem of figures changing from year to year.

- Ratios, of course, are not the final answer: changes in ratios over different accounting periods will just indicate that we need to investigate why those ratios have changed and to rationalize the changes by reference to different economic conditions prevailing in each accounting period, different product mixes or the strategy the organization is pursuing in relation to its goals.

- Ratios are thus not an end in themselves; they are an indicator of change or movement that prompts further questions and further action to correct unfavourable movements or to take further actions to maintain the positive trend.

REFER BACK To illustrate the ratios discussed in this and the next chapter we will use the statement of financial position, statement of profit or loss and statement of cash flows for Bunns the Bakers presented in Chapters 2, 3 and 4. You should refer to Illustrations 2.1, 3.1 and 4.1 in these chapters or refer to the copies available in the **online workbook** as you work through the rest of this chapter and the next.

Profitability ratios

Now that we have considered the role of ratios in conjunction with the financial statement figures, it is time to look at the specific ratios used in analysing organizations' profitability. While we have already looked at a simple example of a profitability ratio earlier in this chapter (Example 6.2), we will now think about profitability ratios in much more depth and detail and consider the ratios presented in Figure 6.1.

As we noted in Chapter 3 (Introduction), profit is one of the most discussed numbers in any set of financial statements. However, to put profit into context, we have to know whether profits are higher or lower and how these profits compare with results from previous accounting periods. In money terms: is the profit of an organization rising or falling? In relative terms: is the entity making more or less profit per pound of sales than in previous years? Profitability ratios compare the various profit figures shown in the statement of profit or loss to the revenue for the year in order to make this assessment.

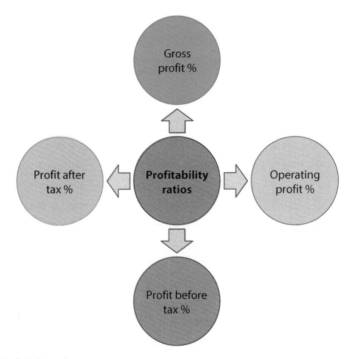

Figure 6.1 Profitability ratios

Bunns the Bakers' statement of profit or loss (Illustration 6.1) shows the revenue and profit figures for the years ended 31 March 2019 and 31 March 2018.

Illustration 6.1 Bunns the Bakers: revenue and profit figures for the years ended 31 March 2019 and 31 March 2018

	2019	2018
	£000	£000
Revenue	10,078	9,575
Gross profit	5,543	4,979
Operating profit	895	767
Profit before tax	760	614
Profit for the year	547	442

Following the principle above that we must consider both the ratios and the absolute figures, we should first highlight the trends in the revenue and profits in Illustration 6.1 before we calculate any ratios. All the figures given for the revenue and for the different profits for 2019 are higher than the revenue and profits in 2018. This looks good: in money terms, revenue and profits are rising. However, as we have already noted, these raw figures only tell us that Bunns the Bakers has made more profit on the back of higher revenue in the current year, but do not tell us whether the company is more *profitable*. To assess profitability, we need to compare the various profit figures to the sales made by the organization to see whether more or less profit is being generated per £ of sales through the calculation of various ratios.

Gross profit percentage

As we saw in Chapter 3 (Different categories of profit), gross profit is the profit left over after deducting from sales the direct costs of production of the goods sold or, in Julia's case, after deducting the costs of buying in goods for resale. This ratio is very useful when assessing how effectively the organization is controlling its costs of production or costs of buying in goods for resale. This ratio is calculated as follows:

$$\text{Gross profit}\% = \frac{\text{Gross profit}}{\text{Revenue}} \times 100\%$$

Looking at Illustration 6.1, the company has made a gross profit in the year to 31 March 2019 of £5,543,000 from revenue of £10,078,000. This gives the organization a **gross profit percentage** for 2019 of:

$$\frac{£5,543,000}{£10,078,000} \times 100\% = 55.00\%$$

Conventionally, ratios are calculated to two decimal places.

Have Bunns the Bakers achieved a higher ratio in 2019 compared with 2018? Let's calculate the gross profit percentage for 2018 to see whether 2019's gross profit percentage is higher or lower than 2018's. Gross profit in the statement of profit or loss (Illustration 6.1) for the year ended 31 March 2018 is £4,979,000 from revenue of £9,575,000, so this gives a gross profit percentage for 2018 of:

$$\frac{£4,979,000}{£9,575,000} \times 100\% = 52.00\%$$

WHY IS THIS RELEVANT TO ME? Gross profit percentage

To enable you as a business professional and user of accounting information to:

- Find information relevant to the gross profit percentage calculation in the financial statements
- Calculate your own gross profit percentage figures from statements of profit or loss presented to you

---

MULTIPLE CHOICE QUESTIONS Totally confident you can calculate a gross profit percentage from a given set of financial information? Go to the **online workbook** and have a go at Multiple choice questions 6.1 to test out your ability to calculate this ratio.

Interpretation of the results

The increase in gross profit percentage is encouraging. Bunns the Bakers are making 55 pence of gross profit from each £1 of sales in 2019 compared to a gross profit of 52 pence from each £1 of sales in 2018. However, as we noted earlier, just calculating the ratios is not enough: in your role as a business professional, you will be expected to investigate and explain why ratios have changed when compared with the previous year. The way to do this is to consider and enquire into possible reasons for the changes or to rationalize these changes by reference to the economic factors affecting the organization both locally and nationally.

Why might Bunns the Bakers be generating a higher gross profit percentage in the current year compared to the previous year? It is important to explain this change as it might be expected that each sale less the cost of sales will generate the same gross profit percentage every time (for this idea, see Chapter 9, Relevant costs, marginal costing and decision making: assumptions) and the assumption that the contribution (sales – variable costs) from each extra unit of production sold will be the same as for all other units of sales).

There are two aspects to the gross profit of an organization, the revenue and the cost of sales, so either or both of these figures might have been subject to certain changes to give a higher gross profit percentage. Therefore, possible reasons for the increase in 2019 might be as follows:

- An increase in selling prices that is higher than the rise in costs incurred in producing or buying in the goods for sale.
- A change in the types of sales made from lower profitability goods such as bread to higher profitability products such as pies, pastries and ready-made sandwiches.
- A fall in the price of input materials thereby lowering the cost of sales while maintaining selling prices at the same level.
- An increase in the productivity of the workforce, producing more goods per hour or selling more goods per shop than in the previous year.
- The company might have benefited from bulk discounts from suppliers: when goods are ordered in larger quantities, suppliers often give their customers a discount for placing larger orders. Bulk discounts received reduce the cost of raw materials in the production process thereby lowering the cost of sales and increasing the gross profit.

These are just some of the possible reasons for the change in the gross profit percentage and you can probably think of other perfectly valid reasons to explain this improvement. As a business professional you will be expected to calculate the ratios and then think about and offer reasons why ratios are changing in order to understand and explain the economic trends underlying the movements in these figures.

6

WHY IS THIS RELEVANT TO ME? Interpretation of the results

As a business professional and user of accounting information, you should appreciate that:

- You will be expected to think about changes in ratios and present reasons why those ratios are changing
- Senior managers and other users of accounting information will want to know why the gross profit percentage is changing: they will not just accept the changes without any explanation
- Business leaders and other users of accounting information do not have to be told that ratios are changing, they want to know why they are changing so that action can be taken to extend favourable or to correct unfavourable movements

GO BACK OVER THIS AGAIN! How easily could you determine the causes of rises and falls in the gross profit percentage? Go to the **online workbook** and have a go at Exercises 6.5 to make sure you can distinguish between factors that will cause the gross profit percentage to rise and factors that will cause it to fall.

Other profitability ratios

As well as the gross profit figure, Illustration 6.1 gives statement of profit or loss figures for operating profit, profit before tax and profit for the year (= profit after tax). Profitability ratios can be calculated for these figures as shown in Table 6.2.

Table 6.2 Profitability ratios for operating profit, profit before tax and profit for the year

Ratio	Calculation	What does this ratio tell us?
Operating profit %	$\dfrac{\text{Operating profit}}{\text{Revenue}} \times 100\%$	Determines profitability on the basis of revenue less all operating costs, before taking into account the effects of finance income, finance expense and taxation
Profit before tax %	$\dfrac{\text{Profit before tax}}{\text{Revenue}} \times 100\%$	Bases the profitability calculation on profit before taxation to eliminate the distorting effect of changes in tax rates. The profit before tax percentage is the profitability of the entity after deducting all costs incurred and taking into account income earned from all sources, both trading and investment
Profit after tax %	$\dfrac{\text{Profit for the year}}{\text{Revenue}} \times 100\%$	Calculates profitability for the period after adding all income and deducting all expenses and charges for the period under review

Using the figures for revenue and for profits in Illustration 6.1, we can calculate the other profitability percentages for Bunns the Bakers for the two years ending 31 March 2019 and 31 March 2018. These figures are shown in Table 6.3.

Table 6.3 Other profitability percentages for Bunns the Bakers for the two years ending 31 March 2019 and 31 March 2018

	2019 Calculation	Ratio	2018 Calculation	Ratio
Operating profit %	$\dfrac{£895,000}{£10,078,000} \times 100\%$	8.88%	$\dfrac{£767,000}{£9,575,000} \times 100\%$	8.01%
Profit before tax %	$\dfrac{£760,000}{£10,078,000} \times 100\%$	7.54%	$\dfrac{£614,000}{£9,575,000} \times 100\%$	6.41%
Profit after tax %	$\dfrac{£547,000}{£10,078,000} \times 100\%$	5.43%	$\dfrac{£442,000}{£9,575,000} \times 100\%$	4.62%

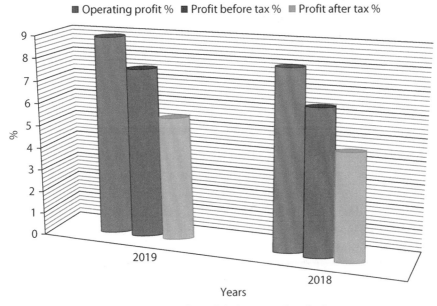

■ Operating profit % ■ Profit before tax % ■ Profit after tax %

Figure 6.2 Bunns the Bakers' operating profit, profit before tax and profit after tax %s

These profitability ratios have risen, too, so it is quite clear that Bunns the Bakers is more profitable in 2019 than it was in 2018, as shown in Figure 6.2. The rise in gross profit is part of the explanation for the increase in the calculated ratios. There is now more gross profit from which to pay all the other operating and finance expenses and still leave a larger profit for the year. Cost control will also be a factor and we can investigate which costs are lower or higher than in the previous year and determine how these rises and falls have affected profits and profitability in the current year. However, we can also investigate the efficiency with which assets are being used within the business. The greater the efficiency and productivity of these assets, the higher the revenue and profits will be.

WHY IS THIS RELEVANT TO ME?   Profitability ratios

As a business professional and user of accounting information, you will be expected to:

• Understand how ratios relevant to assessing profitability are calculated

• Calculate those profitability ratios yourself

• Use the calculated profitability ratios as a foundation on which to build explanations for changes in the ratios in comparison to previous years

---

MULTIPLE CHOICE QUESTIONS   Think that you can calculate operating profit, profit before tax and profit after tax percentages? Go to the **online workbook** and have a go at Multiple choice questions 6.3 to test your ability to calculate these ratios.

Efficiency ratios

Efficiency ratios consider how effectively and productively the resources of the organization are being used to create both revenue and profit. An organization's resources fall into two categories. First, non-current assets used in the production and sale of goods and services and, second, the employees engaged within the business, as illustrated in Figure 6.3. Various ratios can be calculated to demonstrate how efficiently these resources are being used within an organization and these ratios should also help to explain the improved profitability of Bunns the Bakers in the year to 31 March 2019.

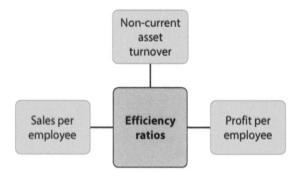

Figure 6.3 Efficiency ratios

Non-current asset turnover

This ratio compares the sales achieved by an organization with the non-current assets in use in that organization to determine how many £s of sales are produced by each £ of non-current assets. Ideally, this ratio will rise over time as non-current assets are used more efficiently to generate increased revenue.

This ratio is calculated as follows:

$$\text{Non-current asset turnover} = \frac{\text{Revenue}}{\text{Non-current assets}}$$

We have already seen that Bunns the Bakers has revenue of £10,078,000 for the year ended 31 March 2019 and revenue of £9,575,000 for the previous financial year. From the statement of financial position in Illustration 2.1, total non-current assets at

31 March 2019 and 31 March 2018 are £11,865,000 and £11,355,000 respectively. This gives the following figures for **non-current asset turnover**:

$$2019: \text{Non-current asset turnover: } \frac{£10,078,000}{£11,865,000} = £0.85$$

$$2018: \text{Non-current asset turnover: } \frac{£9,575,000}{£11,355,000} = £0.84$$

The figures show a slight improvement over the year. In 2018, each £1 of non-current assets generated revenue of 84 pence and in 2019 this has improved to 85 pence. Our conclusion from this ratio would be that non-current assets are being used more efficiently to generate revenue for the business as more revenue is being produced per £ of non-current assets.

However, a word of caution is needed at this point. As we saw in Chapter 2 (How are assets and liabilities valued?), users have to be careful when using information on assets employed within an organization. The amount at which assets are recorded in the statement of financial position may be increased by restating these assets to current values. Conversely, this amount may be too low because assets bought many years ago are still being used within the business. When such assets are still recorded at their original cost less any depreciation charged, these figures will now be seriously out of date and produce much less meaningful comparisons.

Similarly, when an organization leases assets, a situation common in the retail industry as shops are often rented from landlords, these leased assets will not currently appear on the statement of financial position at all as the organization does not control them. Therefore, retailers' non-current assets might be misleadingly low on account of the absence of these leased assets from their statements of financial position (this situation will change for financial statements for accounting periods commencing on or after 1 January 2019: the IASB has issued a new financial reporting standard requiring leased assets to be included in the non-current assets figure in the statement of financial position). Despite the potential shortcomings in this ratio, the non-current asset turnover figure does present users with relevant information on how effectively the organization is using its long-term assets to generate revenue.

6

MULTIPLE CHOICE QUESTIONS Sure that you can calculate non-current asset turnover ratios? Go to the **online workbook** and have a go at Multiple choice questions 6.4 to test your ability to calculate this ratio.

Revenue and profit per employee

Unlike non-current assets, employees are not recognized in financial statements due to the very high level of measurement uncertainty associated with their valuation

(Chapter 2, Assets). However, employees are a vital part of every organization and how they perform during their working hours will determine how successful and how profitable organizations are. Increased productivity on the part of employees, generating more output or selling more goods during the hours worked each week, will have a significant impact upon both revenue and profitability. Employees are usually paid a fixed weekly wage, so the more they produce for that fixed weekly wage, the more profit entities will make. As an example of this, think about Bunns the Bakers' shop employees. They will be paid the same amount each week for selling 10 sandwiches or 400 sandwiches, but the latter sales figure will lead to much higher profits in each shop. Increasing sales while keeping input costs the same inevitably leads to higher profits. This principle holds where any cost is fixed: the more production or the more sales that can be generated from this fixed cost, the more profitable organizations will be.

NUMERICAL EXERCISES   Are you convinced you understand how increasing output while keeping input costs the same can lead to higher profits? Visit the **online workbook** Numerical exercises 6.1 to reinforce your understanding of how this is true.

If employees are not given a monetary value within financial statements, how can we assess whether they have been more or less productive during each accounting period? In many jurisdictions, organizations must disclose the average number of employees during each financial reporting period in the annual report and financial statements. You may have to search for this information in the notes to the financial statements, but it will be there and you will be able to use this information to make meaningful comparisons of the revenue and profit per employee across different years. The higher the revenue and profit per employee, the more efficiently organizations are working to generate returns to satisfy the business's objectives of profit and revenue growth. Where these ratios are falling, management can look into the reasons for declining revenue and profit per employee. Are operations overstaffed and is there scope to reduce employee numbers to improve the efficiency, productivity and profitability of operations?

These measures of employee efficiency are calculated as follows. While operating profit per employee is calculated below, you could just as easily calculate per employee figures for gross profit, profit before tax or profit after tax (= profit for the year). Whichever measure you use, you must be consistent in your calculation of the ratio so that you are comparing like with like across different accounting periods. Similarly, the measure calculated below is based on all employees, but the ratios could be calculated using just production employees or production plus retail employees or any other combination of employee numbers deemed suitable, provided that the calculation continues to be consistently applied.

$$\text{Revenue per employee} = \frac{\text{Total revenue}}{\text{Total number of employees}}$$

$$\text{Profit per employee} = \frac{\text{Operating profit}}{\text{Total number of employees}}$$

From the notes to Bunns the Bakers' accounts, it can be determined that the average number of employees in the year to 31 March 2019 was 120 and 112 in the year to 31 March 2018. Using these figures and the figures for revenue and operating profit in Illustration 6.1, the following efficiency ratios can be calculated:

$$2019\text{: Revenue per employee} = \frac{£10,078,000}{120} = £83,983$$

$$2018\text{: Revenue per employee} = \frac{£9,575,000}{112} = £85,491$$

$$2019\text{: Operating profit per employee} = \frac{£895,000}{120} = £7,458$$

$$2018\text{: Operating profit per employee} = \frac{£767,000}{112} = £6,848$$

While **revenue per employee** has fallen in 2019, operating profit per employee has risen by £610, a rise of 8.91% ((£7,458 − £6,848)/£6,848 × 100%). This increase suggests that costs have been well controlled this year and that the company's employees are working effectively to generate increased profit for the business. This increase in profit per employee might also go some way to explaining the increased profitability noted earlier in this chapter: more profit has been generated per unit of resource employed, possibly due to higher productivity, and, as a result, a higher profit and higher profitability percentages have been produced.

6

WHY IS THIS RELEVANT TO ME? Efficiency ratios

To enable you as a business professional and user of accounting information to:

- Understand ratios that are relevant to determining the effectiveness of asset utilization
- Calculate and apply these ratios yourself
- Appreciate that the more revenue and profit that can be generated from a fixed cost resource, the more profitable and successful an organization will be

MULTIPLE CHOICE QUESTIONS Do you reckon you can calculate revenue and profit per employee ratios? Go to the **online workbook** and have a go at Multiple choice questions 6.5 to test your ability to calculate these ratios.

SUMMARY OF KEY CONCEPTS Certain you can remember the formulae for non-current asset turnover, revenue per employee and profit per employee? Take a look at Summary of key concepts 6.5–6.7 to reinforce your understanding.

Sales and profit per unit of input resource

One further aspect of efficiency merits our attention at this point. It is common practice in the retail sector to measure sales and profits per square metre or square foot of selling space (where shops differ greatly in size from superstores down to small high street outlets) or per shop (where shop size does not vary significantly). When these figures rise year on year, then more has been produced from the same unit of resource: input resources have been used more effectively and efficiently to produce more sales and hence more profits. Let's see if Bunns the Bakers are producing more sales and profits from their resources by calculating asset utilization ratios (Figure 6.4).

Bunns the Bakers had 19 shops all of similar size open to the public in the year to 31 March 2018. During the year to 31 March 2019, an additional shop was opened on 1 October 2018, exactly six months into the current year. During the year to 31 March 2019, then, Bunns the Bakers had $19 + (1 \times 6/12) = 19.5$ shops selling the company's goods and products. Dividing the figures for the number of shops into the revenue for each year will give us the following results for revenue per shop:

$$2019: \text{Revenue per shop:} \frac{£10,078,000}{19.5} = £516,821$$

$$2018: \text{Revenue per shop:} \frac{£9,575,000}{19} = £503,947$$

These figures tell us that Bunns the Bakers has achieved higher sales per shop and so is using the company's resources much more efficiently, squeezing more output from

Figure 6.4 Asset utilization ratios

the same unit of resource. A similar calculation can be undertaken to find out whether more profit has been generated from the resources used. The focus of our attention here will be the operating profit per shop, the sales less all the operating costs of the business.

2019: Operating profit per shop: $\dfrac{£895,000}{19.5} = £45,897$

2018: Operating profit per shop: $\dfrac{£767,000}{19} = £40,368$

Again, just as in the case of the employees, higher profits per shop have been generated in 2019 when compared to 2018. More revenue and more profit have been generated from the same resources and so the business is more profitable in comparison to the previous year.

GO BACK OVER THIS AGAIN!   Quite sure you understand how increasing income per unit of input resource leads to higher profits? Visit the **online workbook** and look at Exercises 6.6 to prove to yourself that this is true.

A real-life example of increasing sales from the same inputs resulting in higher profits can be seen in Give me an example 6.2. As discussed, Ted Baker generated higher sales from each unit of retail space resulting in increased operating profit per unit of input resource.

6

GIVE ME AN EXAMPLE 6.2

Ted Baker's annual report and accounts for the 52 weeks to 28 January 2017 present the following figures:

	52 weeks ended 28 January 2017	52 weeks ended 30 January 2016
Retail revenue	£328.4 million	£294.9 million
Operating profit	£67.0 million	£59.4 million
Average square footage of retail space	387,373 square feet	357,096 square feet

Retail revenue and operating profit have certainly increased since the end of the previous financial year, but is the retail space being used more efficiently and productively to generate higher revenue and operating profit from each unit of input resource? Using the figures presented, we can calculate the retail revenue per square foot of retail space. In the 52 weeks to 28 January 2017, the sales per square foot of retail space were £847.76 (£328,400,000 ÷ 387,373 square feet) while in the 52 weeks to 30 January 2016 sales generated per square foot of retail space were £825.83 (£294,900,000 ÷ 357,096 square feet). Thus, more sales per unit of resource have been achieved in the 52 weeks to 28 January 2017 when compared to the 52 weeks to 30 January 2016. The available retail space has been used more effectively and efficiently to produce higher sales per unit of input resource. But has this greater productivity resulted in

→

higher profits from each square foot of retail space? Operating profit per square foot of retail space has risen from £166.34 in the 52 weeks to 30 January 2016 (£59,400,000 ÷ 357,096 square feet) to £172.96 in the 52 weeks to 28 January 2017 (£67,000,000 ÷ 387,373 square feet) so higher sales per unit of input resource have resulted in higher profits as more sales and hence more profit have been squeezed out of each unit of selling space.

WHY IS THIS RELEVANT TO ME? Sales and profit per unit of input resource

To enable you as a business professional and user of accounting information to:

- Appreciate that increasing sales per unit of input resource is often the key to improving an organization's profitability
- Devise suitable efficiency ratios to measure output per unit of input resource to see if this is rising, falling or staying the same

GO BACK OVER THIS AGAIN! Can you identify ways in which to increase sales and profit per unit of input resource? Go to the **online workbook** and have a go at Exercises 6.7 to test your understanding of how this works.

Performance ratios

These ratios, illustrated in Figure 6.5, are of particular interest to an entity's shareholders. Shareholders invest money into the shares of a company with a view to earning dividends from the profits made by that business. The various ratios considered under

Figure 6.5 Performance ratios

this heading first compare the profits generated to the number of shares in issue and then think about the dividends paid out on each share. Comparisons of dividends to the market price of each share tell shareholders what their return is on that share. In this way they can assess whether they could earn more by investing their money in alternative investments, while comparing dividends paid with profits generated helps investors to decide how safe their future dividend income will be.

Earnings per share (EPS)

The first **performance ratio** that shareholders consider is the **earnings per share** (this is frequently abbreviated to **EPS**). This figure is produced simply by dividing the profit for the year by the number of ordinary shares in issue. This figure represents the dividend that would result if all the profits for the period were paid out to ordinary shareholders as dividends. As we noted in Chapter 5, such a pay-out is most unlikely as the directors hold back some of the profits each year from which to finance future investment in the company.

EPS is calculated as follows:

$$\text{Earnings per share} = \frac{\text{Profit after taxation and after preference dividends}}{\text{Number of ordinary shares in issue}} \times 100 \text{ pence}$$

The profit after taxation is equivalent to the profit for the year. In situations in which an entity has preference shares in issue, any dividends paid on those preference shares will be paid out before any dividends are paid to ordinary shareholders. Therefore, this prior claim on the profits of an entity has to be deducted from profit for the year before the profits available for distribution to the ordinary shareholders can be determined. Note that EPS is always expressed in pence per share.

Looking at the figures for Bunns the Bakers, the profit after taxation (= profit for the year) for 2019 is £547,000 and £442,000 for 2018. The number of shares in issue can be observed in the statement of financial position. As shown in Illustration 2.1, Bunns the Bakers had 2,500,000 £1 shares in issue in the year to 31 March 2019, while in the previous year there were only 2,400,000 £1 ordinary shares. The increase in the number of shares indicates that additional shares have been issued during the year to 31 March 2019. The calculations for EPS for the two years under consideration are thus:

$$2019: \text{Earnings per share} = \frac{£547,000}{2,500,000} \times 100p = 21.88 \text{ pence}$$

$$2018: \text{Earnings per share} = \frac{£442,000}{2,400,000} \times 100p = 18.42 \text{ pence}$$

Bunns the Bakers has no preference shares in issue, so there are no preference dividends to deduct from the profit for the year before the EPS figures can be calculated. Therefore, the EPS calculation is simply based on the profit for the year divided by the number of ordinary shares in issue. Given the rise in EPS, shareholders will be pleased and the stock market will give the shares a higher valuation based on these increased returns.

MULTIPLE CHOICE QUESTIONS   Are you quite confident that you can calculate an earnings per share figure? Go to the **online workbook** and have a go at Multiple choice questions 6.6 to test your ability to calculate this ratio.

EPS is a key figure in the evaluation of an entity's performance by the stock market and by stockbrokers and traders. A review of the financial press will show you that where profits and thus EPS are expected to increase, the share price rises ahead of the announcement of earnings for the financial period under review. Similarly, where an entity's actual profits and EPS do not meet market expectations, share prices of that entity are marked down by the market. This reduction in the market price of the shares arises first from the fact that the results are a disappointment and second because the flows of cash to shareholders in the form of dividends from that entity are likely to be lower than expected. Ideally, the EPS figure should keep rising each year. Where this is the case, the share price will keep rising too and a rising share price is a source of happiness to shareholders as such rises indicate increasing wealth. In reality, EPS rise and fall in line with the economy: during periods when the economy surges, profits and hence EPS rise, but when the economy contracts and slows down, profits reduce causing EPS and share prices to fall. Similarly, when companies' results and EPS are better than expected, share prices rise, but when they fall or are expected to fall, then the share price falls, too. Give me an example 6.3 provides two examples to illustrate these share price movements.

GIVE ME AN EXAMPLE 6.3   The effect of profits on share prices

The online fashion retailer Boohoo.com saw pre-tax profits for the year to 28 February 2017 rise 97% to £30.9m. Over the same time period, revenue rose 51% to £294.6m. The share price, which stood at 49.75 pence on 27 April 2016, rose almost 3.80 times to 188.75 pence over the course of the year to 26 April 2017.

Sources: *Financial Times*, 27 April 2017 and This is Money.co.uk http://www.thisismoney.co.uk/money/markets/article-4446616/Boohoo-s-profits-rise-97-year-amid-share-price-hike.html

At the close of business on 24 April 2017, Whitbread plc's shares stood at 4,307 pence. At the start of business on 25 April 2017, the share price had fallen 6.66% to 4,020 pence as a result of slowing sales growth, profits that rose less strongly than expected and worries about reduced consumer spending. Profit before tax for the 52 weeks to 2 March 2017 was up 5.7% to £515.4m against a market expectation of £554m. The share price fall occurred despite an increase in the final dividend of 6% to 95.80 pence.

Source: ShareCast News, Whitbread warns of tough consumer outlook, 25 April 2017 http://sharecast.com/news/whitbread-warns-of-tough-consumer-outlook/25844885.html

Price/earnings ratio (the P/E ratio)

The price/earnings ratio is linked to the EPS. This ratio divides the EPS into the current market price of that share. This gives a number that is an indicator of how many years of current period earnings are represented in the share price today. Alternatively, you can look at this ratio as the amount that a shareholder would be willing to pay today for every £1 of current earnings made by a company. A quick glance at the financial pages will show you that every listed company has a different P/E ratio (as shown in Give me an example 6.4), some higher and some lower than others. Typically, shares in companies with steady or rising profits have a higher P/E ratio as the earnings are perceived to be more secure and enduring than from other shares. On the other hand, shares in companies whose earnings are expected to be subject to lower or negative growth rates have lower P/E ratios as the earnings in these companies are expected to be much less secure and so P/E ratios for shares in these companies are lower. You might say that the P/E ratio is an indicator of the market's confidence in a particular company and its ability to maintain or grow its current earnings: the more likely it is that a company will continue to produce profits, earnings and dividends for shareholders, the higher the P/E ratio of that company will be.

6

GIVE ME AN EXAMPLE 6.4 Differing price/earnings ratios

A glance at the *Financial Times* Share Service for Monday 12 February 2018 shows the following information for three companies:

Company	P/E ratio
Debenhams	7.27
Next	11.05
Ted Baker	26.61

Source: *Financial Times* for Monday 12 February 2018

→

Ted Baker has a high P/E ratio indicating that shareholders are willing to pay £26.61 for every £1 of today's earnings. Ted Baker markets itself as a global lifestyle brand that designs and sells clothing and fashion accessories to men and women who value something different. The company has very strong UK and international branding and more than doubled revenue and profits from 2012 to 2017. There is a very clear expansion strategy in place and the company's worldwide presence and strong products have encouraged investors to anticipate much higher profits, earnings per share and dividends in the future. The share price reflects these future expectations and investors' confidence that the directors' long-term strategic goals will be achieved.

Next plc conducts almost all of its business in the UK. The market is worried that the rising cost of living and the failure of the growth rate in wages to match inflation over the medium term future will reduce sales of clothing and accessories at Next as consumers cut back on non-essential purchases. While Next generates its sales from both bricks and mortar stores and online, many shoppers today prefer to buy goods online thereby endangering the future of sales on the high street. In addition, there has been a trend away from spending on clothing to spending on experiences and services. All these factors contribute to an expectation of lower growth in sales, profitability and cash at Next in comparison to its online competitors. All these expectations are reflected in the lower P/E ratio of 11.05.

Debenhams is a retailer of general merchandise. The company has suffered various problems in recent years, resulting in downgrades to profit expectations, and has lost sales and customers to other retailers and to online sellers owing to the undifferentiated nature of the products it sells. As a result, the P/E ratio of the company suggests that investors expect the future performance of the business will deliver low returns to shareholders with little prospect of growth in profits and cash inflows.

The P/E ratio is calculated in the following way:

$$\text{Price/earnings ratio} = \frac{\text{Market value of one ordinary share}}{\text{Earnings per share}}$$

Share prices for Bunns the Bakers, when their results were released for the years ended 31 March 2019 and 31 March 2018, were 310.7 pence and 254.2 pence respectively. These prices and the EPS calculated previously give P/E ratios as follows:

$$2019: \text{Price/earnings ratio} = \frac{310.7}{21.88} = 14.2$$

$$2018: \text{Price/earnings ratio} = \frac{254.2}{18.42} = 13.8$$

The share price has risen as the EPS have increased in 2019. Given the rise in EPS in the current financial year, the stock market would expect future earnings to be more secure (and that a higher dividend will be paid from higher earnings) and so the P/E ratio has also risen. Given the nature of Bunns the Bakers' products, investors would also expect customers to continue buying such products in the foreseeable future.

Indeed, they might even buy additional treats to cheer themselves up during a difficult economic period. A higher level of confidence in the shares to continue producing an enduring earnings and dividend stream is thus being shown by the higher P/E ratio.

GO BACK OVER THIS AGAIN! Do you really understand the relationship between price and earnings in the price/earnings ratio? Go to the **online workbook** and have a go at Exercises 6.8 to test your understanding of this relationship.

MULTIPLE CHOICE QUESTIONS How easily can you calculate price/earnings ratios? Go to the **online workbook** and have a go at Multiple choice questions 6.7 to make sure you can calculate this figure.

Dividend per share (DPS)

This ratio is used by shareholders to determine how much dividend is being paid on each share. As in the case of EPS, the ideal situation for shareholders is for the dividends to keep rising each year. Such increases indicate confidence in the company's ability to continue generating rising profits into the future. In addition, higher dividends result in rising share prices as expectations of future dividend increases feed into the market's valuation of the shares. The **DPS** can be compared to the EPS to calculate the pay-out ratio, the percentage of the EPS that have been distributed as dividend to the shareholders over the year.

The DPS figure is worked out in almost exactly the same way as EPS, but the total dividends paid out are substituted for the profits after taxation and after preference dividends. This ratio is calculated as follows:

$$\text{Dividend per share} = \frac{\text{Total ordinary dividends}}{\text{Number of ordinary shares in issue}} \times 100 \text{ pence}$$

From the statement of cash flows in Illustration 4.1, we can see that the dividends paid out in the year to 31 March 2019 were £90,000 compared with £72,000 in the year to 31 March 2018. This gives DPS figures for the two years as follows:

$$2019: \text{Dividend per share} = \frac{£90,000}{2,500,000} \times 100p = 3.60 \text{ pence}$$

$$2018: \text{Dividend per share} = \frac{£72,000}{2,400,000} \times 100p = 3.00 \text{ pence}$$

Comparing these figures to the EPS for the two years gives a pay-out ratio (DPS as a percentage of earnings per share for the year) of:

$$2019: \text{Pay-out ratio} = \frac{3.60 \text{ pence}}{21.88 \text{ pence}} \times 100\% = 16.45\%$$

$$2018: \text{Pay-out ratio} = \frac{3.00 \text{ pence}}{18.42 \text{ pence}} \times 100\% = 16.29\%$$

6

DPS has risen and this represents a higher pay-out ratio as well. The company has thus paid out more DPS this year as a percentage of EPS, but has still retained a significant proportion of the earnings (over 83% in both years under review) with a view to re-investing these into the business to generate further expansion in the future and to increase both sales and profits.

Dividend yield

Shareholders invest in companies firstly to generate income in the form of dividends and secondly to increase their wealth through the capital appreciation (the increase in the market price of a share over the year) of their shares' value. These same share-holders could just as easily invest their cash in the safety of bank or building society accounts and earn interest on their deposits. Is the dividend and capital appreciation they are earning on their shares sufficient compensation for the risk they are taking by investing in the stock market?

The dividend earned by shareholders is compared with the market price of a share to give the dividend yield. This figure is calculated as follows:

$$\text{Dividend yield} = \frac{\text{Ordinary dividends per share}}{\text{Current market price of one ordinary share}} \times 100\%$$

For Bunns the Bakers, the **dividend yield** for the financial years ended 31 March 2019 and 31 March 2018 is as follows:

$$2019: \text{Dividend yield} = \frac{3.60 \text{ pence}}{310.7 \text{ pence}} \times 100\% = 1.16\%$$

$$2018: \text{Dividend yield} = \frac{3.00 \text{ pence}}{254.2 \text{ pence}} \times 100\% = 1.18\%$$

The dividend yield does not appear to be very high at present, though it compares well with the Bank of England base rate of 0.50%. By investing in a building society account with a more favourable interest rate, shareholders could gain a much better monetary return of around 1.50% to 2.00%. However, using this building society interest rate as a benchmark would ignore the fact that the share price has risen from 254.2 pence a year ago to 310.7 pence today, a rise of 22.23% ((310.7 − 254.2)/254.2 × 100%). This capital appreciation, along with the dividends received, represents the total return to shareholders over the year. When looking at the dividend yield, it is important to re-member that a low return does not necessarily indicate a poorly performing share. Both the capital appreciation in the share price and the dividend actually received have to be taken into account.

Dividend cover

This ratio measures how many times the current year ordinary dividend could be paid from the profit for the year. Dividend cover looks at the profit after taxation and after any preference dividends that have to be paid first. This ratio is a measure of the security of the dividend that has been paid: the higher the ratio, the more secure the dividend. A dividend cover of 1.0 would indicate that all the EPS were being paid out as dividends with no retention of profits within the entity to finance future expansion and development. Whereas a dividend cover of 3.0 would indicate that the current year dividend could be paid out three times and that two-thirds of the profit for the year is being retained within the business.

The dividend cover ratio is calculated in the following way:

$$\text{Dividend cover} = \frac{\text{Profit after tax and after preference dividends}}{\text{Total ordinary dividends}}$$

Looking at Bunns the Bakers, the dividend cover ratio for the two financial years that concern us is:

$$2019: \text{Dividend cover} = \frac{£547,000}{£90,000} = 6.08 \text{ times}$$

$$2018: \text{Dividend cover} = \frac{£442,000}{£72,000} = 6.14 \text{ times}$$

As Bunns the Bakers have no preference shares in issue, the relevant number to use in this calculation is the profit for the year as given in the statement of profit or loss. From the results of the above calculations, the ratio has fallen slightly, but a dividend cover of over six times is very safe indeed and shareholders can anticipate that their dividend will continue to be paid for the foreseeable future.

WHY IS THIS RELEVANT TO ME?   Performance ratios

As a business professional and user of accounting information, you will be expected to:

• Understand ratios relevant to investors and the stock market

• Understand how these ratios are calculated

• Be able to calculate these ratios yourself

GO BACK OVER THIS AGAIN!   Sure that you can distinguish between the five performance ratios? Go to the **online workbook** and have a go at Exercises 6.9 to test your understanding of which ratio does what.

Evaluation of performance

How has Bunns the Bakers performed this year? Will the company's shareholders be happy with their company's performance? Shareholders will consider the following factors:

- EPS and DPS are both higher than in 2018.
- The increase in the P/E ratio indicates the market's expectation that the company will continue producing rising earnings and dividends for shareholders into the foreseeable future.
- While the dividend yield fell very slightly from 1.18% to 1.16%, the increase in the share price over the year will have more than compensated for this reduction.
- Taken together, the dividend yield and the increase in the share price have comfortably exceeded the returns on what are perceived to be safer investments (bank and building society deposit accounts).
- Shareholders will therefore be happy with the dividends paid and the increase in the market value of their shares.
- The dividend cover indicates that future dividends should be easily affordable from profits.
- The low dividend pay-out ratio indicates that the company is keeping plenty of profit back with which to finance future growth and expansion.
- While shareholders might want profits, earnings, dividends and share price to be even higher, they can be satisfied with the company's performance in the year ended 31 March 2019 when comparing this performance with the previous year.

WHY IS THIS RELEVANT TO ME? Evaluation of performance ratios

As a business professional and user of accounting information, you will be expected to:

- Appreciate what factors shareholders and the stock market will take into account when assessing an entity's performance
- Be able to make an objective assessment of an entity's performance yourself

Return on capital employed

A common ratio that you will find in other introductory books on accounting is the **return on capital employed** (abbreviated to **ROCE**). This ratio is calculated as follows:

$$\frac{\text{Profit before interest and tax}}{\text{Capital employed}} \times 100\%$$

Capital employed is defined as the equity of an entity plus the long-term borrowings. Looking at the statements of financial position of Bunns the Bakers at 31 March 2019 and 31 March 2018 (Illustration 2.1), equity totals up to £8,459,000 and £7,767,000 respectively. Long-term borrowings (included in non-current liabilities) at the two accounting dates are £2,700,000 and £3,000,000. Profit before interest and tax is equivalent to the operating profit line in Illustration 6.1, and this amounts to £895,000 for the year to 31 March 2019 and £767,000 for the year to 31 March 2018. This gives us the following figures for return on capital employed for the two years as follows:

$$2019: \text{ROCE} = \frac{£895,000}{(£8,459,000 + £2,700,000)} \times 100\% = 8.02\%$$

$$2018: \text{ROCE} = \frac{£767,000}{(£7,767,000 + £3,000,000)} \times 100\% = 7.12\%$$

What is this ratio trying to do? ROCE is used to compare the different profits of different companies that have different capital structures. As we saw in Chapter 5, some companies raise their finance solely through share capital while others rely on loans and still others use a mixture of both share and loan capital to finance their businesses. In this way, the operating profits generated by these different capital structures can be compared to determine which entities produce the highest returns from their capital structures. Investors can then determine the entities in which they will invest their money to produce the highest returns. Return on capital employed is often used to compare returns available from companies with interest rates available from banks and building societies to decide whether it would be safer to invest in these much less risky investments rather than in a particular company.

However, the ROCE ratio suffers from a number of problems. We saw in Chapter 2 that not all the assets of an entity are reflected in organizations' statements of financial position. Similarly, the figures presented on the statement of financial position are not necessarily as up to date as they might be. The equity of an entity is made up of share capital that may have been issued many years ago along with retained earnings that have been accumulated over many different accounting periods. These figures would need to be adjusted for changes in the purchasing power of the pound to bring all the pounds tied up in equity up to current day values for this ratio to be meaningful. After all, the profit before interest and tax has been earned in the current year, but this is being compared to share capital and retained earnings from previous years when the value of each pound was very different from what it is today. As noted in Give me an example 6.5 dealing with Ryanair, this is tantamount to comparing apples and pears so that the comparison loses its validity.

It should be possible to restate all the share capital and retained earnings figures to current values (for example by multiplying the market value of each share by the total number of shares in issue) to produce a suitable figure for equity. However, this is a time-consuming exercise and users of accounts might prefer to look at the total shareholder return as represented by the dividend yield and the increase in the market value of shares over the year as the best indicator of the returns available from each company. Users are completely free to use the ROCE ratio as they see fit, but they must be fully aware of the severe limitations that this ratio presents and how these limitations will affect their perceptions of the returns available from each entity.

6

WHY IS THIS RELEVANT TO ME?   Return on capital employed

To enable you as a business professional and user of accounting information to understand:

- The way in which return on capital employed is used by entities and individuals

- The limitations of the return on capital employed ratio

- That total shareholder return represents a more effective way in which to distinguish between different investment opportunities

---

The importance of calculating and presenting ratios consistently

Emphasis has been placed throughout this chapter on the need to calculate and present ratios consistently year on year. Why is this consistency so important? Failure to calculate and present ratios consistently from year to year will mean that comparisons are distorted and figures misleading rather than being accurate portrayals of the financial position compared to previous accounting periods. The dangers of trying to compare information that is not consistently presented and the distortions that this gives rise to are illustrated in Give me an example 6.5.

GIVE ME AN EXAMPLE 6.5 Ryanair's Stansted spin

Michael O'Leary's ability to spin a tale has reached a new level this week. Along with the gullibility of parts of the media in accepting it. Hook, line and sinker.

'Ryanair cuts Stansted winter capacity by 40%,' claimed his press release. The assertion was patently rubbish. But it is almost universally already accepted as fact. On the most charitable assessment, he is planning to cut Stansted winter capacity by 14 per cent. The probability is that the year-on-year decline in Ryanair passenger numbers at Stansted will be much lower even than that. BAA, Stansted's owner, is forecasting a drop of 6–7 per cent.

To get to the claim of a drop of 40 per cent Mr O'Leary is comparing an apple with a pear. He is comparing the number of aircraft he is operating from Stansted, his biggest base, this summer (40) with the number he plans to deploy in the winter (24). But the airline industry is highly seasonal. Comparing Ryanair's summer capacity with its winter capacity at any airport is about as useful as saying 'ice-cream sales to fall by 40% this winter' or 'temperature to fall by 40 per cent'. Shock horror.

Last winter Ryanair operated between 26 and 28 aircraft at Stansted. This year it is planning

to operate 24, a decline of at most 14 per cent year on year and a long way from the claimed fall of 40 per cent. The decline will doubtless be even less in the number of flights operated year on year. Mr O'Leary chose to describe only the number of aircraft overnighting at Stansted. He gave no numbers for the volume of weekly flights that includes services operating in and out of Stansted from other Ryanair bases.

The summer/winter capacity comparison is about as silly as comparing profits/losses between different quarters of the year rather than year on year. Not even Ryanair has yet adopted that approach as a new accounting standard.

This week's spin was egregious even by Mr O'Leary's standards. A year ago, when he staged the same show over cutbacks at Stansted, at least he had the good grace to compare an apple with an apple. But the result was much less impressive.

Brian Groom, Lombard

Financial Times 23 July 2009.

Source: Kevin Done, 2009, 'Ryanair's Stansted spin,' *Financial Times* Used under licence from the *Financial Times*. All Rights Reserved.

6

WHY IS THIS RELEVANT TO ME? The importance of calculating and presenting ratios consistently

To enable you as a business professional and user of accounting information to:

- Understand why it is important to ensure your reports do not present misleading and biased data
- Appreciate that all data presented must be compiled and calculated consistently in order to produce fair and valid comparisons between different reporting periods
- Be aware of the dangers of not comparing like with like

How well are we doing? Comparisons with other companies

So far we have just looked at the financial statements and ratios of Bunns the Bakers. The company seems to be moving in the right direction with increased profits and profitability, improved efficiency leading to rising revenue and shareholders who should be content with the returns they are receiving. However, we have looked only at internal information with no benchmark against which to compare our company's results. Therefore, we cannot say how well Bunns the Bakers is doing in comparison with the market, whether it is doing better, worse or just as well as its peer companies.

To determine the company's relative success in comparison to other bakery sector companies, we need to compare Bunns the Bakers' figures and ratios with those of a competitor or a series of competitors. In this way, we can benchmark the financial performance of our company against a company in the same line of business to decide whether Bunns' ratios are in line with the sector or whether they are lower or higher. Ratios are a relative measure and, as such, they can be compared with other relative measures from other companies to highlight differences and trends. Such comparisons make ratios especially useful in understanding the profitability, efficiency, performance, liquidity and long-term financial stability of several organizations and in providing individual business entities with a target to aim for.

Ideally, when making inter-company comparisons of ratios and financial statement figures, we should only compare:

- Similar businesses
- Of similar size
- In a similar industry
- In a similar location
- Over the same accounting period

in order to eliminate random variances arising from differences in activities, size, industry, geographical location and economic factors. All comparative data should be consistently prepared to avoid distortions and bias in the analysis. In addition, organizations can also compare:

- Budgeted or planned performance data to see where the plan went well or went off course (see Chapters 10 and 11)
- Industry data and averages for the same accounting period

when making assessments of their own profitability, efficiency and performance.

WHY IS THIS RELEVANT TO ME? **How well are we doing? Comparisons with other companies**

As a business professional and user of accounting information, it is important for you to:

- Appreciate that a full evaluation of an entity's profitability, efficiency and performance cannot be made just from looking at data generated from internal sources

- Understand how comparative data from outside an entity can be used to assess and evaluate that entity's profitability, efficiency and performance

- Source comparative data to make assessments of an entity's profitability, efficiency and performance

Undertaking comparisons

One company that is in the same industry as Bunns the Bakers is Greggs plc. Greggs is engaged in bakery retail throughout the United Kingdom and has 1,854 shops supplied by 11 regional bakeries (Greggs Annual Report for the 52 Weeks Ended 30 December 2017, page 12). To test your knowledge and your ability to calculate and interpret the ratios of another company, you will now need to turn to the online workbook, Numerical exercises 6.2, to undertake the analysis of the financial statements of Greggs plc and to compare Bunns the Bakers' 2018 results with this competitor company.

6

NUMERICAL EXERCISES Think you can calculate profitability, efficiency and performance ratios for Greggs Plc and interpret them in a meaningful way? Think you can use the ratios you have calculated to draw conclusions about Bunns the Bakers' profitability, efficiency and performance in comparison to a competitor? Have a look at Numerical exercises 6.2 which present extracts from the financial statements of Greggs Plc and then have a go at the various exercises linked to the two companies in the **online workbook**.

Appendix: ratios considered in this chapter

To assist your learning, the ratios we have considered in this chapter are summarized in Table 6.4.

Table 6.4 Profitability, efficiency and performance ratios

	Calculation	What does this ratio tell us?
Profitability ratios		
Gross profit %	$\dfrac{\text{Gross profit}}{\text{Revenue}} \times 100\%$	Calculates profitability after deducting all the direct costs of goods sold from sales to determine how effectively an entity is controlling its costs of producing goods for sale or buying in goods for resale.
Operating profit %	$\dfrac{\text{Operating profit}}{\text{Revenue}} \times 100\%$	Determines profitability on the basis of revenue less all operating costs, before taking into account the effects of finance income, finance expense and taxation.
Profit before tax %	$\dfrac{\text{Profit before tax}}{\text{Revenue}} \times 100\%$	Bases the profitability calculation on profit before taxation to eliminate the distorting effect of changes in tax rates. The profit before tax percentage is the profitability of the entity after deducting all costs incurred and taking into account income earned from all sources, both trading and investment.
Profit after tax %	$\dfrac{\text{Profit for the year}}{\text{Revenue}} \times 100\%$	Calculates profitability for the period after adding all income and deducting all expenses and charges for the period under review.
Efficiency ratios		
Non-current asset turnover	$\dfrac{\text{Revenue}}{\text{Non-current assets}}$	Calculates the £s of sales from each £1 of non-current assets to determine how effectively, efficiently and productively non-current assets are being used to generate revenue.
Revenue per employee	$\dfrac{\text{Revenue}}{\text{Total number of employees}}$	Determines how productively employees are working to generate sales for an entity: the higher the sales per employee figure, the higher the organization's profitability will be.
Profit per employee	$\dfrac{\text{Operating profit}}{\text{Total number of employees}}$	Determines how much profit each employee generates during an accounting period. The higher the profit per employee, the more productively employees are working to fulfil the business's objectives of profit generation.

6

	Calculation	What does this ratio tell us?
Sales per unit of input resource	$$\frac{\text{Revenue}}{\text{Total units of input resource}}$$	Focuses on the productivity of each unit of resource employed in generating sales for the business.
Profit per unit of input resource	$$\frac{\text{Operating profit}}{\text{Total units of input resource}}$$	Indicates how productively each unit of resource is employed to generate profits for the organization.
Performance ratios		
Earnings per share	$$\frac{\text{Profit after taxation and after preference dividends}}{\text{Number of ordinary shares in issue}} \times 100 \text{ pence}$$	Represents the profit in pence attributable to each ordinary share in issue for a given accounting period.
Price/earnings ratio	$$\frac{\text{Market value of one ordinary share}}{\text{Earnings per share}}$$	Indicates the price an investor is willing to pay for £1 of earnings in a company today or the number of years of profit represented in the current share price.
Dividend per share	$$\frac{\text{Total ordinary dividends}}{\text{Number of ordinary shares in issue}} \times 100 \text{ pence}$$	The dividend paid out on each ordinary share in issue.
Dividend pay-out ratio	$$\frac{\text{Dividend per share}}{\text{Earnings per share}} \times 100\%$$	Determines the % of earnings per share paid out as dividends together with the % of earnings held back for future investment in the business.
Dividend yield	$$\frac{\text{Ordinary dividends per share}}{\text{Current market price of one ordinary share}} \times 100\%$$	Expresses the dividend paid out on each share for an accounting period as a % of the current share price.
Dividend cover	$$\frac{\text{Profit after tax and after preference dividends}}{\text{Total ordinary dividends}}$$	Assesses how many times the total dividend could be paid out of current year profits after deducting all prior claims on those profits.
Return on capital employed	$$\frac{\text{Profit before interest and tax}}{\text{Capital employed}} \times 100\%$$	Capital employed = equity + long-term borrowings. This ratio is used to determine the profitability of a business to facilitate comparisons with the return on capital employed of other businesses which have different capital structures.

6

CHAPTER SUMMARY

You should now have learnt that:

- Financial statement figures are an absolute performance measure while ratios are a relative performance measure

- Financial statement figures and ratios interact in the interpretation of profitability, efficiency and performance

- Ratios are a very good way in which to understand the changing relationship between two figures

- Managers use ratios to understand and improve the operations of a business

- Profitability ratios are calculated by dividing revenue into gross profit, operating profit, profit before tax and profit after tax

- Ratios are just a starting point in identifying the reasons for changes in financial statement figures year on year

- Efficiency ratios comprise non-current asset turnover, revenue per employee and profit per employee

- Efficiency ratios can be used to understand changes in profitability

- Increasing the revenue from each unit of fixed resource employed in the business will increase an entity's profits

- Performance ratios are calculated for earnings per share, dividends per share, dividend yield and dividend cover

- The price/earnings ratio compares the current price of a share with the earnings per share

- Performance ratios are used by shareholders to assess how well an organization has performed over an accounting period

- Assessments of an entity's profitability, efficiency and performance should never take place in a vacuum but should be compared with measures from other companies in the same industry to provide a better understanding of how an entity's results compare to those of peer companies in the market

QUICK REVISION Test your knowledge with the online flashcards in Summary of key concepts and attempt the Multiple choice questions, all in the **online workbook**. www.oup.com/uk/scott_business3e/

END-OF-CHAPTER QUESTIONS

Solutions to these questions can be found at the back of the book from page 475.

❯ DEVELOP YOUR UNDERSTANDING

❯ **Question 6.1**

Cuddles Limited produces teddy bears. The statements of profit or loss for the years ended 30 April 2019 and 30 April 2018 are presented below.

	2019	2018
	£000	£000
Revenue	34,650	29,360
Cost of sales	15,939	14,093
Gross profit	18,711	15,267
Distribution and selling costs	5,355	4,550
Administration expenses	3,654	3,083
Operating profit	9,702	7,634
Finance income	150	75
Finance expense	750	650
Profit before tax	9,102	7,059
Income tax	2,182	1,694
Profit for the year	6,920	5,365

Other information for the two years 30 April 2019 and 30 April 2018:

	2019	2018
Total dividends paid for the year	£4,400,000	£3,700,000
Number of shares in issue during the year	20,000,000	18,500,000
Number of employees during the year	275	250
Non-current assets at the financial year end	£21,655,000	£18,820,000

Cuddles Limited had no preference shares in issue in either of the two years ended 30 April 2019 and 30 April 2018.

For Cuddles Limited, calculate the following ratios for the years ended 30 April 2019 and 30 April 2018 (all calculations should be made to two decimal places):

- Gross profit percentage
- Operating profit percentage
- Profit before tax percentage

- Profit after tax percentage
- Non-current asset turnover
- Revenue per employee
- Operating profit per employee
- Earnings per share
- Dividends per share
- Dividend pay-out ratio
- Dividend cover

> **Question 6.2**

The following information has been extracted from the financial statements of DD plc for the years ended 30 June 2019 and 30 June 2018:

	2019	2018
Profit for the year	£8,622,350	£7,241,330
Number of ordinary shares in issue during the year	37,192,500	36,197,500
Number of preference shares in issue during the year	22,000,000	20,000,000
Ordinary dividend for the year	£3,347,325	£2,895,800

Further information for the two years 30 June 2019 and 30 June 2018:

- The preference shares have a par value of 50 pence each and a dividend rate of 4%.
- Market values of one ordinary share:

30 June 2017	220 pence
30 June 2018	260 pence
30 June 2019	325 pence

For DD plc calculate the following ratios for the years ended 30 June 2019 and 30 June 2018:

- Earnings per share
- Dividends per share
- Dividend pay-out ratio
- Dividend cover
- Dividend yield
- Growth in the share price over the course of each year

You should make all your calculations to two decimal places.

▶▶ TAKE IT FURTHER

>> **Question 6.3**

Extracts from the income statements (= statements of profit or loss), statements of financial position and notes to the financial statements for Bovis Homes Group plc (years ended

31 December 2017 and 31 December 2016, www.bovishomesgroup.co.uk/investors/reports-and-presentations), Persimmon plc (years ended 31 December 2017 and 31 December 2016, https://www.persimmonhomes.com/corporate/investors/results-presentations-and-financial-reports) and Crest Nicholson plc (years ended 31 October 2017 and 31 October 2016, https://www.crestnicholson.com/investor-relations/reports-results-and-presentations) are presented below. All three companies build residential housing in the UK.

	Bovis Homes Group plc		Persimmon plc		Crest Nicholson plc	
	2017	2016	2017	2016	2017	2016
	£m	£m	£m	£m	£m	£m
Revenue	1,028.2	1,054.8	3,422.3	3,136.8	1,043.2	997.0
Cost of sales	843.6	845.8	2,350.6	2,265.4	768.3	731.2
Gross profit	184.6	209.0	1,071.7	871.4	274.9	265.8
Operating profit	121.2	160.0	955.1	770.5	211.6	203.8
Profit before tax	114.0	154.7	966.1	774.8	207.0	195.0
Profit for the year	91.3	120.8	786.9	625.3	168.6	156.8
Non-current assets	15.7	57.6	542.1	482.9	110.0	118.7
Dividends for year (total)	63.8	60.4	416.6	338.3	84.3	70.3

	2017	2016	2017	2016	2017	2016
	Number	Number	Number	Number	Number	Number
Average number of employees during the year	1,297	1,186	4,535	4,526	905	849
Shares in issue (million)	134.661	134.522	308.856	308.498	255.760	254.364
Houses sold in the year	3,645	3,977	16,043	15,171	2,935	2,870

None of the three companies had any preference shares in issue in either of the accounting periods shown above.

Required

For the three companies for both 2017 and 2016 calculate:

- Gross profit percentage
- Operating profit percentage
- Profit before tax percentage
- Profit after tax percentage
- Non-current asset turnover
- Revenue per employee
- Operating profit per employee
- Earnings per share
- Dividends per share
- Dividend pay-out ratio
- Dividend cover

Make your calculations to two decimal places other than for revenue per employee and operating profit per employee, which should be made to the nearest whole £.

>> Question 6.4

Using the ratios you have calculated in Question 6.3 for the three companies:

- Suggest reasons for the changes in profitability over the two years for all three companies.
- Evaluate the performance of the three companies from the point of view of the shareholders.

>> Question 6.5

From the financial press or internet, track the share price of the three companies given above for one week and calculate the average share price for each company.

Using your average share price, the earnings per share and the dividends per share from the answers to Question 6.3, calculate:

- Dividend yield
- Price/earnings ratio

Using a share price tracker on the internet, look back to the same week you have chosen a year ago and track the share price for that week. Average the share price for that week a year ago and then calculate the percentage increase or decrease in the share price over the past year. Which of the three companies has produced the best total return over the year?

Ratio analysis 2: liquidity, working capital and long-term financial stability

LEARNING OUTCOMES

Once you have read this chapter and worked through the questions and examples in both this chapter and the online workbook, you should be able to:

- Understand what is meant by the term 'liquidity'

- Appreciate that the length of the cash flow cycle varies for different types of business

- Calculate the current ratio and the quick ratio and explain what each of these ratios tells you about the short-term liquidity of an organization

- Understand the shortcomings of current and quick ratios in the assessment of entities' short-term liquidity

- Define the term working capital and state its components

- Calculate ratios for inventory days, receivables days and payables days and discuss what these ratios tell you about the short-term liquidity of an entity

- Calculate the cash conversion cycle and explain what this means for a particular entity

- Show how organizations manage to meet their liabilities as they fall due from year end cash and from future cash inflows from sales despite having current and quick ratios that fall well below the expected norms

- Calculate the gearing ratio, debt ratio and interest cover and explain what these ratios tell us about the long-term solvency and financial stability of an organization

Introduction

The previous chapter considered profitability, efficiency and performance ratios in the interpretation and evaluation of the financial results of each accounting period's trading and operations. These ratios concentrated on the statement of profit or loss as the source of data on which to build these ratios and the evaluations based upon them. Chapter 4 discussed the importance of cash flows and how cash flows and their timing are the key to the survival of any entity. The cash flows of an organization are extremely important in your evaluation of the liquidity of that organization and you should quickly go over the lessons of Chapter 4 again before reading further in this chapter. This is to ensure that you fully appreciate the importance of cash flow information in the assessment of an entity's financial position and its financial stability.

This chapter will look at liquidity ratios and the related analysis provided by **working capital** ratios. Liquidity ratios and working capital ratio assessments are built upon the information contained in the statement of financial position. In addition, we will consider how an entity's capital structure contributes to an assessment of that entity's long-term financial stability. We saw in Chapter 5 that businesses issue shares and take on borrowings with which to finance their activities: the proportions in which share capital and borrowed funds finance an entity have a bearing on the ability of that entity to continue operating when economic conditions become less favourable. We will look at the key ratios in the assessment of entities' capital structures as well as evaluating organizations' ability to survive with high levels of borrowings.

The International Accounting Standards Board (IASB) recognizes the critical importance of information on an organization's liquidity, solvency, cash flow generating capacity and its ability to raise additional funds with which to finance operations:

> Information about the nature and amounts of a reporting entity's economic resources and claims can help users to identify the reporting entity's financial strengths and weaknesses. That information can help users to assess the reporting entity's liquidity and solvency, its needs for additional financing and how successful it is likely to be in obtaining that financing . . . Information about priorities and payment requirements of existing claims helps users to predict how future cash flows will be distributed among those with a claim against the reporting entity.
>
> Source: IASB *Conceptual Framework for Financial Reporting*, paragraph 1.13

Analysis of these aspects is critical to any assessment of an entity's short- and long-term survival prospects. It is these aspects and the analysis of this information that will form the main subject of this chapter.

REFER BACK To illustrate the ratios discussed in this chapter we will use the statement of financial position, statement of profit or loss and statement of cash flows for Bunns the Bakers presented in Chapters 2, 3 and 4. You should refer back to Illustrations 2.1, 3.1 and 4.1 in these chapters or look up the copies available in the **online workbook** as you work through this chapter.

Liquidity and the cash flow cycle

Liquidity refers to the ability of an entity to raise cash to pay off its liabilities as they become due for payment. Any company that is unable to generate this cash with which to meet its debts will be unable to survive and will file for bankruptcy; in this situation, an administrator is appointed to sell the company's assets and the cash raised from these asset sales is used to pay at least some of what is owed to the company's creditors. Insolvent companies have more liabilities than assets, so it is unlikely that the liabilities of such companies will be repaid in full as shown in Give me an example 7.1.

GIVE ME AN EXAMPLE 7.1   Insolvent companies failing to repay all their debts

On 15 January 2018 the Official Receiver was appointed as liquidator of the Carillion Group of companies. At that date the group owed £900m to its lenders but had only £29m in cash. Around 30,000 small businesses are owed money by the group and it is feared that many of these small businesses could themselves become insolvent as a result of Carillion's inability to pay them what they are owed. Up to 43,000 employees across the world could lose their jobs unless other firms step in to take up the group's contracts. Government contracts proved much less profitable and cash generative than the group had expected when bids for those contracts were placed and accepted. Check the internet for the latest on the liquidation to see how much creditors have been paid and how much they have lost as a result of Carillion's collapse.

Source: https://www.theguardian.com/business/2018/jan/15/carillion-what-went-wrong-liquidation-staff

---

How do business entities generate cash from their operations? Some businesses sell their goods for cash so they immediately have money with which to pay suppliers and other parties (such as employees or banks) what they are owed. Other entities sell goods to customers on credit, allowing their customers time in which to pay. In this case, organizations will have to wait for payment, but the cash will be expected to flow in eventually to meet the demands of creditors as they become due. What effect do these two different approaches to selling goods have on the length of the cash flow cycle? The **cash flow cycles** for retailers and manufacturers are illustrated in Figures 7.1 and 7.2.

Figure 7.1 shows that the retailing cash flow cycle is very short: goods are purchased on credit from suppliers, sold on for cash to customers and are then paid for. Figure 7.2 shows that the manufacturing cash flow cycle is much longer. Raw materials bought on credit from suppliers first have to be converted into finished goods inventory. These finished goods are then sold to customers, but they ask for time in which to pay. In the meantime, suppliers will be demanding payment and will most likely have to be paid well before customers have settled what is owed. A store of cash will thus have to be retained within the business to meet the demands of suppliers and of other claims

Figure 7.1 The cash flow cycle for retailers

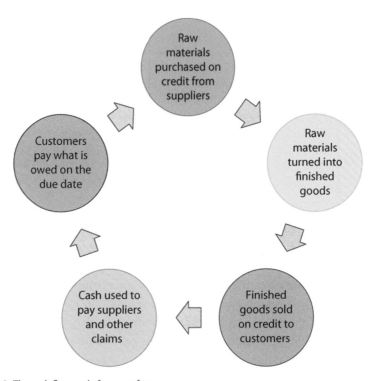

Figure 7.2 The cash flow cycle for manufacturers

upon the business while waiting for customers to pay what is owed. There are thus many delays in the manufacturing cash flow cycle, first in producing the goods and then in waiting for the cash from customers. We shall consider the effect these different business cycles have on our assessment of a business's liquidity when we look at working capital management. However, you should appreciate at this early stage how the cash flow cycle operates and how it is vital for entities to have cash available to meet liabilities as they fall due.

WHY IS THIS RELEVANT TO ME?   Liquidity and the cash flow cycle

To enable you as a business professional and user of accounting information to:

* Appreciate that different businesses have different cash flow cycles

* Evaluate the speed at which different types of business generate cash from their operations with which to pay their debts

* Understand that the faster an entity converts its sales into cash, the more liquid that business is

---

GO BACK OVER THIS AGAIN!   Convinced you understand how vital the cash flow cycle is to businesses? Go to the **online workbook** and look at Exercises 7.1 to enable you to appreciate the need to ensure that there are cash inflows from which to pay liabilities as they fall due.

Liquidity ratios

Have a look at Bunns the Bakers' current assets (Illustration 2.1): these are made up of inventory, trade and other receivables and cash. Now look at the current liabilities, which show the current portion of long-term liabilities, that part of borrowings that is due for repayment within one year, trade and other payables (the amounts due to suppliers and for other liabilities such as rent, business rates and electricity among others) and current tax liabilities. Along with the cash and cash equivalents already available, the other current assets are used to generate cash from sales of inventory and receipts from receivables to pay off the current liabilities. Short-term assets are thus used to meet short-term liabilities: this is the liquidity, the availability of cash in the near future, referred to in the IASB's *Conceptual Framework for Financial Reporting* quoted earlier (this chapter, Introduction). How is the ability of short-term assets to meet short-term liabilities assessed? Not surprisingly, the first step in this assessment will be through the calculation of ratios.

Current ratio

The first ratio that we will look at compares current assets to current liabilities in an attempt to determine whether an organization has sufficient short-term assets from which to meet short-term liabilities. This ratio is called the **current ratio** and is calculated as follows:

$$\text{Current ratio} = \frac{\text{Current assets}}{\text{Current liabilities}}$$

This figure is expressed as a ratio and tells us how many £s of current assets there are for each £ of current liabilities. Calculating the current ratio for Bunns the Bakers at 31 March 2019 and 31 March 2018 gives us the following results:

$$2019: \text{Current ratio: } \frac{£334,000}{£840,000} = 0.40{:}1$$

$$2018: \text{Current ratio: } \frac{£319,000}{£707,000} = 0.45{:}1$$

What do these ratios mean? At 31 March 2019, Bunns the Bakers has 40 pence of current assets for each £1 of current liabilities, while at 31 March 2018 the company had 45 pence of current assets for each £1 of current liabilities. This might not sound very good as the company does not seem to have much in the way of current assets with which to meet liabilities as they fall due.

However, remember that the statement of financial position is just a snapshot of the financial position at one day in the year: the position will change tomorrow and the next day and the day after that as goods are produced, sales are made, cash flows in and liabilities are paid. The current ratio also ignores the timing of the receipt of cash and of the payment of liabilities.

How quickly is cash received by the business? If this is immediately at the point of sale then the entity will have a very positive cash inflow from which to meet its liabilities. If cash is received from trade receivables some time after the sales were made then a much more careful management of cash inflows and outflows will be required. The current ratio's logic assumes that all the liabilities will be due for payment on the day following the statement of financial position date; this is highly unlikely and we will investigate the likely payment pattern for liabilities later on in this chapter to show that, contrary to appearances, Bunns the Bakers is a very liquid, cash generative business indeed (this chapter, Current liabilities: the timing of payments).

WHY IS THIS RELEVANT TO ME?   Current ratio

To enable you as a business professional and user of accounting information to:

- Understand what the current ratio represents and how it is used in the assessment of short-term liquidity
- Calculate current ratios for organizations
- Appreciate the shortcomings of the current ratio as a key measure in short-term liquidity assessment

---

GO BACK OVER THIS AGAIN!   Do you really understand what the current ratio is trying to do and what factors you have to take into account when using it? Go to the **online workbook** and have a go at Exercises 7.2 to check your understanding.

MULTIPLE CHOICE QUESTIONS Sure that you can calculate a current ratio from a given set of financial information? Go to the **online workbook** and have a go at Multiple choice questions 7.1 to test out your ability to calculate this ratio.

Quick (acid test) ratio

This ratio is a modification of the current ratio and ignores inventory in its assessment of an entity's ability to pay its short-term liabilities. Why is inventory taken out of the calculation? There is always a chance that inventory produced by an organization will not be sold quickly, so that this inventory cannot be counted as convertible into cash in the near future. Therefore, the **quick (acid test) ratio** only takes account of current assets that are cash or that are readily realizable in cash: trade receivables are readily convertible into cash as the entity has a contractual right to receive the money due for sales already made to customers. The quick (acid test) ratio is calculated as follows:

$$\text{Quick (acid test) ratio} = \frac{(\text{Current assets} - \text{Inventory})}{\text{Current liabilities}}$$

Using Bunns the Bakers' statement of financial position at 31 March 2019 and 31 March 2018, the following quick ratios can be calculated:

$$2019: \text{Quick ratio:} \ \frac{(£334{,}000 - £60{,}000)}{£840{,}000} = 0.33{:}1$$

$$2018: \text{Quick ratio:} \ \frac{(£319{,}000 - £55{,}000)}{£707{,}000} = 0.37{:}1$$

These ratios are inevitably lower than the current ratios calculated previously as inventory is taken out of the current assets with no corresponding decrease in current liabilities. Again, this paints a very gloomy picture of Bunns the Bakers' short-term liquidity as the company only has 33 pence of readily realizable current assets per £1 of current liabilities at 31 March 2019, a figure that has fallen from 37 pence per £1 of current liabilities at 31 March 2018.

How realistic is the assumption that inventory will not sell quickly? It all depends upon the particular activity in which an entity is engaged. A moment's thought should convince you that the quick ratio is completely irrelevant to any assessment of Bunns the Bakers' short-term liquidity. The company sells freshly baked goods from their shops in towns. People usually get up too late to make their own sandwiches or snacks to take to work (or are too lazy to do so!) and will go out at lunch time to buy the company's products, which will sell quickly rather than being stockpiled for several weeks or months before they are sold. Therefore, what is produced today is sold today and cash is received immediately from cash paying customers at the till. Even if there are sandwiches, pies and pastries left towards the end of the day, shop staff will discount the prices in order to tempt customers to buy up the left over inventory so only very small amounts of the goods produced will be wasted.

The quick ratio may be much more relevant in a manufacturing situation. The swift pace of change in markets and products means that any advance production might result in such goods becoming obsolete or out of fashion so that entities are unable to sell them to recover the costs of producing or buying them. As a result of this risk, many companies today only produce to order rather than manufacturing goods in the hope that they will sell. Such an approach removes the risk of goods becoming obsolete and the losses that disposal of such goods will incur as, first, discounts are given on the original selling price and then goods have to be scrapped as interest in them finally runs out. It is particularly important only to produce goods to order in the high-tech sector; new developments are taking place every few minutes so that products are being improved all the time and earlier models quickly become outdated. As a result, high-tech goods such as laptops, tablets, mobile phones and other electronic devices are produced as orders come in to avoid the losses that would arise if several months' advance sales of such goods were produced all at once.

Give me an example 7.2 presents the differing experiences of Next plc and Ted Baker plc with regard to the effect of old stock on their profit margins.

GIVE ME AN EXAMPLE 7.2 Out of date goods and their effect on profit margins

In the 52 weeks to 28 January 2017, Ted Baker plc reported an increase in the gross profit margin from 59.9% to 61.0%. This increase in gross profit margin was attributed to 'improved full price sell through'. This means that fewer goods were discounted in the sales resulting in more goods being sold at full price which generated higher margins overall.

By contrast, in the 52 weeks to 28 January 2017, Next plc reported a decrease in its retail operating profit margin from 16.9% to 14.7%. Next notes that stock for sale was up 17% on the figures for 2016, which explains 0.7% of the fall in the operating margin over the year. Higher discounts offered on goods thus had the effect of lowering profit margins.

Sources: Ted Baker's annual report and accounts: http://www.tedbakerplc.com; Next plc annual report and accounts: http://www.nextplc.co.uk

---

Where entities are subject to this kind of unpredictable pattern of demand that can suddenly be turned off or interrupted by, for example, an economic downturn, a change in consumer tastes or technological developments, your evaluation of liquidity will be much more cautious. If an organization does not enjoy steady demand for its products then that organization is at much higher risk of suffering liquidity problems and you would expect that entity to maintain much higher current and quick ratios as well as operating a very sophisticated forecasting system to stop production of its goods at the first sign of a decline in demand. In Bunns the Bakers' case, office workers will keep visiting their outlets at lunch time and shoppers will drop in throughout the day as they seek out the company's value for money products, so declines in demand will not be a problem for this organization.

WHY IS THIS RELEVANT TO ME?   Quick ratio

As a business professional and user of accounting information, you will be expected to:

- Understand what the quick ratio represents and how it is used in the assessment of short-term liquidity
- Understand the situations in which inventory obsolescence is a risk and those in which it is not
- Calculate quick ratios for organizations
- Appreciate the situations in which the quick ratio is applicable and not applicable in an assessment of short-term liquidity

---

GO BACK OVER THIS AGAIN!   How well have you grasped what the quick ratio is trying to do and what factors you have to take into account when using it? Go to the **online workbook** and have a go at Exercises 7.3 to check your understanding.

SUMMARY OF KEY CONCEPTS   Can you remember the formulae for the current and quick ratios? Take a look at Summary of key concepts 7.1 and 7.2 to reinforce your understanding.

MULTIPLE CHOICE QUESTIONS   Are you totally confident that you can calculate a quick ratio from a given set of financial information? Go to the **online workbook** and have a go at Multiple choice questions 7.2 to test out your ability to calculate this ratio.

Current and quick ratios: the traditional view

Convention has it that a business entity needs a current ratio of 2:1, £2 of current assets for every £1 of current liabilities, and a quick ratio of 1:1, £1 of trade receivables and cash for every £1 of current liabilities, in order to be able to survive financially. On a conventional reading of the figures for Bunns the Bakers, then, the assessment would be that the company is heading into bankruptcy. Bunns the Bakers has nowhere near current and quick ratios of 2:1 and 1:1, so the question must be asked how the company manages to survive quite happily on much lower ratios than convention dictates.

Working capital

A much more effective way in which to assess liquidity is to look at the working capital cycle, the time it takes for an entity to turn raw materials into goods for sale, sell these goods, collect the cash and then pay suppliers for goods and raw materials supplied. The length of this working capital cycle is determined through the use of the three working capital ratios presented in Figure 7.3. We looked at the cash flow cycle at the start of this chapter for both retailers and manufacturers, but it is now time to look in more detail at the components of working capital and how to use these as a guide to the liquidity and cash flow generating capability of an organization.

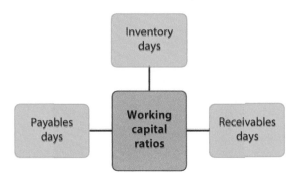

Figure 7.3 The three working capital ratios

First, though, what is working capital? The basic definition of working capital is as follows:

Working capital = current assets − current liabilities

Working capital thus comprises:

- Inventories of raw materials for use in production, of finished goods ready for sale or of goods purchased for resale to customers
- Trade receivables from customers of the business who have been provided with a credit facility by the entity
- Cash in the bank or in hand that is held to meet day-to-day needs
- Trade payables of the business which require settlement on a daily basis. For the purposes of the working capital calculation, amounts due to lenders and money due to settle tax liabilities are ignored as these (as we shall see later, this chapter, Current liabilities: the timing of payments) do not require payment on a day-to-day basis, being settled on a monthly or three-monthly basis.

Working capital ratios

In order to evaluate the efficiency of working capital management, the ratios in Table 7.1 are used.

Table 7.1 Working capital ratios, how they are calculated and what they tell users

Ratio	Calculation	What does this ratio tell us?
Inventory days (also known as stock days)	$\dfrac{\text{Inventory}}{\text{Cost of sales}} \times 365$	• This ratio measures the average stockholding period, how long an entity holds goods in inventory before they are sold • The more quickly inventory turns over the better, as inventory is turned into sales (and hence into cash) much more quickly while obsolete inventories and the risk of deterioration (and hence loss of future cash inflows from the sale of this inventory) are minimized • However, when calculating their optimum level of inventory holding, businesses should consider future demand (no inventory, no sale), any anticipated shortages or price rises, discounts available for buying in bulk, storage, insurance and any other costs involved in holding inventory
Receivables days (also known as debtor days)	$\dfrac{\text{Trade receivables}}{\text{Credit sales}^1} \times 365$	• This ratio indicates the average credit period taken by customers, the length of time it takes for credit customers to pay what they owe • Evaluates the efficiency of the credit control system and the speed with which credit sales are turned into cash • Where this ratio is increasing, steps can be taken to speed up payments (e.g. by offering early payment discounts) to minimize the funds tied up in receivables: it is better to have cash in our bank account than in our customers' bank account
Payables days (also known as creditor days)	$\dfrac{\text{Trade payables}}{\text{Cost of sales}^2} \times 365$	• This ratio measures how quickly the business is paying off its purchases made on credit • Ideally, the receivables days and payables days should be equal: as cash is received, it is used to pay off liabilities • Paying trade payables before trade receivables have paid usually has a negative impact upon cash flow: see the profit ≠ cash example for Start Up in Example 4.1 in Chapter 4

[1]Strictly, this ratio should use only credit sales in the calculation of receivables days: sales made for cash have already been settled and thus no cash is outstanding from these transactions. Therefore, cash sales should be omitted in the determination of receivables days, the number of days of credit allowed to credit customers. However, in practice, companies do not disclose separate figures for their cash sales and their credit sales, so it is normal just to use total sales in this calculation.

[2]Again, while trade payables should be compared to purchases of goods on credit, entities do not publish details of their credit purchases, so cost of sales is used to approximate the cost of purchases. In reality, cost of sales may include the wages and salaries of production operatives in the manufacturing part of a business, which should not strictly be classified as purchases on credit, but the cost of sales is a useful substitute for the credit purchases of a business.

As long as you are consistent in your calculations (as noted in Chapter 6, The importance of calculating and presenting ratios consistently), the relationships and ratios produced should provide a suitable like-for-like basis on which to assess the working capital strengths or weaknesses of a business.

The working capital ratios for Bunns the Bakers are as follows:

2019: Inventory days/inventory turnover: $\dfrac{£60,000}{£4,535,000} \times 365 = 4.83$ days

2018: Inventory days/inventory turnover: $\dfrac{£55,000}{£4,596,000} \times 365 = 4.37$ days

Trade and other receivables for Bunns the Bakers at 31 March 2019 and 31 March 2018 from the statement of financial position are £62,000 and £75,000, respectively. By looking at the notes to the financial statements we can determine that the actual trade receivables, as distinct from other receivables and prepayments, are £25,000 at 31 March 2019 and £35,000 at 31 March 2018. This will give us the following receivables days for the two accounting periods:

2019: Receivables days: $\dfrac{£25,000}{£10,078,000} \times 365 = 0.90$ days

2018: Receivables days: $\dfrac{£35,000}{£9,575,000} \times 365 = 1.33$ days

This ratio is very low, but, as most sales will be made for an immediate cash payment from customers in the shops, this is not at all surprising. As we noted in Chapter 2 (Current assets), credit sales will be limited to a small number of credit customers such as supermarkets.

The rest of the sales will be made for cash to customers as they come into the shops and make their purchases, so a very low receivables days ratio would be expected in such a situation.

Trade and other payables for Bunns the Bakers at 31 March 2019 and 31 March 2018 from the statement of financial position are £390,000 and £281,000 respectively. By looking at the notes to the financial statements we can determine that the actual trade payables, as distinct from other payables, are £300,000 at 31 March 2019 and £220,000 at 31 March 2018. This will give us the following payables days for the two accounting periods:

2019: Payables days: $\dfrac{£300,000}{£4,535,000} \times 365 = 24.15$ days

2018: Payables days: $\dfrac{£220,000}{£4,596,000} \times 365 = 17.47$ days

---

WHY IS THIS RELEVANT TO ME? Working capital ratios

As a business professional and user of accounting information, you will be expected to:

- Understand what working capital ratios are and what they represent
- Be able to calculate working capital ratios for organizations

---

GO BACK OVER THIS AGAIN! Certain you can distinguish between the three working capital ratios? Go to the **online workbook** and have a go at Exercises 7.4 to make sure you can make these distinctions.

SUMMARY OF KEY CONCEPTS Do you remember the formulae for the three working capital ratios? Take a look at Summary of key concepts 7.3–7.5 to reinforce your understanding.

MULTIPLE CHOICE QUESTIONS Certain you can calculate working capital ratios from a given set of financial information? Go to the **online workbook** and have a go at Multiple choice questions 7.3 to test out your ability to calculate these ratios.

What do these figures tell us? First, that, in 2019, inventories are sold within 4.8 days, a very slight increase on the 4.4 days it took to sell inventory in 2018. Much of Bunns the Bakers' inventory will comprise raw materials ready for use in the production of bread, pies, pastries and other bakery goods. Finished goods themselves will probably represent only one day's production as goods are produced fresh and ready for delivery and sale the next day. Certain other inventories, such as soft drinks, which have a longer shelf life, can be kept in storage for several weeks or months before they are out of date, but most of the company's raw materials will be delivered on a daily basis and turned into finished goods for sale on the same or the next day.

This is a very low inventory days ratio and indicates that stocks are turned into sales very quickly indeed. As most of these sales are for cash, the receivables days are also very low. However, trade payables are settled every 24 days in the year to 31 March 2019 (an increase on the previous year) so Bunns the Bakers is holding on to the cash received from customers before they pay their suppliers with this available cash. Money is received at the point of sale, but the company holds on to the cash until the time to pay their suppliers comes around.

The cash conversion cycle

The ratios shown in Figure 7.3 enable us to calculate the **cash conversion cycle** (sometimes referred to as the **operating cycle** or **working capital cycle**). The cash conversion cycle tells us how quickly inventory is turned into trade receivables and how quickly trade receivables are turned into cash with which to pay trade payables (Figure 7.4). The shorter this cycle, the better the working capital is being managed and the more readily cash is available with which to meet liabilities. Conversely, the longer

Figure 7.4 The cash conversion cycle

this process, the higher the investment required in working capital and the higher the emergency sources of cash will need to be (e.g. financing by an agreed short-term over-draft from the bank) to pay liabilities as they fall due.

The cash conversion cycle is calculated in the following way:

Inventory days + receivables days – payables days

For Bunns the Bakers, the cash conversion cycle for the two years under consideration is as follows:

2019: Cash conversion cycle: 4.83 inventory days + 0.90 receivables days
– 24.15 payables days = –18.42 days

2018: Cash conversion cycle: 4.37 inventory days + 1.33 receivables days
– 17.47 payables days = –11.77 days

The calculations above and Figure 7.5 show that the cash conversion cycle figures for both years are negative. This means that Bunns the Bakers are converting their sales into

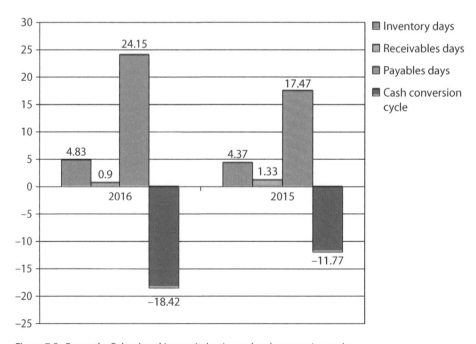

Figure 7.5 Bunns the Bakers' working capital ratios and cash conversion cycle

cash well before they have to pay their suppliers. The negative cash conversion cycles also mean that the company is holding onto this cash for several days before it is paid out and this will enable the company to use this cash to generate additional finance income (interest receivable) on their surplus bank deposits. This additional interest may not amount to much in total in the statement of profit or loss, but it is an important extra source of income for the company and this spare cash is being used effectively to generate additional profits for the shareholders. From Bunns the Bakers' point of view, the increase in the cash conversion cycle this year means that they are taking an extra 6.65 days (18.42 days − 11.77 days) in which to pay their suppliers, indicating that they are holding onto their cash for longer. By using the credit facilities provided by their suppliers, Bunns the Bakers do not have to rely on a short-term bank overdraft to finance their working capital: this finance is in effect being provided by the company's suppliers.

WHY IS THIS RELEVANT TO ME?   Working capital ratios and the cash conversion cycle

To enable you as a business professional and user of accounting information to:

- Calculate additional ratios with which to evaluate short-term liquidity
- Calculate the length of the cash conversion cycle
- Appreciate how working capital ratios and the cash conversion cycle help to supplement the current and quick ratios in liquidity analysis

---

GO BACK OVER THIS AGAIN!   Quite sure that you understand what the cash conversion cycle is telling you? Go to the **online workbook** and have a go at Exercises 7.5 to check your understanding.

MULTIPLE CHOICE QUESTIONS   How easily can you calculate the cash conversion cycle from a given set of financial information? Go to the **online workbook** and have a go at Multiple choice questions 7.4 to test out your ability to undertake the required calculations.

Why is working capital so important?

Organizations need short-term finance to enable them to buy raw materials with which to produce goods to sell to customers. As indicated in Figure 7.2, a firm's suppliers cannot wait for payment until the raw materials have been turned into finished goods, sold on credit and then paid for by that firm's customers. Such a period would be too lengthy and the supplier might well have gone bankrupt while waiting for payment. Therefore, manufacturers and their suppliers rely on short-term credit provided by banks in the form of overdrafts. These overdrafts are used to finance the purchase of materials and the payment of wages to workers to tide them over the short-term lack of funds that arises when waiting for products to be manufactured and sold and for customers to pay. Such short-term working capital allows organizations to build up momentum with this short-term finance being paid back when projects are up and running and cash inflows from customers are financing cash outflows to suppliers. As organizations expand, they receive more orders from customers which require more materials from suppliers and increasing numbers of workers. Customers still want time in which to pay for the goods supplied so companies have to source ever increasing amounts of working capital to finance their commitments to suppliers and to their workforces. Management of payables, receivables and inventory thus requires a very careful balancing act to ensure that working capital continues to flow into the company to finance all the obligations as they fall due.

> **WHY IS THIS RELEVANT TO ME?** Why is working capital so important?
>
> To enable you as a business professional and user of accounting information to appreciate that:
>
> • Entities need short-term finance with which to finance growth and to start up new projects
>
> • That short-term finance has to come either from cash saved within the entity or from outside sources such as bank overdrafts

Current liabilities: the timing of payments

Our calculations in the current ratio section earlier showed that at 31 March 2019 Bunns the Bakers has only 40 pence of current assets for each £1 of current liabilities. At that point we also noted that the current and quick ratios take no account of when liabilities are actually due for payment and make the assumption that all liabilities might call in the money owed to them at the statement of financial position date. Let us now think about how much of Bunns the Bakers' current liabilities might actually be due for payment on the day after the statement of financial position date so that we can assess how liquid the company really is and how easily it can afford to pay its debts from the current assets it already owns.

Bunns the Bakers' statement of financial position shows the following current liabilities at 31 March 2019:

	£000
Current portion of long-term borrowings	300
Trade and other payables	390
Current tax liabilities	150
	840

At 31 March 2019, Bunns the Bakers has £212,000 of cash with which to meet these current liabilities. This does not appear to be a good position to be in, as current liabilities exceed the cash available with which to pay them. However, by thinking about when these liabilities will actually fall due we will be able to see that the company can meet its liabilities very easily from the cash it has at the year end together with all the cash generated from sales in the days and weeks after the year end.

First, let us think about when the current portion of long-term borrowings will be payable. When an entity borrows money from a bank under a formal loan agreement, the entity and the bank sign a contract. This contract governs the loan terms, the terms of repayment and the interest that is payable on the loan. As long as the borrower does not breach the terms of the contract (e.g. by failing to pay either any interest due or a loan instalment by the agreed date), then the bank cannot demand its money back immediately and has to wait for the borrower to meet each repayment as it becomes due. The £300,000 due at 31 March 2019 probably represents 12 monthly payments of £25,000 each so that the most that could be due on 1 April 2019 would be £25,000. The other monthly repayments would be due one month after this, two months after this and so on. This is a very pessimistic assumption: most loan instalments are payable at the end of the month rather than at the beginning, giving the company up to 30 days to save up for the next payment. But for now we will assume that loan repayments are due on the first day of each month so that £25,000 is repayable on 1 April 2019.

While bank loans are covered by contracts in this way, bank overdrafts are not. Should the entity you are evaluating have an overdraft with its bank, do remember that overdrafts are repayable on demand so that all of the overdraft should be added in to the calculation of immediate liquidity on the day after the statement of financial position date.

Turning now to what is owed to suppliers, we saw above that trade payables amount to £300,000 and that this represents 24.15 days of purchases. We noted above that suppliers of raw materials will deliver to the company each day so that the ingredients going into the bread, sandwiches, pies and pastries are always fresh. Therefore, the total amount due to trade payables on 1 April 2019 would be £300,000/24.15 = £12,422, with £12,422 due on 2 April, £12,422 on 3 April and so on. In reality, these amounts will not be spread so evenly, but the £12,422 is a useful average to work with, based on the payables days we calculated earlier (this chapter, Working capital ratios). The other payables of £90,000 (£390,000 − £300,000 trade payables) will probably be payable to a variety of different creditors at different times over the next two to three months. However, as we are cautious accountants, let us assume that one-quarter of this amount is due tomorrow, the day after the financial year end, which represents £90,000/4 = £22,500 payable immediately.

Tax liabilities for limited liability companies in the UK are payable in quarterly instalments three months, six months, nine months and twelve months after the statement of financial position date, so the earliest that any of the £150,000 tax is due would be 30 June 2019, three months after 31 March 2019. Therefore, none of the tax liabilities will be due on 1 April 2019.

Summarizing our results below tells us that we have only a fraction of the total current liabilities at 31 March 2019 to pay on 1 April 2019. The figures below may be seriously overestimated as the long-term borrowings are probably repayable at the end of April 2019 rather than at the beginning of the month and it is unlikely that 25% of the other payables is actually due one day after the year end:

	£
Current portion of long-term borrowings	25,000
Trade payables	12,422
Other payables	22,500
Current tax liabilities	—
Total payable on 1 April 2019	59,922
Cash available at 31 March 2019	212,000
Surplus cash available on 1 April 2019 (£212,000 – £59,922)	152,078

Thus, when it comes to determining how liquid a company is and how easily it can meet its current liabilities when they fall due, timing is critical. In addition, we should not forget that cash will be coming into the business on 1 April 2019 as sales are made at the tills. How much will this be? Given that annual sales are £10,078,000 and that there are, say, 300 trading days a year, this would give daily sales of £33,593. As this cash will come into the business on every trading day of the year, there is always going to be plenty of cash available from which to meet debts as they become payable. Therefore, the current and quick ratio, while giving a good idea of how many £s of current assets are available to meet each £ of liabilities, should not be used as the final indicator of how easily a company can meet its liabilities as they fall due. You must think about the timing of receipts and payments of cash and the way in which an entity manages its cash inflows and outflows to make a full evaluation of an entity's short-term liquidity.

To illustrate the truth of this approach, just think about your own situation for a moment. If we all drew up our own personal statement of financial position at the end of each calendar year and included everything that we had to pay for in the next twelve months and compared this to what cash we had available at the start of the year, we would all be in despair. However, we know that all our liabilities for the next twelve months are not due immediately on 1 January and that we have monthly inflows of cash from our salaries that will gradually pay what we owe throughout the year. Cash outflows are matched by cash inflows and, with a bit of luck, we will be able to save some cash towards a holiday or towards some other treat for ourselves. We do not worry that we do not have enough cash today to pay off everything that is due in the next twelve months and neither do businesses.

WHY IS THIS RELEVANT TO ME?　The timing of payments and the shortcomings of the current and quick ratios

To enable you as a business professional and user of accounting information to:

- Appreciate that an entity's current liabilities will never all be due for payment at the same time unless that entity is in liquidation

- Calculate the amounts due for payment on the day after the statement of financial position date as part of your assessment of an entity's liquidity

- Forecast monthly cash outgoings for the next year to determine whether entities can meet those monthly outgoings from current trading

- Appreciate how timing of payments analysis helps to overcome the shortcomings of the current and quick ratios in liquidity analysis

---

GO BACK OVER THIS AGAIN!　Sure you understand how the timing of payments is critical to an assessment of short-term liquidity? Go to the **online workbook** and look at Exercises 7.6 to enable you to appreciate that not all liabilities are due for payment immediately and that the assumptions of the current and quick ratios are invalid when assessing an entity's ability to meet its short-term liabilities.

Capital structure ratios: long-term solvency and financial stability assessment

7

Working capital, cash conversion cycle and current and quick ratios measure short-term liquidity and the ability of entities to pay their debts on a short-term (within the next 12 months), day-to-day basis. But just as there are ratios with which to measure short-term liquidity, there are also ratios to determine long-term solvency and financial stability (Figure 7.6). As we saw in Chapter 5, companies have a choice of financing models through which to raise the capital required to finance their operations for the long term. They can either raise the necessary funds through an issue of share capital or they can raise the money from borrowings from the bank or the money markets. Many companies combine both share capital and borrowings in their long-term financing. The combination of the two will have implications for our assessment of how easily entities will be able to repay those borrowings while still servicing that long-term capital from profits either through distribution of dividends to shareholders or the payment of interest on borrowings. This is the solvency, the availability of cash in the longer term, referred to in the IASB's *Conceptual Framework* quoted earlier in this chapter.

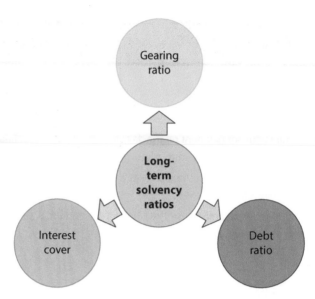

Figure 7.6 Long-term solvency and financial stability ratios

When assessing long-term solvency and financial stability, the ratios in Table 7.2 are used.

Table 7.2 Long-term solvency and financial stability ratios, how they are calculated and what they tell users

Ratio	What does this ratio tell us?
Gearing ratio $= \dfrac{\text{Long and short-term borrowings}}{\text{Equity}} \times 100\%$	• The gearing percentage is often seen as a measure of risk: companies with higher borrowings are supposedly more risky than those with lower borrowings
Debt ratio $= \dfrac{\text{Total liabilities}}{\text{Total assets}}$	• This ratio measures the £s of liabilities per £1 of total assets • The lower the ratio, the more secure the entity
Interest cover $= \dfrac{\text{Profit before interest and tax}}{\text{Interest}}$	• Assesses how many times interest payable on borrowings is covered by operating profits (in the same way that dividend cover measures how many times the ordinary dividend is covered by profit for the year) • The higher the figure, the better, as a high figure indicates an ability to continue meeting interest payments from profits in the future

> **WHY IS THIS RELEVANT TO ME?** Capital structure ratios: long-term solvency and financial stability assessment
>
> As a business professional and user of accounting information, you will be expected to:
>
> - Understand what gearing, debt and interest cover ratios are telling you about an entity's long-term solvency and financial stability
> - Be able to calculate gearing, debt and interest cover ratios for organizations
> - Evaluate the results of gearing, debt and interest cover ratio calculations to produce an assessment of an entity's long-term solvency and financial stability

Gearing ratio

Looking at the statement of financial position for Bunns the Bakers (Illustration 2.1), the company has borrowings of £300,000 in current liabilities and borrowings of £2,700,000 in non-current liabilities, giving a total borrowings figure of £3,000,000 at 31 March 2019. At 31 March 2018, the figures are £300,000 and £3,000,000 giving total borrowings of £3,300,000. Equity in the statement of financial position in Illustration 2.1 is £8,459,000 at 31 March 2019 and £7,767,000 at 31 March 2018. Using these figures we can calculate gearing percentages as follows:

$$2019: \text{Gearing \%:} \quad \frac{£3,000,000}{£8,459,000} \times 100\% = 35.47\%$$

$$2018: \text{Gearing \%:} \quad \frac{£3,300,000}{£7,767,000} \times 100\% = 42.49\%$$

Gearing has fallen this year as borrowings represent a lower proportion of equity than in previous years. This fall is partly due to the repayment of £300,000 during the year to 31 March 2019 and partly due to the increase in equity as a result of the issue of new share capital and the profits retained for the current year. The statement of cash flows (Illustration 4.1) shows us that the company has repaid £300,000 of their borrowings over each of the past two years, so this debt seems to be very manageable. The percentage of borrowings to equity is low and, given the consistency of the trade in which Bunns the Bakers are engaged and the constant demand that their products enjoy, it would be perfectly logical to draw the conclusion that the company's long-term financing strategy is very stable and poses no solvency risk to the organization.

MULTIPLE CHOICE QUESTIONS How easily do you think you can calculate gearing from a given set of financial information? Go to the **online workbook** and have a go at Multiple choice questions 7.5 to test out your ability to calculate this ratio.

Debt ratio

Total assets and total liabilities just have to be read off the relevant lines of the statement of financial position (Illustration 2.1). The company has total assets of £12,199,000 at 31 March 2019 and total assets of £11,674,000 at 31 March 2018. Similarly, total liabilities at 31 March 2019 amount to £3,740,000 and £3,907,000 at 31 March 2018. Comparing the total liabilities with the total assets gives us the following results:

$$2019: \text{Debt ratio: } \frac{£3,740,000}{£12,199,000} = 0.31:1$$

$$2018: \text{Debt ratio: } \frac{£3,907,000}{£11,674,000} = 0.33:1$$

Bunns the Bakers has 31 pence of total liabilities for every £1 of total assets at 31 March 2019 compared to 33 pence of total liabilities for every £1 of total assets at 31 March 2018. This is not a high figure and it would be reasonable to conclude that the company is highly solvent and financially stable.

MULTIPLE CHOICE QUESTIONS   Quite confident you can calculate the debt ratio from a given set of financial information? Go to the **online workbook** and have a go at Multiple choice questions 7.6 to test out your ability to calculate this figure.

7

Interest cover

The gearing percentages and debt ratios are not high, but how easily can the company meet its interest obligations? To determine the interest cover, we will need to turn to the statement of profit or loss in Illustration 3.1. This statement tells us that the finance expense (= interest payable) for the years to 31 March 2019 and 31 March 2018 was £150,000 and £165,000 respectively. This expense now needs matching to the operating profit (the profit before interest and tax) of £895,000 and £767,000 for the two years that concern us.

$$2019: \text{Interest cover: } \frac{£895,000}{£150,000} = 5.97 \text{ times}$$

$$2018: \text{Interest cover: } \frac{£767,000}{£165,000} = 4.65 \text{ times}$$

Increased profits and reduced finance expense in 2019 mean that this ratio has improved greatly this year. Given that interest is covered nearly six times by the operating profit, we can conclude that Bunns the Bakers is a very secure company indeed, with low gearing, low total liabilities to total assets and with a very strong interest cover ratio that indicates that the company will be able to keep servicing its long-term borrowings into the foreseeable future.

SUMMARY OF KEY CONCEPTS   Can you remember the formulae for the three long-term solvency and financial stability ratios? Take a look at Summary of key concepts 7.6–7.8 to reinforce your understanding.

MULTIPLE CHOICE QUESTIONS   Totally confident you can calculate interest cover from a given set of financial information? Go to the **online workbook** and have a go at Multiple choice questions 7.7 to test out your ability to calculate this ratio.

When are borrowings risky?

How much borrowing is too much? The answer to this question is, 'it all depends'. Provided that an organization has sufficiently strong cash inflows from operations and can afford to keep paying the interest as well as saving money towards the repayment of borrowings, then that organization will be able to borrow as much as it likes. Profitability, remember, is not enough: we saw in Chapter 4 that, without the associated inflows of cash from operations, profit means nothing. Many profitable companies have gone out of business because they were unable to generate the necessary cash flows from which to repay borrowings they had taken on.

Let's illustrate these issues with Give me an example 7.3 and 7.4.

GIVE ME AN EXAMPLE 7.3   Next plc

At the end of January 2018, Next plc had borrowings of £1,088.5 million and equity of £482.6 million. The gearing ratio based on these figures is 225.55% (£1.088.5m/£482.6m × 100%). Looked at in isolation, this figure would suggest that Next plc has seriously over-borrowed and is in imminent danger of collapse. And yet, the company is still trading and lenders are falling over themselves to lend the company money: of the total borrowings of £1,088.5 million, £135.0 million was lent to the company on an unsecured basis during the 52 weeks ended 27 January 2018. Clearly, lenders would not continue to provide this amount of funding unless they had cast iron confidence in Next's ability to repay this debt. Therefore, several additional factors must be taken into consideration before we can draw a conclusion on the long-term solvency position of Next plc.

Affordability
Is this debt affordable? Next plc had an operating profit of £759.9 million and interest payable of £35.0 million for the 52 weeks ended 27 January 2018, giving interest cover of 21.71 times (£759.9m/£35.0m). This level of interest is thus very affordable and sales and profits would have to collapse to very low levels before the interest on the borrowings could not be covered by profits from operations.

Repayment dates
When are the borrowings repayable? Of the total borrowings, only the bank overdrafts and short-term borrowings of £45 million and the unsecured loans of £135 million are due for repayment in the next 12 months. The remainder of the borrowings is made up of bonds, of which £328.4 million is due in 2021, £280.1 million is repayable in 2026 and £300.0 million is due for repayment in 2028, so the company has plenty of time in which to save up the necessary cash to meet these repayment dates. The interest rates on the three bonds are fixed at 5.375%, 4.375% and 3.625% respectively, so the company will

7

not suffer higher interest charges if there were to be a sudden increase in bank base rates.

Operating cash inflows

How easily can this debt be repaid? Cash inflows from operations amounted to £721.2 million for the 52 weeks ended 27 January 2018. With annual cash inflows this strong, there is little doubt that the company has the operating cash inflows to meet these liabilities when they become due.

In reality, the group's bankers will probably offer the company new loans with which to repay their existing loans when they are due for payment, fixing the interest rates on these new loans for a further five to ten years. Much public company borrowing is rolled over in this way: borrowings are not actually repaid, they are just swapped for new borrowings at rates of interest fixed at a suitable level given the prevailing market rate of interest at the time the new borrowings are taken out.

Consistency of product demand

As a clothing retailer appealing to the 16–35 age group, Next has a consistency of demand for its goods ensuring a steady stream of profits and cash flows for the foreseeable future. There is nothing risky in its business and nothing to suggest that its products will suddenly go out of fashion. This would not be the case for a mobile phone manufacturer, for example, whose products might suddenly become obsolete if a revolutionary new technology were to be introduced to the market by a competitor.

Source: Next 2018 report and accounts www.nextplc. co.uk

GIVE ME AN EXAMPLE 7.4 **The dangers of borrowing too much**

The private equity firm Terra Firma bought EMI plc in 2007 for £4.2 billion. Despite turning the ailing music business round and generating much improved profitability, with operating profit rising to nearly £300 million, by late 2010 it was clear that Terra Firma had paid far too much for EMI. Interest on the borrowings used to fund the acquisition could not be met from the improved operating cash inflows, resulting in Citigroup, Terra Firma's lender, taking control of EMI in February 2011. Organizations that do not keep within their borrowing capacity will not survive, so it is important for entities to borrow only as much as they can afford to service through interest payments and to repay when the debt becomes due. Contrast Terra Firma's situation with that of Next, whose interest cover of 21.71 times and operating cash inflows of £721 million from which to meet annual interest payments of around £35 million indicate that their borrowings are highly affordable.

Source: *Guardian* news 5 February 2010; *Financial Times* news 14 February 2010

What lessons can we draw from Give me an example 7.3 and 7.4? First, as with the current and quick ratios, you should never jump to conclusions based on isolated figures. An apparently unhealthy gearing ratio turns out to be perfectly sound when all the facts are taken into consideration. When evaluating long-term solvency and financial stability, you should look at:

- The interest cover to determine how affordable the borrowings are: does the business generate sufficiently high profits from which to meet interest payments?

- The dates on which repayments are to be made: the more distant the repayment date, the higher the chance the business has of meeting its commitments by that date.

- The strength of the operating cash inflows from the statement of cash flows: high operating cash inflows indicate that there will be sufficient cash on hand both to repay borrowings when they become due for payment and the annual interest payable on those borrowings.

- The consistency of demand for a company's products: the more consistent the demand, the less likely the company will be to face financial difficulties in the future and be unable to meet its liabilities when they become due. You should also think about the likelihood of new products from different firms replacing the current market leader's products: the more likely this is, the riskier the business will be and the higher the possibility that they could eventually default on their borrowings.

WHY IS THIS RELEVANT TO ME? When are borrowings risky?

To enable you as a business professional and user of accounting information to:

- Appreciate that apparently high levels of borrowings do not always indicate potential problems for an organization in meeting repayments when these become due

- Evaluate the affordability of long-term borrowings and the ability of entities to repay those borrowings from current resources and cash inflows

- Consider the consistency of demand for a business's products and the impact that replacement products would have on a business's long-term solvency and financial stability

7

NUMERICAL EXERCISES Think you can calculate long- and short-term solvency and financial stability ratios, working capital ratios and evaluate the cash conversion cycle and timing of payments for a real company? Do you think that you can interpret these ratios in a meaningful way? Have a look at Numerical exercises 7.1 dealing with the financial statements of Greggs plc and then have a go at the various exercises linked to this example in the **online workbook**.

Appendix 1: more wide ranging assessments of company performance: the balanced scorecard

Our investigations in Chapters 6 and 7 have considered the ratios and the assessments which users of financial statements will make based on the financial information presented by companies in their annual reports and accounts. However, a focus on just the financial results is rather limiting and ignores many other key areas of company performance. Management set the strategy and the goals of organizations, but those goals are not limited to purely financial outcomes. As well as the financial results, users should also be interested in how companies are achieving both their short-term and their long-term strategic objectives and how they are fulfilling the expectations of all stakeholder groups not just the expectations of shareholders. In order to make these assessments, management adopts a balanced scorecard approach.

The balanced scorecard sets out the key strategic objectives of the organization as a whole and provides an overview of the extent to which these are being met. The balanced scorecard seeks to avoid a narrow focus on just financial measures and so considers both financial and non-financial information. At the same time, the balanced scorecard provides an internal as well as an external appraisal of the business focusing on four aspects of an entity's performance. These four aspects cover the financial perspective, the customer perspective, the internal business perspective and the innovation and learning perspective. The overview provided by these different perspectives thus ranges from a short-term assessment and evaluation of current performance to a much longer term consideration of future strategy and goals. While current profitability, sales growth and customer satisfaction targets may have been met, the business needs to grow and develop in order to survive. Therefore, current operations are subjected to a rigourous appraisal in the internal business perspective with a view to future improvement and enhancement. At the same time, the ability of the business to innovate with new products and processes and to build the human capital and products required to meet the challenges of the future is evaluated in the fourth perspective. The format for a balanced scorecard is not fixed. This provides plenty of flexibility for organizations to develop their own goals and performance measures through which to assess their attainment of their key strategic objectives. An example of a balanced scorecard is presented in Figure 7.7. The outcomes on which each perspective is

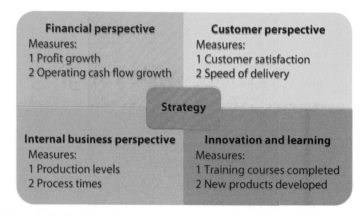

Figure 7.7 An example of a balanced scorecard

measured should be limited to those overriding indicators of success and should not present very large numbers of results which will overload the management with data.

Why is this scorecard balanced? External measures relating to financial outcomes and customers are balanced by assessments of internal business processes and development. Equally, past outcomes are balanced by development and innovation for the future. And finally, easy to measure financial and customer satisfaction outcomes are balanced by more difficult to determine internal measures of development and improvement.

You will come across the balanced scorecard in both your future studies and your career in business.

Appendix 2: ratios considered in this chapter

To assist your learning, the ratios we have considered in this chapter are summarized in Table 7.3.

Table 7.3 Liquidity, working capital and long-term solvency ratios discussed in this chapter

	Calculation	What does this ratio tell us?
Liquidity ratios		
Current ratio	$\dfrac{\text{Current assets}}{\text{Current liabilities}}$	The current ratio presents the £s of current assets per £1 of current liabilities. The ratio shows us whether an organization has sufficient short-term assets with which to meet all short-term liabilities immediately.
Quick (acid test) ratio	$\dfrac{(\text{Current assets} - \text{inventory})}{\text{Current liabilities}}$	This ratio removes inventory from current assets and then compares the resulting figure with current liabilities. Inventory is removed from current assets on the assumption that it is not readily convertible into cash in the near future. The quick ratio compares current assets that are cash or that are readily realizable in cash (trade receivables) with current liabilities in an attempt to determine whether an entity is able to cover immediately all its short-term commitments from readily realizable current assets.

7

Table 7.3 *Continued.*

	Calculation	What does this ratio tell us?
Working capital ratios		
Inventory days	$\dfrac{\text{Inventory}}{\text{Cost of sales}} \times 365$	This ratio measures the average stockholding period, how long an entity holds goods in inventory before they are sold. The shorter the inventory holding period the better, as inventory is turned into sales (and hence into cash) much more quickly while obsolete inventories and the risk of deterioration (and hence loss of future cash inflows from the sale of this inventory) are minimized.
Receivables days	$\dfrac{\text{Trade receivables}}{\text{Credit sales}} \times 365$	This ratio indicates the average credit period taken by credit customers. This is the length of time it takes for credit customers to pay what they owe.
Payables days	$\dfrac{\text{Trade receivables}}{\text{Cost of sales}} \times 365$	This ratio measures how quickly the business is paying off its suppliers for purchases made on credit. Ideally, the receivables days and payables days should be equal: as cash is received, it is used to pay off liabilities.
Cash conversion cycle	Inventory days + receivables days − payables days	The cash conversion cycle tells us how quickly inventory is turned into trade receivables and how quickly trade receivables are turned into cash with which to pay trade payables. The shorter this cycle, the better the working capital is being managed and the more readily cash is available with which to meet liabilities as they fall due.
Long-term solvency (financial stability) ratios		
Gearing %	$\dfrac{\text{Long and short-term borrowings}}{\text{Equity}} \times 100\%$	The gearing percentage compares all borrowings to the equity of an entity. This ratio is often seen as a measure of risk: companies with higher borrowings are supposedly more risky than those with lower borrowings.

Table 7.3 *Continued.*

	Calculation	What does this ratio tell us?
Debt ratio	$$\frac{\text{Total liabilities}}{\text{Total assets}}$$	This ratio measures the £s of liabilities per £1 of total assets. The lower the debt ratio, the more secure the entity.
Interest cover	$$\frac{\text{Profit before interest and tax}}{\text{Interest (finance expense)}}$$	Assesses how many times interest payable on borrowings is covered by operating profits to determine the affordability of monies borrowed. The higher the figure, the better, as a high figure indicates an ability to continue meeting interest payments from profits in the future.

CHAPTER SUMMARY

You should now have learnt that:

- An entity's liquidity depends upon how quickly goods produced or purchased are turned into cash
- Current and quick ratios express the relationship between current assets and current liabilities at an arbitrary point in time, the statement of financial position date
- Current and quick ratios make the misleading and unrealistic assumption that creditors will demand the payment of all monies owed on the day immediately following the accounting period end
- Careful working capital management is vital to an organization's short-term liquidity
- Working capital ratios are used to determine the speed of an entity's cash conversion cycle
- A full appreciation of the short-term liquidity of an organization must be based upon an assessment of the timing of cash receipts and cash payments
- Long-term solvency and financial stability depends upon an entity's ability to repay interest and borrowings from operating cash flows

QUICK REVISION   Test your knowledge with the online flashcards in Summary of key concepts and attempt the Multiple choice questions, all in the **online workbook**. www.oup.com/uk/scott_business3e/

END-OF-CHAPTER QUESTIONS

Solutions to these questions can be found at the back of the book from page 484.

❯ DEVELOP YOUR UNDERSTANDING

> **Question 7.1**

Samoco plc operates a chain of in town grocery convenience stores and edge of town supermarkets across the UK. The company is expanding rapidly and is adding new stores every year. Below are the statements of profit or loss for the company for the years ended 31 May 2019 and 31 May 2018 together with statements of financial position at those dates.

Samoco plc: statements of profit or loss for the years ended 31 May 2019 and 31 May 2018

	2019	2018
	£m	£m
Revenue	13,663	12,249
Cost of sales	12,570	11,330
Gross profit	1,093	919
Distribution and selling costs	121	108
Administration expenses	240	225
Operating profit	732	586
Finance income	20	15
Finance expense	104	84
Profit before tax	648	517
Income tax	162	129
Profit for the year	486	388

Samoco plc: statements of financial position at 31 May 2019 and 31 May 2018

	2019 £m	2018 £m
Assets		
Non-current assets		
Property, plant and equipment	6,040	5,150
Current assets		
Inventories	485	500
Other receivables	45	40
Cash and cash equivalents	122	99
	652	639
Total assets	6,692	5,789
Liabilities		
Current liabilities		
Current portion of long-term borrowings	240	216
Trade payables	830	790
Other payables	150	140
Dividends	200	180
Current tax	170	150
	1,590	1,476
Non-current liabilities		
Long-term borrowings	2,230	2,024
Pension liabilities	756	524
	2,986	2,548
Total liabilities	4,576	4,024
Net assets	2,116	1,765
Equity		
Called up share capital	110	100
Share premium	145	140
Retained earnings	1,861	1,525
Total equity	2,116	1,765

Notes to the above financial statements:

- Samoco plc's sales are made on an entirely cash basis, with no credit being allowed to customers at its convenience stores and supermarkets. Therefore, at 31 May 2019 and 31 May 2018 there were no monies owed by trade receivables.

- Finance expense is made up entirely of interest payable on the long-term borrowings.
- Samoco plc's long-term borrowings are repayable by equal annual instalments over the next 10 years.

Required

(a) Using the financial statements for Samoco plc calculate for both years:

- Current ratio
- Quick ratio
- Inventory days
- Payables days
- The cash conversion cycle
- Gearing %
- Debt ratio
- Interest cover

(b) Using the ratios you have calculated and the financial statements, evaluate the liquidity, working capital and long-term solvency and financial stability of Samoco plc at 31 May 2019.

> **Question 7.2**

A colleague who has just started studying accounting has read in another book that companies without current ratios of 2:1 and quick (acid test) ratios of 1:1 will find it difficult to meet their current liabilities as they fall due. She has just noticed your current and quick ratio calculations for Samoco plc in Question 7.1 and has concluded that the company is about to collapse. Using the information in Question 7.1, ratios that you have already calculated and details of when liabilities can be assumed to be due for payment presented below, calculate the maximum amount of the current liabilities of Samoco plc that could be due for repayment on the day after the statement of financial position date (1 June 2019 and 1 June 2018). Draw up arguments to put to your colleague to show her that a simple reliance on current and quick ratios as an indicator of short-term liquidity fails to address all the relevant issues.

For the purposes of this exercise you should assume that current liabilities are due for payment as follows:

- Bank loans: repayable in 12 monthly instalments
- Trade payables: repayable according to your payables days calculations in Question 7.1
- Current tax: due in four instalments: three months, six months, nine months and twelve months after the statement of financial position date
- Other payables: assume that 20% of this figure is payable immediately
- Dividends: due for payment in August 2019 and August 2018

You can assume that there are 360 days during the financial year on which Samoco plc's shops are open and trading.

▶▶ TAKE IT FURTHER

▶ Question 7.3

Listed below is information relating to four companies:

- Ted Baker is a global lifestyle brand that operates through three main distribution channels: retail, which includes e-commerce, wholesale and licensing, which includes territorial and product licences. The company offers a wide range of fashion and lifestyle collections.
- Nichols is a producer of still and carbonated soft drinks.
- The Weir Group is an engineering company which focuses mainly on the production and maintenance of pumps and valves for use in the mining, oil and gas industries.
- National Express is a leading public transport operator with bus, coach and rail services in the UK, Continental Europe, North Africa, North America and the Middle East.

	Ted Baker	Nichols	Weir Group	National Express
Year ended	27/01/2018	31/12/2017	31/12/2017	31/12/2017
Income statement (= statement of profit or loss)	£m	£m	£m	£m
Revenue	591.7	132.8	2,355.9	2,321.2
Cost of sales	230.9	72.2	1,619.2	1,405.1
Operating profit	70.7	28.7	223.1	197.9
Finance expense	3.3	—	38.2	44.6

	Ted Baker	Nichols	Weir Group	National Express
Year end date	27/01/2018	31/12/2017	31/12/2017	31/12/2017
Statement of financial position	£m	£m	£m	£m
Total assets	449.2	127.4	3,593.5	3,451.5
Total liabilities	225.1	28.1	2,122.4	2,285.1
Current assets				
Inventory	187.2	4.8	586.8	24.9
Trade receivables	42.7	31.3	492.9	238.8
Other receivables	22.8	3.4	179.2	134.4
Cash and cash equivalents	16.7	36.1	284.6	314.3
Current assets (total)	269.4	75.6	1,543.5	712.4

7

	Ted Baker	Nichols	Weir Group	National Express
Year end date	27/01/2018	31/12/2017	31/12/2017	31/12/2017
Statement of financial position	£m	£m	£m	£m
Bank overdrafts	76.0	—	0.1	—
Bank loans	5.5	—	388.3	167.4
Trade payables	36.3	6.8	341.7	258.5
Other current liabilities	59.0	16.8	383.6	500.8
Current liabilities (total)	**176.8**	**23.6**	**1,113.7**	**926.7**
Total equity	224.1	99.3	1,471.1	1,166.4
Total borrowings	128.5	—	1,127.8	1,225.4

Using the above financial information, calculate for all four companies:

- Current ratio
- Quick ratio
- Inventory days
- Receivables days
- Payables days
- The cash conversion cycle
- Gearing percentage
- Debt ratio
- Interest cover

» Question 7.4

Given the activities of each company, comment on how you would expect each company to generate its cash inflows together with an assessment of the liquidity, solvency and long-term financial stability of each company. Your answers should address the following issues, among others:

- The current and quick ratios of the four companies.
- The cash conversion cycles of the four companies.
- Why do the inventory, receivables and payables days vary so much in the four companies?
- The gearing levels in the four companies and whether these are manageable.

Part 2

Cost and management accounting

Product costing: absorption costing

8

LEARNING OUTCOMES

Once you have read this chapter and worked through the questions and examples in both this chapter and the online workbook, you should be able to:

- Define cost and management accounting and explain its role in organizations
- Define costing
- Understand the importance of costing to business organizations in making pricing decisions
- Explain what is meant by the terms direct costs and indirect costs
- Explain the distinction between fixed costs and variable costs
- Construct simple costing statements to determine the total cost of products on an absorption (full) costing basis
- Draw simple graphs to illustrate fixed, variable and total cost behaviour in a business context
- Outline the limitations of absorption costing approaches in allocating overheads to products
- Apply activity-based costing to overhead allocation problems
- Discuss the assumptions on which costing is based

Introduction: cost and management accounting v. financial accounting

In the first part of this book we have looked at financial accounting, how the three key financial accounting statements are put together, the information they contain and their usefulness in understanding a business's past performance. As we have seen, financial accounting reports summarize accounting data, usually on an annual basis, for presentation to interested parties. It is important to appreciate the historical aspect of these financial accounts, how they report on what has happened not on what might or is expected to happen in the future. They are thus not specifically designed to be used for planning purposes although users of these financial accounts might use them as a basis for making investment decisions, to buy, hold or sell shares in an entity. Financial accounts are prepared for parties outside the business and summarize all the transactions that have taken place, together with information relevant to a specific accounting period.

But accounting has other uses. If you worked out your expected income and what you expected to spend during your first year at university, you have already undertaken a management accounting exercise: you prepared a forecast to enable you to determine when you might need additional income to meet your spending plans or you will have reduced your planned expenditure to stay within your expected level of income. Comparing what you have actually spent with what you expected to spend will enable you to modify your income and expenditure plans to enable you to keep within your budget or to find ways in which to earn extra income to meet those plans.

In the same way, businesses use budgeting to model how they expect money to flow into and out of the business, to identify cash shortfalls or surpluses. They can then plan to borrow money from their bank or to invest surplus cash to earn interest for the organization. At the simplest level of planning, organizations will calculate the expected costs of making or buying a product and the expected income from selling that product to other parties. Comparisons will be made between expectations and actual outcomes to enable the organization to plan more effectively in the future and to provide more relevant information to management about how the organization is performing and how it is expected to perform.

What does cost and management accounting do?

Cost and management accounting thus presents information to parties internal to the business and aims to provide data that is relevant to making business decisions now and in the future. The starting point of this information is not a summary of all trans-

8

actions but a detailed analysis of individual cost components of products and services with a view to determining selling prices for those products and services. This detailed information can then be used to plan what the business will do and what decisions it will make to enable it to operate profitably in the future. For planning and control purposes, this detailed information will be summarized into budgets for a particular period of time and these budgets will be used to compare actual performance with budgeted performance as a way of controlling the operations of the business. Costing and its use in making decisions and how costing information is used in budgeting and planning will form the basis of the next four chapters of this book and of the exercises and presentations in the online workbook.

Given the characteristics of cost and management accounting outlined above, it is clear that management accounting information is forward looking, broken down initially into its smallest component parts and used by management to guide and control the business's internal operations. Such guiding and controlling is undertaken with a view to enabling the achievement of an entity's short- and long-term aims. Without a plan no-one, whether an individual or a business, will achieve anything. Without monitoring actual outcomes against the plan entities will be unable to determine whether their plans are reaching fulfilment or not.

WHY IS THIS RELEVANT TO ME? **What does cost and management accounting do?**

As a business professional and user of accounting information, you should appreciate:

- The critical role that cost and management accounting plays in the planning, evaluation, management and control of business activities
- That no matter what your particular business specialism, knowledge of the techniques and practice of cost and management accounting will be crucial to your success in that specialist role

---

GO BACK OVER THIS AGAIN! How well have you understood the differences between financial and cost and management accounting? Go to the **online workbook** and complete Exercises 8.1 to make sure you understand the distinction.

SUMMARY OF KEY CONCEPTS Quite sure you understand what cost and management accounting involves? Take a look at Summary of key concepts 8.1 and 8.2 to reinforce your understanding.

This chapter will look at the basic building blocks of management accounting information: costs. We will consider what costing involves, what types of cost a business will incur in its operations and how this costing information is used to inform that most critical management decision, what prices to charge for products and services so that an organization can make a profit.

Why is it important to know about costs?

Businesses exist to make a profit. Without knowing what costs a business will incur in producing goods for sale or in providing a service, it will not be possible for that business to set a selling price higher than the costs incurred. When selling price exceeds the costs, a profit is made. Should selling price be lower than the costs, then a loss will be made and the business will soon be in financial trouble. We saw in Chapter 3 that revenue (income, sales) − costs = profit. All businesses will be seeking to increase their profits over time 'to create, protect, preserve and increase value for the stakeholders of for-profit and not-for-profit enterprises in the public and private sectors' (*CIMA Official Terminology*, The Chartered Institute of Management Accountants, 2005). There are two paths an entity can take when it wishes to increase profits: either revenue has to increase or costs must decrease. Let's prove this in Example 8.1.

EXAMPLE 8.1

Henry buys T-shirts for £5 and sells them for £10 each. Currently he sells 1,000 T-shirts a year on his market stall. He wishes to increase his profits.

Given his current level of sales, Henry now has a profit of:

	£
Sales 1,000 × £10	10,000
Cost of sales 1,000 × £5	5,000
Profit	5,000

If Henry could buy 1,000 T-shirts for £4 while still selling them for £10 his profit would be:

	£
Sales 1,000 × £10	10,000
Cost of sales 1,000 × £4	4,000
Profit	6,000

Henry has reduced the cost of the goods he sells without reducing his selling price and so his profit has increased from £5,000 to £6,000.

Alternatively, by increasing his sales to 2,000 T-shirts, while still buying them at £5 each, his profit will be:

	£
Sales 2,000 × £10	20,000
Cost of sales 2,000 × £5	10,000
Profit	10,000

Reducing costs or increasing sales are thus the two ways in which businesses can increase their profits.

WHY IS THIS RELEVANT TO ME?   Costs and pricing

- No matter what field of commercial or not-for-profit activity you are engaged in, as a business professional you must know about costs and income
- Knowing about your costs will enable you to determine a selling price to cover those costs and to generate a profit/surplus for your organization
- Knowledge of an activity's costs will enable you as a business professional to devise strategies by which to increase profit, whether by reducing costs or increasing income

---

GO BACK OVER THIS AGAIN!   Happy that you understand the relationship between selling price, costs and profit? Go to the **online workbook** Exercises 8.2 to make sure you understand these relationships.

Give me an example 8.1 shows how both cost reductions and a rise in income increase profits.

GIVE ME AN EXAMPLE 8.1   Agricultural Bank increases its profit

Agricultural Bank of China increased its net profit in the three months to 30 September 2016 by 0.65%. The increase in profit was the result of both increased fee income and a reduction in expenses. Staff reductions in the 6 months to June 2016 caused a fall in expenses of 12%.

While lending was weaker, reducing interest income by 9.3%, fees and commission income rose 9.8%.

Source: http://www.scmp.com/business/banking-finance/article/2041056/agricultural-banks-q3-profit-rises-65pc-lifted-reduced

---

8

Costs and costing

We have seen that costs are important to businesses, but what costs will a business consider in making its decisions? The type and number of costs will depend upon the complexity of each business. Very simple businesses will have very simple costing systems and very few costs, while more complex businesses will have many costs and very complex costing systems to inform management decisions. Consider Example 8.2.

EXAMPLE 8.2

Anna is a self-employed carpenter working at home producing handmade wooden dining chairs. During the month of June, she produced 30 chairs. At what price should she sell her chairs? She provides you with invoices showing the costs of the materials she used in June:

	£
Wood	540
Glue	18
Screws	30
Sandpaper	12

Totalling up the costs above, Anna has spent £600 on making 30 chairs. Dividing the costs by the 30 chairs made gives a cost of £20 per chair.

Setting a selling price

As long as Anna sells her chairs for more than £20 each, then she will make a profit on each sale. However, what other considerations should she bear in mind when setting her selling price? First, she will think about what a reasonable profit on each chair sold would be. If each chair takes her an hour to make, she would probably consider a profit of £30 to be a reasonable reward for the time and effort she has put into making each chair. The selling price for each chair would then be £50: £20 costs plus £30 profit. If each chair takes Anna five hours to make, then she would want significantly more profit and a significantly higher selling price to reflect the time spent on producing each chair.

While considering her own internal perspective, the profit she would like to make based on her time spent on making chairs, she will also need to consider the external market. She will thus take into account the prices her competitors are charging for the same type of chair; if she charges more than her competitors, she will not have many sales as buyers in the market like to buy goods as cheaply as possible. Alternatively, if she sets her selling price lower than her competitors, then she will expect to have a lot of orders from her customers, all of whom will want to buy her chairs at her lower price. However, can she fulfil all those orders? Does she have the time to produce as many chairs as her customers will demand?

Setting a selling price is thus a complex decision that needs to factor in many considerations. While cost is only one of those considerations it is now time to look in much more detail at the types of cost that organizations incur in their operations.

Direct costs, variable costs and marginal costs

In our example above, each one of Anna's costs can be attributed directly to each chair she produces. If she were to produce 31 chairs, we would expect her to incur costs of £600 ÷ 30 chairs × 31 chairs = £620. That is, for each additional chair she produces she will incur an additional £20 of materials cost. These costs are called the **direct costs** of production, the costs that are directly attributable to each unit of output. In Anna's case, these direct costs vary directly in line with each unit of output that is produced and are therefore her variable costs of production. Variable costs reflect the additional costs that are incurred by a business in producing one more unit of a product or service. Borrowing a term from economics, these variable costs are also known as the marginal cost of production, the costs that are incurred in producing one more unit of a product or service. However, as we shall see, not all direct costs of production are variable costs.

SUMMARY OF KEY CONCEPTS Quite sure about what direct cost, variable cost and marginal cost mean? Go to the Summary of key concepts 8.3–8.5 to check your understanding.

Direct costs can be of three types. The first direct cost is materials. In Example 8.2 the wood, glue, screws and sandpaper are all materials used in the production of each chair. The second direct cost is labour, the amount paid to workers for making products. Direct labour may be paid to workers on the basis of an agreed amount for each unit of product produced so that the more the workforce produces, the more they are paid. In this case, direct labour is a variable cost of production. Where production workers are paid a fixed salary that does not depend upon the number of goods produced, this is still a direct cost of production, but it is not a variable cost as salary costs do not rise or fall in line with production. The final type of direct cost is direct expense, costs other than material and labour that can be traced directly to the production of each unit of product. An example of a direct expense would be the electricity required to power machinery to produce one unit of production: the total amount of electricity used by a piece of machinery can be measured precisely and the total cost of electricity divided by the number of units of production to determine a per unit expense for electricity. Example 8.3 illustrates the three types of direct cost.

8

EXAMPLE 8.3

To illustrate the three types of direct cost, material, labour and expense, let us consider the costs incurred in the bread making section of Bunns the Bakers' central bakery. Think about each cost and decide whether it is an example of direct material, direct labour or direct expense.

Cost:

- Flour
- Gas used to heat the ovens
- Bakers' wages paid on the basis of the number of loaves of bread produced
- Ingredient mixing costs
- Equipment cleaning costs after each batch of loaves is produced
- Yeast

- Bakers' productivity bonus
- Olive oil
- Packaging for loaves
- Water

Which of these costs are direct material, direct labour and direct expense? We can allocate these costs to each heading, as shown in Table 8.1.

Table 8.1 Cost allocation

Cost	Direct material	Direct labour	Direct expense
Flour	✓		
Gas used to heat the ovens			✓
Bakers' wages paid on the basis of the number of loaves of bread produced		✓	
Ingredient mixing costs			✓
Equipment cleaning costs after each batch of loaves is produced			✓
Yeast	✓		
Bakers' productivity bonus		✓	
Olive oil	✓		
Packaging for loaves	✓		
Water	✓		

Flour, yeast, olive oil, water and packaging are clearly materials used in each loaf, while the bakers' wages and productivity bonus are labour costs. The gas used to heat the ovens is a direct expense used in production of each loaf as, without the gas to heat the ovens to bake the loaves, there would be no product to sell. The gas is not a material as it is not part of the finished loaf. Similarly, the ingredient mixing costs (by machine rather than by hand) are expenses: the cost of mixing ingredients together is essential to the production of the loaves but is neither direct labour nor direct material. Cleaning the equipment after each batch of loaves is produced is another expense that has to be incurred in the production of bread. Each time a batch of loaves is produced, more cleaning costs are incurred so the cleaning costs are the direct result of production.

GO BACK OVER THIS AGAIN! Can you distinguish between direct materials, direct labour and direct expenses? Go to the **online workbook** Exercises 8.3 to make sure you understand what types of cost fall into each category.

Variable cost behaviour: graphical presentation

In costing, the variable costs of production are assumed to behave in a linear fashion. This mathematical term just means that the variable costs of production rise precisely in line with the number of units produced. For each additional unit of production, the additional cost of producing that additional unit (the marginal cost) will be exactly the same as for all the previous units of production. In Example 8.2, the additional cost of producing one more chair is £20, which is exactly the same cost as all the other chairs Anna has produced.

The relationship between the variable costs of production and the number of units produced can be illustrated graphically, as shown in Figure 8.1.

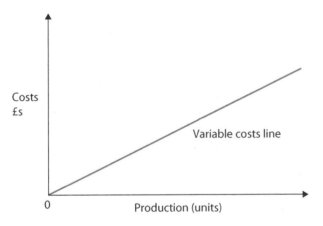

Figure 8.1 Graph showing the effect of production on variable costs

As production increases, variable costs rise directly in line with that production. Production of one chair costs Anna £20 in materials. Production of two chairs costs her £40 and so on. As each chair costs exactly the same to produce as the previous one, the total variable costs of production on the graph will rise in a straight line. If Anna produces no chairs, she will incur no variable costs and so the variable costs line starts at zero.

Fixed costs

However, not all costs incurred by a business are variable, marginal costs. There are also costs that are fixed, which do not vary in line with production. These costs are called **fixed costs** because, for a given period of time, they are assumed to remain the same whether zero units, 10 units or 1,000 units of product are produced. Fixed costs can be direct costs of production (such as the fixed salaries of production workers) or they may be general overheads incurred in the running of the business, costs that cannot be directly attributed to specific products or services. Fixed costs come in many forms, but let us start with the following simple example (Example 8.4).

EXAMPLE 8.4

Anna is so successful in her chair-making enterprise at home that she decides to expand and set up a workshop from which to produce her chairs. She starts renting a small workshop at an annual rental cost of £6,000. Business rates on the workshop amount to £1,000 per annum and the workshop heating and lighting bills amount to £800 for the year. In addition, she takes on two employees who are paid £25 for each chair that they make. Anna now concentrates on running the business rather than crafting chairs herself. How would you classify these additional costs? Which of these new costs do not vary directly in line with production and which will rise or fall precisely in line with the number of chairs produced?

Rent and business rates on the workshop are totally fixed as Anna has to pay these costs whether the employees make no chairs in the year or whether they make 10,000. Thus, her workshop can produce as few or as many chairs as she likes without incurring any additional rent or business rate costs. The rent and business rates are thus both fixed costs. They are also the indirect costs of production: the workshop is essential to the production of the chairs, but the rent and business rates cannot in any way be attributed directly to each chair produced.

By contrast, the employees are a direct cost of production as each additional chair that is made by each employee incurs a further cost of £25, this cost varying directly in line with production. Thus, £25 is a completely variable cost of production, the marginal labour cost of producing one more chair. This £25 will be added to the £20 material costs to give the total direct cost of one chair of £45.

The heating and lighting bills are a little trickier to classify. How much is paid for lighting will depend on how many days the workshop is open. If the workshop is closed, then the lights will not be turned on and no cost will be incurred. Similarly, if no one works in the workshop for the whole year, there will be no need to turn on the lights or the heating and the heating and lighting costs will be £nil. However, even if the workshop is open and the lights are turned on, there is no guarantee that a consistent level of production will be achieved each day. The two employees might be able to produce eight chairs in a day between them, but if either of them is unwell and absent from work, then only four chairs will be produced, assuming that they each make four chairs a day. However, the lighting cost would still be the same for four chairs as it was for eight chairs. If the weather is hot, then the employees will work more slowly and only six chairs a day might be produced. In the same way, more lighting will be used in winter than in summer and this variability is also true of the heating costs: a very cold winter will mean a higher heating bill than when the winter weather is milder. Given this difficulty in allocating the costs of heating and lighting to individual units of production, it is safer to treat these costs as a fixed cost for the year.

Can we illustrate the relationship between fixed costs and production as we did for variable costs in Figure 8.1? Yes we can and this relationship is shown in Figure 8.2.

The fixed costs line is a straight line just like the variable costs line. However, the fixed cost line shows that fixed costs are the same for all levels of production over a given period of time. As we noted earlier, the fixed costs are the same whether no chairs or 10,000 chairs are produced. Thus, the fixed cost line does not pass through

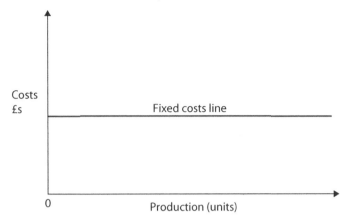

Figure 8.2 Graph showing the effect of production on fixed costs

zero but starts at the level of the fixed costs on the cost axis and continues as a straight line across the graph as there is no variation in the level of fixed costs. Even when no chairs are produced, the fixed costs are still incurred and have to be paid.

WHY IS THIS RELEVANT TO ME?   Direct costs and indirect costs

In your role as a business professional and user of accounting information, you will need to:

- Identify those costs that are directly attributable to units of production or to services provided
- Identify those costs that vary in line with increased business activity
- Identify those costs that do not vary in line with increased business activity
- Possess the knowledge required to identify costs that are relevant in decision making (discussed further in Chapter 9)

8

GO BACK OVER THIS AGAIN!   Quite certain you appreciate the difference between fixed and variable costs? Go to the **online workbook** Exercises 8.4 to make sure you understand this distinction.

Variable costs, fixed costs and total costs

Total costs for an accounting period are the total variable costs incurred in producing goods or services plus the total fixed costs incurred in that same time period. This is illustrated graphically in Figure 8.3.

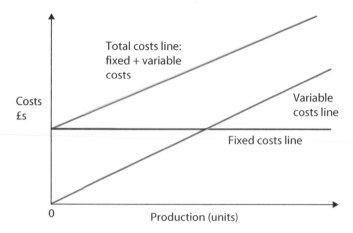

Figure 8.3 Graph showing the effect of production on variable costs, fixed costs and total costs

The variable cost and fixed cost lines are drawn on the graph as before in exactly the same positions. The total cost line adds together the variable and fixed costs for a period to give the total costs incurred by an organization. At a zero level of production, variable costs are zero, so total costs are the same as fixed costs. However, as production takes place, variable costs are incurred and the total costs line rises as these variable costs are added to fixed costs. As production increases, the average total cost of each product produced will fall as the fixed costs are spread across more units of production. To prove that this is the case, consider Example 8.5.

EXAMPLE 8.5

Using the facts from Examples 8.2, 8.3 and 8.4, let's work out the average cost per unit for levels of production of Anna's chairs at 100 units, 200 units, 300 units and 400 units. Remember that variable costs are materials (£20) + labour (£25) = £45 per chair while the fixed costs of the workshop are £6,000 (rent) + £1,000 (business rates) + £800 (heating and lighting) = £7,800.

As Table 8.2 shows, the average total cost per chair falls as production increases and the fixed costs are gradually spread over an increasing number of chairs.

Table 8.2 Anna's average cost per chair at different levels of production

(a) Units of production	(b) Variable cost per unit	(c) = (a) × (b) Total variable costs	(d) Fixed costs	(e) = (c) + (d) Total costs	(f) = (e) ÷ (a) Average total cost per chair
100	45	4,500	7,800	12,300	123.00
200	45	9,000	7,800	16,800	84.00
300	45	13,500	7,800	21,300	71.00
400	45	18,000	7,800	25,800	64.50

How well have you appreciated that higher levels of production mean a smaller average total cost for each product produced? Go to the **online workbook** and complete Numerical exercises 8.1 to prove to yourself that this is still true for higher levels of production in Anna's workshop.

Allocating fixed overhead costs to products: absorption costing

We noted earlier in this chapter that organizations need to know the total cost of their products or services so that they can calculate a suitable selling price to enable them to make a profit on their activities. As we have seen, the costs involved are the direct and indirect costs of production and organizations will take both of these types of cost into account when setting their selling prices. Typically, a cost card will be drawn up for each product that shows the direct costs for one unit of production. Anna's cost card for one chair is shown in Example 8.6.

However, how should the indirect costs of production be allocated to products? Organizations have to take into account their indirect costs when setting a selling price for a product otherwise they might set the selling price too low and fail to cover their indirect as well as their direct costs. But different levels of production will result in different allocations of indirect costs to products and in different total costs for products. Anna has indirect costs of £7,800 for her rent, rates, heating and lighting. As we saw in Table 8.2, at different levels of production the average total cost for each product rises or falls depending on how many or how few products are produced. How can Anna set a selling price for her chairs if actual numbers of chairs produced are not known?

The answer to this problem is that entities will estimate the normal, expected level of production achievable within an accounting period and use this normal level of production as the basis for allocating indirect costs to products. Thus, an allocation of indirect costs is made to each unit of production on the basis of this expected production level so that the indirect costs are recovered with each unit of production sold. This technique is called absorption costing: indirect costs are absorbed into (allocated to) each unit of production to give a total cost for each product. At the same time, the indirect costs are recovered (essentially, paid for by the customer) as each unit of production is sold. Let us see how this will work in the case of Anna's chairs in Example 8.6.

8

EXAMPLE 8.6

Anna decides that her workshop will be capable of producing 1,000 chairs in the next year. She now needs to calculate the total cost for one chair based on the figures given in Examples 8.2, 8.3 and 8.4 so that she can decide upon her selling price. Her cost card for one dining chair is shown here.

Cost card: wooden dining chair	£
Direct production costs	
Wood £540 ÷ 30 (Example 8.2)	18.00
Glue £18 ÷ 30 (Example 8.2)	0.60
Screws £30 ÷ 30 (Example 8.2)	1.00
Sandpaper £12 ÷ 30 (Example 8.2)	0.40
Direct labour (Example 8.4)	25.00
Prime cost (total direct cost of production of one chair: direct material + direct labour + direct expenses)	45.00
Indirect production costs (overheads)	
Rent £6,000 ÷ 1,000 (Example 8.4)	6.00
Business rates £1,000 ÷ 1,000 (Example 8.4)	1.00
Heating and lighting £800 ÷ 1,000 (Example 8.4)	0.80
Total production cost of one chair	52.80

Direct costs of production are split into their component parts (direct material, direct labour and direct expense). The total direct production cost is called **prime cost** (Figure 8.4), the direct cost of producing one dining chair. Indirect (overhead) costs are then allocated to each item of production on the basis of what production is expected to be, the normal level of production. Thus, each element of indirect costs is divided by the total expected production of 1,000 units to give the overhead cost that should be allocated to each unit of production. Adding the indirect (overhead) costs per unit of production to the total direct cost (prime cost) gives the total **production cost** of one chair (Figure 8.5).

Figure 8.4 The components of prime cost

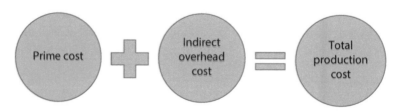

Figure 8.5 The total production cost of one unit of production

---

SUMMARY OF KEY CONCEPTS   Can you define prime cost and production cost? Go to the Summary of key concepts 8.6 to reinforce your understanding.

WHY IS THIS RELEVANT TO ME?   Prime cost and production cost

As a business professional and user of accounting information, you should understand that:

- Setting a selling price to achieve a profit requires knowledge of all the costs incurred in the production of a good or service

- Indirect overhead costs as well as direct costs of production have to be taken into account when setting a selling price

- A suitable method of allocation of indirect overhead costs to products has to be found in order to build the indirect costs incurred into the cost of each product produced and sold

NUMERICAL EXERCISES   Quite sure you can allocate direct and indirect costs to a product or service? Go to the **online workbook** and complete Numerical exercises 8.2 to make sure you can apply this technique.

Setting the selling price

As management accounting is about informing operational decisions as well as costing, in Example 8.7 Anna will now consider what selling price she ought to charge for each chair and how much profit she will make.

EXAMPLE 8.7

Given that each chair is expected to incur a total production (absorption) cost of £52.80, Anna decides that a selling price of £85 is reasonable and will meet market expectations. How much profit will she make if she sells all of the 1,000 chairs produced? The detailed profit calculation is shown below.

8

	£	£
Sales 1,000 × £85		85,000
Direct costs		
Wood 1,000 × £18	18,000	
Glue 1,000 × £0.60	600	
Screws 1,000 × £1	1,000	
Sandpaper 1,000 × £0.40	400	
Direct labour 1,000 × £25	25,000	
Prime cost (total direct cost for 1,000 chairs)		45,000
Rent 1,000 × £6	6,000	
Business rates 1,000 × £1	1,000	
Heating and lighting 1,000 × £0.80	800	
Indirect production costs		7,800
Total expected profit for the year		32,200

Rather than drawing up the detailed costing statement shown, you might have taken a short cut to determine Anna's expected profit for next year. You could have taken the selling price of one chair of £85 and deducted the total production cost of one chair of £52.80 to give you a profit per chair of £32.20 (£85.00 − £52.80). Multiplying this profit per chair of £32.20 by 1,000 chairs produced and sold would give you the same answer of £32,200.

NUMERICAL EXERCISES How well have you understood the calculation of profit from a given set of costing data? Go to the **online workbook** Numerical exercises 8.3 to make sure you can apply this technique.

Absorption costing and inventory valuation

At the end of each accounting period, most organizations will hold unsold items of production. The question that arises is how such inventory should be valued. In Chapter 3, Julia's retail business valued her inventory at the cost to the business, the costs charged by suppliers for goods sold to the business (Chapter 3, Closing inventory). This is an acceptable method of inventory valuation in a retail trading business as this is the cost of the inventory to the business. However, accounting standards allow organizations to value their inventory on an absorption costing basis, the direct production costs of a product plus a proportion of the indirect production overheads incurred in each product's manufacture. Therefore, it is important for organizations to be able to calculate the costs associated with each item of production both in terms of its direct costs and the proportion of indirect production overhead costs attributable to each unit of product.

In Anna's case, any unsold chairs at the end of the accounting period would be valued at £52.80 each, the direct costs of £45 per chair plus the attributable overheads of £7.80 allocated to each chair. These costs would be carried forward under the accruals basis of accounting (see Chapter 3, Closing inventory) to match against sales made in the following accounting period.

Give me an example 8.2 reproduces Rolls-Royce Holdings plc's accounting policy on inventory valuation: note how direct materials, direct labour and overheads are included in the valuation of inventory.

GIVE ME AN EXAMPLE 8.2   **Overheads included in inventory valuation**

Inventories

Inventories and work in progress are valued at the lower of cost and net realizable value on a first-in, first-out basis. Cost comprises direct materials and, where applicable, direct labour costs and those overheads, including depre- ciation of property, plant and equipment, that have been incurred in bringing the inventories to their present location and condition.

Source: www.rolls-royce.com

NUMERICAL EXERCISES   Happy with how to calculate the value of inventory at the end of an accounting period? Go to the **online workbook** Numerical exercises 8.4 to make sure you can calculate an inventory valuation.

> **WHY IS THIS RELEVANT TO ME?**   Inventory valuation
>
> As a business professional and user of accounting information, you should understand that:
>
> - Not all production will be sold by the end of an accounting period
> - This inventory has to be valued to determine the profit for the accounting period and to match costs to products actually sold
> - To comply with relevant accounting standards inventory should be valued at direct cost plus a proportion of the indirect production overheads incurred

Anna's business is simple, with just three indirect overhead costs to allocate to production units of one product. How would these indirect overhead costs be allocated in a more complex organization in which more than one product is produced?

Absorption costing: overhead allocation

In reality, manufacturing and service organizations have many indirect production overhead costs and many different products and services. Entities will seek to allocate these overheads to departments and then to products on the most appropriate basis. This will enable organizations to absorb these overheads into products or services on the way to determining a selling price for each product or service. Commonly, each overhead is determined in total and it is then apportioned to departments. The overhead total for each department is then divided up into an hourly rate on the basis of the number of labour hours or the number of machine hours used in each department (Figure 8.6).

Where labour is the key input to a production process, overheads will be allocated on the basis of the number of labour hours worked in a year. Service industries such as car maintenance, delivery services or catering will allocate overheads on the basis of labour hours as the provision of the service is based on employees rather than on machines. Where a production process is highly mechanized, as is the case in most manufacturing industries, then machine hours will be used as the basis for overhead allocation.

8

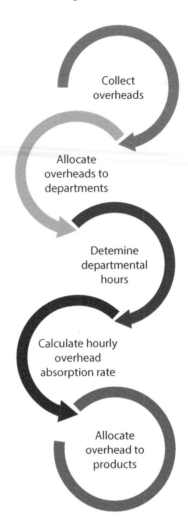

Figure 8.6 The overhead absorption process

How will the number of hours of labour or machine time be calculated? Businesses will first determine their operating capacity, the number of hours that production employees work or the number of hours that production machinery operates during a year. Once capacity has been determined, then overheads will be totalled up and divided by the number of hours of capacity to give an hourly overhead absorption rate.

As an example of this technique, suppose that a car maintenance operation has ten employees who each work a 40-hour week for 48 weeks of the year (allowing for four weeks of holidays for each employee). The labour hour capacity of the business in one week is 10 employees × 40 hours = 400 hours. The labour hour capacity of the business for the year is then 400 hours in one week × 48 working weeks = 19,200 hours. Annual overheads incurred in the car maintenance operation will be totalled up and this total divided by the 19,200 available hours in the year to determine an overhead recovery rate for each job that the operation quotes for. If the total overheads of the business come to £288,000, then the hourly allocation rate will be £288,000 ÷ 19,200 labour hours = £15 per hour. If a job is expected to take five hours, then an overhead cost of £15 × 5 hours = £75 will be added to the direct cost estimate for that job when the customer is quoted a price. Remember that direct costs plus overhead costs give the total cost of providing a service and will be used as a basis on which to determine a selling price that will result in a profit on each job.

The car maintenance operation is a simple example. In more complex situations, the stages in overhead allocation will be to:

1. Determine each overhead cost from invoices and payments.

2. Allocate overhead costs to departments on the most appropriate basis.

3. Total up overhead costs for each department.

4. Determine a labour hour or machine hour absorption rate for departmental overheads.

5. Allocate overheads to products or services on the basis of labour or machine hours used in the production of each product or provision of each service.

Think about how steps 1–5 are applied in Example 8.8.

EXAMPLE 8.8

Information relating to the Picture Frame Company is presented in Table 8.3. You have been asked to allocate the costs to two departments, machining and finishing. The directors of the Picture Frame Company want to absorb overheads in each department into products on the basis of machine hours used in each department, as they consider that this basis will best reflect the way in which departmental overheads are incurred. The Picture Frame Company sells its products at absorption cost plus 20%.

Table 8.3 The Picture Frame Company's annual overhead costs and machine hours

Annual costs	Total £	Machining	Finishing
Rent	100,000	Floor area: 1,800 square metres	Floor area: 1,200 square metres
Business rates	25,000		
Depreciation	40,000	Machinery value: £160,000	Machinery value: £240,000
Heating	15,000	Departmental volume: 10,000 cubic metres	Departmental volume: 5,000 cubic metres
Directors' salaries	80,000	Percentage of directors' time spent in department: 37.5%	Percentage of directors' time spent in department: 62.5%
Machining department manager	29,000		

→

Table 8.3 *Continued.*

Annual costs	Total £	Machining	Finishing
Finishing department manager	34,000		
Employee salaries	270,000	Number of employees in department: 9	Numbers of employees in department: 6
Repairs: machining	19,000		
Repairs: finishing	35,000		
Water rates	20,000	Departmental water usage: 1,800,000 litres	Departmental water usage: 1,200,000 litres
Lighting	18,000	Number of lights in department: 3,600	Number of lights in department: 1,800
Service department	50,000	Departmental usage: 20% of service department	Departmental usage: 80% of service department
	Total hours	**Machining**	**Finishing**
Machine hours	195,000	75,000	120,000

This mass of information might look daunting, but the application of common sense to how these overheads should be allocated to machining and finishing should enable you to determine the total overheads for each department. When allocating overheads, you should use any systematic basis that will result in a fair and equitable allocation of overheads to each department. Taking rent as an example in Table 8.3, the total floor area for the two departments is 1,800 square metres in machining and 1,200 square metres in finishing, a total of 3,000 square metres. The total rent cost is £100,000 so £100,000 × 1,800/3,000 = £60,000 allocated to machining and 1,200/3,000 × £100,000 = £40,000 allocated to finishing.

Using the additional information on departmental usage of each particular production overhead cost and department specific details on particular production costs, overheads can be allocated to the machining and finishing departments as shown in Table 8.4.

Table 8.4 The Picture Frame Company's annual costs allocated to machining and finishing

Annual costs	Total £	Machining £	Finishing £	Notes
Rent	100,000	60,000	40,000	Total floor area: 3,000 sq metres, split both rent and rate costs 1,800:1,200
Business rates	25,000	15,000	10,000	Split on the basis of total floor area 1,800:1,200
Depreciation	40,000	16,000	24,000	Split according to machinery value, 160,000:240,000
Heating	15,000	10,000	5,000	Split according to volume heated, 10,000:5,000

→

Table 8.4 *Continued.*

Annual costs	Total £	Machining £	Finishing £	Notes
Directors' salaries	80,000	30,000	50,000	£80,000 split according to usage, 37.5%:62.5%
Machining department manager	29,000	29,000	—	Actual departmental cost
Finishing department manager	34,000	—	34,000	Actual departmental cost
Employee salaries	270,000	162,000	108,000	£270,000 split 9:6 on the basis of the number of employees in each department
Repairs: machining	19,000	19,000	—	Actual departmental cost
Repairs: finishing	35,000	—	35,000	Actual departmental cost
Water rates	20,000	12,000	8,000	Split according to water usage, 1,800:1,200
Lighting	18,000	12,000	6,000	Split according to number of lights, 3,600:1,800
Service department	50,000	10,000	40,000	Split according to usage, 20%:80%
Totals	735,000	375,000	360,000	

SHOW ME HOW TO DO IT Are you happy with how these allocations were calculated? View Video presentation 8.1 in the **online workbook** to see a practical demonstration to reinforce your understanding of how this overhead allocation between departments was carried out.

8

Now that overheads have been allocated to each department, we can work out an overhead absorption rate, the amount to be charged per hour of resource consumed within the department. As noted in Example 8.8, the directors have chosen to allocate overheads to products on the basis of machine hours as the most appropriate method of overhead allocation and absorption.

In the machining department, £5 of overhead will be allocated to products per machine hour (£375,000 ÷ 75,000 hours), while in finishing, products will absorb £3 of overhead per machine hour (£360,000 ÷ 120,000 hours).

Let us assume that the 50 × 60 centimetre gilt edged frame has a direct material, direct labour and direct expense cost of £56 and requires four hours of machining department time and eight hours of finishing department time. The total absorption cost for 50 × 60 centimetre gilt edged frames is then as follows:

	£
Direct material, direct labour and direct expense cost (prime cost)	56
Machining department overhead absorbed: 4 hours at £5/hour	20
Finishing department overhead absorbed: 8 hours at £3/hour	24
50 × 60 centimetre gilt edged frame total absorption cost	100

The selling price for 50 × 60 centimetre gilt edged frames will be £100 absorption cost × 120% (100% cost + 20% of the absorption cost) = £120.

WHY IS THIS RELEVANT TO ME? Overhead allocation, overhead allocation rates

As a business professional and user of accounting information, you should understand how to:

- Allocate total overheads between different operating departments with a view to determining overhead allocation rates for each department
- Use overhead allocation rates to determine the overhead absorbed by particular products or services
- Set a selling price on the basis of the total absorption cost of a product or service

NUMERICAL EXERCISES Quite convinced you could carry out this kind of overhead allocation exercise for yourself? Go to the **online workbook** Numerical exercises 8.5 to practise this technique.

Give me an example 8.3 illustrates the level of overhead allocation practices in businesses across the world.

GIVE ME AN EXAMPLE 8.3 The use of overhead allocation in business

The July 2009 CIMA report, *Management accounting tools for today and tomorrow*, surveyed the current and intended usage by business of more than 100 management accounting and related tools based on a questionnaire completed by 439 respondents from across the globe. The seventh most commonly used technique in practice was overhead allocation. When used as an operational tool, overhead allocation was undertaken by 66% of respondents, the second most popular operational tool in use behind variance analysis on 73%. The survey discovered that the larger the organization, the more likely it was that overhead allocation would be in use in determining product cost.

Source: www.cimaglobal.com

Allocating service department overheads

Service departments do not produce products or make sales of services to outside parties, but they are an essential support activity in many business operations. Service department costs are allocated to production departments on the basis of each department's usage of each service department. In this way, service department costs are allocated to products and thus built into product selling prices to enable all costs incurred to be recovered through sales of products and services. In the example of the Picture Frame Company, the service department's overheads were allocated on the basis of usage by the two departments, machining and finishing. But what happens in cases where one service department provides services to another service department? In situations such as this, costs are apportioned between production departments and service departments until all the overheads have been allocated. Consider how this approach works in the following example (Example 8.9).

EXAMPLE 8.9

Alpha Manufacturing has three production departments, welding, sanding and painting, and three service departments, parts, set up and repairs. The costs and overheads of the six departments together with the usage made of each of the service departments by the production and service departments are presented in Table 8.5.

Table 8.5 Alpha Manufacturing's production and service department costs and overheads and service department usage percentages

	Production departments			Service departments		
	Welding	Sanding	Painting	Parts	Set up	Repairs
Costs and overheads	£94,200	£86,200	£124,200	£40,000	£24,000	£26,400
Percentage usage of parts	25%	30%	25%		20%	
Percentage usage of set up	20%	40%	10%			30%
Percentage usage of repairs	40%	25%	35%			

You are required to reallocate the overheads for the three service departments to the welding, sanding and painting departments to determine the total costs and overheads for each of the three production departments.

Method

The parts department's overheads of £40,000 will be allocated to each of the three production departments in the proportions indicated in Table 8.5 (25% to welding, 30% to sanding and 25% to painting) and then 20% of the £40,000 overheads will be allocated to the set up department. This will now give overheads in the set up department of £24,000 + (£40,000 × 20%) = £32,000. The set up department's new overheads of £32,000 will now be allocated in the proportions given in the question to the production departments (20% to welding, 40% to sanding and 10% to painting) while 30% of the set up department's overheads will be allocated to the repairs department. The repairs department now has overheads of £26,400 + (£32,000 × 30%) = £36,000 to allocate to each of the three production departments in the proportions 40% to welding, 25% to sanding and 35% to painting.

These calculations are shown in Table 8.6.

Table 8.6 Alpha Manufacturing's service department overheads reallocated to production departments

	Production departments			Service departments		
	Welding	Sanding	Painting	Parts	Set up	Repairs
	£	£	£	£	£	£
Costs and overheads	94,200	86,200	124,200	40,000	24,000	26,400
Parts costs reallocated	10,000	12,000	10,000	(40,000)	8,000	—
Set up costs reallocated	6,400	12,800	3,200	—	(32,000)	9,600
Repairs costs reallocated	14,400	9,000	12,600	—	—	(36,000)
Total costs and overheads	125,000	120,000	150,000	—	—	—

All the service department costs and overheads have now been reallocated to production departments. The overhead recovery rates can be determined on the basis of labour or machine hours in those production departments and overheads allocated to products produced in the welding, sanding and painting departments.

SHOW ME HOW TO DO IT   Quite sure you understand how service department overheads are reallocated to production departments? View Video presentation 8.2 in the **online workbook** to see a practical demonstration of how this reallocation between service and production departments is carried out.

WHY IS THIS RELEVANT TO ME?   Absorption costing: overhead allocation, allocating service department overheads

As a business professional and user of accounting information, you should:

- Understand how costs relating to non-production service departments are allocated to production departments

- Appreciate that this reallocation process is necessary to ensure that all production overhead costs are absorbed into products and services to provide a solid basis on which to determine selling prices

---

NUMERICAL EXERCISES   Quite convinced you could carry out this kind of overhead reallocation exercise for yourself? Go to the **online workbook** Numerical exercises 8.6 to practise this technique.

Administration overheads, marketing overheads and finance overheads: period costs

So far, we have considered the costs of production, direct and indirect, fixed and variable. However, all business entities incur overhead costs through administration activities, marketing activities and the costs of financing their operations.

It is possible that marketing activities will incur certain costs that vary in line with sales: such costs might be the commission paid to sales representatives to reward them for the sales they generate, as higher sales would incur higher commission. However, most marketing costs such as advertising, brochures, product catalogues, the salaries of marketing staff, the costs of running delivery vehicles and of running sales representatives' cars will all count as fixed costs.

Administration, marketing and financing fixed costs are known as period costs and they relate only to the period in which they are incurred. Therefore, while these costs are not taken into account in the valuation of inventory, it is still important to set the production levels and selling prices of products and services in order to cover these costs. Thus, these additional period costs will be built into the cost price of products in the same way as indirect production costs are allocated to products.

8

GO BACK OVER THIS AGAIN!   An example of a cost card for a product that includes all costs and the determination of a selling price is presented in Exercises 8.5 in the **online workbook**.

Problems with absorption costing

Absorption costing seems like an easy and effective way in which to build costs into products to determine first the total cost of the product and then its selling price. However, absorption costing has come in for criticism in recent years. The technique was originally developed as a way to cost products during the early part of the twentieth century. Each factory would turn out products that were all alike for undiscerning customers. Production runs were long and it was easy to spread fixed overheads over many products using the traditional absorption costing technique.

But times have changed. Modern manufacturers are no longer suppliers of goods to a passive market that accepts mass produced products lacking any individual distinction. Today's producers work assiduously to meet and fulfil customer demands and expectations. Production runs are now very short and products are individualized and tailored to each customer's specific requirements. Markets are not easily satisfied: customers have very specific requirements and, if their regular supplier is unable to meet those requirements, there are plenty of other businesses that will. Costs are thus no longer incurred in a steady, easy to allocate way. Lots of different organizational activities give rise to costs as businesses seek to fulfil each order's very specific requirements. As a result, the simplistic allocation of costs to particular products on an absorption costing basis may no longer be the most appropriate method. A different approach has to be found to allocate overheads to products so that a more accurate cost and a more competitive selling price for each product can be determined.

Commentators have criticized absorption costing on the following grounds:

- The allocation of costs to products on either a labour or machine hour basis is too simplistic and does not reflect the actual costs incurred in the provision of specific goods and services.

- Traditional absorption costing fails to recognize the demands made by particular products on an entity's resources.

- Overheads arise not in proportion to direct labour and machine hours but as a result of the range and complexity of products and services offered.

- Selling prices calculated on the basis of absorption costs may be wrong in one of two ways:

  - overhead is either underallocated to products that consume more activities resulting in underpricing of these products, or

- overhead is overallocated to products consuming lower levels of activity and so overprices these products.

- As a result of these misallocations, some products are subsidized by others rather than making a profit in their own right.

WHY IS THIS RELEVANT TO ME? Problems with absorption costing

To enable you as a business professional and user of accounting information to appreciate that traditional absorption costing:

- Is not the only way in which costs can be allocated to products
- May not provide accurate product or selling prices
- May not be particularly well suited to allocating overhead costs to products in modern manufacturing environments

---

GO BACK OVER THIS AGAIN! Confident you understand the limitations of traditional absorption costing? Go to the **online workbook** Exercises 8.6 to make sure you appreciate these shortcomings.

SUMMARY OF KEY CONCEPTS Quite sure that you can state the limitations of traditional absorption costing? Take a look at Summary of key concepts 8.7 to reinforce your knowledge.

Overhead allocation: activity-based costing

As we have seen, the aim of costing is to allocate costs to products and services to enable businesses to determine selling prices for those goods and services so that entities generate profits. Absorption costing works well in the case of mass produced, indistinguishable products, but modern manufacturing approaches require a more sophisticated cost allocation mechanism. Activity-based costing has been put forward as a way of providing this more sophisticated, more precise method of costing products and services to enable businesses to produce more accurate costs and hence more realistic selling prices.

How does activity-based costing work?

Traditional absorption costing adds together all the indirect production overheads incurred by a business and then allocates them across products on the basis of labour or machine hours. Activity-based costing recognizes that activities cause costs: the more activity that is undertaken, the more cost is incurred. Under activity-based costing, costs are allocated to products on the basis of activities consumed: the more activities that are associated with a particular product, the more overhead is allocated to that product and so the higher its cost and selling price will be.

Activity-based costing allocates overheads to products using the following two-step approach.

Step 1: establish cost pools

- Rather than lumping all indirect production overheads into **cost centres** (departments), activity-based costs are allocated to **cost pools**.
- Cost pools reflect all the different activities incurred in the production of goods and services.
- Examples of cost pools might be design costs, set up costs, quality control costs, material ordering costs and production monitoring costs.
- The number of cost pools will depend upon the complexity or simplicity of an entity's operations: the more complex the operations, the greater the number of cost pools will be.

Step 2: allocate costs to products and services

- Once cost pools have been established, a systematic basis on which to allocate those costs to products and services has to be found.
- The most logical method of allocating costs is on the basis of **cost drivers**: cost drivers reflect the level of activity associated with each cost pool.
- For example, if there were 50 machine set ups in a year, then the total cost in the machine set ups cost pool would be divided by 50 to give the cost per machine set up.
- Costs in the cost pools are then allocated to products on the basis of the activities consumed by those products. In our set up costs example, if a product used five machine set ups in the year, then the cost for five machine set ups would be allocated to that product.
- Where product costs turn out to be very high, management can take steps to reduce the activities consumed by those products as a way to lower costs and improve price competitiveness.

It is important to remember that activity-based costing is used to allocate overhead costs to products. Direct costs are still allocated to products in the usual way. Any costs directly linked to a product are still allocated to and form part of the prime cost of that product.

WHY IS THIS RELEVANT TO ME? Activity-based costing

To enable you as a business professional and user of accounting information to:

• Understand how activity-based costing works

• Appreciate the terminology used in activity-based costing and what each term means

GO BACK OVER THIS AGAIN! Do you really understand the differences between traditional absorption costing and activity-based costing? Go to the **online workbook** Exercises 8.7 to make sure you can distinguish between these two methods of overhead allocation.

SUMMARY OF KEY CONCEPTS Think you can state the steps involved in activity-based costing? Take a look at Summary of key concepts 8.8 to reinforce your knowledge of these steps.

Having dealt with the theory and logic behind activity-based costing, let's look now at Example 8.10 to see how overheads allocated under both the traditional absorption costing and activity-based costing methods produce different results.

EXAMPLE 8.10

Cookers Limited assembles microwave ovens and traditional electric cookers from parts produced by various suppliers. The following information relates to the costs and production of the two products:

	Microwave ovens	Electric cookers
Direct materials	£30	£52
Direct labour	£24	£48
Direct labour hours	3	7
Annual production in units	5,000	15,000
Annual number of set ups	15	30
Number of parts suppliers	14	6

Overheads	£
Output related overheads	160,000
Quality control	60,000
Set up related overheads	90,000
Supplier related overheads	50,000
Total overheads	360,000

The directors of Cookers Limited have traditionally allocated overhead costs to the two products on an absorption costing basis based on total labour hours. They have heard of activity-based costing and are wondering whether this would make a difference to the costing of their products. Selling prices for the company's two products are set at total absorption cost plus 25%, rounded to the nearest whole £.

Absorption costing

On an absorption costing basis, the first task will be to determine the total labour hours as the basis on which to allocate overheads: 5,000 microwaves each take three hours while 15,000 cookers each take seven hours of labour time to produce. Total labour hours are thus $3 \times 5,000 + 7 \times 15,000 = 120,000$ hours. The overhead absorption cost per labour hour is thus £360,000 ÷ 120,000 labour hours = £3 per labour hour. Using this absorption cost rate gives us the following product costs on a traditional overhead absorption basis:

	Microwave ovens	Electric cookers
	£	£
Direct materials	30	52
Direct labour	24	48
Production overhead: $3 \times £3/7 \times £3$	9	21
Total cost	63	121
Selling price (cost + 25%, rounded)	79	151

Activity-based costing

In this question, our overhead costs have already been allocated to cost pools for output, quality control, set up and supplier related overheads. In order to allocate the costs in these cost pools to products, we now need to determine the cost drivers of each particular overhead cost pool.

Output related and quality control overhead costs will most logically be driven by the number of production units. The more of a particular product that is produced, the more that product drives those particular categories of overhead costs as more output is achieved and more quality control inspections take place.

Production units total up to 20,000 units (5,000 microwaves + 15,000 electric cookers) so the output related overhead per unit of production is £8 (£160,000 ÷ 20,000 units of production). Here, 15,000 × £8 = £120,000 output related overhead will be allocated to electric cookers and 5,000 × £8 = £40,000 will be allocated to microwaves.

Similarly, quality control costs are allocated over 20,000 units of production. The quality control overhead per unit of production is £3 (£60,000 ÷ 20,000 units of production). In this case £45,000 of quality control costs will be allocated to electric cookers (15,000 × £3) and £15,000 to microwaves (5,000 × £3).

The unit cost for set up overheads will be based upon the number of set ups consumed by each product. Microwaves have 15 set ups in the year and electric cookers have 30, so the total set up related overhead of £90,000 is divided by 45 (15 + 30) set ups to determine the cost per set up of £2,000. Thus, 15 × £2,000 = £30,000 set up related costs are allocated to microwaves and 30 × £2,000 = £60,000 set up costs are allocated to electric cookers.

In the same way, supplier related overheads will be driven by the number of suppliers for each product. The more suppliers or parts there are for a particular product, the more overhead cost will be incurred in ordering, handling and processing those parts from the different suppliers. There are 14 parts suppliers for microwaves and 6 for electric cookers, a total of 20 suppliers. The total supplier related overhead of £50,000 is divided by 20 to determine the cost per supplier of £2,500 and then 14 × £2,500 = £35,000 of supplier related costs allocated to microwaves and 6 × £2,500 = £15,000 supplier related costs allocated to electric cookers.

Summarizing the above calculations, the total overhead cost allocated to each product is as follows:

Overhead	Allocation basis	Unit cost £	Microwave ovens £	Electric cookers £
Output related	Production	8	40,000	120,000
Quality control	Production	3	15,000	45,000
Set up related	Set ups	2,000	30,000	60,000
Supplier related	Number of parts suppliers	2,500	35,000	15,000
			120,000	240,000

These total overhead costs are now divided by the number of units of production and allocated to product costs to determine the total cost price of each product. The 5,000 microwaves drive £120,000 of related costs, so £24 is added to the cost of each microwave (£120,000 ÷ 5,000); £240,000 of overhead cost is driven by electric cookers, so £240,000 ÷ 15,000 = £16 is added as the unit overhead to the cost of electric cookers. These overhead allocation rates now give the following costs and selling prices.

	Microwave ovens £	Electric cookers £
Direct materials	30	52
Direct labour	24	48
Production overhead	24	16
Total cost	78	116
Selling price (cost + 25%, rounded)	98	145

As the above calculations demonstrate, overheads have been underallocated to microwaves and overallocated to electric cookers under the traditional absorption costing approach. When allocating overheads using activity-based costing, microwaves carry a much greater load of overhead cost compared to electric cookers and should sell for a much higher price. Once management are aware of this overhead cost burden attaching to microwaves, they can begin to think about reducing these costs. Most obviously, they should start by sourcing parts for microwaves from fewer suppliers to reduce the supplier related overheads allocated to this product and so lower the cost and selling price.

WHY IS THIS RELEVANT TO ME?   Traditional absorption costing v. activity-based costing overhead allocation

To enable you as a business professional and user of accounting information to:

- Allocate overheads to products using both absorption costing and activity-based costing
- Make recommendations for ways in which product costs could be lowered to improve profitability and make product pricing more competitive

---

SHOW ME HOW TO DO IT   Quite sure you understand how overheads are allocated to products using the activity-based costing methodology? View Video presentation 8.3 in the **online workbook** to see a practical demonstration of how this allocation of overheads was carried out.

NUMERICAL EXERCISES   How effectively could you allocate overheads using the activity-based costing methodology? Go to the **online workbook** and complete Numerical exercises 8.7 to test out your ability to apply your knowledge to activity-based costing problems.

What advantages does activity-based costing bring in practice? Give me an example 8.4 provides a summary of a case study that illustrates the benefits of adopting an activity-based costing approach to product costing.

GIVE ME AN EXAMPLE 8.4   The practical benefits of implementing activity-based costing

Dr Lana Yan Jun Liu of the University of Newcastle in the UK and Professor Fei Pan of the Shanghai University of Finance and Economics in China studied the implementation of activity-based costing (ABC) at Xu Ji Electric Co. Ltd, a large Chinese manufacturing company (*Activity based costing in China: Research executive summary series*, vol. 7(13), 2011, CIMA). An ABC pilot was implemented in one of the main production divisions in December 2001, with two further attempts to expand the use of ABC in a subsidiary and in its sales functions in 2005 and 2008. The subsidiary ran trials with the system in 2009 and then in 2010 reported a record annual sales increase of 50% over 2009 together with a net profit margin increase of 13%. Following the introduction and roll out of the ABC system, management expressed confidence in the accuracy of the company's product costs while the marketing department was able to compete more quickly and more effectively in its market as quotes could now be given instantly. The cost information presented by the new system made staff much more aware of cost savings and the ways in which to achieve them while top management were able to use the ABC information to exercise informed control over sales expenses.

Source: www.cimaglobal.com

The limitations and assumptions of costing

So far, we have taken it for granted in this chapter that fixed and variable costs are easily identifiable and that they behave in exactly the way we have described. Thus, it has been stated that variable costs vary directly in line with production and that fixed costs for a period (usually one year) are fixed and do not vary at all in that period. However, as we shall see, these assumptions should be challenged and it is important to understand the limitations of costing analysis when you are considering what price to charge for a product or service.

Assumption 1: fixed costs are fixed

In all of our examples so far we have assumed that fixed costs will remain at the same level for all levels of production over that period. However, this might not be the case. Once a certain level of production is reached, additional fixed costs might have to be incurred to cope with the increase in capacity. Thus, once Anna's production reaches, say, 2,000 chairs in a year, she might have to rent additional workshop space in which to increase production to more than 2,000 chairs. This would entail more rent, more business rates and more heating and lighting costs causing her fixed costs to jump when production reaches 2,001 units. This increased level of fixed costs would stay the same until production reached 4,000 chairs, at which point Anna would need to rent even more workshop space to produce 4,001 chairs or more. Fixed costs thus rise in steps, staying the same up to a certain level of production and then rising to a new level once the limit of production capacity is reached.

Fixed costs might thus behave in a stepped fashion as shown in Figure 8.7. In this figure, costs remain fixed for a given range of production and then they rise

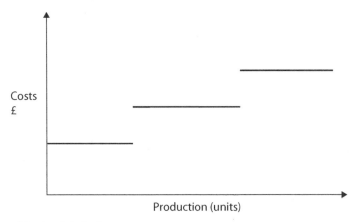

Figure 8.7 Stepped fixed costs behaviour

to a new level once the original range of production is exceeded, remaining steady over the next range of production. Once this increased range of production is exceeded, the fixed costs rise again. Thus, it might not be true to say that fixed costs remain fixed for a given period of time; they might only be fixed for a given range of production.

GO BACK OVER THIS AGAIN! Totally confident you understand how fixed costs might rise in steps? Visit the **online workbook** and work through Exercises 8.8 to see how fixed costs may rise in steps as production increases.

Assumption 2: variable costs remain the same for all units of production

Our analysis in this chapter has been based on the assumption that variable costs remain the same for all units of production. A moment's thought should enable you to see that this assumption will probably not be true in the real world. Increased purchases of materials from suppliers will earn quantity or bulk discounts from those suppliers. The higher the level of direct material purchases, the bigger the discounts and so the lower the average price of those materials will become.

Similarly, we have assumed that the unit cost of labour for each item produced will remain constant. However, this assumption, too, will not hold in the real world as increased productivity will earn productivity bonuses for employees, thereby pushing up the average cost of each unit of production.

GO BACK OVER THIS AGAIN! Reckon you understand how bulk discounts and productivity bonuses might affect the variable cost of materials and labour per unit of production? Try Exercises 8.9 in the **online workbook** to see how variable costs can change at different levels of production.

In situations in which production facilities use materials that fluctuate in price, such as metals and oil, the price of these direct materials can rise and fall during an accounting period. This makes forecasting very difficult but, again, it illustrates our point that variable costs will not necessarily remain the same for all units of production during an accounting period.

It is thus quite likely that the variable costs of production will not behave in the truly linear fashion we have assumed and that variable costs will not be represented by a sloping line of a perfectly even gradient, as shown in Figures 8.1 and 8.3.

Assumption 3: costs can be determined with the required precision

An underlying assumption of all the discussions thus far has been that the costs of products and of activities in making those products can be determined with the necessary degree of accuracy in order to produce accurate selling prices. This is highly unlikely in practice as there are often under or over estimations of the time it will take to complete a given task, of the cost of materials used in the production of goods and of the amount of direct expenses used to make products. Material costs will vary in line with market prices or become cheaper or more expensive depending on the current supply of those materials to the market. Labour may become more expensive if the required skills are in short supply and so push up the direct labour cost of production.

In the same way, your estimate of how quickly you expected to work through this chapter and the online workbook may have proved completely wrong. Whatever your original estimate, it is likely to have been rather different from the actual time taken. Similarly, you may over or under estimate how much you will spend on a night out with your friends; again, though you have been out with them many times before, your expectations of what each evening out will cost will be very different from the costs in reality.

Cost accountants in industry may not achieve complete accuracy in their calculations and they may under or over estimate the cost of direct materials, the time that it will take direct labour to produce each unit of production and the overheads that will be incurred in a given period. Absolute accuracy is not going to be achieved and the best that can be done is a reasonably close estimate. As we shall see in Chapter 10, standard costing makes assumptions about what the costs of production should be and then uses variance analysis to explain the differences between what costs and income were expected to be and what they turned out to be in reality.

8

WHY IS THIS RELEVANT TO ME?   The limitations and assumptions of costing

As a business professional and user of accounting information, you should:

- Appreciate that product costing is not an exact science
- Understand the bases of product costing and how these give rise to its limitations
- Be equipped with the tools to critique solutions that are produced by product costing analysis in a real-world context

CHAPTER SUMMARY

You should now have learnt that:

- Direct costs are those costs directly attributable to products or services

- Direct costs of production may be variable or fixed

- Variable costs are assumed to vary directly in line with levels of activity

- Fixed costs are assumed to be fixed for a given period of time

- Product and service costing is used by business organizations in making pricing decisions

- A cost card for a product is drawn up by splitting product costs into direct and indirect production costs

- Indirect production costs (overheads) are apportioned to departments to determine total overhead costs for each production department

- Overhead recovery rates for products are calculated on the basis of total departmental overheads and expected levels of production

- Service department overheads are reapportioned to production departments as part of each production department's total overheads

- Simple graphs can be drawn up to illustrate fixed, variable and total cost behaviour in a business context

- Using traditional absorption costing to allocate overhead costs to products may no longer be relevant in modern manufacturing environments and may result in the mispricing of products

- Activity-based costing allocates overhead costs to products on the basis of resources consumed by each product

- Costing is based on the assumptions that:
  - Fixed costs are and remain fixed for a given period of time or range of production
  - Variable costs remain the same for all units of production
  - Costs can be determined with the required precision

QUICK REVISION Test your knowledge with the online flashcards in Summary of key concepts and attempt the Multiple choice questions, all in the **online workbook**. www.oup.com/uk/scott_business3e/

END-OF-CHAPTER QUESTIONS

Solutions to these questions can be found at the back of the book from page 491.

❱ DEVELOP YOUR UNDERSTANDING

❱ Question 8.1

Mantinea Limited manufactures various kitchenware products. The following direct costs are incurred in producing a batch of 2,000 food processors.

	£
Materials	22,500
Direct labour	16,500
Direct expenses	13,000

The factory overheads for the year are £3,000,000. Total machine hours for the year are 750,000 and each processor takes 4.5 hours of machine time to produce. The selling price of food processors is total absorption cost plus 50%.

Required
Calculate the total absorption cost of one food processor together with the selling price for each food processor produced by Mantinea Limited.

❱ Question 8.2

Printers Limited has been asked by the local university press to quote for the printing of a new book. The print run will be for 2,000 books of 400 pages each. The costing records of Printers Limited contain the following information:

- Paper is bought from a local supplier. The local supplier provides paper at a price of 2,500 sheets for £9.
- Printing ink costs £57.50 per gallon, which is sufficient to print 20,000 pages.
- Covers for each book will be bought in at a cost of 66 pence for each book.
- Finishing costs per book are 50 pence.
- Production workers are paid an hourly rate of £12.50. The costing records show that a print run of 2,000 books would require 200 hours of production labour time.
- Printers' total production overheads for the year are £500,000 and the normal production level of the business is 50 million pages per annum.
- Printers Limited's pricing policy is to set selling price at total absorption cost plus 25%.

Required
Calculate the price that Printers Limited should charge the local university press for the print run of 2,000 books.

⏩ TAKE IT FURTHER

» Question 8.3

Applokia Limited is a manufacturer of smart phones. The company has the following costs for the month of September:

	£000
Factory rent	100
Factory manager's salary	38
Administration salaries	85
Marketing costs	50
Plastic smart phone covers	250
Quality control staff salaries	75
Production line workers' salaries*	500
Chip assemblies for smart phones produced	1,498
Administration office rent	25
Marketing office rent	20
Factory rates	47
Power for production machinery	50
Factory lighting and heating	43
Administration lighting and heating	5
Marketing lighting and heating	4
Marketing department salaries	51
Batteries	242
Production machinery depreciation*	37

* These costs remain the same no matter how many or how few smart phones are produced and sold in the month

Required

(a) For the above costs, state whether they are:

- Fixed or variable
- Direct production costs, production overheads or period costs

(b) Draw up a table that summarizes the above costs into prime cost, production cost and total cost.

(c) If Applokia produces 130,000 smart phones in a month and selling price is total cost + 25%, calculate the selling price for each smart phone produced in September.

(d) If rival companies are selling similar products for £27, what margin will Applokia make on its costs per smart phone if it sells its smart phones at the same price as its rivals?

» Question 8.4

Folly Limited produces novelty products. The products are produced on machines in the manufacturing department and they are then hand painted and finished in the finishing department. Folly Limited has forecast the following indirect production overheads for the year ended 31 January 2020:

	£000
Machinery maintenance staff salaries (manufacturing department)	100
Employees' salaries (painting and finishing department)	300
Employers' national insurance contributions for both departments	40
Rent and rates	60
Heating (the manufacturing department is not heated)	25
Lighting	25
Machinery depreciation	75
Canteen expenses*	56
Electricity for machinery	50
Insurance: machinery	25

* The canteen is in a separate building. The canteen rent, rates, heating, lighting, insurance and staff costs are all included in the figure for canteen expenses.

The manufacturing department has a capacity of 96,000 machine hours and 2,000 labour hours. The painting and finishing department has a capacity of 4,000 machine hours and 80,000 labour hours.

Additional information:

Recovery/absorption bases	Manufacturing	Painting and finishing
Area (square metres)	4,800	1,200
Value of machinery	£360,000	£15,000
Number of employees	5	15

Required

(a) Using the information provided, calculate the total production overheads to be allocated to the manufacturing and painting and finishing departments.

(b) Calculate the most appropriate overhead recovery/absorption rate for the manufacturing and painting and finishing departments and justify your choice of machine or labour hours as an absorption basis for the two departments.

(c) Using the rates you have calculated in (b), calculate the cost of the following job:

Novelty Christmas pixies: 5,000 units

Direct materials and packaging	£10,000
Direct labour	£1,000
Machine time: manufacturing department	500 hours
Labour time: manufacturing department	5 hours
Machine time: painting and finishing department	10 hours
Labour time: painting and finishing department	1,000 hours

» Question 8.5

Metal Bashers Limited produces steel fabrications for the construction industry. Steel girders and supports are cut to size and welded in the welding department and then painted in the paint shop before proceeding to the finishing department. Details of the overheads incurred by the three production departments are given below along with information on the two additional departments, the canteen and the service department. The canteen is used by all the employees of Metal Bashers Limited but the canteen staff are too busy to make use of the canteen facilities themselves. The service department repairs and cleans the machinery used in the three production departments. External catering equipment maintenance contractors service the canteen equipment.

	Welding	Painting	Finishing	Canteen	Service
Overheads	£100,000	£75,000	£43,000	£60,000	£42,000
Number of employees	15	5	6	2	4
Percentage usage of service department	40%	30%	30%		
Department labour hours	30,000	12,500	10,000		

Metal Bashers Limited is currently quoting for Job No 12359 which will require £1,500 of direct material, £2,000 of direct labour and £500 of direct expenses. It is estimated that job 12359 will use 120 hours of labour in the welding department, 50 hours in the painting department and 25 hours in the finishing department. Overheads are absorbed into jobs on the basis of direct labour hours in each department. The selling price for jobs is the total production cost of each job plus 40% of cost.

Required

(a) Calculate overhead recovery rates for the welding, painting and finishing departments.

(b) Calculate the production cost and selling price of job 12359.

» Question 8.6

Playthings Limited produces two dolls houses, the standard and the deluxe. The direct costs and overhead information relating to these two dolls houses are listed as follows.

	Standard	Deluxe
Direct materials	£50	£76
Direct labour	£30	£42
Labour hours	5	7
Annual production	2,500	1,000
Direct materials orders	400	600
Employees	5	10
Machine hours	10,000	5,000
Annual number of set ups	15	35

Overheads	£
Machining	45,000
Factory supervisor	30,000
Set up related overheads	50,000
Purchasing department costs	25,000
Total overheads	150,000

Playthings currently absorb their total overheads into their dolls houses on the basis of machine hours. The selling price of dolls houses is total absorption cost plus 50%. The directors are concerned about a build up in the warehouse of standard dolls houses. Deluxe models are still selling well and the current price charged by Playthings is the most competitive in the market: their nearest rivals are selling the same type of dolls house for £300. Investigations have shown that competitors are selling comparable standard dolls houses for £165. You have been asked for your advice on the current costing system at Playthings and whether you can suggest a better way in which to allocate overheads to products together with any other suggestions you are able to provide.

Required

(a) Calculate the current total absorption cost and selling price for standard and deluxe dolls houses based on the absorption of total overheads on a machine hour basis.

(b) Determine suitable cost drivers for the four overhead cost pools.

(c) Calculate the activity-based cost of standard and deluxe dolls houses and determine the selling price of each based on activity-based cost plus 50%.

(d) Given your results in (a), advise the directors on how they might reduce the cost of deluxe dolls houses in order to compete more effectively in the market.

8

9 Relevant costs, marginal costing and short-term decision making

LEARNING OUTCOMES

Once you have read this chapter and worked through the questions and examples in both this chapter and the online workbook, you should be able to:

- Define contribution
- Use the distinction between fixed and variable costs to determine the costs that are relevant and those that are irrelevant in making short-term decisions
- Understand how analysis of contribution is used to make short-term decisions
- Undertake break-even analysis and determine the margin of safety
- Use marginal costing and contribution analysis to make a range of decisions aimed at maximizing short-term profitability
- Understand the assumptions upon which marginal costing analysis is based

Introduction

The previous chapter discussed the various types of costs that organizations incur in their activities. These costs can be variable or fixed and can be categorized as direct costs of production, indirect costs of production and period costs. We also saw how fixed production overheads are absorbed into products to enable organizations to make pricing decisions to set the selling price at the right level so that an overall profit is generated from operations.

SUMMARY OF KEY CONCEPTS Not quite sure about the terminology here? Revisit Summary of key concepts 8.3–8.5 to revise direct, variable and marginal costs.

In this chapter, we will expand the analysis of costs to enable us to use this costing information in making decisions that will be valid in the short term (a period of one year or less). This analysis will be used to show which costs are relevant in short-term decision-making situations and which costs are not. In making these decisions, the profitability of the organization will always be uppermost in our minds and we will be seeking to maximize the profits that can be made.

Decision making: not just selling price

Our focus in Chapter 8 was on determining a product's costs to make just one decision: what our selling price should be to enable us to cover all our expenses and make a profit. However, there are other decisions that entities need to make. For example:

- What minimum level of production and sales is required to ensure that all costs are covered and that losses are not incurred?
- What level of production would be required to make a certain target profit?
- How profitable will our business be if the economy takes a downturn and sales and profits fall?
- If we lowered our selling price as a marketing strategy, would we make more or less profit?
- Will orders from new customers be profitable if these customers are looking to buy our products at a price lower than our usual selling price?
- Is it more profitable to make components for our products ourselves or to buy those components in the open market?

• If there are several products that could be made, but there are only sufficient resources to make some of them, which product(s) should be made in order to maximize the short-term profits of the organization?

The first step on the road to using costing to help us make these additional decisions is to look at the calculation and definition of contribution, the surplus that arises from the production and sale of one unit of product or service. As we shall see, contribution is a highly relevant consideration in the decision-making process and is a crucial step in determining those costs that are relevant and those costs that are irrelevant in a short-term decision-making context.

Contribution

We noted in the last chapter that fixed costs are assumed to be fixed over a given period of time and that variable costs vary with production or service delivery. Variable costs thus rise and fall directly in line with rises and falls in production as more or fewer goods or services are produced. However, no matter what the level of production is, fixed costs remain the same. Contribution for one unit of production and sales is the selling price less the variable costs of production (Figure 9.1). Example 9.1 illustrates Anna's contribution from each dining chair that her workshop makes and sells.

Figure 9.1 Contribution

EXAMPLE 9.1

Taking the example of Anna from Chapter 8 (Example 8.6), the contribution from making and selling one dining chair is as follows:

	£	£
Selling price for one dining chair		85.00
Materials (wood, glue, screws and sandpaper)	20.00	
Direct labour cost to produce one chair	25.00	
Total variable cost		45.00
Selling price – variable costs = contribution		40.00

So, with a selling price of £85 and a total variable production cost of £45, Anna is making £40 contribution from each dining chair that she sells. Contribution is very similar to the gross profit that we considered in Chapter 3 (Different categories of profit), the selling price less the directly attributable costs of making that sale.

WHY IS THIS RELEVANT TO ME?   Contribution

- To provide you as a business professional and user of accounting information with know-ledge of the basic building blocks used in marginal cost decision making
- As a business professional, you will need to appreciate that contribution = selling price – the variable costs of production/service provision

---

SUMMARY OF KEY CONCEPTS   Use Summary of key concepts 9.1 to remind yourself of how contribution is calculated throughout your reading of this chapter.

Marginal v. absorption costing

But hold on, you might say. In Chapter 8, we used absorption costing and a production level of 1,000 dining chairs per annum to work out the total cost of one chair at £52.80, which would give a profit per chair of £85 − £52.80 = £32.20. This is different from the analysis undertaken above. Why is this?

The answer to this question lies in the distinction between fixed and variable costs. The variable costs rise and fall directly in line with production whereas the fixed costs do not. Remember that Anna set her production level at 1,000 chairs per annum and absorbed her fixed costs into each chair on this basis to enable her to set a selling price. However, the rate at which Anna absorbed her fixed costs into her production was based on a purely arbitrary assumption that production would be 1,000 chairs each year. To illustrate the effect that this decision has had on the absorption cost of one chair, consider the following alternative scenarios in Example 9.2.

9

EXAMPLE 9.2

Anna's total fixed cost of £7,800 means that each of the 1,000 chairs was allocated a fixed cost element of £7,800 ÷ 1,000 chairs = £7.80. Anna could just as easily have set her production level at 2,000 dining chairs per annum and she would then have absorbed her fixed costs into production at the rate of £7,800 ÷ 2,000 chairs = £3.90 per chair. Alternatively, Anna might have been less optimistic about the level of production her workshop could achieve and set her expected production level at 500 chairs. In this case, her fixed costs would have been absorbed into production at the rate of £7,800 ÷ 500 chairs = £15.60 per chair.

The total fixed costs remain the same, but the rate at which they are absorbed into the cost of products changes depending on the assumptions made about the normal level of production.

The absorption rate adopted is a decision for management, a decision that is a matter of judgement completely dependent upon management's expectations of what represents a normal level of production over a given period of time.

Have a look now at Example 9.3. What are the differences between the two production and sales scenarios in this example? The fixed costs have not changed, but have remained the same for both the original and the increased levels of production and sales. Sales, however, have increased by the selling price of one additional dining chair (£85) and variable costs have increased by the cost of materials (£20) and the cost of direct labour (£25) for one additional dining chair. This has had the effect of both increasing contribution by £40 (selling price of £85 – materials cost of £20 – direct labour cost of £25) and increasing profit for the year by £40. Fixed costs have already been more than covered by the contribution generated by sales of 1,000 chairs per annum, so every additional unit of production and sales will add all of the contribution to the profit for the year.

EXAMPLE 9.3

While fixed costs in total are fixed, sales, variable costs and profits change with each additional unit of production and sales. To prove that this is true, consider what the profit would be if Anna produced 1,001 chairs rather than 1,000 chairs in a year.

	Selling 1,000 chairs in a year		Selling 1,001 chairs in a year	
	£	£	£	£
Sales: 1,000 × £85/1,001 × £85		85,000		85,085
Materials 1,000 × £20/1,001 × £20	20,000		20,020	
Direct labour 1,000 × £25/1,001 × £25	25,000		25,025	
Total variable costs		45,000		45,045
Selling price – variable costs = contribution		40,000		40,040
Fixed costs (rent, rates, heating and lighting)		7,800		7,800
Profit for the year		32,200		32,240

This approach, as we saw in Chapter 8 (Direct costs, variable costs and marginal costs), is called marginal costing: the costs and revenues of producing and selling one more or one fewer unit of product or service and the contribution that results from this increased or decreased activity at the margin. The contribution from each unit of production and sales contributes towards meeting the fixed costs of the organization. The higher the sales, the higher the contribution and the more easily a business can generate a net profit (sales less all fixed and variable costs) by covering its fixed costs and providing a profit on top.

WHY IS THIS RELEVANT TO ME?   Marginal v. absorption costing

As a business professional and user of accounting information, you need to be aware:

- That a product's absorption cost depends upon the production level used to absorb fixed costs into products or services
- That fixed costs do not change in line with production and sales over a given period of time
- That variable costs and contribution vary directly in line with production and sales
- Of the distinction between contribution and the absorption cost profit per unit of production and sales
- That, once fixed costs are covered, the contribution from every additional unit of production and sales is pure profit

GO BACK OVER THIS AGAIN!   Can you really distinguish between fixed and variable costs? Go to the **online workbook** and complete Exercises 9.1 to make sure you understand the distinction.

SUMMARY OF KEY CONCEPTS   Quite sure you understand contribution and marginal cost? Take a look at Summary of key concepts 9.1 and 9.2 to reinforce your understanding.

Relevant costs and sunk costs

Contribution and marginal costing analysis helps us to consider the short-term costs that are relevant and those that are irrelevant when a choice between two alternatives has to be made. Relevant costs are those costs that we will incur if we decide to follow a certain course of action. Relevant costs are the costs that influence our decision making.

As we have already seen, entities incur both fixed costs and variable costs in their activities. Costs that have already been incurred cannot influence future decision making as this money has already been spent and nothing you subsequently do will change those costs. Costs that have already been incurred and that do not influence future decisions are known as sunk costs. Sunk costs are past costs and have no further influence on decisions to be made in the future. To illustrate this idea of sunk costs, let us consider Example 9.4.

EXAMPLE 9.4

You are on holiday for a week in a seaside town. Your train fare has been paid and cost you £70 for a return ticket. Your hotel bill for the week is £500, which you have paid in advance. Now you have arrived you are free to decide what you want to do during your week. You have the option of going to the beach, going walking in the hills, visiting the local historical sites or travelling to another local town that is staging a sporting event you are keen to attend. You have £300 spending money for the week. What are the relevant costs and the sunk costs in this situation?

Your train fare and your hotel bill are sunk costs, costs that have been paid and that have no further bearing on how you will spend your week. The only costs you will take into account now are the different costs of the four options in front of you and how much of your spending money each of these activities will use up. Going to the beach and going walking in the hills are likely to be less expensive alternatives compared with visiting the historical sites or attending the sporting event: both of the latter two options will require the purchase of entrance tickets whereas the former two options will not.

The past sunk costs will have no influence upon your decisions about how to spend your time and money and so are disregarded when you consider your future options and actions. What counts now and what will influence your decisions are the costs and benefits that will be incurred enjoying any one of the four options available to you and the relative costs of each.

In the same way, costs that an entity incurs, whether any activity takes place or not, or which it has already incurred are irrelevant to its short-term decision making. Costs relevant in short-term decision making are those costs that will be incurred as a result of making decisions and implementing a particular course of action. In Anna's case, the relevant costs are the variable costs of producing a larger or smaller number of dining chairs. The rent, rates and heating and lighting costs are all fixed and will be incurred regardless of the number of chairs produced and sold. All Anna has to do is to decide what level of production she needs to achieve in order to cover her fixed costs and what additional revenue she will generate and what additional costs she will face in doing so.

WHY IS THIS RELEVANT TO ME? Relevant costs and sunk costs

As a business professional and user of accounting information, knowledge of relevant and sunk costs will enable you to:

- Distinguish between those costs that are relevant and those costs that are irrelevant in a decision-making context
- Appreciate that costs that do not change as a result of a decision have no bearing on that decision
- Understand that fixed costs are irrelevant in short-term decision making

---

GO BACK OVER THIS AGAIN! Certain you can identify sunk costs and costs relevant to a decision? Go to the **online workbook** and complete Exercises 9.2 to reinforce your understanding of this distinction.

SUMMARY OF KEY CONCEPTS Confident you understand what relevant costs and sunk costs represent? Take a look at Summary of key concepts 9.3 and 9.4 to reinforce your understanding.

Relevant costs: opportunity cost

Another relevant cost that has to be taken into account is **opportunity cost**. This is the loss that is incurred by choosing one alternative course of action over another. Opportunity cost only applies when resources are limited: when there is no shortage of a resource, then there is no opportunity cost. This might seem like an academic exercise, but a moment's reflection will enable you to see that opportunity cost is involved in many everyday choices. See how the idea of opportunity cost works in Examples 9.5 and 9.6.

EXAMPLE 9.5

Before you started your university course, you were faced with a choice. You could spend three years gaining your degree or you could start work immediately and earn money straight away. Choosing to study for your degree involves the loss of income from employment for three years and the loss of being able to spend that money on whatever you wanted. However, by deciding to start work immediately, you faced the loss of three years studying a subject you enjoy and the improved personal and career prospects that such study would have brought to you. Time is limited and you can only make one of the two choices, so making either choice for your time involves an opportunity cost.

EXAMPLE 9.6

In a decision-making context in business, opportunity cost will be the next best alternative use for a resource. In a manufacturing business, raw materials can either be used for one project or another. That piece of steel that cost £100 could be used to produce a new steel fabrication to sell to a customer for £5,000 or it could be scrapped for £20. The opportunity cost of using the steel in the new fabrication is the next best alternative to using it, which is scrapping it. Therefore, the opportunity cost of using the steel in the fabrication is £20. The £100 purchase cost is irrelevant as this is a past cost, a sunk cost and a cost that has no further bearing on your decision. Your choice lies in using the steel in the fabrication to sell to a customer or scrapping it and receiving £20.

9

WHY IS THIS RELEVANT TO ME? Relevant costs: opportunity cost

As a business professional and user of accounting information:

- You should appreciate that the opportunity cost of a decision is the next best alternative use for the resource used in that decision
- You need to be able to identify the opportunity cost of a resource as a relevant cost in a decision-making context

GO BACK OVER THIS AGAIN! Opportunity cost sounds like a difficult concept, doesn't it? Go to the **online workbook** and complete Exercises 9.3 to see if you can decide what the opportunity costs of various decisions are.

SUMMARY OF KEY CONCEPTS Sure you understand what opportunity cost represents? Take a look at Summary of key concepts 9.5 to reinforce your understanding.

As we have discovered earlier, relevant costs are those costs that affect short-term decision making. Let us now see how marginal costing and relevant costs are used in decision making by businesses.

Contribution analysis and decision making

Break-even point

Anna's first concern when setting up her business was to determine the selling price of her dining chairs. Her second concern (and the concern of many new businesses when they start up) is to calculate the number of units of production she will need to sell to cover all her costs, both fixed and variable. The point at which the revenue from sales = the total costs (Figure 9.2) is known as the **break-even point**, the level of sales that produces neither a profit nor a loss. Contribution analysis is relevant in determining break-even point. As we have seen, each additional unit of production and sales adds contribution towards the fixed costs so each sale is a further step towards covering those fixed costs. This is very similar to walking up a hill: the hill does not move (fixed costs) and each step you take (contribution) brings you closer to the top of the hill. Just as all your steps take you to the top, so the contribution from each sale takes an entity closer and closer to the break-even point.

This knowledge enables us to calculate the break-even point as:

$$\frac{\text{Total fixed costs}}{\text{Contribution per unit of sales}} = \text{Break-even point in sales units}$$

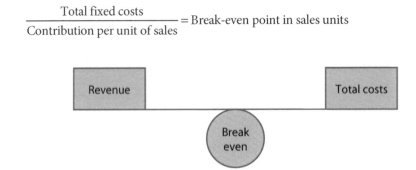

Figure 9.2 Break-even point: revenue = total costs

EXAMPLE 9.7

How many dining chairs does Anna need to sell to break even? We know from our calculations in Example 9.1 that the contribution from the sale of one chair is £40. We also know from our examples in Chapter 8 that Anna's annual fixed costs for her workshop are £7,800 (annual rent of £6,000, annual business rates of £1,000 and heating and lighting costs of £800, see Example 8.4).

Using the break-even formula, Anna's break-even point is thus:

$$\frac{£7,800}{£40} = 195 \text{ Dining chairs}$$

Anna needs to sell 195 chairs in order to break even. Using this figure, let's prove that she does in fact break even if she sells 195 chairs in the year.

	£	£
Sales of 195 dining chairs at £85 each		16,575
Materials cost for 195 dining chairs at £20 each	3,900	
Direct labour cost for 195 dining chairs at £25 each	4,875	
Total variable cost		8,775
Selling price – variable costs = contribution		7,800
Fixed costs (rent, rates, heating and lighting)		7,800
Profit/loss for the year		—

The above calculations prove that our formula for break-even point works and gives us the correct answer. For Anna, at the break-even point, her sales of £16,575 are exactly equal to her variable costs for the break-even level of sales (£8,775) plus the fixed costs that she is incurring during the year (£7,800). She makes neither a profit nor a loss at this point. Once she sells 196 chairs, the additional £40 of contribution is pure profit as there are no further fixed costs that must be covered before a profit can be made.

9

WHY IS THIS RELEVANT TO ME? Break-even point

As a business professional and user of accounting information, knowledge of break-even point analysis will enable you to:

- Appreciate that a business breaks even when all of its costs, both fixed and variable, are exactly covered by the revenue from sales
- Calculate the break-even point in sales units and sales value in £s for different products and services
- Determine break-even points for a new product or service that your company intends to introduce

Break-even point: graphical illustration

Just as we drew graphs to illustrate the behaviour of fixed, variable and total costs in Chapter 8, so, too, we can draw a graph to show the break-even point. Break-even charts require three lines to be drawn: the line representing sales revenue, the line representing fixed costs and the line representing total costs (fixed costs + variable costs). Fixed costs remain the same throughout the period under review just as we saw in Chapter 8 (Fixed costs), but sales revenue and total costs both rise directly in line with the level of sales and production activity. The point at which the sales revenue line and total costs line intersect is the break-even point, as shown in Figure 9.3. Beneath the break-even point losses will be made while above the break-even point profits are made.

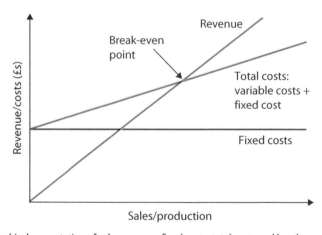

Figure 9.3 Graphical presentation of sales revenue, fixed costs, total costs and break-even point

The margin of safety

As we have seen, the break-even point in sales tells us how many units of production we have to sell in order to cover all our fixed costs and make neither a profit nor a loss. However, it also tells us how far our projected sales could fall before we reach a break-even position. In Anna's case, we found that she needs to sell 195 chairs before she breaks even. As her projected sales are 1,000 units for the year, she has a

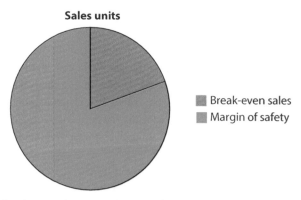

Sales units

- Break-even sales
- Margin of safety

Figure 9.4 Anna's break-even sales units and margin of safety

margin of safety of 1,000 − 195 = 805 chairs (Figure 9.4). This means that her projected sales could fall by 805 chairs before she reaches her break-even point. The higher the margin of safety, the less an organization is exposed to the risk of a fall in sales that could result in a loss-making situation. In Anna's case, even if her projected sales fell to 500 units, she would still make a profit as sales of 500 chairs are still well above the break-even point of 195 chairs.

WHY IS THIS RELEVANT TO ME? Margin of safety

To enable you as a business professional and user of accounting information to:

- Calculate the margin of safety for a product or service
- Appreciate that the larger the margin of safety, the less likely it is that a business will make a loss

---

SUMMARY OF KEY CONCEPTS Can you say what the margin of safety represents? Take a look at Summary of key concepts 9.7 to test your knowledge.

MULTIPLE CHOICE QUESTIONS Happy you can calculate break-even point and the margin of safety? Complete Multiple choice questions 9.2 in the **online workbook** to reinforce your learning.

Sensitivity analysis

Knowledge of the break-even point enables us to determine the profit or loss from any given level of sales, as demonstrated in Example 9.8.

EXAMPLE 9.8

Anna knows that selling her chairs at £85 each will give her a contribution per chair of £40. Her break-even point is 195 chairs, so what will her profit or loss be if she sells 180 chairs or 300 chairs?

We could calculate individual profit and loss accounts for sales of 180 chairs and 300 chairs to determine profit or loss at the two sales levels. However, as we know that the break-even point is 195 chairs, we can calculate Anna's profit or loss by subtracting the break-even point from the projected sales units and then multiplying the difference by the contribution per unit of sales.

Thus, using our previous calculations, the loss at sales of 180 chairs will be (180 − 195) × £40 = £600. Is this right? Contribution of £40 per chair will result in total contribution from sales of 180 chairs of 180 × £40 = £7,200. After deducting the fixed costs of £7,800, Anna's loss will be £7,200 − £7,800 = £600 so our calculation using the number of chairs from the break-even point is correct.

Similarly, at sales of 300 chairs, Anna's profit will be (300 − 195) × £40 = £4,200. Proof: 300 × £40 = a total contribution of £12,000. Deducting fixed costs of £7,800 gives a profit of £12,000 − £7,800 = £4,200.

WHY IS THIS RELEVANT TO ME? Break-even point and sensitivity analysis

As a business professional and user of accounting information, knowledge of break-even point and sensitivity analysis will:

- Enable you to calculate the profit or loss at any given level of sales

- Show you that the profit or loss depends on how far the level of sales differs from the break-even point

- Provide you with a useful analysis tool when evaluating the profit or loss from different levels of sales of products or services

---

SUMMARY OF KEY CONCEPTS Certain you can state the relationship between break-even point and the profit or loss at a given level of sales? Take a look at Summary of key concepts 9.8 to test your knowledge.

MULTIPLE CHOICE QUESTIONS How well can you use break-even analysis to determine profits and losses at a given level of production? Complete Multiple choice questions 9.3 in the **online workbook** to reinforce your learning.

Target profit

Example 9.9 shows how break-even analysis can be used to calculate a target profit.

EXAMPLE 9.9

If Anna sells 1,000 chairs she will make a profit of £32,200 (Chapter 8, Example 8.7). However, she might consider that this profit does not compensate her sufficiently for the time and effort she has put into the business. She might decide that a profit of £40,000 is much more acceptable. How many chairs would she need to sell to achieve this target profit?

Break-even analysis will enable us to calculate the number of sales units required to achieve this target profit. Anna makes a contribution per chair sold of £40. Sales of her first 195 chairs will cover her fixed costs and enable her to break even. Therefore, she will need to sell a further £40,000 ÷ £40 = 1,000 chairs to make a net profit of £40,000. Adding these two figures together means that Anna will have to sell 1,000 + 195 = 1,195 chairs to make a profit of £40,000.

Is this right? Let's check. 1,195 chairs produce a total contribution of 1,195 × £40 = £47,800. Deducting the fixed costs of £7,800 gives a net profit for the year of £47,800 − £7,800 = £40,000, so our calculations above are correct.

WHY IS THIS RELEVANT TO ME?   Break-even point and target profit

As a business professional and user of accounting information, knowledge of break-even analysis will:

- Enable you to calculate a target profit
- Provide you with the technique to calculate the number of units of sales required to achieve a target profit

---

SUMMARY OF KEY CONCEPTS   Can you state the relationship between break-even point and the target profit? Take a look at Summary of key concepts 9.9 to test your knowledge.

MULTIPLE CHOICE QUESTIONS   Certain you can use break-even analysis to determine a target profit? Complete Multiple choice questions 9.4 in the **online workbook** to reinforce your learning.

Cost-volume-profit analysis

The techniques we have considered so far in this chapter are examples of **cost-volume-profit (CVP) analysis**. CVP analysis studies the relationship between costs, both fixed and variable, the level of activity, in terms of sales, and the profit generated. Do entities actually use these techniques in practice? Give me an example 9.1 describes the findings of a CIMA sponsored survey into the use of management accounting practices in small and medium sized entities in the UK.

GIVE ME AN EXAMPLE 9.1   Break-even point and CVP analysis

Management accounting practices of UK small–medium-sized enterprises, published in July 2013, investigated the management accounting techniques and practices used by a sample of small and medium sized enterprises in the UK. All of the small and medium sized enterprises used break-even analysis with managers having a rough idea of their fixed costs and the level of sales revenue required to cover these. However, while all of the medium sized entities surveyed used CVP analysis, this technique was only used by a few of the small organizations in the survey: the view was taken that, as small entities are unable to exercise much control over the selling price that they can charge or the variable costs that they pay for inputs, respondents considered that they would gain little benefit from trying to evaluate alternative scenarios based on selling and cost prices.

Source: www.cimaglobal.com

9

High and low fixed costs

Anna has very low fixed costs and, consequently, a high margin of safety given that she aims to make sales of 1,000 units in a year. However, many businesses have very high fixed costs with very low levels of variable costs. Such businesses will have a very high break-even point and, as a result, a very low margin of safety. Such businesses are thus very vulnerable during a downturn in the economy and, if they do not collapse, they will incur very large losses before the recovery enables them to reach their break-even level of sales. Example 9.10 provides an example of a high fixed costs industry.

EXAMPLE 9.10

Premier League football clubs are an example of businesses with very high fixed costs. Players' wages are a very high proportion of each club's total costs. These wages are fixed and do not vary in line with the number of paying customers who support the team each week. Therefore, Premier League clubs need to fill their stadia for every match in order to cover these fixed costs and still make some sort of profit. Thus, their margin of safety is very low and they have made regular losses in recent seasons. However, changes in the rules imposed by football's governing body have forced clubs into cutting costs in order to make a profit, as shown in Give me an example 9.2.

GIVE ME AN EXAMPLE 9.2 Premier League football clubs make their first collective profit for 15 years

Premier League football clubs made a collective pre-tax profit in the 2013–2014 season of £190m. This was the first profit that the clubs had made as a group since 1997–1998, when the combined surplus before tax was £49m. Ever increasing payments for broadcast rights from television companies had been spent on steeply rising salaries for players as the clubs fought to attract the talent necessary to win trophies or just to stay in the League. However, figures compiled by the accounting firm Deloitte from the clubs' annual reports and financial statements for 2013–2014 showed player wage costs rising just 6% compared to 2012–2013. Measured as a percentage of revenue, player wage expenses were at their lowest level since the 1998–1999 season. Financial fair play rules introduced by UEFA require clubs to break-even instead of allowing wealthy owners to spend more than the clubs generate in revenues in their bid for success. These new rules had had a dampening effect on player wages as the clubs worked hard to comply thereby enabling them to generate a combined profit from this reduction in costs.

Source: the *Financial Times*, 28 March 2015, page 14

Contribution analysis, relevant costs and decision making

Marketing and selling price

Can marginal costing be used to inform other business decisions? The information provided by a knowledge of fixed and variable costs and contribution can be used in a variety of business situations. Firstly, Example 9.11 illustrates how contribution and relevant costs analysis can be used in making marketing and selling price decisions.

EXAMPLE 9.11

Anna is currently selling her chairs at £85 each. A friend who is in marketing and who knows the market well has looked at her chairs and has suggested that she should reduce the selling price to £70. Her friend estimates that this reduction in selling price will enable her to increase sales by 50%. As the workshop has spare capacity, there would be no need to take on any additional workshop space and so fixed costs will not increase as a result of this decision. Similarly, the costs of materials and labour will not increase and will remain the same at £20 and £25 per chair respectively. Anna is now trying to decide whether this marketing strategy will increase her profits or not.

To help her make this decision, we can draw up two costing statements as follows to assess the profits produced by the two different strategies, one for the original level of sales of 1,000 chairs at £85 and one for the expected level of sales of 1,500 chairs (1,000 × 150%) at £70.

	Selling 1,000 chairs at £85 each		Selling 1,500 chairs at £70 each	
	£	£	£	£
Sales 1,000 × £85/1,500 × £70		85,000		105,000
Materials 1,000 × £20/1,500 × £20	20,000		30,000	
Direct labour 1,000 × £25/1,500 × £25	25,000		37,500	
Total variable costs		45,000		67,500
Selling price − variable costs = contribution		40,000		37,500
Fixed costs (rent, rates, heating and lighting)		7,800		7,800
Profit for the year		32,200		29,700

However, if you have been following the argument so far, you will have realized that you could have used contribution analysis to solve this problem much more quickly. A selling price of £70 and a variable cost per chair of £45 gives a revised contribution of £70 − £45 = £25. Selling 1,500 chairs at £70 each would give a total contribution of 1,500 × £25 = £37,500. Fixed costs will not change, so the profit for the year after deducting fixed costs will be £37,500 − £7,800 = £29,700, lower than the current strategy of selling 1,000 chairs at £85.

How many chairs would Anna need to sell to make the new strategy as profitable as the current strategy? Again, contribution analysis will help us to determine the answer to this question. Current contribution from selling 1,000 chairs at £85 each is £40,000. The contribution per unit in the new strategy will be £70 – £45 = £25. To produce a total contribution of £40,000 from selling the chairs at £70 each would thus require sales of £40,000 ÷ £25 = 1,600 chairs. This is a large increase on current sales and Anna might well decide that she is quite happy selling 1,000 chairs at £85 each rather than taking the risk of trying to increase production by 60% for no increase in the profit generated.

WHY IS THIS RELEVANT TO ME?   Relevant costs and the profitability of marketing strategies

- As a business professional and user of accounting information, you will be involved in making pricing decisions for products
- Knowledge of relevant costs and contribution will enable you to evaluate different marketing strategies in terms of their relative profitability and to choose the profit-maximizing pricing strategy

---

GO BACK OVER THIS AGAIN!   Happy you can use contribution analysis to determine the profit that will arise from different marketing strategies? Have a go at Exercises 9.4 in the **online workbook** to make sure you can use contribution analysis in analysing such decisions.

Special orders

Thus far, we have assumed that selling prices will remain the same for all customers and for all of an organization's output. In reality, this is rather unrealistic and most organizations will have different selling prices for different customers. When a new customer approaches an entity with a price they would be willing to pay for goods or services, the organization has to decide whether to accept the new order or not at the customer's offered price. Again, contribution analysis will enable us to determine whether the new order is worth taking and whether it will add to our profit or not. Examples 9.12 and 9.13 illustrate the techniques and considerations involved in making these decisions.

EXAMPLE 9.12

Anna receives an enquiry from a charity that wishes to place an order for 50 dining chairs. They have seen examples of Anna's chairs and are very impressed by the quality of the workmanship and the sturdiness of the chairs, but they have been put off by the £85 selling price. They can only afford to pay £50 for each dining chair and have asked Anna whether she would be willing to sell the chairs at this lower price. Anna looks at her cost card for one chair (see Chapter 8, Example 8.6) and discovers that her absorption cost price per chair is £52.80. Her first thoughts are that if she sells the chairs at £50 each, she will be making a loss of £2.80 per chair. The workshop has spare capacity and the order could be accommodated without incurring any additional costs other than the variable costs of producing each chair. This additional order will not affect Anna's current production of 1,000 chairs. As the price offered by the charity is £2.80 less than the absorption cost per chair, Anna is considering refusing the order. Is she right to do so?

Let's see what Anna's total profit will be if she accepts the new order for 50 chairs at £50 each.

	£	£
Current sales: 1,000 chairs at £85 each		85,000
Additional sales: 50 chairs at £50 each		2,500
Total sales		87,500
Variable costs of production		
Materials: 1,050 chairs at £20 each	21,000	
Direct labour: 1,050 chairs at £25 each	26,250	
Total variable costs		47,250
Total contribution		40,250
Fixed costs (rent, rates, lighting and heating)		7,800
Profit for the year		32,450

Anna's original production level of 1,000 chairs produced a profit of £32,200. Accepting the new order alongside the current production of 1,000 chairs increases profit by £250 to £32,450. Anna expected to make a loss of £2.80 per chair (£50.00 selling price – £52.80 absorption cost per chair) so why is her profit not lower if she accepts the new order?

The answer again lies in the fact that the fixed costs are irrelevant to this decision; fixed costs are fixed for a given period of time and do not change with increased levels of activity. The only relevant costs are those that do change with the increase in the level of activity. These are the variable costs relating to production and the selling price for each additional chair produced. The selling price of £50 is £5 higher than the variable costs of production which are £45. Each additional chair in the new order adds £5 of contribution (and a total additional contribution and profit of £5 × 50 chairs = £250), the selling price less the variable costs, so, as the new order generates more profit for Anna, she should accept.

EXAMPLE 9.13

The decision in Example 9.12 was made on the basis that Anna has spare capacity in her workshop and can easily add the new order to her existing level of production. Would your advice have been different if the additional order for 50 dining chairs had meant giving up 50 chairs of current production? Again, let's look at the effects of this decision and consider the relevant costs of making this decision to decide whether accepting the new order would be worthwhile in terms of the overall effect on profit.

If the new order were to be accepted and 950 full price chairs and 50 special price chairs produced, Anna's profit for the year would be as follows.

	£	£
Full price sales: 950 chairs at £85 each		80,750
Discounted sales: 50 chairs at £50 each		2,500
Total sales		83,250
Variable costs of production		
Materials: 1,000 chairs at £20 each	20,000	
Direct labour: 1,000 chairs at £25 each	25,000	
Total variable costs		45,000
Total contribution		38,250
Fixed costs (rent, rates, lighting and heating)		7,800
Profit for the year		30,450

As we can see, the decision now would be to reject the new order as profits fall by £1,750 from £32,200 for 1,000 full price chairs to £30,450 for 950 full price chairs and 50 special price chairs. How has this fall occurred? Our 50 special price chairs generate a contribution of £5 each, but to generate this contribution of £5, a contribution of £40 has been given up on each of the 50 full price chairs that this order has replaced. This has led to the fall in profit of £1,750 as follows: (£40 (contribution per chair given up) − £5 (contribution per reduced price chair gained)) × 50 chairs = £1,750. Thus, from a profitability point of view, no additional contribution is generated and so the order should be declined. More profitable production would have to be given up to take in a less profitable order so the charity would be turned away if there were no spare capacity in the business.

WHY IS THIS RELEVANT TO ME?   Relevant costs and special orders

To enable you as a business professional and user of accounting information to:

- Use contribution analysis to evaluate the profitability of new orders with a selling price lower than the normal selling price

- Appreciate that new orders should be accepted if they give rise to higher total contribution, add to total profits and make use of spare capacity

- Understand that where more profitable production is given up, orders at a special price should not be accepted

---

SUMMARY OF KEY CONCEPTS   Not sure whether to accept a special order or not? Take a look at Summary of key concepts 9.10 to review the criteria you should apply when evaluating such decisions.

NUMERICAL EXERCISES   Think you can use contribution analysis to determine whether a special order should be accepted? Have a go at Numerical exercises 9.1 in the **online workbook** to test your grasp of the principles.

Special orders: additional considerations

Other than additional income and costs and the effects on overall profit, what other considerations should be taken into account when making these special order decisions? First, as we have seen, entities faced with this choice should have spare capacity with which to fulfil orders at a lower selling price. Entities operating at full capacity have no idle resources with which to meet new orders at lower selling prices and so will not accept them. To do so would be to replace production generating higher contribution with production generating lower contribution. As a result, profits after fixed costs will fall.

Second, entities must also consider how easily information about a special price for a new customer could leak into the market. If existing customers found out that dining chairs are being supplied to a charity at £50 when they are paying £85, they are likely to demand a similar discount and this would have a very severe effect on Anna's profitability in the long run. Where information is likely to be available in the wider market, special orders should thus be declined as long-run profits will suffer as all customers will demand special prices.

In order to avoid rejected orders and hence lost profits, organizations can adopt a product differentiation strategy. Rather than producing and selling all their production under one label, producers have a quality label and an economy label to enable them to overcome the problem of all customers demanding the same reduced price. In the same way, supermarkets sell branded products from recognized manufacturers and they also sell goods with the supermarkets' own label at lower prices. Both quality and economy products might have been manufactured in the same production facility, but they are marketed in different ways.

On the positive side, should Anna accept the order from the charity, she might well receive some welcome publicity for her dining chairs as the charity recommends her business by word of mouth. This would amount to free advertising in return for her cutting the selling price for this special order and, in her attempts to expand her business, she might consider this short-term reduction in profits to be a worthwhile sacrifice for the longer-term growth of the business as a whole.

In such special order situations, after taking into account the additional considerations, the short-term decision will always be to accept the new order when this increases contribution and to reject the order when this results in a reduction in contribution.

9

WHY IS THIS RELEVANT TO ME? Relevant costs and special orders: additional considerations

To enable you as a business professional and user of accounting information to:

- Appreciate that additional profit is not the only consideration in deciding whether to accept or decline a special order
- Understand the non-accounting, business related considerations involved in making special order decisions
- Discuss and evaluate the non-accounting aspects relating to special order decisions

Outsourcing (make or buy) decisions

Relevant costs can also be used in making decisions on whether it is more economical to buy goods and services from external parties or whether it will be more profitable to produce or provide these goods and services in-house. Again, when making this decision, only those costs that change with the level of activity will be considered. Think about these issues in Example 9.14.

EXAMPLE 9.14

Anna is expanding rapidly and has more orders for dining chairs than she can currently fulfil with two employees in her workshop. She has annual orders now for 1,500 dining chairs at a selling price of £85 each. She is considering whether to take on a third employee to help with these additional orders. Taking on this third employee will not increase her fixed costs as she has spare capacity in her workshop to accommodate another two workers and the new employee will be paid at the same rate for producing chairs as the existing employees. Another dining chair producer, Wooden Wonders, has offered to make the additional 500 dining chairs for Anna and to sell them to her at a cost of £49 each. Anna is delighted as this £49 cost is lower than her absorption cost per chair of £52.80, so she is expecting to make an additional profit of £1,900 (500 × (£52.80 – £49.00)) by buying in the chairs. She is ready to accept Wooden Wonders' offer, but, knowing how your advice has proved invaluable in the past, she has asked you whether it will be more profitable to take on the new employee or to contract out the manufacture of the dining chairs to Wooden Wonders.

Let us solve this problem in both a long and short way to show that both approaches give us the same answer and to provide you with a quick method of calculating the alternatives where profit maximization is the objective. First, let us look at a comparison of Anna's sales, costs and profits if she either makes all of her production in-house or if she makes 1,000 chairs in her workshop and contracts out the additional 500 chairs to Wooden Wonders.

	Making and selling 1,500 chairs at £85 each		Making 1,000 chairs, buying in 500 chairs and selling 1,500 chairs at £85 each	
	£	£	£	£
Sales 1,500 × £85		127,500		127,500
Materials 1,500 × £20/1,000 × £20	30,000		20,000	
Direct labour 1,500 × £25/1,000 × £25	37,500		25,000	
Buying in 500 chairs at £49 each	—		24,500	
Total variable costs		67,500		69,500
Selling price – variable costs = contribution		60,000		58,000
Fixed costs (rent, rates, heating and lighting)		7,800		7,800
Profit for the year		52,200		50,200

Anna's expectation was of £1,900 more profit, gained by buying in 500 chairs at £49 each along-side the in-house production of 1,000 chairs. However, this option results in a profit for the year that is lower by £2,000 in comparison with making all the chairs in-house. How does this difference arise?

Using marginal costing and contribution analysis, you could have solved this problem much more quickly. Contribution from in-house production is £40 (£85 selling price less the £20 material costs less the £25 labour cost) whereas contribution from the bought in chairs is £36 (£85 selling price less the £49 purchase cost from Wooden Wonders). The difference in contribution per chair of £4 (£40 – £36) multiplied by the 500 chairs that are bought in from Wooden Wonders explains the £2,000 lower profit if the second alternative course of action is chosen.

Fixed costs are again irrelevant in making this decision as these do not change with the level of production: only those costs that change with the decision should be taken into account alongside the contribution that will be gained from each alternative. Anna had forgotten that the fixed costs had already been covered by the production of 1,000 chairs and that the only relevant costs in this decision were the additional variable costs that she would incur. These would either be £45 if she produces the chairs in her own workshop or £49 if she buys them in from an outside supplier. Given that the outside supplier charges more for the chairs than Anna's employees can make them for, Anna will engage the third employee in the workshop as this is the more profit-able solution to her production problem.

WHY IS THIS RELEVANT TO ME?   Relevant costs and outsourcing (make or buy) decisions

To enable you as a business professional and user of accounting information to:

- Use contribution analysis and relevant costs to determine whether outsourcing decisions are more or less profitable than in-house production

- Appreciate that where profit maximization is the only consideration, products should be bought in when additional contribution is generated by outsourcing production

---

SUMMARY OF KEY CONCEPTS   Quite sure you understand the relevant costs in making outsourcing decisions? Take a look at Summary of key concepts 9.11 to review the criteria you should apply when evaluating such decisions.

NUMERICAL EXERCISES   Convinced you can use contribution analysis and relevant costs to determine whether production should be outsourced or not? Have a go at Numerical exercises 9.2 in the **online workbook** to test your grasp of the principles.

Outsourcing (make or buy) decisions: additional considerations

While profit maximization is a valid aim for many organizations, costs saved and ad-ditional profit will be only one of the considerations in an outsourcing (make or buy) situation. There are also various qualitative factors that have to be taken into account when making decisions of this nature, as shown in Figure 9.5.

Figure 9.5 Factors to consider in outsourcing (make or buy) decisions

First, we will need to consider the products or services that the external provider will be offering us. Will these products or services meet our quality standards? Will the product or service be of the same quality or at the same level as our own in-house employees provide? Should the level of quality be lower, then further costs will arise. Products that use lower quality outsourced parts will break down more often and require more maintenance visits or refunds to dissatisfied customers. Services such as cleaning might not be carried out to the same exacting standards as the organization sets for its own staff, leading to an increase in complaints and a loss of customers as they transfer their business to other product or service providers who are providing the quality that customers demand.

While the product or service might look cheaper to buy in now, there are longer-term hidden costs that have to be considered. These longer-term costs might be much more damaging for the organization in terms of loss of reputation and they will often outweigh the benefit of saving a few pounds at the present time. In Anna's case, she would need to determine whether the chairs bought in from Wooden Wonders will be made to the same standards and with the same care and attention as that given by her own employees. Where the chairs are not made to the same standards, Anna will want to ensure that her own reputation for quality chairs is maintained by producing all her chairs in-house.

Second, the price might be cheaper now, but will it always be cheaper? Once our new supplier has captured our custom and we have closed down our own production facility, will the price rise and wipe out all the previous savings? Contracts for the supply of goods and services have to be drawn up very carefully to ensure that a short-term advantage is not suddenly eroded by a change in price.

Organizations will also need to consider their willingness to be reliant upon another entity. In this case, one organization relies upon the other to maintain continuity of supply and continuity of quality. This may not always happen and disruptions at a supplier very soon affect production and sales to customers. Where components are produced in-house, there is a much greater level of control over production and, hence, sales. Organizations might prefer to maintain their self-reliance rather than handing over responsibility for their parts, sales and production to other businesses.

Similarly, handing over production to another organization will lead to a loss of skills within the business and an inability to reintroduce production at a later date should the current supply contract prove inadequate. Entities will lack in-house knowledge of how their products work and be unable to provide customers with advice on these products. When an organization closes down part of its production facility and makes workers redundant, there is a knock-on effect on other workers. Job losses weaken employee morale, job satisfaction and productivity. These knock-on effects also have an effect on profitability as the current workforce becomes demoralized and more concerned about their own job security than completing the work in hand. Anna's two employees might become concerned about the continuity of their employment with Anna if production is outsourced. Concerned employees are distracted employees and they will not be concentrating on the quality of what they are producing but on whether they will still be employed in a year's time.

However, with the appropriate attention to detail and close cooperation and collaboration between the contracting parties, outsourcing can work very well indeed. Give me an example 9.3 shows how Toyota overcomes the potential difficulties of outsourcing through very close relationships with its suppliers.

GIVE ME AN EXAMPLE 9.3   Outsourcing at Toyota

The Japanese car company, Toyota, prizes high quality at a low price. However, the company outsources 70% of the components for its cars to suppliers and produces just 30% of the components in its own production facilities. In order to ensure the quality of the products produced by its suppliers, Toyota adopts a policy of strong relationships and collaboration with its suppliers through the Toyota Production System. Toyota's high quality has been achieved as a result of the collaborative advantage it enjoys with its suppliers. Toyota regularly evaluates its suppliers' performance and provides suggestions on how they could improve their operations. However, this is not a one way relationship: the company also invites its suppliers to evaluate Toyota and to provide their suggestions for operational improvement. This continuous improvement approach enables the Toyota Production System to deliver the high quality products demanded by both Toyota and its customers despite the fact that most of its car parts are not manufactured in-house.

Source: www.scribd.com/doc/53016595/Vertical-Integration-or-Outsourcing-Nokia-Ford-Toyota-IBM-Intel-Toshiba-Matsushita#scribd

9

> **WHY IS THIS RELEVANT TO ME?**   Relevant costs and outsourcing (make or buy) decisions: additional considerations
>
> As a business professional and user of accounting information, you should:
>
> * Appreciate the additional strategic factors that must be taken into account when an outsourcing decision is being made
> * Understand that cost reduction and profit are not the only grounds on which to base make or buy/outsourcing decisions
> * Be able to discuss and evaluate non-accounting, business related considerations when undertaking make or buy/outsourcing decisions

Limiting factor (key factor) analysis

Contribution analysis can also be used in making decisions to maximize short-term profits where organizations are facing a shortage of direct material or direct labour. In this situation, contribution analysis can be used to determine which products generate the highest contribution per unit of material or labour input in order to maximize profits. Those products that generate the highest contribution per unit of limiting factor will be produced, while those that produce a lower contribution per unit of limiting factor will be discontinued in the short term. Limiting factor analysis is only relevant where two or more products are produced. If only one product is produced, then there is no decision that has to be made, manufacturers will just produce their one product up to the maximum number that they can based upon the limitations imposed by the shortage of direct materials or direct labour. Let us consider how this would work and the steps that would be undertaken to determine which products produce the highest level of contribution per unit of limiting factor in Example 9.15.

9

EXAMPLE 9.15

Anna's business has grown and is now a very successful producer of wooden dining chairs, small wooden coffee tables and wooden kitchen cabinets. However, a new government has come to power in the country from which she sources her supplies of wood. This new government has introduced restrictions on the export of timber as new environmental policies are put in place to preserve rather than exploit the local forests. Anna is thus currently facing a shortage of wood from her suppliers because of these restrictions. While she investigates new production methods to enable her to use wood from other sources, Anna is looking to maximize her short-term profit and needs help in deciding which products she should make to achieve this.

The selling price and variable costs for her three products are as follows:

	Dining chairs	Coffee tables	Kitchen cabinets
	£	£	£
Selling price	85.00	50.00	80.00
Materials: wood	(18.00)	(12.60)	(10.80)
Materials: other	(2.00)	(5.40)	(9.20)
Direct labour	(25.00)	(18.00)	(30.00)
Contribution	40.00	14.00	30.00

All three products use the same type of wood at a cost of £1.80 per kg. The new government in the country of her supplier has allocated Anna a maximum of 12,600 kg of wood for the next three months. Anna has thought about the figures for her three products and is considering diverting all her production into dining chairs as these provide the highest total contribution of the three products and she thinks that producing just chairs will maximize her profit for the period. Is Anna right? If she is not right, which (or which combination) of the three products should she produce to maximize her profits in the next three months?

In problems of this nature you should work through the following three steps.

Step 1: calculate the quantity of limiting factor used in the production of each product

In order to maximize contribution when there is a limiting factor, the first step is to determine the usage that each unit of production makes of that limiting factor. Given that wood costs £1.80 per kg and using the product costing details above, each of the three products uses the following amounts of material:

> Dining chairs: material usage: £18.00 ÷ £1.80 = 10 kilograms
> Coffee tables: material usage: £12.60 ÷ £1.80 = 7 kilograms
> Kitchen cabinets: material usage: £10.80 ÷ £1.80 = 6 kilograms

Step 2: calculate the contribution per unit of limiting factor delivered by each product

The next step is to determine how much contribution each product generates per unit of limiting factor. This calculation divides the total contribution for each product by the number of units of limiting factor used in the production of each product. The products are then given a ranking: the highest contribution per unit of limiting factor is placed first and the lowest contribution per unit of limiting factor comes last.

9

Using the information about Anna and our calculations in Step 1, the three products generate the following contributions per unit of limiting factor:

Contribution per unit of limiting factor		Ranking
Dining chairs	£40/10 kg per unit = £4 of contribution per unit of material used	2
Coffee tables	£14/7 kg per unit = £2 of contribution per unit of material used	3
Kitchen cabinets	£30/6 kg per unit = £5 of contribution per unit of material used	1

As the above calculations show, the highest contribution per unit of limiting factor is delivered by kitchen cabinets. These use 6 kg of material in each finished unit and deliver a total contribution of £30 per product. Dining chairs are ranked second with the second highest contribution per unit of limiting factor, while coffee tables are ranked last out of the three products, with a contribution per unit of limiting factor of only £2.

Step 3: calculate the contribution-maximizing production schedule

If Anna wishes to maximize her contribution and profit, she will now need to determine how much of the limiting factor is available to use and the most profitable products to produce. In Anna's business, if demand for each product is not limited, then she would just produce kitchen cabinets as each kitchen cabinet delivers £5 per unit of limiting factor used. A more likely scenario would be that demand for each product would be limited and so the contribution-maximizing production schedule will involve producing all of the product delivering the highest contribution per unit of limiting factor first, then producing the product delivering the second highest contribution per unit of limiting factor next and so on until all of the limiting factor is used up.

Anna estimates that demand for each product for the next three months will be as follows:

Dining chairs:	580 units
Coffee tables:	500 units
Kitchen cabinets:	900 units

What will the profit-maximizing production schedule be? Anna should produce as many kitchen cabinets as she can, as this product gives her the highest contribution per unit of limiting factor. She should then produce as many dining chairs as possible and finally produce coffee tables up to the total amount of material available, the limiting factor. Her production schedule and contribution will look like this:

	(a)	(b)	(c) ((a) × (b))	(d) (12,600 − (c))	(e)	(f) ((b) × (e))
Product	Kg of material per unit	Quantity produced	Kg of material used	Kg of material remaining	Contribution per unit	Total contribution
	kg	units	kg	kg	£	£
Cabinets	6	900	5,400	7,200	30	27,000
Chairs	10	580	5,800	1,400	40	23,200
Tables	7	200	1,400	—	14	2,800
Total material used (kg)			12,600	Total contribution		53,000

The production schedule shows that demand for kitchen cabinets and chairs can be met in full as there is sufficient material to make the 900 kitchen cabinets and 580 chairs that customers require. However, there is only sufficient material remaining to produce 200 of the 500 coffee tables that customers are looking to buy, so production of these will be limited if Anna adopts a profit-maximizing strategy. This strategy will produce a total contribution of £53,000.

SHOW ME HOW TO DO IT! Are you sure that you understand how the above allocation of limiting factor was made to the three products? View Video presentation 9.1 in the **online workbook** to see a practical demonstration of how this allocation between the three products is carried out.

What of Anna's intention to produce only chairs? How much contribution would this production scheme have produced? As there are 10 kg of wood in each chair, 12,600 kg of wood would have produced 1,260 chairs. The contribution from one chair is £40, so 1,260 chairs would produce a total contribution of 1,260 × £40 = £50,400. This is a good contribution, but it is not as high as the contribution forecast by using the contribution per unit of limiting factor calculated above. Given that demand for dining chairs is only 580 units, Anna will have a lot of chairs in stock at the end of the three months and these unsold chairs, too, will limit her profit for the three-month period.

The above production schedule shows what the maximum profit could be, given the limiting factor and the current maximum demand. However, in reality, it would be very difficult for Anna to stick to this schedule as her customers will be ordering her products in the expectation that she will fulfil all those orders. It would not be easy to refuse an order for coffee tables from a current customer on the grounds that she could not produce those products as they were not profitable enough. Such an excuse would lead to the loss of that customer, who would then source coffee tables from another supplier. In the longer term, the loss of customers could lead to a loss of reputation

9

with all the attendant effects that this would have on sales and profits. Therefore, while the profit-maximizing schedule is a useful technique to determine what maximum profit could be in times of shortage, considerations other than cost and profit will tend to determine what is produced to meet customers' expectations of the organization.

WHY IS THIS RELEVANT TO ME?   Relevant costs and limiting factor analysis

To enable you as a business professional and user of accounting information to:

- Use contribution analysis and relevant costs to devise contribution and profit-maximizing strategies when resources are scarce
- Understand that this technique has certain limitations in the real world

SUMMARY OF KEY CONCEPTS   Do you remember the steps to follow when calculating profit-maximizing strategies in a limiting factor situation? Take a look at Summary of key concepts 9.12 to review the steps you should follow when making such decisions.

NUMERICAL EXERCISES   Can you use contribution analysis and relevant costs to determine which products should be produced to maximize contribution when resources are scarce? Have a go at Numerical exercises 9.3 in the **online workbook** to test whether you have fully grasped the techniques involved.

Relevant costs, marginal costing and decision making: assumptions

The decisions discussed and illustrated previously all seem to be very straightforward and easy to apply. However, in practice, difficulties will be encountered. This is because of the assumptions upon which marginal costing analysis is based. These assumptions can be summarized as follows:

- First, it has been assumed that the variable costs of a product can be identified by a business with the required level of precision to enable accurate calculations to be made.
- Second, fixed costs for a period are assumed to be completely predictable and unchanging.
- Variable costs are assumed to be linear, that is, variable costs vary directly in line with production. In reality, the purchase of more materials will result in bulk discounts causing the average cost of materials used in each product to fall (see Chapter 8, Assumption 2: variable costs remain the same for all units of

production). Similarly, additional units of production might well entail the payment of overtime premiums or bonuses to existing staff, causing the direct labour cost to jump when higher levels of production are reached.

- Prices have been assumed to be stable whereas, in reality, prices of materials change all the time depending on whether there is a shortage or an oversupply of those materials in the market. For example, in a delivery business, the price of fuel to run delivery vans changes on a daily basis.

- In break-even analysis, it is assumed that only one product is produced. Once two or more products are produced, the techniques behind break-even analysis are invalidated by the presence of two sets of variable costs and two contributions, making it impossible to determine the break-even point for one set of fixed costs.

Nevertheless, despite these limitations, relevant cost analysis does have some application in practice, as illustrated in Give me an example 9.4.

GIVE ME AN EXAMPLE 9.4   Relevant costing for decisions in practice

The July 2009 CIMA report, *Management accounting tools for today and tomorrow*, surveyed the current and intended usage by business of more than 100 management accounting and related tools based on a questionnaire completed by 439 respondents from across the globe. The findings indicated that relevant costing for decisions was used by small (43%), medium (48%), large (50%) and very large (44%) companies worldwide. However, product/service profitability analysis was the preferred profitability analysis tool across all companies surveyed. Of those intending to introduce relevant costing for decisions in the coming year, only a small percentage of UK respondents aimed to adopt this technique while a much higher percentage of respondents across all regions were planning to introduce product/service profitability analysis.

Source: www.cimaglobal.com

9

WHY IS THIS RELEVANT TO ME?   Relevant costs, marginal costing and decision making: assumptions

To enable you as a business professional and user of accounting information to:

- Appreciate the assumptions upon which marginal costing and decision-making analysis are based

- Develop an insight into the limitations posed by these assumptions

CHAPTER SUMMARY

You should now have learnt that:

- Contribution per unit = selling price per unit − variable costs per unit
- The concept of opportunity cost is used to determine the benefits lost by using a resource in one application rather than in another
- Fixed costs are not relevant when making short-term decisions as these costs do not vary with changes in the level of activity in the short term
- The only costs relevant in short-term decision making are those that change in line with levels of activity
- The break-even point is calculated by dividing fixed costs by the contribution per unit
- The margin of safety is the number of units of sales above the break-even point: the higher this number, the higher the margin of safety
- Knowledge of the break-even point enables entities to calculate the profit or loss from any given level of sales
- Contribution analysis enables entities to determine the effect of different pricing strategies on short-term profits
- Special orders should be accepted when they increase contribution
- Make or buy decisions can be made on the basis of the marginal costing technique
- Calculation of the contribution per unit of resource enables entities to devise profit-maximizing strategies when resources are limited
- Users of the costing techniques discussed in this chapter have to be aware of the advantages and limitations of marginal costing

QUICK REVISION   Test your knowledge with the online flashcards in Summary of key concepts and attempt the Multiple choice questions, all in the **online workbook**. www.oup.com/uk/scott_business3e/

9

END-OF-CHAPTER QUESTIONS

Solutions to these questions can be found at the back of the book from page 501.

❯ DEVELOP YOUR UNDERSTANDING

❭ **Question 9.1**

Define the following terms

(a) Contribution

(b) Relevant costs

(c) Irrelevant costs

(d) Sunk costs

(e) Opportunity cost

(f) Break-even point

(g) Margin of safety

(h) Target profit

> **Question 9.2**

Podcaster University Press is a small publishing company producing a range of introductory textbooks on a variety of academic subjects for first year undergraduate students. The company's marketing department is considering reducing the selling price of textbooks to generate further sales and profit. The company's textbooks currently retail at £30 each. Variable production costs are £10 per book and Podcaster University Press has annual fixed costs of £3,000,000. Current sales of textbooks are 200,000 per annum. The marketing department has forecast that a £5 reduction in the selling price of each textbook will boost annual sales to 275,000 books whereas decreasing the selling price to £21 would increase annual sales to 360,000 books.

Required

Using contribution analysis, evaluate the proposals of the marketing department and advise the company on whether the two proposals would be financially beneficial or not.

⏩ TAKE IT FURTHER

⟫ **Question 9.3**

Big Bucks University is planning to offer a series of professional accounting course classes. The fee payable for this professional accounting course is £400 per student per module. The university has already allocated lecturers currently employed at the university to each class and has determined that lecturers are being paid £60 per hour for the 60 hours required to deliver each module. The lecturers will be paid whether any students are enrolled on each module or not and they can be diverted to other classes if the professional accounting course modules do not run. Books and handouts are provided to each student at a cost of £100 per student per module. The university allocates £1,200 of central overhead costs for the year to the room used in the provision of each module. The university has asked for your help in deciding on the number of students that should be recruited to each module.

Required

(a) State which costs are relevant to the decision as to how many students to recruit to each module.

(b) Determine how many students the university should recruit to each module to ensure that each module breaks even.

(c) What is the margin of safety if the university recruits 25 students to each module?

(d) Calculate the profit or loss the university will make on each module if 14 students or 30 students are recruited to each module.

(e) What will the break-even point be if the university decides to charge £340 per module instead of £400?

» Question 9.4

Gurjit Limited produces and sells ink jet printers. The selling price and cost card for each printer are as follows:

	£	£
Selling price		40.00
Direct materials	9.50	
Direct labour	11.25	
Direct expenses	3.65	
Fixed overhead	5.60	
Total cost of one ink jet printer		30.00
Profit per ink jet printer sold		10.00

Currently, production and sales are running at 5,000 printers per annum. The fixed overhead allocated to each printer has been based on production and sales of 5,000 units. However, because of the popularity of the product and a strong advertising campaign, the directors of Gurjit Limited are expecting sales to rise to 10,000 units. The directors are currently reviewing the costs and profits made by printers along with their expectations of future profits from the increased sales. One option open to Gurjit Limited is to outsource production of their printers to another company. It is estimated that any outsourcing of production would lead to an increase in total fixed overheads of £40,000 to enable Gurjit Limited to ensure the quality of printers produced outside the company. The directors have a quote from Anand Limited to produce all 10,000 ink jet printers for £200,000. The directors of Gurjit Limited are considering whether to accept this offer and have asked for your advice.
In order to advise the directors of Gurjit Limited on whether to accept the offer from Anand Limited, you should:

(a) Calculate the current profit made at a level of sales and production of 5,000 ink jet printers per annum.

(b) Calculate the profit that will be made if sales and production rise to 10,000 printers per annum.

(c) Calculate the profit that will be made if sales and production rise to 10,000 printers and production of printers is outsourced to Anand Limited.

(d) Advise the directors of Gurjit Limited whether to outsource production to Anand Limited and what additional factors they should take into account in this decision other than costs and profit.

» Question 9.5

Diddle Limited produces ornamental statues for gardens whose selling price, costs and contribution per unit are as follows:

	Clio	Diana	Athena
	£	£	£
Selling price	81	58	115
Materials (clay)	(30)	(12)	(42)
Direct labour	(15)	(27)	(30)
Variable overheads	(6)	(3)	(8)
Contribution	30	16	35

The same specialized clay is used in all three statues and costs £6 per kg. The company faces a shortage of this clay, with only 3,000 kg available in the next month. The board of directors is therefore considering which statues should be produced in order to maximize contribution in the coming month. The sales director has suggested that production should concentrate on Athena as this statue has the highest contribution of the three products. Is the sales director right?

Maximum predicted demand for the three products for the coming month is as follows:

Clio: 198 units

Diana: 900 units

Athena: 200 units

10 Standard costing and variance analysis

LEARNING OUTCOMES

Once you have read this chapter and worked through the questions and examples in both this chapter and the online workbook, you should be able to:

- Appreciate that a standard cost is an expected cost rather than an actual cost
- Determine how a standard cost is calculated
- Calculate direct material total, price and usage variances
- Calculate direct labour total, efficiency and rate variances
- Calculate sales volume and price variances
- Calculate fixed overhead expenditure variance
- Calculate variable overhead total, expenditure and efficiency variances
- Discuss the function of standard costing as an accounting control device
- Understand that variances are merely an indication of a problem that requires further management investigation to establish and rectify the causes

Introduction

In the last two chapters we have looked at the different types of cost that organizations incur in their operations and how the distinction between fixed and variable costs can be used to make decisions that aim to maximize the short-term profitability of an organization. It is now time to turn to the second function of cost and management accounting: planning. Initially, this involves the use of accounting data to make predictions and forecasts for the future. Once actual outcomes are known, then comparison of actual results with these forecasts is used as a means to control an organization's operations. The next chapter will consider budgeting in much greater detail and look at how the use of budgets and the comparison of outcomes with expectations enable an entity to control its operations, to enhance positive trends and to take action to correct problems as they arise. In this chapter we will consider the use of the related technique of standard costing and how the analysis of divergences from the standard can be used to identify problems requiring management's attention.

What is standard costing?

As we saw in Chapter 8, the product costing process takes up a lot of time as information is gathered about the inputs of direct material, direct labour, direct expenses and indirect production overheads and costs are allocated to products and services. This information is then used to determine selling prices for products so that a profit is made. However, prices of inputs change rapidly. The cost of materials rises and falls as users demand more or less of a particular raw material, wages rise each year, electricity and gas prices go up and down as the weather warms or cools. To change all these prices on a daily or weekly basis would be time consuming in the extreme and the task would eventually overwhelm the individuals performing this role. What is needed is an efficient, predictive tool that provides a reasonably accurate estimate of what the cost of a product or service should be over a given period of time. Variations from this estimate can then be analysed to determine whether the estimate needs revising or not. This reasonably accurate estimate can be provided by standard costing.

10

A standard cost card will include all the direct materials, direct labour, direct expenses, variable overheads and an allocation of fixed overheads that go into a product or service. These standard costs are the expected costs of that product and the standard cost card will also include the expected selling price for each product, along with the standard profit. Standard costs are derived from numerous observations of an activity over time and represent an expectation of costs incurred by and income generated from mass produced products and services. As the number of observations increases, so the standard is revised and the accuracy of the estimate becomes much closer to the actual cost of each product.

Standard costs recognize that goods are made up of a fixed set of inputs, whether material, labour or overheads. These inputs are measured and costed and then summarized to present the total costs of producing one item of output. As an example, consider this book. Variable costs will include the paper, the ink, the covers, the binding, the power to drive the printing machinery and the handling of each book as it comes off the press. Fixed costs to be allocated across each print run will include typesetting, editing, development, website construction and maintenance, advertising and marketing. All these costs can be readily determined as a result of Oxford University Press's vast experience of printing books and the staff's detailed knowledge of the costs of book production. All the costs involved can be summarized to calculate the cost of one book and this is then the standard cost of that book. Management will set an expected selling price based on the costs incurred and the anticipated market for the book and this becomes the standard selling price.

WHY IS THIS RELEVANT TO ME? Standard costing

To provide you as a business professional and user of accounting information with:

- A basic understanding of what standard costing involves and how it works
- A predictive accounting tool you can use in the future to forecast the costs and profits of mass produced products and services

GO BACK OVER THIS AGAIN! Confident you can say what standard costing is? Go to the **online workbook** and complete Exercises 10.1 to make sure you understand the aims and objectives of standard costing.

Variance analysis

Standard costs just represent expectations, the expected costs and revenues from each product produced and sold. What happens when the reality turns out to be different from the expectation? When the actual costs and revenues are known, then a comparison of the standard expected results and the actual results is undertaken. The differences between the standard costs and revenues and the actual figures are known as variances. These variances are calculated and then used to explain the difference between anticipated and actual outcomes. In the case of book production, the cost of materials might be more than expected as a shortage of the expected quality of paper might have resulted in more expensive paper being used. Ink prices might have been higher or lower than forecast, a rise or fall in power costs might have resulted in changes to the anticipated printing cost, the selling price might have been set higher to cover these additional costs and so on. Explanations for variances will be sought as a means of controlling operations. Where actual costs are significantly different from the standard, the standard can be updated to produce more accurate information in the future.

What use do organizations across the world make of variance analysis? Give me an example 10.1 describes the findings of a 2009 CIMA survey.

GIVE ME AN EXAMPLE 10.1   Variance analysis

The July 2009 CIMA report, *Management accounting tools for today and tomorrow*, surveyed the current and intended usage by business of more than 100 management accounting and related tools based on a questionnaire completed by 439 respondents from across the globe. The fourth most commonly used technique in practice was variance analysis. When used as a costing tool, variance analysis was undertaken by 73% of respondents, the most popular costing tool in use. Over 60% of small companies in the survey used variance analysis while more than 80% of large companies employed this technique.

Source: www.cimaglobal.com

WHY IS THIS RELEVANT TO ME?   Variance analysis

To enable you as a business professional and user of accounting information to:

- Understand how expected and actual costs and revenues are compared to explain deviations from forecast performance

- Appreciate that variances between expected and actual costs and revenues can lead to improvements in standards

- Have an initial appreciation of the roles that standard costing and variance analysis perform in the control of business operations

---

GO BACK OVER THIS AGAIN!   How well have you grasped what variance analysis is? Go to the **online workbook** and complete Exercises 10.2 to make sure you understand how variance analysis works and what it aims to achieve.

10

Different standards

The different types of standards are shown in Figure 10.1. Setting standards requires thought about expectations and what you want to achieve through the use of standards. You might hope that your favourite sports team will win all its matches, win all the trophies for which they are competing and play perfectly in every match. This would be an ideal standard, the best that can be achieved. However, ideal standards

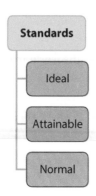

Figure 10.1 The hierarchy of different standards

are unrealistic and unachievable as they would only ever be attained in a perfect world. In the real world, your team will lose some matches and draw others, play poorly yet win and play well but still lose. Therefore, a degree of realism is required in setting standards. **Attainable standards** are those standards that can be achieved with effort and you might set your team the attainable standard of winning one trophy during the coming season: it can be done, but winning that trophy will require focus, concentration and special effort. Alternatively, you might just set a **normal standard**, which is what a business usually achieves. Your team might finish in the middle of the table each year, avoiding relegation yet not playing particularly well or winning any trophies and you might settle for this as this is what is normally achieved. Anything beyond this is a bonus!

In the same way, businesses will set standards based on what they consider to be achievable under normal circumstances, with anything beyond this basic level of achievement being seen as a bonus for the business. Alternatively, directors can set performance targets to encourage staff to put in more effort to generate higher levels of productivity. Staff will be incentivized with the prospect of additional rewards to work towards these attainable standards.

WHY IS THIS RELEVANT TO ME? Different standards

To give you as a business professional an appreciation of the different performance standards that can be set by businesses and what these different performance standards involve

GO BACK OVER THIS AGAIN! Sure you can summarize what ideal, attainable and normal standards are? Go to the **online workbook** and complete Exercises 10.3 to make sure you understand the different standards of performance that can be set.

Setting the standard

We have already considered Anna's cost card, the revenue and costs for one dining chair. This is reproduced below. This cost card can be seen as an example of a standard cost card, the expected costs of each input into each chair along with the revenue that each chair is expected to generate.

Standard cost card: wooden dining chair	£
Variable costs	
Wood	18.00
Glue	0.60
Screws	1.00
Sandpaper	0.40
Direct labour	25.00
Prime cost (total variable cost)	45.00
Rent	6.00
Business rates	1.00
Heating and lighting	0.80
Total production cost of one chair	52.80
Standard selling price	85.00
Standard profit per dining chair	32.20

The standard cost card shows the direct inputs into a product, together with an allocation of fixed overhead to each product. Anna will use this standard cost card to measure actual outcomes and to analyse variances from her expectations. These variances could be positive (**favourable variances**), resulting in lower costs or more revenue than expected, or negative (**unfavourable variances**), arising from higher costs or lower revenue than anticipated. Unfavourable variances are sometimes called **adverse variances** but we will stick with the term unfavourable in this book.

To illustrate how standard costing and variance analysis work, let us consider a comprehensive example (Example 10.1).

10

EXAMPLE 10.1

Anna has completed her first year of dining chair production. Things have gone well and her workshop has made and sold 1,100 chairs over the first 12 months of operations. While happy with her success, Anna is puzzled. She has used her original standard cost card to produce a forecast of the profit she should have made based on production and sales of 1,100 chairs. This calculation is shown in Illustration 10.1. However, her actual results are somewhat different from this forecast and these actual results are shown in Illustration 10.2.

Illustration 10.1 Anna: expected sales income, costs and profit for the first year of trading based on the standard cost card for sales and production of 1,100 dining chairs

	£	£
Sales 1,100 chairs at £85		93,500
Direct materials: wood 1,100 chairs at £18	19,800	
Direct materials: other 1,100 chairs at £2	2,200	
Direct labour 1,100 chairs at £25	27,500	
Total variable costs		49,500
Total contribution (sales – variable costs)		44,000
Fixed costs		
Rent	6,000	
Rates	1,000	
Heating and lighting	800	
Total fixed costs		7,800
Expected profit for the year		36,200

Illustration 10.2 Anna: actual sales income, costs and profit for the first year of trading from the production and sale of 1,100 dining chairs

	£	£
Sales		92,400
Direct materials: wood	19,720	
Direct materials: other	2,200	
Direct labour	28,644	
Total variable costs		50,564
Total contribution (sales – variable costs)		41,836
Fixed costs		
Rent	6,000	
Rates	1,000	
Heating and lighting	600	
Total fixed costs		7,600
Actual profit for the year		34,236

Given that her calculations show that she should have made a profit of £36,200 from the sale of 1,100 dining chairs, Anna is disappointed that her actual income and sales statement above shows a profit of only £34,236, a difference of £1,964. She has asked you to investigate how this difference has arisen.

A comparison of the two statements will enable us to determine where the differences between expected and actual profit lie. A comparison table can be drawn up, as shown in Illustration 10.3.

Illustration 10.3 Anna: comparison of actual and expected sales, expenses and profit for the first year of trading from the production and sale of 1,100 dining chairs

	Actual for 1,100 chairs	Expected for 1,100 chairs	Total variance
	£	£	£
Sales	92,400	93,500	(1,100)
Less:			
Direct materials: wood	19,720	19,800	80
Direct materials: other	2,200	2,200	—
Direct labour	28,644	27,500	(1,144)
Rent	6,000	6,000	—
Rates	1,000	1,000	—
Heating and lighting	600	800	200
Profit for the year	34,236	36,200	(1,964)

What is this comparison telling us? We can summarize our conclusions as follows:

- Sales revenue from the sale of the 1,100 chairs is £1,100 lower than it should have been had Anna sold all her output at £85 per chair.

- The wood for chairs cost £80 less than it should have done based on a wood cost per chair of £18.

- Direct labour cost Anna £1,144 more than it should have done for the production of 1,100 chairs.

- Heating and lighting cost £200 less than expected.

- All other expenses (direct materials: other, rent and rates) cost exactly what Anna had expected them to.

- The positive reductions in spending on wood and heat and light are deducted from the lower sales income and the overspend on direct labour to give the net difference between the two profits of £1,964.

WHY IS THIS RELEVANT TO ME?   Expected costs v. actual costs and calculation of total variances

As a business professional and user of accounting information, you will be expected to understand:

- How standard costs can be used to calculate a statement of expected revenue and costs at any given level of production and sales
- How to compare actual revenue and costs with expected revenue and costs
- How to produce a variance statement comparing actual and expected outcomes
- That each total variance is the difference between the expected revenue and costs of actual production and sales and the actual revenue and costs of actual production and sales

10

NUMERICAL EXERCISES   Quite happy that you could use a standard cost card to:

- Produce a statement of expected costs and revenue

- Compare this to a statement of actual costs and revenue and

- Calculate total variances from this comparison?

Go to the **online workbook** and attempt Numerical exercises 10.1 to make sure you can undertake these tasks.

You explain these differences to Anna, but she is still not satisfied. Why has sales revenue fallen from what she expected it to be and why has so much more been spent on labour than she expected? You ask Anna for her accounting records for the year in order to investigate these differences. Once you have undertaken your investigations, you make the following discoveries:

- The average selling price for each dining chair was not £85, but £84.

- The wood was bought in at a cost of £1.70 per kg instead of the expected cost of £1.80 per kg (Chapter 9, Example 9.15).

- The expected usage of wood for 1,100 chairs should have been 10 kg per chair (Chapter 9, Example 9.15, Step 1) × 1,100 chairs = 11,000 kg whereas actual usage was 11,600 kg.

- Anna expected each chair to take two hours to make and she expected to pay her employees £25 for each chair produced. In fact, she decided to pay her employees an hourly rate of £12.40 instead of a payment for each chair produced.

- The 1,100 chairs should have taken 2,200 hours to produce (1,100 × 2), but her wages records show that her two employees were paid for a total of 2,310 hours.

- Because of the autumn and winter weather being milder than anticipated, the heating costs came in at £200 lower than expected.

How can this information be used to explain the differences between the actual results and the expected results based on the increased levels of production and sales?

10

Direct material price and usage variances

We saw above that the wood for 1,100 chairs cost £19,720 against an expected cost of £19,800 (1,100 × £18 per chair in Anna's original estimates). This gave a total variance of £80. This is a favourable variance as Anna spent £80 less on the wood used in production of her dining chairs. However, our additional investigations revealed two facts relating to the wood used in the chairs. First, the purchase price of wood was £1.70

Figure 10.2 Direct material variances

per kg instead of the expected £1.80 and 11,600 kg of wood were used instead of the expected 11,000 kg. So the material was cheaper than expected but the usage was more than expected. Do these two differences explain the total variance of £80?

Standard costing calls these two differences the **direct material price variance** and the **direct material usage variance** (Figure 10.2). The price variance shows how much of the difference is due to a higher or lower cost for direct materials while the usage variance shows how much of the difference is due to the quantity of material used varying from what the standard says should have been used.

The direct material price variance is calculated in the following way:

	£
11,600 kg of wood should have cost (11,600 × £1.80)	20,880
11,600 kg of wood actually cost	19,720
Direct material price variance	1,160

Does this make sense? The standard cost for wood is £1.80 per kg, whereas Anna paid £1.70 per kg, a difference of £0.10 per kg. Anna's employees used 11,600 kg of wood, so 11,600 × £0.10 = £1,160, the same answer as above.

Is this variance favourable or unfavourable? To answer this question you should ask whether the cost is higher or lower than the standard cost says it should be. In this case, the actual quantity of material used cost less than the standard says it should have done, so this is a favourable variance. Anna has spent less on wood for her chairs than the standard says she should have done.

However, while Anna has spent less on wood for her chairs than her standard says she should have spent, her employees have used more material than anticipated in the standard. Each chair should use 10 kg of wood and so 1,100 chairs should have used 11,000 kg in total. As actual usage was 11,600 kg, Anna's employees have used 600 kg more than expected. The usage variance is calculated as follows:

	kg
1,100 chairs should have used 10 kg of wood × 1,100 chairs	11,000
1,100 chairs actually used	11,600
Direct material usage variance in kg	(600)

	£
Direct material usage variance in kg × standard price per kg (600) × £1.80	(1,080)

10

Again, we can ask whether this variance is favourable or unfavourable. More material has been used than the standard says should have been used, so this variance is unfavourable. Anna's employees have used more wood than they should have done and this has meant that her profit has been reduced as a result of this over usage.

Direct material total variance

How do the price and usage variances relate to the total variance that we calculated earlier? This total variance was a favourable variance of £80 (£19,720 actual cost of the wood compared to £19,800 expected cost of wood for 1,100 chairs). Summarizing our two variances above will give us this £80 total variance thus:

	£	Favourable/ (Unfavourable)
Direct material price variance	1,160	Favourable
Direct material usage variance	(1,080)	(Unfavourable)
Direct material total variance	80	Favourable

WHY IS THIS RELEVANT TO ME?   Direct material price variance, direct material usage variance and direct material total variance

To enable you as a business professional and user of accounting information to:

- Appreciate that variations in both the price and the usage of material should be used to explain the total direct material variance
- Calculate the direct material price variance and direct material usage variance
- Demonstrate that the total direct material variance is the sum of the direct material price variance and the direct material usage variance

10

SUMMARY OF KEY CONCEPTS   Can you state the formulae for the direct material total variance and the two sub-variances, direct material price variance and direct material usage variance? Revise these variances with Summary of key concepts 10.1.

MULTIPLE CHOICE QUESTIONS   Confident that you can calculate the direct material total variance and the sub-variances, direct material price variance and direct material usage variance? Go to the **online workbook** and have a go at Multiple choice questions 10.1 to test out your ability to calculate these figures.

Direct material variances: information and control

We have calculated our variances, but what do they tell Anna and what use can she make of them? Our investigations and calculations show that cheaper material has been purchased and that this has saved Anna money on the material acquired. However, this money seems to have been saved at a cost. While the material is cheaper, more has been used than should have been and this suggests that the wood may not have been of the expected quality. Lower quality materials tend to lead to more wastage as they require more work to shape and fit them into the final product. This additional working has resulted in a higher usage as material was lost in the production process. Anna now needs to conduct further investigations to determine whether this lower cost material really is of lower quality. If so, she should in future demand only material of the requisite quality to minimize wastage and to guarantee the quality of the finished product.

Alternatively, Anna's employees might just have been careless in the way they handled the wood. More careful handling and more thoughtful workmanship might have resulted in less wastage and bigger savings from using this cheaper material. If this is the case, then her workers may need additional advice or training on how to make the best use of the material they are provided with so that wastage is reduced and profits increased. Price and usage variances thus point the way towards the areas that require further investigation to determine the reasons behind these variances and the means to resolve the problems arising.

WHY IS THIS RELEVANT TO ME? Direct material variances: information and control

To enable you as a business professional and user of accounting information to appreciate that:

- Unfavourable material variances are only indicators of problems that require management investigation, intervention and action to correct them
- Management must consider possible reasons for the variances that have arisen, along with potential solutions to ensure that unfavourable material variances do not persist

10

GO BACK OVER THIS AGAIN! Do you think you can identify reasons for changes in the direct material price and usage variances? Go to the **online workbook** and complete Exercises 10.4 to test your skill in this area.

Direct labour rate and efficiency variances

Figure 10.3 Direct labour variances

Our summary table of expected and actual costs in Illustration 10.3 shows that direct labour cost £28,644 against an expected cost to produce 1,100 chairs of £27,500. This is an unfavourable variance as Anna has incurred £1,144 more in direct labour costs than she expected to. Let's look first at the additional information uncovered by our investigations. Anna's employees were paid not for the dining chairs that they produced but at a fixed rate per hour. This hourly rate was £12.40 instead of the expected £12.50 and the actual hours used in producing 1,100 chairs were 2,310 against an expected 2,200. Again, can these two differences explain the total variance of £1,144?

Just as for direct material, we can also calculate sub-variances for direct labour (Figure 10.3). The **direct labour rate variance** performs the same function as the direct material price variance by taking into account the unit cost of each hour paid for production. The **direct labour efficiency variance** looks at the time taken to make the actual goods and compares this with the hours that were expected to be used for that level of production. Where the hours taken are lower than they should have been, workers have been more efficient in producing goods. However, where more hours have been used to make the production than were expected, this will mean that labour has been less efficient than expected. In just the same way, the standard time to work through this chapter might be set at ten hours, but different students will have very different experiences of how long studying this chapter will take them!

Direct labour rate variance is calculated in the following way:

	£
2,310 labour hours should have cost (2,310 × £12.50)	28,875
2,310 labour hours actually cost	28,644
Direct labour rate variance	231

Direct labour cost is lower than the standard says it should be for the hours actually worked, so this variance is favourable. This would be expected as the actual rate at which labour is paid is £12.40 per hour compared to the standard rate of £12.50 per hour. Thus, you could have calculated this variance by taking the difference between the two hourly rates of £0.10 (£12.50 − £12.40) and multiplying this by 2,310 hours to give you the same answer of £231 less than 2,310 standard hours should have cost.

10

Again, while Anna has spent less on labour for her chairs than her standard says she should have done, her workers have also used more hours than they should have spent in making the actual production. Each chair should use two hours of direct labour and so 1,100 chairs should have used 2,200 labour hours. As actual labour hours were 2,310, Anna's employees have taken 110 hours more than they should have done to make the actual production. The direct labour efficiency variance is calculated as follows:

	Hours
1,100 chairs should have used 1,100 × 2 hours	2,200
1,100 chairs actually used	2,310
Direct labour efficiency variance in hours	(110)
	£
Direct labour efficiency variance in hours × standard rate/hour (110) × £12.50	(1,375)

This variance is unfavourable as more labour hours have been used than the standard says should have been used in the production of 1,100 chairs. This means that Anna has incurred more cost and made a lower profit as a result of this increased usage and lower than expected efficiency of the workforce.

Direct labour total variance

The sum of the direct labour rate and direct labour efficiency variances should equal the total variance that we calculated in Illustration 10.3. This total variance was £1,144 (£28,644 actual cost of direct labour compared to a £27,500 expected direct labour cost for 1,100 chairs). Summarizing our two variances will give us this £1,144 total variance thus:

	£	Favourable/(Unfavourable)
Direct labour rate variance	231	Favourable
Direct labour efficiency variance	(1,375)	(Unfavourable)
Direct labour total variance	(1,144)	(Unfavourable)

WHY IS THIS RELEVANT TO ME? Direct labour rate variance, direct labour efficiency variance and direct labour total variance

To enable you as a business professional and user of accounting information to:

- Appreciate that variations in both the rate at which labour is paid and the speed at which employees work should be used to explain the total direct labour variance
- Calculate the direct labour rate variance and the direct labour efficiency variance
- Realize that the total direct labour variance is the sum of the direct labour rate variance and the direct labour efficiency variance

10

SUMMARY OF KEY CONCEPTS   Are you sure you know how to calculate the direct labour total variance and its associated sub-variances, direct labour rate variance and direct labour efficiency variance? Check your understanding of how these variances are calculated with Summary of key concepts 10.2.

MULTIPLE CHOICE QUESTIONS   Quite confident that you can calculate the direct labour total variance and its associated sub-variances, direct labour rate variance and direct labour efficiency variance? Go to the **online workbook** and attempt Multiple choice questions 10.2 to check your ability to calculate these figures.

Direct labour variances: information and control

Again, merely calculating the variances is not enough: these variances have to be investigated and the causes, once identified, used to improve operations with a view to improving efficiency and making additional profit.

It seems that Anna can employ workers at a slightly lower hourly rate than she had expected. This is helpful as a small amount shaved off the labour rate means additional profit for the business. Unfortunately, her employees have taken rather longer than they should have done to make the 1,100 chairs over the course of the year. Why might this be? Under our analysis of the direct material variance (this chapter, Direct material variances: information and control), we suggested that the wood used in the chairs might be of lower quality and hence require more working and shaping before it could be incorporated into the finished chairs. If this were the case, then the additional hours taken in the production of the chairs could be accounted for by this additional working and shaping. Anna should therefore discuss this issue with her employees to find out why these additional hours were worked and whether there is a problem with the wood that is being used. A lower price for direct materials is always welcome, but if this lower price is causing additional costs to be incurred elsewhere in the production cycle, then higher quality materials at a higher price should be acquired. In this way, the higher quality material will pay for itself as lower labour costs will be incurred in making goods and more profit will be generated. Alternatively, Anna's employees might just have worked more slowly to increase the number of hours they worked, thereby increasing their pay. To avoid this problem, Anna needs to think about incentivizing her staff to work to the standard while still producing goods of the expected quality.

10

WHY IS THIS RELEVANT TO ME?   Direct labour variances: information and control

As a business professional and user of accounting information, you should understand:

- That direct labour rate and efficiency variances are only indicators of problems that require management investigation, intervention and action
- How to suggest possible reasons for the labour variances that have arisen, along with potential solutions to ensure that unfavourable variances do not persist

GO BACK OVER THIS AGAIN! How easily can you identify reasons for changes in the direct labour rate and efficiency variances? Go to the **online workbook** and complete Exercises 10.5 to test your skill in this area.

Variable overhead variances

Anna does not incur any variable overheads in her business. If she did incur such overheads, the variances between standard and actual would be calculated in exactly the same way as for direct material and direct labour. First, there would be the variable overhead total variance, the total cost of variable overheads for actual production compared to the standard cost of variable overheads for actual production. This total variance would then be split down into the variable overhead expenditure variance and the variable overhead efficiency variance. To avoid disrupting the flow of our comparison and analysis of Anna's actual and expected profit, further discussion and an example of variable overhead variances is given at the end of this chapter (see Appendix: variable overhead variances).

Fixed overhead expenditure variance

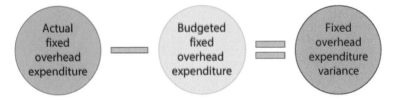

Figure 10.4 Fixed overhead expenditure variance

Fixed overheads are, of course, fixed. Therefore, the only relevant consideration in analysing this variance is the expected expenditure compared to the actual expenditure (Figure 10.4). In Anna's case, she expected her fixed costs to be £7,800 (rent: £6,000, rates: £1,000, heating and lighting: £800) whereas the actual outcome was £7,600 (rent: £6,000, rates: £1,000, heating and lighting: £600). As we discovered from our investigations into Anna's accounting records, £200 less was spent on heating and lighting during the year as a result of milder than expected winter weather. This £200 fixed overhead expenditure variance is favourable as less was spent on fixed costs than was expected.

10

SUMMARY OF KEY CONCEPTS Reckon you can calculate the fixed overhead expenditure variance? Check your understanding of how this variance is calculated with Summary of key concepts 10.4.

Fixed overhead expenditure variance: information and control

As fixed overheads are fixed, businesses usually experience only small variations between expected and actual fixed costs. Organizations will not normally investigate fixed overhead variances in depth. There is little that can be done to reduce fixed costs that are mostly imposed from outside the business. On the other hand, since material, labour and variable overheads are driven directly by internal business activity, time will be spent on investigating these variances as much more can be done to reduce unfavourable variances arising from operations under the direct control of management.

WHY IS THIS RELEVANT TO ME? Fixed overhead expenditure variance

As a business professional and user of accounting information, you should appreciate that:

- Fixed overhead expenditure variance is the difference between total budgeted fixed overhead expenditure and actual fixed overhead expenditure
- Fixed overheads are largely outside the control of businesses
- Management time and effort will therefore focus upon investigating unfavourable material, labour and variable overhead variances as businesses can take action to control and eliminate or exploit these variances

Sales variances

10

Our final variances relate to income, the sales variances.

Sales price variance

The first of these is the sales price variance (Figure 10.5). Anna's expectation was that she would sell her dining chairs for £85 each. However, further investigation revealed that her average selling price was only £84, a reduction of £1 per chair sold. Anna sold 1,100 chairs, so her sales price variance was $1,100 \times £1 = £1,100$. This is unfavourable as she received less income per chair than budgeted.

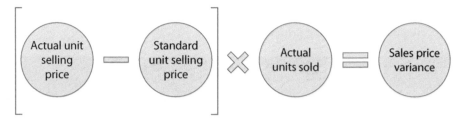

Figure 10.5 Sales price variance

Sales volume variance

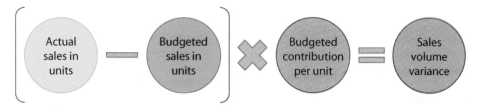

Figure 10.6 Sales volume variance

We have now explained all the variances between Anna's expected and actual profit from the sale of 1,100 chairs as shown in Illustration 10.3, but there is one more variance we need to consider. Anna's original expectation was that she would sell 1,000 chairs and make a profit of £32,200. Her actual results show that she sold 1,100 chairs and made a profit of £34,236. The additional sales of 100 chairs give rise to another variance, the **sales volume variance** (Figure 10.6). This variance takes the additional standard contribution from each sale and multiplies this by the additional number of units sold to reflect the increased contribution arising from higher sales. This is logical as each additional sale will increase revenue by the selling price of one unit, but will also increase variable costs by the standard cost of direct material, direct labour and variable overhead for each additional unit of production and sales. Therefore, the contribution, the selling price less the variable costs, is used in this calculation. This variance is calculated as follows:

	Units
Actual units sold	1,100
Budgeted sales in units	1,000
Sales volume variance	100
	£
Sales volume variance at standard contribution $100 \times £40$	4,000

Is this variance favourable or unfavourable? As more sales have been made and more contribution earned, this is a favourable variance.

Anna will want to know why she is selling more chairs than budgeted and so she will investigate this increase with a view to selling even more. Similarly, she will also be keen to find out why her selling price is lower than budgeted and what factors in the market are pushing her selling price down.

WHY IS THIS RELEVANT TO ME? Sales price variance and sales volume variance

To enable you as a business professional and user of accounting information to:

- Appreciate that variations in the selling price and in the volume of sales will have an impact upon the actual profit made compared to the expected profit
- Calculate the sales price variance and sales volume variances

SUMMARY OF KEY CONCEPTS Are you sure you know how to calculate the sales price variance and the sales volume variance? Check your understanding of how these variances are calculated with Summary of key concepts 10.5.

MULTIPLE CHOICE QUESTIONS Quite confident that you can calculate the sales price variance and the sales volume variance? Go to the **online workbook** and attempt Multiple choice questions 10.3 to check your ability to calculate these figures.

Variances: summary

We can now summarize all our variances and reconcile Anna's forecast to her actual profit as follows. Anna's original expectation was that she would sell 1,000 dining chairs at £85 each and generate a profit of £32,200 so our starting point is this original expected profit.

	Unfavourable £	Favourable £	Profit £
Expected profit from selling 1,000 chairs at £85			32,200
Sales price variance	(1,100)		
Sales volume variance		4,000	
Direct material price variance		1,160	
Direct material usage variance	(1,080)		
Direct labour rate variance		231	
Direct labour efficiency variance	(1,375)		
Fixed overhead expenditure variance		200	
Total variances	(3,555)	5,591	
Add: favourable variances			5,591
Deduct: unfavourable variances			(3,555)
Actual profit for the year			34,236

10

WHY IS THIS RELEVANT TO ME? Summary of variances and reconciliation of expected to actual profit

To enable you as a business professional and user of accounting information to:

- Present all your variances in summary form to explain the difference between expected and actual profit

---

NUMERICAL EXERCISES How confident do you feel about handling extensive variance analysis questions? Go to the **online workbook** and have a go at Numerical exercises 10.2 to see how effectively you have absorbed the lessons of this chapter and how well you understand standard costing and variance analysis.

SHOW ME HOW TO DO IT This chapter has involved a lot of tricky calculations and ideas. View Video presentation 10.1 in the **online workbook** to reinforce your knowledge of how standard costing and variance analysis is undertaken.

Standard costing: limitations

Standard costing is a useful technique in comparing expected with actual financial performance. Where variances arise, these can be investigated to determine their causes and to identify ways in which unfavourable variances can be reduced and favourable variances maintained or enhanced. While setting standards encourages improvement and change for the better over time, standard costing also suffers from the following limitations:

- You will agree, I am sure, that this is a very complicated system and that this complexity can be discouraging when you first come across standard costing and variance analysis.

- It is also a time consuming system: a great deal of time will be needed to gather information from which to set the standards, to collect data from which to monitor standards against actual performance and to produce and evaluate variances.

- Time will also be needed to update standards for changes in costs owing to rising or falling material prices, wage costs, changes in overheads and selling prices.

- The information produced by variance analysis can be extensive and management may be overwhelmed by the volume of data presented to them.

- Standard costing systems tend to be rigid and inflexible: lack of flexibility should be avoided in the modern, ever changing business environment.

- However, modern computer systems should be able to assist management with the production of standard costs and variance analysis and in highlighting those

10

variances that indicate that operations are out of control rather than within set tolerance limits. Profitability improvement depends upon careful cost control and such cost control is one of the key functions of business managers.

Given these limitations, it is probably not surprising to find that small and medium sized companies make no use of standard costing variance analysis. Give me an example 10.2 describes this failure to adopt this approach.

GIVE ME AN EXAMPLE 10.2 Adoption of standard costing variance analysis by small and medium sized companies in the UK

Management accounting practices of UK small–medium-sized enterprises published in July 2013 investigated the management accounting techniques and practices used by small and medium sized enterprises. While all the organizations surveyed undertook product costing, break-even analysis and working capital measures, none of the respondents engaged in standard cost variance analysis. However, the researchers considered that the failure to use this technique was appropriate for small and medium sized enterprises on cost benefit grounds as the costs of obtaining the information were substantial while the benefits gained were very limited.

Source: www.cimaglobal.com

Appendix: variable overhead variances

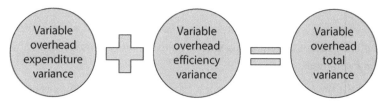

Figure 10.7 Variable overhead variances

Variable overheads are absorbed into products on the basis of the number of hours of activity incurred to produce one unit of production. The standard cost for variable overheads will estimate the number of hours products take to produce on either a labour or machine hour basis (see Chapter 8, Absorption costing: overhead allocation, to refresh your memory on how absorption cost bases work) and then allocate the variable overhead to each product on the basis of the standard number of hours required to produce one unit multiplied by the standard variable overhead cost per hour.

Variable overhead variance calculations divide the total variance into variable overhead expenditure and variable overhead efficiency variances (Figure 10.7), in much the same way that the total direct labour variance is divided into labour rate and labour efficiency variances. The expenditure variance measures the difference between the variable overhead that should have been incurred for the level of production achieved and the actual expenditure paid. The variable overhead efficiency variance compares the difference between the actual hours taken to produce the actual production and the standard hours that actual production would have been expected to take. Think about how these variances are calculated in Example 10.2.

EXAMPLE 10.2

The Ultimate Chef Company manufactures food processors. Variable overhead incurred in the production of each food processor is set at 2½ hours at £6 per hour. During September, 1,000 food processors were produced. The employees of the Ultimate Chef Company were paid for 2,450 hours. The variable overhead cost for September was £14,540. Calculate:

- The variable overhead total variance
- The variable overhead expenditure variance
- The variable overhead efficiency variance

State whether each variance is favourable or unfavourable.

Variable overhead total variance

This is the difference between what the actual production should have cost and what it did cost.

	£
1,000 food processors should have cost 1,000 × 2½ hours × £6	15,000
1,000 food processors actually cost	14,540
Variable overhead total variance	460

The variable overhead total variance is favourable as the actual variable overhead cost is lower than the expected cost for the given level of production.

Variable overhead expenditure variance

This is what the variable overhead should have cost compared with what it did cost for the actual hours worked.

	£
2,450 hours should have cost (2,450 × £6.00)	14,700
2,450 hours actually cost	14,540
Variable overhead expenditure variance	160

The variable overhead expenditure variance is favourable as less cost was incurred than expected for the actual number of hours used in production.

Variable overhead efficiency variance

This is how many hours should have been worked and how many were actually worked for the actual level of production.

	Hours
1,000 food processors should have used 1,000 × 2½ hours	2,500
1,000 food processors actually used	2,450
Variable overhead efficiency variance in hours	50
	£
Variable overhead efficiency variance in hours × standard rate/hour 50 × £6.00	300

The efficiency variance is favourable as fewer hours were used than expected for the level of production achieved.

The variable overhead expenditure variance and the variable overhead efficiency variance can be summarized as follows to give the variable overhead total variance:

	£	Favourable/(Unfavourable)
Variable overhead expenditure variance	160	Favourable
Variable overhead efficiency variance	300	Favourable
Variable overhead total variance	460	Favourable

WHY IS THIS RELEVANT TO ME? Variable overhead expenditure variance, variable overhead efficiency variance and variable overhead total variance

As a business professional and user of accounting information, you should now:

- Appreciate that variations in both the variable overhead expenditure and the speed of working should be used to explain the variable overhead total variance
- Be able to calculate the variable overhead total variance, variable overhead expenditure variance and variable overhead efficiency variance
- Understand that the variable overhead total variance is the sum of the variable overhead expenditure variance and the variable overhead efficiency variance

10

SUMMARY OF KEY CONCEPTS Are you sure you know how to calculate the variable overhead total variance and the associated sub-variances, variable overhead expenditure variance and variable overhead efficiency variance? Check your understanding of how these variances are calculated with Summary of key concepts 10.3.

MULTIPLE CHOICE QUESTIONS Happy that you can calculate the variable overhead total variance and its associated variances, variable overhead expenditure and variable overhead efficiency variances? Go to the **online workbook** and attempt Multiple choice questions 10.4 to check your ability to calculate these figures.

CHAPTER SUMMARY

You should now have learnt that:

- Selling price, materials, labour, direct expenses, variable overhead and fixed overhead are the components that make up a standard cost

- Standard cost is an expected rather than an actual cost

- Standard costs are used in the planning and evaluation of operations

- Total variances between what should have been achieved and what was achieved explain the difference between actual and expected profits

- Variance analysis splits total variances into their constituent sub-variances arising from:
  - Price (material), rate (labour) and expenditure (variable overhead) and
  - Usage (material) and efficiency (labour and variable overhead)

- Sales variances are split into sales price and sales volume variances

- Variances help identify problems requiring further investigation and analysis to assist in the control of operations

QUICK REVISION Test your knowledge with the online flashcards in Summary of key concepts and attempt the Multiple choice questions, all in the **online workbook**. www.oup.com/uk/scott_business3e/

END-OF-CHAPTER QUESTIONS

Solutions to these questions can be found at the back of the book from page 506.

❯ DEVELOP YOUR UNDERSTANDING

> **Question 10.1**

There are 30 apple trees in the orchard attached to Bill's farm. Bill reckons that each tree will be given five doses of fertilizer each year at a cost of £4 per tree and that 10 hours of labour will be required to pick the apples from and prune each tree. Workers are paid £7.50 per hour.

At the end of the apple picking season, Bill calculates that the 30 trees only received four doses of fertilizer, although these cost £4.50 for each tree, and that the picking and pruning was undertaken at a cost of £8 per hour for 270 hours of labour.

Required

Calculate:

(a) The total expected costs of the orchard for the past year

(b) The actual total costs of the orchard for the past year

(c) Material total, price and usage variances

(d) Labour total, rate and efficiency variances

State whether the variances are favourable or unfavourable.

⟩ Question 10.2

Fred bakes cakes. His budget indicates that he will produce and sell 1,000 cakes during March at a selling price of £15 each. At the end of March he calculates that his selling price was £15.50 for each cake produced and sold and that he has generated £14,725 in sales. His standard cost card for each cake shows that his variable cost of production is £6 per cake.

Required

Calculate for Fred for March:

(a) The sales price variance

(b) The sales volume variance

State whether the variances are favourable or unfavourable. Assuming that Fred's actual production costs are £6 per cake, prove that the sales price and sales volume variances explain fully his additional contribution for March.

⟩⟩ TAKE IT FURTHER

⟩⟩ Question 10.3

Sanguinary Services carries out blood tests for local hospitals, surgeries and doctors. The standard cost card for each blood test is given below.

	£
Chemicals used in blood tests: 10 millilitres at 50 pence/ml	5.00
Laboratory worker: 15 minutes at £16 per hour	4.00
Fixed overhead of the testing centre	2.00
Total cost	11.00
Charge for each blood test	15.00
Standard profit per blood test	4.00

The centre has fixed overheads of £72,000 per annum and plans to carry out 36,000 blood tests every year at the rate of 3,000 tests per month.

10

In April, the following results were recorded:

	Number
Blood tests carried out	3,600

	£
Chemicals used in blood tests: 33,750 millilitres at 48 pence/ml	16,200
Laboratory workers: 925 hours at £16.20 per hour	14,985
Fixed overhead of the testing centre	7,500
Total cost	38,685
Charge for each blood test 3,600 at £15.50	55,800
Profit for April	17,115

Required

(a) Calculate the profit that the centre expected to make in April, based on the original fore-cast of 3,000 blood tests in the month.

(b) Calculate the following, stating whether each variance is favourable or unfavourable:

- Sales volume variance
- Sales price variance
- Direct material total variance
- Direct material price variance
- Direct material usage variance
- Direct labour total variance
- Direct labour rate variance
- Direct labour efficiency variance
- Fixed overhead expenditure variance

(c) Prepare a statement reconciling the expected profit to the actual profit for April.

» Question 10.4

10

Smashers Tennis Club runs coaching courses for its junior members. Each course lasts for ten weeks and is priced at £70 for each junior member. Smashers expects each course to attract 12 junior members. Each course is allocated 20 tennis balls for each participating junior at an expected cost of £10 for 20 balls. A professionally qualified tennis coach undertakes each hour-long coaching session over the ten weeks at a cost of £30 per hour.

The club administrator is reviewing the costs and income for the latest junior coaching course and she is trying to understand why the surplus from the course is £438 instead of £420. She tells you that the course actually attracted 16 juniors instead of the 12 expected and that a total of 400 balls had been allocated to and used by juniors on the course. Balls for the latest coaching course had cost 60 pence each. The coach had received an increase in her hourly rate to £33 per hour. The price for each course had been reduced by 10% on the original price in order to attract additional participants.

Required

(a) Calculate the original expected surplus from the coaching course.

(b) Calculate the expected surplus from the coaching course given that 16 juniors were enrolled.

(c) Calculate the actual income and costs for the course.

(d) Calculate variances for income and expenditure and present these in tabular form to reconcile the original expected surplus to the actual surplus.

» Question 10.5

Vijay Manufacturing produces garden gnomes. The standard cost card for garden gnomes is as follows:

	£
Plastic: 2 kg at £2.25 per kg	4.50
Labour: 0.5 hours at £8 per hour	4.00
Variable overhead: 4 machine hours at £0.75 per hour	3.00
Fixed overhead	1.00
Total cost	12.50
Selling price to Plastic Gnome Painters Limited	15.00
Standard profit per garden gnome	2.50

Fixed overheads total £24,000 and are allocated to production on the basis that 24,000 gnomes will be produced each year, 2,000 each month.

Vijay is reviewing the actual production and sales for the month of June. The weather has been wet and garden gnome sales have fallen from their normal levels. Consequently, the company has had to reduce the selling price in June to £14 per gnome in order to keep production and sales moving. Production and sales for the month were 1,800 gnomes. The input price per kg of plastic was £2.50 as a result of a sharp rise in the oil price but, because of reduced wastage and careful material handling, only 3,500 kg of plastic were used in June. Owing to the high level of unemployment in the area, Vijay has been able to pay his employees at the rate of £7.50 per hour. Total labour hours for the month were 950. Total machine hours for the month were 7,000 and the fixed and variable overheads totalled £1,600 and £5,500 respectively. Vijay has been trying to understand why his profit has fallen from its expected level for the month and has asked for your help. You are meeting him later on today to discuss his figures and to show him how his expected profit has fallen to the actual profit for the month.

10

Required

Draft figures for your meeting later on today with Vijay. Your figures should include:

(a) Calculations to show the profit Vijay expected to make from the production and sale of 2,000 garden gnomes in the month of June.

(b) Calculations to show the profit Vijay might have expected to make from the production and sale of 1,800 garden gnomes for the month of June.

(c) Calculations to show the profit Vijay actually did make for the month of June.

(d) A reconciliation statement showing all the necessary favourable and unfavourable variances to explain the difference between the expected profit for June calculated in (a) and the actual profit calculated in (c).

11 Budgeting

LEARNING OUTCOMES

Once you have read this chapter and worked through the questions and examples in both this chapter and the online workbook, you should be able to:

- Discuss the ways in which budgets perform planning, communicating, coordinating, motivating and control functions

- Prepare budgeted monthly statements of profit or loss for an entity

- Determine the timing of cash inflows and outflows from budgeted income and expenditure

- Prepare a month-by-month cash budget for an entity

- Draw up a budgeted statement of financial position at the end of a projected accounting period

- Undertake comparisons between budgeted and actual income and expenditure to highlight variances in expected and actual financial performance

- Undertake sensitivity analysis to assess the effect that any changes in budget assumptions will have

Introduction

The word budget is all around us, every day. There are constant reminders of the national budget, individuals' budgets and business budgets. You yourself may have drawn up a budget for what you expected to spend during your first year at university. This budget might have been quite basic to start with, but, as you thought more about the costs you would be likely to incur, your budget would have been refined and become a more realistic means of planning your anticipated expenditure and its timing. However, budgeting can occur at a much simpler level. When you go out for the evening, the amount of money you take with you is your budget for that evening. In both cases, actual expenditure is likely to be very different from your original plan due to unforeseen costs—an expensive book or field trip for your course or a taxi home when you missed the last bus. This does not mean that the exercise was not worthwhile: planning ahead is important for both individuals and business organizations. Experience helps us to refine our future budgets so that the actual outcomes gradually become closer to our budgeted expectations.

What is budgeting?

For business people, a budget is the expression of a plan in money terms. That plan is a prediction of future income, expenditure, cash inflows and cash outflows. Once each stage of the plan is completed, then the actual results can be compared to expectations to determine whether actual outcomes are better, worse or the same as anticipated. As we saw in Chapter 10 on standard costing, such comparisons are a means of controlling an organization's operations and taking action to reduce or eliminate unfavourable divergences from the plan while finding out the ways in which better than expected performance can be maintained and built upon.

WHY IS THIS RELEVANT TO ME?   What is budgeting?

As a business professional and user of accounting information:

- You need to appreciate that all businesses undertake budgeting
- You will be expected to take part in the annual budgeting process no matter what your particular business specialism is
- Building an awareness of what budgeting is, what it involves and how to budget in practice will be essential business knowledge

11

SUMMARY OF KEY CONCEPTS   Can you define budgeting? Revise the definition with Summary of key concepts 11.1.

Give me an example 11.1 highlights the importance accorded to budgeting and forecasting by the business community.

Budget objectives and the budgeting process

Everyone has objectives, both individuals and organizations. It is not enough to have a vague hope that everything will work out and that objectives will be achieved without any planning, positive actions and a great deal of hard work being undertaken. Thus, individuals and organizations have to decide how they will achieve their objectives through careful planning on a step-by-step basis. A well-known phrase among university tutors is 'failing to plan is planning to fail'. This is just as true when you are writing an essay as it is when making projections for what a business will achieve in the next 12 months.

Budgets and the budgeting process thus assist organizations to focus upon achieving and the means to achieve their objectives in the ways shown in Table 11.1.

Table 11.1 The objectives of the budgeting process

Planning	Budgeting forces entities to look ahead and plan. Planning helps organizations think about the future and what they want to achieve, as well as helping them anticipate problems to determine how these will be overcome.
Communication	The directors will have plans to achieve certain objectives. However, if they do not tell everyone else involved in the organization about those objectives, then they will not be achieved. Budgets communicate information to those persons and departments involved in achieving objectives to tell them what level of performance they have to attain to fulfil their part in reaching the desired goal.
Coordination and integration	Different departments have to work together to achieve objectives. The directors have to tell marketing what level of sales they need to achieve to reach the profit goal. Marketing then have to liaise with production to make sure that production can produce this number of goods and to the required timescale. Production has to make sure that purchasing is buying in the necessary raw materials to enable production to take place on schedule while personnel have to recruit the necessary workers to make the goods. Budgets thus coordinate and integrate business activities to give the organization the best chance of achieving its goals.
Control	Budgeting enables an organization to control its activities and check its progress towards achieving objectives by regularly comparing actual results with budgeted outcomes. Differences can then be investigated and action taken either to bring operations back on track or to exploit favourable trends further.
Responsibility	Responsibility for different parts of the budget is delegated to individual managers. One person alone cannot achieve everything on their own, so various managers work as part of a team, each with their own responsibility for hitting the targets assigned to them in the budget. These managers are then assessed and rewarded on the basis of their ability to meet their agreed objectives. Breaking down one big task into various smaller tasks and then making several managers responsible for achieving each of these smaller targets is a very good way to get things done.
Motivation	Budgets are used as motivating devices. Something too easy is not motivating and managers need to be challenged to achieve more. In the same way, your degree is challenging so that achieving your qualification motivates you and makes it worthwhile. As an incentive to achieve challenging budget targets, managers will be rewarded with bonuses. However, it is important to make sure that the targets are not completely unrealistic as impossible targets will result in managers giving up before they have even started.

11

SUMMARY OF KEY CONCEPTS   Certain you can summarize the objectives of budgeting and the budgeting process? Revise these objectives with Summary of key concepts 11.2.

GO BACK OVER THIS AGAIN!   Convinced you understand the objectives of budgeting and the budgeting process? Go to the **online workbook** and attempt Exercises 11.1 to make sure you have fully grasped the principles.

GO BACK OVER THIS AGAIN!   Do you really understand how the budgeting objectives and the budgeting process work in practice? Go to the **online workbook** Exercises 11.2 and consider the scenario there to see how budgeting objectives and the budgeting process operate in everyday life.

Budgeting: a comprehensive example

Now that we have defined a budget and considered what the organizational objectives in preparing budgets are, let's look in detail at the process of actually setting a budget through a practical example. This process involves several steps, which we will think about one by one.

Anna is considering the expansion of her business. She is planning to move her operations to a bigger workshop and has asked her bank for a loan with which to finance this expansion. In connection with her application for the loan, the bank has asked Anna to produce a budget covering sales, costs and cash flows for the next 12 months, together with a budgeted statement of financial position at the end of those 12 months. Anna has made a start on her projections and has produced information for the first three months of the next financial year. However, she is finding budgeting difficult and has asked for your assistance in helping her to complete the remainder of the required information.

Step 1: setting the strategy and deciding on selling prices

Anna first has to decide what she wants to achieve and whether there are any obstacles she must overcome or which will stand in the way of her achieving her goals. She wants to expand, but she feels that the lack of finance is holding her back. However, her products are selling well and her customers are pleased with the quality of her output. Will she be able to finance her proposed expansion from current operations if the bank is not willing to help her? Budgeting will help her to answer this question and Figure 11.1 illustrates the first step in the budgeting process.

11

Figure 11.1 Budgeting step 1: set the strategy and the selling prices

Her first decision will be to set her selling prices. Should she raise these, leave them at the same level or reduce the selling prices of each product? She has gone back to the costings for her three products that she presented in Chapter 9 (Limiting factor (key factor) analysis). These are reproduced in Illustration 11.1. Can she justify raising her selling prices? This will first depend on whether her costs are rising.

Illustration 11.1 Anna: selling prices and variable costs for dining chairs, coffee tables and kitchen cabinets

	Dining chairs	Coffee tables	Kitchen cabinets
	£	£	£
Selling price	85.00	50.00	80.00
Materials: wood	(18.00)	(12.60)	(10.80)
Materials: other	(2.00)	(5.40)	(9.20)
Direct labour	(25.00)	(18.00)	(30.00)
Contribution	40.00	14.00	30.00

Anna tells you that she has discussed the price of wood and other materials with her suppliers. They have reassured her that there are no price rises or material shortages anticipated in the next 12 months. This tells Anna that there will be no supply difficulties which will need to be planned for over the course of the coming year. At the same time she now knows that there are no expected increases in the cost of inputs to her products which would need to be built into her selling prices in order to pass these cost increases on to her customers.

Her workforce is loyal and they have stated that they have no intention of leaving in the next 12 months. Anna has looked into the current rates she is paying her workers and these are in line with market rates. The furniture makers' trade association informs her that labour costs are likely to remain steady over the course of the next year. Again, Anna now knows that she should not encounter any shortages of labour or pay rises which she would have to build into her budget for the coming year.

As her direct costs should remain unchanged for the next 12 months, it will be difficult for Anna to change her selling prices. She is happy with the levels of profit her sales are currently generating and, as she does not want to lose her customers through pitching her selling prices too high, she decides to leave the selling prices of each of her three products at the same level for the next 12 months.

11

WHY IS THIS RELEVANT TO ME?   Setting the strategy

To enable you as a business professional and user of accounting information to appreciate that:

- Before the detailed budgeting process can begin, businesses have to decide what their objectives and strategy are
- The strategy is directly responsible for the budgeted income and costs, cash inflows and cash outflows
- Setting targets for sales, profits or market share will determine the selling prices of products and services and these targets in turn will feed into the costs of providing those products and services

Step 2: the sales budget

Now that the pricing decision and the supply of materials and labour are clear, Anna's next thoughts will focus on her sales. Once decisions on strategy and prices have been made, this is exactly the right place to start the budgeting process as so many other costs and cash flows depend upon the volume of sales achieved. As we discovered in Chapters 8 and 9, Anna's direct costs for wood, other materials and labour will depend directly upon the number of products she sells: the more products she makes and sells, the more direct materials and direct labour cost she will incur. However, she will be unable to determine her material and labour budgets until she has set her sales budget in terms of units produced and sold. Figure 11.2 outlines this process.

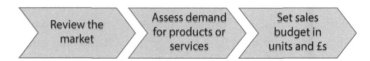

Figure 11.2 Budgeting step 2: setting the sales budget

Anna has been talking to her customers to see how many of her products they propose buying in the near future. She has managed to determine that orders from customers for the first three months of the year are likely to be as shown in Illustration 11.2.

Illustration 11.2 Anna: budgeted sales in units of product for January, February and March

	January	February	March	Total
	number	number	number	number
Dining chairs	150	200	350	700
Coffee tables	100	250	300	650
Kitchen cabinets	300	350	400	1,050

From these budgeted units of sales, Anna can now produce a sales budget in £s. This sales budget is presented in Illustration 11.3.

Illustration 11.3 Anna: budgeted sales in £s for January, February and March

	January	February	March	Total
	£	£	£	£
Dining chairs	12,750	17,000	29,750	59,500
Coffee tables	5,000	12,500	15,000	32,500
Kitchen cabinets	24,000	28,000	32,000	84,000
Total sales for month	41,750	57,500	76,750	176,000

How did Anna arrive at the above figures? Monthly sales for each product are calculated by multiplying the monthly expected sales in units in Illustration 11.2 by the selling price for each product in Illustration 11.1. Thus, Anna expects to sell 150 dining chairs in January at a selling price of £85. This gives her a sales figure of $150 \times £85 = £12,750$ for this product line in January.

WHY IS THIS RELEVANT TO ME? The sales budget

To enable you as a business professional and user of accounting information to understand:

- How a sales budget is prepared
- The influence of projected sales on the direct costs of making and selling products and providing services

NUMERICAL EXERCISES Totally confident you can produce a sales budget? Work your way through the figures in Illustrations 11.1–11.3 again to confirm your understanding of how the monthly sales figures for each product were calculated and then go to the **online workbook** and attempt Numerical exercises 11.1 to make sure you can produce a sales budget from monthly budgeted sales units and budgeted selling prices.

Step 3: calculate the direct costs of budgeted sales

Now that the sales budget has been set, the direct costs associated with those sales can be calculated. As already noted, direct costs are dependent upon the level of sales. In Anna's case, the more of each product her workshop makes, the more wood will be used, the more other materials will be consumed and the more direct labour will be needed. Figure 11.3 outlines this process.

11

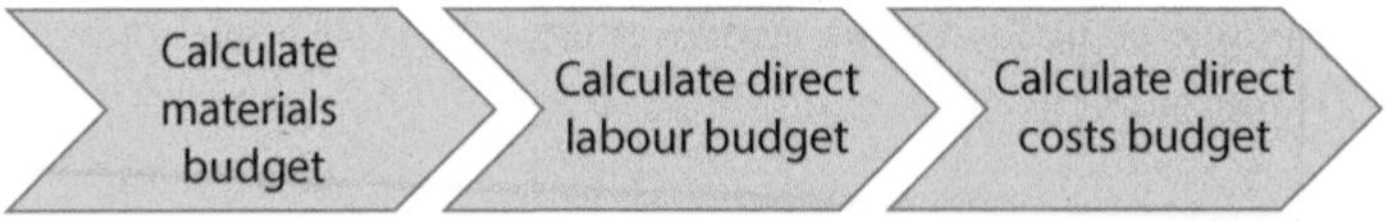

Figure 11.3 Budgeting step 3: setting the direct costs budget

Budgeted sales income for each month was calculated by multiplying the selling price by the number of units produced and sold. In the same way, budgeted direct costs are found by multiplying the direct materials and direct labour costs per product by the number of units of sales. This gives the budgeted material costs for wood shown in Illustration 11.4.

Illustration 11.4 Anna: budgeted costs for wood in January, February and March

	January	February	March	Total
Direct materials: wood	£	£	£	£
Dining chairs	2,700	3,600	6,300	12,600
Coffee tables	1,260	3,150	3,780	8,190
Kitchen cabinets	3,240	3,780	4,320	11,340
Total direct materials (wood) for month	7,200	10,530	14,400	32,130

Illustration 11.2 tells us that Anna expects to sell 150 dining chairs in the month of January, while Illustration 11.1 shows us that the wood for each chair costs £18.00; 150 chairs × £18.00 gives a total cost of wood for dining chairs in January of £2,700. Using the budgeted sales in Illustration 11.2 for each product and the product costs for wood in Illustration 11.1, check the calculation of the budgeted materials costs for wood in Illustration 11.4 to reinforce your understanding of how we arrived at these costs.

In the same way and using the information in Illustrations 11.1 and 11.2, the budgeted costs for other materials and direct labour for each product for each month have been calculated in Illustrations 11.5 and 11.6. Other materials used in dining chairs amount to £2 per chair. Multiplying this cost of £2 per chair by the 150 chairs Anna expects to sell in January gives us a budgeted cost for other materials of £300 in that month. Similarly, labour costs of £25 per dining chair are multiplied by the 150 chairs budgeted for January to give a total budgeted labour cost for dining chairs in that month of £3,750.

Illustration 11.5 Anna: budgeted costs for other materials in January, February and March

	January	February	March	Total
Direct materials: other	£	£	£	£
Dining chairs	300	400	700	1,400
Coffee tables	540	1,350	1,620	3,510
Kitchen cabinets	2,760	3,220	3,680	9,660
Total direct materials (other) for month	3,600	4,970	6,000	14,570

Illustration 11.6 Anna: budgeted costs for direct labour in January, February and March

Direct labour	January £	February £	March £	Total £
Dining chairs	3,750	5,000	8,750	17,500
Coffee tables	1,800	4,500	5,400	11,700
Kitchen cabinets	9,000	10,500	12,000	31,500
Total direct labour for month	14,550	20,000	26,150	60,700

WHY IS THIS RELEVANT TO ME?   The direct costs of budgeted sales

To provide you as a business professional and user of accounting information with the knowledge and techniques to:

• Prepare budgets for direct costs based on budgeted sales

• Understand how direct cost budgets are compiled

NUMERICAL EXERCISES   Think you can produce a direct costs budget for materials and labour? Work your way through the figures in Illustrations 11.1, 11.2 and 11.4–11.6 again to confirm your understanding of how we arrived at the budgeted materials and labour cost figures for each product and then go to the **online workbook** and attempt Numerical exercises 11.2 to see if you can produce a direct materials and direct labour budget from monthly budgeted sales units and budgeted cost prices per unit.

Step 4: set the budget for fixed costs

The fixed costs budget will be different for every organization and will depend upon what sort of resources are consumed by each entity, as shown in Figure 11.4.

Anna expects her fixed costs and her capital expenditure for the next three months to be as follows:

• Rent on the new workshop of £3,000 will be paid in January to cover the months of January, February and March.

• New machinery and tools will cost £15,000 and will be delivered and paid for in January. These new non-current assets will have an expected useful life of five years and will be depreciated on the straight line basis.

• Anna anticipates that she will receive and pay an electricity bill in March covering the period 1 January to 15 March. She expects that this bill will be for around £1,500. Anna estimates that the new workshop will use a further £300 of electricity

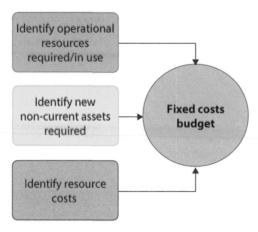

Figure 11.4 Budgeting step 4: setting the fixed costs budget

between 16 and 31 March. Each month of operation should be allocated an equal amount of electricity cost.

- An invoice for business rates of £1,200 on the new workshop will be received and paid on 15 February. These rates will cover the six-month period to 30 June.

- The insurance company requires a payment of £1,500 on 1 January to cover all insurance costs for the whole year to 31 December.

Step 5: draw up the budgeted monthly statement of profit or loss

Anna can now draw up her budgeted monthly statement of profit or loss from the information gathered together in steps 1–4 (Figure 11.5). This budgeted statement of profit or loss is presented in Illustration 11.7.

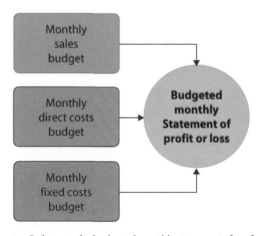

Figure 11.5 Budgeting step 5: draw up the budgeted monthly statement of profit or loss

Illustration 11.7 Anna: budgeted statement of profit or loss for January, February and March

	January	February	March	Total	Note
	£	£	£	£	
Sales	41,750	57,500	76,750	176,000	1
Cost of sales					
Direct material: wood	7,200	10,530	14,400	32,130	2
Direct material: other	3,600	4,970	6,000	14,570	3
Direct labour	14,550	20,000	26,150	60,700	4
Cost of sales	25,350	35,500	46,550	107,400	
Gross profit (sales – cost of sales)	16,400	22,000	30,200	68,600	
Expenses					
Rent	1,000	1,000	1,000	3,000	5
Rates	200	200	200	600	6
Machinery and tools depreciation	250	250	250	750	7
Electricity	600	600	600	1,800	8
Insurance	125	125	125	375	9
Net profit (gross profit – expenses)	14,225	19,825	28,025	62,075	

How did Anna calculate the budgeted results in Illustration 11.7? The following notes will help you understand how she determined the numbers in her budgeted statement of profit or loss:

1. The monthly sales are derived from Illustration 11.3.

2. Similarly, the direct materials for wood are presented in Illustration 11.4.

3. Figures for other direct materials are given in Illustration 11.5.

4. Direct labour costs were calculated in Illustration 11.6. Check back to Illustrations 11.3–11.6 to make sure that the numbers in the budgeted statement of profit or loss have been correctly transferred from these workings.

5. While the rent of £3,000 was paid in January, this payment relates to three months, so the total expense is spread equally over the three months to which it relates. If you are unsure of why this expense is presented in this way, you should revise this allocation of costs in Chapter 3 (The accruals basis of accounting).

6. In the same way, the rates payment relates to the six months from January to June. The total cost of £1,200 is therefore divided by six months and £200 allocated as the rates cost to each month. The total cost for rates for the three months amounts to £600. How is the remaining £600 (£1,200 paid – £600 charged to the statement of profit or loss) classified in the accounts? Chapter 3 (Prepayments and accruals) covers the subject of prepayments—expenses paid in advance that belong to a future accounting period.

7. Depreciation was another expense we tackled in Chapter 3 (Depreciation). The total cost of £15,000 is divided by five years, giving an annual depreciation charge

on these new assets of £3,000. As there are 12 months in a year, a monthly depreciation charge of £3,000 ÷ 12 = £250 is allocated to each of the three months considered here.

8. The total electricity charge for the three months will be the £1,500 bill received and paid in the middle of March plus the £300 that has been used in the last two weeks of March. This £300 will be treated as an accrual (see Chapter 3, Prepayments and accruals), an expense incurred by the end of an accounting period giving rise to a liability and an expense that has not been paid by that period end date. The total electricity expense for the three months is thus £1,800. Dividing this figure by three gives us an expense of £600 for each month of the budgeted statement of profit or loss.

9. While the total insurance payment is £1,500, this cost covers the whole 12-month period. Therefore, the monthly charge for insurance in our budgeted statement of profit or loss will be £1,500 ÷ 12 = £125 per month, the remaining £1,125 (£1,500 − £375) being treated as a prepayment at the end of March.

WHY IS THIS RELEVANT TO ME?   The budgeted monthly statement of profit or loss

To enable you as a business professional and user of accounting information to understand how:

- Budgeted statements of profit or loss you will be presented with have been drawn up
- To prepare your own budgeted monthly statements of profit or loss

---

NUMERICAL EXERCISES   Perfectly happy you could put together a budgeted statement of profit or loss for a given time period using budgeted sales, materials, labour and fixed overheads? Work through Illustration 11.7 again to confirm your understanding of how we arrived at the figures in the budgeted statement of profit or loss and then go to the **online workbook** and attempt Numerical exercises 11.3 to make sure you can produce a budgeted statement of profit or loss from the sales, materials, labour and fixed overhead budgets.

SHOW ME HOW TO DO IT   Did you really understand how this budgeted statement of profit or loss in Illustration 11.7 was put together? View Video presentation 11.1 in the **online workbook** to see a practical demonstration.

Step 6: calculating cash receipts from sales

The budgeted statement of profit or loss for the first three months of the year in Illustration 11.7 shows that Anna expects to make a healthy profit of £62,075. However, as we have already seen in this book, profit does not equal cash (Chapter 4, Profit ≠ cash). The main concern of both entities and their banks will always be the cash flowing in

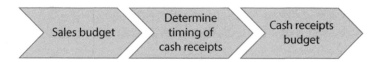

Figure 11.6 Budgeting step 6: cash receipts from sales budget

and the cash flowing out, so it is important in any budgeting exercise to prepare the cash budget alongside the budgeted statement of profit or loss (Figure 11.6).

As we saw in Chapter 3 (Determining the amount of income or expense), sales are recognized as sales in the months in which they occur, but cash from those sales will not necessarily be received in those same months. Where goods are sold on credit, there is a time lag between the date of the sale and the day on which cash from that sale is received.

Based on her past experience and knowledge, Anna expects 30% of her customers to pay in the month of sale and the remaining 70% to pay in the following month. These expected monthly cash receipts from sales are shown in Illustration 11.8.

Illustration 11.8 Anna: budgeted cash receipts from sales in January, February and March

	January	February	March	Total
	£	£	£	£
30% of sales received in month	12,525	17,250	23,025	52,800
70% of sales received next month	—	29,225	40,250	69,475
Total cash receipts per month	12,525	46,475	63,275	122,275

How were these cash receipts calculated? Anna expects to make total sales in January of £41,750 (Illustration 11.3); 30% of £41,750 is £12,525 received in January, the month of sale. Cash from the remaining 70% of January's sales will be received in the following month, February. This amounts to £29,225. You could calculate this number as 70% of £41,750 or just deduct the £12,525 already received from £41,750 to give you the same result. Work through the other sales and cash receipts in Illustrations 11.3 and 11.8 to ensure that you understand how the budgeted cash inflows from sales were calculated on the basis of Anna's expectations of when her customers will pay for the goods they have received.

Anna expects to make sales of £176,000 in the three months to the end of March (Illustrations 11.3 and 11.7). However, she has only collected £122,275 in cash (Illustration 11.8), a difference of £53,725. What does this difference represent and where should it be recorded in the budgeted accounts? Remember that this figure represents trade receivables due to the company, a current asset (Chapter 2, Current assets), which will be posted to Anna's forecast statement of financial position at 31 March.

> **WHY IS THIS RELEVANT TO ME?**   Calculating cash receipts from sales
>
> To enable you as a business professional and user of accounting information to understand:
>
> - That, unless an entity sells for cash, sales do not equal cash receipts in the months in which the sales are recognized
> - How to prepare budgets for receipts of cash from sales made to customers on credit terms

---

NUMERICAL EXERCISES   Totally convinced you could produce a statement of budgeted cash inflows from sales? Work through the figures in Illustrations 11.3 and 11.8 again to confirm your understanding of how we arrived at the budgeted cash receipts from sales and then go to the **online workbook** and attempt Numerical exercises 11.4 to make sure you can produce a statement of budgeted cash inflows from sales.

Step 7: calculating cash payments to direct materials suppliers and direct labour

Just as Anna's customers do not pay for their goods immediately, so Anna, as a customer of her materials suppliers, does not pay for all her direct materials in the month she receives them. Therefore, cash payments to suppliers have to be worked out in the same way as cash receipts from customers (Figure 11.7).

Anna expects to pay for her purchases of wood as follows:

- 50% of the wood used in each month will be paid for in the actual month of use
- 30% of the wood used each month will be paid for one month after the actual month of use
- 20% of the wood used each month will be paid for two months after the actual month of use

Illustration 11.9 shows Anna's budgeted cash payments for wood.

Illustration 11.9 Anna: budgeted cash payments for wood for January, February and March

	January	February	March	Total
	£	£	£	£
50% of wood used in month	3,600	5,265	7,200	16,065
30% of wood used one month ago	—	2,160	3,159	5,319
20% of wood used two months ago	—	—	1,440	1,440
Total cash payments per month	3,600	7,425	11,799	22,824

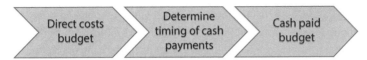

Figure 11.7 Budgeting step 7: cash payments from direct costs budget

How were these cash payments for wood calculated? Anna's direct materials budget (Illustrations 11.4 and 11.7) shows that she expects to use wood costing £7,200 in January. This will be paid for as follows:

- 50% in month of use (January): £7,200 × 50% = £3,600
- 30% one month after the month of use: £7,200 × 30% = £2,160
- 20% two months after the month of use: £7,200 × 20% = £1,440
- Check: £3,600 + £2,160 + £1,440 = £7,200

On top of these payments for January's wood made in February and March are payments for wood used in those months, as well as March's payment for the wood used in February.

Illustration 11.9 shows that Anna will be paying £22,824 in cash for her wood purchases in the three months to 31 March, while her statement of profit or loss (Illustration 11.7) shows that she is incurring total direct materials costs for wood of £32,130. She therefore still has £9,306 to pay (£32,130 − £22,824), made up of £2,106 (20% of February's usage (£10,530 × 20%)) and £7,200 (50% of March's usage (£14,400 × 50%)). This figure of £9,306 represents a liability incurred and due to be paid to her suppliers. This amount will be recorded as a trade payable in Anna's forecast statement of financial position at 31 March.

As well as her suppliers of wood, Anna also buys in other direct materials for use in producing her furniture. She intends to pay the suppliers of these other materials in the month in which these materials are used in production. Similarly, she will be paying her employees in the month in which production and sales are made. The cash outflows for other direct materials and direct labour in her monthly cash budget will be the same as the expenses already presented in Illustrations 11.5–11.7.

WHY IS THIS RELEVANT TO ME?   Calculating cash payments for direct materials and direct labour

To enable you as a business professional and user of accounting information to understand:

- That, unless an entity pays cash for all its direct materials and other purchases, direct materials do not equal cash payments in the months in which the costs are recorded

- How to prepare budgets for payments of cash to suppliers of direct materials and other purchases where these goods are purchased on credit terms

11

Quite confident you could put together a budgeted statement
of cash outflows for direct materials and direct labour? Work through the figures in Illustrations 11.4–11.6, 11.7 and 11.9 again to confirm your understanding of how we calculated the
budgeted cash outflows from payments for direct materials and direct labour and then go to
the **online workbook** and attempt Numerical exercises 11.5 to see how accurately you can
produce a budgeted statement of cash outflows for direct materials and direct labour.

Step 8: draw up the monthly cash budget

Anna now has all the information from which to draw up her month-by-month cash
budget. To do this she will look at the timing of her cash inflows from sales, the timing
of her cash payments for direct materials and labour, together with any other payments
or inflows of cash, as shown in Figure 11.8. Details of other outflows of cash were given
in step 4, the budget for fixed costs. In addition, Anna decides that she will be paying
£10,000 of her own money into her business bank account on 1 January and that she
will be drawing out £2,000 a month for her own personal expenses.

Anna's monthly cash budget for January, February and March is presented in Illustration 11.10.

Illustration 11.10 Anna: cash budget for January, February and March

	January £	February £	March £	Total £	Note
Cash received					
Sales	12,525	46,475	63,275	122,275	1
Capital introduced	10,000	—	—	10,000	2
Total cash receipts	22,525	46,475	63,275	132,275	
Cash paid					
Direct material: wood	3,600	7,425	11,799	22,824	3
Direct material: other	3,600	4,970	6,000	14,570	4
Direct labour	14,550	20,000	26,150	60,700	5
Rent	3,000	—	—	3,000	6
Machinery and tools	15,000	—	—	15,000	7
Electricity	—	—	1,500	1,500	8
Rates	—	1,200	—	1,200	9
Insurance	1,500	—	—	1,500	10
Drawings: personal expenditure	2,000	2,000	2,000	6,000	11
Total cash payments	43,250	35,595	47,449	126,294	
Cash receipts – cash payments	(20,725)	10,880	15,826	5,981	12
Cash at the start of the month	—	(20,725)	(9,845)		13
Cash at the end of the month	(20,725)	(9,845)	5,981		14

11

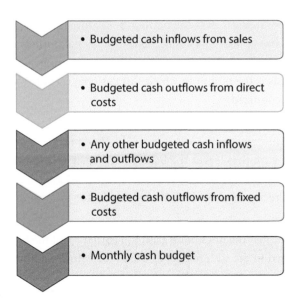

- • Budgeted cash inflows from sales

- • Budgeted cash outflows from direct costs

- • Any other budgeted cash inflows and outflows

- • Budgeted cash outflows from fixed costs

- • Monthly cash budget

Figure 11.8 Budgeting step 8: drawing up the monthly cash budget

How did Anna produce her monthly cash budget for January, February and March? The following notes explain the numbers in each line of the cash budget.

1. The budgeted cash receipts from sales were calculated in Illustration 11.8.

2. Anna is paying in £10,000 of her own money on 1 January as noted.

3. The budgeted cash payments to suppliers of wood were presented in Illustration 11.9.

4. Anna is paying her suppliers of other direct materials in the month in which the other direct materials are used, so the cash payments to these suppliers are the same as the budgeted costs in Illustrations 11.5 and 11.7.

5. Likewise, direct labour is paid in the month in which production and sales take place so these cash payments are the same as the costs given in Illustrations 11.6 and 11.7.

6. Step 4 tells us that the rent is paid on 1 January. Although the cost of this rent is spread across the three months to which it relates in the statement of profit or loss (Illustration 11.7), the actual cash payment is budgeted to take place in January, so the whole £3,000 is recognized in the January cash payments.

7. In the same way, the cash outflow to buy the machinery and tools occurs in January so the whole of the £15,000 cash payment is recognized in January. Remember that depreciation is not a cash flow, just an accounting adjustment (Chapter 4, The indirect method, and Table 4.1) that spreads the cost

11

of non-current assets over the periods benefiting from their use, so depreciation does not appear in a cash budget. The actual outflow of cash to pay for the machinery and tools is £15,000 and this occurs in January so, just like the rent, this is the month in which this cash payment for these non-current assets is recognized.

8. Step 4 explains that the electricity bill received in March will be for £1,500 and that this electricity bill is paid in that month. Thus, £1,500 is the amount of cash that leaves the bank in March. The additional £300 accrual in the statement of profit or loss will be paid in a later period so no cash outflow is recognized in these three months for this amount which has not yet been paid.

9. Step 4 notes that the rates bill is paid in February and the full £1,200 payment is recognized in the cash budget as this is the actual amount paid in February regardless of the amounts that are allocated to each month in the budgeted statement of profit or loss.

10. Similarly, the insurance for the year is paid in January, so the whole cash outflow of £1,500 is shown in January's column even though the cost in the statement of profit or loss is spread over the next 12 months.

11. Anna withdraws £2,000 a month from which to meet her personal expenditure so she recognizes this as a cash outflow each month.

12. After totalling up the cash receipts (inflows) and the cash payments (outflows), the receipts – payments line is presented. For January, total receipts in Illustration 11.10 are £22,525 while payments total £43,250. Thus, £22,525 – £43,250 = –£20,725, which means that there is a shortfall of cash in January and Anna's bank account will be overdrawn. January thus shows payments greater than receipts of cash, while both February and March show a net inflow of cash, receipts in both months being greater than payments.

13. Cash at the start of the month is the cash balance at the end of the previous month. In the first month of a new business venture, as in Anna's case, this will be £Nil. In continuing businesses, this will be the budgeted or actual cash figure at the end of the last financial period.

14. The cash at the end of the month is the net cash inflow or outflow for the month plus or minus the cash or overdraft at the start of the month. In January, the net outflow for the month is £20,725 while the cash at the start of January is £Nil so (£20,725) +/– £Nil = (£20,725). At the end of February, there is a net cash inflow of £10,880 (total cash receipts of £46,475 – total cash payments of £35,595). Adding this positive inflow of £10,880 to the negative balance at the start of the month (£20,725) gives us a lower overdraft at the end of February (£9,845), which then forms the opening balance at the start of March.

11

WHY IS THIS RELEVANT TO ME?   The monthly cash budget

To enable you as a business professional and user of accounting information to understand:

- How cash budgets you will be presented with have been drawn up
- How to prepare your own monthly cash budgets

NUMERICAL EXERCISES   Reckon you could draw up a cash budget? Work through Illustration 11.10 again to confirm your understanding of how the monthly cash budget was constructed and then go to the **online workbook** and attempt Numerical exercises 11.6 to make sure you can produce these budgeted statements.

SHOW ME HOW TO DO IT   How easily did you follow the preparation of Anna's monthly cash budget? View Video presentation 11.2 in the **online workbook** to see a practical demonstration of how the monthly cash budget in Illustration 11.10 was put together.

The importance of cash budgets

The cash budget is the most important budgeted statement that you will ever produce. We have already seen in this book that cash generation is the critical task for businesses as, without adequate cash inflows, a business will be unable to meet its liabilities as they fall due and will collapse. Give me an example 11.2, from the Entrepreneur column in the *Financial Times*, emphasizes how business professionals must continue to produce cash budgets no matter how high up an organization they climb. If they do not, they are risking the very survival of their organizations.

GIVE ME AN EXAMPLE 11.2   Custodians of finance make the difference

The weak link in many failed companies is the finance director. Better custody of borrowed or invested money by them would so often have prevented disaster. In most cases their words betray them as much as the numbers. I am indebted to John Dewhirst of Vincere, the turn-around specialists, for collecting some of the classic lines I discuss below.

'I don't do cash forecasts. I've never found them useful.'

A lack of focus on cash is perhaps the greatest sin. A finance professional who does not pre-pare reasonably accurate projections of liquidity on a rolling basis is guilty of dereliction of duty. Often FDs drop such nitty gritty as they ascend the ranks, while some have historically enjoyed a cash cushion and never felt the pressure. They are the ones exposed when conditions deteriorate.

11

Step 9: draw up the budgeted statement of financial position

The final step in the budgeting process is to draw up the budgeted statement of financial position at the end of the budget period using the budgeted information already produced, as shown in Figure 11.9. As we saw in Chapter 2, this statement summarizes the assets and liabilities of an entity at the end of an accounting period, whether actual or budgeted. We have already looked at all the numbers that will go into Anna's statement of financial position when we prepared the budgeted statement of profit or loss and cash budget. Anna's budgeted statement of financial position is presented in Illustration 11.11, together with notes reminding you of the sources of the figures.

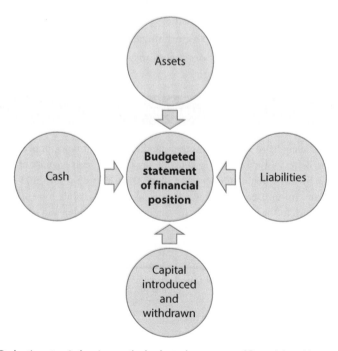

Figure 11.9 Budgeting step 9: drawing up the budgeted statement of financial position at the period end

Illustration 11.11 Anna: budgeted statement of financial position at 31 March

	£	Note
Non-current assets		
Machinery and tools	14,250	1
Current assets		
Trade receivables	53,725	2
Insurance prepayment	1,125	3
Rates prepayment	600	4
Cash at bank	5,981	5
Total current assets	61,431	
Total assets	75,681	
Current liabilities		
Trade payables for wood	9,306	6
Electricity accrual	300	7
Total current liabilities	9,616	
Net assets: total assets – total liabilities (£75,681 – £9,616)	66,075	
Capital account		
Capital introduced	10,000	8
Net profit for the three months	62,075	9
Drawings	(6,000)	10
	66,075	

Notes to Anna's budgeted statement of financial position:

1. Machinery and tools cost £15,000. Depreciation of £750 has been charged in the budgeted statement of profit or loss for the three months to the end of March (Illustration 11.7), so the carrying amount (cost – depreciation) of these assets is £15,000 – £750 = £14,250.

2. The cash not collected from customers by the end of March. We calculated this figure in step 6.

3. The payment of £1,500 covers 12 months of insurance; £375 has been charged against profits as the insurance cost for the three months in the budgeted statement of profit or loss to the end of March (Illustration 11.7), so there is an insurance prepayment of nine months. Therefore, the insurance prepayment is £1,500 × 9/12 = £1,125.

4. Similarly, the payment of £1,200 covers six months of rates expenditure. At 31 March only three of the six months paid for have been used up and charged as an expense in the budgeted statement of profit or loss (Illustration 11.7), so there is a prepayment at 31 March of £1,200 × 3/6 = £600. This £600 represents

the rates cost to be charged as an expense in the statements of profit or loss for April, May and June.

5. The cash at bank must equal the closing cash figure in the cash budget (Illustration 11.10).

6. This trade payables figure was calculated in step 7.

7. The electricity accrual is the expense incurred but not yet paid.

8. Anna introduced £10,000 to the business on 1 January in the cash budget.

9. Net profit for the three months is read off the budgeted statement of profit or loss in Illustration 11.7.

10. Drawings are the total amount that Anna has withdrawn from the business bank account for her own personal expenditure over the course of the three months. This figure appears in the cash budget in Illustration 11.10.

WHY IS THIS RELEVANT TO ME? The budgeted statement of financial position

To enable you as a business professional and user of accounting information to understand how:

- The budgeted statement of financial position is compiled from the budgeted statement of profit or loss and cash budget
- To prepare your own budgeted statements of financial position

---

NUMERICAL EXERCISES Quite certain you can draw up a budgeted statement of financial position? Work through the figures in Illustration 11.11 again to confirm your understanding of how the statement of financial position was constructed and then go to the **online workbook** and attempt Numerical exercises 11.7 to make sure you can produce this statement.

SHOW ME HOW TO DO IT How well did you understand how Anna's budgeted statement of financial position was put together? View Video presentation 11.3 in the **online workbook** to see a practical demonstration of how this statement was prepared.

Conclusions: financing expansion

What has Anna learnt from her budgeting exercise? At the start of the process, she had approached the bank for finance to start her new workshop. The bank asked her to undertake a budgeting exercise. By producing her budgets she now knows that, if everything goes exactly to plan, she will need to borrow a maximum of £20,725 (Illustration 11.10) from the bank as a result of her expansion. Happily, her cash budget also shows that this maximum borrowing of £20,725 will be paid off by the end of March, so any financing she needs will be very short term. A short-term overdraft with the bank would be the most appropriate form of financing for Anna.

Budgeting flow chart summary

We have now looked in detail at the budgeting process, the steps that are followed and the order in which those steps proceed. We can summarize the budgeting process in a flow chart. This flow chart is shown in Figure 11.10. Look back at the earlier sections of this chapter and relate each step to what you have learnt during our study of the budgeting process so far.

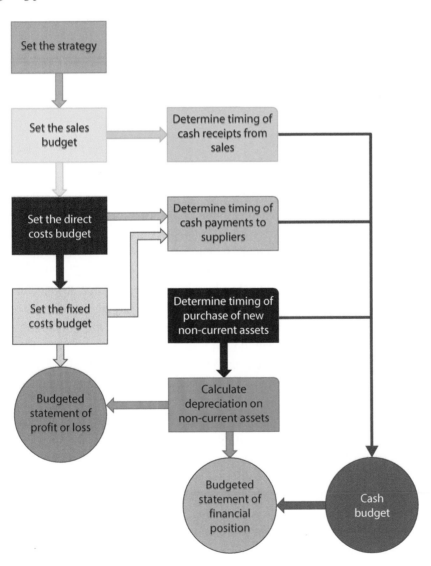

Figure 11.10 The budgeting process

WHY IS THIS RELEVANT TO ME? Budgeting flow chart summary

To provide you as a business professional and user of accounting information with a:

• Map to help you draw up budgets and budgeted financial statements

• Logical step-by-step guide to the production of budgeted information

• Quick overview of the budgeting process to determine where each activity fits into the overall budgeting framework

GO BACK OVER THIS AGAIN! A copy of this budgeting flow chart summary (Figure 11.10) is available in the **online workbook**: you might like to keep this on screen or print off a copy for easy reference while you revise the material in this chapter to provide you with a route map through the budgeting process.

Budgetary control: statement of profit or loss

As we noted earlier in this chapter, budgets are used for control purposes. Once each month of actual activity is complete, comparisons are made between what was budgeted to occur and what actually happened. Figure 11.11 illustrates this process. It is important to undertake this comparison activity every month so that variances from the budget can be determined and their causes investigated. It would be pointless waiting to complete a whole year of activity before any comparisons were made. By then it would be too late to undertake the necessary action to correct budget deviations. In the same way, you do not wait until the end of the academic year to review feedback on your coursework, but instead look at the feedback on each assignment as it is returned so that you can make the necessary improvements in your next piece of assessment.

Monthly comparisons are an example of relevant accounting information (Chapter 1, What qualities should accounting information possess?). Monthly data is provided on a timely basis with a view to influencing managers' decisions in terms of, for example, what products to continue selling, whether to discount products that are not selling or to seek out cheaper sources of material if direct material prices from the current supplier are now too high. Comparisons are also confirmatory as well as predictive. The closer budgeted figures are to actual results in a month, the more likely budgeted figures for future months are to predict future outcomes accurately.

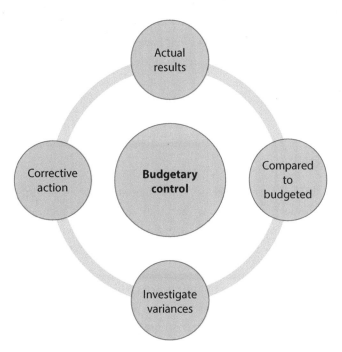

Figure 11.11 The budgetary control process

As an example, let's look at Anna's budgeted and actual results for January. These are shown in Illustration 11.12.

Illustration 11.12 Anna: budgeted v. actual statements of profit or loss for January

	January budget	January actual	January variances
	£	£	£
Sales	41,750	43,000	1,250
Cost of sales			
Direct material: wood	7,200	8,000	(800)
Direct material: other	3,600	3,550	50
Direct labour	14,550	14,500	50
Cost of sales	25,350	26,050	(700)
Gross profit (sales – cost of sales)	16,400	16,950	550
Expenses			
Rent	1,000	1,000	—
Rates	200	200	—
Machinery and tools depreciation	250	300	(50)
Electricity	600	600	—
Insurance	125	125	—
Net profit (gross profit – expenses)	14,225	14,725	500

11

In Illustration 11.12, numbers in brackets in the January variances column are classified as unfavourable, those variances that have reduced the budgeted profit, whereas figures without brackets are favourable, those variances that have increased the budgeted profit.

Now that we have produced our budget v. actual comparison, we can make the following observations.

Higher sales

- Sales are higher than budgeted. This suggests that the original estimates of product sales were a little lower than they should have been. If more products have been sold, Anna should find out why this has occurred and determine whether she can continue to exploit this favourable trend to make higher sales in the future.

- Alternatively, selling prices might have been higher than budgeted because of increased demand pushing prices up. Anna should do her best to maintain any higher selling prices as she will make more profit as a result.

- As there are two possible explanations for this sales variance, Anna will have to conduct further investigations to determine which of the two options is correct or whether it is a combination of both. The sales variance tells her to investigate further, but does not tell her the cause of this variance.

Direct costs

- The cost of wood used in production of goods sold rose in January. This, in itself, is not a surprise as higher production and sales will require more raw material input. However, Anna will need to investigate whether the price of wood has increased or more wood than expected was used in production.

- Other direct material cost less than expected, suggesting lower prices than budgeted or more efficient usage by the workforce.

- Similarly, the cost of labour was lower despite the increased production and sales, suggesting that the workforce has been more productive than budgeted.

- Anna should try to encourage more efficient working as this will increase productivity and lower the costs per unit of production, resulting in the generation of higher profits.

- To encourage this higher productivity, Anna might introduce a bonus scheme for her workers to give them a share in any increased profits. However, she will need to make sure that the bonus scheme does not encourage the workforce to work with less care and attention to detail so that the finished production, while taking less time to produce, is of lower quality.

Fixed costs

- Rent and insurance overheads should be as budgeted as these costs should be easily predictable in advance.

- The rates and electricity budget and actual figures are currently the same as we do not have any actual bills to work from. Remember that the rates bill is expected in February and the electricity bill will arrive in March. Once the actual bills are received Anna will be able to determine whether these costs are higher or lower than budgeted.

- The higher than budgeted depreciation figure suggests that the machinery and tools cost Anna more than anticipated, resulting in a higher monthly depreciation charge. Anna will need to check the actual payment for machinery and tools.

Net profit

- Overall, actual profits for January were higher than budgeted by £500.

- Based upon her investigations of the causes of the variances in January, Anna will aim to correct any unfavourable variances in the cost and usage of wood, while attempting to exploit the favourable variances in the sales to sell more goods or to sell goods at a higher price.

WHY IS THIS RELEVANT TO ME?   Budgetary control: statement of profit or loss

As a business professional and user of accounting information, you will be expected to:

- Take on responsibility for your departmental budget and explain variations between budgeted and actual results
- Produce actual v. budget comparisons on a monthly basis
- Ask relevant questions when evaluating actual v. budget comparisons

---

GO BACK OVER THIS AGAIN!   Could you suggest reasons for changes in budgeted v. actual sales and costs? Go to the **online workbook** and have a go at Exercises 11.3.

Budgetary control: cash budget

As well as comparing her budgeted and actual statements of profit or loss, Anna will also undertake a comparison of her budgeted and actual cash flows. As we noted at the start of this chapter, Anna needs additional finance from the bank to expand her business and move into the larger workshop. Her initial cash budget suggested that she would only need to borrow a maximum of £20,725. Because of the critical nature of cash inflows and outflows in her business operations, both Anna and her bank will be watching her cash position very closely to make sure that she does not exceed her borrowing capacity or her borrowing limits.

Anna produces her budgeted and actual cash flow comparisons for January in Illustration 11.13.

Illustration 11.13 Anna: budgeted v. actual cash inflows and outflows for January

	January budget	January actual	January variances
	£	£	£
Cash received			
Sales	12,525	13,760	1,235
Capital introduced	10,000	10,000	—
Total cash receipts	22,525	23,760	1,235
Cash paid			
Direct material: wood	3,600	4,000	(400)
Direct material: other	3,600	3,550	50
Direct labour	14,550	14,500	50
Rent	3,000	3,000	—
Machinery and tools	15,000	18,000	(3,000)
Electricity	—	—	—
Rates	—	—	—
Insurance	1,500	1,500	—
Drawings: personal expenditure	2,000	2,000	—
Total cash payments	43,250	46,550	(3,300)
Cash receipts – cash payments	(20,725)	(22,790)	(2,065)
Cash at the start of the month	—	—	—
Cash at the end of the month	(20,725)	(22,790)	(2,065)

What does this budgeted v. actual cash flow comparison tell Anna? She can draw the following conclusions:

- Her customers are paying more quickly than she expected. While she anticipated that 30% of her customers would pay in the month of sale, 32% of actual sales have paid in January (£13,760 ÷ £43,000 (actual sales from the statement of profit or loss in Illustration 11.12) × 100%). Anna should try to persuade her customers to continue paying more quickly as this will improve her cash inflows and thereby reduce her borrowings more rapidly.

- While £400 more has been paid out for wood, this is consistent with Anna's intention that she would pay for 50% of the wood she used in the month of usage. As her actual usage was £8,000 (Illustration 11.12), she has paid half this amount in January.

- Payments for both other materials and labour are £50 less than expected, but these are the actual amounts used in January according to the budgeted v. actual statement of profit or loss (Illustration 11.12). Cash payments are thus in line with Anna's policy of paying in full for labour and other materials in the month in which they were used.

- Machinery and tools were budgeted to cost £15,000 but in fact cost £18,000. This is consistent with the increase in depreciation shown in the statement of profit or loss in Illustration 11.12. The machinery and tools are expected to have a five-year life, which gives an annual depreciation charge of £3,600 per annum (£18,000 ÷ 5) which equates to £300 per month (£3,600 ÷ 12). Anna tells you that the machinery and tools had been imported from Germany and that the increased cost was because of a fall in the value of the pound against the euro at the time the machinery and tools were bought and paid for.

- All other inflows and outflows of cash were as budgeted.

- As a result of the above differences in her planned cash inflows and outflows, Anna has borrowed an additional £2,065 from the bank in January. The sole cause of this problem was the payment for her machinery and tools. Her aim now will be to pay off this additional borrowing as quickly as possible by encouraging her customers to pay more promptly or trying to sell more products each month to increase her cash inflows while keeping outflows of cash as low as possible.

WHY IS THIS RELEVANT TO ME? Budgetary control: cash budget

As a business professional and user of accounting information, you must appreciate that:

- Cash is the lifeblood of business and without it businesses will run out of money and collapse

- Monitoring budgeted v. actual cash is thus just as (if not more) important than comparing budgeted v. actual profits

---

NUMERICAL EXERCISES   Positive you could produce a comparison of budgeted v. actual cash flows? Go to the **online workbook** and have a go at Numerical exercises 11.8.

Sensitivity analysis

Anna has produced her budgets for the first three months of operations and predicted her maximum borrowings from the bank. However, what if her budgets don't turn out as she expects? How will this affect her profits and her cash flows? Given questions such as these, it is usual when budgeting to conduct sensitivity analysis to assess how profits and cash flows would turn out if certain expectations are changed. Thus, for example, a reduction in budgeted sales units might be applied, or an increase in direct costs of 10% or a fall in selling price of 10%. Spreadsheets make these 'what if?' calculations easy to undertake.

As an example, let's see what would happen to profits and cash flows if budgeted unit sales of Anna's products fell by 10% while keeping selling prices the same. We will adopt various short-cuts in producing our figures here, but all the calculations will be available in the online workbook.

First, let's look at the statement of profit or loss showing a 10% fall in numbers of products sold compared with Anna's original plans. This is presented in Illustration 11.14.

Illustration 11.14 Anna: budgeted statement of profit or loss for January, February and March assuming a 10% fall in the number of products sold while keeping selling prices the same

	January	February	March	Total	Note
	£	£	£	£	
Sales	37,575	51,750	69,075	158,400	1
Cost of sales	22,815	31,950	41,895	96,660	2
Gross profit (sales – cost of sales)	14,760	19,800	27,180	61,740	
Expenses					
Fixed costs	2,175	2,175	2,175	6,525	3
Net profit (gross profit – expenses)	12,585	17,625	25,005	55,215	

Notes on the above budgeted statement of profit or loss:

1. Sales volumes reduce by 10%, which results in sales 10% lower than those shown in Illustrations 11.3 and 11.7.

2. As sales volumes fall by 10%, cost of sales (direct costs) also fall by 10% as Anna's direct costs in producing 10% fewer goods will be 10% lower.

3. Budgeted fixed costs are made up of £1,000 (rent) + £200 (rates) + £250 (depreciation) + £600 (electricity) + £125 insurance to give total budgeted fixed costs per month of £2,175. These are the same costs that we used in Illustration 11.7. Remember that fixed costs do not change with different levels of sales and production, so these costs are the same for the original budgeted sales and the revised budgeted sales volumes of 10% lower than originally planned.

Anna's original budgeted profit of £62,075 in Illustration 11.7 has now fallen to £55,215 given a 10% fall in sales volumes.

However, Anna's main concern was with finance and how much she would need to borrow from the bank. Surely the effect of this fall of 10% in sales volumes will increase the size of her projected overdraft? The effect of the 10% fall in sales volumes on the cash budget is shown in Illustration 11.15.

Illustration 11.15 Anna: budgeted cash inflows and outflows for January, February and March assuming a 10% fall in the number of products sold while keeping selling prices the same

	January	February	March	Total
Cash received	£	£	£	£
Sales	11,273	41,827	56,947	110,047
Capital introduced	10,000	—	—	10,000
Total cash receipts	21,273	41,827	56,947	120,047
Cash paid				
Direct material: wood	3,240	6,683	10,619	20,542
Direct material: other	3,240	4,473	5,400	13,113
Direct labour	13,095	18,000	23,535	54,630
Rent	3,000	—	—	3,000
Machinery and tools	15,000	—	—	15,000
Electricity	—	—	1,500	1,500
Rates	—	1,200	—	1,200
Insurance	1,500	—	—	1,500
Drawings: personal expenditure	2,000	2,000	2,000	6,000
Total cash payments	41,075	32,356	43,054	116,485
Cash receipts – cash payments	(19,802)	9,471	13,893	3,562
Cash at the start of the month	—	(19,802)	(10,331)	
Cash at the end of the month	(19,802)	(10,331)	3,562	

Budgeted payments for rent, machinery and tools, electricity, rates, insurance and drawings across the three months under review do not change, so these stay the same in both Illustrations 11.10 and 11.15. Receipts from sales fall, but planned payments for wood, other materials and direct labour fall by more than the reduction in sales receipts. This has the effect of actually reducing the expected borrowings at the end of January from £20,725 to £19,802, so, even with lower sales volumes, Anna is borrowing less. Her cash balance at the end of three months is lower at £3,562 compared to the £5,981 shown in Illustration 11.10, but she still pays off the borrowings by the end of March as in her original budget.

The assumptions on which Anna's original budgets were based can be relaxed further to see what effect these changes will have on her budgeted statement of profit or loss, cash budget and projected statement of financial position and you can have a go at some of these in the online workbook.

The following extract, in Give me an example 11.3, from the Audit Committee's report in the annual report and accounts of Greggs Plc, shows how sensitivity analysis is used in practice to test the assumptions on which financial plans and forecasts are based and to determine whether these forecasts and plans are realistic and achievable.

11

GIVE ME AN EXAMPLE 11.3   Sensitivity analysis

The significant areas of judgement considered by the Committee in relation to the financial statements for the 52 weeks ended 28 December 2013 are set out below. These significant areas of judgement are principally borne out of the strategic review which took place during the year, the results of which were announced in August 2013. The strategic review took place as a response to declining like-for-like sales and reduced profitability. The impact of the suggested measures was reflected in a five-year financial plan and liquidity forecasts which were presented to the Board along with sensitivities for each scenario. The assumptions underlying each scenario were challenged robustly by the Committee which concluded that they represented an appropriate and prudent position.

Source: *Greggs Plc Annual Report and Accounts for the year ended 28 December 2013*, page 44

WHY IS THIS RELEVANT TO ME?   Sensitivity analysis

To enable you as a business professional and user of accounting information to:

- Appreciate that original budgets will be subjected to sensitivity analysis to determine the effect of changes in budgeted numbers on budgeted profits and cash flows

- Undertake sensitivity analysis on budgeted information prepared by yourself and others

---

GO BACK OVER THIS AGAIN!   How readily did you understand how the figures for Anna were calculated for the reduction in sales volumes of 10%? Visit the **online workbook** Exercises 11.4 to view all the calculations involved in this exercise.

NUMERICAL EXERCISES   Quite convinced you could undertake sensitivity analysis on a set of budgeted figures? Go to the **online workbook** and have a go at Numerical exercises 11.9 to see what effect various changes would have on Anna's budgeted statement of profit or loss and cash budget for January, February and March.

CHAPTER SUMMARY

You should now have learnt that:

- Budgets perform planning, communicating, coordinating, motivating and control functions within organizations

- The sales budget is the starting point for all other budgeted figures and statements

- Entities prepare budgeted statements of profit or loss and cash budgets on a monthly basis

- Monthly comparisons are made between budgeted income and expenditure and budgeted cash receipts and payments to ensure that operations are under control

- Businesses undertake comparisons between budgeted and actual income and expenditure to highlight variances in expected and actual financial performance

- Sensitivity analysis is applied to assumptions made in budgeted financial statements to determine how easily an entity could make a loss or require overdraft financing

---

QUICK REVISION Test your knowledge with the online flashcards in Summary of key concepts and attempt the Multiple choice questions, all in the **online workbook**. www.oup.com/uk/scott_business3e/

END-OF-CHAPTER QUESTIONS

Solutions to these questions can be found at the back of the book from page 517.

❯ DEVELOP YOUR UNDERSTANDING

❯ Question 11.1

Dave is planning to start up in business selling ice cream from a van around his local neighbourhood from April to September. He wants to open a business bank account, but the bank manager has insisted that he provides a cash budget together with a budgeted statement of profit or loss for his first six months of trading and a budgeted statement of financial position at 30 September. Dave is unsure how to put this information together, but he has provided you with the following details of his planned income and expenditure:

- Dave will pay in £5,000 of his own money on 1 April to get the business started.

- He expects to make all his sales for cash and anticipates that he will make sales of £3,500 in April, £5,500 in May, £7,500 in each of the next three months and £2,500 in September.

- He will buy his ice cream from a local supplier and expects the cost of this to be 50% of selling price. Dave has agreed with his supplier that he will start paying for his ice cream in May rather than in the month of purchase.

- Dave intends to sell all his ice cream by the end of September and to have no inventory at the end of this trading period.

- Ice cream vans can be hired at a cost of £1,500 for three months. The £1,500 hire charge is payable at the start of each three-month period.

- Van running costs are estimated to be £250 per month payable in cash each month.

- Business insurance payable on 1 April will cost £500 for six months.

- Dave will draw £1,000 per month out of the business bank account to meet personal expenses.

Required
Provide Dave with:

- A cash budget for his first six months of trading.

- A budgeted statement of profit or loss for his first six months of trading.

- A budgeted statement of financial position at 30 September.

11

› Question 11.2

Hena plc has a division that manufactures and sells solar panels. Demand for solar panels has picked up recently and the company is looking to increase its output. Hena plc's division currently manufactures 600,000 solar panels annually and is looking to double this capacity. A new factory has become available at an annual rent of £600,000 per annum payable quarterly in advance. New plant and machinery would cost £1.8 million, payable immediately on delivery on 1 January. This new plant and machinery would have a useful life of ten years and would be depreciated on a straight line basis with £Nil residual value. The directors of Hena plc are now wondering whether they should go ahead with the new solar panel factory. They have produced the following projections upon which to base their budgets.

Hena plc sells each solar panel for £150. Demand for the increased output is expected to be as follows:

- January: 20,000 panels
- February and March: 30,000 panels per month
- April: 40,000 panels
- May to August: 80,000 panels per month
- September: 60,000 panels
- October and November: 40,000 panels per month
- December: 20,000 panels
- All panels are sold to credit customers, 10% of whom pay in the month of sale, 60% in the month after and the remaining 30% two months after the month of sale.

Details of production costs are as follows:

- Materials cost is 30% of the selling price of the panels. Materials suppliers are paid in the month after production and sales have taken place.
- Production labour is 20% of the selling price; 70% of this amount is payable in the month of sale and the remainder, representing deductions from production wages for tax and national insurance, is paid to HM Revenue and Customs one month after production and sales have taken place.
- Other variable production costs of 10% of selling price are paid in the month of sale.

Fixed costs are estimated to be £50,000 per month and are to be treated as paid in the month in which they were incurred. Hena plc manufactures to order and sells all its production and has no inventories of solar panels at the end of the year.

Required

Using a spreadsheet of your choice, prepare the following statements for the next 12 months:

- A sales budget
- A production costs budget
- A monthly cash budget
- A monthly budgeted statement of profit or loss
- A budgeted statement of financial position at the end of the 12 months

Advise the directors of Hena plc whether they should go ahead with the proposed expansion or not.

⟩ Question 11.3

The directors of Hena plc are impressed with your spreadsheet and your recommendation. However, they have new information that they would like you to build into your projections. The directors now expect that the selling price of panels will fall to £120 in the near future because of new competitors entering the market. Production materials, due to high levels of demand, will rise to 58% of the new selling price, while employees will have to be given a 5% pay rise based on production labour costs originally calculated in Question 11.2 to encourage them to stay. Other variable production costs will now fall to 10% of the new selling price. All other expectations in Question 11.2 will remain the same. The directors are now wondering if your recommendation would be the same once you have incorporated the above changes into your budget projections.

Required

Using the spreadsheet you have prepared for Question 11.2, prepare the following statements for the next 12 months on the basis of the directors' new expectations:

- A sales budget
- A production costs budget
- A monthly cash budget
- A monthly budgeted statement of profit or loss
- A budgeted statement of financial position at the end of the 12 months

Advise the directors of Hena plc whether they should go ahead with the proposed expansion or not given the new information that has come to hand.

▶▶ TAKE IT FURTHER

⟫ Question 11.4

It is now August 2019. You have been asked by your head of department to prepare the monthly budgeted statement of profit or loss and the monthly cash budget for the 12 months ending 31 December 2020 together with a budgeted statement of financial position at that date. You have been provided with the following details to help you in this task:

(a) Positive cash balances at the end of each month will earn interest at the rate of 0.5% of the month end balance and this interest will be receivable in the following month.

(b) Negative cash balances at the end of each month will be charged interest at the rate of 2% of the month end balance and this interest will be payable in the following month.

11

(c) Cash of £30,000 will be spent in March 2020 on new plant and equipment. The new plant and equipment will be brought into use in the business in the month of purchase.

(d) Your company produces three products: shirts, dresses and skirts. The cost cards for each product are as follows:

	Shirts	Dresses	Skirts
	£	£	£
Direct materials	10.00	12.00	6.00
Direct labour	12.00	15.00	7.50
Variable overhead	3.00	5.00	1.50
Total variable cost	25.00	30.00	15.00

(e) Selling prices are 140% of total variable cost. Payments for direct labour are made in accordance with note (i). 60% of the cost of materials is paid for one month after the month in which the materials were used in production, with the other 40% of materials being paid for two months after the month in which they were used in production. Where purchases of direct materials are greater than £20,000 in any one month, a 2.5% discount is given on all purchases of direct materials in that month. When purchases of direct materials are greater than £25,000 in any one month, a 3.5% discount is given on all purchases of direct materials in that month. Variable overhead is paid for in the following month.

(f) The marketing department has estimated that sales of each product for the year will be as follows:

2020	Shirts Number	Dresses Number	Skirts Number
January	500	300	800
February	600	350	900
March	750	400	700
April	900	700	650
May	1,000	800	500
June	1,000	1,200	400
July	800	1,000	350
August	700	600	200
September	950	400	500
October	650	300	600
November	850	450	750
December	1,100	600	850
Total	9,800	7,100	7,200

Your company sells its products directly to retailers. Retailers pay for the goods purchased as follows: 10% on delivery, 25% one month after delivery, 50% two months after delivery and the remaining 15% three months after delivery. All goods produced in the month are sold in the month and there are no inventories of finished goods or raw materials at the start or end of each month.

(g) The company rents its factory and offices and currently pays a total of £30,000 a year in rent. A rent review in March 2020 is expected to increase the annual factory rent to £36,000 from 1 August 2020. Quarterly rental payments in advance will be made on 1 February, 1 May, 1 August and 1 November 2020.

11

(h) Business rates for the six months to March 2020 will be paid on 1 October 2019 and the prepayment relating to January, February and March is shown in the forecast statement of financial position at 1 January 2020 below in note (k). Business rates of £7,500 per half year will be payable on 1 April 2020 and 1 October 2020. These business rates will cover the year from 1 April 2020 to 31 March 2021.

(i) Administrative and supervisory staff salaries are expected to total up to £9,000 a month. 68% of staff salaries and direct labour costs are payable in the month in which they are incurred with the remaining 32% representing deductions for tax and national insurance being paid to HM Revenue and Customs in the following month.

(j) An insurance premium of £6,000 is payable on 1 May 2020 covering all the insurance costs of the business for the year to 30 April 2021.

(k) The forecast statement of financial position at 1 January 2020 is as follows:

	£
Non-current assets	
Plant, equipment and fittings: cost	120,000
Plant, equipment and fittings: accumulated depreciation	(36,000)
	84,000
Current assets	
Trade receivables (owed by customers)	122,000
Rent prepayment	2,500
Rates prepayment	3,600
Insurance prepayment	1,800
Bank interest receivable	17
Cash at bank	3,395
	133,312
Total assets	217,312
Current liabilities	
Trade payables (materials)	29,400
Trade payables (variable overhead)	7,200
Tax and national insurance (direct labour)	8,570
Tax and national insurance (admin and supervisory salaries)	2,752
Corporation tax payable	3,200
Dividend payable	5,000
Total liabilities	56,122
Net assets	161,190
Equity	
Share capital	50,000
Retained earnings	111,190
	161,190

11

Notes to the forecast statement of financial position at 1 January 2020:

(i) Plant, equipment and fittings have a useful economic life of five years. Depreciation on these assets is charged monthly on the straight line basis.

(ii) Sales for October, November and December 2019 are budgeted to be £60,000, £70,000 and £75,000 respectively.

(iii) Purchases of materials totalled £20,000 in November 2019 and £21,400 (net of the 2% discount) in December 2019.

(iv) The dividend payable is scheduled for payment in April 2020 and the corporation tax is due for payment on 1 October 2020.

Required
Prepare the monthly budgeted statement of profit or loss and monthly cash budget for your company for the 12 months ended 31 December 2020 together with a budgeted statement of financial position at 31 December 2020.

» Question 11.5

Your friend is proposing to make a bid for a manufacturing business that has come onto the market. The business makes white plastic patio chairs. The purchase price for this business is £240,000. This purchase price is made up of plant, equipment and fittings (£180,000) with a useful life of five years, an inventory of raw materials (£20,000) and finished goods (£40,000). A delivery van will be purchased for £24,000 as soon as the business purchase is completed. The delivery van will be paid for in full in the second month of operations.
The following plans have been made for the business following purchase:

(a) Sales (before discounts) of plastic patio chairs, at a mark up of 60% on production cost (see (b) below), will be:

Month	January	February	March	April	May	June	July
Planned sales (units)	10,000	12,000	14,000	20,000	24,000	22,000	18,000

30% of sales will be for cash. The remaining sales will be on credit with 60% of credit sales being paid in the following month and the remaining 40% paying what is owed two months after the month of sale. A discount of 10% will be given to selected credit customers, who represent 25% of gross sales.

(b) Production cost is estimated at £5.00 per unit. The estimated production cost is made up of:

• Raw materials: £4.00

• Direct labour: £1.00

Production will be arranged so that closing inventory of finished goods at the end of every month is sufficient to meet 60% of sales requirements in the following month. The valuation of finished goods purchased with the business is based upon the planned production cost per unit given in (a) above.

(c) The single raw material used in production will be purchased so that raw material inventory at the end of each month is sufficient to meet half of the following month's production requirements. Raw material inventory acquired on purchase of the business is valued at the planned cost per unit as given in (b). Raw materials will be purchased on one month's credit.

(d) Costs of direct labour will be paid for as they are incurred in production.

(e) Fixed overheads are as follows: annual rent: £21,000, annual business rates: £8,100, annual heating and lighting: £7,500 and annual insurance: £1,500. Rent is payable quarterly in advance from 1 January. The business rates bill for January to March has been estimated at £1,800 and will be payable on 15 February while the rates bill from April to September has been estimated at £4,200 and will be payable by monthly instalments from 1 April. Heating and lighting will be payable quarterly in arrears at the end of each three-month period. Annual insurance will be payable on 1 January.

(f) Selling and administration overheads are all fixed and will be £114,000 in the first year. These overheads include depreciation of the delivery van at 25% per annum on a straight line basis.

(g) Selling and administration overheads will be the same each month and will be paid in the month in which they are incurred.

Required
Prepare a monthly cash budget and a budgeted monthly statement of profit or loss for the first six months of operations together with a budgeted statement of financial position at the end of June. As part of your budget, you should also produce a monthly production budget to calculate raw material purchases and a monthly sales budget to calculate both monthly sales and monthly cash receipts from sales.

12 Capital investment appraisal

LEARNING OUTCOMES

Once you have read this chapter and worked through the questions and examples in both this chapter and the online workbook, you should be able to:

- Understand what is meant by the term capital investment

- Understand why businesses undertake capital investment appraisal when making long-term investment decisions

- Explain how the four main capital investment appraisal techniques work

- Apply the four main capital investment appraisal techniques to capital investment decisions

- Explain the advantages and limitations of each of the four main capital investment appraisal techniques

- Understand the idea of the time value of money

Introduction

In the last few chapters, we have looked at the costing of products and services and the role of cost accounting in various short-term decision-making and planning techniques as well as considering the management of short-term working capital in Chapter 7. These short-term decision-making techniques and working capital management aim to maximize contribution and profits over periods of a few weeks or months. What techniques should be applied if we want to maximize our value over the long term? This question arises when businesses want to make long-term investment decisions involving the outlay of significant amounts of capital. What contribution and profits will any new investments make to the business? Will the new investments be valuable in the long run rather than just being profitable over short periods? Will the contribution and profits be higher than the returns we could generate from alternative investment options or from just putting the money into an interest paying bank account? These are important questions to ask when businesses are considering the investment of considerable sums of money in new projects and ventures. Businesses want to know if the contribution generated by these new investments will return their original cost and more. If a long-term investment fails to return the money originally invested, there would be little point undertaking the project in the first place.

What is capital investment?

In Chapter 2, we considered the distinction between non-current assets and current assets. As we discovered, current assets are short-term assets (inventory, receivables and cash). In Chapter 7, we looked at how the cash arising from sales of inventory and the cash received from trade receivables is used to fund a business's short-term working capital requirements. Inflows of cash from the sale of inventory and receipts from trade receivables pay for the day-to-day expenditure that arises in running a business, such as payments for wages, rent, rates, electricity and heating bills as well as paying short-term liabilities as they become due.

However, non-current assets also require funding in order to maintain or expand a business's operations. Assets wear out or become outdated. Failure to replace and renew assets means that businesses are operating less efficiently and less profitably than they should. Without investment in new assets and new projects, businesses will not survive over the long term. When new investment is undertaken, this gives rise to new non-current assets that will be used to generate revenues, profits and cash over several years. Expenditure on these new non-current assets is termed capital expenditure, spending money now to benefit the future through the acquisition of these long-lasting, long-term assets. Consider Example 12.1.

12

EXAMPLE 12.1

If you were in charge of a haulage business, every few years you would need to invest in a new fleet of lorries. This fleet of lorries would then be used to generate revenue for several years before they themselves were replaced with a new fleet. Paying for these new vehicles would require long-term investment today. If the company did not currently have the cash on hand with which to pay for these new assets, these long-term funds would be provided by lenders in the form of loans (non-current liabilities, as we saw in Chapter 2) or by shareholders in the form of new share capital subscribed by the shareholders (considered in Chapter 5).

Businesses undertake **capital investment appraisal** to determine whether new investments will be worthwhile and whether they will generate more cash than they originally cost.

WHY IS THIS RELEVANT TO ME? Capital investment

To enable you as a business professional and user of financial information to:

- Appreciate the need for businesses to invest continually in new long-term assets from which to generate increased revenue, profits and cash

- Reinforce your ability to distinguish between short-term working capital management and long-term capital investment

---

GO BACK OVER THIS AGAIN! Can you distinguish between short- and long-term investment decisions? Go to the **online workbook** Exercises 12.1 to make sure you can make these distinctions.

Why is capital investment appraisal important?

Capital investment appraisal is essential when considering investments in new projects or in new assets. Without this appraisal, we will not be able to decide whether our investment is likely to be worthwhile in financial terms. Think about the points raised in Example 12.2.

EXAMPLE 12.2

When choosing the university at which you wanted to study, you might have weighed up the benefits and drawbacks from your current course compared with the benefits and drawbacks of choosing another programme at another university. Your thoughts will have centred not just on financial considerations: you might have reflected on the nightlife, the sporting facilities and the academic reputation of your chosen university among many other things. But at some point you will have taken into account the costs of studying at a particular college compared with the costs of studying elsewhere and the likely career and salary opportunities that would be open to you upon completion of your chosen course.

In the same way, businesses will want to know whether proposed investments are likely to represent a valuable addition to current operations and whether a positive return will be generated for shareholders. If not, there is no point in undertaking the project. Businesses will want to take on all projects that capital investment appraisal techniques suggest will make a positive return. However, cash for investment purposes, like many other resources, is often in short supply. Therefore, entities will undertake capital investment appraisal to determine which one of the several options competing for funds is the most valuable project in which to invest, given the levels of risk involved. Again, a simple example (Example 12.3) will illustrate these ideas.

EXAMPLE 12.3

If you have spare cash to invest, there are many banks, building societies and other investments competing for your money. You will weigh up each of the available options on the basis of which investment will give you the highest rate of interest, but also consider which investment is likely to be the safest home for your savings. It would be pointless putting your cash into an investment paying a high rate of interest if you were likely to lose all your money when the investment collapsed into liquidation.

Finally, the future is uncertain. What might seem like a good investment now might not look like such a good idea two years down the line. Therefore, managers have to exercise due care and attention when investing shareholders' money into projects in the expectation that they will produce the best outcomes for investors and other stakeholders. Capital investment appraisal is a further example of managers exercising control over an entity's operations, as illustrated in Give me an example 12.1.

GIVE ME AN EXAMPLE 12.1 Capital investment appraisal

The following extract from the published report of Rio Tinto plc illustrates the rigorous approach adopted by company management to evaluating new investment opportunities.

We have strengthened our investment assessment criteria, our levels of independent review of opportunities and our investment approval processes. We approve investment only in opportunities that, after prudent assessment, offer attractive returns that are well above our cost of capital.

Source: *Rio Tinto plc Annual Report and Accounts 2014, Strategic Report*, page 11. www.riotinto.com

12

As a business professional and user of financial information you will be expected to:

- Understand the importance of evaluating long-term investment projects and what they will contribute to your organization

- Be involved in capital investment decisions and appraise both the financial and non-financial aspects of these decisions

- Undertake the necessary capital investment appraisal of long-term projects you are proposing yourself

---

GO BACK OVER THIS AGAIN! Confident you can describe capital investment appraisal and explain why it's needed? Go to the **online workbook** Exercises 12.2 to make sure you appreciate what capital investment appraisal involves.

What financial information will I need to undertake capital investment appraisal?

Capital investment appraisal relates to future events, so a substantial amount of estimation is required when undertaking this technique, as shown in Figure 12.1. All costs and revenues associated with a proposed project are expressed in terms of cash inflows and cash outflows.

The first piece of information required will be the cost of the new capital investment in £s. This is easily acquired as this cost will be readily available from the supplier of the new assets. In our haulage business example (Example 12.1), the capital investment will be the cost of the new lorries. This could be the list price or the list price less a discount for the purchase of several vehicles, but it is an easily ascertainable cost. If the capital investment involves the construction of a new building, then cost will be the cost of acquiring the land plus the construction costs. Again, the cost of the land will be a verifiable fact from the price the seller requires for the land, while the cost of the building will be the contract price determined by the engineers and designers at the construction company chosen to complete the project.

More difficult will be the estimates of revenue and costs arising from the new investment in each year of the proposed project's life. Demand for the new product or service will have to be determined along with the associated costs of providing the service or producing the product. Current demand and current revenue arising from

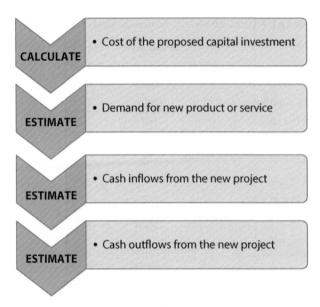

Figure 12.1 Steps in the capital investment appraisal process

that demand can be calculated quite easily, but future demand and future revenue will depend upon many uncertainties. Demand might fall to zero very quickly as a result of superior services and products from competitors or it might rise very rapidly as the business becomes the leading provider in the sector. Technology might reduce costs very quickly or costs might rise as a result of demand for particular raw materials that are in short supply. Whatever the revenues and costs, they will be subject to a high degree of estimation and in many ways will just represent a best guess.

Capital investment appraisal techniques: a comprehensive example

To illustrate the capital investment appraisal techniques that are used in practice we will now turn to a comprehensive example.

Anna is looking to expand by diversifying into different areas of business. She currently has £500,000 to invest in acquiring the assets of an existing business from its owners. She has identified a stonemason, a furniture workshop and a garden design and build company as possible targets for her new investment. Market research and costings indicate that the net cash inflows (revenue − expenditure) into the three businesses over the next five years are expected to be those shown in Illustration 12.1.

12

Illustration 12.1 Anna: cash flows from the three possible capital investment projects

	Stonemason	Furniture workshop	Garden design and build
	£000	£000	£000
Investment cost (an outflow of cash)	(500)	(500)	(500)
Net cash inflows in year 1	160	190	50
Net cash inflows in year 2	160	180	100
Net cash inflows in year 3	160	170	150
Net cash inflows in year 4	160	160	250
Net cash inflows in year 5	160	150	350
Cash inflow from sale of the investment at the end of year 5	200	100	300
Total net cash inflows	1,000	950	1,200
Total net cash inflows – investment cost	500	450	700

All three businesses require the same initial investment, but produce differing total cash inflows after deducting the cost of the original investment. One business is expected to provide a steady income throughout the five years, one produces high initial cash inflows, but these then decline, while the final opportunity starts with very low net cash inflows, which then grow rapidly. How will Anna choose the business in which she should invest? Initially, it would appear that Anna will choose the garden design and build business for her investment as this produces the highest net cash inflow over the five years along with a higher resale value for the assets. However, the majority of the cash inflows from the garden design and build operation occur towards the end of the five years. Later cash inflows are much less certain (and hence riskier) than cash inflows that occur earlier in the other projects' lives. The following capital investment appraisal techniques can be used to help Anna make her decision.

Capital investment appraisal techniques

There are four commonly used techniques when undertaking capital investment appraisal. These are:

- Payback
- Accounting rate of return (ARR)
- Net present value (NPV)
- Internal rate of return (IRR)

We will look at each of these techniques in detail to show how each of them works and what each of them tells us about the positive or negative financial returns from each project.

Payback

This method calculates the number of years it will take for the cash inflows from the project to pay back the original cost of the investment. An investment of £1,000 into a deposit account that pays 5% interest per annum would provide you with annual interest of £50 (£1,000 × 5%). To repay your initial investment of £1,000 would take 20 years (£1,000 ÷ £50). In the same way, businesses assess how long the cash inflows from a project would take to repay the initial invest-ment into the project.

GO BACK OVER THIS AGAIN! Convinced you can calculate a simple payback period? Go to the **online workbook** and have a go at Exercises 12.3 to make sure you can undertake these calculations successfully.

Looking at Anna's investment opportunities, let's consider the payback from the first option, the stonemason. To calculate the payback period, a payback table is drawn up to show how long the project will take to pay back the original investment. The first column of the table (see Table 12.1) lists the annual cash inflows and outflows, while the second column presents the initial investment outflow less the cash inflows received each year.

Table 12.1 Anna: payback table for the investment in the stonemason business

	Cash flows	Cumulative
	£000	£000
Initial investment year 0	(500)	(500)
Net cash inflows year 1	160	(340)
Net cash inflows year 2	160	(180)
Net cash inflows year 3	160	(20)
Net cash inflows year 4	160	140
Net cash inflows year 5	160	300
Cash inflow from sale of the investment at the end of year 5	200	500

In Table 12.1 the investment of £500,000 is made at the present time and so is shown as the initial outflow of cash from the project. Investments made at the start of a project, the present time, are conventionally referred to as being made in year 0 or at time 0. As cash flows into the project, so the initial investment is paid back and the investment in the project not yet paid back falls.

At the end of year 1, after deducting the first year's cash inflows of £160,000, there is £500,000 − £160,000 = £340,000 still to be recovered from the project before the full £500,000 is paid back. In year 2, the project generates another £160,000, so at the end of year 2 there is still £340,000 − £160,000 = £180,000 required from the project before the initial investment is repaid in full. This process is repeated until the cumulative cash flows show £Nil or a positive number. At this point, the initial investment has been completely paid back by cash inflows into the project.

Table 12.1 shows that the stonemason project would repay the initial investment of £500,000 at some time between the end of years 3 and 4 as the cumulative cash flows (original investment − net cash inflows) turn positive by the end of year 4.

However, we can be more precise. Only £20,000 out of the £160,000 cash inflow in year 4 is required to repay the investment in the project that has not yet been repaid by the cash inflows in years 1, 2 and 3. Therefore, the exact payback period for an investment in the stonemason business would be:

$$3 \text{ years} + \frac{£20,000}{£160,000} = 3.125 \text{ years}$$

As 0.125 years is roughly equivalent to 1½ months (12 × 0.125), the initial investment of £500,000 at time 0 is fully repaid after 3 years and 1½ months.

NUMERICAL EXERCISES Think you can calculate a payback period for a project? Work your way through the figures in Table 12.1 again to confirm your understanding of how we arrived at the payback period for the stonemason project and then go to the **online workbook** and attempt Numerical exercises 12.1 and 12.2 to make sure you can apply this investment appraisal technique to the other two investments that Anna is considering.

Payback: the decision criteria

When using the payback method of capital investment appraisal, the project chosen is always the investment that pays back its initial cash outlay most quickly. In Anna's case, on the basis of payback, she would choose to invest in the furniture workshop as this repays the initial outlay of £500,000 in less than three years while the other two projects repay the same initial investment in more than three years, as shown in Figure 12.2.

Would this be a good decision? If Anna is concerned with just the speed of her cash recovery, then the furniture workshop would be the correct choice as her initial investment is returned to her in the shortest possible time. The payback calculation

Figure 12.2 Payback periods in years of the three investment opportunities available to Anna

is easy to make and easy to understand, but it does not consider the **time value of money** (see this Chapter, The time value of money). It also ignores the cash flows after the payback period is complete. In the case of the furniture workshop, a further £450,000 is generated from this project after the initial investment is paid back, whereas the garden design and build project yields a further £700,000 after payback, £250,000 more than the cash inflows from the preferred investment on the basis of the payback period.

Should the payback period be the sole criterion upon which to base an investment decision? The answer to this question is 'no'. Payback will be just one of the criteria upon which any investment decision is based. Further decisions have to be made about the long-term revenue generation prospects of the investment. You probably noticed that the cash inflows from the furniture workshop are reducing year by year and that the resale value of the assets of this business is significantly lower than the resale value of the assets in the other two projects under consideration. Any further investment in this business after the five-year period will probably generate lower cash inflows than the other two options, so, from a longer-term point of view, an investment in the furniture workshop is probably not the best use of Anna's money if she wants to maximize the potential returns on her investment.

Looking at the other investment options, the garden design and build, while presenting the longest payback period, shows rising cash inflows each year that accelerate towards the end of the five-year period. Therefore, this might well be a better investment for the longer term as demand for this business's services seems to be rising sharply and might be expected to increase even further after the end of year 5. The stonemason business shows steady inflows of cash each year, but no increase or decrease in demand. This would seem to be the safest investment, but it is not one that will perform beyond expectations.

> **WHY IS THIS RELEVANT TO ME?** Payback method of capital investment appraisal
>
> To enable you as a business professional and user of financial information to:
>
> - Calculate a payback period for a proposed investment
> - Understand the criteria on which to take an investment decision based on payback
> - Understand the advantages and limitations of the payback method
> - Appreciate that capital investment decisions have to be based on not just one but several criteria

---

SUMMARY OF KEY CONCEPTS Totally happy you understand how payback works and what its advantages and limitations are? Revise payback with Summary of key concepts 12.1.

Accounting rate of return (ARR)

This investment appraisal method averages the projections of accounting profit to calculate the expected rate of return on the average capital invested, as summarized in Figure 12.3. Accounting profit is represented by the net cash inflows of the project over its life less the total depreciation (remember that depreciation is not a cash flow—refer back to Chapter 4, The indirect method, to revise this point—but is treated as an expense in arriving at accounting profit). The total accounting profit projections are divided by the number of years the project will last to give the average profit over the life of the investment. This is then divided by the average capital employed over the life of the project to determine the ARR.

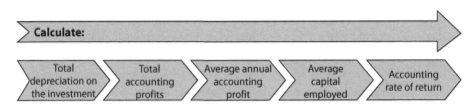

Figure 12.3 Steps in calculating the accounting rate of return (ARR) on an investment

Let's see how the ARR would be calculated for the stonemason business and then you can practise this technique on the other two potential investment opportunities.

ARR step 1: calculate the total depreciation on the investment

First, we will need to calculate the total depreciation on the investment in the stonemason project. Remember that the total depreciation provided on non-current assets is given by the assets' cost – the residual value of those assets (Chapter 3, Residual value and the annual depreciation charge).

From Illustration 12.1:

- The cost of the assets is £500,000

- The residual value is the cash inflow from the sale of the investment at the end of year 5 of £200,000

Therefore, total depreciation over the five years of the project's life is:

£500,000 (cost) – £200,000 (residual value) = £300,000

ARR step 2: calculate the total accounting profits

Total accounting profits are the total net cash inflows – the total depreciation. Total net cash inflows into the stonemason project are £160,000 for five years, a total of £800,000. The resale value of the assets is not included in the net cash inflows as this figure is used to calculate both the total depreciation on the project's assets and the average capital investment over the project's life.

Total accounting profits are thus £800,000 (net cash inflows) – £300,000 (depreciation) = £500,000.

ARR step 3: calculate the average annual accounting profit

The average annual accounting profit is then £500,000 ÷ 5 years = £100,000 per annum.

ARR step 4: calculate the average capital employed

The average capital employed in the stonemason project is found by adding together the original cost of the investment and the resale value of the assets at the end of the project and dividing this total figure by 2.

From Illustration 12.1:

- The cost of the assets is £500,000

- The residual value is the cash inflow from the sale of the investment at the end of year 5 of £200,000

Therefore, average capital employed in the stonemason business over the five years is:

(£500,000 (cost) + £200,000 (residual value)) ÷ 2 = £350,000

ARR step 5: calculate the accounting rate of return

The ARR is then the average annual accounting profit divided by the average capital employed in the project:

$$\frac{£100{,}000 \ (\text{average annual profit})}{£350{,}000 \ (\text{average capital employed over the five years})} \times 100\% = 28.57\%$$

NUMERICAL EXERCISES How confident are you that you can calculate an accounting rate of return (ARR) for a project? Work your way through the ARR calculations again to confirm your understanding of how we arrived at the ARR for the stonemason project and then go to the **online workbook** and attempt Numerical exercises 12.3 and 12.4 to make sure you can apply this investment appraisal technique to the other two investments that Anna is considering.

Accounting rate of return: the decision criteria

The investment decision based on the ARR requires us to choose the proposed investment with the highest ARR, provided that this meets or exceeds the required ARR of the business. Assuming that the ARR meets Anna's target rate of return, the project that she will choose will be the garden design and build project as it produces an ARR of 35% compared with the furniture workshop, which has an ARR of 30%, as shown in Figure 12.4. This approach produces a quite different decision when compared to the payback method of investment appraisal.

While the ARR is easy to calculate and is based on accounting profits, it does suffer from some serious limitations:

- As with the payback method of investment appraisal, the ARR ignores the time value of money.

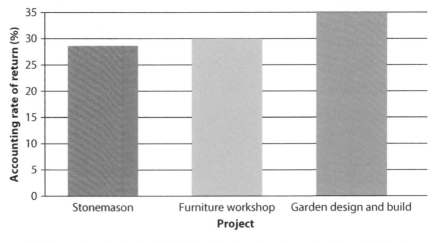

Figure 12.4 Accounting rate of return (ARR) of the three investment opportunities available to Anna

- The ARR is a percentage rather than the total profits generated by an investment, so projects with the same ARR could have hugely different cash flows, one with very low net cash inflows and one with very large net cash inflows. Managers will always prefer larger cash flows to smaller ones, but reliance on the relative measure of ARR might lead to the selection of a project with a higher rate of return but lower net cash inflows. In Anna's case the project with the highest ARR and the highest cash inflows is the same, but this may not always be the case.

- ARR does not differentiate between projects (as payback does) that have the majority of the net cash inflows in the early stages of the project's life. As we have already noted, early cash inflows can be predicted with more accuracy and so are preferred by businesses as the money is in the bank rather than just being a potential future inflow of cash.

WHY IS THIS RELEVANT TO ME? Accounting rate of return method of capital investment appraisal

To enable you as a business professional and user of financial information to:

- Calculate the ARR for a proposed investment
- Appreciate the criteria on which to make an investment decision based on the ARR
- Understand the advantages and limitations of the ARR method of capital investment appraisal

---

SUMMARY OF KEY CONCEPTS Can you remember how the accounting rate of return is calculated and what its advantages and limitations are? Check your knowledge with Summary of key concepts 12.2.

GIVE ME AN EXAMPLE 12.2 Companies' use of payback and accounting measures in evaluating investment opportunities

Do companies use payback and accounting based measures in practice to evaluate investment opportunities? The following extract from Next plc's Annual Report and Accounts for the 52 weeks to 27 January 2018 shows that they do.

The profitability of the portfolio of stores opened or extended in the last 12 months is forecast to be 21% of VAT inclusive sales and payback on the net capital invested is expected to be 24.8 months. The new store portfolio marginally missed its sales target, largely because many of the targets were set some time ago at the point we negotiated terms for these properties; a time when prospects for retail stores were more benign. Payback is forecast to be slightly higher than our 24 month goal.

Source: *Next plc Annual Report and Accounts 2018*, page 8

12

The time value of money

Before we consider the final two investment appraisal techniques, net present value (NPV) and the internal rate of return (IRR), we need to think about the time value of money. We noted earlier in this chapter that both the payback and ARR methods of capital investment appraisal ignore this aspect of the investment decision. So why is the time value of money so important? And what do we mean when we talk about the time value of money? This approach to investment appraisal recognizes that £1 received today is worth more than £1 received tomorrow. There are various reasons why today's money is more valuable than tomorrow's.

Firstly, inflation will reduce the value of our cash: £1 will buy more today than it will buy this time next year. For example, if a litre of petrol costs £1.40 today, we can buy 30 litres of petrol for £42 (30 × £1.40 = £42). However, if the inflation rate is 5% per annum, this means that in one year's time, one litre of petrol will cost £1.47 (£1.40 × 1.05). Our £42 will now only buy us 28.57 litres of petrol (£42 ÷ £1.47), as the purchasing power of our £42 has fallen as a result of inflation. Therefore, given that inflation reduces the value of our money and what we can buy with it, it makes sense to receive cash today rather than receiving cash tomorrow.

We can combat the effects of inflation by investing our money to generate interest to maintain our purchasing power. £1 invested today at an annual interest rate of 5% will give us £1.05 in a year's time, our original £1 plus 5% interest. If the inflation rate over the same period has been 5%, we will be no worse off and our purchasing power will have remained the same. In our example above, £42 today invested at a rate of 5% would give us £44.10 (£42 × 1.05) in one year's time. With this £44.10 we could buy £44.10 ÷ £1.47 = 30 litres of petrol so the purchasing power of our money has been maintained.

However, if we can invest our £1 for a year at an interest rate of 5% while inflation is only 3%, at the end of the year we would need our original £1 plus a further 3p to buy the same goods in a year's time that £1 will buy today. We will thus be 2p better off as our £1.05 is more than the £1.03 we need for consumption in one year's time. If we cannot have our money today, we will demand something in return to compensate us for waiting for cash that is receivable in the future. By investing our money in the bank or in a project, we are missing out on using the cash today so there is an opportunity cost element to this investment. A higher return on the cash is the compensation we expect for forgoing consumption today.

Finally, money that we will receive in the future is more risky than money we receive today because of the uncertainty that surrounds future income. Investing money carries the risk that we will not receive any interest as well as the risk that our original investment will not be repaid in full. Therefore, investors require a particular level of return to compensate them for the risk they are taking by investing their money. In the same way, businesses require a rate of return to compensate them for risking their capital in a particular venture. The riskier the venture is, the higher the rate of return that will be required to invest in that venture, as shown in Give me an example 12.3.

GIVE ME AN EXAMPLE 12.3 Higher risk = higher return

Two bailout packages totalling €240 billion were advanced to the Greek government in May 2010 and October 2011. In April 2015 growing fears that Greece would fail to repay what it owed to its international creditors, thereby forcing the country out of the European single currency, caused the value of Greek bonds to fall dramatically. As a result, anyone investing their money in Greek two-year bonds on 15 April 2015 would have seen the returns on these bonds rise to 27%. This very high return is due to the risk that the Greek government will be unable either to pay the interest or to repay the capital value of those bonds. Clearly, the higher the risk, the higher the return that investors will demand for taking on that risk. By contrast, the price that investors were paying for German 10-year government bonds (which are considered an ultra-safe investment) on the same day meant that their returns from their investment in these bonds are close to zero.

Source: www.wsj.com/articles/greek-government-bonds-plunge-on-ratings-downgrade-1429180492

WHY IS THIS RELEVANT TO ME? The time value of money

To enable you as a business professional and user of financial information to:

- Understand that inflation erodes the value of today's money and reduces its future purchasing power
- Appreciate that money received today has more purchasing power than money received tomorrow
- Appreciate that cash expected in the future is less certain and so riskier
- Understand that investors will require a certain rate of return on money invested in order to compensate them for the risks they are taking in investing their money
- Appreciate that investing money in a project involves an opportunity cost as that money cannot be used for something else while it is invested in the project

GO BACK OVER THIS AGAIN! Certain you have grasped the concept of the time value of money? Go to the **online workbook** and have a look at Exercises 12.4 to make sure you understand this concept and then have a go at Exercises 12.5 to check your grasp of this subject.

MULTIPLE CHOICE QUESTIONS Totally happy you understand the time value of money? Go to the **online workbook** and have a go at Multiple choice questions 12.1 to test your understanding.

Business investment and the time value of money

In the same way, businesses invest money with the expectation that their investments will earn them a return in the future. Businesses will determine an acceptable level of return to compensate them for the risks involved in investing and use this level of return to discount expected future cash inflows and outflows to a **present value**. Present value expresses expected future inflows and outflows of cash in terms of today's monetary values. **Discounting** to present value thus expresses all a project's cash inflows and outflows in the common currency of today, thereby facilitating a fair comparison of projected cash inflows and outflows for different investment proposals.

The acceptable level of return is referred to as the business's **cost of capital** and is sometimes known as the hurdle rate of return. If an investment clears the hurdle—that is, the NPV is greater than or equal to £Nil—then it means that the project will deliver a positive return and generate more cash for the business over time than has to be invested at the beginning of the project.

Net present value

Anna estimates that her expected rate of return is 15%. This is the rate of return that she feels will compensate her for the risk she is taking in investing in a new business of which she has no experience. Applying this rate of return to the stonemason project produces the NPV results shown in Illustration 12.2.

Illustration 12.2 Anna: net present value of the investment in the stonemason business discounted at a rate of 15%

	Cash flows ×	Discount factor =	Net present value
	£000	15%	£000
Cash outflow year 0	(500)	1.0000	(500.00)
Net cash inflows year 1	160	0.8696	139.14
Net cash inflows year 2	160	0.7561	120.98
Net cash inflows year 3	160	0.6575	105.20
Net cash inflows year 4	160	0.5718	91.49
Net cash inflows year 5	160	0.4972	79.55
Cash inflow from sale of the investment at the end of year 5	200	0.4972	99.44
Stonemason investment: net present value of the project discounted at a rate of 15%			135.80

How did we arrive at these figures?

The initial investment is always made at the start of the project, time 0, and so is already expressed in terms of today's money. Therefore, there is no need to discount this figure to present value as today's money is already stated at its present value. This figure is thus multiplied by a discount rate of 1.0000.

All cash inflows are assumed to be received at the end of each year of the project and so are discounted to present value as though they are received at the end of year 1, at the end of year 2, at the end of year 3 and so on, right up to the last expected cash inflow or outflow associated with the project. This is an important convention of the NPV and IRR capital investment appraisal techniques, but is obviously unrealistic as, in reality, cash will flow into and out of projects throughout the year. However, it is an assumption you need to be aware of and this assumption is made to keep the models as simple as possible.

Discount factors are presented in Table 1 in the Appendix. Check that the figures given in Illustration 12.2 are the discount rates for time intervals 1, 2, 3, 4 and 5 for a 15% discount rate. If you ever need to derive your own discount rates, you would divide 1 by $(1 +$ the interest rate being used$)^n$ where n is the number of years into the project. In Anna's case, this is 1 divided by $(1 + 0.15)$ for year 1, 1 divided by $(1 + 0.15)^2$ for year 2, 1 divided by $(1 + 0.15)^3$ for year 3 and so on. Check that these calculations do give you the discount factors shown in Illustration 12.2 by working out these figures on your calculator now. Keep Table 1 in the Appendix handy for the remaining examples in this chapter and when you attempt the various activities in the online workbook.

Just as we saw with statements of cash flows in Chapter 4, cash outflows are shown in brackets while cash inflows are shown without brackets. This convention is also applied when calculating NPVs. Thus the initial investment, which is an outflow of cash, is shown in brackets while the inflows of cash are shown without brackets. Totalling up the NPV of the outflow and the NPVs of all the inflows gives us a positive NPV of £135,800 for the stonemason project.

NUMERICAL EXERCISES Confident you can calculate a net present value (NPV) for a project? Work your way through the above example again to confirm your understanding of how we arrived at the NPV for the stonemason project and then go to the **online workbook** and attempt Numerical exercises 12.5 and 12.6 to make sure you can apply this investment appraisal technique to the other two investments that Anna is considering.

SHOW ME HOW TO DO IT How clearly did you understand the calculation of a proposed project's net present value (NPV)? View Video presentation 12.1 in the **online workbook** to see a practical demonstration of how the NPV calculation is carried out.

Net present value: the decision criteria

Projects discounted at the business's cost of capital resulting in either a NPV of £Nil or a positive NPV are accepted. If a company has several projects under consideration, then all projects with a positive or £Nil NPV are taken on. Where more than one project is competing for investment capital, then the project with the highest NPV is accepted first. If investment capital is available to undertake a further project, then the project with the second highest NPV is accepted and so on until all the available capital for investment has been allocated to projects. Proposed projects with a negative NPV are rejected and are not developed beyond the evaluation stage.

In Anna's case, she can only invest in one of the three projects as her capital for investment is limited to £500,000. Figure 12.5 shows that the garden design and build project gives the highest NPV of £183,850, well above the project with the second highest NPV,

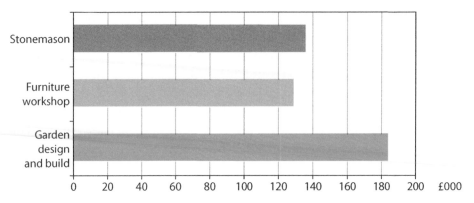

Figure 12.5 Net present value of the three investment opportunities available to Anna

the stonemason business. The furniture workshop, which was ranked first on the basis of payback and second on the basis of ARR, is now the worst performing project on the basis of NPV. Therefore, Anna will accept the garden design and build project on the basis of the evaluation provided by the NPV method of investment appraisal.

Net present value: advantages

The NPV technique has the following advantages:

- Unlike the payback and ARR investment appraisal techniques, NPV does take into account the time value of money. This makes it a superior method of evaluating and differentiating between several projects.
- NPV discounts all cash inflows and outflows from a project into today's money to enable a fair comparison between projects to be made.
- NPV accounts for all the cash inflows and outflows from a project.
- Cash inflows that arise later in the project's life are riskier than cash inflows that arise earlier. The use of discount factors enables users of this technique to reflect this increased risk arising from later cash inflows as these cash inflows are worth less in current money terms.
- The NPV technique can be used in conjunction with the payback approach to determine when NPVs become positive (this chapter, Discounted payback, and Table 12.2). The further into the future this happens, the riskier the project is.

Net present value: limitations

However, as with all investment appraisal techniques, the NPV approach also suffers from the following disadvantages:

- This method is more difficult to understand than the simpler payback method.

• The technique makes the very large assumption that cash inflows and outflows and discount rates can be predicted accurately.

WHY IS THIS RELEVANT TO ME? **Net present value method of capital investment appraisal**

To enable you as a business professional and user of financial information to:

• Calculate a net present value for a proposed investment project

• Appreciate the criteria on which to make an investment decision based on the net present value method

• Understand the advantages and limitations of the net present value method

---

SUMMARY OF KEY CONCEPTS Can you remember how net present value is calculated and what its advantages and limitations are? Revise these with Summary of key concepts 12.3.

Discounted payback

Before we move on to consider the internal rate of return investment appraisal method, it is worth noting that the NPV and payback methods of investment appraisal can be combined to calculate the discounted payback period. This method takes the discounted cash flows under the NPV approach and then determines when those discounted cash flows will turn positive after taking into account the original investment in a project. Table 12.2 presents the discounted payback for the stone mason project.

Table 12.2 Anna: discounted payback table for the investment in the stonemason business

	Cash flows £000	Cumulative £000
Initial investment year 0	(500.00)	(500.00)
Discounted cash inflows year 1	139.14	(360.86)
Discounted cash inflows year 2	120.98	(239.88)
Discounted cash inflows year 3	105.20	(134.68)
Discounted cash inflows year 4	91.49	(43.19)
Discounted cash inflows year 5	79.55	36.36
Discounted cash inflow from sale of the investment at the end of year 5	99.44	135.80

Table 12.2 tells us that the discounted payback period is between 4 and 5 years. Only £43,190 out of the £79,550 discounted cash inflow in year 5 is required to repay the

investment in the project that has not yet been repaid by the discounted cash inflows in years 1 to 4. Therefore, the exact discounted payback period for the investment in the stonemason business would be:

$$4 \text{ years} + \frac{43.19}{79.55} \times 12 = 4.543 \text{ years}$$

0.543 years is equivalent to 6½ months (12 × 0.543), so the initial investment of £500,000 at time 0 is fully repaid after 4 years and 6½ months under the discounted payback approach to investment appraisal.

The discounted payback results are shown in Figure 12.6 together with the original payback results (Figure 12.2). The discounted payback decision would be the same as the payback decision with the furniture workshop paying back the initial investment more quickly than the other two investment opportunities. However, the decision to choose the furniture workshop investment on the basis of the discounted payback period would still suffer from the same limitations as outlined earlier (this chapter, Payback: the decision criteria) so Anna has not gained much additional information as a result of these additional calculations.

NUMERICAL EXERCISES   Are you sure that you can calculate a discounted payback period for a project? Work your way through the figures in Table 12.2 again to confirm your understanding of how we arrived at the discounted payback period for the stonemason project and then go to the **online workbook** and attempt Numerical exercises 12.7 and 12.8 to make sure you can apply this investment appraisal technique to the other two investments that Anna is considering.

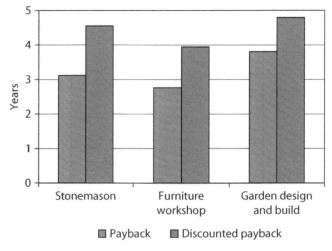

Figure 12.6 Payback and discounted payback for the three investment projects available to Anna

Internal rate of return

The IRR, which is linked to the NPV technique, is the discount rate at which the NPV of the project is £Nil. The IRR is thus the discount rate at which a project breaks even, the discount rate at which the present value of the cash outflows is equal to the present value of the cash inflows.

To calculate the IRR, a process of trial and error is used. Project cash flows are discounted at successively higher rates until a negative NPV is given for that project. The IRR is then estimated using a mathematical technique called interpolation. This technique is illustrated later (this Chapter, Calculating the internal rate of return).

Figure 12.7 illustrates the IRR, the discount rate which gives a NPV of £Nil. The NPV of a project at various discount rates is determined and plotted on the graph. As the discount rate increases, the NPV of the project falls. The point at which the NPV line crosses the x-axis on the graph is the point at which the NPV is £Nil and this is the IRR.

All this may sound very complicated, so let's see how the IRR is calculated using the proposed investment in the stonemason business. We saw in Illustration 12.2 that a discount rate of 15% gave a positive NPV of £135,800 for this project. Using a discount

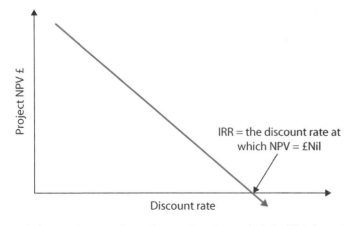

Figure 12.7 Graph showing the internal rate of return, the point at which the NPV of a project is £Nil

rate of 26% to discount the stonemason project will give us the NPV shown in Illustration 12.3.

Illustration 12.3 Anna: net present value of the investment in the stonemason business discounted at a rate of 26%

	Cash flows ×	Discount factor =	Net present value
	£000	26%	£000
Cash outflow year 0	(500)	1.0000	(500.00)
Net cash inflows year 1	160	0.7937	126.99
Net cash inflows year 2	160	0.6299	100.78
Net cash inflows year 3	160	0.4999	79.98
Net cash inflows year 4	160	0.3968	63.49
Net cash inflows year 5	160	0.3149	50.38
Cash inflow from sale of the investment at the end of year 5	200	0.3149	62.98
Stonemason investment: net present value of the project discounted at a rate of 26%			(15.40)

We now know the following facts:

- A discount rate of 15% gives us a positive NPV of £135,800 (Illustration 12.2)
- A discount rate of 26% gives us a negative NPV of £15,400 (Illustration 12.3)
- Therefore, the discount rate that will give us a £Nil NPV lies somewhere between 15% and 26%

Calculating the internal rate of return

This discount rate is given by the following calculation:

$$15\% + \frac{135.80}{(135.80 + 15.40)} \times (26\% - 15\%) = 24.88\%$$

How did we arrive at this IRR of 24.88%?

- We know that a discount rate of 15% gives a positive return, so this will be our starting point
- What we don't know is where the NPV line crosses the x-axis on the graph, the point at which the NPV of the project is equal to £Nil (Figure 12.7)
- Therefore, we have to estimate the discount rate at which the NPV is £Nil
- Our NPV has to fall by £135,800 before we reach the discount rate that gives a NPV of £Nil

- The total difference between the two results is £135,800 + £15,400 = £151,200 whereas we only need our NPV to fall by £135,800 before a NPV of £Nil is reached

- Therefore, if we divide £135,800 by £151,200 and then multiply this fraction by the difference between the positive (15%) and negative (26%) discount rates, this will tell us how far along the line between 15% and 26% the IRR is

- Adding the 15% to this result gives us an IRR of 24.88%

NUMERICAL EXERCISES   Totally confident you can calculate an internal rate of return for a project? Work your way through the above example again to confirm your understanding of how internal rates of return are calculated and then go to the **online workbook** and attempt Numerical exercises 12.9 and 12.10 to make sure you can apply this investment appraisal technique to the other two investments that Anna is considering.

SHOW ME HOW TO DO IT   How easily did you follow the calculation of a proposed project's internal rate of return? View Video presentation 12.2 in the **online workbook** to see a practical demonstration of how the internal rate of return calculation is carried out.

Internal rate of return: the decision criteria

Where a project has an IRR higher than an entity's required rate of return on investment projects, then the project should be accepted. Where projects are competing for resources, then the project with the highest IRR would be selected for implementation. In Anna's case, Figure 12.8 shows that the furniture workshop now comes out on top again with an internal rate of return of 25.31% compared with the garden design and build's IRR of 25.00% and 24.88% on the investment in the stonemason. However, the IRR evaluation requires the project originally selected under the NPV technique to

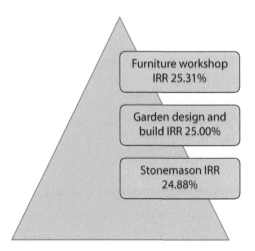

Figure 12.8 Internal rate of return of the three investment opportunities available to Anna

be preferred where the decision under the IRR investment appraisal technique differs from the original NPV outcome. This makes sense as the NPV of the garden design and build investment discounted at a rate of 15% was £183,850 compared with a NPV of £128,890 for the furniture workshop investment discounted at the same rate. As we noted earlier, managers will always prefer a higher to a lower cash inflow.

Internal rate of return: advantages

The IRR has the following advantages:

- As with the NPV technique, the time value of money is taken into account. This gives the IRR the same advantages as the NPV technique when compared with the ARR and payback investment appraisal methods.
- In the same way as NPV, the IRR method accounts for all the cash inflows and outflows from a project and discounts all these figures into today's money.
- Similarly, cash inflows that arise later in the project are riskier than cash inflows that arise earlier in the project. The use of discount factors enables users of this technique to reflect this increased risk arising from later cash inflows as these cash inflows are worth less in current money terms.
- The IRR technique is an absolute value and tells us what the percentage discount rate is that will give a NPV of £Nil, the break-even NPV for a project. Thus, the technique does not require entities to specify in advance what their cost of capital is, but allows users to determine whether the rate of return is acceptable or not.
- The IRR provides more information than the NPV technique in that it tells users which project gives the highest rate of return where all projects have a positive NPV when discounted at the entity's cost of capital.

Internal rate of return: limitations

- Just as you found with the NPV technique, the IRR is difficult to understand! However, with practice and thought you will become familiar with this technique and be able to apply it in practice.
- The IRR, like the ARR, is a % rather than a total figure, so there is a risk that projects with a higher internal rate of return will be accepted even when the NPV of the cash flows from other projects discounted at the entity's cost of capital is higher. Hence the requirement that the IRR does not overrule the original decision under the NPV technique. As we saw in Chapter 6 (Ratios, figures or both?) the magnitude of the figures must be considered alongside any ratios or percentages calculated when making decisions.

- The IRR cannot be used if cash flows are irregular. Where cash flows turn from being inflows to outflows and back again, a project will have two or more internal rates of return as the NPV line will cross the *x*-axis in two or more places (illustration of this is beyond the scope of the present book).

WHY IS THIS RELEVANT TO ME? Internal rate of return method of capital investment appraisal

To enable you as a business professional and user of financial information to:

- Calculate an IRR for an investment project
- Appreciate the criteria on which to make an investment decision based on the IRR
- Understand the advantages and limitations of the IRR method

---

SUMMARY OF KEY CONCEPTS Confident you understand how internal rate of return is calculated and what its advantages and limitations are? Revise these with Summary of key concepts 12.4.

What use do companies make of discounted cash flow measures in practice? Have a look at Give me an example 12.4 to see the ways in which GlaxoSmithKline plc uses discounted cash flow techniques to evaluate investment projects.

GIVE ME AN EXAMPLE 12.4 A company's use of discounted cash flow measures in evaluating investment opportunities

The following extracts from the annual report of GlaxoSmithKline plc illustrate the use of both the NPV and IRR methods of investment appraisal used in evaluating investment opportunities (Note: R&D = Research and Development):

In 2010, we calculated that our estimated R&D internal rate of return (IRR) was 11% and stated a long-term aim of increasing this to 14%. We continue to improve the financial efficiency of our R&D and in February 2014 announced an estimated IRR of 13%. We continue to target 14% on a longer-term basis. Our estimated IRR is an important measure of our financial discipline and our strategic progress to improve the economics of R&D. It also underpins our strategy to

create more flexibility around the pricing of our new medicines.

Source: GlaxoSmithKline plc, Annual Report 2014, page 27

We have a formal process for assessing potential investment proposals in order to ensure decisions are aligned with our overall strategy. This process includes an assessment of the cash flow return on investment (CFROI), as well as its net present value (NPV) and internal rate of return (IRR) where the timeline for the project is very long term. We also consider the impact on earnings and credit profile where relevant.

Source: GlaxoSmithKline plc, Annual Report 2014, page 68

Making a final decision

Which project should Anna choose to invest in? Based on the results from our calculations in this chapter and the results from the Numerical exercises online, we can draw up a table to show us the rankings of the projects based on the outcomes of each of the four capital investment appraisal techniques we have applied to the three proposals. These results are shown in Table 12.3.

Table 12.3 Anna: summary of rankings based on the results of each of the four capital investment appraisal techniques applied to the three proposed investments

Capital investment appraisal technique	Stonemason	Furniture workshop	Garden design and build
	Ranking	Ranking	Ranking
Payback and discounted payback	2	1	3
Accounting rate of return	3	2	1
Net present value	2	3	1
Internal rate of return	3	1	2

The investment in the stonemason fails to come out on top on any of the investment appraisal criteria. Therefore, on purely financial grounds, investment in this project would be rejected. The other two projects are ranked first on the basis of two techniques, second once and third once. However, as already noted under internal rate of return, where the IRR technique gives a different result from the NPV technique, then the original choice under the NPV technique should be the project selected. In this case, the garden design and build will be accepted by Anna on the basis of the capital investment appraisal techniques applied to the three proposals. The garden design and build has the highest NPV and the highest ARR, as well as seeming to offer the highest net cash inflows and the highest growth potential among the projects on offer.

Post investment audit

In previous chapters we have placed emphasis on the need to compare actual outcomes to expectations. Capital investment decisions are no exception to this approach. Once the investment in new non-current assets has been made and cash is flowing in from each new project, then managers will gather relevant information to evaluate how precise or how inaccurate their expectations and forecasts were. A post investment audit will be conducted to compare actual and forecast cash inflows and outflows. The aim of this comparison is to improve the accuracy of future capital investment appraisal proposals in order to minimize unfavourable outcomes. At the end of each project's life, the post investment audit will consider all aspects of the project and compare these with the expectations in the original proposal. Recommendations for improving the capital investment appraisal process will then be made and submitted to management for consideration and implementation.

Sensitivity analysis

In Chapter 11 sensitivity analysis was applied to budgets to determine the extent to which the outcome would change if the assumptions on which the budget was based were relaxed. In the same way, capital investment appraisal can be subjected to sensitivity analysis to see what the result would be if the cash inflows were reduced or increased by 10% or 20%, if the cost of the investment were increased by 10% or 20% and if the cost of capital were increased or decreased. By undertaking these additional calculations, a more informed investment decision can be made.

CHAPTER SUMMARY

You should now have learnt that:

* Capital investment involves the acquisition of new non-current assets or an investment in new projects with the aim of increasing sales, profits and cash flows to the long-term benefit of a business

* Capital investment appraisal is undertaken to evaluate the long-term cash generating potential of investment projects

* Capital investment appraisal of new projects is important in assisting decision makers in allocating scarce investment capital resources to projects that will maximize the profits of the entity in the long run

* Payback, accounting rate of return, net present value and internal rate of return calculations assist in the appraisal of capital investment projects

* All four capital investment appraisal techniques offer both advantages and limitations when used in capital investment decisions

* Money received tomorrow is less valuable than money received today

QUICK REVISION   Test your knowledge with the online flashcards in Summary of key concepts and attempt the Multiple choice questions, all in the **online workbook**. www.oup.com/uk/scott_business3e/

END-OF-CHAPTER QUESTIONS

Solutions to these questions can be found at the back of the book from page 520.

❱ DEVELOP YOUR UNDERSTANDING

Note to Questions 12.1–12.5: don't forget to use Table 1 in the Appendix when calculating the NPV and IRR of an investment project.

❭ Question 12.1

Podcaster University Press is evaluating two book proposals, one in accounting and one in economics. The directors are keen on both books but have funding for only one and they cannot decide which book to publish. Details of the two books are as follows:

Accounting book

The accounting book requires an investment of £450,000 to be made immediately. The book will produce net cash inflows of £160,000 in years 1 to 3 and £100,000 in years 4 and 5. The non-current assets involved in the book's production are expected to have a resale value of £50,000 after five years. It is the directors' intention to sell the non-current assets from this project at the end of year 5 to realize the £50,000 cash inflow.

Economics book

The economics book requires an immediate investment of £600,000. The book will produce net cash inflows of £240,000 in year 1, £200,000 in year 2, £160,000 in year 3 and £105,000 in years 4 and 5. The non-current assets bought to print this book are expected to have a resale value of £100,000 at the end of the project. It is the directors' intention to sell the non-current assets from this project at the end of year 5 to realize the £100,000 cash inflow.

Podcaster University Press has a cost of capital of 10%.

You should use a discount rate of 20% when calculating the IRR of the two book projects.

Required

Evaluate the two book projects using the payback, ARR, NPV and IRR methods of investment appraisal. Which project will you recommend and why will you recommend this project?

❭ Question 12.2

Zippo Drinks Limited is considering an investment in its computerized supply chain with a view to generating cash savings from using the benefits of currently available technology. Two options are under consideration. Option 1 will cost £200,000 and operate for five years, while Option 2 will cost £245,000 and remain operational for seven years. Given the longer implementation period, Option 2 will not realize any cash savings until the end of year 2. Neither investment will have any resale value at the end of its life. Because of the scarcity of investment capital, Zippo Drinks Limited can only undertake one of the supply chain projects. The directors of the company are asking for your help in evaluating the two proposals.

The cash savings from any new investment in the years of operation are expected to be as follows:

	Option 1	Option 2
	£000	£000
Year 1	50	–
Year 2	70	80
Year 3	80	85
Year 4	70	86
Year 5	60	101
Year 6	–	81
Year 7	–	71

Zippo Drinks Limited has a cost of capital of 15%.

For your IRR calculations, you should discount the two projects using a 19% discount rate.

Required

Calculate the payback periods, ARRs, NPVs and IRRs of the two supply chain investment proposals. On the basis of your calculations, advise the directors which of the two investments they should undertake. You should also advise them of any additional considerations they should take into account when deciding which project to adopt.

> ## Question 12.3

You are considering a five-year lease on a small restaurant serving light meals, snacks and drinks. The five-year lease will cost £80,000 and the lease will have no value at the end of the five years. The costs of fitting out the restaurant will be £30,000. After five years, you expect the restaurant fittings to have a scrap value of £2,000. You anticipate that net cash inflows from the restaurant will be £35,000 in the first year, £45,000 in the second year, £60,000 in the third year, £65,000 in the fourth year and £55,000 in the final year of operation. You have been approached by a fellow entrepreneur who is also very interested in the restaurant. She has proposed that you pay the £80,000 to take on the lease while she will fit out the restaurant at her own expense and pay you £40,000 per annum as rent and profit share. You expect a return of 12% per annum on any capital that you invest.

You are now uncertain whether you should fit out and run the restaurant yourself or sub-let the restaurant to your fellow entrepreneur. Running the restaurant yourself results in an IRR of 33.84% while allowing your fellow entrepreneur to run the restaurant and pay you rent and a share of the profits generates an IRR of 41.10%.

Required

Evaluate the above alternatives using the payback, ARR and NPV capital investment appraisal techniques. Which of the two options will you choose? In making your decision, you should also consider any other factors that you would take into account in addition to the purely financial considerations.

▶▶ TAKE IT FURTHER

≫ Question 12.4

Ambulators Limited makes prams and pushchairs. The company is currently evaluating two projects that are competing for investment funds.

The first project is the introduction to the market of a new pram. The new pram will require an initial investment of £3,300,000 in marketing and enhanced production facilities and each new pram will sell for £450 over the life of the product. Market research has shown that demand for the new pram is expected to be 5,000 units in the first year of production, with demand rising by 20% per annum on the previous year's sales in years 2 to 5. At the end of year 5, a new improved pram will have entered production and the investment in the new pram will have a residual value of £Nil.

The second project is a new pushchair. This will require an initial outlay on marketing and enhanced production facilities of £2,200,000. Each new pushchair will sell initially in the first year of production and sales for £220, but the directors expect the price to rise by £10 each year in each of years 2 to 5. Market research has projected that initial demand will be for 6,000 pushchairs in year 1 and that demand will rise by 10% per annum on the previous year's sales in years 2 to 5. At the end of year 5, the production facilities will be used to produce a new pushchair and will be transferred to the new project at a valuation of £500,000.

Both projects are competing for the same capital resources and only one of the projects can be undertaken by the company.

The cost card for the new pram and the new pushchair are as follows:

	Pram £	Pushchair £
Direct materials	150.00	80.00
Direct labour	75.00	40.00
Variable overhead	25.00	10.00
Fixed overhead	50.00	20.00
Total cost	300.00	150.00

Fixed production overhead allocated to the cost of each product is based on 5,000 units of production for prams and 6,000 units of production for pushchairs. Fixed costs do not include depreciation of the new investment in each project.

Ambulators Limited has a cost of capital of 11%.

Required

For the proposed investment in the new pram or pushchair, calculate for each project:

- The payback period
- The ARR
- The NPV
- The IRR

You should round your sales projections to the nearest whole unit of sales.

The directors would like to hear your views on which project they should accept. Your advice should take into account both the financial aspects of the decision and any other factors that the directors of Ambulators Limited should consider when deciding which project to invest in.

» Question 12.5

Chillers plc manufactures fridges and freezers. The company is considering the production of a new deluxe fridge-freezer. The fridge-freezer will sell for £600 and the company's marketing department has produced a forecast for sales for the next seven years as follows:

Year	Units sold
2020	3,500
2021	4,000
2022	4,500
2023	5,250
2024	5,750
2025	5,500
2026	5,250

Variable costs are budgeted to be 40% of selling price. Fixed costs arising from the sale and production of the new deluxe fridge-freezer are expected to be £1,200,000 per annum. Fixed costs exclude depreciation of the new investment.

As a result of the introduction of the new deluxe fridge-freezer, the company expects to lose sales of 2,000 standard fridge-freezers each year over the next seven years. These standard fridge-freezers sell for £350 each with variable costs of 35% of selling price. The reduction in sales of standard fridge-freezers will save cash expenditure on fixed costs of £395,000 per annum.

The initial expenditure on the production line for the new deluxe fridge-freezer has been estimated at £2,000,000. At the end of seven years, this production line will have a scrap value of £100,000.

Chillers plc has a required rate of return on new investment of 13%.

Required
For the proposed investment in the new deluxe fridge-freezer, calculate:

- The payback period
- The ARR
- The NPV
- The IRR

Advise the directors of Chillers plc whether the project should go ahead or not.

Solutions to end-of-chapter questions

Chapter 1

> Question 1.1

Your answers should have included the following points, among others. You may well have been able to think of more points than are given here. In all four cases, figures should be compared with previous years' figures to determine whether current year figures are higher or lower than in the past.

Information required by the trustees of a charity:

- Donations received
- Legacies received
- Money received from fund-raising campaigns
- Ability of the charity to continue to attract financial support
- Expenditure on charitable purposes
- Expenditure on administration
- Expenditure on administration as a percentage of total expenditure/income
- Number of beneficiaries assisted
- Whether the charity made a surplus this year or whether a deficit arose from expenditure being higher than income
- Spare funds to use in an emergency or in the case of a natural disaster

Information required by the managers of a secondary school:

- Number of pupils on roll
- Number of teachers
- Pupils per teacher

- GCSE and A Level results

- Average GCSE and A Level points per pupil

- Number of applications received for new entrants into year 7 next year

- Whether numbers of pupils are rising or falling

- Reputation of the school among parents, pupils and local residents

- Whether the secondary school is staying within its budget or not

- Pupil and parent satisfaction with the educational experience delivered

Information required by the managers of a university:

- Number of applications per course

- Number of offers per course

- Number of students enrolling each year

- Average A Level points or equivalent of students enrolling on courses

- Degree classifications gained by students at the end of their course

- Starting salaries of students entering employment at the end of their course

- Employment rate of students at the end of their course as a percentage of those graduating

- Graduating students still unemployed six months after the end of their course

- Satisfaction ratings from employers with graduates of the university

- Student satisfaction ratings for each course

- Staff/student ratios

- Drop-out rates

- Completion rates

- Surplus or loss generated each year

- Research papers published by staff

- Research grants awarded to staff

- The value of research grants awarded to staff

- Research awards gained by staff

Information required by the managers of a manufacturing business:

- Profit or loss for the year

- Number of products produced and sold in the year

- Selling prices for products whether these are rising or falling

- Demand for products whether this is rising or falling

- Investment in new machinery/facilities

- Number of new/improved products developed this year

- Productivity of employees, products produced per employee

- Number of customer complaints about products

- Health and safety record, number of employees injured while at work
- Financial stability of the business
- Whether the budget for the year was met or not

> **Question 1.2**

Your chart should include the following details (though you may have thought of more points than are given here):

1. Costs

- Transfer fee demanded by potential targets' current clubs
- Weekly wages that new striker is likely to demand
- Signing on fee for new striker
- Agent's fees for handling the transfer
- Length of proposed contract in years

2. On-pitch performance

- Number of career goals
- Number of goals in the last 12 months (to determine current scoring record)
- Goals per game
- Number of yellow and red cards received over career
- Number of yellow and red cards received in the last 12 months (to determine current disciplinary record)
- Number of games missed through suspension in the last 12 months
- Number of minor injuries suffered in the last 12 months
- Number of serious injuries suffered over career
- Number of games missed through injury in the last 12 months

3. Off-pitch performance

- Number of charitable and community activities undertaken in the last 12 months
- Number of clubs played for during career (to gauge loyalty to past clubs)
- Diet
- Alcohol consumption
- Age (to assess the number of playing years left)
- Fitness levels
- Number of non-football related stories in the press about the player in the last 12 months (to gauge the likelihood that the player will get into trouble and damage the reputation of the club)
- Reputation among fellow professionals (scores out of 10)

Chapter 2

> Question 2.1

Resources that are assets

Apply the five criteria to show why the resources in the question are assets of entities and so are recognized on the statement of financial position.

(a) Motor vehicles purchased by an entity

- Is there a present economic resource? Yes, the motor vehicles are a present economic resource.

- Does the entity control the economic resource? Yes, by virtue of purchasing the motor vehicles and registering them in the company's name at the DVLA.

- Is there a past event giving rise to control of that economic resource by the entity? Yes, the purchase of the vehicles.

- Does the economic resource have the potential to produce economic benefits? Yes, the motor vehicles can be used to deliver goods to customers, be used by sales reps to visit customers to generate more sales or for any other business purpose that will result in increasing profits, cash and the production of economic benefits.

- Can the asset be measured and faithfully represented in money terms? Yes, the cost of the motor vehicles can be readily determined from the purchase documents and the cash paid from the bank.

(b) Inventory received from suppliers

- Is there a present economic resource? Yes, the inventory received from suppliers is a present economic resource.

- Does the entity control the economic resource? Yes, by virtue of the contract signed or verbal agreement with suppliers for the supply of goods to the entity.

- Is there a past event giving rise to control of that economic resource by the entity? Yes, the delivery of the inventory by suppliers and the receipt of that inventory by the entity (legally, title to the goods passes on receipt by the customer).

- Does the economic resource have the potential to produce economic benefits? Yes, the inventory can be used in production to produce more goods for sale or, in the case of a retail business, the inventory can be sold at a higher price to customers and so produce economic benefits in the form of cash and profit.

- Can the asset be measured and faithfully represented in money terms? Yes, the cost of the inventory can be readily determined from the invoices from the suppliers and by the cash paid from the bank to suppliers for the goods delivered.

(c) Cash and cash equivalents

- Is there a present economic resource? Yes, cash is a present economic resource.

- Does the entity control the economic resource? Yes, the entity controls the cash through the presence of the cash on company premises or as a result of the cash being deposited into the entity's bank account.

- Is there a past event giving rise to control of that economic resource by the entity? Yes, the receipt of cash in exchange for goods or services sold and deposited in the bank.

- Does the economic resource have the potential to produce economic benefits? Yes, the cash can be used to purchase more goods for use in production or for resale or to repay liabilities upon which interest is being charged thereby saving interest and increasing cash resources in the future still further.

- Can the asset be measured and faithfully represented in money terms? Yes, cash can be measured in terms of the amount of physical cash on the business's premises or by reference to the bank statements if the cash has been paid into the bank.

Resources that are NOT assets

Applying the five criteria to show why the resources in the question are NOT assets of an entity and why they are no longer/not recognized on the statement of financial position of entities.

(a) Redundant plant and machinery

- Is there a present economic resource? No. The plant and machinery is redundant, is no longer used in the business or the industry and has no resale or scrap value.

- Does the entity control the economic resource? Yes, by virtue of purchasing the plant and machinery in the past and using it in the business in prior years to produce goods for sale.

- Is there a past event giving rise to control of that economic resource by the entity? Yes, the purchase of the plant and machinery in the past.

- Does the economic resource have the potential to produce economic benefits? No, the plant and machinery is now redundant and will not produce any more goods or result in a cash receipt when it is sold or scrapped, so there are no more potential economic benefits that can be produced by this piece of plant and machinery. If there are disposal costs for this plant and machinery, you might even be able to make out a case that a liability now exists in relation to this plant and machinery. There would then be a transfer of an economic resource in order to meet the obligation to pay these disposal costs which are unavoidable.

- Can the asset be measured and faithfully represented in money terms? Yes, the cost of the plant and machinery can be readily determined from the purchase documents and the cash paid from the bank.

Result: while the resource meets three of the five criteria, it fails on the first and fourth criteria (no economic resource exists and there is no potential to produce economic benefits) and so the asset, which would have been previously recognized by the entity on its statement of financial position, is now derecognized and is removed from property, plant and equipment.

(b) Trade receivable that will not be recovered

- Is there a present economic resource? No. The trade receivable will not be recovered and so no economic resource now exists.

- Does the entity control the economic resource? Yes, by virtue of delivering goods/providing services to the customer and the customer taking delivery of those goods/services and assuming the obligation to pay for them.

- Is there a past event giving rise to control of that economic resource by the entity? Yes, the delivery of the goods/services to the customer.

- Does the economic resource have the potential to produce economic benefits? No, the customer will not pay the invoice because of its bankruptcy and so there is no longer any potential for this trade receivable to produce economic benefits for the entity.

- Can the asset be measured and faithfully represented in money terms? Yes, the sales invoice from the entity to the customer can be used to measure the value of the trade receivable reliably.

Result: while the resource meets three of the five criteria, it fails on the first and fourth criteria (no economic resource and no potential to produce economic benefits) and so the asset, which would have been previously recognized by the entity on its statement of financial position is now derecognized and is removed from trade receivables.

(c) A highly skilled workforce

- Is there an economic resource? Yes, the highly skilled workforce is an economic resource that gives their employer a competitive advantage in its industrial sector.

- Does the entity control the economic resource? Yes, to the extent that the entity controls the workforce while they are working for the organization, but the entity is powerless to stop any individual worker leaving and joining another company, taking all their skills and knowledge with them.

- Is there a past event giving rise to control of that economic resource by the entity? Yes, each member of the workforce signed their contract.

- Does the economic resource have the potential to produce economic benefits? Yes, the highly skilled workforce will produce goods/services and hence sales, profits and cash for the company into the future.

- Can the asset be measured and faithfully represented in money terms? No: it is not possible to measure or faithfully represent the value of employees to the business due to the subjective nature of such valuations and the wide range of possible outcomes of such a valuation process.

Result: while the resource meets three of the five criteria, it fails on the other two criteria (lack of control and no measurement that would faithfully represent the asset in money terms) and so the asset, which would never have been previously recognized by the entity on its statement of financial position, still cannot be recognized.

> Question 2.2

Oxford Academicals Football Club Limited

This is a further application of the criteria to determine whether entities can recognize assets on their statement of financial position or not. Looking at the five criteria:

- The players are a present economic resource which enables the club to function.

- The football club controls the economic resources, the players, through the contracts that they signed.

- As the club holds the players' registrations and has contracts with the players that they will play exclusively for Oxford Academicals, other football clubs can legally be prevented from employing the club's players in their teams.

- There is a past event, the signing of the contracts by the players and, in the case of those players whose contracts were bought from other clubs, cash paid.

- All the players have the potential to produce economic benefits for the club as spectators will pay to watch the team play, there will be monetary rewards for end of season league position and trophies won and, when the players become surplus to requirements, lose form or fall out with the manager, their contracts can be sold to other clubs for a transfer fee or used in player for player swaps.

- In the case of the players whose contracts have been bought from other clubs, there is a monetary measurement of their cost which can be faithfully represented, the transfer fees of £25 million. In the case of players developed by the club, there is no monetary measure of their cost or value which can result in a faithful representation of this figure in the statement of financial position due to the subjective nature and wide range of values and the very high level of measurement uncertainty connected with this valuation exercise.

Result: the contracts of the bought in players meet all the criteria for asset recognition, so they can be recognized on the statement of financial position at a cost of £25 million. The internally developed players cannot be recognized as assets on the statement of financial position as they only meet four out of the five criteria. This may seem unfair and even illogical, but this is how the accounting rules work.

The player registrations that can be recognized on the statement of financial position will be classed as intangible non-current assets. The players will normally be signed on contracts that exceed 12 months (once a player has one year or less to run on their contract, then these registrations should become intangible current assets as the assets will be used up within one year).

As accounting information is meant to be relevant in order to help make a difference in the decisions made by users, it is quite likely that there will be a note in the accounts explaining that not all player registrations are recognized on the statement of financial position but that the current value of the players not so recognized is estimated by the directors to be so many £million. In this way, an additional disclosure will help users understand all the player resources controlled by Oxford Academicals Football Club.

> Question 2.3

Alma Limited: statement of financial position at 30 April 2019

ASSETS	£000	Note
Non-current assets		
Intangible assets	—	1
Property, plant and equipment	6,500	2
	6,500	

	£000	Note
Current assets		
Inventories	1,000	
Trade receivables	1,750	
Cash and cash equivalents	10	
	2,760	
Total assets	9,260	3
LIABILITIES		
Current liabilities		
Short-term borrowings	1,000	4
Trade payables	1,450	
Current tax liabilities	540	
	2,990	
Non-current liabilities		
Long-term borrowings	1,000	5
Total liabilities	3,990	6
Net assets	5,270	7
EQUITY		
Called up share capital	1,000	
Share premium	1,500	
Retained earnings	2,770	
Total equity	5,270	8

Notes

1. There are no intangible assets in Alma so the total here is zero.
2. (Plant and machinery) £2,000 + (land and buildings) £4,500 = £6,500.
3. Total assets = non-current assets + current assets, so £6,500 + £2,760 = £9,260.
4. (Bank loan due within 12 months) £200 + (bank overdraft: overdrafts are repayable on demand, so due within the next 12 months) £800 = £1,000.
5. Long-term borrowings: the bank loan due seven years after the statement of financial position date on 30 April 2026.
6. Total liabilities = current liabilities + non-current liabilities, so £2,990 + £1,000 = £3,990.
7. Net assets: total assets – total liabilities = £9,260 – £3,990 = £5,270.
8. Total equity: share capital + share premium + retained earnings = £1,000 + £1,500 + £2,770 = £5,270.

Bella Limited: statement of financial position at 30 April 2019

ASSETS	£000	Note
Non-current assets		
Intangible assets	—	1
Property, plant and equipment	28,100	2
	28,100	
Current assets		
Inventories	700	
Trade receivables	3,000	
Cash and cash equivalents	825	3
	4,525	
Total assets	32,625	4
LIABILITIES		
Current liabilities		
Short-term borrowings	400	5
Trade payables	4,000	
Current tax liabilities	1,100	
	5,500	
Non-current liabilities		
Long-term borrowings	10,000	6
Total liabilities	15,500	7
Net assets	17,125	8
EQUITY		
Called up share capital	5,000	
Share premium	7,500	
Retained earnings	4,625	
Total equity	17,125	9

Notes

1. There are no intangible assets in Bella Limited so the total here is zero.
2. (Plant and machinery) £9,500 + (land and buildings) £17,100 + (motor vehicles) £1,500 = £28,100.
3. (Cash at bank) £800 + (cash in hand) £25 = £825.
4. Total assets = non-current assets + current assets, so £28,100 + £4,525 = £32,625.
5. Bank loan due within 12 months of the statement of financial position date.

6. Long-term borrowings: the bank loan due seven years after the statement of financial position date on 30 April 2026.

7. Total liabilities = current liabilities + non-current liabilities, so £5,500 + £10,000 = £15,500.

8. Net assets: total assets − total liabilities = £32,625 − £15,500 = £17,125.

9. Total equity: share capital + share premium + retained earnings = £5,000 + £7,500 + £4,625 = £17,125.

Carla Limited: statement of financial position at 30 April 2019

ASSETS	£000	Note
Non-current assets		
Intangible assets	600	1
Property, plant and equipment	15,900	2
	16,500	
Current assets		
Inventories	800	
Trade receivables	2,750	
Cash and cash equivalents	15	
	3,565	
Total assets	20,065	3
LIABILITIES		
Current liabilities		
Short-term borrowings	1,550	4
Trade payables	1,750	
Current tax liabilities	800	
	4,100	
Non-current liabilities		
Long-term borrowings	1,500	5
Total liabilities	5,600	6
Net assets	14,465	7
EQUITY		
Called up share capital	2,500	
Share premium	4,500	
Retained earnings	7,465	
Total equity	14,465	8

Notes

1. (Goodwill) £400 + (trademarks) £200 = £600.

2. (Plant and machinery) £3,750 + (land and buildings) £10,200 + (motor vehicles) £1,950 = £15,900.

3. Total assets = non-current assets + current assets, so £16,500 + £3,565 = £20,065.

4. (Bank loan due within 12 months) £300 + (bank overdraft: overdrafts are repayable on demand, so due within the next twelve months) £1,250 = £1,550.

5. Long-term borrowings: the bank loan due seven years after the statement of financial position date on 30 April 2026.

6. Total liabilities = current liabilities + non-current liabilities, so £4,100 + £1,500 = £5,600.

7. Net assets: total assets – total liabilities = £20,065 – £5,600 = £14,465.

8. Total equity: share capital + share premium + retained earnings = £2,500 + £4,500 + £7,465 = £14,465.

Deborah Limited: statement of financial position at 30 April 2019

ASSETS	£000	Note
Non-current assets		
Intangible assets	350	1
Property, plant and equipment	14,250	2
	14,600	
Current assets		
Inventories	750	
Trade and other receivables	3,200	3
Cash and cash equivalents	558	4
	4,508	
Total assets	19,108	5
LIABILITIES		
Current liabilities		
Short-term borrowings	—	6
Trade payables	5,600	
Current tax liabilities	—	7
	5,600	
Non-current liabilities		
Long-term borrowings	—	6
Total liabilities	5,600	8
Net assets	13,508	9

	£000	Note
EQUITY		
Called up share capital	3,000	
Share premium	5,000	
Retained earnings	5,508	
Total equity	13,508	10

Notes

1. (Goodwill) £250 + (trademarks) £100 = £350.

2. (Plant and machinery) £4,250 + (land and buildings) £8,750 + (motor vehicles) £1,250 = £14,250.

3. (Trade receivables) £2,950 + (tax repayable: cash will be coming into the business so this is a receivable, hence the title of this total is now trade *and other* receivables) £250 = £3,200.

4. (Cash at bank) £550 + (cash in hand) £8 = £558.

5. Total assets = non-current assets + current assets, so £14,600 + £4,508 = £19,108.

6. There are no short or long-term borrowings in Deborah, so a zero figure is recorded against these headings.

7. Current tax liabilities: this year there is a tax repayment due so this is recorded as a receivable rather than a payable, so the current tax liability is zero.

8. Total liabilities = current liabilities + non-current liabilities, so £5,600 + £nil = £5,600.

9. Net assets: total assets − total liabilities = £19,108 − £5,600 = £13,508.

10. Total equity: share capital + share premium + retained earnings = £3,000 + £5,000 + £5,508 = £13,508.

Eloise Limited: statement of financial position at 30 April 2019

ASSETS	£000	Note
Non-current assets		
Intangible assets	950	1
Property, plant and equipment	21,600	2
	22,550	
Current assets		
Inventories	900	
Trade and other receivables	3,900	3
Cash and cash equivalents	212	4
	5,012	
Total assets	27,562	5

	£000	Note
LIABILITIES		
Current liabilities		
Short-term borrowings	—	6
Trade payables	5,800	
Current tax liabilities	—	7
	5,800	
Non-current liabilities		
Long-term borrowings	—	6
Total liabilities	5,800	8
Net assets	21,762	9
EQUITY		
Called up share capital	4,500	
Share premium	9,000	
Retained earnings	8,262	
Total equity	21,762	10

Notes

1. (Goodwill) £500 + (trademarks) £450 = £950.

2. (Plant and machinery) £5,000 + (land and buildings) £15,000 + (motor vehicles) £1,600 = £21,600.

3. (Trade receivables) £3,100 + (tax repayable: cash will be coming into the business so this is a receivable, hence the title of this total is now trade *and other* receivables) £800 = £3,900.

4. (Cash at bank) £200 + (cash in hand) £12 = £212.

5. Total assets = non-current assets + current assets, so £22,550 + £5,012 = £27,562.

6. There are no short or long-term borrowings in Eloise Limited, so a zero figure is recorded against these headings.

7. Current tax liabilities: this year there is a tax repayment due, so this is recorded as a receivable rather than a payable so the current tax liability is zero.

8. Total liabilities = current liabilities + non-current liabilities, so £5,800 + £nil = £5,800.

9. Net assets: total assets − total liabilities = £27,562 − £5,800 = £21,762.

10. Total equity: share capital + share premium + retained earnings = £4,500 + £9,000 + £8,262 = £21,762.

> Question 2.4

Maria: statement of financial position at 31 October 2019 and 7 November 2019

	Statement of financial position at 31 October 2019	Increase	Decrease	Statement of financial position at 7 November 2019
	£	£	£	£
Non-current assets				
Property, plant and equipment	15,000			15,000
Current assets				
Inventory	20,000	2,500[4]	1,200[3]	21,300
Other receivables	3,000			3,000
Cash and cash equivalents	500	2,000[3]	300[5]	2,200
	23,500			26,500
Total assets	38,500			41,500
Current liabilities				
Bank overdraft	7,000	3,500[1]	10,000[2]	500
Trade and other payables	8,000	2,500[4]	3,500[1]	7,000
Taxation	3,000			3,000
Total liabilities	18,000			10,500
Net assets	20,500			31,000
Capital account				
Balance at 31 October 2019/7 November 2019	20,500	10,000[2]	300[5]	31,000
		800[3]		

Notes

1. Paying trade payables from the bank account will increase the overdraft by £3,500. Money has been paid out of the bank account thereby increasing the amount owed to the bank while reducing the amounts owed to trade payables by the same amount.

2. £10,000 paid into the bank account by Maria will increase the balance in her capital account by £10,000 (this is the owner's own money introduced into the business) and reduce the bank overdraft by £10,000. Less money is owed to the bank but more money is now owed to Maria.

3. Cash goes up by £2,000 as this is money flowing into the business. As inventory has been sold in the first week of November, the inventory will decrease by £1,200. This leaves a difference of £800 which is profit on the sales made (sales made – the cost of making those sales). Profit is

added to the capital account. Any profit retained in the business during the year is added to the capital account as this profit belongs to and is owed to the business's owner.

4. New inventory purchased by the business means that the value of inventory will increase by £2,500. As the inventory was purchased on credit from suppliers (trade payables), trade payables will also increase by £2,500 as more money is now owed to them.

5. The £300 taken out of the business represents a repayment of money owed by the business to the owner. Therefore, the capital account is reduced by £300: the business owes Maria £300 less than it did before this transaction. The £300 was taken out in cash, so cash reduces by £300.

> Question 2.5

Andy Limited: statement of financial position at 30 June 2019 and 7 July 2019

ASSETS	£	Increase £	Decrease £	£
Non-current assets				
Property, plant and equipment	320,000	20,000[2]		340,000
Current assets				
Inventories	50,000	15,000[5]	2,500[4] 7,500[3]	55,000
Trade receivables	75,000	10,000[3]	3,000[1]	82,000
Cash and cash equivalents	20,000	3,000[1] 3,250[4]	2,500[1] 10,000[6]	13,750
	145,000			150,750
Total assets	465,000			490,750
LIABILITIES				
Current liabilities				
Trade payables	80,000	15,000[5]	7,000[6] 2,500[1]	85,500
Taxation	20,000		3,000[6]	17,000
	100,000			102,500
Non-current liabilities				
Bank loan (long-term borrowings)	250,000	20,000[2]		270,000
Total liabilities	350,000			372,500
Net assets	115,000			118,250
EQUITY				
Called up share capital	20,000			20,000
Retained earnings	95,000	2,500[3] 750[4]		98,250
Total equity	115,000			118,250

Notes

- 1 July 2019: the payment of the trade payable reduces both trade payables and cash and cash equivalents by £2,500.

- 1 July 2019: the receipt of cash from a trade receivable reduces trade receivables by £3,000, but increases the cash and cash equivalents balance by the same amount.

- 2 July 2019: both the bank loan and the property, plant and equipment will increase by £20,000. There are £20,000 more assets and £20,000 more liabilities.

- 4 July 2019: inventory of £7,500 has been sold, so inventory decreases by this amount. The buyer has agreed to buy the goods for £10,000 and pay in August, so trade receivables increase by £10,000. The profit on the transaction of £2,500 (£10,000 − £7,500) will increase retained earnings.

- 5 July 2019: similarly, inventory of £2,500 has been sold, so inventory decreases by this amount. The buyer paid cash of £3,250 for the goods and so cash increases by £3,250. The profit on the transaction of £750 (£3,250 − £2,500) increases retained earnings.

- 6 July 2019: both inventory and trade payables increase by £15,000 as there are more goods in stock and there is a bigger liability due to trade payables for goods supplied.

- 7 July 2019: the taxation liability reduces by £3,000 and trade payables decreases by £7,000 as these two amounts have now been paid and are no longer obligations of Andy Limited. The total payment of £10,000 reduces the balance in the bank account by this amount.

> Question 2.6

(a) Frankie Limited: statement of financial position at 31 December 2019

ASSETS	£000	Note
Non-current assets		
Intangible assets	1,000	1
Property, plant and equipment	27,800	2
	28,800	
Current assets		
Inventories	2,500	
Trade receivables	4,910	
Cash and cash equivalents	605	3
	8,015	
Total assets	36,815	4

	£000	Note
LIABILITIES		
Current liabilities		
Short-term borrowings	850	5
Trade payables	6,720	
Taxation payable	1,380	6
	8,950	
Non-current liabilities		
Long-term borrowings	8,500	7
Total liabilities	17,450	8
Net assets	19,365	9
EQUITY		
Share capital	2,000	
Share premium	4,000	
Retained earnings	13,365	
Total equity	19,365	10

Notes

1. Goodwill is an intangible asset, so £1,000,000 is recorded as a non-current asset under this heading.

2. (Land and buildings) £15,500,000 + (fixtures and fittings) £1,670,000 + (plant and machinery) £10,630,000 = £27,800,000.

3. (Cash at bank) £600,000 + (cash in hand) £5,000 = £605,000.

4. Total assets = non-current assets + current assets, so £28,800,000 + £8,015,000 = £36,815,000.

5. Short-term, current borrowings are the borrowings due for repayment within one year of the statement of financial position date, that is, due for repayment by 31 December 2020, so these borrowings are recorded as current liabilities.

6. Taxation payable is a short-term, current liability.

7. Long-term, non-current borrowings are those due for repayment after more than one year from the statement of financial position date. As 31 December 2028 is nine years after the current statement of financial position date, the £8,500,000 is classified as a non-current liability.

8. Total liabilities = current liabilities + non-current liabilities, so £8,950,000 + £8,500,000 = £17,450,000.

9. Net assets: total assets – total liabilities = £36,815,000 – £17,450,000 = £19,365,000.

10. Total equity: share capital + share premium + retained earnings = £2,000,000 + £4,000,000 + £13,365,000 = £19,365,000.

(b) Frankie Limited: statement of financial position at 31 December 2019 and 31 January 2020

	Statement of financial position at 31 December 2019	Increase	Decrease	Statement of financial position at 31 January 2020
ASSETS	£000	£000	£000	£000
Non-current assets				
Intangible assets	1,000			1,000
Property, plant and equipment	27,800	2,500[3]	2,000[8]	28,300
	28,800			29,300
Current assets				
Inventory	2,500	12,200[1]	11,450[2]	3,250
Trade receivables	4,910	15,500[2]	6,450[6]	13,960
Cash and cash equivalents	605	1,500[4]	690[5]	1,955
		6,450[6]	8,210[7]	
		2,500[8]	200[9]	
	8,015			19,165
Total assets	36,815			48,465
LIABILITIES				
Current liabilities				
Short-term borrowings	850		200[9]	650
Trade payables	6,720	12,200[1]	8,210[7]	10,710
Taxation payable	1,380		690[5]	690
	8,950			12,050
Non-current liabilities				
Long-term borrowings	8,500	2,500[3]		11,000
Total liabilities	17,450			23,050
Net assets	19,365			25,415
EQUITY				
Share capital	2,000	500[4]		2,500
Share premium	4,000	1,000[4]		5,000
Retained earnings	13,365	4,050[2]		17,915
		500[8]		
Total equity	19,365			25,415

Notes

1. Inventory has been acquired, so the value of inventory increases by £12,200,000. As the inventory has not yet been paid for, trade payables (= suppliers) will also increase by £12,200,000 as they are now owed this additional amount for the inventory supplied on credit.

2. Sales have been made on credit to trade receivables (= customers), so trade receivables now owe a further £15,500,000 to Frankie Limited and so increase by this amount. The cost of the goods sold by the company was £11,450,000. As this inventory has now been sold, inventory decreases by £11,450,000 to derecognize the asset that is no longer represented on Frankie Limited's statement of financial position. The difference between the selling price of £15,500,000 and the cost of the inventory sold of £11,450,000 is £4,050,000, which represents the profit on the sales transactions. This profit is added to retained earnings.

3. New plant and machinery has been acquired, so property, plant and equipment increases by £2,500,000. The money used to acquire these new non-current assets has been borrowed, so borrowings must also rise by the same amount. The new borrowings are due for repayment in December 2028, which is more than one year after the end of January 2020, so these new borrowings are added to non-current liabilities.

4. Cash has been raised from the share issue, so cash increases by £1,500,000, the total proceeds of the share issue. As £500,000 of the cash raised relates to the share capital, this balance also increases by £500,000. The remaining £1,000,000 of the cash raised relates to share premium, so this balance increases by this amount.

5. Cash has been paid to the tax authorities, so cash must decrease by £690,000. Now that this liability has been discharged, taxation payable also falls by £690,000 as the obligation has been settled and economic resources in the form of cash have flowed out of the company to settle the obligation.

6. Trade receivables have paid £6,450,000 of the amounts owed to Frankie, so trade receivables now decrease by this amount to reflect the realization of this asset through the receipt of cash. Cash will also increase by the same amount as these amounts owed by the trade receivables have now turned into cash.

7. Frankie has discharged obligations owed to trade payables of £8,210,000, so trade payables fall by this amount as the liability has now been paid. As the amounts owed were paid in cash, cash also falls by the same amount to reflect the transfer of economic resources to settle the obligations to trade payables.

8. The sale of the non-current asset results in derecognition of the land as the resource is no longer owned or controlled by Frankie. As a result of the sale of the land, property, plant and equipment fall by the original historic cost of the land of £2,000,000. Cash has now been received of £2,500,000, so cash increases by this amount. The difference between the original cost of the land of £2,000,000 and the selling price of £2,500,000 represents a profit on the sale so this £500,000 profit on the transaction is reflected as an increase in retained earnings.

9. The transfer of cash to settle the obligation to short-term borrowings results in a decrease in short-term borrowings of £200,000 to reflect the settlement of the obligation. As the amounts owed were paid in cash, cash also falls by the same amount to reflect the transfer of economic resources to settle the obligations to short-term borrowings.

Chapter 3

> Question 3.1

1. Abi's capital account balance at 1 September 2018

Remember that assets – liabilities = capital

	£
Assets	
Inventory	2,382
Cash and cash equivalents (= bank balance)	7,342
Total assets	9,724
Liabilities	
Trade payables	3,445
Assets – liabilities = capital	6,279

2. Abi's bank account for the year to 31 August 2019

	Cash in	Cash out
	£	£
Bank balance at 1 September 2018	7,342	
Rent for the year		6,000
Sales for the year	157,689	
Refunds given to customers during the year		3,789
Trade payable at 1 September 2018 paid		3,445
Cash paid for purchases		116,328
Wages paid to assistant 50 weeks paid × £100		5,000
Display stands		600
Drawings 12 months × £1,500		18,000
Bank balance at 31 August 2019 (total receipts – total payments)		11,869
	165,031	165,031

3. Statement of profit or loss by nature for the year ended 31 August 2019 and a statement of financial position at that date

Abi: statement of profit or loss for the year ended 31 August 2019

	£	£	Note
Revenue: £157,689 – £3,789 + £650		154,550	1
Cost of sales			
Opening inventory	2,382		2
Purchases	120,465		3
Closing inventory	(4,638)		4
Cost of sales		118,209	5
Gross profit		36,341	6
Expenses			
Rent	6,000		7
Assistant £5,000 + £200	5,200		8
Depreciation of display stands	190		9
Total expenses		11,390	10
Net profit for the year		24,951	11

Abi: statement of financial position at 31 August 2019

	£	Note
Non-current assets		
Display stands (£600 cost – £190 accumulated depreciation)	410	9
Current assets		
Inventory	4,638	4
Bank balance at 31 August 2019	11,869	
Cash in hand at the year end = unbanked sales	650	1
	17,157	
Total assets (£410 non-current assets + £17,157 current assets)	17,567	
Current liabilities		
Trade payables (£120,465 total purchases – £116,328 cash paid)	4,137	3
Assistant's wages accrual (£5,200 charge for year – £5,000 paid)	200	8
Total liabilities	4,337	
Net assets (£17,567 total assets – £4,337 total liabilities)	13,230	
Equity (capital account)		
Capital account at 1 September 2018 calculated above in 1	6,279	
Add: net profit for the year from the statement of profit or loss	24,951	
Less: drawings (personal expenses) paid from bank	(18,000)	
Capital account at 31 August 2019	13,230	

Notes

1. Revenue is made up of the cash receipts from sales to customers of £157,689 less the refunds to customers for goods returned of £3,789 (= sales returns, the cancellation of a sale) + £650 cash at 31 August 2019 representing sales that had not yet been banked. This £650 cash is added on to sales and is recorded as a cash asset on the statement of financial position at 31 August 2019. This cash represents sales that had taken place during the accounting year and a cash asset at the end of the financial year.

2. Opening inventory is the inventory of £2,382 that Abi held at 1 September 2018.

3. The cost of purchases is the total cost of goods purchased of £120,465, even though Abi has only paid out £116,328. Remember that, under the accruals basis of accounting, transactions are recorded in the accounting period in which they occurred, not in the accounting period in which cash is received or paid. Therefore, as the total cost of purchases for the year was £120,465, this is the amount recognized in the statement of profit or loss for the year to 31 August 2019. While the cost of purchases is £120,465, only £116,328 of this amount has been paid, so there is a liability at the year-end of £120,465 − £116,328 = £4,137. This figure represents the obligation to pay for goods purchased during the year so that a purchase of goods and a trade payable are both recognized for this amount at the end of the financial year.

4. Closing inventory is a deduction from cost of sales and an asset in the statement of financial position. The cost of closing inventory is carried forward to the next accounting period to match against the sales revenue generated from the sale of these goods in the year to 31 August 2020.

5. Cost of sales = opening inventory + purchases − closing inventory.

6. Gross profit = revenue − cost of sales.

7. Rent is the annual cost of the rent paid from the bank account. As Abi has paid all the rent due for the year there is no prepayment or accrual of rent to recognize at the accounting year end.

8. The assistant has been paid for 50 weeks of the year, so £5,000 has been paid out of the bank account. As the assistant has carried out her work for the last two weeks of August, Abi has an obligation at 31 August 2019 to pay for two more weeks of work, so an additional £200 is recognized as a cost incurred in the financial year in the statement of profit or loss and as an accrual in the statement of financial position.

9. Depreciation on the display stands is calculated by deducting the scrap value (= residual value) of the stands from the cost (£600 − £30 = £570) and then dividing £570 by the three years that the display stands are expected to last. £570 ÷ 3 = £190 depreciation for each of the three years that the display stands will be in use in Abi's business. As the display stands have been in use for a whole year in the business (from 1 September 2018 to 31 August 2019) a whole year's depreciation is recognized in the statement of profit or loss. The carrying amount of the display stands at the end of the financial year is £410: £600 cost − the accumulated depreciation at 31 August 2019 of £190 = £410.

10. Total expenses are given by adding £6,000 (rent) + £5,200 (assistant) + £190 (depreciation for the year) to give total expenses of £11,390.

11. Net profit for the year is given by deducting total expenses for the year of £11,390 from the gross profit of £36,341 to give a net profit figure of £24,951.

> Question 3.2

Alison: statement of profit or loss for the year ended 31 December 2019

	£	£	Note
Sales £437,990 (sales) − £17,682 (sales returns)		420,308	1
Opening inventory	27,647		2
Purchases £225,368 (goods purchased) − £5,724 (purchase returns) − £2,324 (discounts received)	217,320		3
Closing inventory	(22,600)		4
Cost of sales		222,367	5
Gross profit		197,941	6
Expenses			
Administration expenses	15,265		
Telephone expenses	5,622		
Rent on warehouse and office unit £15,000 − £3,000	12,000		7
Business rates £9,325 − £1,865	7,460		8
Delivery costs	36,970		
Electricity and gas	8,736		
Insurance	3,250		
Depreciation charge for the year on non-current assets	13,255		
Accountancy costs	1,250		9
Increase in the allowance for receivables in the year £2,740 − £0	2,740		10
Total expenses		106,548	11
Net profit for the year		91,393	12

Alison: statement of financial position at 31 December 2019

	£	Note
Non-current assets		
Racks, shelving and office furniture £33,600 cost – £14,650 accumulated depreciation	18,950	13
Computer equipment £20,775 cost – £13,850 accumulated depreciation	6,925	14
	25,875	
Current assets		
Inventory	22,600	4
Trade receivables £27,400 – £2,740 (allowance for receivables)	24,660	10
Rent prepayment	3,000	7
Rates prepayment	1,865	8
Cash and cash equivalents	52,315	
	104,440	
Total assets (non-current assets £25,875 + current assets £104,440)	130,315	
Current liabilities		
Trade payables	24,962	
Accountancy accrual	1,250	9
Total liabilities	26,212	
Net assets (total assets £130,315 – total liabilities £26,212)	104,103	
Equity (capital account)		
Capital account at 1 January 2019	52,710	
Profit for the year	91,393	12
Drawings	(40,000)	
Capital account at 31 December 2019	104,103	

Notes

Figures that do not change from the list of balances in the question are not discussed further in these notes. Check that you classified these balances correctly as assets, expenses, income, liabilities or capital in the answer given above.

1. Sales are reduced by the sales returns. These returns are treated as a deduction from sales, as the return of goods amounts to the cancellation of a sale.

2. Inventory on the first day of the accounting year, 1 January 2019, is opening inventory. The closing inventory at 31 December 2019 is given in the additional information.

3. Purchases are the purchase of goods for resale, the goods bought in that are sold on to customers. Purchase returns are deducted from this figure as these represent cancelled purchases. Likewise, the discounts received are also deducted from the purchases figure as these discounts received represent a reduction in the cost of purchases made.

4. Closing inventory in the statement of profit or loss is also a current asset in the statement of financial position as the cost of these unsold goods is carried forward to match against sales of these goods in the next accounting period.

5. Cost of sales is calculated as £27,647 (opening inventory) + £217,320 (purchases net of purchase returns and discounts received) − £22,600 (closing inventory) = £222,367.

6. Gross profit = £420,308 (sales) − £222,367 (cost of sales) = £197,941.

7. As £3,000 of the rent is prepaid, £3,000 is deducted from the rent expense for the year and recognized as a current asset in the statement of financial position.

8. Similarly, as £1,865 of rates have been paid in advance, this figure is deducted from the rates expense for the year and recognized as a current asset in the statement of financial position.

9. Accountancy costs have not been taken into account; as they have been incurred in the year, but not yet paid for, they must be recognized as both an expense in the statement of profit or loss and as an accrual, a current liability at the financial year end, in the statement of financial position.

10. The allowance for receivables is calculated as 10% of year end trade receivables. Year end trade receivables stand at £27,400, so 10% of this figure is £2,740. £2,740 is deducted from trade receivables and charged as an expense in the statement of profit or loss. As there was no allowance for receivables at the end of the previous accounting year, the change in the allowance is the allowance now of £2,740 − the allowance at the end of last year of £Nil = £2,740. Trade receivables in the statement of financial position are stated net of the allowance for receivables at a figure of £27,400 − £2,740 = £24,660.

11. £106,548 is the total of all the expenses from administration expenses down to the increase in the allowance for receivables.

12. Net profit for the year is calculated by deducting total expenses of £106,548 from the gross profit of £197,941. This net profit for the year belongs to Alison, so this figure is added to the capital account balance on the statement of financial position.

13. The carrying amount of the racks, shelving and office furniture is calculated by deducting the accumulated depreciation of £14,650 at the end of the current accounting period, 31 December 2019, from the cost of the racks, shelving and office furniture of £33,600.

14. Similarly, the carrying amount of the computer equipment is calculated by deducting the accumulated depreciation of £13,850 at the end of the current accounting period, 31 December 2019, from the cost of the computer equipment of £20,775.

> **Question 3.3**

Volumes Limited: statement of profit or loss for the year ended 30 September 2019

	£000
Revenue (= sales)	4,750
Cost of sales (see working)	(3,550)
Gross profit	1,200
Distribution and selling costs	(200)
Administration expenses	(300)
Operating profit	700
Finance income	25
Finance expense	(100)
Profit before tax	625
Income tax	(250)
Profit for the year	375

Cost of sales working

	£000
Production costs	2,600
Opening inventory at 1 October 2018	100
Production wages	1,000
Closing inventory at 30 September 2019	(150)
Cost of sales	3,550

Cost of sales = opening inventory + production costs − closing inventory. Production wages are also added in to cost of sales in this example as these costs are directly incurred in the production of goods for sale. See the explanation of how cost of sales is made up in Chapter 3, Cost of sales.

Volumes Limited: statement of financial position at 30 September 2019

ASSETS	£000
Non-current assets	
Property, plant and equipment £2,000 (cost) – £800 (depreciation)	1,200
Current assets	
Inventory (= closing inventory in the statement of profit or loss)	150
Trade receivables	430
Cash and cash equivalents	175
	755
Total assets £1,200 (non-current assets) + £755 (current assets)	1,955
LIABILITIES	
Current liabilities	
Trade payables	300
Taxation payable (= income tax charged in the statement of profit or loss)	250
	550
Non-current liabilities	
Borrowings	500
Total liabilities £550 (current liabilities) + £500 (non-current liabilities)	1,050
Net assets: total assets – total liabilities £1,955 – £1,050	905
EQUITY	
Called up share capital	250
Share premium	125
Retained earnings £155 (at 30 September 2018) + £375 (profit for the year)	530
	905

> Question 3.4

Textiles Limited: statement of profit or loss for the year ended 30 June 2019

	£000
Revenue £7,550 (sales) − £150 (sales returns)	7,400
Cost of sales £4,550 (cost of sales) − £80 (purchase returns) − £125 (discounts received) + £600 (plant and machinery depreciation)	(4,945)
Gross profit (revenue − cost of sales)	2, 455
Distribution and selling costs £1,000 + £100 (motor vehicle depreciation)	(1,100)
Administration expenses £700 + £10 (accountancy and audit fees for year) − £15 (prepaid insurance) + £50 (known irrecoverable debt) − £20 (reduction in allowance for receivables)	(725)
Operating profit (gross profit − distribution and selling − administration)	630
Finance expense	(110)
Profit before tax	520
Income tax £520 (profit before tax) × 25%	(130)
Profit for the year	390

Textiles Limited: statement of financial position at 30 June 2019

ASSETS	£000
Non-current assets	
Plant and machinery £3,000 (cost) – £1,200 (depreciation to 30 June 2018) – £600 (depreciation for the year to 30 June 2019)	1,200
Motor vehicles £800 (cost) – £400 (depreciation to 30 June 2018) – £100 (depreciation for the year to 30 June 2019)	300
	1,500
Current assets	
Inventory	300
Trade receivables £1,050 – £60 (allowance for receivables at 30 June 2018) – £50 (known irrecoverable debt) + £20 (reduction in allowance for receivables in year)	960
Insurance prepayment	15
	1,275
Total assets £1,500 (non-current assets) + £1,275 (current assets)	2,775
LIABILITIES	
Current liabilities	
Bank overdraft	200
Trade payables	300
Accruals £10 (audit and accountancy fees for the year)	10
Taxation payable (from the statement of profit or loss: £520 (profit before tax) × 25%)	130
	640
Non-current liabilities	
Borrowings	1,000
Total liabilities £640 (current liabilities) + £1,000 (non-current liabilities)	1,640
Total assets – total liabilities £2,775 – £1,640	1,135
EQUITY	
Called up share capital	200
Retained earnings £545 (at 30 June 2018) + £390 (profit for the year)	935
	1,135

Workings and notes

- The audit and accountancy fees for the year have not been taken into account, so these represent an accrual at the end of the year, adding an expense incurred during the year to costs and liabilities. Administration expenses are increased by £10,000 and a current liability of £10,000 is recognized to reflect the obligation due at the year end.

- The insurance premium represents an expense for part of the year to 30 June 2019 and a prepaid expense for the financial year to 30 June 2020. Six months have been prepaid (July to December 2019), so £30,000 × 6/12 = £15,000 is deducted from administration expenses and added to current assets as a prepayment.

- £50,000 represents a known irrecoverable debt that must be charged as an expense (to administration expenses, not as a deduction from sales) and deducted from trade receivables.

- Trade receivables at the year end now stand at £1,000,000 (£1,050,000 (trade receivables at 30 June 2019) − £50,000 (known irrecoverable debt)); 4% of £1,000,000 = £40,000. The allowance for receivables at 30 June 2018 was £60,000, so there is a reduction in this allowance of £20,000. This reduction in the allowance is added to trade receivables to give a net allowance for receivables at 30 June 2019 of £40,000 (£60,000 at 30 June 2018 − £20,000 reduction in the allowance in the year). The reduction in the allowance of £20,000 is also deducted from administration expenses to reflect the reduction in the allowance during the year to 30 June 2019. Essentially, this reduction in the allowance for receivables is income that reduces expenditure in the current year.

- Depreciation on plant and machinery is to be calculated on the straight line basis. This means that the depreciation charge for the year is based upon the cost of the assets. Plant and machinery cost is £3,000,000, so 20% of this cost is £600,000; £600,000 is deducted from plant and machinery and added to cost of sales. The carrying amount of the plant and machinery is now:

	£000
Cost	3,000
Accumulated depreciation to 30 June 2018	(1,200)
Depreciation charge for the year ended 30 June 2019	(600)
Carrying amount at 30 June 2019	1,200

- Motor vehicle depreciation is to be calculated on the reducing balance basis. As this is not the first year of ownership of the motor vehicles, depreciation cannot be based on cost but must be based on carrying amount, the (cost − accumulated depreciation) at the end of the preceding financial year. The carrying amount at the start of the year is £800,000 − £400,000 = £400,000; 25% of this carrying amount of £400,000 = £100,000. Thus, £100,000 is deducted from the carrying amount of the motor vehicles at 30 June 2019 and added to selling and distribution expenses. The carrying amount of motor vehicles is now:

	£000
Cost	800
Accumulated depreciation to 30 June 2018	(400)
Depreciation charge for the year ended 30 June 2019	(100)
Carrying amount at 30 June 2019	300

• The taxation charge is based upon the profit before tax for the year. Profit before tax totals up to £520,000; 25% of £520,000 = £130,000. Thus, £130,000 is deducted from profit before tax to give a profit for the year of £390,000. As the tax has not yet been paid, a current liability for taxation payable of £130,000 is also recognized on the statement of financial position as a liability due for payment. The profit for the year of £390,000 is now added to retained earnings in the statement of financial position.

> **Question 3.5**

1. Laura's bank account

	Receipts	Payments
	£	£
Cash paid in by Laura	50,000	
Receipts from cash sales	112,000	
Receipts from credit sales	36,000	
Payments for construction materials		38,000
Payment for van		6,000
Payment for construction equipment		5,000
Van running expenses		4,000
Wages paid to part time employees		9,600
Insurance		1,800
Bank charges		400
Bank interest paid		200
Interest received	250	
Drawings 12 months × £2,500		30,000
Drawings: mortgage repayment		90,000
Balance in bank at 31 August 2019		13,250
	198,250	198,250

Remember that the bank account just includes cash receipts and cash payments. If any of your figures are different from the above, check back to the information in Question 3.5 to make sure you have correctly identified the cash receipts and payments rather than cash that had not been received and payments that had not been made by 31 August 2019. The notes at the end of the statement of financial position below also provide further explanations of these figures.

2. Laura: statement of profit or loss for the year ended 31 August 2019

	£	£
Sales: £112,000 (cash sales) + £36,000 (credit sales cash received) + £12,000 (credit sales made but cash not yet received)		160,000
Opening inventory: nil as this is the first year of trading	—	
Purchases: £38,000 (cash paid) + £7,000 (payment still owed for construction materials) − £1,000 (bulk discount received)	44,000	
Closing inventory	(4,500)	
Cost of sales		39,500
Gross profit		120,500
Expenses		
Irrecoverable debt	2,500	
Increase in allowance for receivables: (£12,000 − £2,500) × 10%	950	
Van depreciation: (£6,000 − £600) ÷ 3 years	1,800	
Van running expenses (all paid for in year)	4,000	
Equipment depreciation: (£5,000 − £60) ÷ 4 years	1,235	
Wages of part time employees: £9,600 (paid) + (£9,600 ÷ 12 weeks)	10,400	
Insurance: £1,800 (paid for 18 months) − (£1,800 × 6/18)	1,200	
Bank charges: £400 (paid) + £75 (accrual up to 31 August 2019)	475	
Bank interest paid	200	
Total expenses		22,760
Interest received: £250 (received) + £50 (due for August 2019)		(300)
Profit for the year		98,040

Laura: statement of financial position at 31 August 2019

ASSETS	£
Non-current assets	
Van: £6,000 (cost) – £1,800 (accumulated depreciation charged up to the current year end)	4,200
Construction equipment: £5,000 (cost) – £1,235 (accumulated depreciation charged up to the current year end)	3,765
	7,965
Current assets	
Inventory: (from closing inventory in the statement of profit or loss)	4,500
Trade receivables: £12,000 (invoices not paid) – £2,500 (irrecoverable debt) – £950 allowance for receivables	8,550
Insurance prepayment: £1,800 × 6/18	600
Interest receivable: £50 due for August 2019	50
Cash at bank: (from bank account in part (a))	13,250
	26,950
Total assets: £7,965 + £26,950	34,915
LIABILITIES	
Current liabilities	
Trade payables: £7,000 (payment still owed for construction materials supplied) – £1,000 (bulk discount received)	6,000
Accruals: £800 (wages) + £75 (bank charges)	875
Total liabilities	6,875
Net assets: £34,915 – £6,875	28,040
Capital account	
Capital introduced by Laura	50,000
Profit for the year: from the statement of profit or loss	98,040
Drawings: 12 × £2,500 = £30,000 + £90,000 (mortgage repayment)	(120,000)
Capital account at 31 August 2019	28,040

Notes

- Cash received and paid into the bank from cash sales is £112,000. The sales made on credit amount to £48,000. As these sales all occurred within the financial year to 31 August 2019 they, too, have to be recorded as sales, giving total sales of £112,000 (cash) + £48,000 (credit) = £160,000. Laura has only received cash of £36,000 from her credit customers, so only this amount can be recorded as a cash receipt into her bank. The remaining £12,000 of sales (£48,000 sales – £36,000 cash paid) owed by customers who have not yet paid is recorded as a trade receivable in the statement of financial position. Remember that the accruals basis of accounting says that you must reflect the sales (and expenses) that have occurred in an accounting period regardless of when the cash for those sales was received (or when the cash was paid for expenses).

- Cash paid for construction materials amounts to £38,000. This is the total that is recorded as a payment out of the bank account for construction materials. However, £45,000 of purchases of construction materials took place during the year, so, under the accruals basis of accounting, the total purchases figure is £45,000. The £1,000 bulk purchase discount is a discount received from Laura's supplier. This discount received is deducted from purchases to give a net purchases figure of £44,000 (£45,000 expenditure – £1,000 reduction in costs). The discount relates to purchases within the financial year to 31 August 2019, so this discount is taken into account in this year rather than being taken into the accounting year in which it was received, the year ended 31 August 2020. The remaining £7,000 of amounts owed for construction materials (£45,000 total cost – £38,000 cash paid) is recorded as a trade payable less the £1,000 discount allowed, a net trade payable of £6,000.

- The known irrecoverable debt of £2,500 is deducted from trade receivables in the statement of financial position and recorded as an expense in the statement of profit or loss. This irrecoverable debt is not deducted from sales, but is recorded as an expense. Net trade receivables now stand at £9,500 (£12,000 unpaid sales – £2,500 irrecoverable debt): 10% of these trade receivables is to be recorded as an allowance for receivables; 10% of £9,500 = £950. This amount is deducted from trade receivables and recorded as an expense in the statement of profit or loss (this is not a deduction from sales). There was no allowance at the start of the year as this is the first year of trading, so the statement of profit or loss charge for the movement in the allowance for receivables is the year end allowance of £950 – the allowance at the start of the year of £nil = £950.

- The £6,000 cost of the van is a payment out of the business bank account; £6,000 is recognized as a non-current asset on the statement of financial position. This amount now has to be depreciated. As the van is expected to do 5,000 miles each year, this indicates an even pattern for the consumption of the van's economic benefits, so straight line depreciation will be the most appropriate depreciation method to use. The annual depreciation will be (£6,000 (cost) – £600 (residual value)) ÷ 3 years = £1,800 per annum. This depreciation is deducted from the cost of the van and added as an expense to the statement of profit or loss. The van now has a carrying amount of £6,000 (cost) – £1,800 (depreciation charged in the first year of the business) = £4,200.

- Van running expenses have all been paid from the bank account during the year, so these are recorded as a payment of cash out of the bank and an expense in the statement of profit or loss. There are no adjustments to make to this cost as there are no prepaid or outstanding amounts in relation to these expenses as stated in the question.

- The second-hand construction equipment is a payment out of the business bank account to acquire a non-current asset. As Laura expects to make the same use of these assets in each of the four years, this equipment should be depreciated on the straight line basis. Cost of

£5,000 less residual value of £60 gives a depreciable amount of £4,940. As these assets will last for four years, the annual depreciation charge will be £4,940 ÷ 4 years = £1,235. Thus, £1,235 is deducted from the cost of the construction equipment and added to the statement of profit or loss as an expense. The carrying amount of the construction equipment is now £5,000 (cost) − £1,235 (depreciation charged in the first year of the business) = £3,765.

- £9,600 has been paid out of the business bank account in respect of part time wages. However, £9,600 is not the total part time wages expense. The part time workers were employed for 13 weeks during the summer, but have only been paid for 12. The weekly part time wages were £9,600 ÷ 12 weeks = £800. Therefore, a further £800 expense needs to be recognized in the year to 31 August 2019. The additional £800 cost was incurred during this period, so it must be recognized in the financial statements for this year regardless of whether it was paid or not. The part time wages expense is thus the £9,600 paid during the year + the £800 incurred but not yet paid = £10,400. The £800 not yet paid is then recognized as an accrual, an obligation to make a payment for services received but not paid for by the year end, on the statement of financial position.

- The amount paid out of the bank account in respect of insurance was £1,800. This payment covers 18 months of insurance expense. The financial year to 31 August 2019 is only 12 months long, so 6 out of the 18 months paid for has been prepaid. The prepaid element = £1,800 × 6/18 = £600. This prepayment is deducted from the £1,800 paid to leave a statement of profit or loss charge for insurance of £1,200 (£1,800 paid − £600 prepayment). The prepayment is then recognized as a current asset in the statement of financial position.

- Closing inventory is a deduction in the statement of profit or loss and an asset in the statement of financial position. There is no cash element in respect of this inventory, so no entry is made in the bank account.

- The payment out of the bank for bank charges is £400. This is cash paid and an expense incurred. £75 additional bank charges up to 31 August 2019 have been incurred but not yet paid. Therefore, this additional £75 has to be recognized as an expense in the year to 31 August 2019 as it was incurred in that financial year but paid in the next accounting year. An additional £75 is added to the bank charges expense in the statement of profit or loss and £75 added as an accrual to the statement of financial position as an obligation validly incurred but not yet paid.

- £200 bank interest on the overdraft is the payment out of the bank. No additional bank interest is due, so there are no additional or prepaid expenses relating to bank interest. The £200 is recorded as a payment out of the bank and an expense in the statement of profit or loss.

- £250 interest received from the bank is recorded as a receipt in the bank account and income in the statement of profit or loss. An additional £50 interest has been earned up to 31 August 2019, so, as this income was earned in the accounting period, a further £50 is added to interest received in the statement of profit or loss and a receivable of £50 recorded as a current asset, money due but not yet received from the bank.

- Laura has taken money out of the business each month for her own personal expenses as well as making a large payment off her personal mortgage at the end of the financial year. Total cash withdrawn for personal expenses was £2,500 per month × 12 months = £30,000.

This is a payment out of the bank and a deduction from the capital account in the statement of financial position. Money withdrawn by the owner of a business is not a business expense, but a repayment of capital to the owner, so this £30,000 does not appear in the statement of profit or loss. Similarly, the £90,000 mortgage payment is a payment out of the bank account and a deduction from the capital account, a repayment of capital to the owner of the business not a business expense or the repayment of a business liability.

- £198,250 has been paid into the bank and £185,000 paid out. Therefore £13,250 is left in the bank account. This is recorded on the statement of financial position as a current asset of the business.

Chapter 4

> **Question 4.1**

Abi: statement of cash flows for the year ended 31 August 2019 using the direct method

Cash flows from operating activities	£
Cash received from sales (Note 1)	154,550
Cash payments to suppliers £3,445 + £116,328 + £6,000 (Note 2)	(125,773)
Cash payments for wages (Note 3)	(5,000)
Net cash inflow from operating activities	23,777
Cash flows from investing activities	
Cash paid to acquire display stands (Note 4)	(600)
Cash flows from financing activities	
Cash repaid to Abi (Note 5)	(18,000)
Net cash inflow for the year	5,177
Cash and cash equivalents at 1 September 2018	7,342
Cash and cash equivalents at 31 August 2019 (Note 6)	12,519

Notes

1. As Abi makes all her revenue (sales) for cash, this is the sales figure in the statement of profit or loss. Abi paid £157,689 from cash sales into her bank, but she gave refunds of £3,789 for goods returned. She also had £650 in cash representing unbanked sales at the year end, so her total cash received from sales was £157,689 – £3,789 + £650 = £154,550.

2. Abi paid the £3,445 owing to suppliers at 31 August 2018 in the current accounting year, so this counts as a cash payment to suppliers during the financial year 1 September 2018 to 31 August 2019. She also paid £116,328 of the total purchases during the year of £120,645, so this is also a cash payment to suppliers during the financial year 1 September 2018 to 31 August 2019. During this same financial year, she paid all her rent of £6,000. Therefore, cash payments to suppliers during the financial year to 31 August 2019 were £3,445 + £116,328 + £6,000 = £125,773.

3. Cash paid for wages during the financial year was £5,000 with an accrual (cash not paid, but the expense recognized for services received by the end of the financial year together with a liability for the same amount) of £200 making up the statement of profit or loss figure of £5,200.

4. The actual cash paid to acquire non-current assets (the display stands) was £600. Remember that depreciation is not a cash flow.

5. Abi withdrew £18,000 from the bank for her own personal expenses during the accounting year, so this amounts to a repayment of capital to the owner of the business.

6. Cash at 31 August 2019 is made up of the bank balance of £11,869 + cash from sales unbanked of £650 = £12,519.

Abi: statement of cash flows for the year ended 31 August 2019 using the indirect method

Cash flows from operating activities	£
Profit for the year from Abi's statement of profit or loss	24,951
Add: depreciation charged for the year	190
Deduct: increase in inventory £2,382 – £4,638	(2,256)
Add: increase in trade payables £4,137 – £3,445	692
Add: increase in accruals £200 – £Nil	200
Net cash inflow from operating activities	23,777
Cash flows from investing activities	
Cash paid to acquire display stands	(600)
Cash flows from financing activities	
Cash repaid to Abi	(18,000)
Net cash inflow for the year	5,177
Cash and cash equivalents at 1 September 2018	7,342
Cash and cash equivalents at 31 August 2019	12,519

> **Question 4.2**

Alison: statement of cash flows for the year ended 31 December 2019 using the indirect method

	£	£
Cash flows from operating activities		
Profit for the year from Alison's statement of profit or loss		91,393
Add: depreciation charged for the year		13,255
Add: decrease in inventory £27,647 – £22,600		5,047
Add: decrease in trade receivables £27,200 – £24,660		2,540
Deduct: increase in rent prepayment £2,500 – £3,000		(500)
Add: reduction in rates prepayment £1,965 – £1,865		100
Deduct: decrease in trade payables £24,962 – £30,314		(5,352)
Deduct: decrease in telephone, electricity and gas accruals £1,500 – £Nil		(1,500)
Add: increase in accountancy accrual		1,250
Net cash inflow from operating activities		106,233
Cash flows from investing activities		
Cash paid to acquire new computer equipment	(8,000)	
Cash paid to acquire new racks, shelving and office furniture	(9,600)	
Net cash outflow from investing activities		(17,600)
Cash flows from financing activities		
Cash repaid to Alison		(40,000)
Net cash inflow for the year		48,633
Cash and cash equivalents at 1 January 2019		3,682
Cash and cash equivalents at 31 December 2019		52,315

Note

Check back to Table 4.1 to remind yourself which figures to add and which figures to deduct from operating profit to determine the cash flow from operating activities when preparing statements of cash flows using the indirect method.

> Question 4.3

Laura: statement of cash flows for the year ended 31 August 2019

Cash flows from operating activities	£	£
Profit for the year (Note 1)		98,040
Add van depreciation (Note 2)		1,800
Add construction equipment depreciation (Note 2)		1,235
Deduct increase in inventory (£0 – £4,500) (Note 3)		(4,500)
Deduct increase in trade receivables (£0 – £8,550) (Note 3)		(8,550)
Deduct increase in prepayments (£0 – £600) (Note 3)		(600)
Add increase in trade payables (£6,000 – £0) (Note 3)		6,000
Add increase in accruals (£875 – £0) (Note 3)		875
Deduct interest received (Note 4)		(300)
Add interest paid (Note 5)		200
Net cash inflow from operating activities		94,200
Cash flows from investing activities		
Payment to acquire van (Note 6)	(6,000)	
Payment to acquire construction equipment (Note 6)	(5,000)	
Interest received (Note 7)	250	
Net cash outflow from investing activities		(10,750)
Cash flows from financing activities		
Cash introduced by Laura (Note 8)	50,000	
Cash withdrawn by Laura (Note 8)	(120,000)	
Payment of interest (Note 9)	(200)	
Net cash outflow from financing activities		(70,200)
Net cash inflow for the year		13,250
Cash and cash equivalents at 1 September 2018 (Note 10)		—
Cash and cash equivalents at 31 August 2019		13,250

Notes

Information from the statement of profit or loss and statement of financial position in the answer to Question 3.5:

1. Profit for the year.

2. Depreciation for the year on these two non-current assets.

3. The inventory, trade receivables, prepayments, trade payables and accruals at the start of the year were all £nil as this is Laura's first year of trading. All movements in working capital figures are thus the end of year figures – £nil at the start of the year.

4. Cash inflows from interest received are dealt with under investing activities.

5. Cash outflows from interest paid are dealt with under financing activities.

6. The cash payments actually made to acquire these assets.

7. The cash flow from interest received is the actual cash received: ignore interest due for August as this is cash that has not yet been received so no cash inflow relating to this interest receivable has yet taken place.

8. Laura's cash introduced and cash withdrawn as shown in the bank account.

9. The actual interest paid to the bank during the year.

10. As this is the first year of trading, the cash balance at the start of the business's life was £nil.

> **Question 4.4**

Potters Limited: statement of cash flows for the year ended 30 June 2019

	£000	£000
Cash flows from operating activities		
Operating profit		845
Add: depreciation		800
Deduct: profit on disposal of plant and equipment: £150,000 cash received – £100,000 carrying amount		(50)
Add: amortization of trademarks		20
Add: decrease in inventory: £1,000 – £1,100		100
Deduct: increase in trade and other receivables: £1,800 – £1,550		(250)
Add: increase in trade and other payables: £1,200 – £1,000		200
Cash generated from operations		1,665
Taxation paid		(275)
Net cash inflow from operating activities		1,390
Cash flows from investing activities		
Acquisition of property, plant and equipment	(2,500)	
Proceeds from sale of property, plant and equipment	150	
Net cash outflow from investing activities		(2,350)
Cash flows from financing activities		
Proceeds from the issue of ordinary share capital £2.75 × 200,000	550	
Increase in long-term borrowings: £3,200,000 – £2,600,000	600	
Dividends paid	(100)	
Interest paid	(200)	
Net cash inflow from financing activities		850
Net cash outflow for the year		(110)
Cash and cash equivalents at 1 July 2018		310
Cash and cash equivalents at 30 June 2019		200

> **Question 4.5**

1. **Metal Bashers Limited: statement of cash flows for the year ended 30 September 2019**

	£000	£000
Cash flows from operating activities		
Profit for the year		530
Add: income tax		425
Add: finance expense		870
Deduct: finance income		(100)
Add: depreciation		1,800
Add: loss on disposal of plant and equipment: £250,000 carrying amount – £175,000 cash received		75
Add: amortization of patents		20
Deduct increase in inventory: £1,400 – £1,200		(200)
Add: decrease in trade and other receivables: £2,350 – £2,400		50
Deduct: decrease in trade and other payables: £2,000 – £2,300		(300)
Cash generated from operations		3,170
Taxation paid		(375)
Net cash inflow from operating activities		2,795
Cash flows from investing activities		
Acquisition of property, plant and equipment	(5,000)	
Acquisition of intangible assets	(70)	
Proceeds from sale of property, plant and equipment	175	
Interest received	100	
Net cash outflow from investing activities		(4,795)
Cash flows from financing activities		
Proceeds from the issue of ordinary share capital £3 × 1,600,000	4,800	
Repayment of borrowings (£500 + £6,500) – (£500 + £7,000)	(500)	
Dividends paid	(1,080)	
Interest paid	(870)	
Net cash inflow from financing activities		2,350
Net cash inflow for the year		350
Cash and cash equivalents at 1 October 2018		400
Cash and cash equivalents at 30 September 2019		750

2. **Metal Bashers Limited: statement of cash flows for the year ended 30 September 2019**

	£000
Cash flows from operating activities	
Cash receipts from sales of goods	9,550
Cash payments to suppliers for goods and services	(5,100)
Cash payments to employees	(1,280)
Cash generated from operations	3,170

Chapter 5

> ## Question 5.1

An oil exploration company will set itself up as a public limited company. It will need a lot of investment from a substantial number of shareholders to provide the necessary cash to purchase oil exploration equipment, to hire skilled employees and to buy exploration licences around the world. This size of investment would not be available to sole traders, partnerships or private limited companies.

A taxi driver would set up as a sole trader as driving a taxi is a straightforward operation that will require no major financing or present any other difficulties that might be overcome by adopting a different business format. The taxi driver just needs to buy a car and a hackney carriage licence, all of which expenditure can be met from personal savings. Day to day expenditure, such as petrol and repairs, can be paid for from the receipts from fares.

A family-run knitwear manufacturing business would adopt the private limited company format. As this is a family business, the family will want to maintain control of day to day operations, which would be lost if the business were to set up as a public limited company. The private limited company will be able to borrow money to buy specialized knitwear machinery and equipment while affording the family business limited liability if the business venture were to fail. As a private limited company, the family will be able to concentrate on ensuring that the business will be a commercial success without being distracted by the demands of many outside shareholders.

The business format most suited to the two friends setting up a dance school will be the partnership. Each of the two friends will want to have an equal share in running the school and in contributing to its success. Additionally, both friends will be entitled to share profits in the venture equally. The operations of the dance school will be straightforward with no complexities that would make a different format more suitable.

> ## Question 5.2

Annual interest received on the bond: £200,000 × 5% = £10,000

Annual dividend from the investment in the 50 pence preference shares: £200,000 = 400,000 preference shares of 50 pence each × 3 pence per share = £12,000

Annual dividend from the investment in the 25 pence ordinary shares: £200,000 = 800,000 ordinary shares of 25 pence each × 2 pence per share = £16,000.

Therefore, the investor should invest in the 25 pence shares to maximize income from the £200,000 investment. The investor should also be aware that the ordinary shares are the riskiest of the three possible investments as they may generate no dividend at all and, should the company go into liquidation, the investor may lose all of the £200,000 investment. Alternatively, the dividend per share on the ordinary shares may increase and the value of the shares may also increase, potentially raising the income and capital value of the ordinary shares. The income from the bond and the preference shares, however, will remain the same for each year.

⟩ **Question 5.3**

Borrowing from the bank at 5% per annum: £3,000,000 × 5% = £150,000 annual cost.

Ordinary shares of 40 pence each: number of ordinary shares with a par value of 40 pence each = £3,000,000 ÷ £0.40 = 7,500,000 shares × £0.019 = £142,500 annual dividend.

Preference shares of 60 pence each: number of preference shares with a par value of 60 pence each = £3,000,000 ÷ £0.60 = 5,000,000 shares × £0.0315 = £157,500 annual dividend. Therefore the ordinary shares option will require the lowest cash outlay.

Alternatively, you might have compared the interest or dividend rates on each financing method. The interest on the loan is payable at 5%. The required dividend rate on the ordinary shares is equivalent to a 4.75% return (1.9 pence ÷ 40 pence) while the return on the preference shares is 5.25% (3.15 pence ÷ 60 pence). Therefore the % return on the ordinary dividend is the lowest and will provide the lowest financing cost.

⟩ **Question 5.4**

(a) £1 par value × 6% = £0.06 dividend per share × 100,000 shares = £6,000

(b) 100,000 ordinary shares × 10 pence + 100,000 ordinary shares × 20 pence = £30,000

(c) £45,000 retained earnings at 1 November 2018 + £50,000 profit for the year − £6,000 preference dividend − £30,000 ordinary dividends = £59,000 retained earnings at 31 October 2019

⟩ **Question 5.5**

(a) Amounts to be added to ordinary share capital and share premium in the statement of financial position in respect of the issue of ordinary shares on 1 May 2020:

• Par value of ordinary shares: 50 pence (Question 5.4)

• Issue price per share: £2.50 (£500,000 ÷ 200,000 shares)

• Therefore, the premium on each share issued = £2.50 (issue price) − £0.50 = £2.00

• Additional ordinary share capital: 200,000 shares × £0.50 = £100,000

• Additional share premium: 200,000 shares × £2.00 = £400,000

(b) Total dividends, both ordinary and preference, to be paid in the year to 31 October 2020:

• Preference dividends: no change as no additional preference shares have been issued, so preference dividends remain at £6,000

• Ordinary dividends paid on 15 April 2020: 100,000 shares × £0.15 = £15,000 (new ordinary shares not issued until 1 May 2020, so there were only 100,000 ordinary shares in issue on 15 April 2020)

• Ordinary dividends paid on 15 October 2020: (100,000 shares + 200,000 shares) × £0.25 = £75,000

- Total ordinary dividends for the year to 31 October 2020: £15,000 (15 April 2020) + £75,000 (15 October 2020) = £90,000

- Total dividends, both preference and ordinary, to be paid in the year to 31 October 2020 = £6,000 (preference) + £90,000 (ordinary) = £96,000

(c) Expected balance on retained earnings at 31 October 2020 after dividends for the year have been paid:

- Retained earnings at 31 October 2019 from Question 5.4 (c): £59,000

- + £90,000 (profit for the year to 31 October 2020)

- – £96,000 (total ordinary and preference dividends for the year to 31 October 2020 from (b))

- = £53,000

> **Question 5.6**

Calculate for Halyson plc:

(a) The number of bonus shares to be issued:

- 500,000 ordinary shares currently in issue

- Seven new shares for every two held

- So 500,000 × 7 new shares ÷ 2 = 1,750,000 new shares

(b) The par value of the bonus shares to be added to ordinary share capital:

- 1,750,000 × 25 pence = £437,500

(c) The number of ordinary shares to be issued in the rights issue:

- Number of shares in issue after the bonus issue: 500,000 (original) + 1,750,000 (bonus issue) = 2,250,000 shares

- Rights issue: five new ordinary shares for every three ordinary shares currently held

- Therefore, 2,250,000 ÷ 3 shares × 5 shares = 3,750,000 new ordinary shares issued in the rights issue

(d) The amount to be added to ordinary share capital and share premium as a result of the rights issue:

- 3,750,000 new shares issued in the rights issue from answer (c)

- Par value: 25 pence

- Therefore, par value of shares issued under the rights issue = 3,750,000 × £0.25 = £937,500

- Share premium on each share issued: £0.95 – £0.25 = £0.70

- Total share premium on the issue of 3,750,000 25 pence shares at £0.95 = 3,750,000 × £0.70 = £2,625,000

(e) The preference dividend for the year to 30 June 2020:

• Preference dividend per share: £1 × 0.075 = £0.075
• Total preference dividend on 300,000 shares = 300,000 × £0.075 = £22,500

(f) The ordinary dividend for the year to 30 June 2020:

• Number of ordinary shares in issue at 28 June 2020: 500,000 (before bonus and rights issues) + 1,750,000 (bonus issue) + 3,750,000 (rights issue) = 6,000,000
• Ordinary dividend per share: £0.30
• Total dividend on ordinary shares at 28 June 2020 = 6,000,000 × £0.30 = £1,800,000

(g) The balance on the ordinary share capital account on 30 June 2020:

• 500,000 × £0.25 + £437,500 (b) (bonus issue) + £937,500 (c) (rights issue) = £1,500,000

(h) The expected balance on retained earnings at 30 June 2020:

• Balance at 1 July 2019: £5,200,000
• − £437,500 (b) (bonus issue)
• − £22,500 (e) (preference dividend)
• − £1,800,000 (f) (ordinary dividend)
• − £1,500,000 (loss for the year from the question)
• = £1,440,000

Chapter 6

> Question 6.1

	2019 Calculation	2019 Ratio	2018 Calculation	2018 Ratio
Gross profit %	£18,711/£34,650 × 100%	54.00%	£15,267/£29,360 × 100%	52.00%
Operating profit %	£9,702/£34,650 × 100%	28.00%	£7,634/£29,360 × 100%	26.00%
Profit before tax %	£9,102/£34,650 × 100%	26.27%	£7,059/£29,360 × 100%	24.04%
Profit after tax %	£6,920/£34,650 × 100%	19.97%	£5,365/£29,360 × 100%	18.27%
Non-current asset turnover	£34,650/£21,655	£1.60	£29,360/£18,820	£1.56
Revenue per employee	£34,650/275	£126,000	£29,360/250	£117,440
Operating profit per employee	£9,702/275	£35,280	£7,634/250	£30,536
Earnings per share	£6,920/20,000 × 100 pence	34.6p	£5.365/18,500 × 100 pence	29.0p
Dividends per share	£4,400/20,000 × 100 pence	22.0p	£3,700/18,500 × 100 pence	20.0p
Dividend pay-out ratio	22.0/34.6 × 100%	63.58%	20.0/29.0 × 100 pence	68.97%
Dividend cover	£6,920/£4,400	1.57 times	£5,365/£3,700	1.45 times

> Question 6.2

As DD plc has preference shares in issue, preference dividends will need to be deducted from the profit for the year before earnings per share can be calculated.

Preference dividends for the year ended 30 June 2019: 50 pence × 4% = 2 pence per share × 22m shares = £440,000

Preference dividends for the year ended 30 June 2018: 50 pence × 4% = 2 pence per share × 20m shares = £400,000

	2019 Calculation	2019 Ratio
Earnings per share	(£8,622,350 – £440,000)/37,192,500 × 100 pence	22.00 pence
Dividends per ordinary share	£3,347,325/37,192,500 × 100 pence	9.00 pence
Dividend pay-out ratio	9.0/22 × 100%	40.91%
Dividend cover	(£8,622,350 – £440,000)/£3,347,325	2.44 times
Dividend yield*	9.0 pence/325 pence × 100%	2.77%
Annual growth in share price	(325 – 260)/260 × 100%	25.00%

*Using the end of year share price. You could also use the average share price ((share price at the end of the year + the share price at the beginning of the year) ÷ 2) for the year to calculate this figure. This would give a dividend yield for 2019 of 3.08% (9.00 ÷ ((325 + 260)/2)).

	2018 Calculation	2018 Ratio
Earnings per share	(£7,241,330 − £400,000)/36,197,500 × 100 pence	18.90 pence
Dividends per ordinary share	£2,895,800/36,197,500 × 100 pence	8.00 pence
Dividend pay-out ratio	8.0/18.9 × 100%	42.33%
Dividend cover	(£7,241,330 − £400,000)/£2,895,800	2.36 times
Dividend yield*	8.0 pence/260 pence × 100%	3.08%
Annual growth in share price	(260 − 220)/220 × 100%	18.18%

*Using the end of year share price. You could also use the average share price ((share price at the end of the year + the share price at the beginning of the year) ÷ 2) for the year to calculate this figure. This would give a dividend yield for 2018 of 3.33% (8.00 ÷ ((260 + 220)/2)).

> **Question 6.3**

Ratio calculations and ratios: Bovis Homes Group plc

	2017 Calculation	2017 Ratio	2016 Calculation	2016 Ratio
Gross profit %	£184.6/£1,028.2 × 100%	17.95%	£209.0/£1,054.8 × 100%	19.81%
Operating profit %	£121.2/£1,028.2 × 100%	11.79%	£160.0/£1,054.8 × 100%	15.17%
Profit before tax %	£114.0/£1,028.2 × 100%	11.09%	£154.7/£1,054.8 × 100%	14.67%
Profit after tax %	£91.3/£1,028.2 × 100%	8.88%	£120.8/£1,054.8 × 100%	11.45%
Non-current asset turnover	£1,028.2 /£15.7	£65.49	£1,054.8/£57.6	£18.31
Revenue per employee	£1,028.2 /1,297	£792,753	£1,054.8/1,186	£889,376
Operating profit per employee	£121.2/1,297	£93,446	£160.0/1,186	£134,907
Earnings per share	£91.3/134.661 × 100 pence	67.80p	£120.8/134.522 × 100 pence	89.80p
Dividends per share	£63.8/134.661 × 100 pence	47.38p	£60.4/134.522 × 100 pence	44.90p
Dividend pay-out ratio	47.38/67.80 × 100%	69.88%	44.90/89.80 × 100%	50.00%
Dividend cover	£91.3/£63.8	1.43 times	£120.8/£60.4	2.00 times

Ratio calculations and ratios: Persimmon plc

	2017 Calculation	2017 Ratio	2016 Calculation	2016 Ratio
Gross profit %	£1,071.7/£3,422.3 × 100%	31.32%	£871.4/£3,136.8 × 100%	27.78%
Operating profit %	£955.1/£3,422.3 × 100%	27.91%	£770.5/£3,136.8 × 100%	24.56%
Profit before tax %	£966.1/£3,422.3 × 100%	28.23%	£774.8/£3,136.8 × 100%	24.70%
Profit after tax %	£786.9/£3,422.3 × 100%	22.99%	£625.3/£3,136.8 × 100%	19.93%
Non-current asset turnover	£3,422.3/£542.1	£6.31	£3,136.8/£482.9	£6.50
Revenue per employee	£3,422.3/4,535	£754,642	£3,136.8/4,526	£693,062
Operating profit per employee	£955.1/4,535	£210,606	£770.5/4,526	£170,239
Earnings per share	£786.9/308.856 × 100 pence	255.00p	£625.3/308.498 × 100 pence	202.69p
Dividends per share	£416.6/308.856 × 100 pence	134.88p	£338.3/308.498 × 100 pence	109.66p
Dividend pay-out ratio	134.88/255.00 × 100%	52.89%	109.66/202.69 × 100%	54.10%
Dividend cover	£786.9/£416.6	1.89 times	£625.3/£338.3	1.85 times

Ratio calculations and ratios: Crest Nicholson plc

	2017 Calculation	2017 Ratio	2016 Calculation	2016 Ratio
Gross profit %	£274.9/£1,043.2 × 100%	26.35%	£265.8/£997.0 × 100%	26.66%
Operating profit %	£211.6/£1,043.2 × 100%	20.28%	£203.8/£997.0 × 100%	20.44%
Profit before tax %	£207.0/£1,043.2 × 100%	19.84%	£195.0/£997.0 × 100%	19.56%
Profit after tax %	£168.6/£1,043.2 × 100%	16.16%	£156.8/£997.0 × 100%	15.73%
Non-current asset turnover	£1,043.2/£110.0	£9.48	£997.0/£118.7	£8.40
Revenue per employee	£1,043.2/905	£1,152,707	£997.0/849	£1,174,323

	2017 Calculation	2017 Ratio	2016 Calculation	2016 Ratio
Operating profit per employee	£211.6/905	£233,812	£203.8/849	£240,047
Earnings per share	£168.6/255.760 × 100 pence	65.92p	£156.8/254.364 × 100 pence	61.64p
Dividends per share	£84.3/255.760 × 100 pence	32.96p	£70.3/254.364 × 100 pence	27.64p
Dividend pay-out ratio	32.96/65.92 × 100%	50.00%	27.64/61.64 × 100%	44.84%
Dividend cover	£168.6/£84.3	2.00 times	£156.8/£70.3	2.23 times

> Question 6.4

In the answers to question 6.4, the term income statement = statement of profit or loss

Bovis Homes Group plc

All profitability %s for the company in 2017 are lower than the profitability %s in 2016. Gross profit % in 2017 has fallen in comparison to 2016 from 19.81% to 17.95%. Comments on this fall:

• Is this fall due to lower selling prices or higher cost prices or a combination of both?

• Average price per house sold: £282,085 (£1,028.2m/3,645) v. £265,225 (£1,054.8m/3,977), a rise of 6.36%.

• However, the cost of each house sold was £231,440 (£843.6m/3,645) v. £212,673 (£845.8m/3,977), a rise of 8.82%.

• Costs are thus rising more quickly than selling prices hence the fall in the gross profit %.

• To find out why the company has suffered this adverse result, it would be necessary to consult the annual report and accounts where the reasons for this fall will be presented to shareholders. Given the strength of the housing market during 2017, a fall in the gross profit % seems most unlikely and the company will devote time and effort to explaining this fall.

• On page 12 of the annual report and accounts for the year to 31 December 2017, the chief executive notes the increase in the cost of building houses, sales of properties on older lower margin sites, high levels of investment in the business particularly in customer service (note the large increase in the average number of employees in the year as evidence of this increased investment) and the reorganization of the business as the causes of the reduced profitability %s this year.

• An additional cause of rising costs identified in the annual report and accounts for the year is the shortage of skilled construction labour which will have pushed up the prices paid by the company for workers: these rising costs will have depressed the gross profit %.

Operating profit %, profit before tax % and profit after tax %

- The fall in the gross profit % has fed through into the operating profit, profit before tax and profit after tax %s.

- The income statement on page 115 of the annual report and accounts shows an increase in administrative expenses of £7.550m and non-recurring reorganization costs and advisory fees of £6.812m in 2017. These additional costs will have reduced profitability %s accordingly.

- The fall in gross profit % and the costs of reorganizing the business are thus the main causes of the fall in these other profitability %s.

Comments on the performance of Bovis Homes Group plc from the point of view of the shareholders:

- Earnings per share have fallen as a result of the reduction in profits.

- However, the company has paid a higher dividend for the year as an indicator both of the directors' confidence in the business and of the positive outlook for 2018.

- The dividend cover has fallen from 2.00 times to 1.43 times but, given the robust demand for housing and the housing shortage identified by commentators at the end of 2017 and during 2018, revenue and profits should hold up well in the future justifying the short-term reduction in the dividend cover ratio.

- Shareholders will be disappointed at the reduction in the earnings per share figure but will welcome the rise in the dividend and retain their confidence in the company to build on the reorganization and repositioning of the business undertaken in the year to 31 December 2017.

Persimmon plc

All four profitability %s have risen in 2017 compared to 2016.
Gross profit % has risen from 27.78% in 2016 to 31.32% in 2017. Comments on this rise:

- Is this rise in the gross profit % due to higher selling prices or lower cost prices or a combination of both?

- Average selling price per home was: £213,320 (£3,422.3m/16,043) in 2017 v. £206,763 (£3,136.8m/15,171) in 2016, a rise of 3.17%.

- Average cost price per home fell to £146,519 (£2,350.6m/16,043) in 2017 v. £149,324 (£2,265.4m/15,171) in 2016, a fall of 1.88%.

- Selling prices are higher due to increased demand, a robust housing market and a strong economy while the company has contained cost rises very effectively with the result that the gross profit % for the year has increased sharply.

- Page 1 of the annual report and accounts states that 'Our drive for continual operational improvement, attention to detail and financial discipline results in the Group having excellent margins and profitability, together with a very strong balance sheet. This generates superior returns for our shareholders.'

- Persimmon is a much bigger company than either Bovis Homes Group or Crest Nicholson so may benefit from larger economies of scale in its operations (such as bulk buying and volume discounts) which will also contribute to a lower cost of sales figure and a higher gross profit %.

Rising operating profit %, profit before tax % and profit after tax %:

- The increase in the gross profit % is feeding through into these profit lines.
- Careful cost control as a result of the financial discipline exercised is being felt in the increases in these margins.
- Profit before tax % is higher than operating profit % in both years indicating that finance income exceeds finance expense as a result of surplus cash being invested in interest generating assets to produce additional returns for shareholders.

Comments on the performance of Persimmon from the point of view of the shareholders:

- Earnings per share is up 25.70% in 2017 compared to 2016.
- Dividends are also rising sharply.
- Current dividends are more than covered by the profit after tax, with a slight rise in the dividend cover this year from 1.85 times to 1.89 times. Given the strength of the housing market at the end of 2017 and into 2018 and the rising profits of the company, a dividend cover of less than 2 times is not a cause for concern to shareholders.
- Shareholders will be very pleased with the rising profits, rising earnings per share, rising dividend per share and the strong prospects for the Persimmon group.

Crest Nicholson plc

Gross profit % and operating profit % has fallen in 2017 whereas the profit before tax and profit after tax %s show rises.

Gross profit % has fallen from 26.66% in 2016 to 26.35% in 2017. Comments on this fall:

- Average selling price per home was: £355,434 (£1,043.2m/2,935) in 2017 v. £347,387 (£997.0m/2,870) in 2016, a rise of 2.32%.
- Average cost price per home sold rose to £261,772 (£768.3m/2,935) in 2017 v. £254,774 (£731.2m/2,870) in 2016, a rise of 2.75%.
- Selling prices are rising but not as rapidly as costs which have risen at a slightly higher rate resulting in a fall in the gross profit % in 2017.
- In the annual report and accounts the group finance director attributes this fall in the gross profit % to various factors. Firstly, as for Bovis Homes Group, the shortage of skilled labour resulted in rising wage and salary costs (page 9). Page 10 of the annual report and accounts outlines how lower contributions (= a lower gross profit) were delivered from high margin projects together with reduced margins on sales made in Central London as demand softened (i.e. the lack of demand resulted in the reduction of selling prices while costs remained the same). Shortages of materials have affected the industry this year which has had the

effect of slowing down on site work (page 13) and reducing productivity thereby contributing to the fall in gross profit % in the year to 31 October 2017.

Falling operating profit %:

- The fall in the gross profit % explains the main reason for the fall in the operating profit %.
- However, the decline in the operating profit % is only 0.78% ((20.28 − 20.44) ÷ 20.44 × 100%) whereas the decline the gross profit % is 1.16% ((26.35 − 26.66) ÷ 26.66 × 100%).
- The figures in the income statement show that administration expenses in 2017 are 6.07% of revenue whereas in 2016 these expenses amounted to 6.22% of revenue. Therefore, the reduction in administration expenses as a percentage of revenue has resulted in a lower fall in the operating profit % compared to the fall in the gross profit %.

Both profit before tax % and profit after tax % have risen:

- The figures in the income statement show a £1.5m reduction in finance income and a £1.3m increase in finance expense.
- However, the income from joint ventures which is included in the financing part of the income statement is a positive £3.7m in 2017 compared to a negative £0.7m in 2016 so this increase explains the rise in the profit before tax %.
- Tax as a % of profit before tax has fallen from 19.59% to 18.55% so the increase in income from joint ventures and the lower taxation charge explain the increase in the profit after tax %.

Comments on the performance of Crest Nicholson from the point of view of the shareholders:

- Earnings per share are up 6.94% in the year to 31 October 2017.
- Dividends for 2017 have also risen, but by 19.25% on the dividend per share figure for 2016.
- Current dividends are more than covered by the profit after tax, although the dividend cover has fallen from 2.23 times to 2.00 times. The expectation that demand in the housing market will remain strong and the rising profits of the company indicate that the dividend cover is currently safe.
- Shareholders will be pleased with the rising profits, rising earnings per share, rising dividend per share and the prospect of continued success for the Crest Nicholson group.

> **Question 6.5**

Tracking share prices for the week 23 April to 27 April 2018

	23 April pence	24 April pence	25 April pence	26 April pence	27 April pence	Average pence
Bovis Homes Group plc	1,252.50	1,235.00	1,225.00	1,214.00	1,230.00	1,231.30
Persimmon plc	2,721.00	2,690.00	2,694.00	2,683.00	2,730.00	2,703.60
Crest Nicholson plc	501.50	494.00	486.80	487.40	490.60	492.06

Dividend yield: Bovis Homes: $47.38/1,231.30 \times 100\% = 3.85\%$
Dividend yield: Persimmon: $134.88/2,703.60 \times 100\% = 4.99\%$
Dividend yield: Crest Nicholson: $32.96/492.06 \times 100\% = 6.70\%$
Price/earnings ratio: Bovis Homes: $1,231.30/67.80 = 18.16$
Price/earnings ratio: Persimmon: $2,703.60/254.78 = 10.61$
Price/earnings ratio: Crest Nicholson: $492.06/65.92 = 7.46$

Of the three companies, Bovis has the highest price earnings ratio. This may be something of a surprise as Persimmon is the largest of the three companies with revenue of £3,422.3 million and much higher sales of houses in the year to 31 December 2017. As a very large company, Persimmon would normally be considered to be a stronger investment than the two smaller companies with the ability to sustain its earnings for a longer period of time. However, earnings for Bovis in the year to 31 December 2017 were depressed by one off factors, the reorganization and high levels of new investment coupled with lower margin sales in the year, so the market expects the 2018 results to show a much improved result for the year. Higher earnings for the year to 31 December 2018 will reduce Bovis' price/earnings ratio to a level that is much more in line with that of the other two companies. House building is an economy sensitive activity. When the economy is doing well, house prices rise and building takes place. But when the economy is in recession, consumers save their cash and spend their money on essentials rather than on new houses so that house prices fall and economic activity in the house building sector reduces as a result of this weakened demand. These factors would account for the lower price/earnings ratios in both Persimmon and Crest Nicholson.

Share prices for the week 24 April to 28 April 2017

	24 April pence	25 April pence	26 April pence	27 April pence	28 April pence	Average pence
Bovis Homes Group plc	929.00	926.00	928.00	932.00	920.50	927.10
Persimmon plc	2,284.00	2,267.00	2,286.00	2,340.00	2,330.00	2,301.40
Crest Nicholson plc	595.00	589.50	592.00	601.50	603.50	596.30

Percentage share price changes over the year:

Bovis Homes: $(1,231.30 - 927.10)/927.10 \times 100\%$ = a rise of 32.81%

Persimmon Homes: $(2,703.60 - 2,301.40)/2,301.40 \times 100\%$ = a rise of 17.48%

Crest Nicholson: $(492.06 - 596.30)/596.30 \times 100\%$ = a fall of 17.48%

Total shareholder return over the year:

Dividend yield + share price increase over the past year:

Bovis Homes: 3.85% + 32.81% = 36.66%

Persimmon Homes: 4.99% + 17.48% = 22.47%

Crest Nicholson: 6.70% – 17.48% = –10.78%

Bovis Homes Group has clearly produced the best total return over the year based on the two weeks reviewed.

Chapter 7

> **Question 7.1**

(a) Ratios for Samoco plc

	2019		2018	
	Calculation	Ratio	Calculation	Ratio
Current ratio	652/1,590	0.41:1	639/1,476	0.43:1
Quick ratio	(652 – 485)/1,590	0.11:1	(639 – 500)/1,476	0.09:1
Inventory days	(485/12,570) × 365	14.08 days	(500/11,330) × 365	16.11 days
Payables days	(830/12,570) × 365	24.10 days	(790/11,330) × 365	25.45 days
Cash conversion cycle	14.08 + 0 – 24.10	–10.02 days	16.11 + 0 – 25.45	–9.34 days
Gearing %	(240 + 2,230)/2,116 × 100%	116.73%	(216 + 2,024)/1,765 × 100%	126.91%
Debt ratio	4,576/6,692	0.68:1	4,024/5,789	0.70:1
Interest cover	732/104	7.04 times	586/84	6.98 times

As Samoco plc has no trade receivables, receivables days are zero.

(b) Evaluation of the liquidity, working capital and long-term solvency and financial stability of Samoco plc at 31 May 2019:

- Current and quick ratios are very low.
- However, this is not a problem as Samoco plc sells its goods for cash while trading on credit with suppliers.
- Therefore, goods have been sold well in advance of when they have to be paid for.
- The quick ratio is irrelevant for Samoco plc as inventory is a highly liquid asset, with inventory turning over every 14 days in the 2018/2019 trading year.
- Trade payables are paid after 24 days, so the company is holding on to the cash from sales of inventory for an additional 10 days before this cash is used to pay suppliers.
- The cash conversion cycle results in a negative figure. This means that the trade creditors are financing Samoco plc's working capital requirements.
- The company is paying dividends to the shareholders: this is not something that companies will do if they are short of cash. If Samoco plc were short of cash, the company would be conserving its money and not paying a dividend.
- The borrowings are repayable by equal instalments over the next 10 years. The business seems to be capable of generating the cash required to repay these borrowings as they come up for payment.
- The company trades in essential goods (food), so demand for its products will never fall away.

- This means that sales, profits and cash flows will be generated from which to repay the long-term borrowings as they fall due.

- Gearing might look high at 116.73%, but the interest cover ratio shows that the cost of servicing the interest on the borrowings is easily affordable from the operating profits.

- Gearing has fallen in comparison to the previous year and will continue to fall as the borrowings are repaid each year.

> **Question 7.2**

Amounts due for repayment the day after the year end:

	Calculation	1 June 2019 £m	1 June 2018 £m
Borrowings	240/12: 216/12	(20)	(18)
Trade payables	830/24.10: 790/25.45	(34)	(31)
Other payables	150 × 20%: 140 × 20%	(30)	(28)
Dividends	Not payable until August 2019/2018	(–)	(–)
Current tax	First payment due three months after year end	(–)	(–)
	Total liabilities due for payment on 1 June	(84)	(77)
	Cash and cash equivalents at year end	122	99
	Add: cash from one day's sales on 1 June: 13,663/360: 12,249/360	38	34
	Estimated cash balance at end of 1 June	76	56

Samoco thus has more than enough cash in hand to cover any liabilities due on 1 June in each year.

Problems with relying solely on the current and quick ratios

- Current and quick ratios make the unrealistic assumption that all liabilities will be called in on the day after the statement of financial position date.

- In reality, unless the entity is in liquidation, payment of current liabilities occurs over 12 months not all at once: individuals do not have to consider paying all their debts due over the next 12 months on the first day of the year, so why is this assumption made about business entities?

- Samoco plc is a very large company, so suppliers can be kept waiting for payment until the cash is readily available.

- Contracts govern bank loans, so, unless the company has breached the contractual terms of the loans, lenders cannot demand all their cash back until repayments are overdue.

- Other payables have been assumed to require 20% payment immediately: this is probably a serious overestimate of what is due on the day after the year end, so more cash than estimated is probably available at the end of the first day of the new financial year.

- Similarly, the current portion of long-term borrowings is more likely to be payable at the end of June not at the beginning of the month, so cash outflows on 1 June are, again, probably overestimated.

- Suppliers are happy to trade with such a large organization and will not want to jeopardize their future trading relationships by demanding immediate payments of amounts due. They know they will be paid eventually and are willing to sacrifice cash now for the longer-term certainty of continuing trade with their very large customer.

- When assessing short-term liquidity, timing of payments is everything and liabilities are paid, not immediately, but from cash left over at the end of the previous year and from subsequent cash inflows from daily trading.

- Current and quick ratios are a static measure of liquidity: in reality, the cash keeps flowing in each and every day while amounts due are paid each and every day as current trading pays off past liabilities.

> Question 7.3

Ratio calculations Ted Baker plc

Ted Baker plc	Calculation	Ratio
Current ratio	269.4/176.8	1.52:1
Quick ratio	(269.4 − 187.2)/176.8	0.46:1
Inventory days	187.2/230.9 × 365	295.92 days
Receivables days	42.7/591.7 × 365	26.34 days
Payables days	36.3/230.9 × 365	57.38 days
Cash conversion cycle	+ 295.92 + 26.34 − 57.38	264.88 days
Gearing %	128.5/224.1 × 100%	57.34%
Debt ratio	225.1/449.2	0.50:1
Interest cover	70.7/3.3	21.42 times

Ratio calculations Nichols plc

Nichols plc	Calculation	Ratio
Current ratio	75.6/23.6	3.20:1
Quick ratio	(75.6 − 4.8)/23.6	3.00:1
Inventory days	4.8/72.2 × 365	24.27 days
Receivables days	31.3/132.8 × 365	86.03 days
Payables days	6.8/72.2 × 365	34.38 days
Cash conversion cycle	+ 24.27 + 86.03 − 34.38	+ 75.92 days
Gearing %	0.0/99.3 × 100%	0.00%
Debt ratio	28.1/127.4	0.22:1
Interest cover	N/A: zero borrowings and zero finance expense	

Ratio calculations Weir Group plc

Weir Group plc	Calculation	Ratio
Current ratio	1,543.5/1,113.7	1.39:1
Quick ratio	$(1,543.5 - 586.8)/1,113.7$	0.86:1
Inventory days	$586.8/1,619.2 \times 365$	132.28 days
Receivables days	$492.9/2,355.9 \times 365$	76.37 days
Payables days	$341.7/1,619.2 \times 365$	77.03 days
Cash conversion cycle	$+ 132.28 + 76.37 - 77.03$	+ 131.62 days
Gearing %	$1,127.8/1,471.1 \times 100\%$	76.66%
Debt ratio	2,122.4/3,593.5	0. 59:1
Interest cover	223.1/38.2	5.84 times

Ratio calculations National Express plc

National Express plc	Calculation	Ratio
Current ratio	712.4/926.7	0.77:1
Quick ratio	$(712.4 - 24.9)/ 926.7$	0.74:1
Inventory days	$24.9/1,405.1 \times 365$	6.47 days
Receivables days	$238.8/2,321.2 \times 365$	37.55 days
Payables days	$258.5/1,405.1 \times 365$	67.15 days
Cash conversion cycle	$+ 6.47 + 37.55 - 67.15$	−23.13 days
Gearing %	$1,225.4/1,166.4 \times 100\%$	105.06%
Debt ratio	2,285.1/3,451.5	0.66:1
Interest cover	197.9/44.6	4.44 times

> **Question 7.4**

Assessment of the cash-generating ability, liquidity and solvency of each company:

Ted Baker plc

- The current ratio is very high because of the high levels of inventory maintained by the business.
- High inventories are needed in retail as no stock means no sale.
- With a financial year end at the end of January, new spring and summer season fashions will have just been delivered from suppliers, so high inventories would be expected at this time of year.

- The quick ratio is low because of the high level of inventories at the year end.

- However, this is not a cause for concern. Inventories will be sold in the stores and other outlets each day, so cash will be received on a regular basis with which to pay liabilities and other expenses as they fall due. Remember that inventory in the statement of financial position is shown at cost whereas the goods will sell for a much higher price than this cost (Ted Baker has a gross profit % of 60.98% in the 52 weeks to 27 January 2018) thereby boosting cash inflows on each and every trading day.

- Branded fashion and lifestyle goods have a shelf life of around six months, so inventories will not become obsolete and worthless within a few days of the year end.

- The cash conversion cycle is positive because of the high level of inventories.

- Receivables days are lower than payables days, but most sales will be made for cash in the retail outlets rather than being made on credit.

- Payables days are high as suppliers are willing to allow high levels of credit to the business in order to retain their custom and to develop the business relationship further.

- Gearing is reasonably low at 57.34% and a debt ratio of 0.50:1 indicates that the assets significantly outweigh the liabilities.

- Interest cover of 21.42 times indicates that borrowings are easily affordable.

- Borrowings are in the form of both overdraft and loans, so lenders clearly see Ted Baker as a very solid business with a very high credit rating. The possibility of the bank asking for the overdraft to be repaid immediately is very remote.

- Lenders would not be worried as Ted Baker is a very valuable global brand. This brand does not appear on the statement of financial position, so the breakup value of the group would far exceed the net assets figure as shown in the financial statements.

Nichols plc

- Current and quick ratios are very high at 3.20:1 and 3.00:1 indicating that this is a very solid company indeed.

- As a manufacturer of soft drinks, the company trades on credit with customers, hence the receivables days of 86.03.

- Payables are paid within 34 days.

- However, the very high cash balance of £36.1 million means that the company has plenty of spare money with which to finance its working capital.

- With total cash of £36.1 million and total liabilities of £28.1 million, Nichols could pay off all its liabilities at the year end and still have £8.0 million left over, so this is a company that has no financial problems.

- Soft drinks are a regular purchase for most households, so there is no danger that the business will lose its market.

- The company has no borrowings and is pretty much risk free from a financial viewpoint.

Weir Group plc

- A manufacturer of technical equipment that is sold to other companies for use in their processes.
- Therefore, the company will trade on credit with their customers and allow these customers a suitably long period of time in which to pay.
- The manufacturing cycle for technical equipment is lengthy and the inventory days indicate that this is well over four months.
- With receivables days of around two and a half months, this suggests that the group has to allow around 209 days (132 inventory days + 77 receivables days) from the start of an order to the receipt of the cash.
- Therefore, given the long working capital cycle, current and quick ratios are higher as this working capital has to be financed by the group.
- The cash conversion cycle is positive, indicating that suppliers have to be paid before inventories are turned into finished goods and before cash is received from customers.
- Customers are paying in around 76 days, while suppliers are paid after 77 days.
- While there might be a risk of obsolete stock, the expectation would be that finished goods would be produced for the most part to order for specific customers.
- Gearing is manageable at 76.66%, a debt ratio of 0.59:1 is reasonable and interest cover of 5.84 times indicates that all borrowings are affordable.

National Express plc

- As National Express is a transport operator, cash flows in daily as customers pay for their journeys as they are taken.
- This accounts for the very low current and quick ratios as the company has money flowing in up front from which to pay liabilities and the costs of running the business as they become due.
- The biggest costs in the transport sector are fuel and the wages of employees: fuel is bought on credit from suppliers (though failure to meet the payment terms might result in further supplies of fuel being cut off, bringing operations to a halt) while staff work for a month before they are paid, so the cash is received well in advance of payments being made to suppliers and employees.
- Inventory days are very low as the only inventory at the end of the year will be a few days of fuel in the vehicles and in the bus and train depots and some spares in the vehicle workshops: as long as fuel supplies are guaranteed, this is the only inventory that is required for trading in the transport sector.
- Receivables days at 37.55 might seem high, but these trade receivables will represent money due from local and national governments for grants that are paid as subsidies to operators of bus and train services.

- These receivables are thus guaranteed and there is no risk of irrecoverable debts arising.

- The cash conversion cycle is negative, so suppliers are financing the working capital requirements of the group rather than reliance being placed on short-term bank borrowings.

- Gearing at 105.06% might seem high, but the transport sector finances the purchase of buses and trains it cannot lease by borrowings. Transport is a capital intensive sector that pays for long-term assets (buses and trains) with long-term borrowings. The costs of these borrowings (interest and loan repayments) are met from day to day cash inflows from customers, so the assets are financed by daily income from passengers.

- Interest cover at 4.44 times indicates that borrowings are affordable.

- Transport is an essential sector and one that is likely to grow in importance as governments seek to reduce congestion in city centres and as the need to reduce reliance on other forms of transport to reduce greenhouse gases and global warming increases, so large mass transit operators should be safe companies in which to invest and with which to trade for the foreseeable future.

Chapter 8

> ## Question 8.1

Absorption cost for one food processor

	£
Materials: £22,500 ÷ 2,000 food processors	11.25
Direct labour: £16,500 ÷ 2,000 food processors	8.25
Direct expenses: £13,000 ÷ 2,000 food processors	6.50
Overhead allocation: 4.5 machine hours × £4 per hour*	18.00
Total absorption cost of one food processor	44.00

*Overhead absorption rate: £3,000,000 ÷ 750,000 machine hours = £4 per machine hour

Selling price for one food processor: total absorption cost plus 50% = £44 × 1.5 = £66

> ## Question 8.2

Printers Ltd print run

	£
Paper: 2,000 books × 400 pages = 800,000 pages ÷ 2,500 pages × £9 per 2,500 pages	2,880
Printing ink: 800,000 pages ÷ 20,000 × £57.50	2,300
Covers: 2,000 books × 66 pence per book	1,320
Finishing costs: 2,000 books × 50 pence	1,000
Production workers: 200 × £12.50	2,500
Overheads: £500,000 ÷ 50,000,000 pages × 800,000 printed pages	8,000
Total cost for print run of 2,000 books	18,000

Selling price for printing 2,000 books: £18,000 × 1.25 = £22,500 = £11.25 for each book (£22,500 ÷ 2,000)

> **Question 8.3**

Applokia Limited

Part (a)

	Variable cost	Fixed cost	Direct production cost	Production overhead	Period cost
Factory rent		✓		✓	
Factory manager's salary		✓		✓	
Administration salaries		✓			✓
Marketing costs		✓			✓
Plastic smart phone covers	✓		✓		
Quality control salaries		✓		✓	
Production line salaries		✓	✓		
Chip assemblies	✓		✓		
Administration office rent		✓			✓
Marketing office rent		✓			✓
Factory rates		✓		✓	
Power for production machinery	✓		✓		
Factory lighting and heating		✓		✓	
Administration lighting and heating		✓			✓
Marketing lighting and heating		✓			✓
Marketing department salaries		✓			✓
Batteries	✓		✓		
Machinery depreciation		✓		✓	

Variable costs: these are the costs that will vary directly in line with production. If you were at all unsure about which costs would be variable in this case, the way to determine if a cost is variable is to ask yourself if more of that cost will be incurred if another smart phone, another unit of production, is produced. In Applokia's case, each additional smart phone will require a plastic cover, a chip assembly, a battery and additional power for the production machinery to produce another smart phone. Therefore, these costs of production are entirely variable as they will increase or decrease directly in line with production.

Assembly line workers are paid a salary and, as it says in the question, these remain the same no matter how many or how few smart phones are produced. Thus, the assembly line workers' salaries, while being a direct cost of production (there will be no production without their input), are fixed rather than variable.

All other costs are fixed. Rent and rates will not vary in line with production and anyone paid a salary will receive the same salary no matter how many smart phones are produced or sold. Lighting and heating is best treated as a fixed cost as we noted in the case of Anna (Example 8.4) as it is not possible to allocate these costs to individual units of production.

Part (b)	£000
Prime cost	
Plastic smart phone covers	250
Chip assemblies for smart phones produced	1,498
Batteries	242
Production line workers' salaries	500
Power for production machinery	50
Total prime cost	**2,540**
Production overhead	
Factory rent	100
Factory manager's salary	38
Factory rates	47
Production machinery depreciation	37
Factory lighting and heating	43
Quality control salaries	75
Total production overhead	340
Total production cost (total prime cost + total production overhead)	**2,880**
Period costs	
Administration salaries	85
Administration office rent	25
Administration lighting and heating	5
Marketing lighting and heating	4
Marketing department salaries	51
Marketing office rent	20
Marketing costs	50
Total period costs	240
Total costs for September	3,120

Part (c)

Total costs from part (b): £3,120,000
Total production in September from the question: 130,000 smart phones
Total cost of one smart phone in September: £3,120,000 ÷ 130,000 = £24
Selling price = cost + 25% = £24 + (£24 × 0.25) = £30

Part (d)

If Applokia sells its smart phones for £27, it will make a profit on total cost of £27 − £24 = £3. This is equivalent to a margin on cost of £3 ÷ £24 × 100% = 12.50%. Proof that this is the correct answer: £24 + (£24 × 0.125) = £27

> **Question 8.4**

Part (a) Total production overheads to be allocated to the manufacturing and painting and finishing departments
The first task is to determine appropriate allocation bases for overheads. Using the information from the question, the following overhead bases would be the most suitable for each overhead:

- Machinery maintenance staff salaries and painting and finishing department employee salaries: actual cost for each department.

- Employers' national insurance contributions: these should be allocated on the basis of the salary costs in the two departments as higher salaries will mean higher employers' national insurance costs. Total salaries are £100,000 + £300,000 = £400,000. The manufacturing department is thus allocated (£100,000 ÷ £400,000) × £40,000 = £10,000 and the painting and finishing department is allocated (£300,000 ÷ £400,000) × £40,000 = £30,000.

- Rent and rates should be allocated on the basis of area as the bigger the area occupied by each department, the higher the allocated costs. Total area is 4,800 square metres + 1,200 square metres = 6,000 square metres. Total costs are £60,000, so the manufacturing department is allocated (4,800 ÷ 6,000) × £60,000 = £48,000 and the painting and finishing department is allocated (1,200 ÷ 6,000) × £60,000 = £12,000.

- Heating should be allocated on the basis of actual usage. The manufacturing department is not heated; there is not much point keeping machinery warm! As heat will be generated by the machinery as it is running to keep the manufacturing department heated, all the heating costs should be allocated to the painting and finishing department.

- Lighting is most appropriately allocated on the basis of area. Total costs are £25,000, so the manufacturing department is allocated (4,800 ÷ 6,000) × £25,000 = £20,000 and the painting and finishing department is allocated (1,200 ÷ 6,000) × £25,000 = £5,000.

- Machinery depreciation is best allocated on the basis of machinery value. Total machinery value is £360,000 + £15,000 = £375,000, so the manufacturing department is allocated (£360,000 ÷ £375,000) × £75,000 = £72,000 and the painting and finishing department is allocated (£15,000 ÷ £375,000) × £75,000 = £3,000.

- Canteen expenses should be allocated on the basis of the number of employees. The total number of employees is 5 in manufacturing plus 15 in painting and finishing, a total of 20 employees. Manufacturing department is allocated (5 ÷ 20) × £56,000 = £14,000 and the painting and finishing department is allocated (15 ÷ 20) × £56,000 = £42,000.

- Electricity for machinery should be allocated on the basis of the number of hours usage during the year as the number of hours of running time will determine the power that is used by that machinery. The total number of machine hours for the year is 96,000 in manufacturing and 4,000 in painting and finishing, a total of 100,000 hours. The manufacturing department is thus allocated (96,000 ÷ 100,000) × £50,000 = £48,000 and the painting and finishing department is allocated (4,000 ÷ 100,000) × £50,000 = £2,000.

- Machinery insurance should also be allocated on the basis of machinery value. Given that the total machinery value is £375,000, the manufacturing department is allocated (£360,000 ÷ £375,000) × £25,000 = £24,000 and the painting and finishing department is allocated (£15,000 ÷ £375,000) × £25,000 = £1,000.

The overheads allocated to each department can be summarized in a table along with the allocation bases used.

	Absorption basis	Total	Manufacturing	Finishing
		£000	£000	£000
Salaries	Actual cost	400	100	300
Employers' national insurance	Salaries	40	10	30
Rent and rates	Area	60	48	12
Heating	Actual usage	25	—	25
Lighting	Area	25	20	5
Machinery depreciation	Machinery value	75	72	3
Canteen expenses	Number of employees	56	14	42
Electricity for machinery	Machinery hours	50	48	2
Insurance: machinery	Machinery value	25	24	1
Total production overheads allocated to each department		756	336	420

Part (b) Most appropriate overhead recovery/absorption rate for the manufacturing and painting and finishing departments and justification for choice

- Manufacturing has a high number of machine hours and a low number of labour hours, so the most appropriate basis for the absorption of overheads in the manufacturing department will be machine hours.
- This will give an absorption rate of £336,000 ÷ 96,000 hours = £3.50 per machine hour.
- Painting and finishing has a high number of labour hours and a low number of machine hours, so the most suitable basis for the absorption of overheads in the painting and finishing department is labour hours.
- This will give an absorption rate of £420,000 ÷ 80,000 hours = £5.25 per labour hour.
- Overheads should be absorbed on bases that provide the best approximation of actual costs incurred and spread the costs over as much activity as possible. Thus, where an activity is machine intensive, overheads will be absorbed by products on the basis of machine hours consumed in that activity. On the other hand, where an activity is labour intensive, overheads will be absorbed based on the labour hours used by that activity.

Part (c) The cost of the novelty Christmas pixies will be:

Novelty Christmas pixies: 5,000 units	£
Direct materials and packaging	10,000
Direct labour	1,000
Manufacturing department 500 hours at £3.50	1,750
Painting and finishing department 1,000 hours at £5.25	5,250
Total cost	18,000
Cost per novelty Christmas pixie £18,000 ÷ 5,000	3.60

> **Question 8.5**

Step 1: reallocate service department overheads to production departments. The servicing department overheads can be allocated using the percentage of usage of the service department.

The canteen costs should be allocated on the basis of the number of employees using the canteen as follows:

- Total employees using the canteen: 15 + 5 + 6 + 4 = 30 (canteen employees do not use the canteen so no canteen overheads can be allocated to the canteen)
- Welding department's allocation of canteen overheads: 15/30 × £60,000 = £30,000
- Painting department's allocation of canteen overheads: 5/30 × £60,000 = £10,000
- Finishing department's allocation of canteen overheads: 6/30 × £60,000 = £12,000
- Service department's allocation of canteen overheads: 4/30 × £60,000 = £8,000

Service department costs are allocated on the basis of percentage usage by welding, painting and finishing:

- Service department overhead costs are now £42,000 (given in the question) + £8,000 overhead costs allocated from the canteen = £50,000

- Welding department's allocation of service department overheads: £50,000 × 40% = £20,000

- Painting and finishing departments' allocation of service department overheads: £50,000 × 30% = £15,000 each

	Welding	Painting	Finishing	Canteen	Service
	£	£	£	£	£
Overheads from question	100,000	75,000	43,000	60,000	42,000
Canteen overheads reallocated	30,000	10,000	12,000	(60,000)	8,000
Service overheads reallocated	20,000	15,000	15,000	—	(50,000)
Total overheads allocated	150,000	100,000	70,000	—	—
Department labour hours	30,000	12,500	10,000		
Overhead absorption rate/hour	5.00	8.00	7.00		

Step 2: calculate overhead absorption rates per hour for welding, painting and finishing:

- Welding department overhead absorption rate per hour: £150,000 (total overheads) ÷ 30,000 (total hours) = £5.00 per hour

- Painting department overhead absorption rate per hour: £100,000 (total overheads) ÷ 12,500 (total hours) = £8.00 per hour

- Finishing department overhead absorption rate per hour: £70,000 (total overheads) ÷ 10,000 (total hours) = £7.00 per hour

Step 3: calculate the cost of job 12359 using the information in the question and the overhead absorption rates calculated above.

Job 12359 cost card	£
Direct materials	1,500
Direct labour	2,000
Direct expense	500
Prime cost	4,000
Overhead: welding department: 120 hours × £5/hour	600
Overhead: painting department: 50 hours × £8/hour	400
Overhead: finishing department: 25 hours × £7/hour	175
Production cost	5,175
Selling price: cost + 40% of cost: £5,175 + (£5,175 × 40%)	7,245

> **Question 8.6**

Playthings Limited
Part (a)
First, calculate the overhead to be allocated to each product:

i.   Total machine hours: 10,000 for standard + 5,000 for deluxe = 15,000 hours in total

ii. Total overheads: £150,000

iii. Absorption rate of overheads per hour: £150,000 ÷ 15,000 hours = £10 per hour

iv. Machine hours per standard dolls house: 10,000 total hours ÷ 2,500 dolls houses produced
     = 4 hours per standard dolls house

v.   Overhead allocated to each standard dolls house: 4 hours × £10 per hour = £40

vi. Machine hours per deluxe dolls house: 5,000 total hours ÷ 1,000 dolls houses produced =
     5 hours per deluxe dolls house

vii. Overhead allocated to each deluxe dolls house: 5 hours × £10 per hour = £50

Total absorption cost and selling price for standard and deluxe dolls houses:

	Standard £	Deluxe £
Direct materials	50	76
Direct labour	30	42
Overheads absorbed	40	50
Total cost	120	168
Selling price (cost + 50%)	180	252

Part (b)
Suitable cost drivers for the four overhead cost pools:

* Machining: machine hours would be the most suitable basis for the allocation of these over-heads. The allocation rate will be £45,000 ÷ 15,000 hours = £3 per hour. Machining over-heads of 10,000 × £3 = £30,000 will be driven by standard and 5,000 × 3 = £15,000 by deluxe dolls houses.

* The factory supervisor costs will be driven by the number of employees supervised: the more employees supervised, the more cost is generated by this cost driver. The allocation rate will be £30,000 ÷ 15 employees = £2,000 per employee. Supervisor costs of 5 × £2,000 = £10,000 will be driven by standard and 10 × £2,000 = £20,000 by deluxe dolls houses.

* Set up-related overheads will be driven by the number of set ups: the more set ups there are the more overhead incurred in this cost pool. The allocation rate will be £50,000 ÷ 50 set ups = £1,000 per set up. Set up overheads of 15 × £1,000 = £15,000 will be driven by standard and 35 × £1,000 = £35,000 by deluxe dolls houses.

• Purchasing department costs will be driven by the number of materials orders: the more materials orders there are, the more overhead will be incurred in this cost pool. The allocation rate will be £25,000 ÷ 1,000 materials orders = £25 per order. Purchasing costs of 400 × £25 = £10,000 will be driven by standard and 600 × £25 = £15,000 by deluxe dolls houses.

Overheads allocated to each product on an activity-based costing approach:

	Standard £	Deluxe £
Machining	30,000	15,000
Factory supervisor	10,000	20,000
Set up	15,000	35,000
Purchasing department	10,000	15,000
Total overheads allocated	65,000	85,000
Total production	2,500	1,000
Overhead per unit of production	26	85

Part (c)

Total activity based cost and selling price for standard and deluxe dolls houses.

	Standard £	Deluxe £
Direct materials	50	76
Direct labour	30	42
Overheads absorbed	26	85
Total cost	106	203
Selling price (cost + 50%)	159	304.50

Part (d)

Advice to the directors on how they might reduce the cost of deluxe dolls houses in order to compete effectively in the market:

• Under traditional absorption costing, deluxe dolls houses are not being allocated their full share of overheads and so are subsidized by standard dolls houses.

• Activity-based costing now shows a much more accurate cost for each model of dolls house based on the costs incurred by the activities associated with each product.

• Under activity-based costing, standard dolls houses can now be sold at a much more competitive price (£159 v. the market price of £165) than under traditional absorption costing.

• An activity-based costing approach highlights activities that are causing cost with a view to helping management reduce costs in each particular cost pool, thereby reducing the costs of products in total.

- Machining costs are a necessary part of the manufacturing process and so it is unlikely that any reduction in these costs would be possible or desirable if quality is not to be compromised.

- The role of the factory supervisor could be looked at to determine whether this role is necessary. Employees could be given responsibility for their own production and quality control and incentives given to achieve zero defect production. However, any additional incentives would have to be considered in the total price of each product.

- The number of set ups in the year could be reduced to reduce total costs in this pool and in the amounts allocated to each product.

- Similarly, reducing the number of materials orders would reduce total costs in this pool and in the amounts allocated to each product.

Chapter 9

> ## Question 9.1

(a) Contribution for one unit of production and sales is the selling price less the variable costs of production.

(b) Relevant costs in decision making are the costs that will be incurred if a certain course of action is followed. Relevant costs include opportunity costs.

(c) Irrelevant costs are those costs that will not change whatever course of action is chosen. Irrelevant costs in decision making include fixed costs and sunk costs.

(d) Sunk costs are those costs incurred in the past that have no further influence on decisions to be made in the future.

(e) Opportunity cost is the cost of choosing one alternative course of action over another.

(f) Break-even point is the point at which the revenue from sales = the total costs of the business both fixed and variable. The break-even point in sales units is given by dividing the total fixed costs by the contribution per unit of sales.

(g) The margin of safety is the current sales in units – the break-even point in sales units.

(h) A target profit is the sales in units required to generate a given level of profit. This is calculated by dividing the profit required by the contribution per unit and adding the break-even number of sales units.

> ## Question 9.2

Podcaster University Press
Current profit: selling 200,000 textbooks at £30 each:

- Contribution per book: £30 selling price – £10 variable production costs = £20.
- Current profit: (200,000 sales × £20 contribution) – £3,000,000 fixed costs = £1,000,000.

Option 1: reduce selling price to £25 per book resulting in sales of 275,000 books:

- Contribution per book will now be: £25 selling price – £10 variable production costs = £15.
- Expected profit: (275,000 sales × £15 contribution) – £3,000,000 fixed costs = £1,125,000.

Option 2: reduce selling price to £21 per book resulting in sales of 360,000 books:

- Contribution per book now falls to: £21 selling price – £10 variable production costs = £11.
- Expected profit: (360,000 sales × £11 contribution) – £3,000,000 fixed costs = £960,000.

Option 1, reducing the selling price to £25 to sell 275,000 books per annum, will result in a higher profit whereas option 2 will result in a reduction in profit when compared with the current selling price of £30 and annual sales of 200,000 books. Therefore, Podcaster University Press should consider investigating option 1 further.

> **Question 9.3**

Big Bucks University

(a) Relevant costs

- The lecturer costs are not relevant to the decision on how many students to recruit as the lecturers will be paid whether the modules run or not. The lecturer costs are thus sunk costs and irrelevant to the decision on student recruitment. If new staff were to be recruited to teach these modules, then these costs would be relevant.

- The overhead costs for each room allocated to the modules are also irrelevant as these costs will be incurred whether the courses run or not. Costs that are allocated out of central overheads do not arise from the decision to run the modules and so are not relevant.

- The book and handout costs are relevant as these will vary directly in line with the number of students recruited to each module. For every additional module student recruited, a further cost of £100 for books and handouts will be incurred. These costs, along with the directly variable income from each student recruited to each module, will be relevant to the decision of how many students to recruit to each module in order to break even.

(b) Break-even point for each module

- Contribution per student: £400 module fee − £100 variable cost = £300 contribution

- Fixed costs per module: lecturer: £60 × 60 hours = £3,600

- Fixed costs per module: central overhead costs allocated: £1,200

- Total fixed costs per module: £3,600 + £1,200 = £4,800

- Break-even point: £4,800 (fixed costs) ÷ £300 (contribution per student) = 16 students

(c) Margin of safety if 25 students are recruited to each module

- 25 students recruited

- 16 students required to break even

- Therefore, margin of safety = 25 − 16 = 9 students

(d) Profit or loss at different recruitment levels

- Profit or loss at different recruitment levels will be determined by the number of students above or below the break-even point × the contribution per student

- 14 students recruited = 2 students (14 − 16) below the break-even point

- Loss incurred if 14 students are recruited = 2 × £300 = £600

- 30 students recruited = 14 students (30 −16) above the break-even point

- Profit earned if 30 students are recruited = 14 × 300 = £4,200

(e) Break-even point if the university decides to charge £340 per student per module

- Contribution per student now falls to: £340 − £100 = £240

- Fixed costs are unchanged at £4,800

- Break-even point = £4,800 ÷ £240 = 20 students

> **Question 9.4**

Gurjit Limited

(a) Current profit made at a level of sales and production of 5,000 ink jet printers per annum

	£	£
Sales: 5,000 × £40.00		200,000
Direct materials: 5,000 × £9.50	47,500	
Direct labour: 5,000 × £11.25	56,250	
Direct expense: 5,000 × £3.65	18,250	
Total direct costs of production	122,000	
Fixed overhead: 5,000 × £5.60	28,000	
Total costs		150,000
Profit on sales and production of 5,000 ink jet printers		50,000

(b) Profit expected at a level of sales and production of 10,000 ink jet printers per annum

	£	£
Sales: 10,000 × £40.00		400,000
Direct materials: 10,000 × £9.50	95,000	
Direct labour: 10,000 × £11.25	112,500	
Direct expense: 10,000 × £3.65	36,500	
Total direct costs of production	244,000	
Fixed overhead: 5,000* × £5.60	28,000	
Total costs		272,000
Profit on sales and production of 10,000 ink jet printers		128,000

*No, this is not a misprint! Remember that fixed costs do not change, so, if the overhead absorbed is based on a level of production and sales of 5,000 units, this fixed overhead will not change if production and sales are higher. If you calculated fixed overheads to be £56,000, double the cost for 5,000 units, you should go back over the Marginal v. absorption costing section of Chapter 9 to prove to yourself that fixed costs do not change over a given period, in this case one year.

(c) Profit expected at a level of sales and production of 10,000 ink jet printers per annum and purchasing the finished ink jet printers from Anand Limited

	£	£
Sales: 10,000 × £40.00		400,000
10,000 finished ink jet printers from Anand Limited	200,000	
Additional quality control costs	40,000	
Total incremental costs of the buy decision	240,000	
Fixed overhead 5,000 × £5.60	28,000	
Total costs		268,000
Profit on sales and production of 10,000 ink jet printers		132,000

Expected profit from this option is £132,000, which is £4,000 higher than making the printers in-house. Relevant costs to take into account in this option are the costs of buying the finished products from Anand Limited and the additional quality control costs that will be incurred to make sure that the printers delivered meet the requirements of Gurjit Limited. These incremental costs (the costs that will be incurred if this option is adopted) are £240,000, which is £4,000 lower than the total direct costs of production that Gurjit Limited will incur if the company manufactures the printers themselves.

Therefore, on cost grounds, you would advise the directors of Gurjit Limited to cease in-house production of ink jet printers and transfer production to Anand Limited.

(d) Additional factors that the directors of Gurjit Limited should take into account in this decision, other than costs and profit, and points you might have included and developed further are as follows:

- Loss of internal expertise on the transfer of production to an outside party.

- Loss of control over production of ink jet printers.

- Any interruption to Anand Limited's production of printers through, for example, strikes will mean that the products are not reaching the market and the reputation of Gurjit Limited will suffer damage.

- Additional costs to the reputation of Gurjit Limited should the products produced by Anand Limited fall short of customers' expectations.

- The additional quality control costs are only an estimate and these might be higher than the anticipated £40,000. Any increase in these costs might be greater than the total additional £4,000 profit that the directors expect to make by outsourcing production.

- Loss of confidentiality about product design and manufacture. Anand Limited could take the product and redesign and redevelop it and start producing a more advanced version itself, leading to Gurjit Limited losing all their customers and sales.

> Question 9.5

Diddle Limited

Step 1: calculate the quantity of limiting factor used in the production of each product:

Clio: Material used: £30 ÷ £6 per kg = 5 kg

Diana: Material used: £12 ÷ £6 per kg = 2 kg

Athena: Material used: £42 ÷ £6 per kg = 7 kg

Step 2: calculate the contribution per unit of limiting factor delivered by each product:

	Contribution per unit of key factor	Ranking
Clio	£30/5 kg per unit = £6 of contribution per unit of material used	2
Diana	£16/2 kg per unit = £8 of contribution per unit of material used	1
Athena	£35/7 kg per unit = £5 of contribution per unit of material used	3

The highest contribution per unit of key factor is delivered by Diana statues, which use just 2 kg of material in each unit and deliver a total contribution of £16 per product.

Step 3: calculate the contribution-maximizing production schedule:

Product	Kg of material per unit	Quantity produced	Kg of material used	Kg of material remaining	Contribution per unit	Total contribution
	Kg	Units	Kg	Kg	£	£
Diana	2	900	1,800	1,200	16	14,400
Clio	5	198	990	210	30	5,940
Athena	7	30	210	Nil	35	1,050
Total material used (kg)			3,000	Total contribution		21,390

Adopting the sales director's idea of maximizing production of Athenas:

- 3,000 kg of material ÷ 7 kg per Athena = 428 Athenas produced with 4 kg of material left over.

- Contribution from 428 Athenas = 428 × £35 = £14,890, well below the contribution-maximizing schedule above.

- As demand for Athenas is limited to 200 units, this would also mean that contribution for the month would only be 200 × £35 = £7,000 with 228 Athenas left unsold at the end of the month.

Chapter 10

> **Question 10.1**

(a) The total expected costs of the orchard for the past year

	£
Fertilizer: 5 doses at £4.00 for 30 trees	600
Labour: 30 trees × 10 hours per tree × £7.50 per hour	2,250
Total expected costs of the orchard for the past year	2,850

(b) The actual total costs of the orchard for the past year

	£
Fertilizer: 4 doses at £4.50 for 30 trees	540
Labour: 30 trees × 9 hours per tree × £8.00 per hour	2,160
Total actual costs of the orchard for the past year	2,700

(c) Material total variance

	£
Expected cost of fertilizer	600
Actual cost of fertilizer	540
Total material variance (favourable)	60

Material price variance

	£
4 doses for 30 trees should have cost: 4 × 30 × £4.00	480
4 doses for 30 trees actually cost: 4 × 30 × £4.50	540
Material price variance (unfavourable)	(60)

Material usage variance

	Number
Expected number of doses of fertilizer: 5 × 30	150
Actual number of doses of fertilizer: 4 × 30	120
Material usage variance in number of doses (favourable)	30

	£
Material usage variance in £s: 30 × £4.00 (favourable)	120

(£60) material price variance (unfavourable) + £120 material usage variance (favourable) = £60 material total variance (favourable).

(d) Labour total variance

	£
Expected cost of labour: 30 trees × 10 hours × £7.50 per hour	2,250
Actual cost of labour: 270 hours × £8 per hour	2,160
Total labour variance (favourable)	90

Labour rate variance

	£
270 hours of labour should have cost: 270 × £7.50	2,025
270 hours of labour actually cost: 270 × £8.00	2,160
Labour rate variance (unfavourable)	(135)

Labour efficiency variance

	Hours
Labour hours for 30 trees should have been: 30 × 10	300
Actual labour hours for 30 trees	270
Efficiency variance in number of hours (favourable)	30

	£
Efficiency variance in £s: 30 × £7.50 (favourable)	225

(£135) labour rate variance (unfavourable) + £225 labour efficiency variance (favourable) = £90 labour total variance (favourable).

> Question 10.2

Fred

(a) Sales price variance

- Number of cakes sold: £14,725 ÷ £15.50 = 950.
- Sales price variance: number of cakes sold × (actual selling price per cake − the expected selling price per cake) = 950 × (£15.50 − £15.00) = £475. This variance is favourable as the actual selling price was higher than the expected selling price.

(b) Sales volume variance

- (Number of cakes sold − expected number of cakes to be sold) × the expected contribution per cake.
- (950 − 1,000) × (£15.00 − £6.00) = − £450. This variance is unfavourable as fewer cakes than expected were sold.

Total sales variances: £475 favourable sales price variance – £450 unfavourable sales volume variance = £25 favourable total sales variances.

Proof that £25 favourable is the correct figure for the two sales variances:

	Expected: 1,000 cakes	Actual: 950 cakes	Variances
	£	£	£
Sales: 1,000 × £15/actual sales value	15,000	14,725	275 (U)
Variable costs: 1,000 × £6/950 × £6	6,000	5,700	300 (F)
Contribution/total variances	9,000	9,025	25 (F)

> **Question 10.3**

Sanguinary Services

(a) The profit that the centre expected to make in April, based on the original forecast of 3,000 blood tests in the month:

	£	£
Sales: 3,000 blood tests at £15		45,000
Chemicals used in blood tests: 3,000 × £5	15,000	
Laboratory workers 3,000 × £4	12,000	
Fixed overheads £72,000 ÷ 12 months	6,000	
Total costs		33,000
Expected profit for April		12,000

(b) Variances

Sales volume variance (actual blood tests – standard blood tests) × standard contribution per blood test   Units

Actual blood tests undertaken	3,600
Budgeted blood tests	3,000
Variance (favourable)	600

	£
Sales volume variance at standard contribution 600 × £(15 – 5 – 4) (favourable)	3,600

Remember that the fixed costs are not variable but fixed and so do not form part of the calculation of contribution from each blood test undertaken. Only the costs that vary with the level of activity are deducted from the selling price to give the contribution per unit of sales.

Sales price variance (actual selling price – budgeted selling price) × number of blood tests performed	£
Actual selling price	15.50
Standard selling price	15.00
Variance (favourable)	0.50
Sales price variance at actual sales 3,600 × £0.50 (favourable)	1,800.00

Direct material total variance

Standard quantity at standard cost v. actual quantity at actual cost	£
Chemicals for 3,600 blood tests should have cost 3,600 × £5	18,000
Chemicals for 3,600 blood tests actually cost	16,200
Direct material total variance (favourable)	1,800

Direct material price variance

Actual quantity at standard cost v. actual quantity at actual cost	£
33,750 millilitres should have cost (33,750 × £0.50)	16,875
33,750 millilitres actually cost (33,750 × £0.48)	16,200
Direct material price variance (favourable)	675

Direct material usage variance

(Standard quantity – actual quantity) × standard cost	Millilitres
3,600 blood tests should have used 10 millilitres × 3,600	36,000
3,600 blood tests actually used	33,750
Direct material usage variance in millilitres (favourable)	2,250

	£
Direct material usage variance in millilitres × standard price per ml 2,250 × £0.50 (favourable)	1,125

Labour total variance

Standard hours at standard cost v. actual hours at actual cost	£
3,600 blood tests should have cost (900 hours × £16 per hour)	14,400
3,600 blood tests actually cost	14,985
Direct labour total variance (unfavourable)	(585)

Labour rate variance

Actual labour hours at standard cost – actual labour hours at actual cost	£
925 labour hours should have cost (925 × £16.00)	14,800
925 labour hours actually cost	14,985
Direct labour rate variance (unfavourable)	(185)

Labour usage variance

You should calculate the standard number of hours needed to complete 3,600 blood tests. Each blood test should take 15 minutes, making 4 tests per hour. Therefore, 3,600 blood tests should take 900 hours (3,600 ÷ 4)

	Hours
(Standard hours for actual quantity – actual hours for actual quantity) × standard cost per hour	
3,600 blood tests should have used 900 hours	900
3,600 blood tests actually used	925
Direct labour efficiency variance in hours (unfavourable)	(25)
	£
Direct labour efficiency variance in hours × standard rate/hour 25 × £16.00 (unfavourable)	(400)

Fixed overhead expenditure variance

	£
Standard fixed overhead expenditure – actual fixed overhead expenditure	
Standard fixed overhead expenditure (3,000 × £2) or (72,000 ÷ 12 months)	6,000
Actual fixed overhead expenditure	7,500
Fixed overhead expenditure variance (unfavourable)	(1,500)

(c) Statement reconciling the expected profit to the actual profit for April

	(Unfavourable)	Favourable	Profit
	£	£	£
Expected profit (part (a))			12,000
Sales price variance		1,800	
Sales volume variance		3,600	
Direct material price variance		1,125	
Direct material usage variance		675	
Direct labour rate variance	(185)		
Direct labour efficiency variance	(400)		
Fixed overhead expenditure variance	(1,500)		
Total variances	(2,085)	7,200	
Add: favourable variances			7,200
Deduct: unfavourable variances			(2,085)
Actual profit for April			17,115

> Question 10.4

Smashers Tennis Club

(a) Calculation of the original expected surplus from the coaching course

	£
Revenue: 12 juniors × £70 each	840
Costs: balls: 12 × £10	120
Coach: 10 hrs × £30	300
Expected surplus	420

(b) Calculation of the expected surplus from the coaching course for 16 juniors:

	£
Revenue: 16 juniors × £70 each	1,120
Costs: balls: 16 × £10	160
Coach: 10 hrs × £30	300
Expected surplus	660

(c) Calculation of the actual surplus from the coaching course:

	£
Revenue: 16 juniors × (£70 × 90%) each	1,008
Costs: balls: 400 balls × 60p	240
Coach: 10 hrs × £33	330
Actual surplus	438

(d) Variances

(i) Sales price variance: (£63 − £70) × 16 = £112 (unfavourable) as the price is lower than expected

(ii) Sales volume variance: additional participants: 16 − 12 = 4

Contribution per participant: £70 (price for one junior participant) − £10 (variable cost of balls for each junior member: remember that the cost of the coach is a fixed cost and does not vary in line with the number of juniors participating in the course) = £60

Sales volume variance: £60 contribution × 4 participants = £240 (favourable) as more juniors participated than expected

(iii) Direct material total variance: this relates to the tennis balls:

	£	
Expected cost of balls for 16 participants: 16 × £10	160	
Actual cost of balls for 16 participants 400 × 60 pence	240	
Direct material total variance	(80)	Unfavourable

(iv) Direct material price variance (tennis balls):

	£	
400 balls at 50 pence each	200	
400 balls at 60 pence each	240	
Direct material price variance	(40)	Unfavourable

(v) Direct material usage variance (tennis balls):

	Balls	
16 participants should use 20 balls × 16 participants	320	
16 participants actually used	400	
Direct material usage variance (in tennis balls)	(80)	Unfavourable

	£	
Direct material usage variance: 80 balls × 50 pence	(40)	Unfavourable

The unfavourable direct material price variance of £40 + the unfavourable direct material usage variance of £40 = the total unfavourable direct material variance of £80.

(vi) Fixed expenditure variance (coaching costs): £300 (expected) − £330 (actual) = £30 unfavourable as more cost has been incurred than expected

Reconciliation of expected surplus to actual surplus:

	Unfavourable	Favourable	Surplus
	£	£	£
Expected surplus (part (a))			420
Sales price variance	(112)		
Sales volume variance		240	
Direct material price variance	(40)		
Direct material usage variance	(40)		
Fixed overhead expenditure variance	(30)		
Total variances	(222)	240	
Add: favourable variances			240
Deduct: unfavourable variances			(222)
Actual surplus for the 10-week coaching course			438

> Question 10.5

Vijay Manufacturing

	(a) Sales of 2,000 garden gnomes at standard cost	(b) Sales of 1,800 garden gnomes at standard cost	(c) Sales of 1,800 garden gnomes at actual cost	Variance: (b) – (c) favourable (f) or unfavourable (u)
	£	£	£	£
Sales	30,000	27,000	25,200	(1,800) (u)
Materials	9,000	8,100	8,750	(650) (u)
Labour	8,000	7,200	7,125	75 (f)
Variable overhead	6,000	5,400	5,500	(100) (u)
Fixed overhead	2,000	2,000	1,600	400 (f)
Net profit	5,000	4,300	2,225	(2,075) (u)

(d) Variance analysis and reconciliation statement:

Sales price variance

	£
(Actual selling price – budgeted selling price) × number of gnomes sold	
Actual selling price	14.00
Standard selling price	15.00
Variance (unfavourable)	(1.00)
Sales price variance of actual sales 1,800 × £1.00 (unfavourable)	(1,800)

Sales volume variance
Contribution per garden gnome sold: £15 (selling price) – £4.50 (direct materials) – £4.00 (direct labour) – £3.00 (variable overhead) = £3.50. Remember that fixed overheads are fixed and do not form part of the variable cost of production and so are not part of the contribution calculation.

Actual sales units v. standard sales units	Units
Actual units sold	1,800
Budgeted sales units	2,000
Variance (unfavourable)	(200)

	£
Sales volume variance at standard contribution 200 × £3.50 (unfavourable)	(700)

Direct material total variance

	£
Standard quantity at standard cost v. actual quantity at actual cost	
Material for 1,800 gnomes should have cost (1,800 × £2.25 × 2)	8,100
Material for 1,800 gnomes did cost (3,500 × £2.50)	8,750
Direct material total variance (unfavourable)	(650)

Direct material price variance

	£
Actual quantity at standard cost v. actual quantity at actual cost	
3,500 kg of material should have cost (3,500 × £2.25)	7,875
3,500 kg actually cost (3,500 × £2.50)	8,750
Direct material price variance (unfavourable)	(875)

Direct material usage variance

	Kg
(Standard quantity – actual quantity) × standard cost	
1,800 gnomes should have used (1,800 × 2 kg)	3,600
1,800 gnomes actually used	3,500
Direct material usage variance in kg (favourable)	100

	£
Direct material usage variance in kg × standard price per kg 100 × £2.25 (favourable)	225

Direct labour total variance

	£
Standard hours at standard cost v. actual hours at actual cost	
1,800 gnomes should have cost (1,800 × £4.00)	7,200
1,800 gnomes actually cost	7,125
Direct labour total variance (favourable)	75

Direct labour rate variance

	£
Actual labour hours at standard cost – actual labour hours at actual cost	
950 labour hours should have cost (950 × £8.00)	7,600
950 labour hours actually cost (950 × £7.50)	7,125
Direct labour rate variance (favourable)	475

Direct labour efficiency variance

	Hours
(Standard hours for actual quantity – actual hours for actual quantity) × standard cost per hour	
1,800 gnomes should have used 1,800 × 0.5 hours	900
1,800 gnomes actually used	950
Direct labour efficiency variance in hours (unfavourable)	(50)

	£
Direct labour efficiency variance in hours × standard rate/hour 50 × £8 (unfavourable)	(400)

Variable overhead total variance

	£
1,800 gnomes should have cost (1,800 × £3.00)	5,400
1,800 gnomes actually cost	5,500
Variable overhead total variance (unfavourable)	(100)

Variable overhead expenditure variance

	£
Actual labour hours at standard cost – actual labour hours at actual cost	
7,000 machine hours should have cost (7,000 × £0.75)	5,250
7,000 machine hours actually cost	5,500
Variable overhead rate variance (unfavourable)	(250)

Variable overhead efficiency variance

	Hours
(Standard hours for actual quantity – actual hours for actual quantity) × standard cost per hour	
1,800 gnomes should have used (1,800 × 4 hours)	7,200
1,800 gnomes actually used	7,000
Variable overhead efficiency variance in hours (favourable)	200

	£
Variable overhead efficiency variance in hours × standard rate/hour 200 × £0.75 (favourable)	150

Fixed overhead expenditure variance

	£
Standard fixed overhead – actual fixed overhead	
Standard fixed overhead expenditure	2,000
Actual fixed overhead expenditure	1,600
Fixed overhead expenditure variance (favourable)	400

Statement reconciling the expected profit to the actual profit for June

	(Unfavourable)	Favourable	Profit
	£	£	£
Expected profit (part (a))			5,000
Sales price variance	(1,800)		
Sales volume variance	(700)		
Direct material price variance	(875)		
Direct material usage variance		225	
Direct labour rate variance		475	
Direct labour efficiency variance	(400)		
Variable overhead expenditure variance	(250)		
Variable overhead efficiency variance		150	
Fixed overhead expenditure variance		400	
Total variances	(4,025)	1,250	
Add: favourable variances			1,250
Deduct: unfavourable variances			(4,025)
Actual profit for June			2,225

Chapter 11

> ## Question 11.1

Dave's ice cream van

	April	May	June	July	August	Sept	Total
Cash receipts							
Dave's own cash	5,000						5,000
Sales	3,500	5,500	7,500	7,500	7,500	2,500	34,000
Total cash receipts	8,500	5,500	7,500	7,500	7,500	2,500	39,000
Cash payments							
Ice cream purchases		1,750	2,750	3,750	3,750	3,750	15,750
Ice cream van hire	1,500			1,500			3,000
Van running expenses	250	250	250	250	250	250	1,500
Business insurance	500						500
Drawings	1,000	1,000	1,000	1,000	1,000	1,000	6,000
Total cash payments	3,250	3,000	4,000	6,500	5,000	5,000	26,750
Receipts – payments	5,250	2,500	3,500	1,000	2,500	(2,500)	12,250
Cash at start of month	—	5,250	7,750	11,250	12,250	14,750	
Cash at end of month	5,250	7,750	11,250	12,250	14,750	12,250	

Dave: statement of profit or loss for the six months ended 30 September

	£	£
Sales (all cash receipts)		34,000
Cost of sales (cash paid + outstanding payment for September of £1,250)		17,000
Gross profit		17,000
Expenses		
Ice cream van hire (cash paid)	3,000	
Van running expenses (cash paid)	1,500	
Business insurance (cash paid)	500	
		5,000
Net profit for the six months		12,000

Dave: Statement of financial position at 30 September

	£
Current assets	
Cash and cash equivalents (= cash balance in cash flow forecast)	12,250
Current liabilities	
Trade payable (£2,500 × 50%, ice cream cost for September)	1,250
Net assets (12,250 – 1,250)	11,000
Equity (capital account)	
Cash introduced	5,000
Profit for the six months	12,000
Drawings	(6,000)
	11,000

> **Question 11.2**

Hena plc

- See the spreadsheet for the figures in the online workbook.

- The new venture makes a profit of £34,620,000 and has positive cash at the end of the first year of operation of £29,580,000.

- Therefore, the directors would be advised to go ahead with such a profitable and cash generative operation.

> **Question 11.3**

Hena plc

- See the spreadsheet for the figures in the online workbook.

- Based on the new projections, the venture now makes a profit of £6,540,000 and has year end cash of £2,863,000. However, the cash does not become positive until sometime in October (compared to positive cash from April onwards in the answer to Question 11.2).

- Therefore, the directors would now be advised to undertake careful sensitivity analysis of the figures to determine whether the project is still worthwhile from both a profit and a cash flow perspective.

> **Question 11.4**

Clothing manufacturing company

- See the spreadsheet for the figures in the online workbook.

> **Question 11.5**

Plastic chair manufacturer

- See the spreadsheet for the figures in the online workbook.

Chapter 12

> **Question 12.1**

Podcaster University Press

Payback

	Accounting book		Economics book	
	Annual cash flows	Cumulative	Annual cash flows	Cumulative
	£000	£000	£000	£000
Investment at time 0	(450)	(450)	(600)	(600)
Net cash inflows year 1	160	(290)	240	(360)
Net cash inflows year 2	160	(130)	200	(160)
Net cash inflows year 3	160	30	160	0
Net cash inflows year 4	100	130	105	105
Net cash inflows year 5	100	230	105	210
Year 5 sale of assets	50	280	100	310

Accounting book payback period: 2 years + (130 ÷ 160) × 12 months = 2 years and 10 months

Economics book payback period: 3 years exactly

Payback: considerations

- The Accounting book is clearly preferable on the payback method of investment appraisal, although the Economics book pays back only two months later.

- The Economics book does have net cash inflows of £30,000 more than the Accounting book, although these net cash inflows do rely heavily on the sale of the assets for £100,000 at the end of year 5.

- Without this final inflow of cash from the sale of the assets, the net cash inflows of the Accounting book would be £230,000 (£280,000 − £50,000 cash from sale of the assets) compared with £210,000 (£310,000 − £100,000 cash from sale of the assets) for the Economics book.

Accounting rate of return

Accounting book

- The cost of the assets is £450,000
- The residual value of the assets is £50,000

Therefore, total depreciation is: £450,000 (cost) − £50,000 (residual value) = £400,000

Total accounting profits are £680,000 (cash inflows) − £400,000 (depreciation) = £280,000

Average accounting profit for the Accounting book: £280,000 ÷ 5 years = £56,000

Average investment in the Accounting book over its life: $\dfrac{(£450,000 + £50,000)}{2} = £250,000$

Accounting rate of return for the Accounting book: £56,000 ÷ £250,000 × 100% = 22.40%

Economics book

- The cost of the assets is £600,000

- The residual value of the assets is £100,000

Therefore, total depreciation is: £600,000 (cost) − £100,000 (residual value) = £500,000

Total accounting profits are £810,000 (cash inflows) − £500,000 (depreciation) = £310,000

Average accounting profit for the Economics book: £310,000 ÷ 5 years = £62,000

Average investment in the Economics book over its life $\dfrac{(£600,000 + £100,000)}{2} = £350,000$

Accounting rate of return for the Economics book: £62,000 ÷ £350,000 × 100% = 17.71%

Accounting rate of return: considerations

- The Accounting book has the higher accounting rate of return so would be the preferred project on the basis of this capital investment appraisal technique.

- Average annual profits between the two book projects differ by only £6,000.

- The Economics book requires an additional average capital investment of £100,000.

- Therefore, the additional return of £6,000 per annum for this additional investment might not be considered worthwhile.

Net present value

NPV for the Accounting book

	Cash flow £000	10% Discount factor	NPV £000
Investment at time 0	(450)	1.0000	(450.00)
Net cash inflows year 1	160	0.9091	145.46
Net cash inflows year 2	160	0.8264	132.22
Net cash inflows year 3	160	0.7513	120.21
Net cash inflows year 4	100	0.6830	68.30
Net cash inflows year 5	100	0.6209	62.09
End of year 5 sale of assets	50	0.6209	31.05
		Project NPV	109.33

NPV for the Economics book

	Cash flow £000	10% Discount factor	NPV £000
Investment at time 0	(600)	1.0000	(600.00)
Net cash inflows year 1	240	0.9091	218.18
Net cash inflows year 2	200	0.8264	165.28
Net cash inflows year 3	160	0.7513	120.21
Net cash inflows year 4	105	0.6830	71.72
Net cash inflows year 5	105	0.6209	65.19
End of year 5 sale of assets	100	0.6209	62.09
		Project NPV	102.67

Net present value: considerations

- The Accounting book has the higher net present value, so this book should be accepted instead of the Economics book.
- The Accounting book breaks even on a net present value basis towards the end of year 4.
- The Economics book breaks even on a net present value basis only at the end of year 5.

Internal rate of return

NPV for the Accounting book discounted at 20%

	Cash flow £000	20% Discount factor	NPV £000
Investment at time 0	(450)	1.0000	(450.00)
Net cash inflows year 1	160	0.8333	133.33
Net cash inflows year 2	160	0.6944	111.10
Net cash inflows year 3	160	0.5787	92.59
Net cash inflows year 4	100	0.4823	48.23
Net cash inflows year 5	100	0.4019	40.19
End of year 5 sale of assets	50	0.4019	20.10
		Project NPV	(4.46)

Internal rate of return: Accounting book

$$10\% + \frac{109.33}{109.33 + 4.46} \times (20\% - 10\%) = 19.61\%$$

NPV for the Economics book discounted at 20%

	Cash flow £000	20% Discount factor	NPV £000
Investment at time 0	(600)	1.0000	(600.00)
Net cash inflows year 1	240	0.8333	199.99
Net cash inflows year 2	200	0.6944	138.88
Net cash inflows year 3	160	0.5787	92.59
Net cash inflows year 4	105	0.4823	50.64
Net cash inflows year 5	105	0.4019	42.20
End of year 5 sale of assets	100	0.4019	40.19
		Project NPV	(35.51)

Internal rate of return: Economics book

$$10\% + \frac{102.67}{102.67 + 35.51} \times (20\% - 10\%) = 17.43\%$$

Internal rate of return: considerations

- The Accounting book has the higher internal rate of return.
- This internal rate of return is higher than Podcaster University Press's cost of capital (10%), so the project should be accepted.
- The decision under IRR is consistent with the decision under the net present value appraisal method, which is to choose the Accounting book as this project has the higher net present value of the two books.

Additional considerations:

- The Accounting book is the preferred project under all the investment appraisal methods.
- The Accounting book has a lower capital outlay than the Economics book, which makes the Accounting book less risky as less capital is required to fund the project.
- The Accounting book is the chosen project as this will maximize investors' returns and increase the value of the press when compared with the Economics book.
- If the company has £600,000 to invest in a new project, choosing the Accounting book will leave £150,000, which could be invested to generate additional interest income for the company and its shareholders.

> **Question 12.2**

Payback

	Option 1		Option 2	
	Annual cash flows	Cumulative	Annual cash flows	Cumulative
	£000	£000	£000	£000
Investment at time 0	(200)	(200)	(245)	(245)
Cash savings year 1	50	(150)	—	(245)
Cash savings year 2	70	(80)	80	(165)
Cash savings year 3	80	—	85	(80)
Cash savings year 4	70	70	86	6
Cash savings year 5	60	130	101	107
Cash savings year 6	—	—	81	188
Cash savings year 7	—	—	71	259

Option 1 has a payback period of exactly three years whereas option 2 has a payback period of just under four years. Under the payback method of capital investment appraisal, option 1 would be the chosen project.

Accounting rate of return

Total depreciation for option 1: £200,000 (cost) − £nil (residual value) = £200,000
Total depreciation for option 2: £245,000 (cost) − £nil (residual value) = £245,000
Average accounting profit for option 1: (£330,000 − £200,000) ÷ 5 years = £26,000
Average accounting profit for option 2: (£504,000 − £245,000) ÷ 7 years = £37,000
Average investment in each project over each project's life:

$$\text{Option 1:} \frac{(£200,000 + £Nil)}{2} = £100,000$$

$$\text{Option 2:} \frac{(£245,000 + £Nil)}{2} = £122,500$$

Accounting rate of return: option 1: £26,000 ÷ £100,000 = 26.00%
Accounting rate of return option 2: £37,000 ÷ £122,500 = 30.20%

Under the accounting rate of return approach to capital investment appraisal, option 2 offers the higher rate of return and so would be the chosen project on this criterion.

Net present value

NPV of option 1

	Cash flow £	15% Discount factor	NPV £
Investment at time 0	(200,000)	1.0000	(200,000)
Cash savings year 1	50,000	0.8696	43,480
Cash savings year 2	70,000	0.7561	52,927
Cash savings year 3	80,000	0.6575	52,600
Cash savings year 4	70,000	0.5718	40,026
Cash savings year 5	60,000	0.4972	29,832
		Project NPV	18,865

NPV of option 2

	Cash flow £	15% Discount factor	NPV £
Investment at time 0	(245,000)	1.0000	(245,000)
Cash savings year 1	—	0.8696	—
Cash savings year 2	80,000	0.7561	60,488
Cash savings year 3	85,000	0.6575	55,888
Cash savings year 4	86,000	0.5718	49,175
Cash savings year 5	101,000	0.4972	50,217
Cash savings year 6	81,000	0.4323	35,016
Cash savings year 7	71,000	0.3759	26,689
		Project NPV	32,473

Based on our calculations of net present value, option 2 will be the preferred project as this has a higher net present value when compared with option 1.

Internal rate of return

IRR of option 1

Discounting cash flows at 19%	Cash flow £	19% Discount factor	NPV £
Investment at time 0	(200,000)	1.0000	(200,000)
Cash savings year 1	50,000	0.8403	42,015
Cash savings year 2	70,000	0.7062	49,434
Cash savings year 3	80,000	0.5934	47,472
Cash savings year 4	70,000	0.4987	34,909
Cash savings year 5	60,000	0.4190	25,140
		Project NPV	(1,030)

Internal rate of return: option 1

$$15\% + \frac{18,865}{18,865 + 1,030} \times (19\% - 15\%) = 18.79\%$$

IRR of option 2

Discounting cash flows at 19%	Cash flow £	19% Discount factor	NPV £
Investment at time 0	(245,000)	1.0000	(245,000)
Cash savings year 1	—	0.8403	—
Cash savings year 2	80,000	0.7062	56,496
Cash savings year 3	85,000	0.5934	50,439
Cash savings year 4	86,000	0.4987	42,888
Cash savings year 5	101,000	0.4190	42,319
Cash savings year 6	81,000	0.3521	28,520
Cash savings year 7	71,000	0.2959	21,009
		Project NPV	(3,329)

Internal rate of return: option 2

$$15\% + \frac{32,473}{32,473 + 3,329} \times (19\% - 15\%) = 18.63\%$$

Based on the internal rate of return criteria, the directors should choose option 1 as this has the higher internal rate of return. However, as the internal rate of return gives a different result compared with the net present value calculation, the directors should stick with option 2 as advised by the NPV decision.

Other factors in the decision

- The capital investment appraisal techniques applied favour option 2, with both the accounting rate of return and the net present value suggesting this project should be adopted, whereas only the payback method favoured option 1.

- However, seven years is a long time in technology terms and it is quite possible that better computerized supply chain systems will be developed well before option 2 has completed its useful life resulting in losses from scrapping the system and unrealized cash savings.

- Given the length of the project and the likelihood that new technology will be developed before option 2 reaches the end of its life, the directors of Zippo Drinks Limited should consider the possible obsolescence of option 2's system and any consequences arising from this.

- Cash flows from option 2 do not start until the end of year 2 and are therefore more uncertain than the cash flows from option 1: the directors of Zippo Drinks should factor in the possibility that the cash flows from option 2 do not meet expectations.

> ## Question 12.3

Payback

	Run the restaurant		Rent the restaurant	
	Annual cash flows	Cumulative	Annual cash flows	Cumulative
	£000	£000	£000	£000
Investment at time 0	(110)	(110)	(80)	(80)
Net cash inflows/Rent year 1	35	(75)	40	(40)
Net cash inflows/Rent year 2	45	(30)	40	0
Net cash inflows/Rent year 3	60	30	40	40
Net cash inflows/Rent year 4	65	95	40	80
Net cash inflows/Rent year 5	55	150	40	120
Year 5 sale of assets	2	152	—	120

Running the restaurant yourself results in a payback period of 2½ years, whereas the payback period for renting out the restaurant is just 2 years.

Accounting rate of return

Total depreciation if you are running the restaurant yourself:

£110,000 (cost) – £2,000 (residual value) = £108,000

Total depreciation if you rent the restaurant out:

£80,000 (cost) – £nil (residual value) = £80,000

Average accounting profit:

Running the restaurant yourself: (£260,000 – £108,000) ÷ 5 years = £30,400

Renting the restaurant out:

(£200,000 – £80,000) ÷ 5 years = £24,000

Average investment:

Running the restaurant yourself: $\dfrac{(£110,000 + £2,000)}{2} = £56,000$

Renting the restaurant out: $\dfrac{(£80,000 + £nil)}{2} = £40,000$

Accounting rate of return:

Running the restaurant yourself: £30,400 ÷ £56,000 = 54.29%

Renting the restaurant out: £24,000 ÷ £40,000 = 60.00%

Net present value

NPV: running the restaurant yourself

	Cash flow £000	12% Discount factor	NPV £000
Investment at time 0	(110,000)	1.0000	(110,000)
Net cash inflows year 1	35,000	0.8929	31,252
Net cash inflows year 2	45,000	0.7972	35,874
Net cash inflows year 3	60,000	0.7118	42,708
Net cash inflows year 4	65,000	0.6355	41,308
Net cash inflows year 5	55,000	0.5674	31,207
End of year 5 sale of assets	2,000	0.5674	1,135
		Project NPV	73,484

NPV: renting the restaurant out

	Cash flow £000	12% Discount factor	NPV £000
Investment at time 0	(80,000)	1.0000	(80,000)
Rent year 1	40,000	0.8929	35,716
Rent year 2	40,000	0.7972	31,888
Rent year 3	40,000	0.7118	28,472
Rent year 4	40,000	0.6355	25,420
Rent year 5	40,000	0.5674	22,696
		Project NPV	64,192

Evaluation based on purely financial considerations:

* Renting the restaurant out produces a payback period of 2 years compared with a payback period of 2½ years if you run the restaurant yourself.

* Similarly, the accounting rate of return for the renting option is 60% compared with an accounting rate of return of only 54.29% if you were to run the restaurant yourself.

* The internal rate of return from renting is 41.10% compared with an IRR of 33.84% from running the restaurant yourself.

* The net present value of renting is £9,292 lower (£73,484 − £64,192) than the option of running the restaurant yourself.

* Therefore, given the superiority of the net present value investment appraisal technique, running the restaurant would seem to be the preferred option despite the preference of the other two methods for taking on the renting option.

Other factors in the decision

- Running the restaurant will be very hard work, so you might prefer to take the lower annual income from renting the restaurant out.

- If you were to rent the restaurant out, all the time you would have spent running the restaurant can now be used to undertake other activities to generate cash inflows to replace those lost from running the restaurant yourself.

- Renting the restaurant out is much lower risk as the other entrepreneur is taking on the risk of the restaurant failing to match expectations and generate the anticipated cash inflows.

- Running the restaurant yourself might have been much more profitable than you had expected, so renting it out might result in lost income.

- However, your fellow entrepreneur might not do as well as she expected and this might affect your profit share if this is not guaranteed.

- The problem you face is a common one in investment decisions: a steady, guaranteed income compared with the potentially much higher rewards that might be gained from taking a much bigger risk.

> **Question 12.4**

Ambulators Limited

Before we can undertake any calculations to determine payback, the accounting rate of return, the net present value and the internal rate of return of the two proposed projects, we will have to calculate the expected sales and production together with the estimated net cash inflows (sales − costs) of each project.

Option 1: the new pram: sales, production and net cash inflows

The first step will be to calculate the sales from the new pram for the five years of the project's life. Sales units rise by 20% per annum, so sales units for the five years will be as follows:

Year	Calculation	Sales units
1	—	5,000
2	5,000 × 120%	6,000
3	6,000 × 120%	7,200
4	7,200 × 120%	8,640
5	8,640 × 120%	10,368

Now that the sales and production units are known, the net cash flows (receipts from sales − costs of production) from the production and sales of prams can be calculated.

- Selling price per pram: £450.
- Variable production price per pram: £150.00 + £75.00 + £25.00 = £250.
- Annual fixed overheads for prams: £50 × 5,000 = £250,000.

Remember that fixed costs are fixed and so will not change over the five-year life of the pram project.

Net cash flows per annum:

	Sales units	Gross sales value @ £450 per pram	Variable production costs @ £250 per pram	Fixed costs	Net cash flows
		£000	£000	£000	£000
Year 1	5,000	2,250.00	1,250.00	250.00	750.00
Year 2	6,000	2,700.00	1,500.00	250.00	950.00
Year 3	7,200	3,240.00	1,800.00	250.00	1,190.00
Year 4	8,640	3,888.00	2,160.00	250.00	1,478.00
Year 5	10,368	4,665.60	2,592.00	250.00	1,823.60
Totals	37,208	16,743.60	9,302.00	1,250.00	6,191.60

Option 2: the new pushchair: sales, production and net cash inflows

Projected demand for the new pushchair together with expected selling prices for each year are as follows:

Year	Calculation	Sales units	Selling Price
1	—	6,000	£220
2	6,000 × 110%	6,600	£230
3	6,600 × 110%	7,260	£240
4	7,260 × 110%	7,986	£250
5	7,986 × 110%	*8,785	£260

*Rounded from 8,784.6 to the nearest whole number.

- Selling price per pushchair: as given in the table above with selling prices rising by £10 per annum from a starting price in the first year of £220.
- Variable production price per pushchair: £80.00 + £40.00 + £10.00 = £130.
- Annual fixed overheads for pushchairs: £20 × 6,000 = £120,000.

Remember that fixed costs are fixed and so will not change over the five-year life of the pushchair project.

	Sales units	Selling price per pushchair	Gross sales value	Variable production costs @ £130 per pushchair	Fixed costs	Net cash flows
		£	£000	£000	£000	£000
Year 1	6,000	220	1,320.00	780.00	120.00	420.00
Year 2	6,600	230	1,518.00	858.00	120.00	540.00
Year 3	7,260	240	1,742.40	943.80	120.00	678.60
Year 4	7,986	250	1,996.50	1,038.18	120.00	838.32
Year 5	8,785	260	2,284.10	1,142.05	120.00	1,022.05
Totals	36,631		8,861.00	4,762.03	600.00	3,498.97

Payback

	Pram			Pushchair	
	Cash Flow	Cumulative Cash Flow		Cash Flow	Cumulative Cash Flow
	£000	£000		£000	£000
Investment	(3,300.00)	(3,300.00)	Investment	(2,200.00)	(2,200.00)
Year 1	750.00	(2,550.00)	Year 1	420.00	(1,780.00)
Year 2	950.00	(1,600.00)	Year 2	540.00	(1,240.00)
Year 3	1,190.00	(410.00)	Year 3	678.60	(561.40)
Year 4	1,478.00	1,068.00	Year 4	838.32	276.92
Year 5	1,823.60	2,891.60	Year 5	1,022.05	1,298.97
			Transfer	500.00	1,798.97

Payback period: pram: 3.28 years (3 + 410.00/1,478.00)
Payback period: pushchair: 3.67 years (3 + 561.40/838.82)

Accounting rate of return

Pram

Cost of investment: £3,300,000
Residual value: £nil
Total depreciation: £3,300,000
Total accounting profits: £6,191,600 − £3,300,000 = £2,891,600
Average accounting profit for the pram: £2,891,600 ÷ 5 years = £578,320
Average investment in the pram: (£3,300,000 + £nil) ÷ 2 = £1,650,000
Accounting rate of return: £578,320 ÷ £1,650,000 = 35.05%

Pushchair

Cost of investment: £2,200,000

Residual value: £500,000

Total depreciation: £1,700,000

Total accounting profits: £3,498,970 – £1,700,000 = £1,798,970

Average accounting profit for the pushchair: £1,798,970 ÷ 5 years = £359,794

Average investment in the pushchair: (£2,200,000 + £500,000) ÷ 2 = £1,350,000

Accounting rate of return: £359,794 ÷ £1,350,000 = 26.65%

Net present value

	Pram			Pushchair		
	Cash flow £000	11% Discount factor	NPV £000	Cash flow £000	11% Discount factor	NPV £000
Year 0	(3,300.00)	1.0000	(3,300.000)	(2,200.00)	1.0000	(2,200.000)
Year 1	750.00	0.9009	675.675	420.00	0.9009	378.378
Year 2	950.00	0.8116	771.020	540.00	0.8116	438.264
Year 3	1,190.00	0.7312	870.128	678.60	0.7312	496.192
Year 4	1,478.00	0.6587	973.559	838.32	0.6587	552.201
Year 5	1,823.60	0.5935	1,082.307	1,022.05	0.5935	606.587
Transfer	—	—	—	500.00	0.5935	296.750
	Pram: NPV		1,072.689	Pushchair: NPV		568.372

Internal rate of return

	Pram			Pushchair		
	Cash flow £000	22%* Discount factor	NPV £000	Cash flow £000	19% Discount factor	NPV £000
Year 0	(3,300.00)	1.0000	(3,300.000)	(2,200.00)	1.0000	(2,200.000)
Year 1	750.00	0.8197	614.775	420.00	0.8403	352.926
Year 2	950.00	0.6719	638.305	540.00	0.7062	381.348
Year 3	1,190.00	0.5508	655.452	678.60	0.5934	402.681
Year 4	1,478.00	0.4514	667.169	838.32	0.4987	418.070
Year 5	1,823.60	0.3700	674.732	1,022.05	0.4190	428.239
Transfer	—	—	—	500.00	0.4190	209.500
	Pram: NPV		(49.567)	Pushchair: NPV		(7.236)

*Use the formula $1/(1 + r)^n$ to calculate the 22% discount factors.

Internal rate of return: pram

$$11\% + \frac{1,072,689}{(1,072,689 + 49,567)} \times (22\% - 11\%) = 21.51\%$$

Internal rate of return: pushchair:

$$11\% + \frac{568,372}{(568,372 + 7,236)} \times (19\% - 11\%) = 18.90\%$$

Recommendation:

- On financial grounds, the pram project has the shortest payback period, the highest accounting rate of return, the highest net present value and the highest internal rate of return.
- However, the directors should consider whether sales growth of 20% each year is realistic and achievable.
- Similarly, is a 10% annual rise in the sales of the pushchairs realistic and achievable?
- How realistic is the projection that the price of pushchairs will rise by £10 a year?
- The pram project requires 50% more investment than the pushchair project (£3,300,000 v. £2,200,000) and returns 88.73% more (£1,072,689 v. £568,372) for this additional 50% investment.

Additional factors to consider:

- Projected birth rates over the next five years.

- If these are rising, then the projected growth rates in sales might be achievable.

- If birth rates are expected to fall, then the expected growth rate will probably not be achievable at all.

- Prams and pushchairs produced by other companies and the likely demand for competitor companies' products.

- How competitor company products compare with Ambulators' prams and pushchairs.

- How effectively Ambulators' products will compete with other products on the market.

- Prices charged by competitors and how these compare to the prices charged by Ambulators Limited.

- The possibility that Ambulators will have to reduce their prices in order to compete more effectively against competitors' products.

- An assumption has been made that the cost prices of each product will not change over the five years: this might not be a realistic assumption, so sensitivity analysis should be carried out on the projected results to see what effect any price rises in materials, director labour, variable overheads and fixed costs would have on the results of the calculations.

> **Question 12.5**

Chillers plc

Our first task will be to calculate the annual net cash flows arising from the production of the new deluxe fridge-freezer. Information that we will need to complete this task is as follows:

- Selling price of the new deluxe fridge freezer: £600.

- Variable costs per deluxe fridge-freezer: £600 × 40% = £240.

- Annual fixed costs: £1,200,000.

- Annual value of lost sales of standard fridge-freezers: 2,000 × £350 = £700,000.

- Annual cost savings arising from the lost sales of standard fridge-freezers: (£700,000 × 35%) + £395,000 of annual fixed costs = £640,000.

We can now calculate the annual net cash flows arising from the introduction of the new deluxe fridge-freezer:

Year	Sales units	Sales value	Variable costs	Fixed costs	Lost sales	Costs saved	Net cash flows
		£000	£000	£000	£000	£000	£000
2020	3,500	2,100	840	1,200	700	640	0
2021	4,000	2,400	960	1,200	700	640	180
2022	4,500	2,700	1,080	1,200	700	640	360
2023	5,250	3,150	1,260	1,200	700	640	630
2024	5,750	3,450	1,380	1,200	700	640	810
2025	5,500	3,300	1,320	1,200	700	640	720
2026	5,250	3,150	1,260	1,200	700	640	630
Totals	33,750	20,250	8,100	8,400	4,900	4,480	3,330

Net cash flows are calculated as follows: + sales value – variable costs – fixed costs – lost sales + costs saved. Thus, for 2020, the calculation is + £2,100 – £840 – £1,200 – £700 + £640 = £0.

Payback

	Cash Flow	Cumulative Cash Flow
	£000	£000
Investment	(2,000)	(2,000)
2020	0	(2,000)
2021	180	(1,820)
2022	360	(1,460)
2023	630	(830)
2024	810	(20)
2025	720	700
2026	630	1,330
Scrap value 2026	100	1,430

Payback period: 5.03 years

Accounting rate of return

Cost of investment: £2,000,000
Residual value: £100,000
Total depreciation: £1,900,000
Total accounting profits: £3,330,000 − £1,900,000 = £1,430,000
Average accounting profit: £1,430,000 ÷ 7 years = £204,286
Average investment: (£2,000,000 + £100,000) ÷ 2 = £1,050,000
Accounting rate of return: £204,286 ÷ £1,050,000 = 19.46%

Net present value

	Cash flow £000	13% Discount factor	NPV £000
Year 0	(2,000)	1.0000	(2,000.000)
2020	0	0.8850	0.000
2021	180	0.7831	140.958
2022	360	0.6931	249.516
2023	630	0.6133	386.379
2024	810	0.5428	439.668
2025	720	0.4803	345.816
2026	630	0.4251	267.813
2026 Scrap value	100	0.4251	42.510
		Net present value	(127.340)

Internal rate of return

As the net present value at a 13% discount rate is negative, the internal rate of return must be lower than 13%.

	Cash flow £000	11% Discount factor	NPV £000
Year 0	(2,000)	1.0000	(2,000.000)
2020	0	0.9009	0.000
2021	180	0.8116	146.088
2022	360	0.7312	263.232
2023	630	0.6587	414.981
2024	810	0.5935	480.735
2025	720	0.5346	384.912
2026	630	0.4817	303.471
2026 scrap value	100	0.4817	48.170
		Net present value	41.589

Internal rate of return:

$$11\% + \frac{41,589}{(41,589 + 127,340)} \times (13\% - 11\%) = 11.49\%$$

Should the directors undertake the project?

- Net present value at a discount rate of 13% is negative, so this project does not give a positive return to the company.

- The internal rate of return shows that the rate of return on this project is 1.51% below the required rate of return.

- The project only pays back after five years. This is a long time to wait for the return of the capital invested.

- The project is thus risky because of the length of time it takes to return the capital originally invested.

Therefore, based on the capital investment appraisal figures, this project should not go ahead.

Appendix

Table 1 Present value of £1 at compound interest $(1 \div r)^{-n}$

Periods of n	Discount rate as a percentage									
	1%	2%	3%	4%	5%	6%	7%	8%	9%	10%
1	0.9901	0.9804	0.9709	0.9615	0.9524	0.9434	0.9346	0.9259	0.9174	0.9091
2	0.9803	0.9612	0.9426	0.9246	0.9070	0.8900	0.8734	0.8573	0.8417	0.8264
3	0.9706	0.9423	0.9151	0.8890	0.8638	0.8396	0.8163	0.7938	0.7722	0.7513
4	0.9610	0.9238	0.8885	0.8548	0.8227	0.7921	0.7629	0.7350	0.7084	0.6830
5	0.9515	0.9057	0.8626	0.8219	0.7835	0.7473	0.7130	0.6806	0.6499	0.6209
6	0.9420	0.8880	0.8375	0.7903	0.7462	0.7050	0.6663	0.6302	0.5963	0.5645
7	0.9327	0.8706	0.8131	0.7599	0.7107	0.6651	0.6227	0.5835	0.5470	0.5132
8	0.9235	0.8535	0.7894	0.7307	0.6768	0.6274	0.5820	0.5403	0.5019	0.4665
9	0.9143	0.8368	0.7664	0.7026	0.6446	0.5919	0.5439	0.5002	0.4604	0.4241
10	0.9053	0.8203	0.7441	0.6756	0.6139	0.5584	0.5083	0.4632	0.4224	0.3855
11	0.8963	0.8043	0.7224	0.6496	0.5847	0.5268	0.4751	0.4289	0.3875	0.3505
12	0.8874	0.7885	0.7014	0.6246	0.5568	0.4970	0.4440	0.3971	0.3555	0.3186
13	0.8787	0.7730	0.6810	0.6006	0.5303	0.4688	0.4150	0.3677	0.3262	0.2897
14	0.8700	0.7579	0.6611	0.5775	0.5051	0.4423	0.3878	0.3405	0.2992	0.2633
15	0.8613	0.7430	0.6419	0.5553	0.4810	0.4173	0.3624	0.3152	0.2745	0.2394
16	0.8528	0.7284	0.6232	0.5339	0.4581	0.3936	0.3387	0.2919	0.2519	0.2176
17	0.8444	0.7142	0.6050	0.5134	0.4363	0.3714	0.3166	0.2703	0.2311	0.1978
18	0.8360	0.7002	0.5874	0.4936	0.4155	0.3503	0.2959	0.2502	0.2120	0.1799
19	0.8277	0.6864	0.5703	0.4746	0.3957	0.3305	0.2765	0.2317	0.1945	0.1635
20	0.8195	0.6730	0.5537	0.4564	0.3769	0.3118	0.2584	0.2145	0.1784	0.1486
21	0.8114	0.6598	0.5375	0.4388	0.3589	0.2942	0.2415	0.1987	0.1637	0.1351
22	0.8034	0.6468	0.5219	0.4220	0.3418	0.2775	0.2257	0.1839	0.1502	0.1228
23	0.7954	0.6342	0.5067	0.4057	0.3256	0.2618	0.2109	0.1703	0.1378	0.1117
24	0.7876	0.6217	0.4919	0.3901	0.3101	0.2470	0.1971	0.1577	0.1264	0.1015
25	0.7798	0.6095	0.4776	0.3751	0.2953	0.2330	0.1842	0.1460	0.1160	0.0923

Discount rate as a percentage											
11%	**12%**	**13%**	**14%**	**15%**	**16%**	**17%**	**18%**	**19%**	**20%**	**25%**	**30%**
0.9009	0.8929	0.8850	0.8772	0.8696	0.8621	0.8547	0.8475	0.8403	0.8333	0.8000	0.7692
0.8116	0.7972	0.7831	0.7695	0.7561	0.7432	0.7305	0.7182	0.7062	0.6944	0.6400	0.5917
0.7312	0.7118	0.6931	0.6750	0.6575	0.6407	0.6244	0.6086	0.5934	0.5787	0.5120	0.4552
0.6587	0.6355	0.6133	0.5921	0.5718	0.5523	0.5337	0.5158	0.4987	0.4823	0.4096	0.3501
0.5935	0.5674	0.5428	0.5194	0.4972	0.4761	0.4561	0.4371	0.4190	0.4019	0.3277	0.2693
0.5346	0.5066	0.4803	0.4556	0.4323	0.4104	0.3898	0.3704	0.3521	0.3349	0.2621	0.2072
0.4817	0.4523	0.4251	0.3996	0.3759	0.3538	0.3332	0.3139	0.2959	0.2791	0.2097	0.1594
0.4339	0.4039	0.3762	0.3506	0.3269	0.3050	0.2848	0.2660	0.2487	0.2326	0.1678	0.1226
0.3909	0.3606	0.3329	0.3075	0.2843	0.2630	0.2434	0.2255	0.2090	0.1938	0.1342	0.0943
0.3522	0.3220	0.2946	0.2697	0.2472	0.2267	0.2080	0.1911	0.1756	0.1615	0.1074	0.0725
0.3173	0.2875	0.2607	0.2366	0.2149	0.1954	0.1778	0.1619	0.1476	0.1346	0.0859	0.0558
0.2858	0.2567	0.2307	0.2076	0.1869	0.1685	0.1520	0.1372	0.1240	0.1122	0.0687	0.0429
0.2575	0.2292	0.2042	0.1821	0.1625	0.1452	0.1299	0.1163	0.1042	0.0935	0.0550	0.0330
0.2320	0.2046	0.1807	0.1597	0.1413	0.1252	0.1110	0.0985	0.0876	0.0779	0.0440	0.0254
0.2090	0.1827	0.1599	0.1401	0.1229	0.1079	0.0949	0.0835	0.0736	0.0649	0.0352	0.0195
0.1883	0.1631	0.1415	0.1229	0.1069	0.0930	0.0811	0.0708	0.0618	0.0541	0.0281	0.0150
0.1696	0.1456	0.1252	0.1078	0.0929	0.0802	0.0693	0.0600	0.0520	0.0451	0.0225	0.0116
0.1528	0.1300	0.1108	0.0946	0.0808	0.0691	0.0592	0.0508	0.0437	0.0376	0.0180	0.0089
0.1377	0.1161	0.0981	0.0829	0.0703	0.0596	0.0506	0.0431	0.0367	0.0313	0.0144	0.0068
0.1240	0.1037	0.0868	0.0728	0.0611	0.0514	0.0433	0.0365	0.0308	0.0261	0.0115	0.0053
0.1117	0.0926	0.0768	0.0638	0.0531	0.0443	0.0370	0.0309	0.0259	0.0217	0.0092	0.0040
0.1007	0.0826	0.0680	0.0560	0.0462	0.0382	0.0316	0.0262	0.0218	0.0181	0.0074	0.0031
0.0907	0.0738	0.0601	0.0491	0.0402	0.0329	0.0270	0.0222	0.0183	0.0151	0.0059	0.0024
0.0817	0.0659	0.0532	0.0431	0.0349	0.0284	0.0231	0.0188	0.0154	0.0126	0.0047	0.0018
0.0736	0.0588	0.0471	0.0378	0.0304	0.0245	0.0197	0.0160	0.0129	0.0105	0.0038	0.0014

Table 2 Annuity table: the present value of £1 received or paid per year at a compound rate of interest
$1/r - \{1/[r(1+r)^n]\}$

Periods of n	Discount rate as a percentage									
	1%	2%	3%	4%	5%	6%	7%	8%	9%	10%
1	0.990	0.980	0.971	0.962	0.952	0.943	0.935	0.926	0.917	0.909
2	1.970	1.942	1.913	1.886	1.859	1.833	1.808	1.783	1.759	1.736
3	2.941	2.884	2.829	2.775	2.723	2.673	2.624	2.577	2.531	2.487
4	3.902	3.808	3.717	3.630	3.546	3.465	3.387	3.312	3.240	3.170
5	4.853	4.713	4.580	4.452	4.329	4.212	4.100	3.993	3.890	3.791
6	5.795	5.601	5.417	5.242	5.076	4.917	4.767	4.623	4.486	4.355
7	6.728	6.472	6.230	6.002	5.786	5.582	5.389	5.206	5.033	4.868
8	7.652	7.325	7.020	6.733	6.463	6.210	5.971	5.747	5.535	5.335
9	8.566	8.162	7.786	7.435	7.108	6.802	6.515	6.247	5.995	5.759
10	9.471	8.983	8.530	8.111	7.722	7.360	7.024	6.710	6.418	6.145
11	10.368	9.787	9.253	8.760	8.306	7.887	7.499	7.139	6.805	6.495
12	11.255	10.575	9.954	9.385	8.863	8.384	7.943	7.536	7.161	6.814
13	12.134	11.348	10.635	9.986	9.394	8.853	8.358	7.904	7.487	7.103
14	13.004	12.106	11.296	10.563	9.899	9.295	8.745	8.244	7.786	7.367
15	13.865	12.849	11.938	11.118	10.380	9.712	9.108	8.559	8.061	7.606
16	14.718	13.578	12.561	11.652	10.838	10.106	9.447	8.851	8.313	7.824
17	15.562	14.292	13.166	12.166	11.274	10.477	9.763	9.122	8.544	8.022
18	16.398	14.992	13.754	12.659	11.690	10.828	10.059	9.372	8.756	8.201
19	17.226	15.678	14.324	13.134	12.085	11.158	10.336	9.604	8.950	8.365
20	18.046	16.351	14.877	13.590	12.462	11.470	10.594	9.818	9.129	8.514
21	18.857	17.011	15.415	14.029	12.821	11.764	10.836	10.017	9.292	8.649
22	19.660	17.658	15.937	14.451	13.163	12.042	11.061	10.201	9.442	8.772
23	20.456	18.292	16.444	14.857	13.489	12.303	11.272	10.371	9.580	8.883
24	21.243	18.914	16.936	15.247	13.799	12.550	11.469	10.529	9.707	8.985
25	22.023	19.523	17.413	15.622	14.094	12.783	11.654	10.675	9.823	9.077

				Discount rate as a percentage							
11%	12%	13%	14%	15%	16%	17%	18%	19%	20%	25%	30%
0.901	0.893	0.885	0.877	0.870	0.862	0.855	0.847	0.840	0.833	0.800	0.769
1.713	1.690	1.668	1.647	1.626	1.605	1.585	1.566	1.547	1.528	1.440	1.361
2.444	2.402	2.361	2.322	2.283	2.246	2.210	2.174	2.140	2.106	1.952	1.816
3.102	3.037	2.974	2.914	2.855	2.798	2.743	2.690	2.639	2.589	2.362	2.166
3.696	3.605	3.517	3.433	3.352	3.274	3.199	3.127	3.058	2.991	2.689	2.436
4.231	4.111	3.998	3.889	3.784	3.685	3.589	3.498	3.410	3.326	2.951	2.643
4.712	4.564	4.423	4.288	4.160	4.039	3.922	3.812	3.706	3.605	3.161	2.802
5.146	4.968	4.799	4.639	4.487	4.344	4.207	4.078	3.954	3.837	3.329	2.925
5.537	5.328	5.132	4.946	4.772	4.607	4.451	4.303	4.163	4.031	3.463	3.019
5.889	5.650	5.426	5.216	5.019	4.833	4.659	4.494	4.339	4.192	3.571	3.092
6.207	5.938	5.687	5.453	5.234	5.029	4.836	4.656	4.486	4.327	3.656	3.147
6.492	6.194	5.918	5.660	5.421	5.197	4.988	4.793	4.611	4.439	3.725	3.190
6.750	6.424	6.122	5.842	5.583	5.342	5.118	4.910	4.715	4.533	3.780	3.223
6.982	6.628	6.302	6.002	5.724	5.468	5.229	5.008	4.802	4.611	3.824	3.249
7.191	6.811	6.462	6.142	5.847	5.575	5.324	5.092	4.876	4.675	3.859	3.268
7.379	6.974	6.604	6.265	5.954	5.668	5.405	5.162	4.938	4.730	3.887	3.283
7.549	7.120	6.729	6.373	6.047	5.749	5.475	5.222	4.990	4.775	3.910	3.295
7.702	7.250	6.840	6.467	6.128	5.818	5.534	5.273	5.033	4.812	3.928	3.304
7.839	7.366	6.938	6.550	6.198	5.877	5.584	5.316	5.070	4.843	3.942	3.311
7.963	7.469	7.025	6.623	6.259	5.929	5.628	5.353	5.101	4.870	3.954	3.316
8.075	7.562	7.102	6.687	6.312	5.973	5.665	5.384	5.127	4.891	3.963	3.320
8.176	7.645	7.170	6.743	6.359	6.011	5.696	5.410	5.149	4.909	3.970	3.323
8.266	7.718	7.230	6.792	6.399	6.044	5.723	5.432	5.167	4.925	3.976	3.325
8.348	7.784	7.283	6.835	6.434	6.073	5.746	5.451	5.182	4.937	3.981	3.327
8.422	7.843	7.330	6.873	6.464	6.097	5.766	5.467	5.195	4.948	3.985	3.329

Table 3 Future value of £1 at compound interest $(1 + r)^n$

Periods of n	Discount rate as a percentage									
	1%	2%	3%	4%	5%	6%	7%	8%	9%	10%
1	1.010	1.020	1.030	1.040	1.050	1.060	1.070	1.080	1.090	1.100
2	1.020	1.040	1.061	1.082	1.103	1.124	1.145	1.166	1.188	1.210
3	1.030	1.061	1.093	1.125	1.158	1.191	1.225	1.260	1.295	1.331
4	1.041	1.082	1.126	1.170	1.216	1.262	1.311	1.360	1.412	1.464
5	1.051	1.104	1.159	1.217	1.276	1.338	1.403	1.469	1.539	1.611
6	1.062	1.126	1.194	1.265	1.340	1.419	1.501	1.587	1.677	1.772
7	1.072	1.149	1.230	1.316	1.407	1.504	1.606	1.714	1.828	1.949
8	1.083	1.172	1.267	1.369	1.477	1.594	1.718	1.851	1.993	2.144
9	1.094	1.195	1.305	1.423	1.551	1.689	1.838	1.999	2.172	2.358
10	1.105	1.219	1.344	1.480	1.629	1.791	1.967	2.159	2.367	2.594
11	1.116	1.243	1.384	1.539	1.710	1.898	2.105	2.332	2.580	2.853
12	1.127	1.268	1.426	1.601	1.796	2.012	2.252	2.518	2.813	3.138
13	1.138	1.294	1.469	1.665	1.886	2.133	2.410	2.720	3.066	3.452
14	1.149	1.319	1.513	1.732	1.980	2.261	2.579	2.937	3.342	3.797
15	1.161	1.346	1.558	1.801	2.079	2.397	2.759	3.172	3.642	4.177
16	1.173	1.373	1.605	1.873	2.183	2.540	2.952	3.426	3.970	4.595
17	1.184	1.400	1.653	1.948	2.292	2.693	3.159	3.700	4.328	5.054
18	1.196	1.428	1.702	2.026	2.407	2.854	3.380	3.996	4.717	5.560
19	1.208	1.457	1.754	2.107	2.527	3.026	3.617	4.316	5.142	6.116
20	1.220	1.486	1.806	2.191	2.653	3.207	3.870	4.661	5.604	6.727
21	1.232	1.516	1.860	2.279	2.786	3.400	4.141	5.034	6.109	7.400
22	1.245	1.546	1.916	2.370	2.925	3.604	4.430	5.437	6.659	8.140
23	1.257	1.577	1.974	2.465	3.072	3.820	4.741	5.871	7.258	8.954
24	1.270	1.608	2.033	2.563	3.225	4.049	5.072	6.341	7.911	9.850
25	1.282	1.641	2.094	2.666	3.386	4.292	5.427	6.848	8.623	10.835

				Discount rate as a percentage							
11%	12%	13%	14%	15%	16%	17%	18%	19%	20%	25%	30%
1.110	1.120	1.130	1.140	1.150	1.160	1.170	1.180	1.190	1.200	1.250	1.300
1.232	1.254	1.277	1.300	1.323	1.346	1.369	1.392	1.416	1.440	1.563	1.690
1.368	1.405	1.443	1.482	1.521	1.561	1.602	1.643	1.685	1.728	1.953	2.197
1.518	1.574	1.630	1.689	1.749	1.811	1.874	1.939	2.005	2.074	2.441	2.856
1.685	1.762	1.842	1.925	2.011	2.100	2.192	2.288	2.386	2.488	3.052	3.713
1.870	1.974	2.082	2.195	2.313	2.436	2.565	2.700	2.840	2.986	3.815	4.827
2.076	2.211	2.353	2.502	2.660	2.826	3.001	3.185	3.379	3.583	4.768	6.275
2.305	2.476	2.658	2.853	3.059	3.278	3.511	3.759	4.021	4.300	5.960	8.157
2.558	2.773	3.004	3.252	3.518	3.803	4.108	4.435	4.785	5.160	7.451	10.604
2.839	3.106	3.395	3.707	4.046	4.411	4.807	5.234	5.695	6.192	9.313	13.786
3.152	3.479	3.836	4.226	4.652	5.117	5.624	6.176	6.777	7.430	11.642	17.922
3.498	3.896	4.335	4.818	5.350	5.936	6.580	7.288	8.064	8.916	14.552	23.298
3.883	4.363	4.898	5.492	6.153	6.886	7.699	8.599	9.596	10.699	18.190	30.288
4.310	4.887	5.535	6.261	7.076	7.988	9.007	10.147	11.420	12.839	22.737	39.374
4.785	5.474	6.254	7.138	8.137	9.266	10.539	11.974	13.590	15.407	28.422	51.186
5.311	6.130	7.067	8.137	9.358	10.748	12.330	14.129	16.172	18.488	35.527	66.542
5.895	6.866	7.986	9.276	10.761	12.468	14.426	16.672	19.244	22.186	44.409	86.504
6.544	7.690	9.024	10.575	12.375	14.463	16.879	19.673	22.901	26.623	55.511	112.455
7.263	8.613	10.197	12.056	14.232	16.777	19.748	23.214	27.252	31.948	69.389	146.192
8.062	9.646	11.523	13.743	16.367	19.461	23.106	27.393	32.429	38.338	86.736	190.050
8.949	10.804	13.021	15.668	18.822	22.574	27.034	32.324	38.591	46.005	108.420	247.065
9.934	12.100	14.714	17.861	21.645	26.186	31.629	38.142	45.923	55.206	135.525	321.184
11.026	13.552	16.627	20.362	24.891	30.376	37.006	45.008	54.649	66.247	169.407	417.539
12.239	15.179	18.788	23.212	28.625	35.236	43.297	53.109	65.032	79.497	211.758	542.801
13.585	17.000	21.231	26.462	32.919	40.874	50.658	62.669	77.388	95.396	264.698	705.641

Annotated statements

Illustration 2.1: Bunns the Bakers plc: annotated statement of financial position at 31 March 2019

	2019	2018
	£000	£000
1 ASSETS		
Non-current assets		
3 Intangible assets	50	55
Property, plant and equipment	11,750	11,241
4 Investments	65	59
	11,865	11,355
Current assets		
Inventories	60	55
7 Trade and other receivables	62	75
Cash and cash equivalents	212	189
8	334	319
Total assets	12,199	11,674
LIABILITIES		
Current liabilities		
10 Current portion of long-term borrowings	300	300
Trade and other payables	390	281
Current tax liabilities	150	126
13	840	707
Non-current liabilities		
Long-term borrowings	2,700	3,000
Long-term provisions	200	200
	2,900	3,200
17 Total liabilities	3,740	3,907
Net assets	8,459	7,767
EQUITY		
19 Called up share capital	2,500	2,400
20 Share premium	1,315	1,180
Retained earnings	4,644	4,187
21 Total equity	8,459	7,767

Callout numbers: 1, 2, 3, 4, 5, 6, 7, 8, 9, 10, 11, 12, 13, 14, 15, 16, 17, 18, 19, 20, 21

1 Present economic resources controlled by the entity as a result of past events. An economic resource is a right that has the potential to produce economic benefits. To be recognized on the statement of financial position, the monetary value of an asset must be measurable in such a way that a faithful representation is achieved.

2 Assets not purchased for resale in the normal course of business. Non-current assets are held for long-term use within the business to produce goods or services.

3 Intangible assets have no material substance and include intellectual property rights, patents, licences and trademarks.

4 Assets with material substance including land and buildings, vehicles, machinery, fittings and equipment.

5 Holdings of shares and loans in other companies.

6 Short-term assets whose economic benefits will be used up by the entity within the next 12 months. Current assets change constantly during the trading cycle as inventory is turned into goods for sale and then into cash and new inventories are bought in and turned into more goods for sale and into more cash in an ever repeating cycle.

7 Inventories comprise raw materials for use in the production process and finished goods for sale and goods bought in for resale.

8 Money due from customers for goods supplied on credit terms and other money due from other parties external to the business.

9 Cash held within the business and in bank current and short-term deposit accounts.

10 Present obligations of the entity to transfer an economic resource as a result of past events. To be recognized on the statement of financial position, the monetary value of a liability must be measurable in such a way that a faithful representation is achieved.

11 Short-term liabilities that will be paid within the next 12 months. As with current assets, current liabilities are constantly changing as liabilities paid are replaced by new liabilities incurred.

12 Bank overdrafts and loan instalments due within the next 12 months.

13 Amounts owed to suppliers for goods provided on credit and other money due to other parties external to the business.

14 Tax payable to local taxation authorities on the profits made by the business during the last trading year.

15 Long-term liabilities due to be paid by the business more than 12 months after the statement of financial position date.

16 Loan instalments that are due more than 12 months after the statement of financial position date.

17 Liabilities the entity must meet that are due for payment more than 12 months after the statement of financial position date.

18 The residual interest in the assets of the entity after deducting all of its liabilities. Remember that assets – liabilities = equity.

19 The number of shares in issue multiplied by the par (face) value of each share.

20 Amounts received on the issue of share capital over and above the par (face) value of each share.

21 Profits earned by the business in earlier accounting periods not yet distributed as dividends to the shareholders.

Illustration 3.1: Bunns the Bakers plc: statements of profit or loss for the years ended 31 March 2019 and 31 March 2018

	2019 £000	2018 £000
Revenue	10,078	9,575
Cost of sales	(4,535)	(4,596)
Gross profit	5,543	4,979
Distribution and selling costs	(3,398)	(3,057)
Administration expenses	(1,250)	(1,155)
Operating profit	895	767
Finance income	15	12
Finance expense	(150)	(165)
Profit before tax	760	614
Income tax	(213)	(172)
Profit for the year	**547**	**442**

Note: income and profit figures are shown without brackets while items of expenditure are shown in brackets. This is to help you understand which items are subtracted and which items are added to determine the result (profit or loss) for the year.

1   Revenue, cost of sales, gross profit, distribution and selling costs, administration expenses and operating profit all form the trading part of the statement of profit or loss.

2   Sales income earned in an accounting period. Revenue represents sales made in the ordinary course of business, in this case from selling bakery and related goods.

3   The direct costs of making the sales included in Revenue. These could be the costs of making bakery goods (including ingredients and bakers' wages) or the direct costs of buying in related products for resale.

4   Gross profit = revenue – cost of sales.

5   The costs of selling and distributing goods such as advertising, transporting bakery goods from the main bakery to the shops, costs of running the shops and shop wages.

6   All the costs of running the trading operation that do not fall under any other heading including legal expenses, audit, accountancy and directors' salaries. All these costs are essential in running the business but they cannot be allocated to the costs of making and producing or distributing and selling the goods sold.

7   Operating profit = gross profit – distribution and selling costs – administration expenses.

8   Finance income and finance expense form the financing part of the statement of profit or loss.

9   Interest received and receivable on surplus cash deposited with the company's bank.

10   Interest paid and payable on borrowings used in financing the business's operations.

11   Profit before tax = operating profit + finance income – finance expense.

12   The tax charged on the profit for the year. For UK companies, this tax is called Corporation Tax.

13   Profit for the year (also called profit after tax) = profit before tax – income tax.

Illustration 4.1: Bunns the Bakers plc statements of cash flows for the years ended 31 March 2019 and 31 March 2018

	2019 £000	2018 £000
Cash generated from operations		
Operating profit for the year	895	767
(Increase)/decrease in inventories	(5)	8
Decrease in trade and other receivables	13	9
Increase/(decrease) in trade and other payables	109	(15)
Amortization of intangible non-current assets	5	7
Depreciation of property, plant and equipment	394	362
(Profit)/loss on disposal of property, plant and equipment	(3)	4
Cash from operating activities	**1,408**	1,142
Taxation paid	(189)	(154)
Net cash inflow from operating activities	1,219	988
Cash flows from investing activities		
Acquisition of property, plant and equipment	(910)	(600)
Acquisition of investments	(6)	(11)
Proceeds from sale of property, plant and equipment	10	47
Interest received	15	12
Net cash outflow from investing activities	(891)	(552)
Cash flows from financing activities		
Proceeds from the issue of ordinary share capital	235	148
Dividends paid	(90)	(72)
Repayment of current portion of long-term borrowings	(300)	(300)
Interest paid	(150)	(165)
Net cash outflow from financing activities	(305)	(389)
Net increase in cash and cash equivalents	23	47
Cash and cash equivalents at the start of the year	189	142
Cash and cash equivalents at the end of the year	212	189

Annotation numbers shown around the statement: 1, 2, 3, 4, 5, 6, 7, 8, 9, 10, 11, 12, 13, 14, 15, 16, 17, 18, 19, 20

Note: cash inflows (money coming in) are shown without brackets while cash outflows (money going out) are shown in brackets. Work through the above statement of cash flows, adding the figures without brackets and deducting the figures in brackets to help you understand how the cash inflows and outflows add up to the subtotals given.

1 Cash generated from operations reconciles the operating profit for the year to the cash generated from operating activities in the year by adjusting for certain non-cash transactions in the statement of profit or loss and changes in working capital.

2 = operating profit in the statement of profit or loss (= profit after tax + income tax + finance expense − finance income).

3 (Increase)/decrease in inventories, (increase)/decrease in trade and other receivables and increase/(decrease) in trade payables represent the cash effects of movements in working capital over the course of the accounting year.

4 Depreciation and amortization of non-current assets are not cash flows but an accounting adjustment to reflect the benefits of non-current assets used up in each accounting period. The cash outflow associated with non-current assets is the actual cash paid to acquire them.

5 Profits and losses on the disposal of property, plant and equipment are the difference between sale proceeds and carrying amount and are thus not a cash flow. The cash flow associated with disposals of property, plant and equipment are the actual cash receipts from the sale of the assets.

6 Cash generated from day to day trading activities from which to finance day-to-day operations. Surplus cash can be used for expansion and investment.

7 Taxation arises on profits from operations so taxation paid is deducted from cash flows from operating activities.

8 Cash inflows and outflows from long-term investing.

9 Cash invested in new long-term capacity from which to generate new income by expanding and improving the business.

10 Investment of surplus cash in order to generate interest or dividend income to boost profits.

11 Cash received from the sale or scrapping of non-current assets.

12 Interest received from investing surplus cash in current or non-current asset investments.

13 Cash raised from or paid to long-term providers of finance.

14 Cash raised from the issue of new share capital.

15 Dividends paid to shareholders as a return on their investment in the company.

16 Capital element of long-term borrowings repaid in the year to the providers of long-term debt finance from operating cash inflows.

17 Interest paid on long- and short-term borrowings as a return to lenders for providing debt finance to the company.

18 Net increase in cash and cash equivalents = net cash inflow from operating activities (£1,219) – net cash outflow from investing activities (£891) – net cash outflow from financing activities (£305) = £23.

19 Cash and cash equivalents on the statement of financial position at the end of last year.

20 Cash and cash equivalents at the end of the current year on the statement of financial position.

Terminology converter

Terms used in this book	Equivalent term or terms
Absorption costing	Full costing
Allowance for receivables	Provision for doubtful debts
Capital	Equity
Carrying amount	Net book value
Cash conversion cycle	Operating cycle, working capital cycle
Cost of capital	Hurdle rate of return
Equity	Capital, capital and reserves
Finance expense	Interest payable
Finance income	Interest receivable
Inventory	Stock
Inventory days	Stock days
Irrecoverable debts	Bad debts
Payables	Creditors
Payables days	Creditor days
Receivables	Debtors
Receivables days	Debtor days
Revenue	Turnover, sales
Statement of financial position	Balance sheet
Statement of profit or loss	Income statement, statement of financial performance, profit and loss account

Glossary

Absorption costing The cost of products including all the direct costs of production and a proportion of the indirect costs of production based on normal levels of output.

Accountability Managers provide an account of how they have managed resources placed in their care. In this way, those appointing managers can assess how well their managers have looked after the resources entrusted to them.

Accounting The summarizing of numerical data relating to past events and presenting this data as information to managers and other interested parties as a basis for both decision making and control purposes.

Accounting equation Assets – liabilities = equity or assets = liabilities + equity.

Accounting rate of return An investment appraisal technique that averages the projections of accounting profit to calculate the expected rate of return on the average capital invested.

Accruals Expenses incurred during an accounting period but not paid for until after the accounting period end are recognized as a liability in the statement of financial position and as an expense in the statement of profit or loss.

Accruals basis of accounting All income and expenditure are recognized in the accounting period in which they occurred rather than in the accounting period in which cash is received or paid.

Acid test ratio See quick ratio.

Activity-based costing Overhead costs are allocated to products on the basis of activities consumed: the more activities that are consumed by a particular product, the more overhead is allocated to that product and so the higher its cost and selling price will be.

Actual v. budget comparisons A comparison of forecast outcomes with actual outcomes on a monthly basis as a means of exercising control over operations.

Adverse variances Unfavourable variances.

AGM See annual general meeting.

Allowance for receivables The allowance for receivables is calculated as a percentage of trade receivables after deducting known irrecoverable debts. This allowance is an application of the prudence concept, assuming that not all trade receivables will pay what is owed. Also referred to as the provision for doubtful debts.

Annual general meeting A meeting held every year by limited liability companies at which shareholders consider and vote on various significant resolutions affecting the company.

ARR See accounting rate of return.

Articles of Association A document that covers the internal regulations of a company and governs the shareholders' relationships with each other.

Assets Defined in the IASB's *Conceptual Framework for Financial Reporting* as 'a present economic resource controlled by the entity as a result of past events'.

Attainable standard A standard that can be achieved with effort. This standard is neither too easy nor so difficult as to be unattainable.

Balance sheet Another term for the statement of financial position.

Bond A long-term loan to an organization with a fixed rate of interest and a fixed repayment date.

Bonus issue An issue of shares at par value to shareholders from retained earnings. A bonus issue does not raise any cash.

Break-even point The point at which sales revenue = fixed + variable costs. At the break-even point, an entity makes neither a profit nor a loss. Break-even point can be expressed in £s or units of sales. Break-even point cannot be used when more than one product or service is produced and sold. The break-even point is calculated by dividing total fixed costs by the contribution per unit of sales.

Budget The expression of a plan in money terms. That plan is a prediction or a forecast of future income, expenditure, cash receipts and cash payments.

Budgetary control Comparisons between budgeted and actual outcomes to determine the causes of variances between budgeted and actual results. The causes of differences are then identified to enable remedial action to be taken.

Budgeting The process of drawing up the budget.

Business entity Any organization involved in business. Business entities may be sole traders, companies with limited liability or partnerships.

Business entity convention The business is completely separate from its owners. Only business transactions are included in the business's financial statements.

Capital account The equity part of the statement of financial position for sole traders. The capital account is the sum of the opening capital balance plus the profit for the year (minus a loss for the year) minus any drawings made by the sole trader during the year.

Capital investment The acquisition of new non-current assets with the aim of increasing sales, profits and cash flows to the long-term benefit of a business.

Capital investment appraisal An evaluation of the long-term cash generating capacity of capital investment projects to assist decision makers in allocating scarce investment capital resources to projects to maximize long run profits.

Carrying amount Cost or fair value of a non-current asset − the accumulated depreciation on that non-current asset. Net book value is an equivalent term that you might also come across to describe the result of deducting accumulated depreciation from the cost or fair value of a non-current asset.

Cash budget A detailed summary on a month-by-month basis of budgeted cash inflows and cash outflows.

Cash conversion cycle Inventory days + receivables days − payables days. Also known as the working capital cycle or the operating cycle.

Cash flow cycle The time it takes a business to convert inventory into a sale and to collect cash either at the point of sale or from trade receivables with which to pay trade payables.

Cash flows from financing activities One of the three sections in the statement of cash flows. This section represents the cash raised from the issue of share capital and loans and the cash spent in repaying borrowings and paying interest to lenders and dividends to shareholders.

Cash flows from investing activities One of the three sections in the statement of cash flows. This section represents the cash spent on buying new non-current assets, the cash received from selling surplus non-current assets and the cash received from interest and dividends on investments made.

Cash flows from operating activities One of the three sections in the statement of cash flows. This section represents the cash generated from sales less the cash spent in both generating those sales and in running the organization.

Comparability An enhancing qualitative characteristic of financial information. Information should be comparable over time. The usefulness of information is enhanced if it can be compared with similar information about other entities for the same reporting period and with similar information about the same entity for other reporting periods. Comparability does not mean consistency, although consistency of presentation and measurement of the same items in the same way from year to year will help to achieve comparability. Similarly, comparability does not mean uniformity of presentation.

Consistency The presentation or measurement of the same piece of accounting information on the same basis each year.

Contribution Selling price less the variable costs of making that sale.

Corporate governance The system by which companies are directed and controlled.

Cost allocation The process of allocating costs, both direct and indirect, to products or services.

Cost centre A division of an entity to which attributable costs are allocated.

Cost drivers The level of activity associated with each cost pool used to allocate costs to products under activity-based costing.

Cost of capital The level of return on an investment that is acceptable to a business given the level of risk involved. Also known as the hurdle rate of return.

Cost of sales The direct costs attributable to the sale of particular goods or services.

Cost pools The allocation of indirect costs of production associated with particular activities in an activity-based costing system.

Cost-volume-profit analysis A management accounting technique used to determine the relationship between sales revenue, costs and profit. Abbreviated to CVP.

Costing The process of determining the cost of products or services.

Creditor days See payables days.

Creditors Persons to whom entities owe money. See also payables.

Credits A term used in double entry bookkeeping. Credits represent liabilities, capital and income as well as reductions in assets and expenses.

Current assets Short-term assets that will be used up in the business within one year of the year end date. Examples include inventory, trade receivables, prepayments and cash.

Current liabilities Short-term liabilities due for payment within one year of the year end date. Examples include trade payables, taxation and accruals.

Current ratio Current assets divided by current liabilities. Used in the assessment of an entity's short-term liquidity. This ratio should be used with caution in the evaluation of an entity's liquidity.

CVP See cost-volume-profit analysis.

Debenture A long-term loan to an organization with a fixed rate of interest and a fixed repayment date.

Debits A term used in double entry bookkeeping. Debits represent assets and expenses as well as reductions in liabilities, capital and income.

Debt ratio Total liabilities divided by total assets. An indicator of how reliant an entity is upon external parties to fund its assets.

Debtor days See receivables days.

Debtors Persons who owe money to an entity. See also trade receivables.

Depreciation The allocation of the cost of a non-current asset to the accounting periods benefiting from that non-current asset's use within a business. Depreciation is *not* a way of reflecting the market value of assets in financial statements and it does not represent a loss in value.

Direct costs The costs of a product or service that are directly attributable to the production of a product or the delivery of a service. Direct costs can be fixed or variable.

Direct labour efficiency variance The time taken to make the goods actually produced compared with the standard time that should have been taken to make those goods multiplied by the standard rate per hour.

Direct labour rate variance What labour hours actually cost compared with what the standard says the labour hours should have cost for the actual level of production achieved.

Direct material price variance What the materials for actual production cost compared with what the standard says they should have cost for that level of production.

Direct material usage variance The actual quantity of materials used to make the goods actually produced compared with the standard quantity that should have been used to make those goods multiplied by the standard cost per unit of material.

Direct method An approach to preparing the statement of cash flows that involves disclosing the gross cash receipts from sales and the gross cash payments to suppliers of goods and services.

Directors Persons appointed by the shareholders at the annual general meeting to run a limited company on their behalf.

Discounting Future cash inflows and outflows are discounted to their present value using an entity's cost of capital.

Discounts allowed An allowance given to trade receivables to encourage early payment of amounts owed. Discounts allowed not taken up by customers are added to revenue when customer payments are received.

Discounts received Suppliers reward their customers with discounts either for early payment of what is owed or for bulk purchases. Discounts received are a source of income in the statement of profit or loss, a deduction from cost of sales and a deduction from trade payables.

Distributable reserves Retained earnings available for distribution to shareholders as a dividend.

Distribution The distribution of retained profits to shareholders as a dividend. A distribution is not an expense of a company but a deduction from retained earnings.

Dividend A distribution of profits to shareholders.

Dividend cover A comparison of the total dividend for an accounting period to the profit after taxation and after preference dividends. This ratio is used to assess the expected continuity of dividend payments. The higher the ratio, the more likely the dividend payment will continue into the future.

Dividend per share The total dividend for a period divided by the number of ordinary shares in issue multiplied by 100 to give a figure of dividends per share in pence.

Dividend yield The dividend per share as a percentage of the current share price.

Double entry An accounting methodology which recognizes that every transaction affects two figures in the financial statements.

DPS See dividend per share.

Drawings Amounts taken out of a business by a sole trader for personal rather than business use. Drawings are in effect a repayment of the amounts owed by the business to the owner. Drawings are not an expense of the business but a deduction from capital. Drawings are not permitted in limited liability companies.

Dual aspect The recognition that each accounting transaction has a double effect on the amounts stated in the financial statements.

Duality principle Each transaction has an equal and opposite effect on two or more accounts.

Earnings per share The profit after taxation and after preference dividends divided by the number of ordinary shares in issue multiplied by 100 to give a figure of earnings per share in pence.

Economic resource Defined in the IASB's *Conceptual Framework for Financial Reporting* as 'a right that has the potential to produce economic benefits'.

Efficiency ratios Measures of non-current asset turnover and revenue and profit per employee to determine how well an organization has used its resources to generate profits.

EGM See extraordinary general meeting.

EPS See earnings per share.

Equity The capital of an entity on its statement of financial position. Equity is, in theory, the amount the owners of the business would receive if all the business assets and liabilities were sold and settled at the amounts stated in the statement of financial position. Defined by the IASB's *Conceptual Framework for Financial Reporting* as 'the residual interest in the assets of the entity after deducting all its liabilities'.

Equity share capital This is an equivalent term for ordinary share capital.

Exceptional income Income and expenditure that arise from transactions that are not in the ordinary course of business.

Expenses Defined by the IASB's *Conceptual Framework for Financial Reporting* as 'decreases in assets, or increases in liabilities, that result in decreases in equity, other than those relating to distributions to holders of equity claims'.

Extraordinary general meeting A meeting called by the directors of a limited company to request the approval of shareholders for certain business transactions. An extraordinary general meeting is any meeting of the shareholders as a body other than the annual general meeting.

Fair value The amount at which an asset could be sold or a liability settled in the open market.

Faithful representation One of the two fundamental qualitative characteristics of financial information. Financial information must not only represent relevant economic phenomena (transactions and events), but it must also faithfully represent the phenomena that it purports to represent. Perfectly faithful representation of economic phenomena in words and numbers requires that the information presented must have three characteristics: it must be complete, neutral and free from error.

Favourable variances Differences between actual and budgeted results arising from higher income or lower expenditure.

Financial accounting The reporting of past information to parties external to the organization.

Fixed cost A cost that does not vary in line with production or sales over a given period of time.

Fixed overhead expenditure variance The difference between the actual fixed overhead expenditure incurred and the budgeted level of fixed overhead expenditure.

Gearing ratio Long- and short-term borrowings divided by the total statement of financial position equity figure × 100%. A measure designed to help financial statement users assess whether an entity has borrowed too much money. The gearing ratio should be used in conjunction with the interest cover ratio in making this assessment.

Going concern A business that has sufficient demand for its products and sufficient sources of finance to enable it to continue operating for the foreseeable future.

Gross profit Sales less the direct costs of making those sales.

Gross profit % The gross profit of an organization divided by the sales figure × 100%.

Historic cost The original cost of an asset or liability at the time it was purchased or incurred.

IASB International Accounting Standards Board.

Ideal standard The best that can be achieved. Ideal standards tend to be unrealistic and unachievable as they would only ever be attained in a perfect world.

Income Defined by the IASB's *Conceptual Framework for Financial Reporting* as 'increases in assets, or decreases in liabilities, that result in increases in equity, other than those relating to contributions from holders of equity claims'.

Income statement An equivalent term for the statement of profit or loss.

Indirect cost Costs that cannot be attributed directly to units of production. Also known as overheads.

Indirect method An approach to preparing the statement of cash flows that ignores total inflows and outflows of cash from operations. Instead, the operating profit for a period is adjusted for increases or decreases in inventory, trade receivables, prepayments, payables and accruals and for the effect of non-cash items such as depreciation and profits and losses on disposal of non-current assets in order to determine the cash flows from operations.

Insolvency The inability of an entity to repay all that it owes to its creditors.

Interest cover Trading profit divided by finance cost (interest payable). This ratio shows how many times interest payable on borrowings is covered by operating profits. The higher the ratio, the more likely entities will be able to continue paying the interest on their borrowings.

Internal rate of return The discount rate applied to the cash flows of a capital investment project to produce a net present value for the project of £nil.

Inventory A stock of goods held by a business.

Inventory days Inventory divided by cost of sales × 365 days. This ratio measures the average stockholding period, the length of time an entity holds goods as stock before they are sold.

Irrecoverable debts Trade receivables from which cash will not be collected. Irrecoverable debts are an expense in the statement of profit or loss and are not a deduction from sales. Also known as bad debts.

IRR See internal rate of return.

Key factor = Limiting factor.

Liabilities Defined by the IASB's *Conceptual Framework for Financial Reporting* as 'a present obligation of the entity to transfer an economic resource as a result of past events'.

Limiting factor A scarcity of input resources, such as materials or labour, is referred to as a limiting factor in the production of goods or services. When input resources are scarce, entities calculate the contribution per unit of limiting factor to maximize their profits in the short term.

Liquidity The ability of entities to meet payments to their creditors as they become due.

Loan notes A long-term loan to an organization with a fixed rate of interest and a fixed repayment date.

Management accounting Cost and management accounting is concerned with reporting accounting and cost information to users within an organization to assist those internal users in making decisions and managing the business.

Margin of safety The difference between the current level of sales in units and the break-even point of sales in units.

Marginal cost The additional cost incurred in producing one more unit of product or delivering one more unit of service. Also known as the variable cost of production.

Materiality The IASB's *Conceptual Framework for Financial Reporting* defines materiality thus: 'Information is material if omitting it or misstating it could influence decisions that . . . users . . . make on the basis of . . . financial information about a specific reporting entity. In other words, materiality is an entity-specific aspect of relevance based on the nature or magnitude, or both, of the items to which the information relates in the context of an individual entity's financial report.'

Memorandum of Association This document covers a limited company's objectives and its powers and governs the relationship of the company with the outside world.

Money measurement The measurement of financial results in money terms.

Net present value The total of the discounted future cash inflows and outflows from a project. Projects with a positive net present value are accepted, while projects with a negative net present value are rejected.

Net profit The surplus that remains once all the expenses have been deducted from all sources of income.

Non-current asset turnover Revenue is divided by non-current assets to determine how many £s of sales are generated from each £ of non-current assets.

Non-current assets Assets held within the business for long-term use in the production of goods and services. Non-current assets are retained within the business for periods of more than one year and are not acquired with the intention of reselling them immediately or in the near future.

Non-current liabilities Liabilities due for payment more than 12 months from the statement of financial position date.

Normal level of production The expected level of production achievable within an accounting period. This level is used as the basis for allocating fixed overhead costs to products and in the valuation of inventory at the year end.

Normal standard What a business usually achieves.

NPV See net present value

Operating cycle Another term for the cash conversion cycle or working capital cycle. See Cash conversion cycle.

Operating profit The profit that remains after all the costs of trading, direct (cost of sales) and indirect (distribution and selling costs and administration expenses), have been deducted from sales revenue.

Operating profit % Determines profitability on the basis of revenue less all operating costs before taking into account the effects of finance income, finance expense and taxation.

Opportunity cost The loss that is incurred by choosing one alternative course of action over another, the benefits given up to use a resource in one application rather than taking the next best alternative course of action. Opportunity cost is only a relevant consideration when resources are limited: when resources are unlimited there is no opportunity cost.

Ordinary share capital The most common form of share capital issued by companies conferring on holders the right to receive all of a company's profits as dividends and to vote at company meetings. Also known as equity share capital.

Par value The face value or nominal value of a share.

Payables Amounts owed to suppliers and other creditors for goods and services supplied on credit.

Payables days Trade payables divided by cost of sales × 365 days. This ratio measures the average period taken to pay outstanding liabilities to trade suppliers.

Payback The number of years it will take for the cash inflows from a capital investment project to pay back the original cost of the investment.

Performance ratios Ratios of particular interest to an entity's shareholders as they measure the returns to the owners of the business.

Period costs Fixed costs incurred in the administration, marketing and financing of an entity relating to the period in which they are incurred.

Periodicity The preparation of financial statements for a set period of time, usually one year.

Pre-emption rights The rights of existing shareholders to subscribe for new issues of share capital before those shares can be offered to non-shareholders.

Preference share capital Preference shares receive a fixed rate of dividend that is paid before the ordinary shareholders receive any dividend. Preference share capital is returned to preference shareholders before any amounts are returned to ordinary shareholders on the winding up of a company. However, preference shareholders have no right to vote in company general meetings.

Prepayments Amounts paid in advance for goods and services to be provided in the future. These amounts are recognized as prepayments (a current asset) at the statement of financial position date and as a deduction from current period cash payments for expenses.

Present value The discounting of future cash inflows and outflows to express all cash flows in the common currency of today, thereby facilitating a fair comparison of projected cash inflows and outflows for evaluating different capital investment proposals.

Price/earnings ratio The current market price of a share divided by the latest earnings per share figure. The ratio provides an indicator of how many years of current period earnings are represented in the share price today.

Prime cost The total direct cost of producing one product or one unit of service.

Production cost The total direct costs of producing one product or one unit of service plus the proportion of indirect production overheads allocated to products and services on the basis of the normal level of production.

Profit The surplus remaining after all expenses are deducted from sales revenue.

Profit after tax The profit that remains once all the expenses and charges have been deducted from sales revenue and any other income for the accounting period added on.

Profit after tax % Profit for the year (= profit after tax) divided by revenue × 100%.

Profit before tax Sales – cost of sales – distribution and selling costs – administration expenses + finance income – finance expense.

Profit before tax % Profit before tax divided by revenue × 100%.

Profit for the year Profit after tax.

Profit per employee Calculated by dividing the number of employees during an accounting period into the operating profit for the period.

Profitability An assessment of the profits made during an accounting period by comparing current period profits and profitability %s to those of previous periods.

Prudence The process of exercising caution in the production of financial statements under conditions of uncertainty.

Purchase returns The cancellation of a purchase by returning goods to suppliers. The accounting effect of purchase returns is to reduce purchases in the statement of profit or loss and trade payables in the statement of financial position.

Quick ratio Also known as the acid test ratio. The quick ratio compares current assets that are readily convertible into cash with current liabilities as a measure of an entity's short-term ability to pay what it owes over the next 12 months. This ratio should be used with caution in the evaluation of an entity's liquidity.

Ratio(s) The expression of the relationship(s) between two different figures.

Realization Profits should not be anticipated until they have been earned through a sale.

Receivables Amounts of money owed to an entity by parties outside the organization.

Receivables days Trade receivables divided by sales × 365 days. This ratio measures the average period taken to collect outstanding debts from credit customers.

Reducing balance A method of allocating depreciation on non-current assets to accounting periods benefiting from their use. This method uses a fixed percentage of cost in the first year of an asset's life and then applies the same percentage to the carrying amount of assets in accounting periods subsequent to year 1. The reducing balance method allocates a smaller charge for depreciation to each successive accounting period benefiting from a non-current asset's use. Residual value is ignored when calculating reducing balance depreciation.

Relevance One of the two fundamental qualitative characteristics of financial information. To be relevant, information must be capable of making a difference in the decisions made by users. Relevant information may be predictive and assist users in making predictions about the future or it may be confirmatory by assisting users to assess the accuracy of past predictions. Relevant information can be both predictive and confirmatory.

Relevant costs The costs that will be incurred if a certain course of action is followed. Relevant costs are the costs that influence decision making.

Residual value The amount which the original purchaser of a non-current asset thinks that the asset could be sold for when the time comes to dispose of it.

Return on capital employed Operating profit (profit before interest and tax) divided by the equity of an entity plus any long-term borrowings × 100%. Abbreviated to ROCE.

Revenue Sales of goods and services made by an entity in the ordinary (everyday) course of business.

Revenue per employee Calculated by dividing the revenue for an accounting period by the average number of employees employed during that accounting period.

Rights issues An issue of shares to existing shareholders at a discount to the current market price. This is not the issue of shares at a discount, which would be illegal under the Companies Act 2006.

ROCE See return on capital employed.

Sales = revenue.

Sales price variance The difference between the standard selling price and the actual selling price multiplied by the actual quantity sold.

Sales returns The cancellation of a sale by a customer returning goods. The accounting effect of sales returns is to reduce sales in the statement of profit or loss and trade receivables in the statement of financial position.

Sales volume variance (The actual sales – budgeted sales in units) multiplied by the standard contribution per sale.

Sensitivity analysis Changing the assumptions on which forecasts are based to determine the effect of those changes on expected outcomes.

Share capital A source of very long-term financing for limited companies. All limited companies must issue share capital that will remain in issue for as long as the company exists.

Share premium The amount subscribed for shares in a limited company over and above the par value of each share.

Shareholders Owners of share capital in limited companies. Shareholders may be either ordinary shareholders or preference shareholders.

Standard costing The costs and selling prices of products are estimated with a reasonable degree of accuracy. Comparisons of actual and standard outcomes are then undertaken to determine the variances between expected and actual outcomes with a view to revising standards where necessary.

Statement of cash flows A summary of the cash inflows and outflows of an entity for a given period of time.

Statement of financial position A summary of the assets, liabilities and equity of an entity at a particular point in time.

Statement of profit or loss A statement of income and expenditure for a particular period of time.

Stewardship The process of looking after resources entrusted to a person.

Stock An equivalent term for inventory.

Stock days See inventory days.

Straight line A method of allocating the cost of non-current assets to the accounting periods benefiting from their use. The straight line method allocates the same charge for depreciation to each accounting period benefiting from a non-current asset's use within a business. Residual value is deducted from the cost of non-current assets when calculating the annual depreciation charge on a straight line basis.

Sunk costs Past costs which have no influence on future decision making. Sunk costs represent expenditure that has already been incurred which no future action can change or alter.

Timeliness An enhancing qualitative characteristic of financial information. The decision usefulness of information is enhanced if it is available to users in time for it to be capable of influencing their decisions. While the decision usefulness of information generally declines with time, information that can still be used in identifying trends continues to be timely in the future.

Time value of money Money received today is worth more than money received tomorrow due to the impact of inflation and the uncertainty surrounding the receipt of money in future time periods.

Trade receivables Amounts owed to an entity by customers for goods and services supplied on credit.

Turnover The term used in financial statements in the UK for sales or revenue.

Understandability An enhancing qualitative characteristic of financial information. Understandability should not be confused with simplicity. Financial statements that excluded complex information just because it was difficult to understand would not result in relevant information that was faithfully presented. Reports that excluded such information would be incomplete and would thus mislead users. Readers of financial reports are assumed to have a reasonable knowledge of business and economic activities in order to make sense of what they are presented with but when they are unable to understand the information presented, then the IASB recommends using an adviser. To help users understand information presented, that information should be classified, characterized and presented clearly.

Unfavourable variances Differences between actual and budgeted results arising from lower income or higher expenditure.

Unsecured Loans for which no assets of an entity have been pledged in the event that the entity fails to repay the loan.

Variable cost The costs of a product or service that vary directly in line with the production of a product or delivery of a service. Also known as the marginal cost of a product or service.

Variable overhead efficiency variance The time taken to make the goods actually produced compared with the standard time that should have been taken to make those goods multiplied by the standard variable overhead rate per hour.

Variable overhead expenditure variance The variable overhead actually incurred in the production of goods compared with the standard expenditure that should have been incurred for the level of actual production.

Variances Differences between budgeted and actual financial results.

Verifiability An enhancing qualitative characteristic of financial information that enhances the usefulness of information that is relevant and faithfully represented. Verifiability provides users with assurance that information is faithfully presented and reports the economic phenomena it purports to represent. To ensure verifiability, it should be possible to prove the information presented is accurate in all major respects. The accuracy of information should be capable of verification by observation or recalculation.

Working capital Current assets less current liabilities.

Working capital cycle See cash conversion cycle. This is another term for the cash conversion cycle which is also known as the operating cycle.

Index

Note: Tables and figures are indicated by an italic *t* and *f* following the page number.

We are handed an identity
before having a say in the matter,
and we spend our lives running from it,
pretending we have left it behind,
or grappling with it as Jacob wrestled
with his angel.

—Fenton Johnson, *Keeping Faith*

Acts of Faith,
Acts of Love

Gay Catholic Autobiographies
as Sacred Texts

Dugan McGinley

continuum

NEW YORK • LONDON

2006

The Continuum International Publishing Group Inc
80 Maiden Lane, New York, NY 10038

The Continuum International Publishing Group Ltd
The Tower Building, 11 York Road, London SE1 7NX

Printed in the United States of America

Library of Congress Cataloging-in-Publication Data

McGinley, Dugan.
    Acts of faith, acts of love : gay Catholic autobiographies as sacred texts / Dugan McGinley.
      p. cm.
    Includes bibliographical references and index.
    ISBN 0-8264-1545-8 (hardcover : alk. paper)
    ISBN 0-8264-1836-8 (paperback : alk. paper)
    1. Catholic gays – United States – Biography – History and criticism. 2. Gay men – United States – Biography – History and criticism. 3. Autobiography – Religious aspects – Catholic Church. 4. Homosexuality – Religious aspects – Catholic Church. I. Title.
BX4669.M248 2004
282′.73′086642 – dc22

                                            2003027592

Contents

Acknowledgments

A s with any project of this scale, it cannot be accomplished alone. I want to thank everyone who has helped me in the process of making this book a reality. Lucy Bregman, Rebecca Alpert, Leonard Swidler, Regina Bannan, Katie Cannon, and Laura Levitt were all enormously helpful with guidance, feedback, suggestions, and support over the years, especially in helping me to shape this project. Many others made contributions either directly or indirectly, whether they realize it or not. These include Bob Miailovich, David Floss, Dick Young, Bruce Cory (who all gave me suggestions when I put the word out that I was looking for autobiographies), Nancy Krody (one of the first to put herself on the line to declare the reality of being gay and Christian), Ron Karstetter, Frank DeBernardo and New Ways Ministry, Paul Halsall (whose web page bibliography is an incredible resource for gay Catholics), Sally Bourrie, Kathy Coffey, Jim Mallon, Bill Leahy, Paul Michalenko, Kent Epperson, Maria Fama, and Marian Ronan. A special thanks to Frank Oveis at Continuum for believing in this project and for his input.

I owe a lot to my friends in Dignity, especially Dignity Denver, where I learned how faithful Catholics can maintain an intentional community in the face of the church's opposition, and where I first got my feet wet in the world of church reform activism. I also owe a lot to my friends in the National Association of Pastoral Musicians, where I remain connected to the church at large and find the energy to sustain my ministry as a Roman Catholic liturgist and musician. I thank anyone else along the way who made suggestions and shared with me their relevant insights and perspectives.

In terms of financial support, I was given a boost early on from Eileen Mackin. The Temple University Department of Religion also assisted along the way with scholarships and teaching assistantships. I am also greatly indebted to the Jonathan Lax Scholarship for Gay Men, administered by Philadelphia's Bread and Roses Community Fund, for giving me significant support for two years. I am so grateful to have met Mr. Lax before his untimely death in January 1996.

I also need to thank some of my spiritual mentors who have been my guides at various points along the way: Mary Ann Surges, John Dold,

Deborah Voss, Chris Nyholm, and Dale Coski, each of whom is a manifestation of God's presence in this world. Betsy Kelso gave me much needed personal support and guidance years before I undertook this particular project, planting seeds in me to eventually pursue this work. The St. Vincent de Paul Gay and Lesbian Spirituality Group has provided support and friendship throughout the many years I have lived in Philadelphia. Each time I am with this fine group of faithful individuals, I know my work is important. It is for the sake of holy people like them that I undertook this project. I also write in memory of those I have known who have died of complications from AIDS: Thom, Greg, Richard, John, Scott, Tim, Urban, Sonny, Bill, Merrill, Marty, Kevin, Sam, Lou, Ron, and Gary. Their lives cut short on earth, they now exist and offer guidance in the communion of saints.

Most importantly, thanks to my life partner Scott Roulier. In the over three years I worked on this project from start to finish, a number of things occurred, any of which might have completely derailed any hope of progress: our house was burglarized and my computer and disks were stolen; Scott's father died suddenly, just a few years after the death of his mother; we endured a strenuous process to acquire a lovely old house which had stood vacant for a time and needed lots of loving care; my own father suffered a heart attack and underwent subsequent medical treatment, which compromised his mental and physical health to the point that he passed away after an eight-month struggle; the events of September 11, 2001, took an emotional toll, especially for a New York lover like me; and I was diagnosed with and underwent surgery and treatment for testicular cancer. In the face of such overwhelming life events, my dear partner Scott stood with me through it all, performing countless "acts of love." Never have I met a more generous and forgiving person, who truly knows the meaning of unconditional love. He is a constant reminder and embodied representation of God's love and action in my life. I so appreciate Scott's unwavering faith in my abilities and in the value of this work. I could not have written this book without him and I can confidently say I would never have completed it without his support. I hope whatever fruit this project yields will not only serve to "repay" him but also stand as a testament to the procreativity of our union.

Preface

This book explores gay Catholic identity as narrated in autobiographical texts. It builds upon and has been shaped by a body of scholarship related to gay Catholic studies that has emerged over the past several decades to analyze and respond to church teaching on homosexuality and to paint a more complex picture of gay and lesbian reality in the church. John McNeill was one of the first to challenge the Catholic Church's negative assessment of homosexuality. His 1976 book, *The Church and the Homosexual*, set the foundation for much of the liberatory work that would follow.[1] Subsequent scholars have approached this issue through historical studies to see how the tradition has dealt with sexuality at various points in time. Some have analyzed Roman Catholic teachings on homosexuality through the discipline of moral theology.[2] Others have tried to bring lesbian and gay experience to bear directly on the ethical and theological assumptions underlying official church positions on homosexuality. My work fits most closely in this latter category of scholarship.

Scholars across a broad spectrum of religious traditions and other Christian denominations have been doing similar work and adding to our general knowledge of religion and sexuality.[3] Biblical scholars have also taken up the very important task of critically analyzing scripture to determine what it has to say about homosexuality as we understand it today.[4] All of this has taken place within the context of the rise of feminist consciousness in academia, and a number of feminist scholars have made significant contributions to and been influenced by the study of religion and sexuality.[5] Though this book is neither historical, nor a work of biblical analysis, nor explicitly feminist, I owe a great deal to the theoretical and methodological foundations and insights such scholarship has provided.

The autobiographies examined here are in themselves part of the body of literature on being gay and Catholic that has emerged over the past three-plus decades since Vatican II and the Stonewall riots. The concern in this type of literature is to share a life story (or particular aspects thereof) and not necessarily to deal with church teaching in any systematic way. Indeed, the motivations for a person to engage in writing something autobiographical vary from one to another and this is true even among the

1

authors whose works I will discuss. Certainly, many of these writers are motivated by a perceived need on their part to respond to the conflicted atmosphere within the church and/or society on sexual issues, to insert their own personal stories into the debate. Others simply want to share their personal struggles or discuss important pieces of their spiritual journeys as a way of giving witness to some larger meaning in their lives. Still others are only marginally concerned, if at all, about the role of religion in their current lives and may or may not even self-identify as Catholic at the time of writing their story. Their reasons for writing are probably not spiritual in any meaningful sense of the word. But all of them have been marked in some way by Catholicism and all of them are gay (or at least not heterosexual). These writings have gone largely untapped as a source for critical analysis and as a starting point for overcoming the problems with official church teaching on homosexuality I discuss herein. I use them in this book as the basis for a literary, textual analysis springing from theories of autobiography.[6]

Limits and Terminology

My study is limited in the following ways, which are summed up in the phrase "gay Catholic men." First, I only examine autobiographies written by *men*. Although there is a large body of autobiographical writing by Catholic lesbians, men and women confront different issues in both society and the church, and their life stories need to be analyzed separately. A pervasive tendency in much of the relevant scholarship (and indeed in church teaching itself) is the conflation of gay male and lesbian experiences. The problem is well articulated by Adrienne Rich:

> Lesbians have historically been deprived of a political existence through "inclusion" as female versions of male homosexuality. To equate lesbian existence with male homosexuality because each is stigmatized is to erase female reality once again. . . . I perceive the lesbian experience as being, like motherhood, a profoundly *female* experience, with particular oppressions, meanings, and potentialities we cannot comprehend as long as we simply bracket it with other sexually stigmatized existences.[7]

My intention is not to further marginalize women, as they have been so frequently in Catholicism, but to take gender differences seriously and set limits that will do justice to my analysis and women's experience. This enables me to better address gender issues related specifically to men and masculinities. Ultimately, my hope is that the same liberatory principles of my analysis can be applied similarly to lesbian women's life texts, given that homophobia, antigay bias, and hate crimes do affect all gay, lesbian, bisexual, and transgendered people (though perhaps not in equivalent ways). My conclusions and the impact of my work on church teaching should be beneficial for men and women alike given the conflation of gay men and lesbians in official documents.

Second, I only examine autobiographies written by *gay* men who are self-identified as such. For my purposes, this also includes anyone who identifies himself as bisexual, which is the case in only one of the texts in my survey. It is important to say a few words about the terminology associated with sexual identity because some of these terms have become contentious in both political and academic circles. The debate has to do with how same-sex desire is theorized in relation to the idea of "sexual identity." In his groundbreaking *History of Sexuality,* Michel Foucault charts the nineteenth-century evolution (or devolution, as it might be interpreted) of "sodomy" as a category strictly of forbidden acts to "homosexuality" as a category of persons: "The nineteenth-century homosexual became a personage, a past, a case history, and a childhood. . . . The sodomite had been a temporary aberration; the homosexual was now a species."[8] This could be considered the birth or "invention" of homosexuality as an identity.[9] The use of the term "gay" in place of or as an equivalent to "homosexual" was a strategic move, first deployed in the 1960s, by gay liberationists who viewed it as a counter to the sexual hierarchy that classed heterosexuality as normal and homosexuality as deviant. "Gay" is now widely accepted in popular usage as describing a person with exclusively same-sex desires.[10] It tends to carry a more publicly affirming expediency and linkage to the gay rights movement than the more clinical sounding "homosexual," though both can be politically deployed in different contexts.[11]

The use of "gay" or "homosexual" as identity categories is not entirely unproblematic, however, because as identities the terms become much more restrictive. Consider, for instance, a man who is sexually attracted to women and even maintains a relationship with a woman, but who also engages in occasional sexual encounters with men. He is not likely to identify as "gay" because the popular understanding of that term does not accurately describe his feelings or experience. The category of "bisexual" has been deployed to counter and deconstruct the either/or binary created by the usage of terms like "gay" and "straight" or even the more clinical sounding "homosexual" and "heterosexual"; but some theorists argue "bisexuality" integrates rather than disrupts the binary sexual economy and reifies a third identity category that is still too restrictive and reliant on traditional constructions of gender. Where, for example, does sex-as-recreation or transvestism fit into this model? Much of this hinges on how one understands the concept of sexual identity in the first place. Is it fixed,

natural, and innate — often called the *essentialist* position — or is it fluid
and dependent on social conditioning and available cultural models — the
constructionist position?[12]

Critical theorists offer the term "queer" as a way out of this conundrum. "Queer" is an outgrowth of the constructionist position, founded
on twentieth-century theories which have destabilized "identity" as a self-
evident or natural category. While some might see "queer theory" as the
latest institutional transformation of "gay and lesbian studies," those who
advocate using the term "queer" see it as something much more complicated and hard to define. "Broadly speaking, queer describes those gestures
or analytical models which dramatise incoherencies in the allegedly stable relations between chromosomal sex, gender and sexual desire."[13] The
whole purpose of deploying this term is to resist definitions and boundaries that reinscribe the limitations it seeks to overcome. Its usage is also
a resistance to what many perceive as a normalizing tendency in the gay
rights movement today. Many advances in gay rights realized in the past
few decades are seen as signs "not of progress but of how lesbians and gays
have been assimilated into mainstream culture and values."[14] In this way,
queer advocates would argue, those with marginalized identities are complicit with the identification regimes they hope to counter. By lumping
all "non-normative" sexualities and desires under the umbrella of "queer,"
without drawing boundaries around what that term describes, queer theorists seek to revolutionize the way we think about sexual categories and
identities.

But the use of "queer" is still contested by many to whom the label
may be applied. The openendedness of the term effectively erases real differences between and among those who are grouped under the umbrella,
and potentially effaces injustices and discrimination experienced by some
queers but not all. "Queer" also neutralizes the political efficacy of "gay"
and "lesbian" as gendered identity categories. This is a serious consideration in the realm of Christian theology, where gays and lesbians have
been working hard to assert their equal placement at the "table."[15] While
"queerness" works very well to disrupt the givenness of heterosexuality,
the content of gay identity needs to be recognized on a par with religious
identity before we can destabilize it. Additionally, many gay men and lesbians feel uncomfortable using a term for themselves that has been and
often still is used derogatorily toward them by those who want to denigrate them.[16] By far, the terms "gay" and "lesbian" and even "bisexual" are
still more widely used than "queer" in terms of self-identification.[17] With
few exceptions, the writers of the autobiographies I examine use "gay" to
describe themselves. Some use "queer" in addition to "gay," but in most
cases they use both in terms of sexual *identity*, which strict queer theorists
would resist.

A simple and helpful way of thinking about sexuality is in three component parts: orientation (feelings/desires), behavior, and identification.[18]
I am most concerned with questions of identity and self-identification, so
I will use the term "gay" most of the time because of its popular usage
as an identity category. I do not think "gay" yet represents a category of
assimilation, so I think it still accomplishes the goal of challenging the
heteronormative status quo. I will use "queer" or "bisexual" when it is
more appropriate and if the autobiographer himself uses that term; I will
also use "homosexual" as appropriate, especially to separate church teaching that denies gay identity or when referring to "clinical" descriptions of
same-sex desire or activity. Despite the nuances of these terms, it must
be remembered that in popular usage among gay men these terms are
roughly equivalent. Which term is deployed when is largely a matter of
context, but "gay" remains the popular term at this point in time.

My limitation of using only gay men's life texts by definition excludes
the stories of "ex-gay" men. In spite of my personal misgivings about the
"ex-gay" movement, it is not my intention to simply dismiss their experiences. I do think "ex-gays" have something to say about the fluidity of
sexual identity and their life texts are worth studying in another project.
Indeed, one might theorize "ex-gays" are still "queer" by virtue of their
nonfixed sexuality; but most "ex-gays" identify themselves that way in
conformity with heterosexual norms. In that respect, they desire "straight"
rather than "queer" identity, and an analysis of their autobiographies could
be most helpful in revealing how their life stories have been usurped by
religious right rhetoric. It is important to note that a "bisexual" man's life
story might look sexually similar to "ex-gay" stories if he is not currently
engaging in any same-sex behavior. Again, the crucial difference is in self-
identification. "Ex-gays" define themselves outside of my methodological
paradigm by flatly rejecting gay or even homosexual identity. I do, however, include autobiographies of gay men who (try to) live celibate lives in
accord with current Catholic teaching. Living in chastity is not the same
as trying to "become heterosexual," and the stories of gay celibates are
equally important in my analysis.[19]

My third limitation is using only autobiographies written by gay *Catholic* men. By this, I mean men who were born into or converted to Roman
Catholicism. I exclude those who grew up in or write from a Protestant
tradition that could broadly be called catholic, like the Episcopal Church.
The uniqueness of dealing with Roman authority separates the Roman
Catholic tradition from other sacramental churches. I include autobiographers whose commitment to Catholicism ranges from intense and devout
to marginal or nonexistent. I operate from the assumption that Catholicism is a culture that is formative beyond whatever faith commitments
inhere in the individual.[20] A few of these writers might object that they

are no longer Catholic and would not necessarily want to be included in a study like this, but I believe their stories are essential in addressing the problems with church teaching I will discuss.[21] After all, many gay Catholics leave the church precisely because church teaching on homosexuality does not make sense in their lives. Their life stories are important for the life of the church, embodied both in the hierarchical leadership *and* the people in or out of the pews who call themselves Catholic. As Vatican II defined it, the church is the entire people of God.

My study is further limited by time and place. In terms of time, I only examine autobiographies written by gay Catholic men since 1969. This situates my analysis firmly within the contemporary church and contemporary gay culture, post-Vatican II and post-Stonewall. Life stories written before that would reflect a radically different cultural and religious paradigm. As Ken Plummer notes, "Whilst men and women have been coming out for over a hundred years, it is only since 1970 that the stories have gone very public."[22] In terms of place, I only examine autobiographies written by gay Catholic men living in the United States, or whose stories take place or are influential primarily in an American context. The American Catholic Church has its own dynamics that are different in some ways from the global church, and the U.S. bishops have made their own statements on homosexuality and have dealt with Vatican statements in a particular way. Also, American gay culture has its own history and has developed its own dynamics.

Locating MySelf

In recognition of the supposition that all scholarship is engaged in some degree of advocacy work, and in line with the current trend of scholars being forthright about their own social location, I feel compelled to reveal something about my own life circumstances in relation to this project. In a book concerned with life stories, it would seem somewhat disingenuous not to disclose the pertinent details of my own story. My life text (if I had written one) would fit within the parameters I outlined above. I am a gay American Catholic man. I was born during Vatican II — to a quintessentially Catholic family: six kids, regular churchgoers, Catholic grade schools — so I am essentially what is now called a post-Conciliar Catholic, though I am not quite part of "Generation X." When I was very young, I remember the altar rail separating the priest from the people being removed at my church. Around the same time, when I was in grade school in the 1970s, our parish formed its first folk music group. I was envious of my teenage sisters who were old enough to join, and I quickly followed suit once I was in high school. From my earliest memories of going to church, I have always loved church music. It has nurtured my soul and has proven to be my primary point of connection with the Catholic tradition, almost "singing" it into my bones. The sweeping changes in American Catholicism have been represented in my life by the changes in church music styles that have happened simultaneously with my own coming of age. Throughout my adult life I have continued this deep connection by working as a music director and liturgist at a variety of Catholic parishes. I dearly love the Roman Catholic liturgy and have found in its depths the inspiration and power to work for social justice in the world.

My education was profoundly influenced by the Sisters of Loretto, arguably the most radical congregation of American nuns. Not only did they staff my grade school — though by the time I reached eighth grade, only one remained on the faculty — but they also founded the college I attended. At first, I resisted their progressive and challenging vision of being Catholic. I was comfortable at my church and enjoyed making music there. But I was also something of a late bloomer and as I slowly explored my sexual self, I began to experience my own cognitive dissonance in the church. The values I learned in my Catholic education about praying with an open mind, listening to my inner voice, and searching for answers that make sense spiritually and intellectually propelled me to push for reconciliation between who the church said I should be and who I knew myself to be. "Leaving" the church, or rather letting the church abandon me, never really occurred to me. I found affirmative spaces in the Catholic community through Dignity and progressive parishes, so I remain a deeply committed Catholic; yet I know for myself if I were to stop going to Mass, I would still have Catholicism "singing" in my bones. The critical work I am now doing is the culmination of my quest to have my life experience taken seriously by my church, as I have taken the church seriously throughout my life. May it bear good fruit for all gay Catholics.

Introduction

Whispers from the Housetop

Then, one Sunday during mass, my mind adrift in the sea of colorful light filtering down from the stained glass window above as I recited the Apostles' Creed, I made the inconceivable and irrevocable connection, felt the blazing brand of recognition — as if I had finally been given the gift of life, been filled almost unbearably by what I could only identify as the Holy Spirit: *I* was the degenerate homosexual whom I imagined my Church so despised. I felt I had been chosen and, in the same excruciating moment, obliterated. Suddenly, everything made perfect sense to me, and yet was all the more terribly incomprehensible. — Rafael Campo, *The Desire to Heal*

Gay and Catholic. The very idea of being both at once seems almost absurd. The popular conception of traditional religions like Roman Catholicism seems to preclude any hope of claiming both descriptions for oneself. Indeed, the phrase "gay Catholic" strikes many as an oxymoron; a painful, if not impossible, convergence of identities; a combination both morally untenable and theologically problematic. Yet behind such theoretical assumptions, gay Catholics do exist: persons who occupy the space where these two identities collide; people who feel both "chosen" and "obliterated"; people for whom everything becomes "all the more terribly incomprehensible," just as everything begins to make "perfect sense." Yes, gay Catholics do exist and are increasingly visible at the beginning of the twenty-first century, especially in the American context. This unavoidable reality represents an ethical and pastoral dilemma for Roman Catholicism as it embarks on its journey into the next Christian millennium.

Of all the issues polarizing American society at this point in time, homosexuality is one of the most divisive. One might think the events of September 11, 2001, would have made this issue seem less important to Americans. After watching the harrowing images of people falling to their deaths from the burning World Trade Center buildings, one might think newspaper coverage of a same-sex union with a photograph of two men kissing would not be a big deal. One might hope that images of love

9

and commitment would be welcome in a world filled with terrorism and uncertainty. But as time passes, objections to such images are still raised,[1] and we find ourselves in the same old debates over the moral status of gay relationships. If anything, 9/11 reemphasized how unresolved this issue is: within days, a few conservative religious leaders construed the attacks as God's punishment for allowing gay rights and abortions. (They quickly retracted these statements in the face of public pressure, saying they had been misinterpreted.) Later, longtime gay partners of those who died in the attacks had to take legal action to receive the same benefits automatically accorded to legally married others who may have known their spouses only a short time.

The fact that these kinds of debates and legal challenges are going on could be read as a sign of progress. Forty years ago, questions about gay rights were hardly on the radar screens of most Americans. While gay and lesbian subcultures and movements existed and even thrived through-out the twentieth century, the 1960s and the 1969 "Stonewall Riots" in particular pushed the gay movement to a new level of visibility that has grown exponentially ever since.[2] And is it ever visible today! The open-ing years of the twenty-first century have seen the societal discourse on homosexuality taken to a level that seemed unimaginable even one decade earlier. Gay characters in some form or another find their way into some of the most popular television shows and movies, and gay roles have be-come less risky for actors. When Ellen DeGeneres came out both on her television show and in her personal life in 1997, it caused enough of a stir to make the cover of *Time* magazine. Her show quickly faltered as a result of the fallout. Today, the audience cheers as Jay Leno gets a makeover by the fab-five gay-team boys of *Queer Eye for the Straight Guy* on *The To-night Show*. Of course, gay representation in mainstream programming is, like so much in popular entertainment culture, rarely multidimensional. It is built upon and fuels a host of stereotypes and is usually drained of any meaningful sexual content. But this partial invisibility is a form of visibility nonetheless, and it has made gay people seem no more screwy than other television characters.

None of this means gay people are now firmly accepted in American society, however. Gay visibility in the fantasy world of television is one thing; the reality in the world of law and ethics is another. According to a recent Washington Post/Kaiser Family Foundation/Harvard University poll, 72 percent of respondents feel "gay sex" is "unacceptable," yet 87 percent say homosexuals should have equal rights and opportunities in the workplace.[3] This reveals a striking tension between people's moral evaluation of homosexuality, on the one hand, and their respect for in-dividual rights and equal treatment, on the other. Unfortunately, many people feel pressed to choose one over the other. When the question is phrased differently to ask about the acceptability of homosexuality as an alternative "lifestyle" rather than focusing on "gay sex," people are more evenly divided in their moral evaluation: 54 percent say it is acceptable, while 43 percent say it is not.[4] Alan Wolfe's research suggests Americans are largely tolerant of difference, but the vehement expressions of opinions on homosexuality indicate it is the ultimate test of this tolerance: "The line separating gay America from straight America is a line that an unusually large number of middle-class Americans are unwilling to cross."[5] According to Wolfe, Americans remain deeply divided with regard to homosexuality: "The question of homosexuality reveals two genuinely different moral camps in America, which disagree profoundly about the fundamental nature of what they are contesting."[6]

Today's legislative propositions and judicial pronouncements on a variety of gay civil rights issues represent the public manifestations of people grappling with the moral status of gay and lesbian relationships. On June 26, 2003, in one of the most symbolically meaningful victories for advocates of gay rights, the United States Supreme Court found a Texas anti-sodomy law unconstitutional, thus overturning all such laws in the thirteen states that still had them. Writing for the 6–3 majority, Justice Anthony Kennedy states, "Adults may choose to enter relationships in the confines of their homes and their own private lives and still retain their dignity as free persons. . . . The state cannot demean their existence or control their destiny."[7] The significance of this ruling was lost on no one, and it caused those opposed to gay rights to draw more dramatic battle lines. The Reverend Louis P. Sheldon, of the Traditional Values Coalition, immediately called for an impeachment movement against the justices who had sided with the majority opinion, suggesting they had "ushered in a new form of government in the United States."[8] Matt Foreman, of the National Gay and Lesbian Task Force, was both hopeful and cautious: "This is both the most promising and the most frightening moment in this movement's history. There's nothing to compare it to."[9]

Foreman's trepidation stems from his recognition that the situation will become far more divisive and volatile as gay rights issues continue to come to the fore. This is especially true with regard to gay marriage, an issue all sides seem to interpret as the ultimate step in the normalization of same-sex relationships. Vermont already recognizes same-sex unions without calling them marriages and, as I complete the writing of this manuscript, the Massachusetts Supreme Court is poised to issue a ruling on gay marriages. Only a handful of countries have actually legalized gay marriage, but the fact that the Canadian provinces of Ontario and British Columbia have done so has turned up the heat on this issue in the United States. Those opposed to same-sex marriage have proposed the dramatic step of amending the U.S. Constitution to limit marriage to a union between a man and a woman. Thirty-seven states already have "Defense of Marriage" laws so that they do not have to recognize same-sex unions or marriages from other states. By a strange warp of logic, they believe that if more people want to be married and have access to it, this will somehow harm the institution of marriage. Peter La Barbera, of the Culture and Family Institute, takes it a step further: he says gay marriage "is a signal of moral breakdown" in society.[10]

Needless to say, many of these attitudes are driven by religion, and religious people are, in turn, caught up in this societal conflict. Religious bodies have been rocked and torn apart by issues related to homosexuality — most visibly within Christian churches.[11] Debates swirl throughout Christian communities regarding the appropriate theological and pastoral responses to same-sex orientations and relationships. The most recent and visible example is in the Episcopal Church, where the openly gay and partnered Rev. V. Gene Robinson was recently elected and approved as bishop of New Hampshire. As a result of this action, some bishops in the Anglican communion are threatening a schism, and the archbishop of Canterbury has called an emergency meeting to address the issue. The Episcopal convention also acknowledged that the blessing of same-sex unions has occurred in the ordinary life of the church, which drew equally heavy criticism from some quarters. Here again, the issue of gay marriage has touched off a firestorm, pushing people to "take sides" against each other within their own church community. A Washington Post poll taken after the Supreme Court decision invalidating anti-sodomy laws showed nearly three out of four regular churchgoers opposing the Episcopal convention's decisions, while less frequent churchgoers remain nearly evenly divided.[12] In the words of Alan Wolfe, "Americans are saying, 'We're willing to move pretty far on this issue, we're much more tolerant than we used to be, but don't mix it up with religion and God.'"[13]

But debates over homosexuality are unavoidably about religion and God, especially when the question deals with something sacramental like marriage — a fitting topic through which to introduce the particular context of Roman Catholicism. In light of all the recent advances toward full, legal recognition of same-sex relationships, Catholic hierarchical leaders have launched an aggressive campaign against this movement. In April 2003, the Vatican issued a lexicon designed to clarify church doctrine and define terminology church leaders find problematic or misused in modern political agendas. Besides making the blanket assertion that homosexuality is "without any social value," the document also characterizes legislative bodies that grant legal recognition to same-sex relationships as being filled with "deeply disordered minds."[14] Later, the bishops of Massachusetts, concerned their Supreme Court might decide the state constitution allows same-sex marriage, urged Catholics in the state to lobby for an amendment that would restrict marriage to heterosexual unions.

Most recently, the Vatican issued one of its most emphatic statements on the subject to date: "Considerations Regarding Proposals to Give Legal Recognition to Unions Between Homosexual Persons." Though the document says nothing new in terms of church teaching, it is notable for its sweeping statements and defensive, reactionary posturing. It is a challenge not only to Catholic politicians, but a call for all Catholics "to refuse to cooperate with measures that suggest an analogy between same-sex unions and traditional marriage between a man and a woman."[15] According to the document, "Not even in a remote analogous sense do homosexual unions fulfill the purpose for which marriage and family deserve specific categorical recognition."[16] Although most people, even those opposed to any kind of legal recognition, would acknowledge something at least remotely analogous about gay unions and legally valid marriages, the Vatican absolutely denies it. Seemingly blind to the historical malleability of the reasons and purpose for marriage, the document also assumes there is unanimous agreement as to why (and whether) marriage and family deserve special categorical recognition.[17] Riding the wave of such debatable assertions, and despite the diversity of opinion among other Christians and Catholics, the Vatican insists that denying the recognition of same-sex relationships is not opposed to justice: "On the contrary, justice requires it."[18]

The full reality of Catholic teaching on homosexuality is far less clear cut. Within the Catholic Church, concerned Catholics negotiate a delicate position between Vatican condemnations of homosexual behavior and church teachings affirming the inherent dignity of all human persons. Over the past four decades, the church has left a legacy of teachings on homosexuality that represents developments in understanding and sends decidedly mixed messages to the Catholic faithful. Beginning with the Second Vatican Council, 1962–65, the Roman Catholic Church deliberately turned itself toward engaging with the modern world. Pope John XXIII was explicit in his call for the *aggiornamento* (It., updating) of the Catholic Church and the necessity of the church to constantly renew and reform itself (*ecclesia semper reformanda*). Though primarily pastoral in nature, the Council affirmed the idea that doctrine could develop.[19] This was especially true with the 1965 promulgation of the "Declaration on Religious Freedom" (*Dignitatis Humanae*), which built upon human rights ideals set forth in John XXIII's 1962 encyclical *Pacem in Terris* and radically reversed earlier condemnations of religious liberty. The Council also affirmed the primacy of one's well-formed conscience in moral decision making and religious matters.[20] The confluence of these factors with the heightened visibility of the lesbian and gay movement provided fertile ground for an array of Catholic responses to homosexuality.[21]

Official Catholic teaching since Vatican II has consistently maintained that sexuality in general is properly expressed only within the confines of a sacramentally valid marriage.[22] Even then, sexual acts are circumscribed by the requirement that they must always be both "unitive" and "procreative."[23] Regarding homosexuality in particular, the church has attempted to integrate Vatican II teachings on the innate dignity of all human beings and the mandate to learn from and dialogue with the modern world by marking a difference between homosexual orientation and homosexual acts. This was first emphasized in the 1975 "Declaration on Certain Questions Concerning Sexual Ethics" (*Persona Humana*) by the Congregation for the Doctrine of the Faith (CDF). The separation between acts and orientation has allowed the church to "respect" homosexual people and at the same time "deplore" homosexual behavior. As Andrew Sullivan describes it, church teaching is now directed in two simultaneous and opposite directions: "A deeper respect for and understanding of homosexual persons, and a sterner rejection of almost anything those persons might do."[24] This has been stressed to various degrees and to various ends in all subsequent Vatican statements on the subject. The CDF's 1986 "Letter to the Bishops of the Catholic Church on the Pastoral Care of Homosexual Persons" exploited this difference not only to condemn homosexual acts but also to describe homosexual orientation as an "objective disorder."[25] The split between behavior and orientation is echoed in the 1995 *Catechism of the Catholic Church*, in which Catholics are reminded "homosexual acts are gravely disordered," but homosexual men and women "must be accepted with respect, compassion and sensitivity."[26]

The Bifurcation Problem

Robert Westerfelhaus discusses the Roman Catholic Church's teachings on homosexuality since the Second Vatican Council in terms of a shift in rhetorical stance. Prior to Vatican II, the church condemned both act (homosexual behavior) and actor (homosexual person). That rhetorical stance has been replaced by two distinctly different rhetorics: a moral rhetoric (to condemn the act) and a pastoral rhetoric (to uphold the person). Westerfelhaus argues that this has resulted in an uneasy bifurcation of the institutional church's position regarding homosexuality.[27] Within the frame of this teaching, the church creates a category of persons who — unlike heterosexual persons, whose nonmarital sexual acts are similarly forbidden, and unlike those who have actively chosen to abstain from sex — are required to be celibate simply because of who they are. The peculiar notion of the church that it is okay to be a homosexual as long as you do not act like one reflects an attempt by the church to balance its two rhetorics. The moral and pastoral rhetorics tenuously balance each other like a see-saw waiting to tilt, if it hasn't careened already. The problem is that by simultaneously trying to elevate both rhetorics, "the Church effectively elevates neither."[28]

The Catholic bishops of the United States have upheld the distinction defined by the two rhetorics, but even they do not seem convinced of its efficacy. In 1981, the United States Catholic Conference stated, "The person who is ostracized in his/her own Church community because of a homosexual orientation finds little comfort that the Church distinguishes between homosexual orientation and homosexual activity."[29] Even more tellingly, in a document distributed ten years later designed to reinforce the distinction "between being homosexual and doing homosexual actions," the bishops note that this distinction is "not always clear and convincing."[30] They want to maintain the church's bifurcated position, even as they admit the underlying reasoning for it may not be completely persuasive.

On a practical level, this bifurcation carries some problematic implications. Primarily, it causes the church to assert itself in inconsistent and troubling ways. For example, the *Catechism* argues with respect to gay and lesbian people, "Every sign of unjust discrimination in their regard should be avoided."[31] Yet in 1992, at a time when several American states and cities were considering legislation concerning the civil rights of gays and lesbians, the CDF issued a statement specifically to assert, "There are areas in which it is not unjust discrimination to take sexual orientation into account, for example, in the placement of children for adoption or foster care, in employment of teachers or athletic coaches, and in military recruitment."[32] In their most recent statement on gay rights legislation, the Vatican argues that allowing children to be adopted by persons living in same-sex unions "would actually mean doing violence to these children."[33] Apparently, the moral rhetoric is now so important to church leaders that they would rather ignore the evidence of thousands of children already being raised by gay and lesbian parents.[34] Surely these children deserve the same protections of family and marriage — an important pastoral concern — as children of heterosexual unions, who we know are not immune to violence simply because they have two opposite-sex parents. Similarly, the church's response to AIDS has been implicated in this problem. Although the pastoral rhetoric might support the use of condoms in order to protect the human person, the moral rhetoric absolutely could not.[35]

The tensions in church teaching have been even more evident since the release of the U.S. Bishops' most recent document concerning homosexuality: "Always Our Children: A Pastoral Message to Parents of Homosexual Children and Suggestions for Pastoral Ministers."[36] The original statement clearly emphasizes the pastoral rhetoric in its insistence that parents of lesbian and gay children should do everything possible to show

love to their children. The reasoning is that every child is a gift from
God and a homosexual orientation by itself cannot be considered sinful
because it is not freely chosen. Here, the American bishops acknowledge
the contemporary psychological argument that regardless of what factors
"cause" homosexuality, most people who describe themselves as homosexual experience their orientation as a given.[37] Overall, the message in
their statement is quite positive and accepting, though nowhere does it
negate the moral rhetoric of the church. In fact, in response to those
who favor the moral over the pastoral stance, the document was eventually revised and reissued in July of 1998. In the revision, a footnote was
added to the above passage concerning the neutrality of the orientation:
"This inclination, which is objectively disordered, constitutes for most a
trial."[38] While most Catholic lesbians and gays still view the document in
a mostly positive light, they find the distinction between orientation and
activity confusing and problematic. In the words of Robert Miailovich,
then-President of Dignity USA (the nation's largest organization of lesbian, gay, bisexual, and transgendered Catholics), in a statement released
the same day as the bishops' letter, "This is a distinction that makes little
sense to us and will be a stumbling block in the way of any effective
pastoral program seeking to encompass the letter's recommendations."[39]

As recently as December 2000, an American bishop found himself in
a delicate situation as a result of the mixed messages in church teaching. Baltimore Bishop William Newman commendably presided at an
Advent liturgy for gay/lesbian people, their families, and friends. In the
Spirit of "Always Our Children" and the jubilee year launched by Pope
John Paul II for the millennium, Bishop Newman used his homily to seek
reconciliation between the church and gays and lesbians:

> In this spirit today I lead the Church Community in seeking the
> forgiveness of our loving God for the sins individually and collectively
> the Church has committed against the gay and lesbian community.
> We all are children of God made in God's image and should enjoy
> the dignity of being a human person.[40]

Needless to say, this action by a bishop was greeted with cheers by lesbian and gay Catholics and celebrated in progressive Catholic publications.
After a favorable editorial in the *National Catholic Reporter,* however, the
director of communications of the archdiocese of Baltimore issued a clarification in his own letter to the editor. In his letter, he reiterates the
moral rhetoric by noting the church "does proscribe intimate acts of sexuality that are reserved in God's plan for a man and a woman in union
with one another through marriage." He further notes that the absence of
the moral rhetoric in the bishop's homily "does not signal a withdrawal
from the truth, but recognition that in an ongoing ministry of outreach,

it does not have to be underscored on every occasion."[41] Lesbian and gay Catholics then expressed frustration with the clarification through their own statements and letters. Indeed, one wonders why this clarification was necessary if it is not necessary to underscore the moral rhetoric on every occasion. The clarification from Bishop Newman's office, obviously sent with his authorization, effectively undermined the effort at reconciliation he was putting forth in the first place. Any pastoral ministers in the church will inevitably find themselves between a rock and a hard place attempting to straddle the bifurcated church teaching on homosexuality.

From Bifurcation to Fragmentation: Division in the Church Community

This bifurcation problem negatively impacts those in the church who seek to minister to lesbian and gay Catholics. At the heart of the concept of ministry is the ideal of service. The Roman Catholic Church has a hierarchy of "ministers," both lay and ordained, whose "vocation" or "job" it is to serve the faithful, even as all Catholics are called to be "ministers" to each other and to the world. The goal is for everyone in the church to be served by and through various ministries. Some ministries are based on various church functions and offices (e.g., liturgy, music, education), while others are focused on particular groups of people with special needs (e.g., poor, homeless, youth, elderly). All such ministries are usually called "pastoral ministries" because they are concerned with the spiritual formation and well-being of human persons.

Reflecting the visibility of lesbian and gay people in modern society, there have arisen new ministries designed to reach this group in particular. The nature of these ministries varies according to the ministers' biases and political views about homosexuality and what they perceive is needed. Officially sanctioned ministries, such as Courage,[42] view homosexuality as a problem to be overcome, and they seek to effect a change in the person. They avoid using terms like gay and lesbian because they represent identity categories. Some dioceses maintain various outreach programs for gays and lesbians, grouped under the umbrella National Association of Catholic Diocesan Lesbian and Gay Ministries (NACDLGM). Most of these are designed to keep gay and lesbian Catholics connected to the church by offering opportunities for spiritual enrichment, without challenging church teaching. At the opposite end of the spectrum from Courage, ministries such as Dignity view homosexuality as a reality to which the church must adapt. Founded in 1969, Dignity thrives without official recognition from the church and operates independent of church support. The organization has chapters across the United States offering liturgies and community for gay, lesbian, bisexual, and transgendered Catholics. Dignity publicly dissents from the church's official moral condemnation of homosexual relationships and offers commitment ceremonies to bless same-sex unions.[43]

In 1977, Sister Jeannine Gramick, SSND, and Father Robert Nugent, SDS, cofounded New Ways Ministry in response to a void they perceived in the church's official response to gay and lesbian Catholics. They were also motivated by a sympathetic statement made by the American bishops in 1976.[44] From the outset, they envisioned themselves as bridge-builders between the church, which they "officially" represent as consecrated religious, and lesbian and gay Catholics, with whom they had already developed a pastoral relationship.[45] Their goal was to listen to gay people, communicate their concerns and needs to the church, and thereby begin to bring about reconciliation between the two groups. Their mode of ministry has been primarily educational presentations, seminars, and retreats, in which they discuss church teaching, scripture, and tradition and give participants the chance to voice their concerns. Gramick and Nugent's work has always reflected a recognition that real pastoral ministry must first and foremost demonstrate a true respect for persons as they are in the context of who they believe themselves to be. In that regard, their presentations have always underscored the church's pastoral rhetoric without overemphasizing the doctrinal condemnation of homosexual acts. They have always been clear about the content of the moral rhetoric, but they interpret it as one evolving piece of a multifaceted set of teachings in which the pastoral rhetoric deserves more attention.

In 1984, they were ordered by the Holy See through their community superiors to cease their association with New Ways Ministry and not to "engage in any apostolate or participate in any program or write on any subject concerning homosexuality unless [he/she] makes clear that homosexual acts are intrinsically and objectively wrong."[46] They stopped functioning formally under the auspices of New Ways but continued their ministry as extensions of their work in their own religious congregations. They believed they had adequately addressed the Vatican's concerns; but in 1988, an investigation was launched by the Vatican's Congregation for Religious and Secular Institutes to evaluate the orthodoxy of Gramick and Nugent's ministry. Thus began a long ordeal which would eventually culminate in July 1999, with an order from the Congregation for the Doctrine of the Faith, for Nugent and Gramick to terminate all of their ministry to gays and lesbians. A year later, circumstances had escalated to the point where they were even ordered not to speak about their ministry, the investigation, or anything having to do with lesbian and gay issues.

How did such an ugly situation come to pass for two relatively moderate ministers of the church? Anyone who attended their presentations or read any of their publications would be hard-pressed to characterize Nugent and Gramick as radicals. They even faced some degree of criticism from activist gay Catholics for not insisting on changes in the church's moral rhetoric. I contend the heart of the problem was and is the bifurcated church teaching on homosexuality. The chasm between the moral and pastoral rhetorics cannot reasonably be bridged in a way that makes sense in the lives of those toward whom the teaching is geared or for those who try to carry out a pastoral ministry for their sake. In the appendix, I offer my appraisal of the investigation of Nugent and Gramick by dissecting some of the statements made in the documents related to the case. While myriad problems emerge related to the way the Vatican conducts its business, especially in terms of what constitutes due process, my analysis demonstrates how the underlying dilemma lies in the impossibility of realistically applying church teaching on homosexuality as it currently stands.[47]

As one might expect, the investigation and silencing of Nugent and Gramick caused a considerable uproar in the community, with concerned Catholics caught in the middle and taking sides against each other, mirroring the polarization in American society on the issue of homosexuality in general. Immediately after the initial Vatican notification against Nugent and Gramick, Dignity released a statement denouncing the action. Charles Cox, Executive Director at the time, was quoted as saying, "The CDF's continued use of 'intrinsic evil' to describe homosexual acts, and implicitly homosexual persons, is a chilling reminder of the Church's on-going attempt to marginalize and stigmatize pastoral care for gay men, lesbians, bisexuals, and transgendered persons."[48]

In quick succession, the Gramick and Nugent case became a cause célèbre among Catholic organizations who used it to accentuate their differences with regard to negotiating authority in the church. Reformist Catholic associations like Call to Action circulated petitions asking Catholics to object to the order of silence, while conservative organizations like the Catholic League used it as an opportunity to reiterate the moral rhetoric against homosexual relationships and to urge fidelity to the Vatican. Nugent and Gramick were given awards and were featured speakers at a variety of local and national progressive conferences and retreats,[49] and letters to the editor flooded Catholic publications that covered the story. Responses ranged from outrage and anger toward the Vatican, to demands that Nugent and Gramick follow their religious vows and obey the Vatican orders to the letter.

The case of Nugent and Gramick did not create new tensions; it only exacerbated divisions already in place. The bifurcated teachings have struck a raw nerve among American Catholics, who are more and more likely to be personally acquainted with a gay or lesbian person. The discrepancy between what the church teaches about homosexuals and what some Catholics feel about the lesbian and gay people they know creates a sense of cognitive dissonance.[50] Other Catholics cling to the moral rhetoric as a shield against a creeping secularism that threatens to undermine religious values. Not surprisingly, even the American bishops are divided. While most of them struggle valiantly to walk the narrow line "between Roman authority and American pastoral practice" (see appendix), some are more extreme. I will briefly highlight two of these, arguably the most extremely conservative and the most radically liberal bishops: Fabian Bruskewitz, of Lincoln, Nebraska, and Thomas Gumbleton, of Detroit. When the Nebraska chapter of Call to Action invited Jeannine Gramick to speak at one of their gatherings, Bishop Bruskewitz wrote the following in his diocesan newspaper:

> In a failed attempt to infect decent people with their ideological pathologies, the anti-Catholic sect Call to Action has recently reached into a theological sewer and brought to Nebraska Sister Jeannine Gramick, SSND, an apostle of sexual perversion.[51]

At the other end of the spectrum, Bishop Gumbleton has stated, in reference to church teaching on homosexuality:

> If you tell someone that at the very core of your being you're disordered and you've got a strong inclination [toward sin], what does that do to you? It's cruel to say to anybody. There's no basis to say it to anybody.[52]

While both bishops' statements might be considered inflammatory, they represent a palpable rift in the Catholic community on the issue of homosexuality.

The polarization was starkly visible a few years ago at the fifth annual conference of the National Association of Catholic Diocesan Lesbian and Gay Ministries, held in Rochester, New York, with the full support of Bishop Matthew Clark. A wide variety of speakers talked of hope, love, justice, and reconciliation between the church and its lesbian and gay members. Though none of the speakers at this officially sanctioned event directly challenged the magisterial position on the moral status of homosexual acts,[53] the overall theme of the conference was acceptance and advocacy of lesbian and gay participation in the church. Outside, however, the picture was very different. Protesters made their objections clear by carrying a variety of signs: "Practicing Catholics cannot practice homosexuality"; "Bishop Clark: Love the Homosexual with the Truth";

"Homosexual Persons Are Called to Chastity." The scene was a micro-cosm of the American Catholic Church's "tense and increasingly public struggle over homosexuality."[54]

Less than two months earlier, the Rochester diocese had been the center of yet another controversy related at least partially to the issue of homo-sexuality. This time Bishop Clark appeared to be on the other side of the rift. In late August 1998, Bishop Clark removed Fr. Jim Callan from his position as pastor of Corpus Christi Parish because Callan regularly al-lowed a woman to co-preside at Eucharist and also because he had blessed same-sex unions.[55] The Corpus Christi community had attracted a large number of gays and lesbians since Fr. Callan first came to the parish in 1976, and it had become well known as a place where Catholic lesbians and gays could openly participate and share their gifts. The new pastor was charged with the task of "cleaning up" the parish, bringing it in line with "traditional" norms. Unfortunately, the situation became both divi-sive and explosive, with parishioners voting to protest the removal of their pastor and to continue their inclusive ministries. In December 1998, six parish staff members were fired for "refusal to cooperate with the new pastor."[56] In the meantime, Fr. Callan, originally reassigned to a rural par-ish, was suspended from administering sacraments or celebrating Mass at any parish until he agreed to "abide by Church regulations."[57] The rift in the Corpus Christi community ultimately resulted in a schism and the excommunication of dissident members.[58] Supporters of Fr. Callan have formed a breakaway church and are now functioning independently with their own paid staff, under the name Spiritus Christi. They still claim au-thentic membership in the Catholic community and have ordained two women of their community as priests.[59]

The above examples depict fragmentation on a large and visible scale, but tensions surrounding church teaching on homosexuality can be ob-served at the most localized levels, affecting individuals and families. A case in point involves Anne and Ed Reynolds, parishioners of St. Aedan Parish in Pearl River, New York, since its founding in 1966. The Reynold-ses wrote a letter to their local newspapers in support of Nugent and Gramick in August 1999. Their son Andrew (then twenty-eight years old) is gay and the Reynoldses had attended four retreats led by Nugent and Gramick. In their letter, they voiced their distress over the church's moral rhetoric which labeled their son "objectively disordered": "As par-ents of a gay man, we cannot fully assent to the Church's teaching on homosexuality. To do so would be to deny our son and violate our con-sciences."[60] After the parish pastor received complaints about the letter, he called the Reynoldses into his office and pressured them into resign-ing as eucharistic ministers, a liturgical ministry they had exercised since 1977. They agreed to resign, but were quite shaken by the confrontation and now encounter only tacit support and even disapproval from their fel-low parishioners. Anne and Ed Reynolds represent the most mainstream of American Catholics. They both attended Catholic schools through col-lege, and all eight of their children attended Catholic elementary and high schools; yet church teaching created a moral dilemma for them. "We're not political people, We're both just tired of secrecy and shame. . . . [We] agree with the bishops on so many things. We're really very conservative,"[61] states Ms. Reynolds. She maintains church teaching on homosexuality does not reflect her family's reality, and words like "evil" and "disordered" justify violence against gays and lesbians: "The bishops don't mean to do that, but I don't live in an ivory tower. I live with real people in a real house and I can see how harmful that wording is."[62]

Ms. Reynolds is concerned about the ramifications of church teaching when it seeps into the public square. If church teaching reflects soci-etal prejudices, then it can easily be used to justify and reinforce those prejudices, perpetuating rifts not only in the church but also in society at large. This is an especially important concern when Catholics hold positions of public office and base decisions on their religious beliefs. Re-cently, in an interview held before the Supreme Court's ruling against anti-sodomy laws, conservative Catholic Senator Rick Santorum, R-PA, compared homosexuality to bigamy, polygamy, incest, and adultery, as he expressed his hope that the Court would not overturn the Texas law. He feared that allowing consensual gay sex based on a right to privacy would then open the legal door to a host of other sexual behaviors like those he listed. His remarks touched off the expected storm of objectors and supporters throughout the country and made starkly visible the ruptures in American Catholicism over issues related to homosexuality.[63] When he spoke less than a month later at the St. Joseph's University Com-mencement (a Catholic institution), several students and faculty walked out to protest his remarks, marking further dissension in the Catholic community.

In the same interview, Santorum made remarks echoing the bifurcated church teaching: "I have no problem with homosexuality—I have a prob-lem with homosexual acts, as I would with acts of other [sic] . . . acts outside of traditional heterosexual relationships."[64] Though it is not en-tirely clear, it seems Santorum was trying to draw the same difference church teaching does between gay persons and their behavior. This makes his analogy to other sexual behaviors all the more puzzling. Would he ever say something like, "I have no problem with incest, just incestuous acts"? I doubt it. The confusing separation between homosexual behavior and homosexual orientation, between gay act and gay actor, obscures his real message. Clearly, Santorum does have a problem with homosexuality—

both the acts and the people who do them — otherwise why draw the analogy to other sexual behaviors that do not fit the same mold?

Whose Reality? The Subjectivity Problem

Gay people reject any comparison between homosexuality and any of the sexual behaviors Santorum mentioned because they know being gay involves more than same-sex acts. On this much, Santorum would agree, as his clumsy statements reveal. This is also the reason for the church's distinction between sexual orientation and behavior, and the assumption underlying the bifurcated rhetoric. But the problem is that being gay does in some way involve same-sex acts. Being gay and doing gay are connected. Any clean separation of these aspects does not make sense in the reality of gay existence. From a gay perspective, the bifurcation masks a different reality: the church has a problem with gay persons. Let's say, however, the church sincerely does want to respect gay persons as the pastoral rhetoric states. Why is it not enough for them to say it? What will it take for gay people to believe it and take the pastoral rhetoric seriously?

It is one thing for a public official to say he has no problem with gay people and then denounce the actions that inform gay identity in the first place; but when a church representative says it, it directly implicates church teaching and produces a sort of theological dissonance. Here is where Nugent and Gramick were caught in the middle. The Nugent and Gramick case not only highlights the fragmentation of the Catholic community around this issue but also raises important questions about ministry and the role of ministers. In one of their written responses during the investigation, Gramick and Nugent draw an analogy to other ministries in the church to justify their method:

> Those who minister today to the divorced and remarried are not expected to constantly proclaim the immorality of divorce and remarriage. Hospital chaplains are not expected to constantly proclaim the immorality of neglecting and endangering one's health. Those in prison ministry are not expected to constantly proclaim the immorality of criminal acts. Military chaplains are not expected to constantly proclaim the immorality of war. The expectations of those in lesbian and gay ministry should be similar.[65]

At first glance, this comparison offers an insight into the way Gramick and Nugent view their ministry. For them, pastoral ministry is to some extent always already separate from any moral evaluation of those for whom the ministry exists. In that respect, it would seem their ministry and the others they mention actually rely on some degree of bifurcation. They would assert all people deserve pastoral care regardless of the choices they have made in their lives. In broader Christian circles, especially Evangelical strands, this idea is represented by the phrase, "Love the sinner, hate the sin."

But I do not think the above analogy is helpful in relation to the church's teaching on homosexuality. First, if the church's moral teachings were under fire in relation to any of the above groups, I think church officials would indeed expect pastoral ministers to reiterate the moral doctrines. Second, the church does not recognize soldiers, criminals, hospital patients, and divorced and remarried people in the same way it does homosexuals. Soldiers and divorced and remarried people are not said to have an innate orientation related to these life choices. Criminals and hospital patients may indeed have some inborn inclination or trait which led them to their current situation, but they are then accorded the label of "sick." This is a designation which has been roundly rejected by most lesbian and gay Catholics for themselves. When someone is "sick," their subjective culpability is mitigated and pastoral care becomes an act of charity. Most lesbian and gay Catholics do not want "charity" in place of authentic respect, and they want to take full responsibility for their subjective moral choices.[66]

Nugent and Gramick attempted to build the bridge between the moral and pastoral rhetorics by capitalizing on this distinction between objective immorality and subjective culpability, even as they tried to take seriously the lived experience of gays and lesbians. But this negation of subjective responsibility compounds the bifurcation problem by further separating gay and lesbian persons from their actions. In effect, the gay voice is silenced because gay subjectivity is still lacking. In my usage of these terms, *experience* and *subjectivity* are closely linked to each other and ideally function together, but they are not exactly the same thing. *Experience* is the act and result of participation in one's life as a person with same-sex desires. It informs a self-knowledge that is particular and individual, which is what makes it problematic as a criterion for any moral theology claiming to be "objective." *Subjectivity* is the act and result of being the narrator and interpreter of one's own experience.[67] Experience is communicated through subjectivity. Experience cannot be the only criterion for determining church teaching on sexuality, but it must be one of the criteria.[68] Otherwise, sexual ethics remains entirely theoretical. In fact, gay and lesbian Catholics are increasingly demanding that their experience be taken into account in church teaching.[69] Indeed, their experience should be given priority with regard to moral teachings that directly affect them and about which they are the most knowledgeable. This experience must be ascertained from their own voices, from the kind of subjectivity that is an integral aspect of autobiography.

This focuses attention on the other key problem, integrally related to the bifurcation problem, in official church teaching on homosexuality: the apparent absence of gay subjectivity in the documents. Consistently, "homosexuals" are presented as objects of study, abstractions almost, about whom the teaching is written. As Gramick and Nugent note in reference to the CDF's 1986 "Halloween" Letter, it "obviously did not begin from the experience of being lesbian or gay."[70] It is as if no gay or lesbian people exist either in the group of men who constructed the documents[71] or in the group of people to whom the documents are addressed. Though some of the church documents are addressed only to bishops, most of them are designed to address the church at large, the entire community of believers. The implicit assumption then is that gay and lesbian people are legitimate only outside the Catholic community, or within the community only as disembodied orientations denied realization. Unfortunately (or fortunately, depending on one's rhetorical stance), this does not correspond with the reality of the church community regardless of what the official moral stance would like to dictate.

A sort of hidden gay subjectivity could be said to exist in the documents because some of the writers themselves may be homosexual, but they would not necessarily claim a gay identity, and they certainly would not do so in any remotely public way. They do not write openly from a "sexual subject" position because their own sexuality is displaced and superseded by obligatory celibacy. Of course, the issue of homosexuality within the hierarchy is much more complicated than that. There is certainly homosexual activity going on at all levels of church leadership, the "secrecy" of which is maintained and enhanced by church doctrine on homosexuality. Mark Jordan's recent book, *The Silence of Sodom*, deals with the way Catholic clerical culture simultaneously suppresses and encourages, condemns and elicits, persecutes and instructs homoeroticism. The tension between acceptance and condemnation that plays out in gay Catholic lives and ministries as a result of the bifurcated church teaching actually mirrors an institutional schizophrenia. Indeed, Catholic clerical culture has long offered a relatively safe haven for homosexuals, and the similarities and parallels between that culture and modern gay culture are striking. The power structure provides an arrangement through which same-sex desire can be exercised in secret, without the risks of self-identification, and the official teachings in turn support that structure and its subjective silence.[72]

Jordan's goal is to demystify the Catholic clerical culture which makes church teaching on homosexuality unlikely to change. My goal is to fill in the reality gap in church teaching by introducing gay subjectivity into the equation. Fr. Robert Nugent has suggested gays and lesbians have a *responsibility* to articulate their experiences for the broader community:

"You are the experts in this area . . . and you cannot be silent — for your own good or for the comfort of others."[73] Even the Catholic Theological Society is having discussions about the gap between church teaching and gay experience. At a recent meeting of the Society, Augustinian Fr. Daniel Doyle said Catholic theology "had reached an 'impasse' in its approach to homosexuality, . . . a point where the natural law tradition 'can no longer carry us,' given the insights gleaned from 'the positive experiences of same-sex relationships.'"[74] My analysis of gay Catholic autobiographies — products of gay subjectivity — will carry our theological understanding forward. These first-person narratives represent people who self-identify as gay, for whom sexuality is a defining piece of personal identity, and for whom "objective" teachings on human sexuality are irrelevant by definition. As I have already discussed, the breach in church teaching between the moral and pastoral rhetoric is a void of gay experience, not reflective of reality. Attending to what these autobiographies have to say about gay identity and Catholic identity will help fill in this gap.[75] By doing so, the church community, as Nugent and Gramick state, "will have a more complete understanding of the complex reality of homosexuality as it affects the lives of people in our Church and will be able to respond in a realistic, sensitive and compassionate manner."[76]

For too long, gay Catholic lives have been shrouded in the secrecy advanced by official church teaching. For many gay Catholics, the "closet" remains a powerful metaphor for the secrecy and shame which cause many of us to keep our sexual identity hidden. At times, the decision to stay "in the closet" is carefully calculated and deliberate. At other times, the closet is forced upon us from outside. Yet it is in this context that gay Catholics must reconcile their sexual and spiritual lives. Gay Catholic autobiographical acts reveal the delicate interplay between sexuality, spirituality, and the many other components of identity which make a person unique. These acts of self-disclosure — of confession — stand as revelations of God's intervention and action in gay Catholic lives. I offer a gay interpretation of Matthew 10:27, on open and fearless confession, from which I imagine the framework for understanding these autobiographies as sacred texts. In Jesus's instructions to his apostles, he admonishes them not to be afraid of those who do not welcome them or who would persecute them: disciples of Jesus are not afraid to speak the truth hidden away in their hearts. What gay Catholics learn about themselves and God "in the closet" is revealed in the life narratives they construct and share with the world:

> What I say to you in the dark, tell in the daylight;
> what you hear in whispers, proclaim from the housetops.[77]

When a gay Catholic takes the risk of narrating his gay identity, transforming what was once a secret and publishing it for public dissemination, his autobiographical act becomes a "whisper from the housetop." These autobiographies provide a glimpse of the lives on which the church's twin rhetorics on homosexuality converge and collide, thus creating a space to synthesize and transcend the bifurcation in church teaching and the polarization now being felt over this issue in the Catholic community. Life stories are central to the mythology that creates and legitimates both sexual and religious identities: "All dogma and proof, i.e., formulations and facts of religious belief, are founded deep in autobiography."[78] Spiritual autobiographies have, in fact, played a significant role in shaping the Catholic tradition. Beginning with Saint Augustine's *Confessions*, often considered the founding moment in the Western tradition of an inward autobiographical subject, such writings reflect upon the experience of divine intention in human lives. Gay Catholic autobiographies function similarly and so should be considered sacred texts for the entire Catholic community, voices which must be heard and analyzed in order to paint a more complete picture of what it means to be Catholic.

Overview

In the next chapter, I will survey the many autobiographical works that form the data pool of this study. There are a surprising number of published works out there when one sets his mind to finding them. I bring them together and describe the various styles of autobiographies represented, in addition to briefly introducing the various authors. I also survey some of the most pertinent theoretical concerns associated with this genre of literature, highlighting the peculiarities of using autobiography as a source of analysis.

In the following chapters, I will dwell in the narrative world of these gay Catholic autobiographers in order to become enmeshed in reality as they conceive it. My goal is not to reify any one particular portrait of gay Catholic identity but rather to show its multiplicity and complexity. I will expose trends, patterns, constructions, perceptions, and divergences, and theorize these in terms of identity questions. I am looking for the ways these autobiographies open up the identities of "gay" and "Catholic" and then complicate simplistic conceptions of these categories. In chapter 2, I will focus on the "gay" side of the identity equation. How do these writers experience being gay and how is gay identity performed in these narratives? Is the separation between doing gay and being gay as viable as the bifurcated church teaching would have us believe? What role do gender constructions and masculine expectations play in their lives? In chapter 3, I will focus more on the "Catholic" side of the identity equation, but with an understanding that these religious and sexual identities are deeply entangled. How is gay Catholic identity performed in these narratives? How does Catholicity function both as a "passed on" culture and as a "taught" system of beliefs, and how do both of these dimensions influence the Catholic world view? How and why has problematic church teaching caused some gays to "leave" the church and others to remain?

In chapter 4, I will examine the ethical struggles and decisions of these gay Catholics as a way of bridging the theoretical division between homosexual persons and behaviors that is the foundation for the bifurcated church teaching. When gay people are in relationships with others, be it friends or family or lovers, the concept of "homosexual acts" becomes nebulous. How are the moral and pastoral rhetorics played upon and by gay Catholics as moral agents themselves? How does the integration of sexuality as an identity piece of one's personhood complicate the separation between being and doing? How are these autobiographies moral performances and how is gay Catholic moral agency and conscience reflected in their life texts? My analysis cannot offer the final answers to these questions, nor can it single-handedly "solve" the problems in church teaching, but it is a necessary next step toward the transformation of church teaching. I hope to distill from these autobiographies an intellectual analysis that is useful for and speaks to gay Catholics and the church community at large.

In chapter 5, I will reiterate the need to overcome and adapt problematic church teaching on homosexuality in light of all that has been revealed in this study. I will propose a way forward that relies on the sacramental dimension of life writing. In the encounter between the Catholic reader and these autobiographies, the church has the opportunity to reflect on its own failures. These autobiographers call attention to the ways the church's official teachings and institutionalized attitudes diminish the opportunity for gay Catholics to fully realize their human potential. When gay Catholic autobiographies reveal such failures in human relationships, it is a starting point for reconciliation between the church and its gay members.

Chapter 1

Surveying Autobiographical Acts

We forget the memories that hinder our continuing on; we cherish and embellish those that give us hope. From our stories we each compose our private opera, for playing and replaying to ourselves and others. This is memory's triumph — it filters and shapes the past into a package suitable for remembering. And this is memory's tragedy: All that shaping and filtering is finally so much stage play, for history exacts its dues independent of what memory wants.

—Fenton Johnson, *Geography of the Heart*

When I first embarked on this project and told people I was using autobiographies written by gay Catholics as my primary sources, people would invariably ask, "How many are there?" Their thinly disguised incredulity that there would be an adequate number to propel a project like this initially caused me some anxiety. I knew I had seen several, and I knew the literary world had witnessed an explosion of autobiographical writing in the last few decades. Publishers are only too happy to benefit from our contemporary, tell-all culture, which encourages people to devour the most intimate details of other people's lives. What motivates some people to tell their stories varies according to the type of story being told: ethnic "minorities" in America, for example, may wish to tell their stories in order to preserve their cultural heritage or as a way of resisting the hegemonic norms of "white" America; people facing situations of death and dying may tell their stories to bear witness to a life that has passed on, to report their encounters with the medical system, or to relate their experience of grief;[1] prominent celebrities may tell their stories to attest to their struggle for fame or simply to further their own popularity. But where do gay Catholics fit into this scheme of life storytelling at the cusp of the twentieth and twenty-first centuries, and have they published a sufficient number of autobiographies to justify a study such as mine?

As I set out to find the texts to analyze for this project, I decided to open up the definition of autobiography beyond book-length life stories. After all, the word broken into its roots means *self-life-writing*, and my

aim was to find instances of self-life-writing by gay Catholics. With that
in mind, I decided any such occurrences — whether they are in the form
of essays, articles, chapters, or embedded in novels — would be eligible for
consideration. For this reason, it is helpful to think of these writings as
autobiographical *acts*, not necessarily complete life stories, but moments
of lives enacted textually. An autobiographical act is an animated and
dynamic gesture — to act is to do — a wonderfully proactive method of
exploring the self. And in line with autobiography theory, it is also an "act":
a performance of conscious identity construction. Happily, I was able to
find an ample number of gay Catholic autobiographies, though there are
surely many more to be both found and written. I will begin this chapter
with an overview of these texts in order to understand the rich framework
of data upon which this analysis is built. The reasons each author has for
telling his story inform the style and scope of his autobiographical act.
Although their particular motivations are numerous and varied, and not
always entirely clear, some general patterns and types emerge when they
are studied together. These categories and styles inevitably overlap, but
they also provide a way into the world of these sources.

Surveying the Literature

Given my specific location as a scholar of religion, it makes a certain
sense to begin by discussing the works that are explicitly *spiritual* autobiographies. While this is a slippery term, especially in contemporary
American culture, which labels almost any personal exploration as a "spiritual" project, I am using it here to identify the texts in which the writer
is negotiating his spiritual identity in light of his Catholic background.
Although spirituality and religion are not synonymous terms,[2] each of
these lives begin from a Catholic understanding of ultimate reality, so
the two concepts are unavoidably linked for them. Some remain deeply
engaged with the tradition, some have found ways of refashioning their
relationship with the church, and others have virtually abandoned it in
favor of more eclectic understandings of religion. In any case, the spiritual
struggle forms the core of each of these works. Not surprisingly, the majority of these autobiographical acts are found in anthologies devoted to
this kind of struggle. Foremost among these for my purposes is Raymond
Holtz's *Listen to the Stories*, because every one of the contributors to his
volume comes from a Catholic perspective. Twenty-two gay Catholic men
present their journeys through Catholicism to articulate their current perception of themselves in relation to the church. Each was asked to reflect
on three broad questions and their reflections were then converted to text.
Because many of the contributors belong to Dignity — the organization for
gay, lesbian, bisexual, and transgendered Catholics — their stories tend to

reflect an insistence that gay identity should not be an impediment to membership in the Catholic community.[3]

Another substantive anthology, Brian Bouldrey's *Wrestling with the Angel*, features autobiographical essays on faith and religion in gay lives, eight of whom are Catholic: James Morrison, Andrew Holleran, Kevin Killian, Peter Krask, David Plante, Philip Gambone, Fenton Johnson, and Bouldrey himself. Unlike the Holtz anthology, all of the contributors to this volume are professional writers who not only know how to craft compelling stories but also understand the literary issues at stake in the construction of autobiography.[4] Two Catholic contributors to Catherine Lake's *ReCreations: Religion and Spirituality in the Lives of Queer People* are also gifted writers, one widely published (Daniel Curzon) and the other a graduate student in physics (Brian Utter). Their essays are brief, but focused specifically on spiritual concerns.[5] Andrew Sullivan, who was at one time the editor of the *New Republic,* published an essay on Catholicism and homosexuality in that same magazine in November 1994. It first appeared under the title, "Alone Again, Naturally,"[6] and then was reworked as "Virtually Normal" for Thomas Ferraro's *Catholic Lives, Contemporary America.* Though it was eventually expanded for a book, the essay form remains the most focused on issues of spirituality and religion and consequently fits nicely in this category.

Other anthologies of this type are dedicated specifically to the stories of gay priests and brothers, some of whom write their stories under aliases to avoid the obvious, potential ramifications to their ministries of publicly admitting their sexual activity. Jeannine Gramick's *Homosexuality in the Priesthood and the Religious Life* contains seven autobiographical chapters,[7] and James Wolf's *Gay Priests* contains two essays that explore the particular concerns of gay clergy through autobiographical recollections.[8] Some of the anthologies mentioned earlier in this category also contain contributions by gay priests, and several of them are by ex-priests or former seminarians. Indeed, many of the gay Catholics in this study considered becoming priests at some point in their lives. These details should not be surprising given the homosocial and implicitly homoerotic nature of Catholic clerical culture.[9] The fact that so many of these stories find a link to the "clerical caste" is indicative of how pervasively the issues I am addressing affect and are endemic to the highest levels of the church hierarchy. Furthermore, it signifies how much is at stake in the struggle between sexual and religious identities for many of these autobiographers. I will return to this theme of gay Catholics feeling pulled to the priesthood in later chapters.

In addition to the above kinds of spiritual autobiographies, I have gathered a significant number of short articles written for various magazines and newspapers. Brief and focused in first person on the most particular life issues, these are the most concise of autobiographical acts. Coming from publications as diverse as *Christopher Street*, the *Advocate*, *Equal Times*, *U.S. Catholic*, the *National Catholic Reporter*, *America*, the *Humanist*, *Dignity* newsletters, a university newspaper, and even the *International Journal of Sexuality and Gender Studies*,[10] they represent a range of singular responses to being gay and Catholic and are often written in response to particular issues or questions. Along this line, I have also gathered a number of published interviews with gay Catholics. Interview responses are usually somewhat spontaneous and do not undergo the same textual editing process normally given to written narration; hence, these are the most fragile of autobiographical acts, primarily due to the explicit editorial intervention of the interviewer. I draw on these in my analysis only for purposes of corroboration. Nonetheless, most of these fit in the "spiritual" category. These include three selections from David Shallenberger's *Reclaiming the Spirit*, Mark Thompson's interview with Joseph Kramer in *Gay Soul*, Thomas Stahel's interview with Andrew Sullivan in *America*, and Paul Crowley's interview with Richard Rodriguez in Ferraro's book.[11]

Of the many book-length autobiographies included in this study, the majority do not fit so neatly in this "spiritual" category. John McNeill's *Both Feet Firmly Planted in Midair*, however, is definitively spiritual and is as such reinforced by its subtitle: *My Spiritual Journey*. McNeill is a former Jesuit priest whose publications on Catholicism and homosexuality have been seminal in the field. This autobiography is his most recent book, coming after his trilogy of theological reflections on religious and sexual identities, and telling his life story through the prism of his spiritual struggles. Because of his career as a priest and then a psychotherapist, it could also be called a professional autobiography (a category I will soon address). A good portion of the text not only deals with the way his gay self-awareness influenced his vocational decisions but also recounts many of his struggles with church authorities over his ministry.[12] Fenton Johnson's *Keeping Faith* also belongs here because it focuses on his internal struggle to reconnect with his Catholic roots — via an exploration of Catholic and Buddhist monasticism — after years of anger and alienation.[13] Finally, Brian McNaught's *On Being Gay* and *A Disturbed Peace* fit largely in the "spiritual" category. These books, the first a revised reissue of the second, are not traditional autobiographies in the sense of mapping out a life trajectory. They are, instead, collections of essays organized around issues of growing up gay, coming out to friends and family, building relationships, and being gay in the church. His style, reflective of his experience as a motivational speaker, is to affirm his gay Catholic readers through the telling of his own life experiences.[14]

To the extent McNaught deals with gay culture separate from religious themes, his books might also be positioned in the next category: autobiographies centered around *cultural* concerns. I use the term "culture" in a deliberately broad sense, referring to a terrain of meanings and significations associated with specific communities or identities. Andrew Sullivan's *Love Undetectable* brings together three extended essays interspersed with autobiographical acts, which address ethical issues related to gay identity and culture, especially in light of what it means to be HIV-positive today. Because his work is involved with constructing an ethics for the gay community, his Catholic identity tends to be more explicit than in some of the other book-length autobiographies in this category.[15] James Morrison engages in a sort of gay cultural criticism in *Broken Fever.* A professional academic, he is most interested in the way his gay identity emerged in his childhood and how it continues to emerge and form in the narration of his childhood. His Catholic identity is almost incidental in the text, but present nonetheless.[16] This is also true of Patrick Horrigan's *Widescreen Dreams*, a project very much like Morrison's, but constructed around a set of movies and television shows that both influenced and now reflect his own life trajectory. Horrigan, an English professor, knows how intimately connected are the tasks of autobiography and cultural criticism.[17]

Frank DeCaro accomplishes the same sort of combination in his much more lighthearted autobiography *A Boy Named Phyllis*. His is a cultural criticism of the middle class American suburbia in which he was raised, through the lens of his current life as a New York fashion editor. Again, his Catholic identity is obscured, but integral to his life story.[18] Where DeCaro focuses on suburbia, the four Catholic contributors to Will Fellows's *Farm Boys* all come from a farming background. Like the Holtz anthology discussed earlier, Fellows converts their reflections on growing up gay in farm culture to text. Together, their stories reveal not only the difficulties of being gay in a rural community but also the lifetime impact of agricultural life and appreciation for the work ethic it instills.[19]

Richard Rodriguez also fits in the category of cultural autobiography because of the centrality of his Mexican-Indian-American identity. In *Hunger of Memory* and *Days of Obligation*, Rodriguez, a well-known media commentator, is primarily arguing in his books against bilingual education and affirmative action programs, which he feels work against people of Hispanic background becoming full-fledged Americans. His Catholic identity is configured in a much different way than many of the aforementioned autobiographies by white Americans. Rodriguez recognizes the cultural dimension of Catholicism and thus understands the imprint a Catholic upbringing leaves on one's personality. He knows this from his experience as an ethnic "minority" in America, and the close link between Hispanic ethnicity and Catholicism. A tension between Catholic identity and American identity, along with an ambivalence about what it means for him to be a successful American, underlie his autobiographies.[20] These themes and some of the same material are also reflected in an essay entitled "Irish Catholic," in which he articulates the influence of Irish culture on American Catholicism and the role it played in his own schooling.[21] In Rodriguez's texts, it is his gay identity that is obscured and, early in his writing, camouflaged. Although he has publicly acknowledged and claimed a gay identity, it is not ever mentioned in his first book and he only obliquely deals with it in his essay and the second book. He finally deals with his gayness more directly, but not without his usual nuance and subtlety, in his third book *Brown*.[22] As is true for those whose Catholic identity is obscured in their texts, his gayness and his relationship with his culture's machismo ideals still play an integral role in his life story.

Two anthologies address Italian-American heritage, a culture likewise intimately connected to Catholicism. *Hey Paesan!* features relevant autobiographical essays by Rob Nixon and Tommi Avicolli Mecca; *Fuori* contains a different essay by Mecca and a contribution by Philip Gambone. These are perfect examples of cultural autobiographical acts because Italian heritage is the central axis on which each of the narratives is assembled. Catholic identity is woven intricately into each story, though not as blatantly as it is with Rodriguez; but gay identity is at the fore, particularly in relation to gender concerns and Italian-American expectations of masculinity.[23] Rafael Campo's *The Desire to Heal* combines many of the themes traversed by these "ethnic" writers, in this case from a Cuban-American perspective: what is lost and what is gained in becoming a successful American; how that is affected by the mark of both an ethnic legacy and queer sexual desire; and how one negotiates these seemingly antagonistic identities. Campo is a physician and also critiques the culture of the medical field as he reflects upon his education and practice as a doctor. In addition, he has published three volumes of poetry which are autobiographical meditations on the same themes.[24]

Campo's book might also fit into the next category because he deals with some professional concerns. What distinguishes an *occupational* autobiography is the focus on the writer's professional career and how that career was altered by the acknowledgment of his gay identity. It is the same dilemma faced by gay priests, so these men are, in a sense, their secular counterparts. In some ways, these stories read like celebrity memoirs, but the emerging consciousness of gay identity over the course of their life trajectories makes them more complicated than simple memoirs. Catholic identity is, however, eclipsed by other pieces of their lives, as it is in some of the cultural autobiographies. José Zuniga's *Soldier of the Year* describes his fall from grace as a decorated sergeant in the U.S.

Army after going public with his gay identity. His Mexican heritage figures into the story, but not in any pivotal way except for his relationship with his father.[25] David Kopay's *The David Kopay Story* recounts his career as a professional football player (after a brief stint as a seminarian) and the saga of coming out in the culture of pro sports.[26] Similarly, Dave Pallone's *Behind the Mask* reports the fallout of his umpire career when his sexuality is discovered and he is falsely accused of sexual misdeeds.[27] I should note these latter two books are coauthored with journalists so they are not constructed in the strictest sense by the self about whom they are written. Even so, both Kopay and Pallone claim to have played primary roles in authoring and ultimately approving the final versions of their stories, and their locations as pro athletes lend an important range of experience to my study.

Two autobiographies stand in a category of their own because of their unique forms and the role of AIDS in their stories. The first, Robert Arpin's *Wonderfully, Fearfully Made*, tells his story from childhood to becoming a priest to being diagnosed with AIDS, and how his perspective is influenced by having to confront a fatal illness in himself and in his community. Arpin structures his ruminations in a sort of elaborated diary format, with each entry dated and addressed to particular persons. Most of the entries are addressed to a friend named "D" who, he says, "lives in Las Vegas and is a therapist to the stars." Others are addressed to family members and colleagues. The book then appears to be a series of letters written over six years, but covering his life history.[28] Fenton Johnson's *Geography of the Heart* is a memorial tribute to his partner Larry Rose, who died of complications from AIDS in 1990. Johnson, an extremely gifted writer, artistically weaves his own life story with that of his partner's to demonstrate how their relationship and its subsequent ending forever changed him. The very form of his autobiography acknowledges the way memory both affects and is affected by close interactions with others in our lives.[29]

The last set of autobiographies I examine fall under the heading of *coming out* stories. In a way, this is a problematic category to stand on its own because coming out, either to oneself, to friends or family, or in some public way, is a component in nearly all gay life texts. I will have more to say about the "coming out narrative" and its function in gay lives and communities later in this chapter; but for now, suffice it to say coming out is in reality a complicated journey in any gay life. When gay identity is made the focal point of a narrative, the coming out trajectory becomes isolated and appears more direct and predestined than is often the case. Many of the autobiographies I examine in this study are concerned with other identity markers in addition to gay identity, so the coming out narrative is either downplayed or problematized. Some, however, are explicitly about coming out, and this genre of stories has become extremely popular among gay and lesbian readers. Patrick Merla's anthology, *Boys Like Us*, is a collection of coming out stories by gay writers. The Catholic contributors to the volume are Andrew Holleran, Philip Gambone, Stephen McCauley, and J. D. McClatchy. Happily, all of them are professional writers, so their coming out stories are particularly compelling and creatively written.[30] Many of the best gay fiction writers have published compelling novels that are marketed as coming out stories, but are far from simplistic in their constructions of gay identity. This would be true of Andrew Holleran's *Nights in Aruba* and *The Beauty of Men*, David Plante's *The Catholic*, and Daniel Curzon's *The World Can Break Your Heart*, all of which I mention here because the writers have claimed in interviews that these novels contain autobiographical elements.[31]

These gay Catholic autobiographical acts provide the much-needed element of gay subjectivity that is at present so sorely lacking in the church's understanding of gay people. Taken together, they comprise a rich body of literature from which to theorize the important identity questions that need to be addressed in order to begin to overcome the problems in church teaching on homosexuality. First, however, it is necessary to understand some factors that make autobiography an appropriate, but not uncomplicated, source for this kind of analysis. Keep in mind the "limitations" imposed due to the nature of autobiography as a written genre: this is not a random sample of gay Catholics; it is a sample of gay Catholics who have committed their story to writing. Consequently, those who cannot write or be published, for whatever reason, are excluded. Yet even this limitation is at least partially overcome by some of these authors with the help of editors, in the case of anthologized autobiographical acts, and coauthors, in the cases of Kopay and Pallone. In any case, it should be obvious from the above survey that the life texts I am using in this study do represent a range of class, ethnicity, age, and experience.

Any one of these autobiographical acts on its own has certain things to say about gay and Catholic identity. This genre has, in fact, become one of the most popular ways of expressing and struggling with issues of difference and identity. But one gay Catholic life story is not adequate for seriously debating the kinds of problems I am addressing in this project. They tend to be inward and personal and less conclusive about the larger concerns of culture and society, except as these impact the individual. When these life stories are analyzed and theorized together, however, numerous conclusive possibilities are opened up. In the following section, I describe some of the theoretical implications of using the autobiographical genre as data. It would be simplistic and rather inaccurate to presume I am unproblematically bringing gay "lived experience" to bear on church teaching by using autobiographies. Yes, I am using lived experience (rather than scripture, tradition, or reason) as a tool of analysis and reflection, but it is experience as filtered through textual intervention. Certain conclusive possibilities may be foreclosed in this methodology, but the answers disclosed about identity and self-identification are eminently useful for building a more complex understanding of gay Catholic reality.

Using Autobiography/Surveying Theory

My mother's letter reminds me, too, that the figures I've used in constructing a mythology for myself about who I am and where I came from . . . exceed my grasp, don't do everything I want and need them to do for me, have a life of their own quite apart from the use to which I've put them, can in fact be used against me. And yet, without them, how else would I conceive of myself? What I've made of them is partly a fiction, but I can't live without *some* kind of fiction about who I am. For one thing, I would never be able to communicate my sense of who I am to anyone else without some amount of cutting, pasting, editing, quoting, sampling, shaping, framing — that is, without some kind of fiction-making.

— Patrick Horrigan, *Widescreen Dreams*

The focus in church teaching on sexuality as a "problem" has the effect of isolating and disconnecting one's sexuality from the rest of one's personality and life. Autobiography works against such isolation by revealing a self in context, connected to others in a complex web of personal relationships, living and working in particular places and situations over time. Personal narratives also provide a richer context in which to understand sexuality and sexual ethics. For example, while the public debate often frames the issue of homosexuality as one of "choice" (i.e., does one choose to be gay?), autobiographies reveal selves for whom issues of "free will" and "destiny" are much more complicated and nuanced than the public debate would imply. Indeed, these life texts function to disrupt such simplistic dichotomies and may help reframe the issue in ways which make more sense. Autobiography is also a useful resource for testing and evaluating the truth-claims made about the particular self by other agents. In the case of this study, church teaching can be evaluated in light of how gay Catholics write about their own lives and experiences. How valid, for example, is the split between homosexual orientation and behavior in these life texts? This same analytical eye can in turn be focused on claims made in other realms (political, psychological, societal, etc.), about gay identity.

What is the nature of autobiography and how does it function with regard to concepts of self, identity, truth and memory? Autobiography is an act of constructing both a world in which to make sense out of life events and a unique "self," so there is always a distance between the self of the text and the self who actually lives/lived (the life).[32] Figuring the relationship between the textual self and the life is the starting point of most autobiography theory: How much does the constructed self in the narrative resemble the flesh-and-blood person the narrative claims to be about? What can then be said about personal identity based on a self that is textually constructed? And ultimately, what are the implications of this theory on the position of the autobiographer as the privileged authority of his/her own life? If this self is a construction, what makes this rendering of the self any more authentic or authoritative than another author's rendering of the same character? Both readers and writers of autobiographies take the textual self/real life referentiality for granted; yet, it is helpful to expose these distinctions because we have direct access only to the text, not the person.

The notion of the constructed self in autobiography finds its origins in James Olney's groundbreaking work *Metaphors of Self.* Though each of us has a sense of self that we know privately and intuitively, it is only meaningful at an internal level. The task of the autobiographer is to externalize this self, to make it the subject of a text and impart a sense of that self to the reader through language. Internal consciousness and life experiences mean nothing until we supply a pattern and trajectory to make sense and meaning out of them. For Olney, metaphor provides this connection and meaning:

> The self expresses itself by the metaphors it creates and projects, and we know it by those metaphors; but it did not exist as it now does and as it now is before creating its metaphors. We do not see or touch the self, but we do see and touch its metaphors.[33]

Elsewhere, Olney discusses the complex interplay between the *autos* (self) and the *bios* (life), neither of which are complete or defined at the beginning of an autobiographical project. When the "I" shapes its autobiography, it "half discovers, half creates itself."[34] It is through the act of writing — producing written language — that the self and the life "take on a certain form, assume a particular image and shape, and endlessly reflect that image back and forth between themselves as between two mirrors."[35] When we read autobiography, we know the self not so much by the events and experiences narrated, but by the consciousness brought to that narration through the language of metaphor. For Olney, this process is reciprocal between the self and the life; the formulation of the textual self enables the life's own self discovery and creation.[36]

This separation between the textual self and the life is stressed over and over again by almost all autobiography theorists because it affects the kinds of conclusions we can make about the life behind its representation in the text. This is often depicted as an issue of truth vs. fiction. Some theorists want to disrupt the notion of autobiography as nonfiction and go so far as to insist there is no referentiality at all between the self and the life.[37] Others suggest the concept of a unified self as constructed in an autobiography is a fiction in itself based on modernist assumptions about personal identity.[38] These theories reflect postmodern critiques decentering the subject. One theoretical way around or through these debates is the concept of an autobiographical *persona,* something like a stand-in between the self and the life, which then functions as the subject of the autobiography and avoids conflating the subject and the self. This approach attempts to overcome the problematic terms altogether and still maintain a degree of subjective authority in the text.[39] For my part, I accept that the textual self is a construction and even a function of language, but I do not think this erases its reference to the life or diminishes its subjectivity; quite the contrary, I think it tells us a great deal about the life because the very act of writing one's life text is one of the most self-defining things one can do. My project obviously assumes and relies on the self-life referentiality of autobiographies: these textual selves represent real gay Catholics. These are stories of actual flesh-and-blood lives, most certainly constructed, but by no means fictitious.

So autobiography, as I use and understand it, is an act of representation: a signification of a real life. For Ken Plummer, the "life story" is precisely that: a story, limited by the language and metaphors available when it is constructed:

> *Whatever else the story is, it is not simply the lived life.* It speaks all around the life: it provides routes into a life, lays down maps for lives to follow, suggests links between a life and a culture. It may indeed be one of the most important tools we have for understanding lives and the wider cultures they are part of. But it is not *the* life, which is in principle unknown and unknowable.[40]

While Plummer is here reiterating the distance between the story and the life, he also recognizes the value of the story for getting "into a life." If the life itself is "unknowable," then autobiography provides one of the only points of access into a person's lived experience. I would further suggest it is a source to be privileged. The very creation of the autobiography is a moment of tremendous meaning in a life. Autobiography "does not show us the individual seen from outside in his visible actions but the person in his inner privacy, not as he was, not as he is, but as he believes and wishes himself to be and to have been."[41] Autobiographers present themselves as *subjects,* and their experiences as *they* assess them, in a world *according to them.* Far from being a limitation, this underscores the authority of these texts in relation to the lives they represent; and it makes them doubly useful as sources of data: *how* one presents one's life story can be just as revealing as *what* one presents.

But this still leaves some methodological questions unresolved. How do we assess and apply the truth claims of these life texts since we are dealing with subjective representations and constructed selves? Once we accept the proposition that autobiography is not exactly fiction, in that it references a real life, we need to come to terms with the fact that it is also not simply an historical account of a life or the events surrounding a life. Such historical accounts might be "verified" by a correspondence theory of truth, which would suggest elements of the story can be documented in other sources; but this simplistic approach does not account for the aesthetic dimension of autobiography, which could be said to reveal *narrative truth*. While biography may be assessed using a correspondence theory of truth, the *auto* is what marks these texts in a distinct way. In the words of Philip E. Baruth, "A reader does not go to an autobiography for a referential history; a reader goes to an autobiography for a subjective perspective *by* the author *on* the author."[42] The autobiographical narrative emerges in a sort of reciprocal understanding between the author and the reader, who both know the primary subject of the text is a self-identity that is a product of the author's memory.[43]

Memory is a crucial factor in the production of an autobiographical narrative and an important consideration in a discussion of narrative truth. To begin with, the mind simply cannot remember everything. It edits and selects based on what matters in the context of one's life and it deletes that which is seemingly irrelevant. Unlike a computer, however, which also edits and deletes, human memory is emotionally contingent and inextricably linked with human imagination. In terms of the self, memory looks back on a sense of self that has changed and continues to change over time. As such, the self over time seems fragmented, as exemplified in the oft-heard expression, "I'm not the same person I used to be." In the writing of a life text, however, the autobiographer engages the memory to reassemble the seemingly fragmented self. Yet memory is not static, and the way it activates the past is dependent upon the present. As Olney notes:

> Memory, at least in part, is an adaptive function, with a self-adjusting and self-defining plasticity about it, turning back to the past so as to position itself and us for what is to be dealt with in the future: it adapts continuously to changing circumstances, external and internal, to constitute the self as it is at any given instant.[44]

If memory is thus filtered through all subsequent experience, what does this say about concepts like accuracy and truth? Here again, Olney is useful. For him, these terms do not make sense because memory is by its very nature indeterminate: "To indenture it to its own first perception of how things are would be to deny memory's evident plasticity and its capacity for adaptation."[45] Memory is active. In constructing the life narrative, the autobiographer *remembers* — and reconstructs — the self, and narrative truth emerges. In a way, remembering is more revealing than first perceptions. Georges Gusdorf frames this in terms of truth: "In other words, autobiography is a second reading of experience, and it is truer than the first because it adds to experience itself consciousness of it."[46]

Concepts like truth and falsity become murky in this paradigm, but it is not adequate to simply cast aside concerns related to such concepts. After all, my project is addressing problems in doctrinal pronouncements by the church, and "truth," even with the contingencies I have noted, matters a great deal in the world of moral guidelines. By now, it should be clear it is best not to assess narrative truth in terms of accuracy and factual details; instead, we can shift the focus to other matters. Bregman and Thiermann use internal coherence requirements in their assessment of death and dying autobiographies. They expect consistency between the way characters in the story are portrayed and how their actions reveal them to be. Similarly, they ask for the narrator and the protagonist to bear a reasonable resemblance to each other. Ultimately, the story should not violate basic assumptions about how people behave.[47] In a sense, the life story should "ring true," and when certain elements of the text do not, it provides the opportunity to question why. Such instances of "falseness" can be the most revealing moments in an autobiography because they often signal divergences between ideals and reality. It can also signal divergences between the world views of the reader and the author. In any case, this leads to a complication and reevaluation of assumed perceptions and given truths. Making these divergences visible is one of my primary goals.

Narrative truth needs to be taken on its own terms and recognized for its own value. I tend to align myself with critics like Gusdorf who frame autobiography as a "truer" reading of life experience because it adds consciousness to the experience. It takes advantage of both insight and hindsight — the "If I knew then what I know now" phenomenon — examining one's life trajectory in light of current circumstances. The risk, of course, is the erasure — the forgetting, perhaps — of previously held perspectives and feelings that disrupt and complicate current consciousness; but these are precisely the kinds of divergences that make for a richer analysis. In Ken Plummer's sociological study of sexual stories, he shifts the focus from truth and falsehood to truth and consequence.[48] I want to follow this lead and focus on the implications of these narratives. For gay Catholics to tell their stories at this point in history is a bold challenge to deeply held, traditional beliefs about sexuality and sexual identity. It threatens not only the boundaries of what constitutes morally acceptable relationships but also the boundaries of Catholic identity itself. My hope is that my exploration of these gay Catholic autobiographies will make their truths more consequential by beginning to unravel the assumptions underlying problematic church teaching on homosexuality.

Autobiography, Identity, and Personal Meaning

I see identity now not as a fixed destination, but as the locus of all we've forgotten, all we know, all we'll never know. It's the site of imagination and desire, always on the verge of discovery and fulfillment.
— Rob Nixon, "Avondale"

Since identity questions, both sexual and religious, are central to my project, an examination of narrative identity is in order. In this section, I am interested in something more specific than the self, which I conceive as a collection of identity pieces. Identity here stands for the collective set of characteristics by which a self is known and recognizable as fitting into a particular group, in this case gay and Catholic. Even when an autobiographer's self-identity is presented as a given, the construction of the life text implies a concurrent construction of both self and identity(ies), which could be called the process of self-identification.[49] Let me start here by returning to Olney and his assertion that the self is only known, even to itself, by the metaphors it creates. In Olney's theory, there is a sense of narrative language as a doorway into the self, both realized and constructed. For identity, the pieces of which form the structure of the self, this can be pushed even further. Identity, at once singular and multiple, is formulated entirely through language, and narrative gives it its particular shape and substance.

Paul Ricoeur philosophically discusses narrative identity by distinguishing between two usages of the term identity: "identity as sameness" (*idem*), marked by continuity and permanence over time; and "identity as self" (*ipse*), marked by continuous refiguring and reinterpretation. Noting that human lives become more readable when transformed into narratives, Ricoeur states, "In the application of literature to life, what we transfer and transpose in the exegesis of ourselves is the dialectic of ipse and idem."[50] In Ricoeur's framework, autobiography is configured as a sort of "narrative hermeneutic of the subject," in which the self "cobbles together its identity by constructing a life-story that uses the resources of various narrative fragments."[51] This dialectical process gives rise to a self (con)textualized by narratively configured identity markers.

A key point here is that identity is molded and assembled in context, not only of the self's totality but also in relation to present and past circumstances. This follows Erik Erikson's admonition that autobiographical events need to be fixed in the moment of writing and in the history of the writer and his time.[52] The autobiographers I examine are narrating their stories in a contemporary context in which public discourse and media images have become increasingly sexualized even as Americans remain reticent to talk seriously about sex. It is also a highly politicized atmosphere, in which asserting and claiming a gay identity has become the basis of political action in the gay rights movement. Gay identity takes a particular shape based on expectations of the gay "community" and those who stigmatize it, and telling the story of one's sexual identity has become a way of coming to terms, so to speak, with difference. The availability of gay identity as it is conceived today is not unproblematic with regard to autobiographical narratives. On the one hand, claiming the identity (coming out) is a strategy of information control. By disclosing himself, a gay man no longer has to worry about managing the information of his sexual identity but rather his social situations and relations in light of his disclosed identity.[53] Coming out is, in this sense, a liberating gesture and the gay "community" applauds and almost requires the gesture as a mark of self-esteem.

On the other hand, it is often this coming out imperative which drives and defines the gay life story to the point where gay identity is "standardized." Gay people today can find readily available versions of gay identity in the proliferation of coming out stories and stage theories related to coming out. The whole process of coming out has taken on a mythic narrative structure of its own, with concomitant truth claims about the psychological benefits of doing so.[54] Goffman notes that the voluntary disclosure of a stigmatized identity is usually configured in autobiographies as the final, mature, well-adjusted phase in the self's moral career — "a state of grace."[55] While it provides a framework around which to organize the details of negotiating sexuality in one's life, this coming out narrative can intrude on individual autobiographies and act as a heavy handed interpretive force in the construction of narrative identity. "This model of coming out, by itself, exhibits little concern for how lesbian or gay identities are socially constituted, for how they are intersected by other arenas of difference, or for what sort of collective political action might develop from an assertion of one's lesbian or gay identity."[56]

Of course, people often try to orient their lives toward a model which is presented as an ideal possible "self." In many Christian conversion stories, for example, when the self is reborn with a Christian identity, he/she will strive to imitate the model of Christ. The autobiographer will construct the self after the conversion as close to this ideal as possible, even as the narrative as a whole reveals shortcomings toward the ideal. According to Karl Weintraub, "When a man's inner compass is set on the pursuit of such a model form of being human, . . . The essential contours of his life and personality are prescribed.... The entire objective is to make his being conform, as fully as it can, to its normative ideal."[57] Weintraub's words can be especially applicable to the model of gay identity in the coming out narrative. Gay life stories can be "distorted" by the expectation to narrate a trajectory of coming out that matches the ideal model. Paul Robinson affirms this in his analysis of gay autobiographies. He observes how the narratives of the three contemporary gay autobiographies he analyzes are manipulated by the authors to conform to the standard model. He especially notices a "tendency to paint a blacker picture of the closet years than seems warranted."[58] This is similar to Christian conversion stories in which the preconversion years are painted as more hedonistic than warranted. For the gay "convert," the closet represents the period of time when he was "lost" before being "found." Robinson classifies this as a literary strategy, which it may be, but some writers may not perceive a choice to construct their story in any other way. This can be especially true when the writer comes from a Christian background in which these kinds of narratives have meaningful resonances.

The issue at hand revolves around narrating a unique and individual gay identity in an environment in which the communal gay identity is so powerful and articulated. Individual gay life stories are easily assimilated and subsumed into the story of the group. But this too is a complex matter. Yes, the gay Catholic autobiographies I examine do repeat some of the patterns of the dominant narrative, but they also disrupt the narrative in other ways. This is particularly true of the more gifted writers whose narrative technique overcomes linear models of finding sexual identity. Several of the authors depict a relatively happy childhood; some are still struggling with what it means to live a gay life; some of the writers simply do not fit into the expectations of the "community"; and many express some degree of ambivalence about it. James Morrison resists what he calls the myth of the collective because he perceives the collective as a false entity. His remarks about a gay rights rally he had attended are indicative:

> As much as I long to repeat experiences of collective transcendence such as those I associate with the time of my coming out, I'm suspicious of them, still and always, as the denial of genuine otherness. When you learn that I am gay, you still know nothing of my self, *even of my sexuality*, except what you think you know about gay people; and when I was in that life-sustaining crowd at the rally in Ypsilanti, I was not among people any more "like" me, necessarily, than I was in my sixth-grade classroom.[59]

Such ambivalence is to be expected. When a gay person finds himself in the company of other gay people, he will surely observe differences in himself that complicate his association.[60] If absolutely no ambivalence about the identity exists in the narrative, then it probably does not quite "ring true," and we need to ask why the narrative is ordered in such a way. While it could be construed as conforming to a gay ideal, it could also be interpreted as a resistive response to oppressive church teaching, which functions at the other end of the extreme by completely marginalizing gay identity. My analysis will uncover how normative ideals (both from the church and the gay community) are negotiated in the lives of gay Catholics, how they deal with "falling short" of the ideal, and to what degree these life stories are usurped by such models.

Despite these cautionary notes about communal identity and expectations, I do not wish to diminish the importance of the gay community in making the production of gay life stories and gay identities possible in the first place. For these narratives to be told and to flourish, there must be an interpretive community to hear them. The presence of a more visibly defined gay and lesbian community since the late 1960s has allowed for the creation of a shared history, identity, and politics. Life stories emerge from and contribute to this environment. As Ken Plummer puts it, "The one — community — feeds upon and into the other — story":

> As gay persons create a gay culture cluttered with stories of gay life, gay history and gay politics, so that very culture helps to define a reality that makes gay personhood tighter and ever more plausible. And this in turn strengthens the culture and politics.[61]

These stories represent the stories of a people whose existence was previously ignored. They reveal a communal reality and a set of beliefs about the meaning of gay and lesbian identity at this historical moment. In the words of Olney, "Autobiography renders in a peculiarly direct and faithful way the experience and the vision of a people."[62] This folklore of stories is transmitted from generation to generation, "complete with ritualistic days and marches — Stonewall, Gay Pride, Aids [*sic*] Awareness, etc. — which help to provide a sense of shared history."[63] In this respect, these autobiographies are sacred texts, canonized by the lesbian and gay community. Debates over the real cohesion of this community notwithstanding, the trope of communal identity is ubiquitous, powerful, and meaningful; and the existence of a gay culture — and by extension, a "people" — is undeniable in America today.

The church inadvertently contributes to the cohesion of the gay community by lumping all gay people into one marginalized category, as exemplified in church teaching that treats homosexuality as a singular phenomenon. Collectively, gay Catholic autobiographies depict the multiplicity within that community. They not only fill the void between church teaching and gay and lesbian reality but also replace the silence that would isolate gay Catholics from each other. When a gay Catholic writes his story, he is responding to a need for other gay Catholics and those who love them to know they are not alone. "The call of the human other, the neighbor, for justice and compassion secures the ethical and political aspects of forging a narrative identity."[64] Although the majority of the autobiographers I examine in this study are not aware of the many theoretical concerns related to this genre, they do have a sense that telling one's life story is vital to becoming a self and finding one's voice. In doing so, they challenge those who would marginalize them, and they do justice work for the entire community. "Storytelling from this vantage becomes a sacred act; authority is transferred from external figures and forces, to the newly discovered authentic and interior self."[65] They perform a service by bringing flesh and blood to church teaching that effectively disembodies them, and by giving life to otherwise theoretical moral arguments. In autobiography, they find the space to make personal meaning and express new forms of spirituality, and in the process help both the church and themselves to find their "soul": "To write a life, or to tell a life, is to wager that an exegesis of the self's untold story will pay rich dividends in one's quest for authenticity and integrity."[66]

The dividends of authenticity and integrity found in the narrative self will spill over into the broader Catholic community when we carefully attend to what these autobiographies have to say. These sacred texts collectively reveal what it means to be gay and Catholic in America at this time in history. In so doing, they also reveal how and why church teachings on homosexuality fall short. Examining how gay Catholics construct their life stories and author their own experiences restores a certain level of gay subjectivity to our understanding of sexuality and legitimates representations of gay Catholics as full human beings. The following exploration of sexual and religious identities as these autobiographers narrate them represents an exegesis not only of sacred texts, but of sacred lives as well.

Chapter 2

Narrating Gay Identification

But for another second the rock was still in midair, and it was *that* second when I knew that, whatever else, I thought Craig's *body* was beautiful; that I would have to find a place for such knowledge among whatever other knowledge I could forge; that my future life, which I could not before imagine, would depend on it; that in this way the lack I had perceived within me might yet be overcome.

—James Morrison, "Saved"

In Andrew Holleran's quasi-autobiographical novel *The Beauty of Men*, Lark, the protagonist, decides he needs "something very gay" after visiting his mother in a nursing home. He quickly drives to the weekly session of Gaytalk, a group forum for discussion of gay issues led by a variety of guest speakers. As he scans the mostly middle-aged group of men around him — in a chapter of the book aptly titled "Talking About It" — he ponders how difficult it must be for the facilitator to come up with a new topic every week: "What is there to say about being gay? Coming out is the central story, told over and over again, like people describing how they found Christ."[1] With that statement, Holleran lays down the central question this chapter will address with regard to these gay Catholic autobiographers: what is there to say about being gay? For Holleran's character Lark, there is nothing more to say about being gay. The repetition of coming out stories, each one bearing the "Once I was lost, now I'm found" theme, has become tiresome. The stories do not reveal anything original for him. He is bored and is probably disappointed not to find a young man in the crowd to pursue. After all, being gay is about sexual desire, is it not? What is there to talk about? Yet Lark still attends the meeting and seems to be seeking a different answer to his question than his cynicism would suggest. So, what *is* there to say about being gay? How *does* one talk about it? Is gay identity simply a repetition of the same story over and over, or is it something more complex?

This project is premised on the idea that sexuality can be configured as an identity category, so it is helpful to understand what terminology like *sexual identity* signifies. As I proposed in the previous chapter, "identity" represents the collective set of characteristics by which a self is known and recognizable as fitting into a particular group. A gay man labels himself as such because he *identifies* with other men who experience their sexuality in a similar way, even as he *dis*-identifies with those same men in other ways. This process of identification and dis-identification is a function of language in that it is a way of articulating and defining his erotic desires in relation to the rest of himself. The *self*, then, is comprised of various identities and fragments of identity, which are formulated and (con)textualized entirely through language. The autobiographical project brings this into sharper focus through the construction of the textual self via narrative identities. How gay sexual identity is "narrated" is the subject of this chapter.

At first, it may seem odd to use erotic desire as a factor around which to organize an identity. Why, for example, should men who like to have sex with men want to gather for intellectual discussions, or sing together, or play bridge together, or do any of the vast array of activities available in gay social clubs? The answer lies in understanding how such skepticism about sexual identity is actually reductive of what sexuality is and what it represents. Quite simply, sexuality is more than sex. Sexual *behavior* is usually a component and an expression of one's sexual *orientation*, which is "the preponderance of sexual or erotic feelings, thoughts, fantasies, and/or behaviors one has for members of one sex or the other, both, or neither."[2] Even the Catholic Church recognizes the difference between orientation and acts, as I have already made abundantly clear. The prevailing belief is that sexual orientation is relatively fixed and extremely difficult to change, while what one does with that orientation in terms of sexual behavior is completely a matter of choice. The missing link that helps to overcome this binary economy is found in the realm of sexual *identity*. According to Ritch Savin-Williams, sexual identity "represents an enduring self-recognition of the *meanings* that sexual feelings, attractions, and behaviors have for one's sense of self. This self-labeling occurs within the pool of potential sexual identities that are defined and given meaning by the cultural and historic time in which one lives."[3]

Sexual identity represents an integration of one's sexuality, both orientation and behavior, with one's sense of self. Claiming a gay identity is a way of making sense of and giving meaning to the erotic desires and the intimate connections experienced by men who have same-sex desires. It is first of all an insistence that sexuality is much more than sexual acts. A 1974 study of sexual identity concluded, "The [gay] community provides criteria for locating a sexual identity that differ from that of the stigmatizing society in that they do not specify acts of sex, but *feelings* of romantic or emotional sexuality as the basis of homosexuality."[4] This should not, however, be taken to imply that sexual identity is simply a different way of talking about a core sexual orientation, which is often perceived as immutable and inborn. Yes, a gay man may feel he was "born this way," and many of the autobiographers I study express such a feeling, but adopting a gay sexual identity is something much more and even different.[5] Barry D. Adam interviewed over a hundred men who enjoy sexual encounters with other men, not all of whom position themselves as gay or even bisexual. He concludes that "both gay and nongay men tend to locate themselves in relation to a language of emotional and relational engagement rather than to a sexual 'essentialism' per se."[6] This is significant in that the assertion of a sexual identity represents a moment of profound emotional subjectivity. A gay man locates his sexual identity not only in relation to his interpersonal affiliations but also in relation to available categories of sexual identity, which are invested with various meanings and social connotations.

Postmodern theorists like Foucault are quick to remind us that identity is not a stable category, and sexual identity categories can be restrictive of new pleasures and alliances. For Foucault, sexuality is "produced" through discursive strategies which reflect prevailing power structures. These constructed discourses give rise to "identities," which need to be policed and controlled. The shift in the discourse of sexuality to persons rather than acts is problematic for Foucault because it subjects the person (the "homosexual" and even the "heterosexual") to new regulations and expectations. Even if a gay man experiences his sexuality as a given, it is only because he has internalized the *discourse* of sexual identity.[7] While I find this theoretical framework convincing, I want to resist the tendency of postmodern theory to effectively erase gay subjectivity and agency. While we are all limited to a certain degree by the discourses of sexuality we inherit, we must and indeed do make self-narrative choices within that discursive framework. Deploying these identities may foreclose some possibilities for self understanding, but it also discloses others; narrative identification can be productive and revealing. Foucault remarks, "We must not exclude identity if people find their pleasure through this identity, but we must not think of this identity as an ethical universal rule."[8]

Foucault's words are cautionary because sexual identity might be useful as a descriptive mechanism, but it can too easily become prescriptive, and its effects are deep. In the words of Laurel Schneider, "Regardless of its origins, the individual's assumption of homosexuality as an identity has an effect on social organization and on physical bodies that is both real and enduring."[9] At the same time, identities should not be perceived as fixed entities. They are built upon, added to, fragmented, and even disposed of. I believe most gay people know this intuitively even if they would not theorize it quite this way. Most of these gay autobiographers spent part of their lives identifying as heterosexuals. Their self-definition shifted as they learned more about their sexuality and made different choices about their sexual identity. "Coming out" thus reveals the fluidity and partiality of all identities, and "unbinds us from any sense that we can establish a fixed identity completely and forever."[10] My goal is not to reify any single or static portrait of gay identity but rather to find what these gay Catholic men share in the way they narrate their individual experiences of gay sexuality. Against this backdrop, it will be clear that gay identity is not a singular phenomenon. As Jonathan Alexander says in reference to queer identity, "There remains the simple fact that we are obviously not all the same because we do not configure our specific sexual, emotional, and intimate desires in the same way."[11] And as Brian Utter says, "Categories become merely guide posts and the only definitions that are ultimately meaningful are self-definitions in which we affirm our own identity."[12] This represents a challenge for church teaching, which tries to paint all gay people with the same brush.[13]

Sexual identity is an articulation of the meaning of sexuality in the context of one's values and self-understanding. Some Catholics believe the church has a lot to learn about sexuality from gays and lesbians, who understand that "Sexuality includes interpersonal relations, emotions, our whole way of relating to one another as human bodies."[14] When understood in this way, it becomes clear why gay men would want to gather together in groups to do activities that seemingly have nothing to do with sexual orientation per se. It is important to note that heterosexual people do the same thing and likewise claim sexual identities congruent with the whole of themselves and their experience of sexuality. The heteronormativity of society masks the fact that being straight is as much a sexual identity as being gay — that the two depend upon each other for their definition. Some straight people may, in fact, question why gayness should be an identity at all — "why do you have to flaunt it?" — even as the "in-your-face" hegemony of heterosexual culture marginalizes those with different desires and forces the issue. Gay people are effectively forced into an "other" space in which meaning making and self-definition are a means of survival. This is even more pronounced in the church, where the heteronormativity of sacred texts and traditions leaves a void and thus creates a space for gayness where absence and reality collide.[15] Without a way to make sense of sexual "otherness," that space remains a vacuum. Sexual identity represents a way of making sense in that void.

In the epigraph to this chapter, James Morrison awakens to his emerging gay desire as a "knowledge" for which he knows he will have to find a place within himself. He intuitively knows, even as a fourteen-year-old boy, that the void he senses inside can only be filled with this "knowledge." It is a piece of himself, one of the identities that will form — construct —

his self. His future life "would depend on it." Rob Nixon similarly understands the way desire becomes a place within the self, so much more than just a feeling, but a space where identity resides:

> There are places we visit. There are places we inhabit. There are places we can't go. There are places we can't leave. There are places that exist beyond our imaginings. There are places we dream. There is a longing so real it becomes a place, an identity, a home.[16]

For these autobiographers, being gay is an integral part of who they are. Their sexual desire informs and completes their self-knowledge. It guides them toward the kinds of intimate connections with others that will resonate in their hearts and occupy that place within themselves that feels like home.

So, we are back to the same questions I raised earlier: What *is* there to say about being gay? How *does* one talk about it? Is gay identity simply a repetition of the same story over and over, or is it something more complex? In the world of these particular autobiographies, certain patterns and themes do emerge, and the portrait of gay experience they provide is often strikingly similar in important ways. It is not, however, a monolithic experience, as the texture of their diverse lives reveals. I should reiterate here that these gay men also share a common religious identity, which unavoidably colors the way they experience and narrate their sexual identity. How these men experience being gay is deeply influenced by their Catholic upbringing and many of the examples I cite in this chapter reflect that influence. In a way, it is artificial to isolate one or the other factor because both sexual and religious identities resonate in the core of selfhood and directly concern human fulfillment; and each of these men embody a host of other identity pieces which make them so much more than any one of these pieces alone. On the other hand, given the faulty assumptions about sexuality in church teaching and the ignorance of so many Catholics about the reality of gay experience, a focus on sexual identity is in order. That is what I will examine in this chapter.

Being Gay—Coming to Terms

When the foreigner enters the native's terrain, the lesson *should* be that whatever difference we think has thus intruded was really already there all along, in some other form, but unseen, effaced, or denied. It is a lesson nobody knows as subtly, perhaps, or as powerfully, as the gay child: the child who longs, so deeply, to be like the others, who is taken so readily to be like the others, since the crucial difference is not "visible," but who sees reflected in the difference of others a difference that has already been gleaned, or discovered more fully, with terror, or with wonder, in the self.

—James Morrison, *Broken Fever*

For most of these narrators, any hint of being gay began with an awareness of feeling different when they were young. This sense of difference was not at the time necessarily linked in a conscious way to sexual desire, but many of them link it in retrospect to their emerging sexual identity.[17] Philip Gambone says, "Feeling different is the predominant experience of my childhood and adolescence. Most gay Americans can report the same thing."[18] He attributes this feeling not only to his gayness and his Italian Catholic heritage but also to a host of other factors in his personal history. Another Italian American, Tommi Avicolli Mecca, was convinced he was the only boy in his world who saw boys' faces in his sexual fantasies:

If there was one word to describe my childhood, it is "lonely." An overwhelming, unbearable loneliness. Loneliness walked through my days, became my nightmares. I remember Christmas Days when I sat alone near the tree in the living room, looking into a kitchen full of relatives and family friends, feeling left out and thinking how unwelcome I'd be if they knew I was queer.[19]

Toby Johnson remembers when he was little feeling like he was "from outer space. I think that was the way I sensed my being different — not being part of the human race — being homosexual. There is something about being gay that just doesn't fit."[20] He eventually chose to enter religious life because he felt called to be an "alien" and that was the closest he could get. Frank DeCaro humorously configures his childhood difference in the context of his equally weird suburban family. He likens his family to *The Munsters*, who thought they were completely normal:

In my mind, Frank and Marian [his parents] were Herman and Lily Munster, look-alikes for Frankenstein and Vampira; my grandmother was Count Dracula in a housedress. I was cast — by default — as Eddie Munster, the pointy-eared were-kid with fangs and a Little Lord Fauntleroy suit. But I felt more like Marilyn, the family's ugly duckling cousin. This unfortunate girl, golden-haired, with delicate features, was the blond sheep of the family — totally unlike her relatives, but bound to them nonetheless.[21]

In DeCaro's portrait, he is different, but he feels like the normal one in a strange environment. His use of the Munsters turns his difference back on those around him and affirms his own uniqueness. Patrick Horrigan uses Barbra Streisand in a similar way. He found himself drawn to her when he watched *Funny Girl* as a boy. Horrigan recreates his realization that there was something very special about her as he reviews the plot of the movie. He could tell this "ugly duckling" (Barbra Streisand as Fanny Brice) had an "inner life" that mattered more than what anyone else might say about her, and in fact, it seemed better to be her than anyone else in the world. "In that moment, she made it supremely okay to be cast out. Because of her, being rejected acquired beauty and dignity. She became someone to turn to, someone to emulate."[22] Even though he would still feel different and rejected at times, he had the sense that his difference could be distinctive and even beautiful in its own way. Mark, one of the contributors to *Reclaiming the Spirit* conceives of this "presence of difference, of not really fitting in," as a spiritual gift of being gay. He envisions a spiritual "ancestry" for gay people, through which the legacy of difference allows gay people to be compassionate ministers of healing.[23] While this legacy is certainly double-edged and can induce a sense of cynicism and bitterness, Mark's notion might explain why so many of these men wanted to be priests or join religious communities at some time in their lives.[24] As Fenton Johnson speculates, "Youngest of nine children, a loner in childhood, teased by my classmates...maybe that was the beginning of my consciousness of being a monk."[25]

Almost all of the autobiographers had some sense of their same-sex desire in their childhoods even if they could not name what they were feeling. Some of them date this awareness very early and link it to their feeling of difference. James Morrison explicitly understands how gay identity is socially constructed even as he maintains that this identity might "precede awareness, understanding, or experience of such desire." As such, he can not remember a time in his life when he was *not* gay.[26] Along this line, Frank DeCaro states, "I was *born* gay. It just took sixteen years for me to figure it out."[27] He ultimately "figured it out" in his junior year of high school when he fell in love with a boy from his geometry class.[28] Rafael Campo never allowed himself to fully explore his sexuality until well into his college years and yet he says, "I had been attracted to men as long as I could remember."[29] John McNeill knew he was sexually attracted to other males "even in early childhood," which made him feel hopeless and evil because he knew the church would not accept this.[30] Dave Pallone knew a career in baseball was in his blood — "it was something powerful inside me" — by the time he was in seventh grade; "But something else was in there, too. Something I didn't understand. Something I would later come to think of as 'the other me'."[31] William Hart McNichols felt his calling to the priesthood around age five, "not too much earlier than the time I began to experience a glimmer of my given sexual orientation."[32]

Similarly, Brother Jonathan knew he was attracted to men as early as five years of age: "I have a recollection of this, as well as an equally strong awareness that this was not something I could share. It was my secret."[33]

As a boy, Richard Rodriguez was embarrassed by his sexual imagination. His feelings made him suspect dimensions of the world existed for which he could find no precedent in his own sphere.[34] He learned early on that he would need to guard this part of himself: "For I knew nothing was so dangerous in the world as love, my kind of love":

> ... from an early age I needed to learn caution, to avert my eyes, to guard my speech, to separate myself from myself. . . . Or to reconstruct myself in some eccentric way. . . . My eyes looking one way, my soul another. My motive could not be integrated with my body, with act or response or, indeed, approval.[35]

Rodriguez learned to disguise his feelings and act in ways that would not betray his desires. When he had a boyhood crush on Billy Walker, he threw a rock at Billy's "beautiful face" because he loved him.[36] He did not have any context for dealing with or understanding his attraction to Billy, so he acted against it. Rodriguez wondered when his desire would match the images of love and family he saw depicted in the books he was assigned to read. He would study pictures in history books to find the persons who stood out or looked like they did not belong there. He read books about encounters between peoples in the old American West and read the proximity and convergence of races and continents as erotic: "I was looking for the precedent that made me possible. . . . I was looking for physical inclusion in the world. I was amassing an encyclopedia of exceptionalism for my own use."[37]

Fenton Johnson had known he was drawn to men from the earliest consciousness of his body. He perceived this as a curse by which he had been chosen by God, a sort of special temptation thrown his way to use as a means of proving his virtue. "I felt singled out in that way, except that where the saints always seemed confident that God was on their side, I was alone."[38] In high school, he tried dating girls and he tried to feel some of the heterosexual desire his classmates so vocally effused. "I decided passion was something other people felt. I concluded that I was an aberration, one of a kind, an emotional eunuch with a heart of stone."[39] As a teenager, he came face to face with the deafening silence surrounding the whole idea of homosexuality in his world. His family lived by a monastery in Kentucky and the monks would often visit them for fun-filled evenings of food, drink, and dancing. He was named for one of the monks, Brother Fintan, who abruptly left the monastery when Johnson was young. When Johnson was sixteen years old, however, Fintan (no longer *Brother* Fintan) returned with a male companion for a New Year's Eve Party at his family's home. They were received with the usual hospitality and Johnson eagerly looked forward to hearing more about Brother Fintan's "date":

> Afterward I listened for the customary postparty gossip. Had Fintan arrived with a woman, the household would have been abuzz: *who is she? Might they get married?* Had he brought a mere friend, there would have been idle chatter: *Nice man. Needs a haircut.* But: Nothing. My namesake and his companion might never have sat at our table.[40]

In that moment, Johnson understood why Brother Fintan had been asked to leave the monastery; and while the silence reinforced his sense of isolation, he felt a new kinship with his namesake that made him feel he was not alone.

The silence in childhood and adolescence around homosexuality was deafening in many of these gay lives, so much so that they had little or no context through which to understand and interpret their emerging feelings. For Johnson, he found nowhere to go and no one to turn to, no model of what his feelings might mean in terms of finding someone else to love: "Growing up gay in an isolated hill town, I had never encountered so much as a hint that others might share my particular landscape in the geography of desire. I understood this as the defining fact of my life: the utter invisibility of any resonant construct of passionate adult love."[41] When Lon Mickelsen grew up and heard stories of gay boys meeting in high school, he thought "it must have been on another planet." In his Minnesota farm community, he had no points of reference nor any role models for being gay: "It's not that homosexuality was frowned upon. It simply didn't exist."[42] But this vacuum of gay experience is not peculiar to farm culture and isolated American hill towns; gay boys in cities and suburbs often faced a similar void. Andrew Sullivan, who grew up in a town just south of London, echoes Johnson's experience of a sort of loud absence: "At school, the subject was everywhere and nowhere: at the root of countless jokes and double entendres, but never actualized as a reality or as something that could affect anyone we knew."[43]

Even schools and libraries were inadequate sources of information. Allen Barnett found only three relevant books in his local public library when he was sixteen years old, and the librarian made him feel very uncomfortable when he checked them out.[44] I remember going to the public library in my own home town to find information because there was no one in my life I felt safe asking. All I found were a few paragraphs here and there in books on sexuality in general, and I remember hoping I was just going through a phase because the alternative sounded too abnormal and marginal. For gay boys coming of age in suburban America before the advent of the Internet, the range of information on homosexuality available to children and teens was extremely limited.[45] Any information provided in schools before college usually provided no help at all and sometimes contributed to the unsafe atmosphere for gay boys. Frank DeCaro recalls his high school health class, taught by a male gym teacher who "possessed all the sensitivity of a pit bull with hemorrhoids."[46] When the class reached the chapter in the text on homosexuality, the teacher said, " 'I can't tell you what to think about ho-*mo*-sexuals, . . . Personally, I think they should shoot the bastards.' " DeCaro relates his predicament:

> I hated him, but did nothing. I never reported him to the superintendent or told my parents how his lectures made me feel. How could I? To do that would be to admit that I was gay . . . and I was not yet prepared to stand up and tell everyone. Instead, feeling like an alien in the most familiar of surroundings, misshapen and beleaguered, I suffered in silence.[47]

His teacher may represent an extreme example of blatant intolerance, but DeCaro's feelings are only too representative of the heartbreaking loneliness endured by so many gay boys in school.

Going to college afforded many of these men the opportunity to more freely explore their sexual desires, but their context was still limited and they struggled with what being gay meant in terms of one's identity. James Morrison captures the disparity between homosexual and heterosexual visibility: "What could I know of marriage, then, except what I could learn from all that daily surrounded me, or from every movie in the history of the world? But what could I *ever* know of the joining together of men, except what I might have gleaned from Laurel and Hardy, or else could teach myself?"[48] When Philip Gambone went to Tanglewood for a summer internship, he developed feelings for his roommate Andrew, who would talk about the church's "antiquated" teachings on matters of sex, including homosexuality. "All of this talk was academic, but my heart was pounding with excitement. If Andrew was sending signals in my direction, I didn't know it (after all, I had no context in which to read any signals)," he says. He later realizes in hindsight how full of gay men Tanglewood was that summer.[49] Rafael Campo similarly found himself feeling affection and desire for Jorge, his college roommate at Amherst; but the two of them danced around their desire for a long time:

> Sadly, we did not know enough about who we were from our own experiences even to know that we might call ourselves "gay." The few words we might apply routinely to ourselves, 'faggot,' 'homo,' and

'queer,' were like the few words I occasionally borrowed from Spanish: they felt lost and foreign in my mouth and did not even begin to describe what I hoped might make my life more comprehensible. Internally, we only guessed at the depth of expression available to us in the lost language of our hearts, a language that we knew painfully must exist, but for which we had no teachers.[50]

Campo was aware of his desire, but the terms he heard used to describe people with such feelings seemed to vulgarize something he sensed was deeply meaningful in his soul. He and his friend busied themselves all the more intently with their academic studies as a way of staying close but also to avoid a level of connection that seemed altogether dangerous: "We cultivated as vigorously as we could our identities as premeds — the one thing Jorge and I could be together that was accepted and normal, the one appellation we could safely share."[51]

The derogatory terms these men heard while growing up and even into adulthood made claiming a gay identity even more problematic. Dave Pallone never felt especially "different" as a boy because he enjoyed sports and a certain camaraderie with other boys, but he knew as a teen that boys who "liked" other boys were called names. "During the 1960s, when I was in my teens, those words were used as weapons. Getting labeled a 'faggot,' a 'queer,' or a 'homo' was considered worse than being called a communist."[52] Sadly, not much has changed since then, and these terms are still used to attack young men who are perceived as different. The climate of fear generated by these abusive terms, combined with a reluctance to feel anomalous and outcast, causes many men to resist acknowledging their deepest feelings and desires for a long time. Matthew Bartosik tried to think of himself as bisexual for a while in order to hold on to some form of heterosexuality, even though he did not feel any erotic desire toward women: "I was unwilling to identify myself as gay. I liked being with guys and having sex with guys, but I kept telling myself that I wasn't 'gay,' or a 'fag,' or any of that." He would tell himself he and the guys he was with were "real men." " 'Gay' was something else. I believed that if I didn't say that — even to myself — then I wasn't."[53] James Morrison likewise grasped the significance of naming his sexual identity. Unlike Bartosik, Morrison was always aware of being different from other boys and he never fit the "real man" category. Still, he was reluctant to claim a gay identity, even when the man he loved in college finally came out to him: "I know he wanted me to say that I was gay too, but I was not, in spite of everything, unless I said it."[54]

Many of the autobiographers recount a time when they resisted their gay feelings, even to the extent of trying to be heterosexual or at least appearing to be, and this was usually related to their fears of being perceived as gay. David Kopay found himself in a particularly difficult situation coming to terms with being gay as a professional football player. He had a few obligatory sexual relationships with women, but he never really enjoyed them and he often fantasized about his friend Ted. In fact, he and Ted had been able to have some sexual experiences together when they were drunk. Kopay did not even feel naturally aroused by the one woman with whom he felt comfortable enough to marry. When he was with her, he knew he would have been aroused by another man, "but the fact was I still didn't consciously know how to go about it. And certainly at the time I didn't think of myself as a homosexual any more than Ted did. Homosexuals were the effeminate 'fags' or 'fairies' of my teammates' curses."[55] He could not identify with his stereotypical impression of being gay, so much so that when a female friend of his took him to a gay bar, he reacted furiously at the implication that he might "fit in" there. In truth, he was frightened by the fact that his friend had obviously detected his homosexuality, and he was petrified he might be exposed.[56]

Rafael Campo was struggling to repress and eradicate his sexuality when he was visiting prospective college campuses. Though he tried not to be attracted to any of the handsome men he met, he felt drawn to some of them nonetheless. At Yale, Campo found himself attracted to the student who led the tour and made it a point to speak with him personally; but when the student casually mentioned the active gay and lesbian group and offered to send information, Campo was incensed: "I acted appalled. I told him, abruptly and in my iciest voice, that he was greatly mistaken and that I had long ago decided not to apply to Yale at all, but my parents were forcing me to take the tour anyway."[57] Like Kopay, Campo feared exposure of the sexual identity he was trying so hard to cloak. Andrew Sullivan also worked hard to guard that no one else in school would ever know the truth of his erotic desire: "I learned to kill off sexual yearnings for the boys I cared about and fell for, and to reattach sexual attraction to boys who would never know and never guess." Sullivan reasons this is why it remained so difficult for him to nurture meaningful intimate relationships for many years.[58]

When he was twenty-one years old, José Zuniga developed a brief sexual relationship with a waiter named Russell. It ended shortly after it began because neither of them wanted to think he was a "fag." Zuniga says he closed his heart to love the night their relationship ended. He "escaped" the identity he feared he was becoming by enlisting in the army.[59] While in the army, he fell in love with a fellow soldier named Alex; but the possibility of this kind of love was still too much for him. He was eventually transferred to a different unit and was relieved the relationship could not be pursued. He was determined to avoid his homosexual feelings: "I had shut the door to my heart when I signed my name on a dotted line, swearing my allegiance to the Army. I had made a conscious decision, a promise to myself, to repress any and all sexual and emotional feelings."[60] He was later stationed in San Francisco and allowed himself to begin exploring his same-sex desire behind the camouflage of a marriage of convenience with a lesbian. He hoped that by burying himself in his work he would keep his sexual feelings at enough of a distance to feel safe:

> But my attraction to men was continuous, and it affected me in so many disparate and confusing ways that I felt myself faltering. My life was in emotional upheaval. God, don't let me be wrong. At work I maintained the facade of a happily married heterosexual, wearing the snug straitjacket I'd worn in public since my high school days.[61]

Eventually, Zuniga would find his denial too much to bear, and he would risk his standing in the military in order to openly acknowledge his gayness and escape what he came to conceive of as self-hatred.

Lon Mickelsen dated girls all the way through high school and college, "mostly to be one of the gang." He had his last steady girlfriend in college. Though he dated her about two and a half years and actually loved her, he finally broke up with her because he could not bear the incongruence of his actions and feelings: "I was dating her, but fantasizing about my male roommates."[62] Even Frank DeCaro, one of the most flamboyantly gay of the men in my study, tried to be straight for a time in junior high school: "I would have been happy to make *anyone* my girlfriend. I was so lonely and wanted so desperately to prove to my classmates and my parents — if not to myself — that I could be straight, despite mounting evidence to the contrary."[63] Fenton Johnson fought so hard against his feelings that he believed he had no capacity to give or receive love:

> I had so deeply and profoundly accepted this given that I had no awareness of my own self-contempt. . . . I had never heard words to describe the desires that of their own accord visited me. A man loving a man — I had never read of this or seen images of it; I had never experienced it in any way other than in the recesses of my own desire, a place so ugly (I assumed) it was beyond the pale of words. To defend myself against my desire I constructed an elaborate wall around my heart, so high no one could see in and I could not see out.[64]

Like so many of these men, Johnson tried for a time to be straight but did not succeed.[65] He spent his teen years avoiding physical contact with anyone of either gender. He hoped his first sexual encounter would feel like a gift from God; instead, he felt anger and shame: "On the morning after I first had sex — a few months after my twenty-first birthday — the man with whom I'd gone to bed put his hand on my arm. I shook it off. 'Touch me again,' I said, 'and I'll break your neck.'"[66]

Andrew Holleran relates the push and pull of desire and resistance in a short coming out story. Drafted into the army and stationed in Germany in 1968, he remained sexually inexperienced even though he was surrounded by men who were living gay lives. "Denial is always astonishing in retrospect, that one was able to compartmentalize oneself, to proceed with one part while putting another on ice."[67] On the night he finally allowed himself to have his first homosexual experience, he found himself subsequently washing his mouth out with soap in the shower room, where he would also be likely to see another man's body. After telling his roommate about his experience, he went back to the shower room:

> In truth to wash my mouth out again and wait for somebody else to come in and take a shower; the two instincts (desire and remorse) that would characterize much of my homosexual life to come — a life, I would discover, that was, just as my teenage self had suspected when it retreated into books, easier to read about than live.[68]

This dynamic between desire and remorse, acceptance and resistance, avowal and disavowal, is a recurring theme in the lives of these gay men as their sexual orientation emerges and they try to integrate its meaning into their selves. In large part, the struggle for these men as they come to terms with their sexual identity is how exactly to "be gay" in a world designed for heterosexuals. Feeling odd and alone, they find little guidance, a fragmented context, and no easy answers. Holleran describes the feeling through his character Lark, who finds himself trying to connect with someone (anyone) at the Gaytalk meeting. He wonders why gay men keep trying against all odds:

> Because, he thinks, being a homosexual is like trying to climb Niagara Falls. Eventually you have to admit: The water is going the other way. If you would only go in its direction, Life would take you right along downstream. Heterosexuality is like having a room ready for you at a hotel: The staff is expecting you — everyone knows his role. The homosexual shows up and has no reservation; he ends up outside, quite literally in the bushes.[69]

In narrating his sexual identity and how it has taken its present form, the gay man reserves a space for himself. Together, these autobiographies represent a river going upstream, following a path of new stories by which to navigate one's direction.

Being a Man—Gender Expectations

...Before too long, I'd dance and twirl,
turn diva in my bathroom mirror, ...

. . . .

I didn't care. I knew the melody
would never really set me free, I was
so utterly bereft. Yet *not* alone—

I knew a woman's voice was saving me.

—Rafael Campo, "Diva" in *Diva*

The feeling of difference I explored above is often configured as a failure to live up to masculine gender expectations. It is no surprise gender should play a primary role in narratives about sexual identity given that gender role subversion is an issue in debates about sexual orientation and identity. Heterosexual norms buttress a paradigm in which all same-sex activity goes against what is considered proper and natural for male and female bodies. For example, male bodies have traditionally been understood as active agents and female bodies as passive recipients in sexual acts; but same-sex acts seem to subvert this paradigm and thus become a perceived threat to the moral order of sexuality. So, "men behaving like women" becomes as much of an issue as the fact that men are having sex with each other. Most theorists today separate the construction of gender from the category of "sex," which is the anatomy of bodies as male or female.[70] Gender, which relates to concepts of masculinity and femininity, is a social construction built on top of bodies. This is why we can speak of the concept of *gender identity:* how a person experiences his/her gender and makes meaning out of it in relation to his/her body. The traditional assumption has been that "normal" gender identity occurs when one's expression of gender matches one's anatomical sex. This has, of course, been called into question by those who project gender markers that differ from what is traditionally expected. This conception of gender as a construction on the body casts gender as something people do, rather than something essential about who they are.[71]

The separation of sex and gender allows for a more meaningful understanding of concepts like masculinity and femininity, the performative aspects of gender. As such, being biologically male and "acting like a man" are two very different things. *Masculinity* is the culturally contingent and temporally varied configuration of practices that represent manhood. Though it is often mistaken as natural and given, the content of this category is not monolithic. In our patriarchal culture, masculinity has been associated with practices and attributes that seemingly uphold male dominance in society. Aggression, strength, toughness, power-over, control, muscles, etc., could all be said to be elements of masculinity as conventionally understood. Theorists sometimes refer to this as "hegemonic masculinity," because it exalts and upholds one vision of manhood to the exclusion of all others.[72] This is precisely where gay men encounter trouble: hegemonic masculinity in today's popular American culture relies to a great extent on the repression of male-male eroticism. Gayness then becomes whatever is expelled from hegemonic masculinity. Men who demonstrate enough qualities or attributes that are considered "feminine" — "men behaving like women" — are suspected of being gay, whether they are or not. Gay men then experience any "nonmasculine" traits as doubly marginalizing.[73]

Almost all the autobiographers in my study encountered "trouble" because they failed to live up to masculine expectations. Interestingly, their "feminine" traits (all the ways they were not conventionally masculine) often revealed themselves at an early age, well before these boys were "sexual." This had the effect of alienating them from other boys at a time when they were just beginning to sense an inner attraction for them. The recurring patterns of traits perceived as feminine and the strategies these authors recall for dealing with their resulting alienation are strikingly similar. Patrick Horrigan notes about his school days, "As a rule, guys hated me because I had female friends, I was a sissy, and I was a top student." He also suspects there was something about the way he inhabited his body that made him fodder for other boys' hatred.[74] Like so many young gay boys, he had to face daily insults being shouted his way — "you faggot" — and the embarrassment of it all prevented him from confiding his pain with anyone else. Yet he knew he identified more with girls and women than other boys:

> I resented my effemininity and hated the masculine entitlement other men and boys seemed to flaunt at my expense....I sought revenge in being an excellent student, and I comforted myself by playing the piano with aching sensitivity. But in the tough world of boys and masculinity, those things counted for almost nothing.[75]

Horrigan hits on the key issue here: what counts and what does not in the world of boyhood and adolescent masculinity. Being good at sports and excelling in physical education classes definitely counts; being a good student and preferring aesthetic endeavors usually does not.[76]

Horrigan relates a very telling story from when he was thirteen years old. It was 1976 on the night of the television premiere of *The Sound of Music*. Horrigan had already seen the movie three times in the theater and he could not wait to see it again. That day, however, his family had gone to a Philadelphia Phillies game and got stuck in traffic on the way home.

Horrigan was out of his mind at the thought of missing even one minute of the movie, especially because he had been dragged to a baseball game he did not even really enjoy. Sitting in the car, his mother became exasperated with him. Here they had superbox seats at the stadium — something most boys would love — and all he could do was think about *The Sound of Music*. "All of this meant, somehow, that I wasn't learning to act the way a boy ought to act (preferring Hollywood musicals to baseball games and making a big fuss over it),"[77] Horrigan observes. Boys who would be men were always supposed to be sports fans. Otherwise, something seemed "wrong" with them.

P.E. class was the site where one's "manhood" was put to the test. Several of these autobiographers recall the "Darwinian atmosphere of gym class,"[78] where their masculine inadequacies would be fully exposed for the taunting of their classmates: "Gym entailed games, but its atmosphere could never have been mistaken for that of play. The games were brutal and primal."[79] Frank DeCaro, an otherwise straight-A student, was called a "faggot" every day of school through junior high. He remembers gym class being an exercise in forced humiliation with no remedial help available, especially for an overweight "sissy":

> In English, if you were a nimrod and didn't know that "a lot" is two words, you could get all the catch-up help in the world. But if you couldn't slam-dunk anything but a doughnut, you and your incredible shrinking self-esteem were made, time and again, to prove just how bad you were at balls — kick-, soft-, basket-, and dodge-.[80]

Robert Arpin was also a "fat" kid, so it made playing sports that much worse: "Teasing and being laughed at were part of my life from a very early age."[81] Brian McNaught recalls feeling "paranoia" in gym class, especially in the locker room — "the sacristy of straight male machismo" — where one's masculine "fitness" or lack thereof was on full display. Whenever he goes to the gym as an adult, McNaught thinks about how many upset stomachs he had as a kid, "fearing that I would strike out at bat, drop the fly ball, cry in front of other boys when I hurt myself, get into a fistfight, cross my legs or look at my fingernails in an 'unmanly' manner."[82]

Although most of the autobiographers in my study who discuss their experience with sports and P.E. share this sense of dread and failure, there are a few exceptions — enough to dispel any bizarre notion that sports can "cure" homosexuality. Dave Pallone, for example, fell in love with baseball from an early age. José Zuniga says he "detested sports," especially "battleball" (dodge-ball), and he felt himself an artist at heart, but he was never the stereotypical outcast on the sidelines. By the time he went off to college, he had become a real fan of football.[83] Rick Noss enjoyed track and was captain of his high school basketball team in his senior year.[84]

David Kopay always loved sports, especially football, and he insisted on playing even when his parents discouraged him from doing so because of a knee problem. Kopay's experience on the other side of the sports divide, however, illustrates how tightly interwoven masculine expectations are in games like football. Kopay says from grade school on, "the curse words on the football field are about behaving like a girl. If you don't run fast enough or block or tackle hard enough you're a pussy, a cunt, a sissy."[85] Even more revealing is his discussion of the imagery used to coach the team: "The whole language of football is involved in sexual allusions. We were told to go out and 'fuck those guys'; to take that ball and 'stick it up their asses' or 'down their throats.'"[86] The overt implication is to emasculate the other team by metaphorically making them the passive recipients of homosexual acts. For gay boys who do enjoy sports, this kind of imagery and language only reinforces the fear of appearing feminine or being perceived as gay. The "protection" sports provides in terms of masculine appearances feels thin and contingent on their continuing to follow the "rules." Young gay men intuitively understand their desires are literally dangerous in a world of sports that is constantly policing the boundaries of masculinity.

No wonder so many gay boys find solace in aesthetic and intellectual interests, even as this increases their risk of being perceived as "feminine." Richard Rodriguez would withdraw with five or six "intelligent" but physically clumsy classmates to a distant corner of the field during his high school P.E. classes. From that vantage point, they could engage in witty, sarcastic conversation to scorn the "animal" games being played around them.[87] John McNeill felt very different from his peers when he was a child because of his "total captivation with the beauty of classical music" and his general "sensitivity to the beauty of music," which he interprets in retrospect as God's special gift to him in his gayness.[88] Drama class and theater were Frank DeCaro's salvation in high school, for he finally found a place where his effeminate traits could be applauded as "acting." In the school musical, he was part of an "in" group, and he even found himself abandoning other outcasts who had previously been his friends.[89] He saw in flamboyant performers like Elton John, Charles Nelson Reilly, Liberace, and Paul Lynde the opportunity to take his effeminacy and sell it back to the world as "fabulousness."[90]

Aesthetic interests offer some gay boys and men the chance to turn their difference back on itself and find a niche. Patrick Horrigan's interest in movies offered him an escape from the ordinariness and loneliness of his world. He could imagine possibilities for himself to be transformed from a misfit into a "star." In acting out a role, he could try on different identities and explore who he really was. For Horrigan, drama is a hiding place where one finds oneself: "And once your solitude has turned into drama, in a way you're no longer alone; someone is always bearing witness to you, even when no one else is around, because at least *you* are bearing witness to you. You become your own best friend."[91] Horrigan's words express how the artistic life overcomes loneliness but also relies on it. Clearly, the aesthetic realm provides not only liberation but also a hiding place for some of these autobiographers, even in adulthood. Sometimes the line between finding and avoiding oneself is quite narrow, as James Morrison so eloquently writes:

> The more undeniable my sexual identity became, the more aestheticized I willed my intellectual or emotional or cultural identity to be. It was like so much in my boyhood, a way of asserting and disavowing a gay self, at one and the same time.[92]

Claiming an "artistic" identity is a way of defining oneself as "creative" rather than "weird," and it offers a way to live on the margins of masculinity and still find some level of acceptance and self-empowerment. Richard Rodriguez discusses this rather cynically in his assessment of gay life in San Francisco, where he has made his home as an adult. He reasons that since society condemns homosexuality as being a sin against nature, homosexuals have been forced to find their redemption — a way of ordering their existence — outside nature, in the aesthetic realm. Society has also assumed gays are always childless (increasingly not always the case), so Rodriguez configures the aesthetic impulse as a way for gay people to arrange "a decorative life against a barren state." But he is not sympathetic with this impulse and he makes a point to trivialize the aesthetic, comparing it to a list of ornamental and decidedly unmasculine pursuits: "Homosexual survival lay in artifice, in plumage, in lampshades, sonnets, musical comedy, couture, syntax, religious ceremony, opera, lacquer, irony. . . . The impulse is not to create but to re-create, to sham, to convert, to sauce, to rouge, to fragrance, to prettify."[93] Rodriguez scorns gays who invest themselves in the aesthetic, even as he engages in the aesthetic project of writing his own intellectual autobiographies.

In fact, Rodriguez hides himself to a great extent behind beautifully written literary criticism, flowing rhetoric, and an ever-present preoccupation with the line between public and private selves. Though he has publicly acknowledged his gay sexual identity, he never directly identifies as gay in his first two books.[94] His allusions are always indirect and couched within external observations and related concerns. Just as the content of much of his writing deals with his struggle to balance his Mexican and American identities, his narrative identity reflects his struggle to write intellectually and creatively and still live up to masculine expectations — "machismo" in his cultural background.[95] He discusses the three F's that were expected of Mexican men: *feo, fuerte, y formal* (which he translates as rugged, strong, and steady), and ponders how he may or may not have measured up to the nuances of this definition of manhood. He was often concerned that his education was making him effeminate: "And it seemed to me that there was something unmanly about my attraction to literature."[96]

At the end of his chapter on gay San Francisco, Rodriguez seems to moderate his cynicism about gay aesthetics and shifts it toward himself as he sits in church during a roll call of AIDS support group volunteers. He notices a gay man in his seventies stand when his name is called and we get a glimpse of his own insecurities about how he may be perceived: "Something of the old dear about him, wizened butterfly, powdered old pouf. Certainly he is what I fear becoming."[97] Then, he seems to have a realization as he views these "saints" at the front of the church:

These learned to love what is corruptible, while I, barren skeptic, reader of St. Augustine, curator of the earthly paradise, inheritor of the empty mirror, I shift my tailbone upon the cold, hard pew.[98]

Perhaps there is more to the aesthetic impulse than Rodriguez first expressed. Yes, it may be a survival strategy that provides a veneer of acceptability for a marginalized position; it may be a way of reordering or reinterpreting reality; but it also reflects the human capacity to make life meaningful and to embrace beauty — a love of the "corruptible" in the face of death-dealing circumstances.

Besides the aesthetic and decorative, it is amazing the number of traits and interests that become linked to the feminine in these narratives because of the rigid code imposed by hegemonic masculinity. Gay boys who already know they are "different" become almost hyper-sensitive about the ways they do not meet the code. James Heckman wished he could be at his mother's side to cook, bake, and sew, but "only girls did those things." He had to avoid most of the things that really drew his interest:

Needlework, knitting, and crocheting fascinated me, and I really wanted to do them. But had I done them, I would have been ridiculed for being such a sissy. My uncle would have started it and it would have spread out from there. Even my grandfather would say, "Oh, you don't want to do that. That's girl stuff."[99]

Violations of the masculine code can be found in the smallest details. Both Patrick Horrigan and Brian McNaught recall the requirement for boys to hold their schoolbooks at their side on their hips, even if it was much more comfortable to hold them in their arms.[100] I remember balancing ridiculously large stacks of books on my hipbone in order to meet the code because I did not want to be late by going to my locker between classes, not realizing until later I was violating a different code by carrying around so many books. The boys in these life texts came to understand very early what was okay and what was not. Boys should: maintain emotional boundaries between themselves; always appear in control; enjoy and be good at sports; like to go to camp; not have too many female friends; not enjoy home ec classes; never cry; not be too neat; and most importantly, never appear weak. Violators were sissies.

One of the illusions of hegemonic masculinity is that real men are "perfect men" — tough, sturdy, strong, and most definitely at the top of their fields. While most men do not live up to the ideal, they find ways of accentuating the ways they do, and they can reap the benefits of the ideal by proving their heterosexuality. Since gay boys are constantly told they fall short of the masculine ideal, they often strive to be "perfect" in other ways. Many of these Catholic autobiographers spent their boyhood doing well in school, overachieving, or just being "good boys" in order to please their parents and teachers, to be "on top" in some way, and to redeem themselves from the fate of total ostracism and church condemnation.[101] Andrew Sullivan describes this as being "driven inward." He says many intelligent gay boys harbor grandiose ambitions or display precocious scholarship not because of any intrinsic nature, "but as a form of protection against the taunts and weapons of the people around them."[102] Gerald Allen was an exemplary high achiever: "I got A's in school. I was an altar boy *par excellence*. I was a liturgist and was master of ceremonies for big events. I was active in CSMC (Catholic Students Mission Crusade), Holy Name Society, Boys Club, and 4H Club. I did what the family expected of me and did it well. I did what the church expected of me and did it well."[103] Dan, one of the profiles in *Reclaiming the Spirit*, says, "I was always a good boy. I always did what they told me to do, and never got in trouble."[104] Mark, another of those profiled in this volume, was the one in his family everyone thought should become a priest, which he attributes to winning the admiration of his nun teachers by being a perfect student and always getting straight A's.[105]

The drive to please and be perfect is not without its costs. For many, it was a way of blocking their feelings. For Rafael Campo, it was his way of trying to contain and decipher his "discordant inner reality": "My cardboard report cards, like my bed and all windows and every classroom, were each another in a series of squares that contained me. My parents rewarded me generously for all the A's that were neatly held, like me, in tiny square boxes, and I pretended to be happy."[106] Philip Gambone sublimated his erotic desire for other boys throughout his high school years by busying himself with school work and lots of after-school activities.[107] James Abdo looks back at his own adolescence from his standpoint as a psychologist at a student health center. He fell into the same pattern he frequently sees: He cut himself off from his adolescent energy by doing what everyone in authority hoped he would do. Thus he was a real hit with his parents and teachers, but he suffered the rejection of most of his peers.[108] Similar stories abound. Toby Johnson and Tom Cunningham both talk about being "good boys" in school, doing everything right and developing workaholic study habits.[109] These habits also work effectively to subli- mate erotic desires as adults. Joe Izzo and Larry Sullivan both believe they dove into their careers in such a big way because they were avoiding their homosexual desires and trying to live "normal" looking lives. Eventually, both of them found the "normal" lives they had fashioned for themselves were quite fragile when they acknowledged their erotic attractions.[110]

The drive to be perfect is a running theme in many of Brian McNaught's autobiographical essays. Throughout his life, he was always a "good boy," getting A's in school, doing everything expected of him, and never giving his parents any trouble. He was always trying to prove himself worthy of love and respect. He even tried dating girls in high school and college and "seriously considered getting married on three occasions,"[111] because that's what good, successful Catholic young men should do. When he went to Marquette University, he was a daily Mass-goer and was labeled the "saint." He did not have a sexual encounter of any kind until he was twenty-one. As McNaught reflects on his life, he wonders how much of his life "is an attempt to prove to my folks that they didn't fail. How much of my life is an attempt to prove to the church that I am still worthy of its praise?"[112] McNaught ultimately realizes it did not matter how much he tried to be perfect throughout his life; he would always feel discounted in some way because of his sexual identity. It is tremendously frustrating for him:

> I am a good man, a loyal and loving son and citizen. I smile a lot, say please and thank you and give money to people in need. My home is wonderfully embracing. My relationship with my lover is nourishing and inspiring. My bills are paid; my dog is well-trained; my lawn is mowed; my flowers are the envy of the neighborhood and I always put down the toilet seat when I'm finished, so why do I sometimes hurt so badly? And why am I so angry?[113]

By emphasizing the quotidian ways he is a "good boy," McNaught demon- strates how much he simply wants to be considered "normal." He does not want to be defined solely by his sexual identity and he does not want to be excluded because of it: "My hurt resulted from wanting to be part of the group and knowing that no matter how good I was, how smart, how kind, how generous, I would never really fit in."[114] Although McNaught has now happily claimed his gay identity, there is clearly a part of him that wishes things could be different; but he knows he cannot change who he is and being "perfect" will not change how society views his sexuality. This disen- franchisement in the face of trying so hard to be fully accepted is what drives so many gay men to find spaces where they will fit, as I will discuss shortly.

Richard Rodriguez was also an excellent student and a high achiever. He was an obedient, organized Catholic schoolboy who by the fourth grade shelved his books at home alphabetically.[115] He uses Richard Hoggart's *The Uses of Literacy* to describe himself and to interpret the gains and losses of his academic success. The "scholarship boy," like Rodriguez, comes from a working class, "illiterate" background and finds himself increasingly distanced from his familial and cultural (Mexican-Indian) roots as he attains mastery of his education. The more he achieves at school, for which he is then mocked, the more he keeps to himself at home. The more he pleases his teachers, the more foreign he becomes within his own family and even to himself: "Here is a child who cannot forget that his academic success distances him from a life he loved, even from his own memory of himself."[116] Rodriguez frames this experience entirely in a cultural paradigm (what it means to become an "American"), so he does not consciously link his drive to be a "good boy" to his emerging sexual identity; but he does not ever directly narrate his sexual identity. The similarities of his experience as a "scholarship boy" to other gay "good boy" stories are striking. The quest to prove and find oneself involves the same search for affirmation and subsequent alienation from one's familiar world. For Rodriguez, the world he "lost" in his personal journey was culturally determined, but it was also heterosexually defined. Surely this was also an element in his feeling of difference at home — a factor that would make the divide between him and his parents all the more palpable.

Being at Home — Relating to Parents

My father is another man I love.
I love another man. My father is
A man who loves his parents, wife, and kids.
I am his son. The other man I love
Is someone very much like him, a man
Of honest words. And strong commitment. . . .

. . . .
. . . My father knows I run
Away in his direction. That I love.
That words I make are only words, that sons
And fathers love enough so that a knife
Can grow between two men, and take one's life.
I love my father. I am not alone.

—Rafael Campo, "Love Poem"
in *The Other Man Was Me*

Relating to one's parents as a gay child can be challenging, especially in a Catholic context. The parents in these autobiographies were almost all reared in the pre–Vatican II Catholic generation, when gay people were not as visible in society, much less the church; and when even the pastoral acceptance of celibate homosexuals was unimaginable. A gay boy grows up knowing his parents' feelings about homosexuals and usually believes coming out will cause a rift in his family. The implicit knowledge that his parents will perceive him as "flawed" if he is gay sometimes fuels the drive to compensate by trying to be "perfect" in other ways. In any case, parents may sense something different about their son, and this difference sometimes makes it difficult for one or both of them to connect with their son. As Joseph Kramer says, "We are outside of their frame of reference even before we are explicitly sexual."[117] This in turn may cause the gay son to pull away himself, creating a gradual cycle of ambivalent alienation.[118]

Sometimes parents already know their son is different, and they may even "know" he is gay, but they will not think of him that way until the word is spoken. Once again, sexual *identity* is about language and identification. J. D. McClatchy kept his sexuality a secret from his family until he was in his late twenties and in a relationship. He announced at the dinner table that he had something important to tell about himself, to which his mother replied, "Don't bother, I know what you're going to say." McClatchy's narration of his subsequent realization is so relevant to the material in this chapter, it is worth quoting in full:

> Of course she knew. What else could she have concluded, years ago, from all those afternoons I'd spent listening to Brahms in my room while my father took my sister to the football game, from my wanting to play house with the neighborhood girls when I was young and later insisting on late-night pool parties with the classmates in my all-boys prep school, from my acting out Eve Arden roles in our living room, from the too-glamorous dates I found for the proms — oh, from hundreds of things done and not done, felt and not felt. My parents could see as well as I the texture of my life, like a cobweb on the lawn that if touched anywhere trembles all over, so tender that it feels everything. But what was more important even than my "orientation" was that it not be spoken about. That was what my mother's interruption meant: *Whatever you do, don't put it into words.*[119]

For McClatchy, "Not-speaking-about meant not-dealing-with,"[120] and he wanted the feeling that his identity was no longer disguised; but his parents maintained their silence about it even after his revelation, implicitly refusing to embrace his sexual identity and all that meant for him. His parents preferred the illusion silence gave them; McClatchy wanted revelation and redemption. Yet from that night on, he felt a certain ambivalence about the whole thing and wondered if he had spilled the secret as a way of manipulating what his parents felt.

When Stephen McCauley's mother seemed to figure out the nature of his relationship with an older man who was his lover at the time, she raised the question. His affirmative response was all it took to send her into an emotional frenzy, after which she implored him not to tell the rest of the family. Later, after his father had learned the news and reacted similarly to the point of suggesting he should leave, McCauley wonders whether lying would have been better — if that is what his mother wanted him to do all along — and forever feels a disjunction between who he had been before he named his identity and who he was after.[121] Brother Jonathan felt his relationship with his parents would forever be shallow if he did not disclose what he felt was a vital part of himself. His parents accepted him but never spoke of it again, and he knows they never will have to talk about it as long as he remains in religious life and maintains his vow of celibacy.[122] Paul Albergo states, "My parents' approach to my gayness is denial. If we don't talk about it we don't have to deal with it."[123] The only time his parents did talk about it was when Albergo was president of the Washington, D.C., chapter of Dignity and appeared in a television interview. His parents saw it and told him he should be careful. My own parents stayed silent on the topic in spite of my work in the field. When I was on the board of directors of Dignity Denver and appeared frequently in the news, they never said a word to me about it; but then I never discussed it with them either.

Based on the accounts of the autobiographies in this study, there is no single way to characterize the relationships these men have had with their parents.[124] Growing up Catholic before Vatican II, most of the parents grew up in a church and societal climate that maligned and condemned homosexuals; but Catholic parents are as diverse in their opinions as the general population. Not surprisingly, some parents are supportive and some are not; some need more time than others to come to terms with their son's identity; and some never come to terms with it. Rick Noss came out to his parents in a note he wrote for them to read on their way home after visiting him for Labor Day. "My dad called me at 6:30 the next morning to make sure he caught me, to tell me he loved me and he didn't care." Even with such a positive attitude, there were great periods of adjustment between Noss and his parents. At first, they did not seem to want to meet any boyfriends; but eventually, they made a special trip to meet his boyfriend for Christmas. Today, Noss feels loved and supported by his parents, and knows he always has a home with them: "I can't describe how much they mean to me because of that."[125]

Other stories are not so easy. José Zuniga's father was an officer in the army and ran their home like boot camp. As a boy, Zuniga's toys had to be arranged by height, and no infractions against any of the rules were tolerated.[126] Though he believed his father loved him, Zuniga's father was emotionally unavailable throughout his life; and his rigidity inspired fear. Zuniga tried desperately to please his father, especially in his teenage years. The only time his father ever said "I love you" was when Zuniga was going off to serve in the Gulf War and his mother was gravely ill.[127] Though Zuniga had always felt closer to his mother and he suspected she knew his sexual identity on some level, she died before he came out. When Zuniga did come out and made a splash in the media for being discharged from the military, his father was quoted in the newspaper as saying, "I have no son named Joe."[128] Zuniga felt abandoned and did not speak with his father for over a year. Time, however, has an inevitable way of changing circumstances. In his epilogue, written just two years after coming out, Zuniga reports that he and his father were speaking again — on trivial matters, but speaking nonetheless.

Robert Arpin's parents had a hard time with his coming out. The only thing that moderated their loathing was Arpin's diagnosis with AIDS and their concern for his health.[129] David Kopay's mother became hysterical when he came out to her. In the height of her frustration, she told him, "I created you and I can destroy you, . . . I never want to see you again."[130] They did see each other again and had reached a point of "respect" for each other's positions as of the writing of his narrative.[131] Tommi Avicolli Mecca's experience is illustrative of how parents feel when they too have to "come out." Mecca dealt with his femininity by embracing it and flaunting it. After he came out, he began wearing makeup, dresses, and heels. He walked the streets of South Philadelphia in drag and heard the little old Italian ladies shout, "Don't you know you're killing your mother?" Their husbands would mutter, "If you was my son, I'd give you a good wallop to the head — that'd straighten you out."[132]

Mecca's parents had to face their friends and neighbors who saw their son dressed in drag every day. His father never really got over the shame he felt, but father and son seemed to reach an unspoken truce before the former passed away. Mecca's mother was always more open to learning about her son, but the two of them really became close only after his father died. Eventually, on her deathbed, she took steps to really make peace with him. She revealed a secret that speaks volumes about his father and his own masculine negotiations. His parents and uncle were driving one day and saw Mecca walking in drag on a downtown street:

> My uncle told my father to pull the car over, because he wanted to get out and beat the hell out of me. Momma had to physically restrain him. Poppa did nothing. As she told me this story, I was devastated. The rage I felt was unbearable. I wanted to run out of that hospital and cry, scream, anything. But I sat there listening to her

talk, knowing she had to get it out before she died: the final Mecca aria, that her father sang, her sister sang and I will one day sing.[133]

Mecca constructs this story as the final scene of an Italian opera — with all the passionate emotion of an old Requiem Mass — to convey the drama and tragedy families needlessly face because homosexuality is so stigmatized. In this case, family divisions were only bridged when death finally put everything in perspective.

It was easy for Frank DeCaro to love his father when he was a little boy and masculine differences did not matter so much; but as he grew up, their differences began to matter. DeCaro found more in common with his mother, and the two eventually became quite close. When he finally came out, his mother reacted coldly and became depressed until one of her best friends reacted neutrally to the news her son was gay. With "permission" from her friend to feel okay about it, she ultimately became "gay-positive."[134] His father was yet a different story. When DeCaro came out to him, his father ranted, "You mean all those kids were right all those years!" This hurt DeCaro because his father had always yelled at him for not fighting back. "Now it seemed he was joining my tormentors' ranks, doing to me what they'd always done."[135] Frank, Sr., never understood why his son had to be so open about his sexuality — he preferred that it remain a secret. For years, they found ways to hurt each other:

> I could no longer see the goodness in his heart or the reasons we'd nicknamed him St. Francis when I was a kid. It would be years before we became close again, and by that point, neither of us thought that day would ever come. . . . It turns out my father and I are a lot alike . . . both self-centered, both believing we were always right; each unable to say "I love you" even though we both knew it was mutual and true.
> The fruit *didn't* fall far from the tree after all.[136]

Once again, the stigma of homosexuality added unnecessary walls in a family. Because of the way gayness becomes overdetermined rather than situated among a variety of identity factors, other commonalities among family members get lost. Sadly, these divisions can persist and may only be bridged in times of crisis, if they are at all.

Being Oneself — Finding Home

Coming out, or rather coming *into* a gay identity, involves a sort of reinvention of oneself in response to shifts in one's sexual self-awareness. I want to resist the language that portrays coming out as "finding" oneself;

instead, I like to think of it as a re-narration of the self. For these autobiographers, coming out represents planks in the reconstruction of their
narrative identities. In the process of building their life stories, they fashion a description of sexual identity that makes sense with the whole of
their feelings and experiences. They narrate themselves into gay identities that reflect both their own unique qualities and definitions of sexual
identity currently available to them. If there is a sense of inevitability
in their sexual stories, it is revealed only in retrospect through memory;
but as I discussed in the previous chapter, that is the form and function of autobiography. In rereading the past, the autobiographer brings
a second consciousness to bear on it. The autobiographer refashions his
identity puzzle pieces in a new way that makes more sense with who he
has become.

Part of assembling this puzzle is figuring out where he fits. For several
of these authors, this quest is literally geographical. A recurring theme in
these narratives is the idea of "belonging" somewhere other than his place
of origin. This is not surprising given how many of them felt they did not
"fit in" while they were growing up. Usually, the geography is configured
as a difference between cities and suburbs or small towns. Gay "communities" in America have emerged for the most part in large cities and a few
"remote" tourist destination spots,[137] so other gay people are not usually
as visible outside of these areas. Frank DeCaro fell in love with another
boy in high school, and the two of them became schoolboy friends and
lovers. Of course, they kept their relationship a secret and did not even
really think of themselves as homosexual: "We had no gay identity then,
no sense of a gay community existing beyond the world we knew in Little
Falls."[138] He also recalls his boss at an after-school job and the neighborhood postman, who were both thought to be gay in his suburban town.
Both men ultimately committed suicide — casualties, as DeCaro says, "of
time and place, and the inhospitable nature of the suburban environs we
call home."[139] DeCaro would eventually escape his suburbia and reinvent
himself in the big city. Rafael Campo's moving away to college in Amherst
is comparable to DeCaro's feelings about the suburbs. Campo talks about
leaving "the confines of suburbia" and becoming someone else, a different
person: "The sun seemed a bit less out of reach."[140]

A remarkable number of these autobiographers extol New York as the
place where they feel most at home. In Ric Burns's PBS documentary *New
York*, the narration consistently refers to New York as the place to come
and reinvent oneself, much as the city has done throughout its history.
No doubt many of these autobiographers would understand that message
deeply. Andrew Holleran, whose novels offer a portrait of gay "circuit" life
in 1970s New York City, says of New York: "It was a place where you could
just leave everything behind and create yourself anew." He adds that the

thing that makes gay culture possible in cities is "that kind of anonymity and freedom, that detachment from your origins."[141] Frank DeCaro also mentions the "comfort of anonymity" he feels in New York.[142] This has all the sound and feel of "escape" or even "running away," and to a certain extent it is; however, it would not be accurate to dismiss this migration to the city as a shirking of responsibility or abandonment of one's family. Some of these men lose touch with their families of origin, but this is far from a dominant trend in this set of autobiographies. For most of them, the city atmosphere provides them with a place to feel at "home," which in turn gives them a better vantage point from which to view their families of origin more clearly, without the angst of feeling like the odd man out. Most of them continue to take family relationships seriously, albeit in different ways.

The city represents freedom, community, and refuge for gay men. For Tom Cunningham, choosing to remain in his New York assignment (as a Dominican priest) rather than accept a transfer to South Carolina meant "the end of the good Catholic boy who always does what he is told." It also meant the end of his active ministry as a priest.[143] Joseph Kramer felt liberated in New York: "My authentic self was terrified to express itself until I traveled to New York City at age twenty-eight and met men who were kindred spirits."[144] When Rob Nixon was young, his family moved from their Italian neighborhood in New Jersey to Florida, where he was the only Italian in his school class. In New Jersey, he was "weird"; in Florida, he became "exotic": He was The Italian. Nixon took comfort in being able to "hide" in this identity: "It became my mask, a cover for my oddness, an excuse for my theatricality, my strange way with a gesture or turn of phrase. I mythologized my difference. . . . Even the kids who disparaged me did so, not because I was queer, but because I was from New Jersey. Italian became the lie that saved me from the truth I dared not speak."[145] As an adult, Nixon moved back north to New York and let go of the identity he had fashioned to feel safe in Florida:

> I no longer needed to be a dancing minstrel show of Italianness to be accepted. I had achieved the gleaming city at last. Fully out on the streets of New York, I felt I had arrived somewhere, a destination where what had been hidden, disavowed, was given a name and a public face. . . . I found a physical site to inhabit, an architecture for my existence as a gay male in late twentieth century America. . . . I was gay, and the identity fit like a glove.[146]

Nixon's words reveal much about the relationship between migration and reinvention of the self. His experiences in both Florida and New York represent various strategies of identification — ways of constructing himself in order to feel safe and at home.

New York figures prominently in so many of these stories because of its size and ethos, but it is not the only city, of course. Other cities like San Francisco and Washington, D.C., also figure in these stories and these are described when the geographic move is meaningful to the author. In some cases, the movement is away from the city, and gay people by now have established a variety of lives in a variety of locales across the country. Fenton Johnson, for example, found gay life in 1970s San Francisco (where he too had moved to chart a new arrangement of himself) a bit too fast for him. He escaped to a small Midwestern college town in the early 1980s and remained there for a few years, only to return to a San Francisco changed by AIDS.[147] Some writers remain in surroundings similar to their origins and find other ways of refashioning themselves. James Heckman, for example, grew up on farms in Indiana and still lives among farmers in Wisconsin. He loves to go to New York periodically and knows he could have a "gayer" social life if he moved there, but that is not his home. As he puts it, "Agriculture is my life." For Heckman, farming actually helped him understand his sexual identity: "On the farm, I learned to appreciate nature, and for me being gay is a very natural thing. Some cornstalks do not bear ears of corn, some gilts do not have babies.... On a farm, you accept that some things are out of the ordinary. That has helped me to accept being gay."[148]

Richard Rodriguez moved from his boyhood home in Sacramento to go to college in Stanford — not too far, but far enough to make a difference. More significant to Rodriguez than the actual geography, however, is what his migration represented: "My departure would only make physically apparent the separation that had occurred long before."[149] Couched again in cultural differences, Rodriguez still understands how the migration from home begins before the physical geography changes. In his final chapter, aptly titled "Mr. Secrets," Rodriguez declares that the new version of himself — what he calls the "public person," the successful writer — that he fashioned in the "liberation of the city," would remain "distant and untouchable" to his parents.[150] Inevitably, the public self Rodriguez created when he moved away would also maintain some "private" dimensions, such as his sexual orientation, which would contribute to his feeling of distance.

A Gay New World?

The inner movement to reshape oneself with a gay identity begins prior to and apart from any geographical change that may or may not occur. As these life stories testify, most gay men experience an incongruity between who they are and who they are expected to become well before they can name this difference as something sexual. Claiming the gay identity ultimately becomes a matter of integrity. Though it is often framed and perceived as finding oneself, it reads more like an acknowledgment of an identity piece that has been hidden for some time; hence the imagery of being in the closet and coming out. Though it inevitably causes some pain and entails loss as any change would, coming out is usually narrated as a healthy decision. I suspect this is not only because it feels "true to oneself" — a question of integrity again — but also because it takes more energy to conceal one's sexuality and the relationships that result from it. Concealing it feels deceptive and honesty is freeing. As Brian McNaught says, "I no longer fear being discovered."[151] For McNaught, coming out was more than an issue of integrity; it was a matter of life and death. Hiding himself nearly cost him his life in a suicide attempt, a literal way of undoing the self he had become according to external expectations. He pledged to live according to the geography of his own inner compass and found it liberating: "My freedom began only after twenty-five years of hiding, of keeping my secret, of being what others thought I ought to be."[152]

Coming out and naming oneself as gay is a strategy that takes many different forms in these autobiographies, and an entire book could be written about the choices involved in taking that step. José Zuniga, David Kopay, and Dave Pallone each sacrificed their careers by telling their stories publicly. Though each of them paid dearly for their coming out and express bitterness about what happened to them, they all feel "healthier" and say they do not regret their decision. This says a lot about the centrality of this piece of identity. Coming out need not be a grand and public act; however, it is usually felt most deeply within the dynamics of one's most important relationships. Recall the poignant instances of coming out to parents I discussed above. Fenton Johnson's coming out to his mother is indicative of how significant and transforming these personal interactions can be. When he told her he was gay, when he spoke the word, she responded positively; but even if she had not, Johnson would have been forever changed by naming and claiming his sexual identity: "In that moment I felt our relationship transform itself from parent/child to that of peers. In that moment I acquired a sexual and romantic life. At thirty-two years old I became an adult."[153]

Johnson may have come out in the sense that he revealed a piece of identity he had been hiding, but his mother had already suspected it. Johnson's narrative moment is better described as a *coming into*, as I suggested earlier. In revising his self-image to include a gay identity, he also became a man, despite what hegemonic masculinity might otherwise suggest. He established the geography within himself on which to chart his sexual identity. These inner movements toward being gay are profoundly meaningful. Rafael Campo also uses geographic imagery to depict the inner movement to his gay identity. He writes of his thoughts during a medical lecture about people and diseases in foreign lands, and imagines a homeland for gay people:

> I began to daydream more deeply, instead, about the possibility of a kind of homosexual country of origin, a different and fabulously free New World, a place whose existence seemed plausible to me after so many long and tortured journeys I had made across oceans of disavowal to the deepest reaches of my heart. On each of these journeys, a vast and unexplored continent stretched before me there, in the shape of a man's body. I had the feeling that I was searching for something of tremendous value.[154]

Campo's quest is to find the space where he fits: his home, the place where the puzzle pieces of his identities come together to form himself. One of these pieces is his sexual identity, his desire for other men, which he has denied like "oceans of disavowal." This desire is physical and sensual and is located on the beautiful expanse of the male body.

The core of sexual identity lies in the heart of this erotic desire. For some of these autobiographers, it is in the moment of sexual connection with another man that they know they have arrived in a place where they fit, where the pieces of identity make sense. Philip Gambone experienced this consciousness when he was a boy messing around with another boy: "In some unverbalized way, I understood that erotically touching another boy—being with another boy that way—was going to be a fundamental, inescapable aspect of who I was."[155] Dave Pallone put off having a sexual relationship with a man until well into his adulthood. When he finally found an opportunity and allowed himself to do it, it was a breakthrough moment for him. "And I knew it was the real me touching him: the excited boy who groped with other boys in the shed, not the tortured guy behind the mask with women." Pallone felt in that intimate moment with another man that he was the person he had always imagined himself to be, and for the first time he felt love would be possible for him in the future: "Because now I knew who I was. For the first time in my life, I knew absolutely: *I was gay.*"[156] Peter Krask had his revelation the first night he shared another man's bed. He intuited a new inner harmony when the man kissed him gently on the ear and fell asleep beside him: *"You have changed your life."*[157]

Rafael Campo wrestles throughout his life text with the same-sex desire he had tried so hard to deny, and with its consequences. He spent many years afraid of it, wanting to be "normal," but he was unable to extinguish the desire he felt. When he was drawn to Gary, a flamboyant gay black man on campus, he found ways of dismissing his attraction by stigmatizing Gary: "I had neatly and efficiently converted his campiness into effeminacy, his raucous humor into poor taste, and his sexual confidence into a self-destructive addiction to promiscuous sex."[158] He eventually realized he was mostly afraid of how Gary and he were alike — he was afraid of himself: "Now I realize that for a long time what I had feared was my own humanity.... There is no medication to cure me, and only boxes of my own construction to contain me, whose walls allowed me to smash against them my own head."[159] He needed to find space for his desire within himself, not in some exterior landscape that would feel safer. Once he embraced the erotic attraction he already held inside, the puzzle pieces started to fit, and he could know the pleasure of desire: "Being gay was joyfully not to have a country of origin at all, only a place in my heart where a man was extending his arms toward me."[160] Campo comes upon this revelation in the poetry and stories he writes. He finds in the written word the power to reinvent himself with an identity that reflects his desire. He "finds himself" by narrating himself. It is the same revelation for each of these autobiographers when they finally say the words, even within themselves: *I am gay.*

But being gay also means figuring out where one fits in terms of communal identities. Like Richard Rodriguez, Philip Gambone explores the ways American identity pulls him from his cultural roots. Gambone, however, is more direct about the ways ethnic and sexual identity converge and play upon the person in analogous ways. Gambone writes at length about his Italian background and his Italian American identity, trying to sort out what distinguishes this category and what about it makes him unique. "What part of the whole person I am today is the "real" me, and what part is just the *bella figura* I was taught to present to the real world?" As he grows up and charts his own landscape as an Italian American, different from the path of his parents, there will be some inevitable disconnection from them. He ponders how his sexual identity is also a catalyst in this process:

And what is it like when the world you're being prepared for —
yes, isn't this exactly where the experience of many third-generation
ethnic Americans and the experience of gay Americans intersect —
when the world you take your place in as an adult is not a world your
family can follow you into?[161]

While it is expected that every person will chart a path at least somewhat different from his/her parents, this is further exacerbated for Gambone because of his gayness. He understands, moreover, how this path moves him even farther away from his people. In the process of becoming more "American" and "gay," he will explore a geography not only different from, but largely unfamiliar to the people he has known before. He will effectively find a new people, a new tribe.

One's inner geography is mapped in conversation with the gay communal landscape and all that being gay means — and this is the ultimate coming to terms. For almost every one of the autobiographers in this study, it meant and continues to mean coming to terms with his own difference from the "norm." It means an acceptance of the ways he is not masculine, of the ways claiming this identity will be liberating even as it reinforces his marginalized position. It means identifying — and dis-identifying — with others who are gay. Some gay men experience a certain amount of cognitive dissonance finding their position within the landscape of gay communal life and expectations. Other than the common bond of their sexual identity, they may have little else in common. Several of the autobiographers I examine express reservations about their fit in this larger puzzle. R. Roberts, for example, does so by criticizing gay subculture. When he was first coming out and exploring gay life, he visited bars, bookstores, and dance clubs. "I was struck with two impressions: first, I was very much attracted to the men and being with them; second, there was a subculture that was not attractive. I noticed a superficiality, a slavish conformity, a painful impersonalism."[162] I suspect Roberts was responding more to the ethos of the types of establishments he was visiting, which would feel that way even in a heterosexual setting, than anything endemic to gay culture per se. Larry Ebmeier echoes Roberts's sentiment when he describes "the outgoing, outspoken, socialistic, activist, flamboyant and fast-paced, dishing, camping-it-up type of people who seem to dominate when gays come together in urban areas." Much more the introvert, Ebmeier prefers a less visible segment of the gay community — the people who enjoy staying at home.[163]

For each gay man, the foray into the "gay ghetto" represents another step in the process of locating himself in the larger framework of gay culture. The process of gay identification involves a struggle to both claim the identity, which in some ways feels so right and seems to "fit like a glove," and not be trapped or limited by it. This echoes Foucault's cautions about the traps of identity and the way it can police and control persons. James Abdo seems aware of Foucault's theory and expresses his frustration over the current available descriptions of sexual identity. He notes the lack of definitive content in the categories of "gay" and "straight": "People self-select, and nobody knows on what criteria. . . . But when it comes to their individual identity inside, there is a lot of complexity involved."[164] Rob Nixon felt confined by the available sexual identity categories when he was just an adolescent: "As yet only dimly aware of the traps of identity, of the unnatural suffocation declared by 'us' and 'them,' I straddled worlds, negotiating rules and rites, searching for a geography that could welcome and contain all that I was."[165] Philip Gambone, always the good boy who tried to do everything right — like so many gay Catholic boys — hopes to find the geography that will contain him as he grapples with the expectations of gay identity:

> I still sometimes get too concerned about whether I'm gay enough, too concerned about whether I'm doing the queer thing the way I'm "supposed" to, still too anxious that the boat that will transport me to the fabulous Gay New World is leaving and I'm not on it.[166]

And so we come full circle. The metaphorical search for "home" brings us back to the questions first raised in this chapter. What is there to say about being gay? Is it just the same story told over and over again? The answer appears to be both yes and no. In this chapter, I have explored some recurring patterns and themes that emerge in these narrations of gay identity. These include the feeling of difference while growing up; some sense of sexual attraction at a very early age; the experience of silence on the subject of being gay; being objects of derision in school; the struggle between denial and avowal of sexual desire; various negotiations with masculine gender expectations; stormy relationships with parents, particularly around coming out; and finding a new geography through which to narrate oneself, both literally and figuratively. Yet no single portrait fits everyone. These narratives of gay identity unavoidably complicate simplistic and reductive conceptions of what homosexuality is all about. The fact that the content of American gay identity is amorphous is compounded by the way it continues to shift and change in response to historical circumstances. After all, it has only been some 130 years since "homosexual" was first applied to persons; and it has been less than 100 years since "heterosexuality" attained its popular normative status.[167]

At present, gay identity is marked by particular meanings and contexts, which may or may not resonate with all men who experience same-sex desire. Even so, it is an identity label embraced to some degree by all of the autobiographers whose life texts inform this study. They do so because they live in a cultural context in which powerful forces like the church and lawmakers tell them their erotic attractions matter. They do so in response to societal attitudes and messages designed to marginalize them. As William Glenn says in his reflections on being gay in a Catholic school, "My story is a version of the 'coming out' story of every gay boy or girl, and these stories will continue until the dominant culture, which suffers exquisitely from its own homophobia, withdraws its enormous and blinding sexual shadow."[168] I would like to think we will reach a point when sexual identity does not "matter" as it does now, by which I mean gay persons will be able to celebrate their sexuality and forge their relationships without societal stigma and church condemnation overwhelming them. Perhaps we are seeing movement in that direction as laws change and AIDS becomes less fatal; but the progress is uneven and contingent, so being gay still "matters."[169]

Based on these life texts, being gay is not just about men having sex with men. Yes, it is about erotic desire; but it clearly means so much more and it is performed in myriad ways, not just through erotic activity. It is deeply linked to constructions of gender and informed by a range of normative expectations. These autobiographers show how being gay is deeply embedded in their sense of self, emerging before they become sexual. Indeed, an astonishing number of these men never even had gay sex until well into their adulthoods, yet they recall performing in gay ways throughout their childhoods. The church would like to separate *being* gay from *doing* gay, but it is not that simple according to the life texts examined here. For many of these men, they were "doing gay" before they really came to terms with "being gay." Gay identity bridges the enforced chasm between orientation and acts. It encompasses feelings and behaviors that happen across lifetimes. Gay identity involves relationships, secrets, honesty, fears, hopes, decisions, love, and desire. In the words of Andrew Holleran, sexual identity "is also the thing around which our deep wishes coalesce: the desire for love, trust, fidelity, stability, a home, a companion, a future, all of that."[170]

For men who claim a gay identity, being gay and doing gay are inseparable. The church's monolithic vision of homosexuality seems sorely inadequate to capture the rich experiences of these authors. In the next chapter, I will take up the Catholic piece of these gay lives. My analysis will shed light on the ways being Catholic and being gay intersect and complicate each other. By surveying the way gay Catholic identity is performed in these narratives, I will provide a framework through which to understand how these identities are worked out in reference to each other. Here again, being and doing are not so easily separated.

Chapter 3

Orbiting the Catholic Axis

My mother worries about my association with Larry Faherty. . . . My mother has no reason to fear. I will always be attracted for the same reason that I will never become. Because I am a Catholic.

—Richard Rodriguez, "Irish Catholic"

T alking about religious identity is no less complicated an endeavor than talking about sexual identity. The same theoretical concerns with regard to the concept of identity in general apply. Like sexual identities, religious identities are not fixed but rather are dependent upon available categories which change according to historical and cultural circumstances. Religious identities are similarly worked out and articulated in relation to both self-understandings and communal expectations. This communal dimension, however, is particularly strong with regard to religious identity. Among its many roles and functions, religion is often concerned with boundaries that differentiate insiders from outsiders. Much as with ethnicity, members of religious groups learn what makes "us" distinct from "them," and this consciousness enhances the definition of their religious identity. The idea that religion is also partially a belief system further amplifies this sense of boundedness and consistency, to the point that words like "heretic" and "dissident" are deployed in some religious systems to marginalize those who do not adhere to the prevailing creed and/or code of ethics. But this ideological cohesiveness is illusory and is usually asserted when the boundaries of religious identity are contested by different interpretations of what it means to be a member. Such contestation is further exacerbated by the reality that religion is also deeply "cultural," replete with a variety of socially transmitted practices and customs that inform the way members interact with the world and with others.

For Catholics, the communal identity is reinforced by the strong and visible hierarchical structure of the church, with watchdogs like Cardinal Ratzinger who try to police the boundaries of Catholic identification. Ratzinger would point to ideological factors, such as adherence to certain doctrines or allegiance to the Pope, to define what it means to be Catholic; but this does not take into account the various cultural, political, and psychological factors which also contribute to the formation of Catholic identity. These factors are much more difficult to control and act on persons in subtle ways. This is the Catholicism that is less about adhering to specific beliefs, and more about a living system into which one is born. At this level, Catholic identity is not constructed by those who make the "rules" (i.e., Roman officials and the bishops) but rather is passed on and "learned" through particular Catholic communities and families. It is experienced more than taught. This is the Catholicism that permeates the lives of these gay men. That being said, I do not mean to overdraw a dichotomy between Catholicism that is directly "taught" (i.e., doctrinal) and that which is "passed on" (i.e., cultural). Though not always perfectly harmonized, these aspects are not mutually exclusive. Indeed, it is difficult to imagine one without the other, even for adult converts who study church doctrine but learn Catholic practice and culture within the context of particular parish communities. The question is, how do these aspects inform American Catholic identity today?

It might be helpful to begin this discussion with a dichotomy that is more familiar in the Catholic landscape today: the split between "liberal" and "conservative" Catholics. Although these terms oversimplify more complex positions, they are used and claimed by a wide range of Catholics and those who write about them.[1] The words denote ideological stances, and as such would seem to relate most closely to the doctrinal dimension of Catholicism. "Liberal" Catholics are usually cast as the ones who diverge from church teaching, especially on sexual, reproductive, and gender matters, while "conservative" Catholics are cast as holding to the "party line." But this construction is misleading because "conservative" Catholics are just as likely to dissent from church teachings, often in the seemingly different arenas of socioeconomic justice and liturgical reform. The problem is that the terms are predefined by the bipartisan political atmosphere and are then unevenly applied in the context of church teachings and tradition.[2] Michele Dillon recently studied Catholic identity in relation to members of three groups she calls "pro-change Catholics" because they challenge particular aspects of church teaching: Catholics for a Free Choice, Women's Ordination Conference, and Dignity.[3] Although usually identified as "liberal," these Catholics demonstrate a remarkable variety of positions and opinions, conservative in some ways and liberal in others. Dillon's study demonstrates not only the inadequacy of labels like "liberal" and "conservative," but also the fallacy of assuming pro-change Catholics fit neatly in the liberal category. Some gay and lesbian Catholics, for example, are fiercely conservative regarding church and/or social issues.

In terms of identity, one might be tempted to align "conservative" Catholics more closely than "liberal" Catholics with the doctrinal aspect of Catholicism, but both camps evidence complicated positions in relation to the Catholicism they have been "taught." Consider Supreme Court Justice Antonin Scalia's public dissent from the church's teachings on the death penalty in early 2002. He did not justify his right to dissent based on a notion of individual rights or a uniquely personal faith but rather on the doctrinal technicality that these teachings have not been proclaimed *ex cathedra*.[4] Although Scalia would definitely describe himself as conservative, he uses an argument more often associated with liberal Catholicism. Similarly, in Dillon's study of "pro-change" Catholics, she found that even though they have disagreements with Catholicism as it is officially "taught," they still draw on traditional church teachings (like baptismal equality) to justify their stance:

> Importantly, it is these doctrinal rather than nondoctrinal cultural resources that pro-change Catholics use to legitimate their pro-change projects. Rather than using distinctively American arguments, such as appeals to individual or group rights . . . , the respondents in this study reflexively engage the Catholic tradition.[5]

Despite these efforts to remain in some way aligned with doctrinal Catholicism, these kinds of disagreements inevitably disrupt Catholic identification. It would imply a sort of Protestant fragmentation were it not for all the other ways one "learns" to be Catholic. Catholics faced with the paradox of being Catholic and being at odds with aspects of its ideological dimension usually lay claim to the cultural, "passed on" dimension as a way of getting around what others might perceive as an insurmountable contradiction. Appealing to that aspect of Catholicism provides a way of holding it all together, even when the ideal of a unified Catholic identity is no longer a reality.

Another complicating factor is the way generational differences inform how Catholic identity has been and is negotiated. To understand this facet of the Catholic equation, it is important to situate this discussion within a particular historical context. American Catholicism, though closely tied to and technically governed by the global Roman Catholic Church, has its own unique history and assumes its own kind of identification.[6] Underlying most discussions of American Catholic history is the prevailing understanding that the United States is historically a Protestant country, so Protestantism operates hegemonically in American religious discourse. From this perspective, American Catholicism developed as a religious "outsider" and American Catholic identity has been formed through the mind-set of being different from the Protestant Christian "norm." The theory, as articulated by R. Laurence Moore, is that to be a true American, one has to be an "insider," so the story of American Catholics is a story of struggling to be accepted as insiders — true Americans — while in some way remaining distinctive. At the same time, however, "outsiderhood" is a characteristic way of constructing American identity, so having a unique identity turned against the dominant culture is in itself a mark of being American.[7]

This insider-outsider dialectic is borne out in varying degrees in most surveys and studies of American Catholic history. In this theoretical framework, Catholic identity becomes a strategy for remaining distinct in the face of an inevitable Americanization that threatens to make the boundaries between Catholics and non-Catholics nebulous. For example, beginning especially with the influx of immigrant Catholics in the mid-nineteenth century and lasting until at least Vatican II, hallmarks of Catholic identity included attention to sin, an emphasis on ritual, Marian piety, belief in the miraculous, close contact with the communion of saints, and adoration of the real presence of Jesus in the Blessed Sacrament. Though varied because of the many different cultural versions of Catholicism, such instances of devotionalism and supernaturalism thrived in America precisely because they distinguished Catholics from Protestants.[8] Rather than moderating Catholicism for public consumption, most Catholics chose to assert a distinct identity in the private sphere of devotional life and in particular cultural traditions associated with sacraments and feast days. This dialectic was not lost on church leadership. Robert Orsi and Ann Taves both note how leaders in Rome used their approval and regulation of private devotions as a way of combating Americanist and modernist tendencies in the church of the late nineteenth and early twentieth centuries. This in turn buttressed Roman control and safeguarded Catholic identity against Protestantization.[9]

As time went on, more and more Catholics began to move into the middle class and they began to fashion a sort of Catholic Americanism to replace their ethnic consciousness.[10] This amounted to a sort of Catholic subculture within the dominant American norm. As they began to embrace typical American middle class values, Catholics had to find other ways of maintaining a distinct identity, and scholars have revealed multiple strategies which functioned to that effect. Paula Kane finds Catholics of the early twentieth century achieving mainstream success but also asserting a code of conduct designed to avoid the individualistic philosophical implications of that success. Their efforts to preserve rigid communal boundaries found symbolic representation in church buildings designed to imitate old medieval cathedrals.[11] William Halsey finds Catholic intellectuals sustaining American optimism and innocence after the devastation of the World Wars through the resurgence of Thomistic rationalism.[12]

James Terence Fisher finds Catholics in the same time period identifying with a counterculture based on self-abnegation, the romanticization of the collective, or alternative aesthetics.[13] The diffusion of Catholic identities was further compounded and complicated by other identity components that became increasingly contentious in the American context, such as race and gender.[14]

The establishment of the highly successful parochial school system played a major role in the maintenance of Catholic identity, even as education moved more Catholics into the mainstream. Born in 1945 and coming of age in the 1960s, Richard Rodriguez's life story parallels this broader Catholic movement and reflects the ongoing dialectic of being both American and Catholic, which he constructs in comic/tragic terms. In his Catholic elementary school, the Irish nuns who were his teachers assumed their students' eventual success as Americans. Ambition and optimism were expected in the pursuit of worldly knowledge, in the learning of reading, writing, and American history; but in religion class, the students entered a different world—the "cold bath" of Irish Catholicism:

> The dagger in Mary's heart was sorrow for man's sins. The bleeding heart of Jesus was sorrow for man's sins. . . . *That cross you wear isn't a pretty bauble, Patsy, it's like wearing a little electric chair around your neck.* Christ had instituted a church — a priesthood, sacraments, the mass — and man required all the constant intercession of the saints and the church and the special help of Mother Mary to keep the high road. . . . The nuns never reconciled the faces of comedy and tragedy, and they never saw the need.[15]

Rodriguez's teachers inculcated the necessity of Catholic identity in light of humanity's continual need of redemption. Even American success, by then a given possibility for Catholics, could not obliterate sinful human nature. Besides, the church had consistently been wary of modernity and progress, key factors in the American imagination.

Vatican II and the 1960s, however, brought significant changes in the landscape of American Catholicism. The election of John F. Kennedy to the presidency is often deployed as the symbolic marker of the arrival of Catholics as true Americans. As Catholics attained American insider status, Catholic identity could no longer rely on "ghetto" churches and communities for its maintenance. It could no longer be assumed that Catholic children would attend Catholic schools. As Rodriguez states, "My generation would be the last to be raised with so powerful a sense of the ghetto church."[16] Part of this movement toward American insider status was manifested in the mass movement of Catholics from their urban ethnic enclaves to the suburbs, which began in the 1950s. Though not as quick to make this shift as other middle class Americans, Catholics slowly established themselves in the suburbs where Catholicism was no longer the dominant presence. And they did so in large numbers. In fact, the majority of the autobiographers in my study who are in their forties and younger grew up in the suburbs, which played a definitive role in the way they apprehended their gay identity, as I discussed above.[17] It also influenced how they experienced being Catholic. Anthony Smith theorizes that the mass movement into the suburbs already occurring by Vatican II actually enabled many of the changes of the Council to take hold. He asks, "Did the impact of Vatican II depend as much on the ranch-style housing American Catholics were moving into as it did on *Gaudium et Spes?*" Smith believes these Catholic suburban "pioneers" were already engaging themselves with the changing world and were thus more receptive to the task.[18]

Vatican II's openness to the modern world was marked in several symbolic ways. Church architecture shifted so that Catholic churches became less distinguishable from Protestant ones. The switch from Latin to the vernacular made the liturgy seem less mysterious; communal participation became one of the central features in the celebration of the Mass. Though he mourns the loss of mystery and transcendence in the new liturgy, Rodriguez interprets this change as a necessary permutation in the maintenance of American Catholic identity:

> It reflects and attempts to resolve the dilemma of Catholics just like me. The informal touches; the handshaking; the folk music; the insistence upon union — all these changes are aimed at serving Catholics who no longer live in a Catholic world. To such Catholics — increasingly alone in their faith — the Church says: You are part of a community of believers. You are not single in your faith. Not solitary. We are together, Catholics. *We* believe. We believe. We believe. This assurance is necessary because, in a sense, it no longer is true.[19]

Rodriguez is on to something very important about American Catholic identity today: the boundaries between "us" and "them" have become diffuse; the borders are harder to identify and negotiate. This does not mean, however, that Catholic identity is no longer a component of self definition. It merely means the terms have shifted and Catholic identities have become more varied and less monolithic. Indeed, what Rodriguez mourns throughout his life writings as a loss of contact with his ethnic roots is also a loss of a more defined and distinct Catholic identity.[20]

Rodriguez's experience points back to the way generational identity is an important consideration in the formation of Catholic identity.[21] As American Catholicism has grown and changed throughout its history, so too have the strategies for Catholic identification shifted. Though most of these autobiographies reveal common threads in their experiences of Catholicism, this should not obscure the fact that their life stories do not all follow the same trajectory with regard to American Catholic history. During Vatican II, some were middle-aged, some were growing up, and others were not yet born. Consequently, their experiences of Catholicism varied. As Leslie Scanlon states, "For American Catholics, the church they know now, the church that's emerged from the nearly 40 years in the stewpot with the teachings of Vatican II, embodies a much different kind of Catholic culture than that of their parents' or grandparents' generation."[22] While this is probably an obvious insight, given the rapid changes in American Catholicism this century, it is important to reiterate and explore it. Note that Scanlon says Catholic culture is different; it has not dissolved but rather morphed into something less uniformly definable. There is still something being "passed on."

Some of the differences are born out in a recent article about two Catholic nuns: "fifty-something" Carolyn Osiek and "thirty-something" Laurie Brink. Osiek was raised with the rigid Baltimore Catechism and became a nun at the cusp of adulthood before Vatican II. Like many of her religious sisters who have remained in their orders, she wholeheartedly embraced the promising reforms of the Council. Brink, on the other hand, was raised reading "comic books about St. Francis" and coloring "endless pictures of Jesus in various cardboard settings." Her spirituality sprang out of the folk tunes she learned at Saturday evening Masses, and her decision to join a religious order came well into her adulthood. Many of Osiek's generation were happy to jettison older practices which they had experienced as restrictive or even oppressive, and many of them feel betrayed and angry the reforms did not go as far as they would have liked. Brink, on the other hand, does not understand her older sisters' anger. Her formative experience took place in a church that was already in flux, already embracing new practices and revising older ones. As Brink says, "I did not earn my stripes on the battlefield of change and therefore I do not feel betrayed." Brink's generation is less apprehensive about exploring older aspects of the tradition because they do not have the same oppressive resonances, and in turn, Osiek's generation perceives their younger sisters as being conservative.[23]

In the meantime, the vast majority of Catholics who are not clergy or religious are swept up in their own negotiations of these generational differences. Some wonder if the reforms of Vatican II went too far and want to reemphasize those things that make Catholics different from Protestants. These are the Catholics who want the tabernacle returned to the sanctuary, and who attend Tridentine Masses whenever they are offered.[24] Others have little patience for old practices and feel the reforms of Vatican II have not yet been fully realized. Many others find themselves somewhere in between, feeling nostalgia for a real or imagined Catholic past but also living solidly in the Catholic present.[25] It becomes difficult to characterize any particular generation in any one way. In fact, younger

Catholics seem to come in all stripes. Some appear conservative and seek a certain amount of orthodoxy, but many disagree with some aspect of church teaching and seek creative ways of plugging into the received tradition. Tom Beaudoin, a scholar whose work focuses on "generation X" Catholics (born in the 1960s and 1970s) believes the American Catholic identity of the future will be a deeper mixture of historically Catholic and Protestant understandings of the church. In characterizing the movement toward a more Protestant sensibility, Beaudoin says young Catholics see the church as "ultimately something to be set aside if it interrupts one's relationship to God."[26] I think the operative principle affecting Catholics of all ages today is the idea of choice. Catholics find themselves in a larger culture of choice and now also choose how to be Catholic. The confluence of Vatican II and modern American culture has produced a range of available Catholic identities.

The multiplication of Catholic identities in the late twentieth century indicates many Catholics still share a feature which distinguishes them from Protestants: they do not easily leave to start or join another church. Thus, we have cradle, practicing, lapsed, cafeteria, Tridentine, Conciliar, feminist, orthodox, and a host of other "Catholics" who still claim a Catholic identity. Underlying these divisions is the unfortunate, and in many ways deceptive, dichotomy between liberal and conservative Catholics. This dichotomy, along with the host of other categorical markers dividing Catholics, may be an indication that the insider/outsider dialectic has now moved inside the boundaries of Catholicism. Catholics seem to compete more and more with each other over what constitutes Catholic identity. If Moore is right that outsiderhood is part of the construction of American identity, then perhaps perceiving oneself as a sort of "outsider" within the church is now a part of assembling an American Catholic identity. Indeed, it is striking that all of the autobiographers in my study sense having an outsider status imposed on them because of their gay identity; yet even among those who have "left" the church, the vast majority have not joined another church. Instead, they assert revised Catholic identities, such as "former" or "recovering." The Catholic factor in their lives is deep and formative.

All of the "pro-change" Catholics discussed in Michele Dillon's study (see above) could be said to exist in a sort of "outsider-within" status, yet they remain entrenched in the pool of symbolic resources provided by the Catholic tradition. Her Dignity respondents assert their Catholicity with statements like, "Catholicism is inescapably part of my life," or "Catholicism is an encompassing identity for me."[27] Even their arguments for doctrinal change are built upon other aspects of Catholic doctrine. The point of contestation between these Catholics and others is centered around the question of which teachings allow for a range of interpretation and the possibility of change, and which do not. Dillon's "pro-change"

Catholics are characterized as such because they seek changes in doctrine related to gender and sexuality. Other Catholics who are publicly unyielding on these issues might favor changes or allow for gray areas in doctrine related to war, unions, or capital punishment. Yet all of these Catholics feel at home in the same symbolic universe. One of the most useful aspects of Dillon's study is her comparison of these "pro-change" Catholics with members of the doctrinally conservative Catholic League for Religious and Civil Rights. Dillon finds both groups share a deep attachment to both the sacramental and universal dimensions of Catholicism. Additionally, both sets of Catholics value the idea of a communal identity and the unifying symbolism of the papacy.[28] The commonalities she uncovers speak volumes about the persistence and cohesion of Catholic identity, even in this era of seeming fragmentation.

Dillon's findings are further supported by a number of broader studies. The most recent of these is a 1999 survey of Catholics conducted by the Gallup Organization and supervised by noted sociologists Dean Hoge, William D'Antonio, James Davidson, and Katherine Meyer.[29] They found substantial agreement across a wide range of Catholics, including those who consider themselves marginal or "dormant," regarding what is most central about *being* Catholic (deliberately posed as an identity question). Topping the list is the sacraments, followed closely by a sense of spirituality, concern for the poor, and the spirit of community. Two other studies from 1997 and 1998 similarly found a set of elements or beliefs almost all respondents considered essential to being Catholic.[30] In his summary of the 1997 study, Davidson envisions these factors in a set of three concentric circles in which the core elements are considered the most central. In the inner circle lie the beliefs most widely held across the board to be the essence of Catholicism, such as the Trinity, the Incarnation, the Real Presence, and Mary as Mother of God. The second circle holds the church's social teachings and responsibility to the poor. The third circle contains rituals, such as attending Mass and receiving Holy Communion, the things represented by the phrase "practicing Catholic."[31] Davidson's model is useful in showing how Catholic identity hinges more on sacramental than juridical definitions of the church, and involves more than either holding certain beliefs or the fulfillment of ritual obligations.

Various writers and scholars have tried to address the dimension of Catholic identity that goes beyond the religious externals of creed and cult, the aspect that inheres in a person regardless of their adult faith commitments.[32] Lawrence S. Cunningham, for example, proposes that being Catholic is being part of a "community of memory," involving space, time, silence, prayer, sacraments, story, persons, catholicity, and community.[33] This relates to the sense of history so many Catholics consider a hallmark of Catholicism. But being formed in Catholicism also seems to affect the way one sees the world and negotiates reality. According to Andrew Greeley, the material culture of Catholicism (as found in things like statues, holy water, stained glass, votive candles, saint relics, religious medals, rosary beads, and holy cards) produces and represents an enchanted world and pervasive religious sensibility "which inclines Catholics to see the Holy lurking in creation."[34] In the "Catholic imagination," as Greeley calls it, grace permeates the natural world. "It sees created reality as a 'sacrament,' that is, a revelation of the presence of God."[35] In this paradigm, the world becomes revelatory rather than fallen, and creation takes on a metaphorical quality: "The objects, events, and persons of ordinary existence hint at the nature of God and indeed make God in some fashion present to us."[36] Catholic lives, even gay Catholic lives, then become instances of God's revelation, and autobiographical narratives provide windows into God's imagination and the fullness of ultimate reality.

Rosemary Haughton talks about the Catholic "thing," a "something else" deeper than the visible church and the external representation of Catholicism, which can only be articulated through the lives of individual Catholics.[37] This is the heart of Catholic identity, and autobiography is an ideal interpretive tool for trying to understand it. I want to reimagine Davidson's model of concentric circles to represent how I perceive this Catholic "thing" operating in the lives of these gay men. I envision an axis of Catholic identity grounded in each of their life stories. As their lives orbit this axis, some stay close to the Catholic core; its pull is inescapable, and they experience it as foundational in their lives. Because of its centrality, they struggle with its contradictions and find ways of remaining consciously committed to it. Others struggle with it and decide on a slightly wider orbit because the gravity has worn on them. Still others are in the widest orbit of all: For them, Catholicism plays a role in their life stories, but it is not so "visible" in their narratives. Their lives revolve at a greater distance from this core and other axes are more prominent. In any case, being Catholic is an inescapable and formative component in these gay lives no matter how tight or wide they maintain their orbits.

The Catholic Ethos: Sensual Memories

> I wished her a happy Easter, said nothing about her gloves, or perfume, or colored eggs, and hung up. As I sat there in my silent room I saw these memories would be with me forever, that wherever they were, I was: some part of me. But the life I must begin was my own —
> a separate person's.   —Andrew Holleran, *Nights in Aruba*

As I mentioned in the previous chapter, religious identity and sexual identity are only artificially separated from each other because both resonate in the core of selfhood and are directly concerned with human fulfillment. As such, these autobiographies provide a glimpse of Catholic identity as filtered and interpreted through the lens of gay self-understanding. This is a portrait of *gay* Catholic identity, yet many Catholics would certainly identify with the way they narrate their Catholic experience. Catholic identity begins in a world of sensory stimulation fueled by the materiality of Catholic culture, sometimes called the "smells and bells" of Catholicism. This is the world of sacraments, liturgy, rituals, and mystery that informs the Catholic imagination and teaches us on a subconscious level the answers to ultimate questions about who we are and who God is. It comes alive in Catholic homes, churches, and schools.[38] Brian McNaught compares having a Catholic background with having a Jewish background, "insofar as it involves growing up with rules, rituals and cultural idiosyncrasies which separate you from many of your friends and provide common bonds with others." He goes on to enumerate a few of these signifiers of American Catholic identity as he experienced it as a child:

> The Latin Mass, no meat on Fridays, the rosary, the May crownings, your new St. Joseph Missal, the nun's habits, being an Altar Boy and fainting from the incense, traditional rivalries with the athletic teams of the neighboring public schools, thoughts about entering the seminary or convent, holy cards, the "Decency Pledge" and a variety of other "typically Catholic" traditions are essential ingredients to my past which I share with other persons who grew up Catholic.[39]

David Kopay's childhood home in Chicago was marked as Catholic through and through, "with a Sacred Heart of Jesus over the door and religious figurines and objects in every room." Kopay remembers his parents kept a jar of holy water in the closet and would sprinkle drops of it around the house during storms. His family's life was centered around St. Christina's church, and they never missed going to Mass on Sundays and Holy Days. When he was in fourth grade, his family moved to California and immediately became a part of St. Patrick's church "without missing a mass."[40] Similarly, no matter where José Zuniga's military family lived, his mother walked him and his sister to church every Sunday and Holy Day without fail. Like Kopay's and most of the Catholic families profiled in these life texts, Zuniga's family never missed a Mass. The obligatory and rhythmic repetition of the ritual burned the imagery of Catholicism deep into their senses. It was awe-inspiring, terrifying, and comforting for the young Zuniga: "How portentous the epigrammatic words sounded to an impressionable ten-year-old: *Sin.* Benevolence. *Satan.* Saint Francis of Assisi. *Burn.* Resurrection. *Sinful.* Repentant. *Forever.* Amen."[41]

Fenton Johnson recalls the rhythmic cycle of the church calendar, repeated year after year and ritually echoing the death and rebirth cycle of nature:

> Transmogrified cannibalism, mortification, exaltation — these were re-enacted according to a routine as dependable as sunrise and nearly (it seemed) as old. . . . The gritty rub of ashes on the forehead. Clouds of cloying myrrh ascending to the high-domed ceiling. Mind-numbing mantras mouthed in a tongue at once centuries dead and more evocative than our quotidian English, *ora pro nobis, ora pro nobis, miserere nobis.* Ours was a sensual church, the Opera of Faith, and we were its captive patrons.[42]

He realizes the lasting impression this sensual world left on him: "I acknowledge the shaping hand with gratefulness. Because of it I grasp in some way the incomprehensible magnitude of the mystery of being."[43] Johnson mourns the loss of this kind of spirituality for gays like him who feel alienated from the church. As an adult, he still feels drawn to elements of it and takes comfort in some of the simpler rituals. For example, he stops to light a votive candle whenever he passes a church and has time to stop: "The habit is partly a remnant of Catholic grade school, partly a gift from a culture that valued remembering its past and the names of its dead."[44] Throughout *Geography of the Heart,* he lights the candles for his father and his many friends who had died of complications related to AIDS. Then, as his partner Larry's own disease worsens, the candles offer both of them a measure of comfort. Lighting the candles provided a structure for Johnson's interior prayer that Larry would die a speedy and painless death with him at his side.[45]

Catholic rituals and cosmology afford a sense of security and comfort during difficult moments in these lives. Brian Bouldrey recited the Prayer of St. Francis at night while his dying partner Jeff slept downstairs, too weak to make the trip up. When Jeff died, Bouldrey found solace in knowing Jeff was now a saint in a heaven filled and alive with people like him. Bouldrey still finds himself praying to Jeff at times.[46] When John McNeill was taken captive as a prisoner of war in World War II, he and his captor passed a roadside shrine of the crucified Christ. He asked permission to stop and say a prayer. "I fell to my knees, made an act of contrition, and asked God to protect me and save me from death. . . . I surrendered myself totally to God's mercy, and obviously God had other plans for me."[47] When Tony Laveccia was stabbed by a man he took home whose friends broke into the apartment after they got there, he prayed the Hail Mary over and over ("Pray for us sinners now and at the hour of our death") because he thought he was going to die.[48] And when Scott Trepania learned he was HIV-positive in 1991, he immediately visited the Shrine of the Immaculate Conception in Washington. "I went into the crypt church, lay in front of the tabernacle and prayed the prayer that our Lord prayed in the garden." In light of his diagnosis, Trepania turned to the Mass, saying the rosary, and the stations of the cross to bolster his prayer life and his spirits.[49]

Catholicism provides these men tools and strategies not only for dealing with life's difficulties but also for relating to God in the process. When Dave Pallone's lover Scott died suddenly in a car accident, Pallone had not come out to anyone, and no one knew about their relationship. In his position as a "secret survivor," Pallone could only turn to God. At first, he was understandably angry. He went to his parents' graves and asked for their help in coming to terms with all of it: "Why would God . . . take away the only person in the world that I loved, the only stabilizing force in my life?"[50] Pallone later confided what had happened and the nature of his double life to a priest whom he considered his spiritual advisor. Fr. Piermarini told him to trust himself and to trust God, which gave Pallone the confidence to carry on with his life and be himself. He also found comfort in the idea that Scott was now part of the communion of saints: "Scott's up there saying, 'Life goes on, Dave. Be strong; keep fighting.' "[51]

For Rafael Campo, the Catholicism of his childhood was like a mother who cradled him in her accepting arms. The church provided restitution for all Campo lacked as a Cuban American living in suburban New Jersey, and he took comfort in the fact that the prayers he prayed in New Jersey were the same prayers being offered in far-off Cuba. "The bits of Latin uttered solemnly during mass were so much like Spanish that they implied that even my possibly shameful ethnic heritage was fit to be set to ethereal music."[52] Campo found a sublime and all-embracing poetry in the ordinary, tangible elements of his religious world:

> Poetry flowed in the supple warmth of votive candles lit by the trembling hands of supplicants, whose soft voices mixed with the tenuous light thrown across the highest rafters. Poetry blinded whole congregations in the gleam of the silver chalice raised for God's most precise inspection. The comforting word was present even in the worn and faded velvet lining of the offerings basket, which looked as if it might also serve as a cozy resting place for the neighborhood's stray cats that the priests took in. Any creature was welcome in my romanticized, hymn-drenched Catholic Church — even the most irretrievably lost of wanton souls.[53]

Campo's feelings of safety and acceptance were disrupted only when he grew up and realized the church did indeed consider some souls to be irretrievably lost and they were not necessarily welcome.

Patrick Horrigan also remembers the security being Catholic provided him as a child. He felt it let him in on secrets and truths that non-Catholics would never understand or appreciate. He enjoyed making people who weren't practicing Catholics feel like they were missing out on something.[54] He grew up in a very Catholic world in which the parish priest would sometimes say Masses in his family's home, and the sacraments marked some of life's most important moments. Horrigan recalls the emphasis his mother put on the ritual of First Holy Communion, as important to her as the day she got married and the times she gave birth to Horrigan and his siblings.[55] When he was a little boy, he imagined a movie being made of his life but ending just before the "big First Holy Communion scene." The audience would be devastated to miss it and would cry in vain until the big sequel was made.[56] While reflective of childlike egocentrism, the whole idea of his young life, down to the smallest diurnal details, being compelling material for a movie is indicative of his Catholic sense that whatever one does in this world matters.

Like Horrigan, Richard Rodriguez experienced his childhood Catholicism as something pervasive that marked him distinctively from others: "At home, there were holy pictures on a wall of nearly every room, and a crucifix hung over my bed. My first twelve years as a student were spent in Catholic schools where I could look up to the front of the room and see a crucifix hanging over the clock."[57] Catholicism shaped his whole day, every day, and framed the hours and the seasons. Rodriguez recalls an enchanted quality in his world, punctuated by Catholic rituals and celebrations:

> I felt the air was different, somehow still and more silent on Sundays and high feastdays. I felt lightened, transparent as sky, after confessing my sins to a priest. Schooldays were routinely divided by prayers said with classmates. I would not have forgotten to say grace before eating. And I would not have turned off the light next to my bed or fallen asleep without praying to God.[58]

For Rodriguez, being Catholic gave him tools to navigate a world filled with both good and evil. A prayer to his guardian angel and a sign of the cross aimed in the direction of his window would keep Satan from getting in his bedroom. The seasons of the church year accompanied his journey through time and the sacraments marked his coming of age. Rodriguez sensed how this world and its material sensuality set him apart from others and gave his life substance: "Catholics were mysteriously lucky, 'chosen' by God to be nurtured in a special way." Non-Catholics may have gone to church too, but "there was no incense, no sacred body and blood, and no confessional box. . . . For non-Catholics, it seemed, there was all white and no yolk."[59]

Andrew Sullivan writes at some length about this "yolk" of Catholicism. When he says Catholicism was always sacramental for him, he refers to the way God literally touches and is touched by this world. "By this, I mean that it was not about abstraction but about reality, not about words but about actions, not about the unreachable but about the physicality of the divine." He remembers the carnality of incense, bread, wine, vestments, pews, candle wax, and kneelers, all pointing to the reality and centrality of the Incarnation. "When sexuality burst in upon this boyhood scene, I was not so uninformed as to be guileless, but I was also primed to embrace it as yet another manifestation of a sensualized spirituality. It came easily to me. And not despite my Catholicism, but *because* of it."[60] Rodriguez was similarly affected by the sensual trappings of his Catholic world, noting how the church seemed to "excite more sexual wonderment than it repressed." The irony of it all was not lost on him, especially as he was coming of age in Catholic school: "When we were in eighth grade the priest told us how dangerous it was to look at our naked bodies, even while taking a bath — and I noticed that he made the remark directly under a near-naked figure of Christ on the cross." Rodriguez recalls the carnality of a nun's "wedding ring," pictures of martyrs in physical pain and virgins fallen in death, and the perfume of Easter lilies. His words echo Sullivan's: "At such moments, the church touched alive some very private sexual excitement; it pronounced my sexuality important."[61]

The liturgy, with its attendant ceremony and imagery, provides a host of sensual memories for these autobiographers. Fenton Johnson felt drawn into "a fantastical world — the world, in fact, of theater, where everything stood for something else and everything was or had the potential to be sacred."[62] There is much about the performative and decorative aspects of the Mass that resonates with the aesthetic interests of gay men. Gay men who are attuned to the artistic world can "plug into" the ritual world of liturgical celebration. Patrick Horrigan remembers when he was editor-in-chief of his high school yearbook, he had grand ideas for the special "yearbook mass." In the midst of planning, his faculty advisor warned him, "Patrick! We'll have none of your Cecil B. DeMille productions!"[63] I can relate to Horrigan's desire to choreograph a special liturgy. By the eighth grade, I was helping plan the music for our school Masses, and I have spent all of my adult life working as a liturgist and music director. I have always experienced the liturgy as an important point of connection with the church. Many of these writers who are active in Dignity comment on the importance of the liturgy and take special pride in the fact that their Dignity chapters concentrate on good ritual planning. It affords them an outlet for creativity and artistic expression within the arms of the church.

A number of the autobiographers, however, express some dissatisfaction with the new liturgy. In one respect, this is surprising because one would expect most of them to support the reforms of Vatican II, especially in light of the way these reforms have empowered the people of the church to take ownership and more openly challenge teachings they find problematic. It is not surprising, however, in that the new liturgy is focused more on the immanence of God in the gathered assembly than on the God who transcends this troubled world. As such, the new liturgy can feel less aesthetically refined than the old liturgy for someone wishing to be transported beyond the ordinary. Rob Nixon recalls how "very limp and graceless" the new liturgy seemed when he first encountered it.[64] Richard Rodriguez despised the new liturgy from the start:

> In college chapels I would listen to folk singing and see plain altars draped with bright applique banners: Joy! God is Love . . . one Sunday there would be a rock mass; one Sunday the priest encouraged us to spend several minutes before the Offertory introducing ourselves, while a small bad jazzy combo punched out a cocktail mix. I longed for the Latin mass. Incense. Music of Bach. Ceremonies of candles and acolytes.[65]

No doubt part of the "problem" in Nixon's and Rodriguez's experiences with the new liturgy was bad execution of the new ritual. In their zeal to update and "inculturate" the liturgy, many parishes turned it over to the people without any particular training. The result was a pastiche of ritual activity that reflected American culture of the 1960s and 1970s, more so than any systematic liturgical theology. For gay boys and men who were already feeling marginalized from mainstream culture, this liturgical environment was not necessarily welcoming. It did not feel safe. Many of them felt "robbed" of some of the otherworldliness of Catholicism that afforded a space in which the unfairnesses of this world did not seem so important. When they fondly remember the old liturgy, they reimagine a bulwark of security and solidarity, where one's potentially threatening personal uniqueness would not be noticed. Still, the Catholic world did not disappear; it was merely altered.[66] James Morrison nicely sums up this transformation when he discusses what the new liturgy would now have to be about: "Where formerly I had been susceptible to a kind of effortless transport from the modes of everyday life in church, now I was surrounded by them, and what church would have to be about was the nexus between the ordinary and the extraordinary."[67]

The Catholic world also communicates a host of particular values and ways of interpreting reality, all encircling the idea that what you do in this life, in this world, really matters. Fenton Johnson calls this Catholic world view superstitious fatalism. When his lover Larry was still alive, the two of them would read aloud every night, and Johnson was grateful to read a long book: "So long as we were in the middle of a book, he wouldn't die.

The longer the book, the better."[68] In the Catholic imagination, one has the potential of controlling reality if one "behaves" the right way; yet one also knows the inevitability that something eventually will go wrong. In fact, Toby Johnson says he still experiences the feeling that the way God loves him is to foul up his plans.[69]

Richard Rodriguez constructs this Catholic fatalism on a compass of tragedy: "If I respond to the metaphor of spring, I nevertheless learned, years ago, from my Mexican father, from my Irish nuns, to count on winter."[70] This is why, according to Rodriguez, Catholics need the constancy and mediation of the church in their lives — an ongoing sense of the religious that is not about quick conversion but rather about God's sacramental intervention over time. As he says, "The Catholic part of me — ancient, cynical, feminine — is appalled by the nakedness, the humorlessness, the sweetness of evangelical conversion narratives."[71] Achieving salvation is about finding one's wholeness, and this is a lifetime process. There is something about being Catholic that takes the long view and recognizes the redemptive value of suffering. This piece of Catholic identity is particularly resonant for gay Catholics who feel alienated, and struggle for years to come to terms with their sexuality.

This sense of the long view — of history and memory — is part of what gives Catholic identity its persistent quality. Jim Bussen likens it to an ethnic identity and notes how disaffected Catholics usually just stop going to church rather than becoming something else.[72] Tom Kaun and Kevin Calegari say the same thing in the opposite way: "We are going to be Catholic no matter where we go, even if we join the Lutherans or Episcopalians."[73] Joe McGuire and Father Paul both echo the feelings among many of these gay Catholics that Catholicism is an integral part of their selves, as integral as their sexuality.[74] The rich material culture of Catholicism — the signs and symbols, smells and bells, rituals and sacraments — implanted something deep in their senses and memories.

"I Wanted to Be a Priest"

If I had to pick one phrase or sentence which popped up more frequently than any other in the course of reading these gay Catholic autobiographies, it would have to be, "I wanted to be a priest." Though it could not be said for all of them, enough of them felt this desire at some point in their lives that it deserves discussion. I can also think of no better illustration of the way gay and Catholic identities are fused in these life narratives. The isolation they feel around their sexual identity growing up makes them feel singled out by God. Gay Catholic boys sensing their sexual difference and being baffled by it see in the priesthood an opportunity to be respected while both inhabiting a mysterious world and not being married to a woman. In many ways it seems to answer a dilemma they are not quite able to articulate as boys. It also plugs into so many of the aspects of being gay I discussed in the previous chapter. James Heckman, for example, thought about joining the priesthood from third or fourth grade through high school, in part because priests were not supposed to have girlfriends. There was something intriguing and sexual about it: "I would sometimes have dreams about being with a bunch of guys in a monastery and not having any undergarments on underneath my cassock."[75] While some heterosexual Catholic boys want to be priests too, I do not think this theme would appear as regularly in their life stories, nor would all the reasons for their attraction be the same.[76] In any case, there is clearly something about the priesthood that resonates in a special way with emerging gay Catholic identity.

For a boy, being a priest means being in charge of a magical and important world. Patrick Horrigan remembers being fascinated by a large free-standing gold-papered wall that stood behind the altar of his hometown church, Sacred Heart, where he would eventually become an altar boy. It concealed the entrance to the sacristy and, in a telling bit of symbolism, Horrigan was always curious about "what went on behind that wall."[77] The first thing he wanted to be when he grew up was a priest. It may have been partially about curiosity; but as Horrigan narrates it, his desire to be a priest was wrapped up in ideas about "eternity, uphill struggles, self-sacrifice, and strong leadership."[78] José Zuniga became an altar boy at age eight, which made him feel closer to God. He enjoyed playing a role in the mystical and ancient traditions that were all so ominous to him. He too decided he wanted to be priest, but his military father scoffed at the idea: "He bought me my first pistol the day after I announced my intention."[79] Brian McNaught did not simply want to be a priest; he wanted to be a saint so he could be God's best friend:

> Believing a saint to be a "perfect person," I prayed daily, was obedient to my parents and teachers, never said "damn" or "hell," guarded the refrigerator between noon and 3 p.m. on Good Friday so no one would eat, built elaborate May altars for the Blessed Mother and said home "Masses" by tying a towel around my neck and passing out Necco wafers to my little sister and brother.[80]

I too wanted to be a priest when I was young — in the second grade to be exact. Like McNaught, I said home Masses on Sundays, but I wore a sheet around me and used Ritz crackers for communion. At these young ages, it is the enchantment of the Catholic world that draws boys in. For gay boys who are feeling different, but not yet sexual, the otherworldliness of the church is appealing. It is an alternative space where men wear "dresses" and are "queer" in comparison to other adult men. It is also a space in which being a good boy is not only perceived as normal, but is also expected.

In adolescence, the desire to be a priest becomes much more complicated as boys begin to feel sexual and to understand what the celibacy requirement means. For gay boys, it is even more confusing because they realize their emerging sexual identity is at odds with what the church says is normal. This is enough for some gay young men to abandon any thoughts of becoming a priest. For others, the celibacy requirement provides a potential excuse to avoid confronting their sexuality altogether. Of course, who actually becomes a priest depends upon a host of other practical concerns, and needs to be charted by generations. In the decades before Vatican II, it was almost a given that at least one child in every Catholic family would become a priest or join a religious order. Often, the fact that a sibling or aunt or uncle was a priest or nun was enough to inspire other young Catholics to pursue religious life. Being a priest (or monk or nun) was a noble calling — something of which to be proud — and it was also the path to a higher education at a time when Catholic families could not generally afford it. After Vatican II, the situation changed quickly as massive numbers of men left the priesthood in order to marry. In the following decades, fewer and fewer men went to seminary as becoming a priest came to be seen as more of an anomaly. With regard to the autobiographers who went to seminary in my study, some joined before Vatican II, some in the midst of it, and some at least a decade later. Even though they narrate a similar thread of feelings about the connections between their sexual identity and their call to be priests, it is important to keep in mind how different the connotations of joining the priesthood today are from fifty years ago.[81]

One obvious result of these shifts is a drop in the number of heterosexual priests — the ones who left to get married. That means a higher proportion of gay priests. Father Donald Cozzens, a former seminary rector, has discussed the disproportionately high percentage of gay men in the priesthood and especially among those presently studying in seminaries.[82] It is inherently difficult to pinpoint exact numbers of gay priests, either many decades ago or today, because of the difficulty in obtaining honest responses about priest sexual orientation. Closeted priests are unlikely to be counted because either they do not self-identify as gay or they fear the consequences if they are discovered. Surveys about the presence of gays in seminaries also reflect the particular perspectives of those being interviewed. For example, according to one recent survey of gay priests, those ordained before 1960 remember their seminary as having been 51 percent gay. Those ordained after 1981 put the number at 70 percent. These numbers may be inflated because they are likely including fellow priests whom they perceive as being gay, but who may not ever identify as such.[83] Even so, the most conservative estimates indicate the priesthood is at least 20 percent gay, and the percentage rises among younger priests. Regardless of the exact numbers, it is clear a sort of de facto gay subculture has existed across generations in the priesthood and now thrives even more intensely.[84] For Cozzens, this is one factor in a long list of "problems" the church must address with respect to the changing face of the priesthood. It is not that homosexual orientation is a problem in and of itself but rather that seminaries are not preparing priests well enough to deal with their sexuality in open and healthy ways. Cozzens also fears, rightly I think, that the expanding gay subculture within the ranks will alienate prospective heterosexual candidates.

In any case, the ever-increasing proportion of gay men in the priesthood is a reality deserving widespread discussion. Gay priests do have special gifts to offer the church that are developed largely through the experience of growing up gay. Jesuit Father James Martin considers some of these unique gifts, in response to Cozzens's findings, as a way of spiritualizing the phenomenon by acknowledging that God must be calling gay men to the priesthood for a reason. Martin highlights three particularly relevant aspects of gay experience, all of which I discussed in some way in the previous chapter: First, gay people know what it is like to suffer ridicule and rejection and may then be more sensitive to others who feel marginalized; second, gay people are often drawn inward and may develop a level of self-understanding that allows for a deeper spirituality; and third, the aesthetic and creative interests of gay men can be utilized in service to the liturgy and consequently enhance the liturgical reformation ignited with Vatican II.[85] Even though there is something very stereotypical about these "gay gifts," they are echoed in these autobiographies by gay priests themselves as they ponder the interplay of their gay and clerical identities. While the issue needs further thought and analysis, Martin deserves credit for asserting that gay priests have something positive to contribute to the church.

Given these positive contributions and the number of gay priests populating the clerical ranks, the intransigence of church leaders in refusing to reconsider the church's condemnation of gay relationships is disturbing. And the willingness of gay priests to tow the party line, upholding a system of teachings on sexuality they know does not adequately address the totality of gay experience, is indicative of a pervasive pathology. In rare and extreme cases, this pathology can lead to abuse, as it did for Kevin Killian. When Killian was sexually abused by members of a religious order, he observed a church hierarchy that preached self-denial even as its members indulged their desires: "Within the Church's apparently ascetic structure, the pursuit of pleasure has been more or less internalized. By and large, the pursuit (of violence, danger, beauty) is the structure."[86] For a while, Killian considered becoming a priest. He envied their privilege and entitlement. He saw a haven for queers, in which their love lives were forever shielded by the hierarchy that protected them: "I continue to see the Church as the house of Eros, a place of pleasure and fun, and I continue to regard men in religious costume as possible sex partners, yearning to break free. Such was my training, my ritual life."[87]

Let me be clear that most gay priests do not engage in sexual abuse. In fact, less than 2 percent of all American priests have been implicated in the recent revelations of clergy sexual abuse.[88] I am merely pointing out that gay priests directly participate in a structure and system of teachings that is not liberating for most gay people. I have already mentioned Mark Jordan's exceptional work about the homosexuality endemic to the clerical culture of the Catholic Church, and it is worth reiterating some of his points here. According to Jordan, the present power structure of the church provides a space for gay priests to engage in a culture of same-sex desire and affiliation, without the risks of identifying as gay, while also rewarding their silence with power. Church teachings in turn support this structure, resulting in the startling irony whereby any revision of doctrine that would make gay Catholic identification more visible and morally acceptable would rob gay priests of their hiding place. In other words, clerical culture relies on gay *in*visibility. This is why advocating for change in the realm of moral theology will only get us so far. As for numbers of gay priests, the exact percentage is beside the point:

> It doesn't much matter whether it is 5 percent or 25 percent or 50 percent. The construction and enforcement of rules of silence will operate at any of those levels, because the closet is a collaborative construction of gay and straight.... The recent increase in the perceived number of gay clergy has opened some closet doors, but it has locked others more securely.[89]

Jordan's analysis relies largely on his astute observations of Catholic clerical culture in general, and the parallels with gay culture he finds there. He exposes the "campiness" of the culture — the theatricality of liturgies, fanciful vestments, style wars, lifestyle excesses — all of which are stereotypically perceived as feminine when reflected in gay culture, but are "excused" when associated with priests. A wonderful example of this phenomenon, though not tied as directly to church imagery, is found in Fenton Johnson's autobiography. When he was growing up near the Trappist monastery of Our Lady of Gethsemane, in rural Kentucky, his family's lives became intertwined with those of the monks. The monks were fond of spending evenings at the Johnson home, having dinner, drinking, smoking, and talking late into the night. Brother A. was obviously the "performer" in the bunch:

Brother A. was fond of a fake grass skirt someone had sent my mother from Hawaii. When the moon was right and the whiskey flowing, he donned the skirt and some hot-pink plastic leis, then hoisted my mother to the tabletop and climbed up after. There she sang "Hard-hearted Hannah" ("the vamp of Savannah, G-A!"), while Brother A. swayed his hips and waved his hands in mock hula. Later he launched into Broadway tunes, warbling in falsetto with his arms thrown around one or more of his brethren.[90]

In most situations, Brother A.'s behavior would signify gay campiness in the extreme. Whether Brother A. was actually gay or not is irrelevant. Almost any other man engaging in such a drag performance would have been suspect. His membership in the clerical caste, however, "excused" his conduct and no insinuations were made about him. If it were today's world, with our heightened awareness of gay identity, Johnson's family might have been more "suspicious," but Jordan's point is that within the church, a certain campiness pervades the functions and roles fulfilled by priests. The priesthood provides a space where gay and Catholic identities can be performed simultaneously without being explicitly recognized.

This clerical climate simultaneously evokes and suppresses homosexuality; so it is not surprising young gay Catholic men might be drawn to it, especially if they feel conflicted about their sexuality. This theory is supported by the autobiographies in my study, in which a clear majority of these gay men wanted to become priests at some point in their lives. Some followed through and many went as far as seminary, but most of them at least toyed with the idea as boys and young men. Jordan, borrowing from John Shekleton, offers some insightful reasons why this is so:

> Because they are promised an exchange of their anguished identity as outsiders for a respected and powerful identity as an insider. Because they want to remain in the beautiful, queer space of the liturgy. Because they are drawn to public celebration of suffering that redeems. Because they want to live in as gay a world as the Catholic church offers.[91]

Jordan's reasons represent the kind of allure to the priesthood that simmers at an almost subconscious level. The autobiographers articulate different kinds of reasons for wanting to be priests, usually more in line with James Martin's thoughts on the special gifts gay men have to offer. They consciously experience the desire as a "calling" to serve and help people in some way, which also gives them a sense of purpose. On some level, however, and more in line with Jordan, they are also drawn to find a space where their feelings of difference will not matter so much.

John McNeill dates his vocation to the priesthood from his time as a prisoner of war, when a slave laborer risked his own life to toss the starving young McNeill a potato. He saw the laborer make the sign of the cross, and McNeill interpreted it as a sign to be courageous and work against evil in the world.[92] Though this was a pivotal event in his discernment, he soon realized his vocation was also wrapped up in his gay identity:

> I was still ambivalent about my vocation, which was still based primarily in my fear that as a gay man the only way I could get to heaven was by denying and suppressing my sexuality and my desire for human love and my belief that the only way to accomplish that denial was to enter a religious order, which would provide the environment and the support for a life of celibacy that was possible and meaningful.[93]

In spite of his misgivings, he was ordained in the Jesuits in 1959, when he was thirty-four. Afterward, he felt depression instead of joy because he felt he was still going through the motions of religious life out of a fear of punishment. After some years of travel and his experience of a gay relationship, he ultimately realized complete sexual abstinence was for him "morally evil and psychologically destructive. Discernment of my own experience led me to the conclusion, after many years of struggle, that God was calling me to a ministry to gay and lesbian people but was not calling me to a life of celibacy."[94] McNeill soon met his life partner and tried to remain a Jesuit, but was finally dismissed for his strong and public challenges of church teaching on homosexuality.

McNeill wanted to remain a Jesuit because it was a core identity for him. Not surprisingly, this idea of priesthood as a central identity appears over and over again in the life texts of gay men who are still priests. These are the ones who are also most likely to have "known" they would be priests since they were very young, and who now consider their gay identity as a fundamental aspect of their priesthood. William Hart McNichols, another Jesuit, knew he would be a priest when he was five years old. He constructs his priesthood as something inseparable from his sense of self. It is a seal on his soul that cannot be shed, and being gay is an integral component of it.[95] Matthew Kelty states, "I wanted to be a priest and a monk since the time I knew what the words meant."[96] Kelty found the church and his religious training profoundly inadequate in terms of helping him come to terms with his gayness, so he did so on his own and now agrees with the church that gay men are called in a special way to celibacy. Richard John Cardarelli also knew from a young age that he wanted to be a priest and that he was different from other boys. He joined a conservative community so he could hide his gay identity, but he eventually found it suffocating and left. Becoming involved with Dignity "cured" him of his self-hatred, and he later returned to his religious order.[97] Brother Jonathan was marked early by his teacher nuns as the one in his grade school class who would have a vocation. Though he sensed his attraction to men at age five, he was long reluctant to come out, and remained closeted even when a close friend in his community came out to him. He later came to feel this blocking of his sexuality was blocking his entire emotional life. When he finally "owned" his sexuality, he felt his life and his ministry become whole:

> Sexuality enhanced my religious life, my personal spiritual journey, and also my work for the poor and oppressed. It made me sensitive to others' suffering in my community, to women's issues in church and society, and to the cry of all oppressed and marginalized people.[98]

This theme of gayness enhancing one's ministry recurs over and over again in the narratives of gay priests. Fr. T. Thompson feels being gay is almost revelatory: "Being gay in this culture and church can enable us to experience compassion. Being gay can be the threshold of the reign of God."[99] Father Aelred felt very naive when he entered the seminary and did not begin serious exploration of his sexuality until he was in his thirties. Though his first homogenital experience was with a fellow priest, he still felt like "the only homosexual clergyman in the world." One evening in a gay bar, he spied another priest with whom he had been secretly in love, and the two of them began talking. Before he knew it, and in a moment that confirms Jordan's thesis, he found himself in the company of several gay priests who were in the bar and joined in their conversation. Father Aelred soon found a lover and, with the support of Dignity, decided to remain a priest rather than choose between his priestly and sexual identities. He too feels his experience as a gay man enhances his sensitivity to the suffering of others and enriches his priestly vocation: "I have come to view my own sexual orientation as the source of many important vital traits that are making my ministry more sensitive and increasingly effective."[100]

Robert Arpin wanted to be priest from the time of his earliest memories, and by age five he too was playing priest and saying home Masses using Necco wafers. He associates his desire to be a priest with a need for respect and recognition.[101] Arpin never felt guilty about being both gay and priest because he experienced both as core identities and figured he could not cut himself in two. But it did make him wonder where he fit in terms of community: "So here I am in the middle, too gay for the Church and too Catholic for the gays."[102] When he learned he was HIV-positive, he also had to integrate that into the way he understood himself and his ministry. At the time, he was not certain how it would all fit together, "But I do believe that God is calling me to use my sickness and my sexual orientation in some ministry to those who feel unwanted."[103] Arpin soon found himself needed not only at Dignity but also in various care centers for people with AIDS. One of the most poignant stories he narrates is about his celebrating Mass with men in the hospital participating in drug trials. When he spoke the words, "This is my body" and "This is my blood," the power of those words in the context of what these men were undergoing for the sake of people like him was overwhelming. For Arpin, it made him realize the significance of his own vocation to the priesthood. He remembered the first time he celebrated Mass after his ordination when he felt momentarily frozen: "I was gripped with fear because I realized for the first time what being a priest meant. It was *my* body and *my* blood on the line!"[104]

Arpin's words say a lot about the depth of priestly identity. His experience and that of the other gay priests I have profiled here indicate how embedded are the components of being gay and being a Catholic priest in the way they understand themselves. Their stories reveal how difficult it is to unravel the complex clerical system, illuminated by Jordan, in which these men are both protected and "hidden." The clerical culture provides particular ways for them to be gay within the confines of the priesthood, but it does so at the cost of maintaining a system of teachings that are repressive for gay Catholics in general. Catholic scholars like me would like to see gay priests band together and leave their active ministry, thus depleting the ranks and forcing the church to reevaluate how it envisions the priesthood; but I know this is a fantasy at this point in time. It ignores some important things the life texts of gay priests reveal. Yes, they do reap the dividends of priestly power by participating in the priestly caste of the church, and I would challenge them to seriously examine the ethics and hypocrisy of that aspect of the priesthood; but being a priest is also a core identity for them. It is not just a job from which they can easily walk away, even when their sexual identity is in conflict with their vocation. To make matters worse, the church does not always deal fairly with those who do resign.[105] Perhaps lay Catholics need to take the lead and find ways of helping these men exercise their priesthood outside the official structure of the church.

"Obscene Acts, Alone or with Others"

The hole I had dug in the sand — the sand itself having run through the hourglass of several years — was not as dark as the confessional's velvet gloom. If I felt at home there, it was because I was both reluctant believer and artful dodger. That is to say, I didn't want to "sin,"

but only to enjoy myself. A great part of the enjoyment was confessing the forbidden pleasures, because a great part of the pleasure lay
in the subsequent fall from grace.   —J. D. McClatchy, "My Fountain Pen"

Many of the autobiographers in my study are conscious of the way being
Catholic has given them a sense of the sacramental nature of the created
world.[106] They see a holy world in which God is revealed in bodies and
matter, even if church teachings on sexuality seem to mitigate against
this. David Plante writes about how being Catholic taught him an appreciation of the interconnectedness of body and soul, "and that we are in
the wholeness of our personalities what we are because we are both body
and soul."[107] For Plante, the body finds its fullest sensuality in the soul;
and the soul finds its fulfillment in the body, especially in the resurrected,
glorified, and entirely beautiful body we acquire at the end of the world.
Sexual desire then becomes part of this equation, especially in the context
of the basic Catholic teaching that sex is an expression of love for another
human being. Because of this, Plante trusts his body and his desire:

> If my sexual love for another was not sanctified by marriage, much
> less by heterosexuality, I never doubted, not for a second, that it was
> love, and even if I spent only one night with someone, what that
> person and I had exchanged over the night, in the wholeness of our
> love-making, was love. . . . I have always felt that in making love with
> a body in its wholeness, I was also making love with a soul. This idea
> fills me with the longing to make love, and this idea comes directly
> from my religion.[108]

For all Catholicism teaches about the dangers of the flesh, Plante and other
gay Catholics learned to listen for God in the created reality of the natural
world, which ultimately includes their bodies. This is why so many of
these writers have come to feel the natural law tradition is incomplete if
it does not take seriously the experience of gay people.

Sometimes it is participation in the very ordinariness of the world that
makes it redemptive. As a boy, James Morrison was so enamored with
his friend Craig that he went with him to his Baptist church and even
raised his hand when converts were being called forth, much to Craig's
excitement. After a nervous interview with the minister, however, Morrison knew he would never be a Baptist. He considered how much Craig
seemed sort of like a saint: "He was *in* the world, necessarily, but not *of*
it."[109] For himself, Morrison could not detach from the world. He realized
how comfortable he felt with his other friends who were not so concerned
about being "saved." The Catholic in him sensed that he needed to be a
part of this world in all its earthiness and vulgarity:

It had begun to seem to me that, in any case, the closer I came to exaltation, the further I was from God. Shooting the breeze with Kevin or Ronny, I felt I had come back to them after a long time away. There was something reassuring about their commitment to the known world. ... [110]

Part of this Catholic commitment to the known world involves the idea that one's actions in this world matter, that salvation is not just about *believing* but also about *doing*. As Morrison says to Craig a few days after the night of his "conversion" (and echoing Rodriguez's discomfort with instant salvation), "I don't think it happens that way, being saved. Like, you walk into a church and then all of a sudden you're suddenly saved. ... Going to heaven depends on what you do. It depends on how you act."[111]

This focus on one's actions can be inspiring in terms of social justice and giving meaning to one's daily life, but it also encourages a greater consciousness of the ways one falls short. Many of these writers experience Catholic identity as an awareness of personal sinfulness — an awareness that, when taken to its extreme, can overwhelm any appreciation of one's self as good. This is especially true for young boys with emerging erotic desires. David Kopay remembers the intimidating feelings he had when he had to go to confession during puberty and confess that he had touched himself in "an impure way." One was supposed to be firmly resolved to change the sinful behavior in order to be forgiven, which made it all the more terrifying for the young Kopay. "I would say the words but I also knew I would do it again."[112] He then had to perform the penance prescribed by the priest. Doing the Stations of the Cross was the worst because he had to stare at Jesus suffering, all because he had touched himself "in an impure way." On one occasion of confessing this particular sin, the priest yelled at him through the confessional screen and ordered him to stay silent in his room for the rest of the night. Though the Kopays had friends for dinner that night, the young David stayed in his room and could not even explain to their guests why he had to do so. "In fact I was honestly frightened that I would be struck dead if I broke the penance, and convinced that I would suffer eternal damnation in hell as the priest had said I would." Of course, this all did nothing to curb Kopay's desire to masturbate; it just made him feel bad for it. "I learned a lot about fear and guilt through the church, and very little about compassion and love."[113]

During Fenton Johnson's single hour of sex education in the seventh grade, one of his classmates asked if jacking off was a mortal sin. Father Gettelfinger's uncomfortable nod confirmed Johnson's suspicion that "anything that felt this good must be really, really bad." Unlike Kopay, however, he could not imagine going to confession and admitting he masturbated. Not only had he "done the deed," but he had done it often, and he was constantly devising ways of prolonging and intensifying it. The thought of telling Fr. Gettelfinger in the confessional was for Johnson "as impossible as giving it up."[114] He simply resigned himself to the fact that he would have to live with this mortal sin on his soul. But he didn't feel bad about it as much as he felt angry and betrayed by the mixed messages of his religion. As with Plante, Catholicism had infused Johnson with the sense that God was revealed in the natural world — including the flesh — so the fear and shame around all things sexual felt like a discrepancy:

> This was a contradiction I could not sustain, between the frank sensuality of this most voluptuous of Western Christian traditions and its niggardly attitudes toward the body's rich and varied landscapes. Instinctively I knew that something was seriously amiss in this separation of body from soul, flesh from spirit, though I was unable to express this duality in words. I never went to confession again.[115]

Just as Johnson could not, as an adolescent, articulate the inconsistency and hypocrisy he intuitively sensed, most of the boys in these stores were unable to frame their feelings of shame and confusion as anything but their own problem. Feelings of guilt and personal sinfulness would then compound into the feeling that one is never good enough. Larry Ebmeier knew his same-sex desire did not match what the church said he should feel. When he fell in love with another young man, he was in constant turmoil about sinning. In his words, "I would go from masturbation to confession to masturbation to confession."[116] José Zuniga claims to have written his life story at least partially out of a sense of Catholic guilt and regret. Though he came out publicly as a decorated soldier in the army, and ultimately was discharged for doing so, he writes to talk about his mistakes along the way, and also because he fears "I may still not have done enough in this battle."[117] During one of his earliest sexual experiences with another man, he found himself plagued with thoughts of hell and damnation because of the Catholic prohibitions on sex.[118] When he was younger, he decided to masturbate and sin by himself, rather than risk the greater transgression of desecrating another person's body.[119] Tommi Avicolli Mecca also tried to resist those "near occasions of sin" he was supposed to avoid and which would lead to even worse sins. He writes, "My Catholic upbringing was always in direct conflict with my natural sexual urges." Even so, nature would sometimes win, and then confessing the sin only made him feel lonelier.[120]

Philip Gambone carried his "uptight interpretation of Catholicism" into his adulthood. Even with his first adult boyfriend, he was preoccupied with sorting sins into categories of mortal and venial, as all Catholics learned in the Baltimore Catechism.[121] The worst part of sinning was the feeling that one was disappointing God, and it seems even the youngest boy could upset God by "misusing his body." When Joseph Kramer was a very little boy (he says age three), he already liked the feeling of putting his hands in his underwear and rubbing; but his mother quickly pointed out the gravity of this kind of behavior: "You shouldn't be doing that. God doesn't like when you touch yourself."[122] Thus, a good Catholic boy already struggling with the sinfulness of masturbation also had to struggle with the thought that his behavior was alienating God. For a gay Catholic boy, the feeling of alienation would be magnified; his "abnormal" desires would make his behavior even more disappointing for God. When Richard John Cardarelli first admitted to himself he was probably gay, he felt he had let God down. This in itself made him feel completely unlovable. He felt terrible and internalized the shame: "I hate myself, and if anyone ever finds out, they will hate me, too. *O God, forgive me!*"[123]

Andrew Holleran struggles with his own sinful perception of himself throughout his life writings. For Holleran, growing up Catholic "meant refining what may have been an already intrinsic sense of sin":

> Faced with the list of sins in my missal, as I examined my conscience before Confession, I became a connoisseur of the evil that lurks behind our every act, of the duplicity, the obfuscation with which we hide our true natures. . . . Growing up Catholic meant being intoxicated with the sense of one's own evil.[124]

As has already been indicated, the "cure" for one's sinfulness was the sacrament of Confession. Holleran writes of his satisfaction with this sacrament as a child. Sitting next to the votive candles in the church and going through the list of sins in the "examination of conscience" in his missalette was a way of peeling away the layers of his soul. It made him feel special, devoted, and clean. I remember my own similar encounters with this sacrament when I was growing up. Our parish pastor was far too intimidating, so I would always go to the associate, Fr. Tevington. He made me feel I had made a perfect act of contrition, and I always left with the feeling that my soul was again a clean slate. I shared Holleran's trepidation in that moment: we both left almost afraid to venture into the world again. The commission of new sins was inevitable.

The onset of puberty changed the dynamics of Confession for Holleran. Unlike David Plante, Holleran always felt ashamed of his body, especially his sexual organs, and this shame was magnified when his sexuality was awakened. As for all Catholics, puberty also presented more occasions for sin. Holleran learned to think of his sins as a betrayal of Christ and the reason He had to be crucified:

> This sense of betrayal, of Sin, meant that when puberty arrived in the life of a Catholic idealist and the body asserted itself in a way that

nothing in Catholicism had prepared you for, that single phrase on
the pages of the missalette — "obscene acts, alone or with others" —
was literally breath-taking, heart-constricting, to the child who heard
the screen slide open and knew he was about to say these words to
a priest. "Alone" meant you had jerked off in the bathroom. "With
others" meant you'd compared penises with the boy next door (the
son of a Protestant minister, in my case). Either one was terrifying;
a new order of guilt — so great one started to postpone, and fear, a
sacrament which till then had been eagerly sought.[125]

Slowly but surely, Holleran just stopped going to Confession and his religious fervor dissipated as he became an adult and really explored his
sexual identity. By the time he finally went to bed with another man at
the age of twenty-six, the lateness of which he attributes to his Catholic
upbringing, he thought he had left his Catholic identity behind him; but
as with most of these writers, he found it was not so simple. He found
himself "unwilling to cease the internal dialogue between my Catholic self
and daily life":[126] "It was one thing to say, reasonably, that religion was
only superstition: it was another to extinguish the self that had spent so
many warm, happy hours in church preparing for Confession."[127]

I have already recounted Holleran's story of the first time he spent the
night with another man and subsequently found himself in the shower
washing his mouth out with soap the next morning. As told in his coming out narrative, it was about the dynamic of acceptance and resistance
involved in coming to terms with gay identity. In his essay on Catholic identity, however, the same story has a slightly different resonance.
He refers to his washing action as a "soapy purification of the Temple
of the Holy Ghost," which was also his "first glimpse of the fact that
we never really leave Catholicism behind."[128] The story thus becomes
emblematic of the push and pull of Catholic identity, and a striking representation of the way sexual and religious identities are fused. After his
mouth-washing, Holleran tried celibacy for about a year; but an unbearable loneliness pushed him to question the church's recommendation for
gay people. This marked the beginning of a transformation in the way he
experienced his Catholic identity:

If God is Love, and sex is love, then sex between two people of the
same gender can only be looked upon benignly by God. The real sin
would be to live...without ever having this contact with another
human being, and the relief from isolation it provides. I took my
mantra from St. Augustine — "Love, and do as you will" — and distinguished between a human and a divine church; made my own
list of sins; and became in the process what is known as a cafeteria
Catholic.[129]

With this passage, Holleran ends up in a similar place as Plante in find-ing a core link between sex and God. Whereas Holleran ultimately remains ambivalent about the church and even the existence of God, Plante finally becomes an atheist; yet both maintain a Catholic identity and fill their fiction with Catholic imagery. Holleran, for example, still takes the sacra-mental system so seriously that he expresses reluctance to receive Holy Communion without being in a confessed state of grace.[130] And although Plante describes himself as an atheist, he still calls himself a Catholic writer. Being a Catholic inculcated in him a longing to be with God in eternity. "But," he says, "I think this longing is greater than my believ-ing or not."[131] Plante also says his book *The Annunciation* represents "a deepening of my devotion to my native religion," and even though his book *The Catholic* has the "longest sex scene in literature," he says it is really about being Catholic.[132] As for so many of these autobiographers, the gay and Catholic identities are so entangled, it is difficult to separate the two. Perhaps Plante's conflicted position is best understood in relation to something Dan, the protagonist in *The Catholic*, hears from a voice in his head: "It doesn't matter now if you believe or not, your beliefs are with you whether you want them or not."[133]

Shifting Orbits:
Deconversion and the Revision of Catholic Identity

It was only when I had finally begun to sin in ways I couldn't think how to disguise that I lost my faith in both religion and language.

Of course, language had been my religion all along, and my faith in its powers of salvation was only temporarily shaken. In the end, it was merely the heavy burden of the Church's authority that I had once and for all to shrug off.   —J. D. McClatchy, "My Fountain Pen"

Holleran and Plante seem to affirm the "Once a Catholic, always a Catho-lic" adage, yet their stories demonstrate this is not a static effect. Although Catholic identity remains persistent in their self-definitions, their rela-tionship to Catholicism is dynamic. When a gay Catholic comes to terms with his sexual identity, he inevitably comes to a new set of terms with his religious identity. His relationship to Catholicism and his construction of Catholic identity are tested and reassembled. John Barbour calls this process "deconversion." Barbour recognizes that the standard trajectory for traditional autobiography is the conversion narrative in the pattern of St. Augustine and so many autobiographies that have followed. But every conversion is a result of some kind of deconversion, or loss of faith in something prior. This is especially true for religious identity when a given religious system fails to adequately address the questions arising in the life that is narrated. Often, issues related to gender and sexuality provide the impetus for the deconversion. Barbour focuses primarily on women's life writings in his analysis of gender and deconversion,[134] but he acknowledges that men's life stories can also reflect these concerns. Augustine himself is a case in point: his dissatisfaction with Manicheism and other philosophies "was based partly on their failure to help him understand his anxieties about his sexual life."[135]

The gay Catholic autobiographies I study are prime examples of Barbour's deconversion theory. While Barbour sees his women autobiographers as "revisionists or reformers of traditional Christian assumptions about women," I view my autobiographers in a similar manner. All of these gay Catholics, in their own ways, are reformers of traditional Catholic assumptions about gay men. "In each [of their narratives], an experience of the loss of faith is central to the autobiographer's portrayal of [his] spiritual journey and demonstrates the inadequacy of some traditional Christian attitude, belief, or interpretation of a symbol."[136] For most, the "loss of faith" is not wholesale; rather, it is wrapped up in a complicated dialectic of embrace and abandonment in which repressive aspects of the institutional church are deconstructed. This has already been demonstrated in the texts by Holleran and Plante. The deconversion process is further complicated by the interplay of the doctrinal/ideological aspects of Catholicism with the cultural/"passed on" dimension. It is not simply a matter of remaining Catholic in an ethnic sense and discarding troublesome teachings. As I have been claiming throughout this chapter, Catholic identity involves a complex mixture of doctrines, practices, perspectives, and traditions, all of which are both "taught" in a direct way and "learned" more subtly. As these autobiographers come to terms with the meaning of their sexual identity through life experience and rational discernment, their religious self-understanding inevitably readjusts. They shift the position of their orbit on the Catholic axis. Their autobiographies recount and play out this readjustment, but it is never a finished story.

Rafael Campo uses part of his autobiography to discuss his own "fall from grace," as the church would view his relationship with Catholicism. Campo frames it as a sort of conflicted mutual abandonment. After feeling so comforted and accepted by the church in his childhood, he soon realized his gay identity seemingly placed him outside the community of the redeemed: "I was an abomination to the same God they said had created me, and whose forgiveness at the same time was the only hope for my salvation."[137] This was especially painful and confusing for Campo because he felt condemned for something he never chose, for the part of himself the church called "sin." "Of course, I remembered learning about other so-called sins as a child in Sunday school; they seemed carefully choreographed and intentionally committed, in contrast to the way my heart spontaneously quickened and lurched with a music my teachers said was abhorrent and unnatural."[138] What the church labeled a sin was an instinctive and joyous feeling within Campo, a feeling that would define his loving relationships with others: an identity. Campo was angry at the ironic situation created by church teachings in which sexual acts of any kind could be confessed and forgiven, but if he chose to live in a committed relationship with another man, he would remain separated from the very God who was supposed to be a God of love: "Clearly this horrible benefaction from my creator was to be my test in this life, my sexy crown of sharp thorns to wear."[139]

Gradually, Campo drifted away, and the church did nothing to stop him from straying. He was aware of the pronouncements coming from Rome that seemed designed to push gay people like him farther away. He saw no other recourse but to acquiesce to his exclusion, but this meant giving up another integral piece of himself, his Catholic identity:

> As I gradually relinquished what had been one of the greatest comforts in my life, one of the first things I forfeited was my capacity for believing in miracles. I was just sixteen years old. One day, with hardly a hesitation, I gave to my sister the shiny gold crucifix I had always worn faithfully around my neck. It felt like giving away a part of my body, like a heart valve or an eyelid or a small muscle in my hand.[140]

As so many of these autobiographers discover, shedding the Catholic identity from their selves is not so easy. There is always a part of Campo that clings to the Catholic, the part of him that gets angry when someone assumes he is a Catholic and defensive when someone speaks of Catholics with derision in their voice. When he was still calling himself a Catholic, Campo felt the ambivalence in the wholeness of himself, body and soul: "A queer still desiring and perhaps even needing some form of a relationship with God, I bitterly embodied as deep a schism as any in the Catholic Church's long divisive and blood-soaked history."[141] He would ultimately claim a space for himself "somewhere between what might be called atheism and secular humanism," formalizing in language his loss of faith in the church; yet in his text, he still associates aspects of himself with being Catholic, such as feelings of guilt and his respect for the mysterious workings of the human body and its ability to heal itself.

Philip Gambone writes of his long journey to find and claim a spiritual space that would fit his sense of self, all the while feeling the pull of his Catholic identity. He grew up with a typical letter-of-the-law Catholicism, in which his family always fulfilled the Sunday obligation. As is also typical for these autobiographers, Gambone felt an inner dissonance when he reached puberty. By the time he was twelve, he had added "impure thoughts and actions" to his list of weekly sins in the confessional. In college in the 1960s, he tried to live by the rules and even spent time with students who were affiliated with the ultraconservative Catholic group Opus Dei. Gambone realizes, in retrospect, his attraction to Opus Dei "had as much to do with the physical attractiveness of several of its members...as it did their theology." It was not helping him be a better Catholic: "By the time of Bobby Kennedy's assassination, I had driven myself crazy with ascetic practices — praying the rosary with the Opus Dei boys, going to mass, refraining from masturbation — yet none of these things had put a stop to the sexual urges that kept churning within me."[142] When he finally had a fulfilling sexual experience with another man after his second year at Harvard, his journey "away" from Catholicism began.

For a time, in the 1970s, Gambone tried the Episcopal Church because his boyfriend was Episcopalian. "I did not think of myself as leaving the Church but only of entering into a different (only *slightly* different, I reminded myself) 'communion' — the Anglican communion."[143] When he moved and became involved with his second lover, he began to attend a liturgically conservative Anglo-Catholic parish in Boston with a large gay population. His eventual drifting away from that church along with his drifting away from that lover led him to try a series of Catholic parishes, including Dignity; but by the end of the 1980s, he was fed up with the internal struggles and debates of Catholicism and drifted away once again. He tried a Unitarian-Universalist meeting house in Provincetown for a time, but now considers himself "free-floating." Even so, he still feels the push and pull of Catholicism within him:

> I want to be rigorously unsentimental about this. I want to say that my nostalgia for a sacramental religion is just that, a piece of nostalgia that I must get big enough to overcome. I want to say that the Church as I know it today — the Church of papal encyclicals against homosexuality, the Church of an all-male celibate clergy, the Church in whose name all manner of oppression and intolerance continues to be practiced — that that Church is an irrelevancy in my life. I want to say that I wish it a swift death.
> And yet...[144]

Gambone is wrestling here with the dialectic of embrace and resistance that is so much a part of the gay-and-Catholic identities of these autobiographers. His "And yet..." is his acknowledgment that his journey of deconversion is not clear cut. There is something in him — that Catholic thing — that stays with him in spite of his intellectual objections. As he comments after his sojourn with the Unitarians, he is drawn by the "mystery" of Catholicism: "Yes, I missed that sense of mystery — that sense of the universe as a place that cannot be taken at face value—which seems to be at the heart of what is best in Catholicism."[145]

Like Gambone, Fenton Johnson explored other religions in his spiritual search for a place to fit. He considered atheism, but soon realized he had been "fated" for faith. Though he was attracted to the "easy alliance between democracy and theology" he found in the Protestant churches he visited, he left those Protestant services dissatisfied with their lack of primal mystery: "These services bore the imprints of hands of remembered generations, whereas the services of my childhood church had been shaped by hands outside of memory, embracing and incorporating the ancient rites along with their gods and goddesses of mountains and plains, skies and seas."[146] Johnson knew he belonged in the world of Catholicism, where the liturgies conveyed a connection to an enduring community that seemed to transcend time. "Those collective celebrations of faith were a powerful and binding magic: to have known them in the flesh means never to leave them entirely behind."[147] What he felt in his body, however, was not affirmed by the proverbial "keepers" of the tradition. Though he carried his Catholic identity in his flesh, he did not feel at home in the institution: " . . . I'm a gay man and the Catholic Church has made it clear it has no place for me."[148] Feeling alienated from the church for being gay, yet valuing the Catholic tradition, he spent years feeling angry—so much so that he lost his impulse toward spiritual expression.

Johnson devotes his most recent life text to finding his way through this anger and back to faith—a narration of deconversion and reconversion. The boy who had once imagined the Virgin Mary might appear to him in the Kentucky hills[149] became an adult whose heart pounded with rage when he expected to make the sign of the cross. He still felt fated for faith, but it had been blocked by the institution and it seemed to elude him: "Why don't I have it, and is it possible, this late in the game, that I might acquire some?"[150] In his search, he gives himself over to the disciplines of monastic life by visiting and studying at both a Zen Buddhist monastery and the Trappist monastery near his childhood home. "What would be required of me to form an identity from some place other than my wounds? This was the scary, liberating question arising from zazen."[151] He learns to look inside himself and embrace the faith lessons already learned from his marginalization as a gay man:

My journey among the monks...was bringing me to understand that for me the wellspring of faith resides in the source of my otherness, my homosexuality—the condition that led me, or rather *forced* me, to seize my destiny and determine my own values, even as it taught me to respect the given, those aspects of life over which I had little or no control.[152]

Framing his journey in this way allows Johnson to shift his focus away from the death-dealing institutional church and to examine the inner "demons" that had maintained their white-knuckled grip on his wounds. By the end of his time at the monastery, he came to understand the sign of the cross as a gesture of community in suffering. He writes about that pivotal moment with the same kind of ambivalence expressed by Gambone: "On this my last evening of this stay among the monks, I signed myself a Christian. (*How hard it is for me even now, years later, to write those words.*)"[153] Like Gambone's deconversion, Johnson's "reconversion" is inevitably conflicted.

Richard Rodriguez understands the push and pull of Catholicism, but he remains devoutly Catholic because he senses something at the heart of Catholicism that resonates with his experience of being gay. Though he says he was born a Catholic and embraced it in his childhood without question, he later chose to be Catholic: "I do not wish to live beyond a crucifix. The crucifix does not represent guilt to me, but love."[154] He empathizes with those who "wish to be quit of the church," especially in light of bishops who seemingly hope to "rescue" gay people. Yet he feels a familial bond with these same bishops, rooted in his gay identity: "That which is homosexual in me most trusts the durability of this nonblood lineage. *Trees and their gracious silence.* Though I scorn them sometimes too and I ask forgiveness for my scorn. For none of us has made flesh."[155] Even so, Rodriguez experiences the dialectic of embrace and resistance that holds gay Catholic identity together. When he awakens in the middle of the night with his lover breathing at his side, he knows this breath is what sustains him. He feels angry the church would have him doubt that this is love:

> I turn the pillow to its cool side. Then rage fills me, against the cubist necessity of having to arrange myself comically against orthodoxy, against having to wonder if I will offend, against theology that devises that my feeling for him, more than for myself, is a vanity.[156]

In spite of his anger, Rodriguez lives at the crux of this tension. He calls it his "brown paradox," which he configures in the spirit of Walt Whitman as being brown in a deceptively black-and-white world: "*Of every hue and caste am I.*"[157] His gay Catholic identity, like his ethnic identity, is constructed upon the "impurity" that results when conflicting positions collide. Even though the church tells him his love is wrong and asks that he segment himself like a cubist drawing, it is also the church that taught him how to love in the first place. Ironically, it is the Catholic within him that enables him to trust the love he feels lying next to his lover in bed.

This irony is part of what propelled Peter Krask to enter a monastery just six weeks after spending his first night with a man. He went there for a three-month quest to figure himself out and to explore his vocation. True to the pattern of so many good gay Catholic boys, it did not surprise anyone in his family that he would go and that he might someday join a religious order. Of course, he had not planned on falling in love just before going, but this would also be the catalyst for his own deconversion. One morning, while watching the monks chanting in prayer, with his mind on the man he had left behind, Krask realized he believed so little of what they were singing. He even began to look at some of the monks sexually and developed a crush on one of them. When he finally got up the nerve to tell one of the monks he was gay, the monk did not judge him for it. Krask was able to vent the frustration he had been holding for so long about being gay and trying to be a good Catholic: "Being gay is this sick cosmic joke. How could God be so cruel? That's what makes me the angriest. How unbelievably cruel. Bolt a starving person in a chair and place a plate in front of him. Just out of reach."[158] A few days later, alone in the chapel and feeling the weight of his inner conflict, he stopped fighting himself: "And then the word came from my mouth. Alone, on my knees and terrified, I said yes. Yes to everything. To all of it."[159] All at once, Krask felt weightless. Although accepting his gay identity would mean not living up to his image as the perfect Catholic boy, he would finally be embracing that part of himself he had resisted for so long.

After David Kopay spent eighteen months in the seminary trying to live by the rules, he decided, "I'd had enough of the life." This was only the beginning of his complete break with church. As much as he tried to change it or deny it, he believed he was naturally attracted to other men and that sexual love was a good thing, not a sin. For Kopay, it was a rational and seemingly uncomplicated decision: "The Church couldn't accept me in my natural state so I could no longer accept the church."[160] The church had also caused a rift between Kopay and his parents, who accepted the teachings on homosexuality without question. Kopay felt like Isaac, whose father Abraham was willing to kill him in order to obey God's commands.[161] The church came to represent a God who would create him as a gay man and then sacrifice him for it.

For Kevin Killian, who had been sexually abused in his Catholic boys' high school,[162] his decision to break with the church was also rather uncomplicated. He says it was because of its policies on abortion, women's rights, and gay rights; but he had also been used by the church and found he could neither fight nor hide in its monolithic structure: "I tried to talk to It, but It just sat there, a big unresponsive sack of white sugar. So goodbye." At the same time, something inside him longs for and still pursues the bridging of human and divine that is at the heart of Catholicism: "And yet I suppose I'm a far better Catholic now than then. I dream of this God who took on clothes of man and then stepped forward to strip them off at the moment of humiliation."[163] Killian knows first hand what it is like to suffer degradation from his experience being sexually abused. Like Jesus, he was stripped both literally and figuratively of his pride. His identification with the suffering God-made-human resonates in the core of his Catholic identity. But it is not enough. Clearly wounded by his experience with his Franciscan teachers, Killian has lost faith not only in the institutional church but also in the goodness of human love. "I try to get closer to Christ through work. I tried love for a long time, but it only lengthened the distance between Him and me."[164]

Brian McNaught almost heroically resisted his deconversion. His life writings are part of what was once his larger life project of being a gay Catholic activist. He even spent twenty-four days fasting as a way of calling attention to the church's problematic teachings on homosexuality. He first talks about the old Brian, who spent "many, many years in the confessional feeling guilty about being a homosexual."[165] Later, he came to accept that part of himself as God-given and committed himself to helping gay Catholics recognize their self-worth. His life texts, however, reveal the emotional toll this took on him and his relationship to the church. In April 1979, he was unabashedly proclaiming his devotion to the church in spite of its hurtful teachings: "Lest anyone be confused, I love the Church."[166] Within a year, his writing reflects an overwhelming frustration and anger, due to the church's insistence on forbidding him to be himself, like a parent who secretly beats her child: "Today my pain is stronger than my devotion. Today I can't find the strength to defend [the Church] against the curses of the neighbors and relatives who know. Today I fear I will stand rigid and scream 'I hate the Church! I hate it! I hate it!'"[167] McNaught never again proclaims his love of the church; but he does settle into a revised relationship with the church, somewhere between love and hate, in which he rewards himself for his years of struggle and constancy. This is most tellingly revealed in a letter he wrote a year later designed to be read after his death by his partner Ray:

> If the Church should decide to begin canonization proceedings, don't discourage them! When they start looking for miracles, tell them I grew to my full potential. There is no greater miracle for a gay person today. Tell them, too, that I kept the Faith, which is also no small task. Finally (because they always look for three), tell them how we loved each other selflessly.[168]

McNaught demonstrates how "keeping the faith" for a gay Catholic necessarily involves a parallel loss of faith in the institutional church. The Catholic world may remain an enchanted place in which to dwell, but the enchantment is stripped of illusion. The deconversion is focused primarily on the "keepers" of that world, whose rigid rules and unidimensional view of sexuality do not make sense in the lives of gay Catholics. For Fenton Johnson, the task involves a reclamation of the spiritual legacy by those who have been marginalized by it:

> I have been unable to use traditional language to describe my experiences of the sublime because I associated that language with a world that had failed me. But the fault lies not in the words but in the institutions that abused them. My task — the task of all seekers — is to find a way to reclaim the language of the spiritual life.[169]

For several of these autobiographers, Dignity empowers them to reclaim the language of spiritual life. Dignity represents the kind of revision of Catholic identity that provides a path for gay Catholics to both "keep the faith" and be true to themselves. It could be argued that in the post–Vatican II church, Dignity has made a fully gay and Catholic identity possible. I have already mentioned the role Dignity played in the lives of some gay priests. For other gay Catholics, Dignity is the space in which the deconversion narrative is transformed into a narrative of recommitment, after their relationship to the church hierarchy is revised.

The only way this kind of recommitment is possible is through an acceptance of the fact that the church hierarchy is composed of men who are capable of making errors. In this model, these men get so caught up in wanting the church to appear free of error that they seem to forget they are dealing with a living and growing church. Tony Laveccia says, "My gripe with the institutional church is that they are not interested in gay people as people, but more concerned in upholding rules and regulations."[170] For Gerald Allen, the problem is that church leaders are out of touch with the realities of the people they are supposed to be serving: "Those who are making these decisions are old men who are not married. They do not have families or pay mortgages. There seems to be a real gulf between them and where the people are."[171] Sometimes, seeing the hierarchy for what it is creates too much cognitive dissonance so that any real recommitment to the church is impossible. William G. Storey spent years in close association with church leaders during his long tenure as a professor of liturgy and church history at the University of Notre Dame. He calls the Roman system "false and pernicious" and "the antithesis of the Gospel." He refuses to be associated with it any longer.[172]

The autobiographers who remain committed to the church in their life texts find a way of separating the church from its institutional hierarchy. Even Richard Rodriguez, who finds a certain amount of comfort and stability in the historical lineage of the institutional church, knows the dangers posed by men who "presume to divine, to enforce, to protectively wear the will of God."[173] After reflecting upon his own ambivalent relationship with church leaders, Rodriguez turns to consider the perpetrators of September 11, 2001. He characterizes them as men of "certainty," who were waging a war against "impurity" — men who saw things in black-and-white, rather than brown — in the name of God.[174] Though Rodriguez does not directly draw the analogy, the same could be said of church leaders who maintain a rigid and singular position on homosexuality. They want pure boundaries for sexuality. They resist the "brown." They fear the "impurity" represented by gay Catholics. Yet many gay Catholics continue to keep the faith, and the Catholic tradition goes on despite the human beings who are its administrators. Jim Revak puts it this way:

> My basic feeling is that I am part of the Catholic tradition, and I have just as much right to call myself Catholic as a Pope, a Cardinal, or a Bishop does. . . . I live with the fact that there is a hierarchy that doesn't particularly like me as a gay person.[175]

Dignity was the first group to offer a space for being the kind of gay Catholic described above. By providing liturgies and sacraments — the material culture of Catholicism — in an environment that is openly affirming of gay identity, Dignity salvages the Catholic identity of many of these autobiographers. Tony Laveccia says Dignity has been his salvation.[176] Dignity provided Masses and prayer vigils for Tom McLaughlin when his lover was dying of complications related to AIDS.[177]

Of course, Dignity cannot accommodate all gay Catholics because not all of them want to worship in a separate space; nor is that the answer to the problem of the church's inadequate teachings with regard to homosexuality. Quite simply, the church needs to listen to the life experiences of gay Catholics and develop teachings on sexuality that make sense to them and respect their subjectivity. Their life texts reveal deeply ingrained and formative Catholic identities. Though Catholic identity is culturally constructed and informed, it feels for many of these autobiographers just as natural and essential as their (also constructed) sexuality feels.[178] Their revised versions of what it means to be Catholic also demonstrate the multiplicity and possibilities of Catholic identity, yet I am writing this book at a time when church leaders are increasingly concerned with tightening and policing what defines a Catholic. To pick up on the metaphor I was using at the end of the previous chapter, the church and gay Catholics seem to be seeking different landscapes. As American Catholics move increasingly from cities to suburbs, gay Catholics are seeking spaces for themselves in cities. Is this a literal representation of the reality that gay Catholics and the church seem to be moving in opposite directions?

Being gay and being Catholic are both deeply embedded identities in the lives of these autobiographers. It is a tragedy when gay Catholics are made to feel they have to choose between these two core identities. Jon

Soucy expresses this dilemma succinctly when he remembers his days as a conservative "defender of the faith" while a student at Georgetown University: "I just wish I'd spent less time saving Georgetown's Catholic identity and more time trying to come to terms with my own identity as a gay man."[179] When Catholic identity is displaced, revised, or rejected, it speaks volumes about the deficiency of church teachings on sexuality. Given the strength of the Catholic "thing" in these lives, consider how many of them would be committed and practicing Catholics today if church teaching took their subjectivity seriously. Their involvement and allegiance could only be a boon. Instead, the church insists on bifurcating their personhood by maintaining impossible dualisms. Church teaching falsely maintains a clean separation between sexual orientation and sexual behavior. In the realms of sexual and religious identity, however, it is not so easy to untangle being from doing, act from actor. At face value, this may seem possible; but gay Catholic autobiographies demonstrate how illusory such a separation really is.

Chapter 4

"Homosexual Acts"

The main source of my fear was this: Each time we made love I took from him a little more of his self, and gave in return a little more of my self, binding us together a little more closely. We were becoming married, in fact if not before the law; we were becoming one instead of two.... Each time we made love I gave more of myself to him and took more in return and so enlarged my heart, made it bigger and stronger (like any muscle, the heart grows with exercise). But as we grew more a part of each other, I grew more terrified that when he died, he would take some large part of me with him and that I would fall into the hole he left behind, whose bottom (if it existed) I could not yet begin to fathom. — Fenton Johnson, *Geography of the Heart*

The dialectic of embrace and renunciation that is so much a part of gay Catholic identity as revealed in the previous two chapters is mirrored in the official teachings of the church. The same church telling gay people they are to be accepted with sensitivity, compassion, and respect, simultaneously tells them their sexual orientation is objectively disordered. True, official teaching distinguishes between the person and their sexual expression, but this distinction does not make sense in light of the way the gay men I profile here narrate their sexuality. As my analysis of their life texts reveals, sexuality is such an integral part of their human personhood, it becomes a piece of identity. While this is enhanced by the current historical context in which sexual identities are especially available and viable, this does not make their experience of gay identity any less valid. All identities, including Catholic identity, are culturally conditioned and socially and historically contingent. Indeed, in many ways it is easier to define and discuss gay identity today than it is to pin down Catholic identity, as my analysis also reveals. In any case, gay identity is much too complicated, multivalent, and wrapped up in other identity pieces for it to be summarily dismissed as disordered. Saying it is *objectively* disordered compounds the problem because it presumes sexuality can be evaluated outside of the particular context of persons and their relationships. On some level, of course, church leaders realize this and try to have it both

124

ways. The result is the present bifurcation of church teachings into moral and pastoral rhetorics which attempt to both respect and condemn gay identity.

One troubling ramification of this bifurcation problem is the separation of persons from their acts. In a narrow sense, such a separation is understandable. When a person performs a particular action, it does not necessarily alter who he/she is. A person is not the same as his/her actions. The church rightly recognizes this with respect to human sins, which are construed as aberrations in the course of who we are and what we are supposed to do. This clean separation, however, becomes quite messy when applied to sexuality and sexual identity, which encompasses both being and doing. When these autobiographers discuss being gay, they relate it to a range of feelings, perspectives, *and* behaviors that are deeply interconnected. The same can even be said for the way they talk about Catholic identity. It too is related in these narratives to a host of interwoven perceptions, attitudes, and activities that are separable only on the most simplistic and deceivingly obvious levels. These sexual and religious identities do not inhere in a vacuum, apart from one's actions and relationships.

The church says gay people should be treated with friendship and justice, even as it says homosexual acts are intrinsically evil — love the "sinner"; hate the "sin." In other words, you can be a homosexual as long as you do not act like one. But what does it mean to perform a homosexual act? What *is* a homosexual act? Church officials may think the terminology is obvious, but one must wonder if they are all on the same page in their definitions. Are they thinking only of genital activity or any kind of intimate, physical contact between two people of the same gender? The term can be nebulous. My point, however, is not to urge the church to codify what constitutes a homosexual act (though I have no doubt there are scholars in the Vatican ready and eager to do so) but rather to demand contextualization of the concept. Homosexual acts, like all sexual acts, are always performed in the context of other life experiences and relationships. They cannot be fully evaluated in isolation, as if these acts are free-floating and disconnected from their actors and their complex lives. This is not a foreign idea in Catholic moral theology for actions the church finds problematic in some way. "Just war theory" was developed in order to contextualize the "problem" of war and killing in Christian ethics, and a range of opinion on the subject has been expressed throughout Christian history. Acts must be appraised in relation to actors and their life situations.[1]

One might object that it is impossible to achieve ethical clarity without focusing on acts; that juridical discussions and decisions must be centered on acts in order to achieve a sense of fairness and impartiality; that even personal meanings, motives, and decisions always relate to and result in actions. Of course, acts matter in the realm of sexual ethics, but they are only one piece of the equation, and the church errs when the focus on acts shrouds other mitigating factors. One might contend the church does consider both act and actor when it considers the genders of those involved in a sexual act, but this is not really the case. When the church condemns same-gender sexual acts, it does not care about the persons who inhabit the bodies involved. It is only interested in the way these bodies are anatomically sexed as male or female. It is not even accurate to say the church considers "gender" because that word implies a social meaning layered on the body. In the church's assessment of homosexual acts, homosexual persons are effectively obliterated, no matter how much the pastoral rhetoric tries to gloss it over. At least for heterosexual persons, the church makes some space for the acceptability of their sexual acts by contextualizing them in personal situations. Here too, however, church leaders fail to take seriously the full range of heterosexual lived experience.[2]

Part of the problem which prevents the church from seeing alternative ways of developing sexual ethics is the persistence of procreationism in Catholic moral theology. Procreationism is the assumption that sex is naturally oriented toward creation of human life. Christine Gudorf spells out some of the ways this assumption is manifested in our society. The first is the common view that penile-vaginal intercourse is *the* sexual act. Heterosexual coitus is "real sex" because it is procreative; all other sexual acts are either perversions to be avoided or foreplay. This attitude then leads to the denigration of sexual relationships in which coitus is not possible: "real sex" requires a penetrating and impregnating penis. This works against gay men in fostering the assumption that the primary gay sexual activity is anal intercourse, thus delegitimating other sexual practices like mutual masturbation. It also belittles the sexuality of anyone who is or is perceived to be incapable of coitus. Finally, procreationism too easily supports an understanding of children as the "cost" of sex, which ironically fosters the attitude that sexual activity without contraception is somehow more "moral" than sex with contraception, even when conception is not desirable or advisable.[3] These attitudes, so endemic in the history of Christian moral theology, work against viewing the purposes of sex in new ways.

Twentieth-century and subsequent moral theology has begun to witness the reinterpretation of procreation as a norm for sexual ethics, even among conservative ethicists. Kathy Rudy elucidates a few of the factors contributing to this shift in consciousness. First, there is a recognition that contemporary life does not always allow families to adequately provide for a large number of children. Second, the good of unitivity between sexual partners sometimes conflicts with the end of procreativity, prompting some couples to forego the good of sexual relations in order to limit family size. Third, we now recognize that good parenting is not simply a biological function; the ability to make new life is not as important as the ability to nurture that life. Lastly, and I think most importantly, new reproductive technologies have made reproduction possible without physical, sexual contact.[4] Gays and lesbians have seized upon these last two factors — through methods like adoption, foster care, and artificial insemination — to be procreative in their own way, without necessarily ever having personally experienced penile-vaginal intercourse. If reproduction no longer requires heterosexual coitus, then it is no longer necessary to assume that sex is naturally oriented only toward the creation of human life. We can also then put aside the mind-set that delegitimates sexual acts outside of heterosexual intercourse. Once we have abandoned the necessity of procreativity as a norm for sexual ethics, we can begin to reimagine a Catholic moral theology which includes homosexual acts as legitimate and morally sound expressions of intimacy.

Of course, we also need to overcome the heteronormativity that has similarly constricted the imagination of the Catholic moral tradition. The "heterosexual grid," as it is currently constructed, is based on the same faulty binary economy which is at the root of the church's bifurcated teachings on homosexuality. It posits one sexuality as the norm — the "real" sexuality — and all others as deviant. Mary McClintock Fulkerson suggests that the importance placed on absolutized notions of sexuality which support heterosexism represents a form of idolatry for Christians. It relies on a cultural code to restrict membership in the Christian community, much like some early followers of Jesus sought to do with their insistence that one had to first be circumcised (become a Jew) in order to become Christian. As the early Christians decided after some debate, such a restriction goes against the grain of the Gospel. For Fulkerson, the refusal to accept the heterosexual grid is like the refusal to accept the circumcision requirement.[5] Given that sexual identities are culturally and historically contingent, it is unwise for Catholic moral theology to rely on heterosexual identity as normative. Heterosexual identification is as much a socially constructed phenomenon as gay identification. In fact, heterosexual identity is currently available largely because of gay identity, on which it relies for its definition. Without the constraints of procreationism and heteronormativity, each of which increasingly look like a theological straw man, there is little left to sustain the church's position that all homosexual acts are morally unacceptable.

The blanket condemnation of homosexual acts, whatever that means, results in an ethical vacuum about the "doing" of being gay. Andrew Sullivan calls this an "unethic," which he explains as "a statement that some people are effectively beneath even the project of an ethical teaching."[6] This contributes to the deafening silence so many of these autobiographers experienced growing up gay. Rather than consider the possibility that some homosexual acts might be ethically permissible or even morally sound, the church leadership instead backs out of the conversation entirely. Fortunately, the discussion takes place in spite of them. There is a prevailing awareness among Catholic moral theologians of the inadequacy of the deontological, confession- and act-centered approach to sexual ethics that has traditionally been employed. The newer model situates sexuality in a broad social context by shifting the discussion from an emphasis on acts to an emphasis on the meaning of acts and relationships, forming ethical ideals independent of the genders involved. In this paradigm, new values emerge as the basis for developing sexual norms, such as mutuality, hospitality, maturity, and responsibility.

Margaret Farley is an example of a Catholic moral theologian whose work reshapes the conventional approach to sexual ethics and thus provides a way of rethinking how we understand human acts and desire. Farley builds her sexual ethics on the foundations of justice, commitment, and respect, suggesting all relationships and acts within those relationships need to be assessed according to these kinds of standards. Most useful for my purposes is her discussion of what it means to really respect persons, as the church instructs Catholics to do with regard to gay people. Respect for persons recognizes them in their wholeness and in their context: "We are who we are within social, cultural, linguistic contexts, formed in our understandings and our desires. We do not produce our own meaning out of nothing, nor are our actions wholly our own."[7] As we interact with the world, we become ourselves, and this interaction gives rise to our own actions: "Every action that we choose is for the sake of some love, whether for ourselves or for another, whether for persons or things. When we choose our actions, we ratify, identify with, some of our loves (deferring, or refusing to ratify, other loves that are thereby not expressed in action)."[8] For Farley, true respect of persons affirms their freedom to act on behalf of the loves and desires that arise from their interaction with others.

The same idea about the origin and meaning of our actions is articulated differently and applied directly to homosexual acts by Andre Guindon. Guindon posits that because human sexual activity expresses and communicates emotions and meanings, it should be understood as language. Building on the insights of contemporary linguists like S. I. Hayakawa, he describes language as the way one thinks about and expresses oneself. The meanings of the words one uses to express oneself are always modified by the particular context in which they are deployed, such that no word ever has the same meaning twice. Guindon extends this to the concept of "homosexual acts," which are part of the self-expressive language of gay identity. He criticizes church leaders for assuming "there are specific instances of 'physical behavior' or 'material performances' which, independently of any user's meaning-making operation, have an evil meaning."[9] Gay persons will employ a variety of words and actions, including the language of physical, sexual activity, to express their sexuality and the feelings that go along with it. This shifts the discourse from "homosexual acts" to "gay speech." For Guindon, "Each modulation of self-expression and communication [between gay persons] is a 'homosexual act.'"[10] To say such actions are forbidden is to deny gay persons the capacity to make meaning out of their own language. In effect, it denies gay persons their ability to speak.

We need not look to Catholic theologians, however, for a way out of the ethical conundrum left in the wake of inadequate church teachings on sexual identity; we can look to gay lives themselves as represented in life narratives. Here, the discernment of right and wrong is played out in concrete ways, with real-life consequences. These autobiographies stand as testaments to the untenability of bifurcated church teachings which presume to separate the being and the doing of gay identity. If we are to take seriously gay men's subjectivity as narrators of their own lives, we must also take seriously the conclusions they provide with regard to "homosexual acts." First, homosexual acts are not exclusively physical. What gay people do as a consequence of being gay involves a variety of actions and interactions with themselves and others. Second, these actions represent an integration of gay identity within the whole of themselves and so should be viewed as outgrowths of their personhood, not of some free-floating sexual desire. Third, these are the actions of gay men who are themselves moral agents, who evidence a great deal of discernment and struggle as they decide how to act. This last point, especially, underscores the artificiality and uselessness of a phrase like "love the sinner; hate the sin." As Andrew Sullivan states:

> When you begin to see homosexuality not as some bizarre and willful attempt to practice a specific sex act, but as a deep and complex part of a human person, a person who needs as much love and as much divine love as any other person, then it becomes clear how it is, in fact, impossible to hate the "sin" and love the "sinner." Or how the very formulation is, in fact, a way of denigrating homosexual people, denying their humanity, erasing their integrity. It is as if we were to say that we loved Jews, so long as they never went to a synagogue; or that we welcomed immigrants, so long as they never tried to learn English. It is a rejection masquerading as an acceptance,

and it perpetuates, in the guise of alleviating, the very ethical conflict from which homosexuals are doggedly trying to escape.[11]

Sullivan's words indict church teachings that effectively denigrate and deny the moral agency of gay people even as the church professes to love and respect them. The ethical conflict to which he refers is rooted in the silence gay people face in trying to find any framework for understanding and assessing the choices that result from their gay identity.

Some gay activists might be wary of the implication that there *needs* to be an ethical framework around gay identity. In the earliest days of the gay pride movement after 1969 and through the 1970s, activists emphasized the need to question the values and institutions of mainstream society. As these pioneers saw it, the problem was not that gay people needed to be accepted by assimilating into hegemonic cultural and religious values but rather that these values need to be overthrown. Institutions like marriage and ethical mandates like monogamy simply do not fit the needs of all people. In fact, these societal "values" effectively control and oppress people. These activists viewed attempts to fit gay relationships into conventional norms with skepticism. Would this not serve to reinforce the very structures which had marginalized them in the first place? In the words of Audre Lorde, "The master's tools will never dismantle the master's house."[12] Instead, the value of freedom in desire and pleasure should be the norm for which gay people should strive. This would mean challenging anything designed to restrict sexual freedom in any way, calling into question the need for norms and ethics regarding sexuality.

Successive generations of gay activists have been exploring the viability of this strategy, especially in the face of dramatic shifts in gay visibility in the last three decades of the twentieth century. The AIDS pandemic intensified the dynamics of this debate.[13] Some of the first activist pioneers witnessed the deaths of numerous friends and worried that the emphasis on absolute freedom was killing the gay community. They began to insist on an ethic of *safe* sex, and advocated restrictions which would curtail the practice of risky and deadly behaviors. Some focused on behaviors only, while others went further and found "protection" in conventional norms like monogamy. Others maintained that any return to restrictive, traditional codes would only recreate the situation of marginalization that had initially prompted gay men to engage in covert and risky behaviors. By the late 1990s, gay activists were divided into conflicting positions in the debate, with the extremes identified as radical and neoconservative.[14] The most important thing this debate reveals is not the *need* for an ethical framework around gay identity, but the fact that there *is* always an ethical framework in place. The question is what kind of ethics and how these ethics are formulated and articulated.

The real-life ethical struggles represented in these kinds of debates are played out and applied on a practical level in gay lives. Choices are made and actions are performed against the backdrop of this larger socioethical context, and gay life narratives recount these choices and actions. By and large, the autobiographers in my study do not evidence an ethic based purely on freedom as the overriding norm in their life narratives.[15] These are not stories in which finding and having unencumbered access to sex is the most important theme. Quite the contrary, these are stories of men who grapple with the ramifications of their actions, for themselves and for others, in both their nonsexual and sexual relationships. Yes, they feel sexual desire for other men, and they want to affirm that desire as an integral part of themselves — as a sexual identity; but they also sort out its meanings and implications. I think this is a reflection of the way their Catholic identity informs their sexual identity. Rather than occupying the extremes of the debates I discussed above, these gay Catholic autobiographers reflect a both/and sensibility. As a whole, they make a case for sexual freedom *and* responsibility as norms. They challenge the church's apparent belief that there can or should not be any discussion at all about the ethics of "homosexual acts."[16]

The fact that these life narratives already provide an ethical framework for understanding and assessing the choices that inhere with gay identity is what enables us to recognize these autobiographers as moral agents themselves. The idea of agency, however, has been called into question by postmodern theorists who have deconstructed the notion of the "subject." According to the theory, the subject is not the originator of subjectivity but rather the effect of social and symbolic processes. This would seem to foreclose any possibility of personal moral reflection that does not simply replicate prevailing conventions. Marilyn Gottschall uses Judith Butler's deconstruction of gender to deontologize the subject and then reimagine a moral agency that is consistent with postmodern subjectivity. Following Butler, Gottschall sees agency as being embedded in power and discourse: "The potential to act emerges within the interface between the subject and discursive/cultural injunctions and practices. . . . It is in performativity, the reworking of the discursive processes, that the process of change is opened up."[17] For Gottschall, agency is not found in the world of free will facing infinite possibilities, but paradoxically, within our constraints. It is agency limited by the interaction of the subject and its formation. Once agency is reconstituted in this way, ethical analysis can move beyond the determination of rights and wrongs, toward an inquiry into "the multiple levels of contingency and complexity that accompany the desire to act."[18]

Autobiography seems to be the perfect vehicle for the conveyance of this kind of ethical reflection. It represents in narrative form the interface between the subject and the context of its formation, which Gottschall posits as the site of agency; and it is a window into the "multiple levels of contingency and complexity that accompany the desire to act." Autobiographers are moral agents in their own right and their autobiographies are moral performances of a kind. Diane Bjorklund points out how the construction of the self in autobiography is inextricably linked with moral values:

> Autobiographers offer a public explanation of how they have led their lives. To tell their life stories, they must speak of their beliefs, actions, intentions, choices, and goals. Because they pursued such goals and actions in a social context where others may be harmed or helped, their actions and intentions become moral topics.[19]

When autobiographers account for their choices and actions in their life texts, they are doing so, "not just in terms of personal goals achieved or personal problems solved but also in response to prevailing moral values."[20] The life writer ponders questions about personal responsibility; self-control; the relative importance of will, reason, and emotion in decision making; and the meaning of freedom in terms of human conduct. The resulting life narrative will ultimately help to articulate, sustain, or challenge prevailing ethical norms. According to Bjorklund, an autobiographer whose life narrative challenges conventional norms will also guide the reader to agree with their choices or at least not judge them harshly for it. In this sense, autobiographies are moral performances in which ethical issues are worked out and justified in the context of concrete lives.[21] The autobiographies I analyze are no exception. They challenge the church's narrow meaning of "homosexual acts" and guide us to reconsider traditional assumptions that simplistically sever the connection between doing and being gay. If we are truly to respect these autobiographers as persons, as the church enjoins us to do, then we must take seriously their moral agency as subjects of their actions and relationships as they reconstruct them in their life texts.

"Acts of Faith"

" . . . and homosexual acts saved my life."
— Mr. Friel, in Andrew Holleran's *Nights in Aruba*

Daniel Curzon's largely autobiographical novel begins with his own real-life memories as portrayed through his protagonist Benjy.[22] He then projects, in the progressively older characters of Ben and Benjamin, what his life would have been like had he lived out the heterosexual expectations of the church. In an imaginary scene in a church confessional, Ben (Curzon) is able to take a personal stand against his priest-confessor, who presumes to know what is best for Ben's life based on the teachings of the church:

> "Don't raise your voice; this is a confessional!"
>
> "I know what it is, Father. All my life I've known. It's a place where everything's a *sin!* Everything's a *sin* unless it's done exactly the way somebody else tells me to do it! And now I'm supposed to get up off my knees and walk out of here and go back to my wife and kids and stick with my job selling ads in a magazine and never go to a park again, never play basketball with men again, never think what I really *do* think again!"
>
> "You're committing sins right *here* in the confessional!" Father Agler said severely.
>
> Ben stood up, although his heart was failing, although he felt stunted with fear and anger at what he was saying to the priest. "That's exactly what I mean, Father. To the Church, questioning, living — *everything* — is a *sin!*"[23]

Curzon overturns the oppressive process he felt during confession as a child and seizes his own power and moral agency to determine how he does and does not sin. He is empowered in his narrative to resist the church's deontological, confession- and act-centered moral theology, which so conveniently polices his sexual identity and forbids all "homosexual acts." He is then able to articulate how gay acts are inextricable from gay selfhood. Each of these autobiographers are similarly empowered in their narratives.

My goal in this chapter is to lift up pieces of these life stories that resonate very directly with the concerns I have outlined above. There are particular aspects of these life texts which represent the kinds of choices and struggles that form the nexus of being and doing gay Catholic identity. These moments, especially in the context of valuing oneself and one's relationships, complicate what it means to engage in a "gay act." I want to use these life texts to subvert the church's simplistic usage of the word "acts" with regard to sexuality by extending its meaning.[24] My reading of these life texts in this way can be understood as "queering" the ethics of homosexual acts. I want to further extend this idea by queering the aspect of Catholic prayer life that is also called "acts." When Catholics recite certain formulaic prayers, they engage in acts of a certain kind, according to the title of the prayer and the context in which it is spoken. Wrestling with the ethics of gay identity in the construction of one's life text is another kind of act, a sort of queer prayer of discernment. The acts these autobiographers narrate and the act of narrating them bring alive an ethical world in which the being-and-doing of gay-and-Catholic are deeply entangled. When a gay Catholic comes to terms with the implications of his unique identity, he performs an "act of faith."

Coming to terms with gay identity requires a readjustment of one's self-image. The act of letting go of an old and often destructive image of the self and embracing a new one involves a courageous leap of faith. Fr. Roberts recounts feeling this shift within himself literally exploding in his body. After years of being a successful parish priest and keeping his sexuality suppressed beneath his clean-cut image, he finally reached a point where he could no longer stand the pressure. In the wee hours of the morning, he wandered outside the rectory and began to cry. In anger, he shook his fist toward the sky and at God, feeling like a dirty joke had been played on him. "My whole body convulsed, my head became dizzy, my legs gave way, and I crumpled to the ground in the middle of the church parking lot."[25] In addition to the powerful symbolism of having a nervous breakdown close to, but still outside, the church building, Roberts's episode represents a moment of hitting bottom. He believes "it was a birthing experience, a new awareness of myself, of my sexual identity and sexual desires, my skin hunger and craving for intimate relationship.... It was time for an integration of mind and heart. It was time to deal with my sexuality and my true self."[26] In that moment of physical and emotional agony, Roberts decided it was time to open the door to his gay identity. From then on, his actions would be defined by self-exploration rather than self-denial.

Rafael Campo also felt the destruction of his own self-denial in his body. By the time he went to college and was experiencing the first glimmers of his sexual desire, he had decided to deny himself love and pleasure rather than give in to what his Catholic upbringing had told him was evil. The more he desired anything, or anyone, the less he ate. As his health deteriorated, he became increasingly isolated and fearful of what his desire meant for him: "I fantasized about suicide as the only way out of humiliating my parents...I was fulfilling all their prophecies for homosexuals, and I had not even had homosexual sex. I was unsuccessful even in the expression of my own hideous vice."[27] Eventually, Campo wound up in the hospital with an intense pain in his upper abdomen. He realized as he lay on the examination table that he had reached the threshold between life and death:

> I had located an intersection between my own mortality and the world around me, which was named desire. I wanted to live and to be loved, and at the same time I yearned to erase myself from the face of the earth. I wanted the morgue-like steel and chill of the doctor's office, and the warm hands of another upon my body telling me by their touch that I would endure.[28]

From that moment, Campo took action to cross that threshold "from bodily illness to mental health, from repressed misanthrope to unabashed queer." He made love shortly thereafter with his best friend, the man who would ultimately become his life partner. His decision to embrace his sexual identity literally saved his life. Though he could not articulate this at the time, it was clear to him in retrospect: "I can report now, however, the healing I felt in each kiss, each touch, each murmured word. My body belonged to me again, as soon as I had owned its desire."[29]

Learning to own one's sexual desire is a struggle with ethical ramifications for gay men. To deny one's desire is to deny the wholeness of oneself, which can lead to the kinds of physical and emotional problems recounted above. Wholeness is linked to both body and soul; cutting one off from the other is tragic. As Brian McNaught says, "It is a sad thought to know that you have hated your body."[30] It also leads to a lack of integrity in dealing with others. McNaught confesses to having cooperated in the purging of his college fraternity pledgemaster who was accused of being "queer." He configures this failing in the context of the unresolved anguish he felt about his emerging sexual identity during his college days. When he looks back, he is confronted by memories of a Brian he hardly recognizes, the one who hid behind the "good boy" facade. He would like the people in his past to understand what he was going through, so they could understand why he was so moody; why he did not maintain his heterosexual relationships; why he avoided other men who were perceived as gay. He regrets what that other Brian did back then, but he also understands it was all part of who he has become: "There is the Brian who met others' expectations and the Brian who struggles with his own. I don't understand why I had to go through those painful experiences, but I don't hate the other Brian any more than the butterfly hates the caterpillar."[31] This kind of language is not surprising given the way coming into gay identity often reads like a conversion narrative.

Each of these gay men senses he is somehow not the same person he was before he self-identified as gay. In becoming who he is now, he may have acted in ways he now regrets, but these choices and losses were part of a larger identity project. Writing about this provides a structure for articulating and conceiving this process of self-definition. As Richard Rodriguez introduces his first autobiography, "I turn to consider the boy I once was in order, finally, to describe the man I am now. I remember what was so grievously lost to define what was necessarily gained."[32] Rodriguez knows that the regret that comes with personal growth is wrapped up in loss. José Zuniga also explicitly understands how the gains of "finding oneself" are always beset with losses. He notes the most important lesson he learned about coming out was "that there has to be a certain degree of destruction of familiar structures in order for a person to build at last the very individual structure of his or her own life."[33] In his life text, Zuniga is able to mourn the destruction of the familiar as he navigates his way through the unfamiliar geography of his emerging gay identity.

Though people with heterosexual desires can also struggle with their body image and their emerging sexuality, they are not told their desires are unnatural or disordered as gay people are told in church teachings. Gay Catholics must make an active choice to own their desire, which is an act of faith in oneself and in God. John McNeill calls this "taking a chance on God."[34] While doing so can be scary, as conscientious ethical decisions often are, it also opens the doorway to love. For Fenton Johnson, desire is intimately linked to both faith and love, as the life force that motivates people who seek God: "Desire is to love as belief is to faith: each is a means to an end; each is so easily mistaken for the end."[35] Desire leads to love through faith. Owning one's desire as something given by God in spite of societal messages to the contrary — an act of faith — leads to love. "Desire coupled with reason is what brings us to God, who is love."[36] Passing through the struggle to accept and embrace his desire earned him the "right" to passionately love and to be loved in return. After that, there was no healthy way of going back: "I have, in fact, arrived at the heterosexual take on passionate love, which is to say that I have integrated that love so wholly and completely into who I am that to deny it would be to deny my whole being."[37]

Denying one's self as created by God is certainly a sin according to Catholic moral theology. This is part of the anguish gay Catholics feel whenever they deny or conceal their sexual identity. It may be a strategic decision and it may even protect their safety in dangerous situations, but it does not feel like the honest thing to do. Andrew Holleran compares this self-denial to Peter's denial of Jesus in the Passion. In *Nights in Aruba*, Paul's mother asks him one evening if he is homosexual:

> I jumped up from the sofa, said, "No! Of course not!" in a voice as sharp as my father's when he was angry, and left the room. My heart hammered as I stood in the kitchen, however, thinking of the scene in the Gospels in which Peter denies knowing Christ when the woman asks him if she has not seen him with the Galilean. The comparison was disproportionate but in a sense exact: for if the Gospels told us one would have to leave one's family to follow Christ, the curious thing was that loving men had the same effect.[38]

Gay Catholics are seemingly put in an ethical double bind. Both the denial and the owning of one's sexual identity have potentially devastating consequences. Holleran's narrative highlights how owning one's desire risks the loss of one's family, a potential fate also shared by those who choose to follow Christ.

José Zuniga discusses the risk of losing one's reputation and credibility. When he came out after being named soldier of the year in 1993, he did so to call attention to the problematic policy banning gays and lesbians from serving in the military.[39] When asked if he had ever had sex with another man, he decided to lie rather than risk a court-martial. Subsequent personality features focused on his virginity even more than on the army policy. When a reporter learned of a man named Russell in Zuniga's past, with whom Zuniga had, in fact, had his first gay relationship, she asked Zuniga point blank if he had been his lover. Like Holleran, Zuniga's heart skipped a beat when he was asked, but he did his best to evade answering honestly while still acknowledging his friendship with Russell. When he recounts this in his autobiography, Zuniga also compares his denial with that of Simon Peter; but he turns it around to justify his evasion of the truth:

> The apostle Simon's threefold denial of Jesus, who had been arrested in the courtyard of the Sanhedrin, had been a central doctrine drilled into the pliable minds of Catholic children on the Sunday mornings dedicated to theological study. As far a stretch as it might seem, my conscience had applied this doctrine to my quandary with Russell. Just as Sister Marie Jésus interpreted the Scripture to say Simon's denial had been a morally neutral and prudent act, so too I came to consider my denial.[40]

Even so, Zuniga still wrestled with his ethical dilemma, and the fact that he could not be totally honest caused him great anguish: "The guilt of betrayal flooded my heart. I had come out to stand for honor and integrity, my soul screamed out."[41] Though his decision was strategic and self-protective, the fact that his public image did not reflect the wholeness of his sexual desire and experience felt self-effacing.

As a teenager, Patrick Horrigan created a fantasy wherein he exploded the myth of his public image as a way of coming into his own. Horrigan imagined himself costarring in a movie with Al Pacino and being romantically involved with him both in the movie and in real life. He further imagined a late night TV interview of the two of them with Dick Cavett, in which Horrigan would talk candidly about his role and his love life. Whenever he thought about the interview, he always envisioned them wearing tuxedos:

> Somehow the tuxedos heightened for me the shattering discrepancy between my public image (nice, clean cut, obedient, from a good Catholic family) and what I was doing privately (having sex with men on screen, talking openly about it on TV), between my ostensible identity as an "artist" and the homosexual content of my art. But the tuxedos also domesticated and legitimated, in my mind, the frightful power of my sexuality, of my character's homosexuality.[42]

For Horrigan, the idea of owning his same-sex desire in such a public way was also a way of owning his personhood. It was his way of becoming an adult, taking ownership of himself, and doing what he felt was best for him. He knew it would shock people. He wanted others to feel "disappointment and moral outrage" about him: "I wanted people to think, Patrick's not the boy I used to know."[43] It was his way of dramatically visualizing what it would be like to unleash and simultaneously "tame" that part of him that his good-boy image denied.

Several of these autobiographers explore the ethics of hiding their sexual identity behind the facade of an "acceptable" public image. Sometimes it is directly related to the kinds of careers they have chosen, as with Fr. Roberts (the clergy) and José Zuniga (the military) above. Not surprisingly, this is also a central concern in the life text of Dave Pallone, a professional baseball umpire. As his narrative progresses, his "double life" becomes his biggest problem, and he constantly fears being exposed. Whenever he was out with his lover Scott, Pallone constantly feared being seen by someone who knew him. When Scott traveled out of town for games with Pallone, the two devised strategies to avoid any suspicion they might be more than friends. These included things such as not going to the hotel room at the same time, not sitting together on airplanes, and not meeting each other at the ballpark gate after the game.[44] Later, when Scott died, Pallone could not even share the depth of his loss with any of his colleagues. It all came to a head for him when he was set up and falsely accused of engaging in sex with some teenage boys. He was betrayed by "friends" who knew his secret, and he eventually found himself coming out publicly in the worst possible circumstances. Pallone reflects on the problem of having a "hidden life" and the fact that his "mask" could be yanked off at any time: "The real problem wasn't *being* gay; it was the fear of people *finding out* I was gay."[45] Clearly, if he had to do it all over again, he would not have kept his sexual identity hidden. He thought he was protecting the most important thing in his life — his career as an umpire. In the end, he lost his career anyway, and at the cost of denying his wholeness: "If you live a lie, you're a completely lost soul."[46]

One might raise the objection that everyone keeps parts of their private lives hidden in various contexts and life situations. Some might say it is important to keep private matters out of the public workplace, for example, so hiding one's sexual orientation and preferences in a situation like that is appropriate anyway. But it is clearly not that simple when we are talking about sexual *identity*. Consider the fact that in the current American system, the extent of employee health insurance benefits is usually tied to marriage and family, which are legally, as of this writing, facts of heterosexual identity.[47] Just as the line between doing and being gay is not so well-defined, the clean separation between what is public and private is illusory with regard to one's sexual identity. When things like career, reputation, livelihood, and health coverage are at stake, the message is that sexual identity does matter, whether it should or not. Many advocates of gay rights have built the case for the decriminalization of same-sex acts based on the "right to privacy." As Mark Blasius, asserts, "The 'privacy strategy' for lesbian and gay rights is necessary but has its limits." Ironically, such a strategy actually supports a very flimsy "tolerance" of gay people: "What is least tolerated about homosexuality is not the sex acts themselves (since they are rarely engaged in 'in public view' anyway), but the *appearance,* the social visibility of lesbians and gay people and their affectional relations with each other throughout the fabric of social life."[48] In other words, acceptance is predicated on gay invisibility — and gay identity matters all the more.

Most of these autobiographers know sexual identity matters because they grew up in a societal context in which they were told it does. They write in a societal context that still tells them it matters. Each act they make toward acknowledging their sexual identity is a leap of faith. Andrew Sullivan likens his own faith journey to his coming to terms with his sexuality:

> Like faith, one's sexuality is not simply a choice, it informs a whole way of being; but like faith, it involves choices — the choice to affirm or deny the central part of one's being, the choice to live a life that does not deny but confronts reality, the choice to persist in the adventure of one's own existential journey, despite its destination's being uncertain and its hazards unknown.[49]

The idea that choosing to affirm one's sexuality is an act of faith suggests gay men make this choice knowing some of the potential ramifications of their decision, without fully comprehending where this affirmation will take them. Their life texts reveal not only the difficulties of coming into gay identity but also the hazards of keeping it hidden in the name of abiding by church teachings. As Sullivan recounts it, echoing the warnings of Pallone, Zuniga, Holleran, and Campo, trying to follow the church's teachings on homosexuality "led not to virtue but to pathology"; rather than requiring trust and faith, it required "the first lie in a human life, which would lead to an entire battery of others."[50]

This is an extremely important point with regard to church teaching. The intention is to promote lives of virtue for gay people, but the effect of trying to live according to church teaching on homosexuality is usually the opposite. For example, the church insists upon life-long celibacy for gay people, even though they may not possess the charism necessary for such a commitment. Without the charism, the requirement is no longer life-enhancing but rather death-dealing. It relies on an artificial separation of doing and being gay, and transforms into a bare-bones order of abstinence — a suffering to be offered up, a cross to bear. As Sullivan says, "Abstinence forever; abstinence always; abstinence not for the sake of something else, but for its own sake; abstinence not just from sex, but from love and love's hope and the touch of a lover's embrace. Abstinence even from recognition, acknowledgment, family."[51] This last statement underscores how the pathology spreads beyond just the individual gay person. Families can also cling to unrealistic images of their gay relatives and fail to fully recognize and acknowledge them. Derrick Tynan-Connolly notes how his parents who are normally "the most hospitable, generous and kind people in the world," treat his life partner Jimmy as if he doesn't exist. His parents perceive as evil and sinful a relationship that is based on trust, faithfulness, and commitment, and they condemn what is clearly a central component of their son's identity. They think they can love their son and hate his "sin," but they are clinging to an illusion: "I keep telling them when they say they love me that they don't love me but rather an image in their mind [of] who I should be. I told them that person doesn't exist."[52] Love premised on a false image is a lie.

The imperative to seek wholeness and honesty and to embrace a gay identity with integrity assumes a greater urgency for some of these writers in light of the scourge of AIDS in gay communities in the last two decades. In his San Francisco circle of friends, Richard Rodriguez was always the cautious one, the skeptic who would not fully indulge in the aesthetically rich world they had created for themselves. He watched as each of his friends was diagnosed with AIDS and was especially saddened when his dear friend César was found to be infected too. As César lay on his deathbed, he said Rodriguez would be the only one of his friends who was spared. "You are too circumspect," César told him. Though the sad situation confirmed his cautious reluctance to indulge himself in the material world of his gay community, Rodriguez felt remorse when his wise and loving friend issued his accusation: "It was then I saw that the greater sin against heaven was my unwillingness to embrace life."[53] James Morrison recalls an experience with a friend who was dying of AIDS that powerfully underscores the illusory nature of loving and hating when bodily integrity is at stake. Morrison remembers telling his sick friend Owen how much he hated AIDS, but he was quickly corrected: " 'You *can't*,' Owen said, his clear eyes shining with anger. 'It's *in* me. If you hate it, you hate me.' "[54] Owning our bodies and our desires means owning everything that comes with them. The fullness of gay identity involves body and soul, desires and actions.

With AIDS in the background, the performance of homosexual acts becomes even more significant, especially in the context of physical intimacy. Rafael Campo discusses this resonance in terms of his own identity construction: "I have in the past resisted the simplistic notion that what I do in bed primarily defines my overall identity as a person."[55] He especially resented the many assumptions foisted upon him by homophobic society — that he was not manly enough to be a physician, that he could not maintain a long-term relationship, that he would probably die of AIDS someday — because he was gay. Campo deliberately bucked these assumptions and forged a successful path for himself despite messages that gay men were fated for a certain amount of misery. He decided his "homosexual acts" did not really matter. "So the specific experience of having another man's cock inside my mouth, or having mine inside another man's rectum, had to be trivial, totally irrelevant."[56]

When he began to treat more and more AIDS patients, however, he came to see things differently. He realized how unfairly AIDS attacked those who were already marginalized, even as religious conservatives used AIDS as a symbol of the demise of traditional family values: "How convenient, I thought, that the same terrible disease could be used to decimate minority cultures and simultaneously to destroy the values of the much stronger mainstream."[57] In the minds of those self-appointed protectors of morality, gay people are guilty of crossing hallowed ethical boundaries, just as "illegal aliens" violate the geographical borders of an exalted nation. For Campo, AIDS makes the situation even more palpable and accents the need for gay men to claim the fullness of their sexual identities. Now he perceives the meaning of his homosexual acts differently: "In the face of the AIDS crisis, however, such physical expressions of love have become revolutionary indeed, as revolutionary and as physical for me as the act of writing poetry."[58] Just as writing poetry is embedded in his personhood, so too are homosexual acts intimately linked to gay identity. Campo finally realized:

> that our sexual acts are among the few scraps of identity that we do own, that we must own. The kiss that locates us on a map of the known world, the interlocking legs that are the sextant pointing the way home, the renewing embrace that does not transmit HIV — even if they do not make up our identities entirely, we must give them to ourselves freely and without remorse or encumbrances.[59]

Campo writes this in the name of saving lives. He recognizes that safe-sex admonitions with a focus on "dangerous" acts only serves to perpetuate the negativity that drives such acts in the first place. Focusing on acts in the context of relationships and connections to others validates the personhood and identity of the individual in question. Similarly, the church's focus on acts without context fails to affirm the wholeness of gay individuals. Each of these autobiographers writes his story to save lives — his own and those of other gay Catholics who have tried to bifurcate themselves in order to mirror church teachings, only to find themselves spiritually emaciated. Some of these writers are explicit about the deadly risks of this bifurcation: if a gay man is valued only when he is less than whole, he may feel his own life is worthless. José Zuniga draws a link between the negative attitude toward gay identity and suicide. He mentions the 1989 Department of Health and Human Services report which demonstrated that "lesbian and gay youth are two to six times more likely to attempt suicide than other youth, and they accounted for thirty percent of all completed suicides among teens."[60] Surely these are the kinds of acts we should all be working to eliminate.

James Heckman writes movingly of the circumstances which led to his making a suicide attempt as an adult. He got married when he was twenty-seven because a priest advised him he would grow into it and because "it was time to get married." Though they had children together and he thought of her as "a fine woman," he was clearly not sexually attracted to her. Sex with her eventually became impossible for him and he became visibly despondent: "I had decided to suppress my homosexual feelings, and that I would end my life if they ever came to light." Sure enough, he met a guy when he was about thirty-four and fell "head-over-heels in love." It was all more than he could bear, so he drove his car into the barn on his farm, intending to end his misery. "There was no reason why it failed, except maybe the grace of God. The vent came loose from the tailpipe. I kind of lost consciousness, rolled out of the car, and found myself on the ground when I came to." Heckman finally told his wife he was gay during his third stay in the hospital psych ward. She was hurt but relieved to know what was going on inside him. From that day forward, he was able to move on with his life — no longer burdened by the demands of living a lie.[61]

Richard John Cardarelli shares the story of his own suicide attempt during college, which ultimately led to his becoming a priest and then becoming active in Dignity: "My emotional scars disappeared as I dared to love without fear."[62] Brian McNaught shares the story of his suicide attempt, after which he "vowed never again to live [his] life based upon the expectations of others."[63] It also propelled him into a life of activism and speaking out so that gay and lesbian people would not feel isolated and thus not feel drawn to put themselves in dangerous situations.[64] David Kopay likewise has no regrets about speaking out and putting his career on the line whenever he hears stories of gay people who see no other way out but to kill themselves.[65] Fr. Raymond Calabrese writes about the suicide of a friend from seminary who could not handle the supposed contradiction of being both gay and priest. He shares his own story of being gay in part because he worries his silence contributed to his friend's despair.[66] When gay people acknowledge the fullness of their personhood and share their stories with others, these actions save lives. These are homosexual acts to be celebrated, acts that inspire survival, which can be very brave indeed. In the words of Stephen McCauley, "Let's say it's easiest to believe that you did the best you could at the time, and so did everyone else. It's a blessing even to be alive, an accomplishment, a privilege. Let's leave it at that."[67]

"Acts of Love"

My deciding to take care of Larry as he goes through this is in part a religious decision—a decision to thank the power, or powers, that have granted me life. And it's a humanistic decision—a storing up, I can hope, of grace; if I stand at someone's side during this hard portion of his journey, perhaps, I can hope, I will have someone to stand by me when my time arrives, be that one or five or fifty years away.   —Fenton Johnson, *Geography of the Heart*

The decisions to be in relationship with other human beings and to meet the demands of those associations lay the foundation for gay Catholics to perform acts of love. Whether it be in relationships with friends, parents, lovers, partners, or colleagues, these autobiographers spend their lives invested in ethical situations that require discernment and action (or inaction, which is a kind of action in itself). Homosexual acts are not only about self-care and personal wholeness; they also involve interacting with and potentially loving an other(s). When Richard Rodriguez considers love, he notes, "The way we are constructed constructs the violin. The violin constructs the music." Yet many different kinds of instruments make music, so he is certain music comes first. In turn, he asks if the way we are constructed constructs love? He is similarly assured of his answer: "Love comes first. The first principle comes first. God's love comes first and is not changed, cannot be diminished or turned away by the instrument."[68] Rodriguez knows love functions regardless of the particular bodies that transmit and receive it. We all understand the emotion expressed when Shakespeare says, *"Shall I compare thee to a summer's day? / Thou art more lovely and more temperate."*[69] Like all people, gays and lesbians are drawn to particular others, with whom they engage in loving and hopefully life-enhancing relationships. Their decisions to act within the context of these particular relationships are rooted in the many dimensions of the meaning of love. The men of these life texts manifest their love and caring for others in a variety of ways and, in these gay acts, provide new ways of understanding what love entails.

Fenton Johnson's life text focuses on his relationship with his lover Larry. As time went by in the course of their partnership, Johnson noticed how well-suited the two of them were for each other. At times, they seemed a model of the kind of unitivity espoused in Catholic moral theology as an essential component of a valid marriage.[70] They effortlessly complemented each other in numerous ways. As an example, Johnson notes, "Without my knowing it, our two ways of being engaged each other — my preoccupation with the future; his immersion in this day, this hour, this minute."[71] Johnson weaves his own life story with that of Larry's to represent their interconnection. He also notes the different ways they were engaged in their relationships with their parents. Johnson's parents "released" him and his siblings to make their own ways, as much out of financial necessity as any belief in letting go. Larry's parents, survivors of the Holocaust, clung to their only child who, for them, represented survival and the new life they forged in America. The first time the two men visited Larry's parents, Larry's mother was not comfortable with both of them spending the night there, so they were faced with a decision that would seemingly prioritize one relationship over another. Larry decided he needed to stay alone at his parents' house, so Johnson stayed at a nearby hotel. "Alone in that room, I considered the enormous burdens of love, its two-edged sword, how large and daunting the responsibility of knowing when to cling and when to let go."[72] Both men performed gay acts of love that night. Larry took care of his mother, even though he wanted to be with his lover; Johnson helped his lover out of his predicament by honoring Larry's relationship with his mother and letting him go for the evening.

The biggest issue the two of them had to confront was Larry's HIV-positive condition. Though Johnson felt that love had chosen him rather than the other way around,[73] he still asked himself again and again: "How could I fall in love with someone whom I knew to have a terminal, transmissible disease?" One evening, while they were lying in bed together, he was able to tell Larry his greatest fear — that Larry would die and leave him infected and alone. In the silent moments following, as they held each other, Johnson began to understand the completeness of his love, that he could "speak aloud the unspeakable, secure in the knowledge of the bedrock on which you rest."

> I was beginning to understand how I might love through pain and ugliness, for better or for worse, up to and beyond death. I was beginning to understand how love offers some kind of victory, the thing that enables us to become larger than ourselves, larger than death.[74]

Because their love felt so solid, Johnson knew he would have the courage to stay with and care for Larry, even through the ugliness of AIDS. He could rise to the occasion, an act not so much of courage as of love. It was this love that drove him to keep in touch with Larry's parents after Larry died. It started with weekly phone calls and grew into occasional visits to their home in Santa Monica. He still keeps in touch with Larry's mother, who has come to rely on Johnson even more since the death of her husband. Theirs is a story of how acts of love can build a family, but it also demonstrates how simplistic it is to reduce gay identity to merely sexual acts. Johnson's sexual acts, whatever they are, are embedded in an entire set of acts and choices made between people who came to know what it means to love each other.

Despite the intentions of church teachings, the church inadvertently encourages gay sex acts outside of the context of love and relationship. As John McNeill explains it, according to the pastoral practice of the church, a man could have gay sex one night and then be absolved for his "sin" in confession the next day. If, on the other hand, he fell in love and moved in with another man, he would be denied absolution unless he broke off the relationship. This is how he experienced his own coming to terms with homosexuality as a Catholic: "Ironically, the church fostered promiscuity and felt that the enemy was not gay sex but gay love."[75] Fortunately, McNeill disregarded these messages when he met Charlie, who would become his life partner. Like Johnson in his relationship with his partner, McNeill eventually found himself taking risks in the name of love. For McNeill, the risks were financial. Charlie had a series of heart attacks beginning in 1990 that forced him into early retirement and required serious long-term medical care. They had to sell their dream house at half its value just to pay off their debts. For McNeill, this meant having no savings of his own for retirement, since his dismissal from the Jesuits left him with virtually nothing. He knows now that if Charlie dies ahead of him, he will live in poverty because he will not be eligible for Charlie's pension or social security (yet another societal unfairness against gay couples). Despite this, McNeill performs his act of love without question; he is committed to Charlie for better or for worse.

In trying to live up to the expectations of the church and society, a few of these men made commitments "for better or for worse" to a woman within the framework of a heterosexual engagement or marriage. They usually do so in the hopes of somehow regulating or covering their gay identity, but this creates conflict when they realize they cannot turn off that part of themselves or the false image becomes too much to bear. We have already seen how a situation like this led James Heckman to attempt suicide. Fortunately, when he finally told his wife he was gay, she found a way to accept it and helped them both move forward. In fact, when Heckman later told his parents he was gay, his wife told them "that if they wanted their grandchildren to be a part of their lives, they would have to accept their son for who he was.[76] His honesty and her acceptance of his sexual identity in the name of his personal wholeness represent acts of love.

Dave Kopay told his girlfriend Mary Ann he was gay before they ever decided to marry. He felt it was important for her to know why he "couldn't do more for her in bed."[77] She said it did not matter to her as long as she was the only woman in his life. Kopay eventually decided it would be expedient to marry her, especially in light of his pro football career. It was only a short time, however, before he realized he had made a mistake. He felt that "no matter how much we could do for each other in some ways, I just wasn't capable of the deeper emotional commitment with her I felt I could have with another man."[78] The emotional fallout for Mary Ann was devastating. She was initially suicidal and felt she was a failure. On some level, she had hoped to change Kopay and believed they could "live happily ever after." Kopay, on the other hand, seemed to know their marriage was doomed from the beginning. He regretted the whole thing. He stayed with her a while until she was more stable and then continued to help her financially in the hopes of making amends: "I didn't know what else to do for her. I did know I could no longer go on trying to change into the husband she wanted and needed."[79] Kopay's attempt to "live a heterosexual life" put him in an ethical double-bind and created a tragic situation in which both he and Mary Ann suffered.

Dave Pallone dated a woman named Linda, to whom he was attracted in most every way except sexually. He felt very comfortable with her and liked the idea of having a girlfriend because he felt society's pressure was off as long as he was with a woman. He also thought she might be able to "change" his sexual desire: "I ignored reality and hoped against hope that I would eventually be physically attracted to her. It was the most terrible thing I could have done to anybody, including myself."[80] As time went on, he feared losing her if he did not make a firm commitment, so he proposed to her. While she "heard bells" and said yes, he heard alarm bells and immediately felt he may have made a mistake. Two months later, he finally summoned the courage to break it off with her, but he was not able to tell her the real reason why. He knew telling her he was gay would likely make it easier for her to understand, but he feared her reaction and had not yet come out to anyone else. After he broke up with her, he still called her now and then because he felt so bad about hurting her, but it only strung her along and made her angry. They parted with bitterness between them and Pallone felt ashamed and sorry: "I promised myself that I would never hurt anyone again like I'd just hurt Linda. To this day, I hate thinking about what I did to her. I consider it my ultimate sin against another human being."[81] In this confessional moment, Pallone comes to terms with the negative effects of trying to maintain a romantic relationship that went against the thrust of who he knew himself to be. His acts of love, however well-intentioned, became acts of harm.

Situations like that of Pallone and Kopay are not uncommon among gay Catholic men who try to bifurcate themselves in order to have a relationship sanctioned by the church. Church teachings that say in effect, "a heterosexual relationship or no relationship at all," prompt many gay Catholics to seek such connections. Many of these autobiographers also came of age at a time when they did not see many other options for themselves because gayness was not as visible as it is today. Some of them got married, had children, and tried for a long time to make things work out because they sincerely loved their wives and wanted to honor their commitments. Larry Sullivan threw himself into work to escape his feelings until he met a younger man and began a passionate affair with him. "I didn't know what to do about it. I loved my wife and my kids, but I felt more fulfilled this way."[82] He felt tremendously guilty for his dishonesty and finally told his wife everything, which led to their divorce and coming out to his kids. They handled it well enough, but he always wished things could have been different. He felt lonely, stressed, and absent in his marriage, but happy and present to himself once he acknowledged his gay identity. William Storey went through a similar experience, being married and having seven children before coming to terms with his sexual identity. Though he now enjoys a fulfilling, long-term relationship with another man, he too regrets how acts of love can be double-edged: "The only sadness I feel periodically is that I did not discover my sexual identity earlier in life and that I had to wound my wife and children in becoming who I am."[83]

Some of these autobiographers have tried, with varying degrees of success, to restructure the terms of their relationships in the hope of being gay and remaining married. James Abdo was in his mid-twenties and married several years when he had his first sexual experience with a man. He felt compelled to explore this part of himself but did not want to just break up his marriage: "It was clear that my marriage and my responsibility to that marriage came first. That was tremendously influenced by my Catholicism."[84] They tried opening their relationship so that both of them could have other sex partners, but this plan ultimately failed and they ended their marriage as adversaries. Abdo still weighs the decisions he made and is disappointed he was unable to balance his marriage and gay identity: "I certainly don't perceive that I could have denied my homosexuality and remained healthy, and particularly spiritually healthy. But it has cost me a lot."[85] Gerald Allen, on the other hand, provides an example of a gay man who, with the help of his wife, did manage to hold his marriage together. Allen is a lector in his parish and serves as vice-president of the parish council. As of the writing of his life text, he had been married to and in love with the same woman for twenty-five years. He did not act on his homosexual desires until he was thirty years old, and he kept his behavior a secret from his wife for at least a decade. Eventually he found the pressure of the dual life too much to endure, so he told his wife he was involved with another man. They both found support groups to help them through this and they stayed together. It seems to have worked out remarkably well for him: "My wife and my lover are good friends. The two of them have helped me solve some of my own problems."[86]

The above stories demonstrate there is no single, correct solution to the ethical problems of being gay and married. In all of these cases, however, the men were driven to act with honesty. Being honest was an act of self-love that relieved them of the burdens of a heavy secret, yet it also created a burden for their wives. While it might be fair enough to interpret their actions as selfish and harmful, these men were also motivated by a sense of respect for their wives. They knew their wives deserved honesty and the option to decide for themselves if they would rather be with a man who could be totally devoted to them, emotionally and physically. These men tested the boundaries of relationship and found the best possible resolution in their circumstances.

James Morrison feels being gay should be all about testing boundaries and forging new ways of structuring relationships. Since gay people are already marginalized for their intimate relationships and erotic desires, they are in the position to question all conventional norms. He feels gay people can lead us to explore new frameworks for understanding what constitutes an act of love. "Gay men will have accomplished nothing, I believe, if we do not create new kinds of relation — to one another, and to others, and to ourselves — different from the ones we have been given."[87] As an adult, Morrison found himself being abandoned by a man he loved because the man wanted a conventional relationship and he did not. He questioned if committing to an exclusive, monogamous pairing was really the best way to be in a loving relationship with another man.

Other autobiographers contemplate these kinds of issues too. Gerald Allen, above, found a way to balance two important relationships at the same time — with his wife and with his lover. José Zuniga tried for a time to maintain a three-way relationship with his friends Dave and Laurie, who were themselves romantically involved. He was always sexually and emotionally attracted to Dave; at the same time, he loved Laurie and their physical acts together were an outgrowth of their spiritual intimacy.[88] Then there are those who, like Morrison, wonder if monogamy is necessary for building a healthy relationship. Brian McNaught used to think monogamy was the only appropriate choice to legitimate a committed relationship. He learned, however, from gay friends of his in open relationships, that there are other forms of "monogamy" that matter just as much if not more. Physical, sexual monogamy does not guarantee emotional fidelity and intimacy. As McNaught says, "If having a consistent sex partner is all a relationship is about, it would be smarter to find a young whore."[89] Just as the church fixates on a narrow set of acts in order to condemn all gay relationships, it is a mistake to emphasize sexual monogamy as the primary glue for holding two people together. Obsessing over sexual acts misses the point:

> If, on the other hand, your ideal relationship is based on deep love; if your dream is to share yourself as a friend and companion with another; if your life course is to grow and discover, be sick and healthy, rich and poor in the company of a particular one whose devotion and whose growth prompt an internal peace, then seek out a person who shares your ideal, and don't settle for less. Sex will take its appropriate place.[90]

The point, of course, is to find an arrangement that honors the needs of all persons in relationship. McNaught and his partner Ray decided physical monogamy was the right thing for them. Fenton Johnson and his partner Larry argued over Johnson's sexual forays in other cities, which he sought whenever he traveled. Larry wanted Johnson to be monogamous; but Johnson wanted to keep other doors open, knowing Larry would die before him. They worked out an arrangement allowing Johnson to have sex with other men only when he traveled out of town, as long as he told Larry about it afterward. Johnson writes about this arrangement with a certain amount of ambivalence. He knows their relationship was founded on an emotional monogamy, but he also realizes how his position blocked a channel of intimacy:

> In refusing what he wanted, in denying us both this commitment, I kept some doors open, but at the expense of other, more sumptuous rooms. Monogamy, or the lack of it, would not break us up — we were too much in love, both of us, to break up. But after this conversation Larry held a part of himself in reserve, however small, a protected place where he did not allow me to go.[91]

In retrospect, Johnson would have handled things differently in order to be as close to Larry as possible. Since Larry died, he has the privilege of writing about his acts of love from the perspective of having lost the one he loved. He now knows the importance and value of honoring the needs of the other, which in turn pushes the self to grow: "To advance into our lives, to open new doors, we have to shut old doors behind us."[92]

The death of his lover also taught Johnson the urgency of love. James Morrison learned this lesson too late with a close friend in college. He knew he loved Nicholas and that Nicholas loved him, even though neither of them had yet come to terms with being gay. When Nicholas came out to him, hoping for a reciprocal utterance from his friend, Morrison could not say the words. He did not want to say he was gay and he did not want to say he loved him because that would imply his homosexuality. Instead, he put it off:

> I would tell him in the springtime, I thought, and meanwhile I would love him, in a language definite as speech, and hope that he knew. It was not so long a time, and the innocence before experience has experience in it too, just as the fullness before loss has loss in it, and the loss after, fullness.[93]

By the springtime, however, it was too late. Nicholas was gone, seemingly killed in an accident, though Morrison leaves the details unclear. The time before the end is what matters most. Indeed, acts of love are not as freely given after a relationship ends, yet Morrison realizes urgency is a luxury. Most of us who love are faced with making commitments which must last a very long time. Morrison knew from what he had observed in his life, "that vows of allegiance or resolution were always followed by obtuse breadths of time that made those vows hard to keep, and that this very phenomenon was what life was mainly about."[94] Even though Morrison advocates finding new ways of relating, he recognizes both the centrality and the difficulty of commitment, regardless of its specific content and form.

Within the context of important relationships, commitment is bolstered by love, which is reflected in actions. Whenever these autobiographers discern and act on their responsibilities to themselves and to their "significant others," they perform acts of love. Sometimes these "homosexual acts" are physical and sometimes they are not, but they are performed within the particular context of a loving and committed relationship. To ignore the context is to ignore the person, whose gay identity is a combination of being *and* doing. To deny gay people their acts is to deny them love; and if we believe God is love, as Catholics do, then to deny them love is to deny them God. Church teaching on homosexuality should then be considered not only inadequate or insufficient but also sinful and idolatrous. These gay Catholics have loved as deeply and intensely as anyone, and in that love have attained glimpses of the holy. When Philip Gambone was intimate with his first lover, it was about much more than sex: "I wanted to do everything for him, give him everything, surrender totally, the way the saints had surrendered to God."[95] William Storey cannot imagine a relationship more loving and fulfilling than the one he has with his life partner: "We enjoy a spousal relationship that is a true marriage of minds, hearts, and bodies in every way—except legally!"[96]

It is these kinds of connections and relationships — manifestations of divine love — that matter the most in human lives, especially in the face of death. Rafael Campo learned about the power of love and forgiveness in an encounter with a close friend who was dying of complications from AIDS. Gary was a fellow writer Campo had met through a teacher who had inspired them both. Campo writes about Gary as a man who was not afraid of his sensuality. In sharing their poetry with each other, Campo learned from Gary how to explore the dimensions of his sexuality he had previously held beneath his surface consciousness. When Gary's condition began to worsen, it was overwhelming for Campo. The link between desire and disease was too much to fathom, so he withdrew from the situation entirely. Campo did not return phone calls and he ignored the messages that Gary might be dying. When Gary was brought into the ICU where Campo was working, Campo still avoided contacting him. He did not know how to be both friend and doctor for this man who represented so much for him. One night, he finally visited Gary. Though Gary was angry at Campo for having kept his distance, he offered his forgiveness and understanding. In that moment of reconciliation — made possible by Gary's act of love — Campo felt the grace-filled touch of a man who not only had forgiven himself and his body but had also transcended the boundaries that limit and constrict:

> He forgave me my own needs, understanding at once my preoccu-
> pation and fascination with his death and my fear of it consuming
> me. In that tiny hospital room, on my own turf and surrounded
> by devices familiar to and workable only by me, fairy-godmotherly
> Gary orchestrated with the sweep of his pen my salvation. Capable
> of levitating above his bed, lashed down only by the chest tube that
> attached him to the mortal world I inhabited, he made me feel fab-
> ulously and unabashedly queer, made me want to sing the soothing
> Spanish lullabies whose words I knew but had never learned.[97]

In that grace-filled moment, Campo felt the touch of liberation to embrace the fullness of himself, the self he knew inside but had never learned to contact. His encounter with his friend Gary helped Campo to embrace his gayness on his own terms. Gary's act of love, expressed by granting forgiveness of his friend, was redemptive for both of them.

In old Catholic practice, we were encouraged to *seek* forgiveness when faced with our own deaths — to make an act of contrition. It represented the need for our souls to be pure when coming face to face with our eternal judgment. The focus was on our sins, our actions and inactions in which we failed to live according to God's will. While Catholics probably still hope for purity of soul at the time of death, as symbolized in the sacrament of anointing of the sick, contrition is no longer the dominant theme. Love seems to take priority. Catholics have followed other Americans in being less concerned about sin and judgment at the hour of death, and more concerned about connecting with loved ones. Eugene Kennedy notes how the fateful events of September 11, 2001, as recorded in countless phone calls and voice messages, provide a portrait of what people do when they believe they are going to die: "Hearing death's door unlatch where preachers had warned them the ghosts of judgment waited for them, they did not enter a plea of mercy to God but instead pledged their love to their wives and children, their families, and their friends."[98] Now, while it is true some of them may indeed have implored God's mercy in their final moments, the point is they wanted to be sure others knew they loved them. They wanted their final acts to be acts of love. They knew that in love, they would find God.

Just as these people facing death sensed that acts of love would help ease their passage from this life into the spiritual realm, these gay Catholic autobiographers know love — of self and in intimate relationships with others — is part of finding salvation. Fenton Johnson, whose relationship with his lover Larry has played such a prominent role in this part of the chapter, captures the connection between gay acts of love and the realm of the holy:

> In caring for my lover I came to understand the tautological relationship between God and love. My lover's love for me and mine for him made me into something better, braver, more noble than I had imagined myself capable of being. I was touched by the literal hand of God, for this is what love is, in a way as real as I expect to encounter in this life.[99]

In loving and nurturing his partner, Johnson achieved a new level of wholeness and holiness — a touch of salvation. The wholesale denigration of gay acts of love by the church presumes to sever this important connection to the divine, yet it is in these very acts that redemption is found. If gay people are not allowed to love as deeply and intensely as everyone else, then their acts will, of necessity or despair (the greatest sin of all), become acts of harm:

> What is the cost of cutting love from the heart? I have spent a good deal of time considering that question, and this is part of what I have learned: The cost translates into acts that can be counted and tallied and for which we all finally pay. Violence against others, violence against oneself; bigotry, drug addictions, suicides, assaults, murders, or the simple, dull passing of a life given to self-pity, self-denial, and

bitterness; contempt for others, so as to reduce them to something like the contempt one feels for oneself.[100]

The church's refusal to view homosexual acts in the context of particular situations and relationships is death-dealing. Being gay and doing gay are inseparable, so our survival is linked both to who we are and what we do. The church needs to recognize that homosexual acts are inextricable from gay selves. If church leaders really grasped this, they could reshape the tradition and dialogue with gay Catholics to help us discern when our acts lead to good and when they lead to harm. Instead, the church has withdrawn from *any* conversation about the potential goodness of homosexual acts, so gay Catholics have begun to develop their own sexual ethics. This is most appropriately where the conversation should begin anyway, with the lived experience of those who have been marginalized for their sexual identity. As Johnson says, "We are in the earliest stages still of creating a community, which is to say a stable set of values against which we may measure and reward or correct our conduct."[101] These life texts provide the initial transcripts of the conversation. They are narrative portraits of gay-and-Catholic identity, written by persons whose authorship of their own lives is at the same time their claim to authority over those lives.[102]

And what of this question of authority? Critics inevitably make the charge that when gay people call for a revision in church teaching, they are trying to "conform the truth to fit their lives rather than conforming their lives to the truth." But this seemingly clever turn of phrase is nothing more than word play. It creates an artificial dichotomy in a relationship that is more realistically symbiotic. If "truth" is to be more than an abstraction, it can only be apprehended through real lives. It is wonderful when people find a truth that works for them and answers whatever is unresolved in their lives, but it is a problem when they decide this "truth" must work for everyone. Insomuch as "truth" is reflective of societal norms, it always represents and "fits" the lives of those considered normative, which by extension are those who have the power to set the definitions. Thus, to some degree, people always conform the truth to fit their lives, or at least to what they need or desire in their lives. To insist that the whole church in all its diversity must live by that partial "truth" is to conform the truth to people's lives. Instead, we need always to be seeking the fullness of truth. The "truths" we have received through church teachings about sexuality are not complete because they do not account for the experience of all sexual lives. Gay Catholic autobiographies reveal a different "truth." In these sacred texts, we observe men who try very hard to conform their lives to the heterosexual norm, but who eventually realize this is not their truth. It does not include their reality. If church teachings on sexuality are to be "truthful," they must encompass the moral universe found in these life narratives and reflect an understanding that the best authorities on sexuality are those who live sexual lives.

Gay Catholics are ready and willing to develop a gay moral theology in a dialogue of mutual accountability with the church, but only if the church takes gay lived experience seriously.[103] It would not be enough for the church to simply subsume gay people into the present system of sexual ethics, in which the wisdom of many sexually active Catholics is already discounted or ignored entirely. Taking lived experience seriously means listening to more than just those people for whom the traditional rules work. Gay people have long been shut out of the traditional system of sexual ethics, and we must not replicate the same disenfranchisement when we develop a gay moral theology. Laurel Schneider cautions us against "advocating 'good' homosexuals who incidentally look and act a great deal like good heterosexuals at the expense, perhaps, of many of the rest of us."[104] It may be true that many gay people want to assimilate and mimic heterosexual norms, or minimally desire the benefits of those norms, as the strength of the gay marriage movement might indicate. But such norms will still exclude those who structure their moral lives in other ways, a point queer theory has made abundantly clear. As I discussed earlier in this chapter, there is always an ethical framework in place, even among those whose life texts do not look traditional. The gay Catholic autobiographers at the heart of this book are both blessed and cursed by the church's exclusion of their lives: cursed because the church does not take their experience seriously, but blessed because their marginal position gives them the perspective to explore a range of ethical options. Their life texts can help us move toward the dismantling of the oppressive categories that cause exclusion in the first place. As Schneider says, "In the end, full inclusion may mean that neither homosexuality nor the heterosexual norm will be left intact."[105]

In one of his autobiographical essays, Andrew Holleran devotes much of his thoughts to a reconsideration of what constitutes sin in his life. He does so in light of the church's condemnation of all homosexual acts as sins. All gay Catholics ultimately face the same dilemma: we all must discern if our gay acts, which we experience as actions of love and faith, are truly the sins our church tells us they are. Holleran comes to the conclusion that homosexual acts are not among the sins that have characterized his life, but "[t]he way I've treated others because of the conflict between my religion, society, culture and those acts may well be, however."[106] Until the church overcomes its fear of "homosexual acts," gay Catholics will have to reshape the tradition themselves. We will continue to reappraise what constitutes sin in light of our experience of being gay.

These autobiographies, texts infused with gay subjectivity, show us gay identity manifested in acts with ethical ramifications — acts that are not "intrinsically evil" but rather integral to full personhood. As such, they provide a necessary foundation for a realistic discussion of gay sexual ethics and the revision of problematic church teachings on homosexuality. The church would do well to join in the conversation.

Chapter 5

Reconciliation

So when I came to be asked, later in life, how I could be gay and Catholic, I could answer only that I simply was. What to others appeared a complete contradiction was, in reality, the existence of these two inextricably connected, yet sometimes parallel, experiences of the world. It was not that my sexuality was involuntary and my faith chosen and that therefore my sexuality posed a problem for my faith; nor was it that my faith was involuntary and my sexuality chosen so that my faith posed a problem for my sexuality. It was that both were chosen and unchosen continuously throughout my life, as parts of the same search for something larger.

— Andrew Sullivan, "Virtually Normal"

My goal in the previous chapter was to profile some examples of the choices and relationships that inform the ethical world of these autobiographies and to place these in the context of my discussion of gay Catholic identity. Within that context, we find these gay men already engaging in the work of moral discernment and performing their actions accordingly. Respecting these autobiographers as persons requires that we respect their subjectivity as narrators of their own moral agency. While this material is already a kind of moral teaching that provides fertile soil for developing a gay sexual ethics, my book is not explicitly a work of moral theology. My intention, for example, has not been to analyze gay acts according to the technicalities of moral theology, with an eye toward evaluating whether these acts are good or evil.[1] My analysis does demonstrate the inadequacy of church teaching on homosexuality, particularly in the way its moral and pastoral bifurcation falsely separates the doing and being of gay Catholic identity. This makes a strong case for the reconsideration and revision of these teachings. But working through the field of moral theology will only provide limited success at this point in time. A great deal of ethical analysis has already been done by notable Catholic moral theologians, but we are still stuck with the same teachings and sometimes even retrenchments in this these teachings. I agree with Mark Jordan that moral and doctrinal analysis alone will not change

156

toxic church teachings on homosexuality until the current structure and culture of the clerical caste is unraveled:

> Correcting Catholic teachings on homosexuality is not only or mainly a matter of proposing amendments to specific documents. The official doctrine is more deeply embedded than that. It is more intimately connected to old arrangements of institutional power. Changing the language without reforming institutional arrangements would be useless, even if it were possible. The most important relations between Catholicism and homosexuality are not embedded in official propositions about homosexuality, nor even in official regulations for homosexual behavior. The forces at work here are not only the forces of words.[2]

So where do we go from here? As I have been saying throughout this book, the church needs to listen to the experience and wisdom of its gay members. We need to move gay life texts to the center of the church's conversation about human sexuality. Gay Catholic autobiographies need to be primary sources in the tradition — sacred texts in their own right, revealing divine intention in the lives of people who have been marginalized for their sexual identity. This is the first step in overcoming the lack of gay subjectivity that is so problematic in the church's understanding of homosexuality. To accomplish this, we will need to engage the Catholic imagination and view these autobiographical acts as "sacramental" events: as grace-filled moments of self-expression and self-understanding, as representations of selves in search of wholeness, integrity, and meaning. Here, I am using the principle of sacramentality in its broadest sense: the notion that "all reality, both animate and inanimate, is potentially or in fact the bearer of God's presence and the instrument of God's saving activity on humanity's behalf."[3] Recall from my discussion in chapter 3, that sacramentality is considered a primary element of Catholic identity across the range of American Catholics, while moral teachings are widely disputed. It seems reasonable then that a more fruitful way forward and a more "convincing" approach to the problems I am addressing will bear this in mind. Reading gay Catholic autobiographies as instances of revelatory grace taps into this dimension.

Gay Catholic autobiographies reflect many qualities of sacramentality as it might be broadly interpreted. They are written in the context of a community that makes gay identification possible; and they aid in the creation of that community, which in turn empowers the life writer to speak his truth in the name of liberating the wholeness of his being. They recount and attest to encounters with the divine that are rooted in loving, interpersonal relationships and encounters. They are metaphorical representations that facilitate self knowledge and allow gay Catholic reality "to be there" for the sake of the whole church. The experience they narrate transcends binaries and bifurcations that separate the ambiguous elements of being and doing gay and Catholic. The early church applied the Greek word *mysteria* to early liturgical practices, such as the reenactment of the Lord's Supper, initiation of new members, the laying on of hands, and practices of public repentance — practices which would later be called sacramental.[4] The use of such a word as *mysteria*, which means mysteries, or "secrets whispered by God," indicates how beyond definition early Christians considered these actions. It is this sense of sacrament I want to link with gay Catholic autobiographical acts. As Doris Donnelly explains, sacraments "are the places where God's story and the human story connect. Not only do we need to tell the human story; we need to hear the human story *first*."[5] When these life writers narrate their gay Catholic identities through autobiography, they proclaim "from the housetops" their own "secrets whispered by God."

In the written narrative, these autobiographers find a space to share intimate, private information with us about how they experience their sexuality. Such information needs a public hearing if church teaching is to be reconciled with the reality of gay lives. Writing provides a kind of "shield" between the autobiographer and the forces that would have him policed and silenced, so that he can discuss his sexual desire:

> The act of writing functions as a buffer between private and public discourse. [Autobiographies] mediate intimacies. They transform inarticulate experiences into speech, body into voice. They are a safe way to acknowledge the woundedness which men may not otherwise admit. There is no immediate other to dispute the retrospective construction and interpretation of the male self.[6]

The "safety" of uncoerced writing lies in the absence of a policing confessor who would attempt to edit previously unspoken desires of which others may not approve. Such uncensored intimacies may make readers uncomfortable. We see what these life writers hold within themselves, and it forces us to reassess what we previously took for granted as ethically normative. We observe both their moral victories and their moral failures, yet we must identify with their human struggle and quest for integrity. As Stephen Spender notes, "Self-revelation of the inner life is perhaps a dirty business. Nevertheless, even in its ugliest forms we cannot afford altogether to despise anyone who — for whatever reasons — is the humblest and ugliest servant of truth."[7]

These gay Catholic autobiographers are indeed "servants of truth." In writing their life narratives, they engage us in a sacramental encounter with the reality of their identities. Their texts provide a tangible form

through which we can make contact with their lives. Ron Hansen explains
how the art of writing is holy and reciprocal: "Writing not only gives form
and meaning to our sometimes disorderly existence, but gives the author
the chance for self-disclosure and communion with others, while giving
readers a privileged share in another's inner life that, perhaps impercep-
tibly, questions and illuminates their own."[8] This is the foundation of
reconciliation, which is one of the effects of sacramental grace. At this
point, we are very much in need of reconciliation — between the church
and its gay members, and for gay Catholics themselves, whose identities
have been ruptured by teachings and attitudes that ignore their authentic voices and the fullness of their personhood. Because of this rupture,
the journey to reconciliation is a struggle — one that can feel like a battle
against internal and external demons. Fenton Johnson notes that writing
is his battleground and "the prize in the struggle is nothing more or less
than life, which is to say love, which is to say God."[9]

In the aesthetic process of writing their life texts, these gay Catholics
reconcile their seemingly conflicting sexual and religious identities. Or at
least they find a way of holding the two together. For Richard Rodriguez,
it is a matter of accepting his inner plurality. When asked how he can
call himself both gay and Catholic, he takes this as "a question about
the authenticity of the soul": "When you slice an avocado, the pit has to
go with one side or the other, doesn't it?" But Rodriguez is not either/or,
or black/white; instead, he is both/and — what he calls *brown*. His is a
mixed soul, which has to do "with the irreconcilability of questions and
answers." Thus, he finds a better analogy in the image of a wishbone that
is tugged on, but still held together in tension: "The tension I have come
to depend upon. That is what I mean by brown. The answer is that I
cannot reconcile. I was born a Catholic. . . . I was born gay."[10]

The reconciliation afforded for gay Catholics in the autobiographical
process is not based on resolution but rather on a coming to terms that is
founded on a deeper self-awareness. Their life texts represent a discovery
and acknowledgment of divine intention in their lives. By the time they
write their texts, their "conversion" or self-healing has already begun to
occur. In a sense, the autobiography reenacts this process. It is a sort of
"ritualizing" of the transformation that has already begun to transpire in
a life. The autobiographical act gives birth to the constructed self of the
text, a representation of who the autobiographer imagines himself to be.
As the life writer moves through his "rebirth," he begins to tell his story
differently. Part of healing is imagining how he wants his life to look.
The past is rethought and reworked through memory in order to redeem
the present and forge a new self-concept, a process that is intrinsically
sacramental.

For true reconciliation to occur between gay Catholics and the church, both sides have important roles to play. Mark Jordan insists gay people must continue to be pioneers of identity and try to move beyond those terms altogether. We must not be satisfied with familiar categories and constructs of sexual identities, which, as generated by the church, have been "officially sin-identities, identities of condemnation." "The identity was conceived precisely as lacking human fullness, as a deficiency, as a permanent human poverty." Jordan suggests gay Catholics need to repent of having ever put on the identities made for them in the first place. "We should feel contrition for having pretended to have a sexual identity, when what we had were desires, memories, loves."[11] By shifting the terms of the debate, once again taking it out of the realm of moral theology, we begin to ask new questions. We begin with our own subjectivity — that sacramental encounter with God's design in our lives — rather than relying on preconceived notions. In the sacramental process, we touch the whole community. We queer the church. As Jordan states, "We want to queer Catholicism so that we can be queerer than 'homosexuals' were ever supposed to be."[12]

Gay Catholic autobiographers call attention to the inadequacy of the objective moral system itself. They help us revise what needs policing in the first place and name the kinds of sins that have kept us from realizing our human potential. The prophetic task for gay Catholics is to open the eyes of the church community to its own sinfulness, and thereby participate in a sort of institutional "examination of conscience." Their autobiographies represent an important way of carrying this out. The lives narrated in these texts are filled with examples of the way church teaching on homosexuality can be damaging. These life texts move us away from hypothetical theories about sexuality toward a deeper grasp of the reality of gay identity and experience. We observe in these autobiographies the impossibility of being a gay person "without acting like one." We observe the church's denigration of loving relationships and commitments in the name of condemning a particular subset of acts that are integral to those same relationships. We observe gay men coming to terms with their own failure to live with integrity, even as we observe these same men overcoming debilitating teachings that would have them neglect and deny important dimensions of themselves. In taking these stories seriously, as true respect demands, we Catholics come face to face with our own failures as the people of God.

The gay men of these autobiographies may experience pockets of reconciliation in particular church communities that welcome them as full persons — Dignity chapters and "gay friendly" parishes, for example — but in general, their experience of the institutional church is one of alienation and rupture. Whenever the church excludes people from the eucharistic table, or communicates that there is a hierarchy among us in terms of gender, sexuality, vocation, lifestyle, etc., it runs the danger of participating in societal sins of injustice, the "sin of the world." When the church paints itself as the perfect society against the backdrop of a perceived "culture of death," it is failing to see the plank in its own eye and the lovable-ness of God's world. Kathleen Hughes brilliantly expresses how such an attitude works against reconciliation:

> The difficulty is this: there can be no reconciliation until there is recognition of need, of rupture, of alienation, of sin, of being drawn to conversion and a new life. If you are a member of the perfect society you have no need of conversion and little need for adequate rituals to express healing. Who needs healing if you aren't broken? . . . How difficult it is to stand in need of the mercy of God if some in the community think they are able to define it and mete it out. Reconciliation cannot happen in a community where the majority believe that they don't need it and that the minority don't deserve it.[13]

The way to overcome this obstacle to reconciliation is to maintain a stance of inclusivity. As much as exclusion is participation in the "sin of the world," inclusion, or the valuing of a high degree of diversity, reconnects us to community. The "sin of the world" prevents us from recognizing the other (those who are different or "queer") as gift. To be authentically Catholic, on the other hand, is to embrace pluralism (both/and rather than either/or), to unite without erasing differences.

This is the role the church community must play if reconciliation is to take place. Such a stance of inclusivity is an example of what Toinette Eugene calls "reconciliatory emancipation." Eugene draws on James Lopresti to discuss marginalized people who tell the truth of their stories and themselves over and against the sin of the community. Such people are the "prophetically alienated." Eugene argues that true reconciliatory emancipation must not just proclaim deliverance and forgiveness for individuals, but it must do so "through a redress of specific social and public expressions of oppression and repression in our era of church and world history, from which profound and prolific deliverance is needed."[14] "The two elements expressed in the term 'reconciliatory emancipation' work together to structure the salvific communal dynamic of sacramental realities toward an end of alienating and destructive responses to human difference and of oppressive forms of domination."[15] We have a model for the inclusive embrace of human difference in St. Paul's analogy of the Body of Christ with the human body:

> As it is, God has put all the separate parts into the body as he chose. If they were all the same part, how could it be a body? As it is, the

parts are many but the body is one. The eye cannot say to the hand, "I have no need of you," and nor can the head say to the feet, "I have no need of you."

What is more, it is precisely the parts of the body that seem to be the weakest which are the indispensable ones. . . . If one part is hurt, all the parts share its pain. And if one part is honoured, all the parts share its joy.[16] (1 Cor. 12:18–21, 26)

Reconciliatory emancipation is necessarily about communal liberation. Raymond-Jean Frontain points out that beleaguered cultures often survive oppression through storytelling. Autobiographical narratives assist in this task. According to Frontain, "Memory is driven by the will to survive. If narrative is both the product of and the stimulus to memory, then narrative, in its richest form, can enact the hope of redemption."[17] Similarly echoing Eugene's injunction, Walter Holland states, "Gay autobiography employs various strategies to validate homosexual identity, depathologize it, and move it toward a political construction of identity, community, and a liberationist ethic."[18] As gay autobiographies expose the political nature of the church's construction of "homosexual" identity, à la Jordan, the reality of gay existence in all its diversity and its full dimensions of being and doing can be revealed.

As members of the church encounter these narratives and take them seriously, the opportunity arises for reconciliation. Then, the long work of healing can begin. Narrating one's life story thus lays the foundation for conversion, or *metanoia*, not just within individuals but also in the church and in the world. As Georges Gusdorf points out in his discussion of the interface between memory and autobiography, "In becoming conscious of the past, one alters the present."[19] When the church community reads these life texts and identifies with their common humanity, we can begin the work of putting aside those long-held attitudes and beliefs that effectively dehumanize particular members of the church. Perhaps then we can move forward to heal the ruptures in gay Catholic lives and create a space within the church for gay Catholics to realize their fully human and embodied potential.

One of the central themes in the stories of gay Catholic identity is regret for the times we failed to be ourselves by trying to live up to others' expectations and images of who we should be, rather than existing as we are with our own unique thoughts, feelings, memories, and desires. Mark Jordan suggests the first step, not only in coming to terms with this failure but also in redefining the terms of self-identification altogether, should be repentance by gay Catholics: "The 'invisibility' of our sexual orientation, the possibility of keeping it as an open secret, has tempted us with silent collaboration for centuries."[20] This silent collaboration only serves to perpetuate damaging church teachings which are designed to erase, or at least hide, gay existence. James Morrison is explicit about why he wrote his autobiography: "I wrote this book to know myself better, and maybe to help certain children, or the grown-ups who tend them, or the adults they grow into, to understand that they exist."[21]

Fenton Johnson notes the irony of the church's reluctance to affirm gay existence in light of its past errors in validating reality. It makes gay people a kind of modern Galileo, whom the church only recently "forgave" for his assertion that the earth was not the center of the universe. "Yet here we are, living, omnipresent evidence of a fact of life far more obvious than the heliocentric planetary system... but apparently just as difficult for Christianity to accept."[22] Perhaps these grand gestures of reconciliation begin on the smallest level, when those who read these autobiographies realize, one by one, their common humanity with these gay Catholics. Then we can begin to imagine the rejection and abandonment of church teachings that effectively turn fellow Catholic Christians into alien "others." Then we can heal a rupture in the mystical Body of Christ. As Rafael Campo says so well:

> I want to be mistaken for your brother, or your son; I want to remind you of your daughter, your mother, your sister. I want to give you something, not a disease, but perhaps a cure. I want you to look into the liquid mirror of my eyes, and see someone you recognize. Someone you have always known, someone you might even love.
> Yourself.[23]

Acts of Contrition?

> Every time I pass a crucifix I wonder, what if it had been me up there instead, could I have said, *Father, forgive them, for they know not what they do?* I don't think I'm so special, not any more. At the church here in San Francisco, I bow down and make the sign of the cross, the logo of the Church, an imprint deep within forces me to replicate this logo. Up, down, left, right, the hand that seeks, then pulls away frustrated. The hand tightens, becomes a fist, the fist is raised to the sky, on the desert's edge, angry and queer.
> —Kevin Killian, "Chain of Fools"

Recent events have created a stormy context for the appearance of a book dealing with Catholicism and homosexuality. While I was working on the final chapters of this project, the Catholic Church in America was being rocked by numerous revelations of sexual abuse by clergy over the past several decades, causing even more ruptures in the church community and within individuals. Kevin Killian's anger stems from his own experience of being abused by members of a religious order. Such abuse leaves the deepest of scars. When those who are supposedly God's representatives violate the trust of their position and perpetrate acts like this, it is yet another blow to Catholicism's institutional integrity and credibility. It calls the moral authority of church leaders into question. As Fenton Johnson remarks with due frustration, "A reasonable observer might comfortably characterize the history of the institutionalized church as a series of greater and lesser blunders, and yet its priests and ministers and bishops still claim the authority to judge the realities of our lives."[24] The need for church leaders to listen to the experience and acknowledge the authority of the laity — people who live sexual lives — is apparently more urgent than ever.

Almost equally upsetting as the fact that sexual abuse by priests occurred at all is the way such cases typically were handled by the bishops in charge. In a flood of reports touched off by the criminal trial of priest serial abuser John Geoghan in Boston, the mainstream media uncovered case after case in which the priests in question were reassigned to parish work and then continued their abusive patterns.[25] Staggering sums of money were spent in dioceses across the country to settle these cases without notification of civil authorities and to keep the victims isolated and quiet. The concern with protecting the status and reputation of the clerical caste seems to have taken precedence over the well-being of the faithful. No longer able to control the information related to these cases, the bishops have been forced to confront this issue and deal with the reality of their collective moral failure.[26] In their first official response to this situation, the bishops not only acknowledged their mistakes and apologized for "too often failing victims and our people in the past" but also affirmed their concern with regard to "issues related to effective consultation of the laity and the participation of God's people in decision making that affects their well-being."[27] While it remains to be seen how such a general statement of concern will actually be realized, it is an ideal and standard to which they must be held for the good of the people of God.

The bishops' actions in most of these cases are reflective of an organizational structure in which the top is severed from the bottom. In such a paradigm, the leaders are not answerable to those whom they are "leading." Acting as if they have been granted a sort of "divine right" to rule, the bishops of the church have long operated out of this medieval model. The current crisis illustrates the disastrous results of this kind of unchecked power. Catholic historian R. Scott Appleby notes this scandal "has never been just about the incidence of sexual abuse. It's been about a culture of secrecy, clericalism, a lack of trust and confidence in the laity, a lack of transparency and accountability in the church, and an arrogance that is used to dominate and not to serve."[28] Overcoming these problems will require an "opening up" of the hierarchical structure. In light of the current situation, Catholics on the right and left seem united in recognizing the need for lay Catholics — especially those who live and work with children — to be more involved in church governance.[29] The bishops need to be accountable to us, the laity of the church. It is our children and families who have been put in harm's way and it is our financial contributions they used to "settle" so many of these cases.

The sexual abuse crisis is not only one of unchecked authority and misuse of power with regard to church administration, however; it also illustrates the bishops' inability to fully appreciate and address matters related to sex and sexuality. To put it more bluntly, their understanding of human sexuality needs a "reality check." This crisis is a result of priests dealing with their sexual desire in inappropriate ways, and the bishops have obviously been confounded by the problem. Within their insular system, the bishops have not adequately understood reality as lay, noncelibate people see it. They need to listen to Catholics who are raising families and are responsible for the healthy formation of children and teenagers. They need to listen to Catholics who are actively engaged in sexual relationships, people who can help them understand a dimension of human life in which we can assume the clergy are not the most experienced.[30] The bishops also need to hear the voices of gay and lesbian Catholics, who know the difference between sexual identity and sexual abuse. As Andrew Sullivan states, "We have attempted to explain the moral lessons we have learned in the real world of family and sex and work and conflict. But so many church leaders — from the Pope on down — do not seem to hear or even care."[31]

At various points throughout the unraveling of this crisis, there has been an unfortunate and dangerous tendency on the part of some Catholic leaders to conflate homosexual orientation and pedophilia, in spite of the fact that psychologists mark the former as a natural variation in human sexuality and the latter as a function of arrested sexual development. Some church leaders voiced their opinion that gay priests were *the* problem. In the Vatican's first public comments on the current crisis, papal spokesman Joaquin Navarro-Valls said men who are homosexually inclined "just cannot be ordained," and he even suggested annulling the existing ordinations of gay men.[32] Archbishop Tarcisio Bertone, secretary of the Vatican's doctrinal congregation said that "persons with a homosexual inclination should not be admitted to the seminary."[33] Philadelphia's Cardinal Anthony Bevilacqua remarked, "We feel a person who is homosexual-orientated is not a suitable candidate for the priesthood, even if he has never committed any homosexual act."[34] Even celibacy is not enough to make a gay man worthy in Bevilacqua's eyes — never mind current church teaching to the contrary.

Why would men who would ordinarily claim absolute fidelity to church teaching make remarks which so clearly deviate from it? And why the quick connection to homosexuality in the first place? Let me start with the second question. Given the sexual nature of these crimes, I think it is fair to take the sexuality of these priests into account, but only as one piece in the larger puzzle of this problem.[35] While pedophilia in the strictest sense does not correlate with the sexuality of the perpetrator, not all of these cases are about pedophilia. According to the information currently available, a large percentage of these cases involved teenagers, which experts agree is more accurately called ephebophilia. Adults who find adolescents sexually attractive usually experience this desire according to their sexual orientation, especially when the teenager is clearly maturing into a young adult.[36] In our overly sexualized culture, we are bombarded with images of teens portrayed as sexual objects, particularly in movies and marketing. Indeed, it is almost normative in hegemonic heterosexual masculinity to "want" teenage girls, as long as they are "legal."[37] Inasmuch as this kind of sexual attraction tends toward a "disorder," particularly when it is manifested in an obsessive, multiple, or compulsive manner, it is certainly not what we think of as pedophilia, which turns prepubescent children into sexual objects regardless of gender. The fact, then, that the majority of the teenagers abused by priests were male makes gay priests seem especially culpable, even though ephebophilia is not just a gay issue.[38] Experts also observe more women slowly coming forward to reveal their past abuse by priests, so we do not yet have all the facts we need to accurately assess the problem (if we ever will).[39]

In April 2003, eight internationally recognized psychiatric and medical experts were invited to a symposium at the Vatican to discuss the sexual abuse problem. These experts told church officials that "banning homosexuals from the priesthood would not solve the problem." One of the experts said there is no evidence "that a homosexual orientation, specifically sexual attraction to another adult man, increases the risk of sexual molestation or repeated sexual offenses." Another expert reminded church leaders that "most male homosexuals do not molest children or adolescents," so the presumption of any one-to-one correlation between homosexual identity and abuse is unfounded. They indicated homosexuality is only one of many "risk factors," but that is far different than a "cause" of abusive behavior. More salient risk factors for abuse include access to children, intimacy deficits in adulthood, antisociality, and an exaggerated sense of self-worth. According to one expert, a more central issue in Catholic seminaries is "whether or not students have a mature understanding of their own sexuality."[40]

All of this leads me back to the first question. The reason some church leaders would stray from church teaching that insists on the "worthiness" of celibate gay priests is that it is easier to lay the blame on gay priests than to seriously examine the underlying factors contributing to this situation. As I discussed in chapter 3, the Catholic priesthood contains a disproportionate number of gay men. By now, this is relatively common knowledge in church circles. To suggest there are none in a particular diocese or seminary is naive at best; and to propose the nullification of their ordinations (if one could actually identify which priests really are gay) is outrageous, if only for the impact in terms of numbers. Church leaders who blame gay priests do not want to examine the obvious connections between an all-male, celibate clergy, on the one hand, and church teaching that "requires" celibacy of gay men, on the other.

Let me briefly articulate some of these connections. Gay Catholics are expected to completely sever the *being* from the *doing* of sexuality, a separation most of them find untenable on a permanent basis, as these autobiographers attest. Some gay men (and even some heterosexual men) turn to the celibate priesthood in the hopes of escaping the integration of orientation and acts that would enable a healthy sexual identity. In their striving to be faithful to church teaching, they avoid a healthy sexual formation and an open embrace of their sexuality. In the priesthood, they find an all-male atmosphere, which ironically promotes a culture of homosexuality. These same men traditionally have had unfettered access to young people, young men in particular, who were effectively at the same level of sexual development and experience as the priests themselves. Given this kind of access and their level of sexual immaturity, it is not surprising some of these men might seek carnal experiences with other "boys," sadly violating their position of trust and authority.[41]

Church leaders must share the blame for what has happened — not just for the way they handled the cases, but for maintaining teachings and a structure which implicitly supported occurrences of this kind of abuse. Some conservative commentators are using this crisis to assert the necessity of reinforcing current church teaching on human sexuality.[42] They feel ideals of chastity, abstinence, and celibacy have become diluted and even lost in the midst of a promiscuous popular culture. While it is reasonable enough to frame the issue in this way, I do not agree it captures the real problem: current church doctrine does not reflect the full range of sexual reality and ethical possibilities. Rigid, one-size-fits-all teachings on sexuality inevitably lead to the duplicity we now see with regard to sexuality and the priesthood. Yes, there are many priests, including gay priests,

who live celibate lives, but many do not.[43] Strategies for being celibate
and still embracing one's sexual self, which seminaries are supposedly
emphasizing, simply do not work for everyone. Thus, we have cases of
sexual abuse, priests having affairs, and an active homosexual culture in
the priesthood.

Minimally, the bishops need to understand that healthy sexuality formation must integrate both *being* and *doing* — orientation *and* acts.
Celibacy works only if it too is both orientation and act: an interior
charism and a choice freely sought and embraced for as long as it nourishes
the soul. In other words, celibacy and priesthood are distinct vocations.[44]
When celibacy is forced, it becomes a preoccupation with avoiding all
things sexual, which in turn makes it a greater risk factor in terms of
sexual abuse.[45] Dropping the celibacy *requirement* and letting women be
ordained will not eliminate cases of clerical sexual abuse, but changes like
this could go a long way toward solving the problem. It is time for church
leaders to abandon old ideas about gender and sexuality and learn from
lay people whose experience communicates a different reality. It is not
enough to frame this crisis exclusively as an administrative problem, in
which bishops are called to accountability in the way they deal with personnel. They also must be accountable in terms of their moral and pastoral
teaching. Especially with regard to sexuality, lay people simply have more
experience than the celibate clergy has.[46] And no one has more to teach
about gay identity than gay people themselves. That is why heeding the
lessons of these autobiographies is so important.

Behind the scapegoating of gay priests in this crisis lies an antigay
agenda. Catholic lay people need to check not only the bishops' power
and lack of expertise but also the bishops' biases and homophobia. It is an
animus against gay people which prompts men like Cardinal Bevilacqua
and papal spokesman Navarro-Valls to issue a wholesale condemnation
of gay men — even to the extent of making remarks that do not accurately reflect church teaching or the reality of the priesthood. The depth
of societal enmity toward being gay makes these autobiographies even
more consequential. I hope my analysis of these "sacred texts" will enlighten the church to the reality of gay lives and lay bare the inadequacy
and injustice of current church teaching on homosexuality. These life
texts offer a corrective to simplistic constructions of what it means to
be gay and to act gay. The "homosexual lifestyle," as naysayers like to
call it, is no more or less complex, rich, and varied than the "heterosexual lifestyle." These autobiographies represent the lives of real people
making sense of the various identities with which they have been dubbed
in the present social and religious context, a challenge we all share in
different ways.

Conclusion: An Act of Hope

So, we are obliged to live out the telling of our individual stories, and then we are obliged to attempt to tell the church secrets that begin to appear through them.
— Mark Jordan, *Telling Truths in Church*

I write this book as an act of hope: I hope my work will be a contribution to the ongoing and worthy effort to destigmatize being gay in the church. As it is now, even though the church teaches respect and justice for gay people, the bifurcated and confusing teaching interferes with the realization of that goal. Consider the case of celibate gay priests. According to church teaching, they should be able to share the truth of their sexual identity with their parishioners; but we know this is rarely the case. Ignorance and misconceptions about being gay work against an honesty that would no doubt be life-saving for some of their congregants. The same can be said of gay teachers in Catholic schools. One risks one's job if one comes out; yet, consider how meaningful it would be for a student with an emerging gay identity to have a positive Catholic role model. One gay Catholic man who attended a high school seminary recalls being counseled by his spiritual director, a priest whom he later learned was gay: "[Being gay] was still something I was trying to figure out, I was struggling with, and all he could do was listen to me."[47] Just imagine the positive interaction which might have occurred if the priest/director had been able to share his own sexual identity with a student who likely felt alone. The church needs visible gay role models, but fear on all sides buttresses the closet walls. I hope my opening up of these gay life stories will help lower the fear factor that functions to overdetermine the differences in our sexual identities.

My biggest hope lies with gay Catholic students. I hope work like this will alert school administrators to the way their institutions reinforce heteronormative assumptions that marginalize sexual minorities. Catholic schools should be places where the values of respect, friendship, and justice for gay people are clearly communicated. This too is not generally the case. In his recent book, *Being Gay and Lesbian in a Catholic High School*, Michael Maher documents through personal interviews and two survey studies the many ways lesbian and gay Catholic high school students still experience what he calls "dis-integration." The integration of student, studies, family, community, and faith that is a mark of Catholic education is not happening for students who are gay. Catholic educators who attempt to rectify this situation by providing supportive experiences for gay students often find themselves facing a storm of criticism from parents and colleagues. Maher's conclusions about the double message of church teaching on homosexuality mirror my own. Maher asks in his conclusion, "Can most people defend the rights of gay and lesbian people and at the same time condemn the actions they take in expressing love?" He answers, "In my 1995 survey study, I found that most adolescents cannot hold both of these views simultaneously."[48] The students who agreed with statements based on the church's moral rhetoric were less likely to agree with statements based on the pastoral rhetoric. The opposite was also true. It seems even teenage Catholics find the bifurcated church teaching on homosexuality sends a mixed and confusing message.

Mixed messages like this have serious repercussions within schools and in society at large. Although surveys disclose a majority of America's high school students tend to hold more liberal, "pro-gay" opinions than previous generations have held, high schools remain largely hostile environments for gay students. In a recent poll conducted by Zogby International, half of high school students surveyed admitted having witnessed gay students being called "faggot," "homo," or "dyke" to their faces, and an astounding 88 percent of those polled used the phrase, "That's so gay," to describe something they do not like.[49] Happily, Catholic students in the survey stand out as a group in having particularly liberal opinions with regard to gay civil rights and marriage issues, so something positive is getting across; but direct harassment of gay students persists. This paradoxical behavior reflects the contradictions inherent in bifurcated church teaching and presumptions that it is realistically possible to love a person but hate the actions that help define who they are in the first place. These schizophrenic attitudes contribute to the higher rate of gay teenage suicides. In April 1997, an eighteen-year-old football player named Marcus Wayman killed himself after a police officer stopped him and a male friend and threatened to out him.[50] I hope my work will help to enlighten more people to the full reality of gay experience so we can work to save the lives of young men like him.

American society is increasingly divided over the issue of homosexuality and lesbian and gay rights. Instances of harassment and violence toward gays and lesbians have been on the rise in recent years. The church is not entirely to blame for this volatile atmosphere, but it must own its share of responsibility for the ambiguous message and attitudes its teachings promote. It denounces violence against gay people even as it calls into question their relationships. I hope this book will help move the societal debate forward in a productive and nonviolent way by taking us beyond the constraining assumptions religious institutions have fostered about gay people. We need to see gay people not as a category about which simplistic generalizations are to be made, but as complex individuals dealing with multiple concerns in their lives. Gay people want the same social recognition as heterosexual people for their loving relationships and families.

On October 16, 2000, Robert Daniel was admitted to a Shock Trauma center in Baltimore for complications arising from AIDS. His partner Bill

Flanigan was not allowed to see Daniel or confer with Daniel's physicians, even though he had a Durable Power of Attorney for Health Care Decisions. It was only after Daniel's mother and sister arrived four hours later that Flanigan was allowed access or information. By that time, Daniel was unconscious with a breathing tube he would not have wanted. He died shortly thereafter without ever having been able to say goodbye to his partner.[51] I hope my work will highlight the validity of gay relationships and the importance of giving them the same protection and benefits as heterosexual partnerships. Then, men like Robert and Bill will not have to be separated from each other when they need each other the most.[52]

This kind of social change will require a conversion of heart on the most personal levels, so I return to my hope for reconciliation. It is a difficult task because it is not only a matter of memory, healing, and forgiveness, but also, as Robert Schreiter says, "about changing the structure in society that provoked, promoted and sustained violence."[53] Yet gay Catholics continue to seek reconciliation with the church. In these life texts, gay autobiographers engage in an exercise of self-examination which discloses not only their own personal struggles and shortcomings but also the ways the church has failed them. My analysis of these texts reveals that church teaching on homosexuality is not just inadequate but also injurious in the way it bifurcates human beings. On this level, these autobiographies are confessions of the "sinned against," stories of the way church teaching has victimized gay people. When gay Catholics tell their life stories, they stand as alienated prophets. James Lopresti links the term "prophetic alienation" with those

> who take a stance over against the community because of what they claim to be the community's own failure or sin. In its classic forms, such alienation resulted in schism, the separation of the churches. In contemporary forms, while schism may not be publicly acknowledged, that is the private experience of the prophetically alienated. In the past, doctrinal or juridical questions may have caused the separation. Today it is usually a matter of disagreement about moral principles, the acceptability of variant lifestyles, or disputes over the roles of church leadership.[54]

Church leaders need to take the steps to overcome this de facto schism. They need to listen to the life stories of gay people and take seriously their moral agency and life experience. They need to recognize that the pastoral rhetoric about respecting gay persons is meaningless when the associated moral rhetoric undercuts gay personhood. Consider the case of Bill Stein, who was fired from his job as Music Director at Holy Family Parish in Rockford, Illinois. Though Stein had worked at the parish for five years and had performed with the church choir for the pope in Italy, he was fired for refusing to end his relationship with his partner of ten years. According to news reports, Stein had never hidden nor flaunted his relationship; it only became an issue when parishioners learned he and his partner were planning to adopt a child.[55] Something is terribly amiss when a person who has competently served his community for several years is fired for loving another human being and wanting to care for a child in need of a home. Such an action on the part of the church in no way signifies the respect and justice that is supposed to be accorded gay people. Quite the contrary, the church is participating in a grave injustice when it imposes a penalty — the loss of one's livelihood — for remaining in a committed and loving relationship. In the collision of the moral and pastoral rhetoric, it seems the church is more than happy to take advantage of gay people and to use their talents as long as they do not act like full human beings.

Gay Catholic autobiographies reveal what it means for a gay person to be a full human being. In light of the complexity of gay lives, it is untenable to make sweeping condemnations of gay acts and relationships that are directly linked to gay identity. It is no longer admissible for church leaders to ignore the unitive and procreative aspects of so many gay relationships, and it is absolutely unacceptable for church leaders to blame gay people for problems like clergy sexual abuse. Just as listening to the stories of abuse victims prompted the bishops to take action and make changes in policy, listening to gay life stories should prompt a similar *metanoia* on their part.

In a recent apostolic letter, the pope stated, "It is clear that penitents living in a habitual state of serious sin and who do not intend to change their situation cannot validly receive absolution."[56] Whereas the pope was likely referring in part to gay people who reject the church's ban on homosexual acts, I would turn his statement back on church leaders who, despite overwhelming testimony by faithful Catholics, refuse to consider any modification of the church's teachings on homosexuality. We cannot absolve church leaders of their sin until they demonstrate a serious intention to change their situation. As Richard Rodriguez declares, "I predict the Vatican will one day apologize to homosexuals, just as Rome has needed to apologize to Jews, for centuries of moral cowardice."[57] I will not hold my breath for such an apology in the near future, but this book is a testament to my belief that things can and eventually must change.

Once I had finished the first draft of this book, my partner and I decided to paint one of the bedrooms in our house in anticipation of a visit from my mother. As we worked, I realized how much more difficult it was to paint inside the closet than in the rest of the room. It required all sorts of bending and a great deal of discomfort to make the inside of that closet as pretty as the rest of the room. Taping off corners in there was twice as difficult because the light was poor and the space was cramped. The irony of this image was not lost on me in light of having read and analyzed so many gay autobiographies. There is so much more room to move outside of the closet, but church teaching would have us remain still rather than moving as the Spirit might will us. I hope for a day when gay identity does not have to matter so much, when our whispers from the housetop become full-throated and joyous proclamations.

In order for gay identity to no longer matter, we as Catholics will have to recover a sense of what matters most in terms of Christian identity. We need to unravel the categories and assigned meanings that stand in the way of recognizing our common baptismal bond. To be baptized is to be a member of the mystical body of Christ. This is the communion we should experience whenever we participate in the Eucharist. It is the bond that gives meaning and purpose to our gathering for liturgy. It is the reason gay Catholics like Fenton Johnson continue to participate in the life of the church: "I receive [communion] in part because so few gestures remain that bind me to the stranger, that declare that our common fate, which is to be human, transcends distinctions of race or gender or sexuality or economic or social class."[58] This is *koinonia* — the vision of true reconciliation. Once again, the view of a Catholic youth is instructive and hopeful. As a recent graduate of a Catholic high school says about his experience being gay as a teenager:

> On the one hand, I was hiding it. But on the other hand, I knew it was not *the* most important thing at the time. That's what messes you up, because, rationally, you know, "This isn't the most important thing about me, necessarily." But then you get all this information and background that it's bad, so it just kind of blows it out of proportion. It should be an important part of you, but it shouldn't have to be inflated.[59]

From his mouth to God's ears! I hope for a day when coming out does not have to overshadow everything else. I hope someday research like mine will not be so vital — when being gay will simply be something to be celebrated along with so many other human traits.

Appendix

The Gramick and Nugent Investigation: A Test Case for Church Teaching

Sister Jeannine Gramick, SSND (now SL), and Father Robert Nugent, SDS, began their official ministry to gay and lesbian Catholics in 1977 with the founding of New Ways Ministry. Under pressure from the Holy See, they disassociated themselves from New Ways (which still operates with the same mission) but continued to minister to lesbian and gay Catholics. In 1988 an investigation was launched by the Vatican's Congregation for Religious and Secular Institutes, to evaluate the orthodoxy of their ministry. After some preliminary communications between the Congregation for Religious and Secular Institutes, Nugent and Gramick, and their superiors regarding who would be on the investigative commission and how it would proceed, there was no word from the commission again until January 1994. In fact, Gramick's and Nugent's religious communities believed the whole thing had been dissolved. Apparently, however, they had been conducting a "study phase" of Gramick and Nugent's ministry. It seems there was a great deal of pressure brought to bear on the Congregation for Religious and Secular Institutes (now called the Congregation for the Institutes of Consecrated Life and Apostolic Societies) by Cardinal James Hickey of Washington, D.C., who was Sister Jeannine's local bishop, to proceed as quickly as possible with the inquest. He had written them "many times concerning this matter" and had clearly already decided that she (and Nugent, by extension) was guilty of "ambiguity with regard to the wrongness of homosexual activity."[1]

After some discussions about the process, Gramick and Nugent were eventually sent a series of questions about their work and texts from their book *Building Bridges: Gay and Lesbian Reality and the Catholic Church,* which they earlier had acknowledged was most representative of their approach to this ministry. They mailed written responses to the questions on June 24, 1994, and discussed them in person with the commission on July 26, 1994. The Maida commission's questions and concerns reveal its attention to the moral rhetoric of the church's teaching on homosexuality,

174

while Gramick and Nugent's responses illustrate their persistent emphasis on the pastoral rhetoric, which they characterize as portraying the full range of church teaching on the subject.

Nugent and Gramick begin by describing the basic purpose of their workshops and writings: "The basic purpose of our ministry is to serve as bridge builders between the church and its gay and lesbian members. We accomplish this as advocates for both groups to be reconciled."[2] With regard to the church, they state they are advocates by presenting

> the full range of teaching on homosexuality and homophobia [a word the Vatican does not use] to lesbian and gay persons. Although Catholics are knowledgeable about the teaching on the objective immorality of homogenital acts, they are largely unaware of the other teachings on homosexuality: the personhood and human dignity of gay and lesbian people, social justice and civil rights, the immorality of unjust discrimination and violence toward homosexual persons, and the mandate for authentic pastoral care.[3]

With regard to lesbian and gay persons, they are advocates by "listening to their experiences, by articulating their concerns, and by being present to them pastorally in their efforts to integrate their sexuality and their faith lives."[4] They state one of their goals is to provide "responsible, balanced, and contemporary information," which includes not only the official teachings of the Roman Catholic Church but also "positions and studies from other Christian denominations, and relevant data from the empirical and social sciences on human sexuality, sexual identity, and sexual orientation."[5] They further nuance this by saying they distinguish between doctrinal affirmations which require assent from Catholics and those which allow for differing judgments. This is a strategy often deployed by progressive Catholics to underscore the fact that very few church pronouncements carry the official distinction of being infallible. In fact, none of the church's teachings on homosexuality could be considered officially infallible. Members of the hierarchy will say these teachings are "definitive," but that in itself is a rhetorical tactic designed to muffle dissenting voices, and it is a category lacking solid canonical grounding. Needless to say, these discursive strategies feed on each other and lead to a combative tension that is difficult to reconcile.

When asked if their goal is to draw people to an acceptance and practice of the official teaching of the church on homosexuality, Nugent and Gramick respond affirmatively, with the caveat that this includes the "full range" of teachings as described above. They are admirably adamant about maintaining this emphasis on including the pastoral rhetoric over and against the commission's obvious preoccupation with the moral rhetoric. The commission notes that the two have been charged in the past with "ambiguity" regarding their treatment of the prohibition on homosexual relationships because they present other theological opinions (regarding the acceptability of homosexual acts) as viable. They do indeed present other views, but Nugent and Gramick claim these are not offered as viable alternatives to magisterial teaching.[6] As the investigation unfolded, the way they handled these "dissenting" opinions became a key sticking point between them and the commission. Interestingly, the commission admittedly had on record letters from five Roman Catholic bishops who had attended Gramick and Nugent's workshops and determined them to be orthodox.[7] This was still not sufficient to assuage the concerns of the commission.

The specific passages of Gramick and Nugent's book, *Building Bridges*, selected by the commission further illustrate the commission's fixation on the moral rhetoric of church teaching. Much fuss is made over the use of the word "natural," which Nugent and Gramick use to describe homosexual feelings and orientation. They use the term in accordance with church teaching that homosexual orientation is innate and unchosen, and to incorporate the position of most modern psychologists. The church also uses the term "disordered," in relation to the orientation, but Nugent and Gramick resist this term for pastoral reasons. They defend themselves by turning on itself the Vatican's argument that "ambiguity" on this subject confuses the faithful. Gramick and Nugent note:

> The layperson, even if well-educated, is not aware of the different technical uses which philosophers and theologians have made of the word "natural" and of the continuing debate about natural law. So, it is somewhat confusing to such a person to hear statements which appear to contradict contemporary scientific claims.... It would be less problematic for the ordinary faithful and for the *pastoral* minister if theologians and philosophers were more sensitive to the way words are generally understood in contemporary society.[8]

In the same document, Gramick and Nugent are asked to discuss their criticism of the 1986 "Letter to the Bishops of the Catholic Church on the Pastoral Care of Homosexual Persons," from the Congregation for the Doctrine of the Faith. One of their primary points relates directly to the bifurcation problem I have been delineating. They state, "Most of the document is concerned with explicating the *moral* evaluation of homogenital activity. As such, it would more adequately be characterized as *doctrinal*, rather then *pastoral*."[9] The bifurcation problem is further implicated, albeit with different words, in one of the book passages the commission wants clarified: "We may have to choose between 'defending Church teaching' and proclaiming Jesus' message of love."[10] Yet another selected passage from *Building Bridges* reconfigures the bifurcation under the guise of American (pastoral) versus Roman (moral) concerns: "Attempting a delicate balancing act, the U.S. hierarchy is trying to demonstrate to lesbian and gay Catholics a sense of care and compassion while, at the same time, trying to maintain loyalty to Roman expectations."[11]

On October 4, 1994, the commission issued a lengthy report of its findings, and on January 12, 1995, Nugent and Gramick submitted an equally lengthy response analyzing the commission's report. Looking at the two documents together, I see the same fundamental sticking point solidifying: the commission is seeking unequivocal emphasis on the moral condemnation of homosexual acts and relationships; Nugent and Gramick continue to deemphasize the moral rhetoric because they feel that aspect of church teaching is already "well-known and clear."[12] The commission insists this moral teaching "is a crucial question for the moral choices that affect the human person, and, therefore, it cannot be considered incidental."[13] This is an essential and legitimate point, which undergirds my argument about the bifurcation of church teaching. Lesbian and gay persons cannot be separated from the actions and choices which flow directly from their sexual identity. The church recognizes this reality (at least narrowly) with heterosexual persons by enunciating a moral theology of what constitutes good sexual expression and relationships. For homosexual persons, however, all sexual expression is denied, in spite of the assertion that they are to be accorded the dignity and respect due all people, and despite the theological understanding of celibacy being a special charism not granted to everyone. The commission investigating Nugent and Gramick is right: the moral rhetoric cannot be incidental. Nugent and Gramick's ministry is problematic because, in the name of building a bridge, they gloss over the "well-known" moral rhetoric that denies full personhood to gays and lesbians. They know they cannot harmonize the moral and pastoral rhetorics. The commission, on the other hand, marginalizes the pastoral teaching to fully respect gays and lesbians by fixating on the moral condemnation of gay relationships. They too know they cannot harmonize the moral and pastoral rhetorics.

The commission is especially bothered by Gramick and Nugent's reluctance to clearly use the term "disordered" in relation to homosexual orientation. In a strange distortion of logic — an attempt to put a pastoral spin on the moral rhetoric — they insist that the use and precise explanation of the word "may conceivably lead those who are offended by the perceived meaning of the word to cease being offended."[14] It is as if the pastoral component of church teaching exists only to make us feel better about the moral rhetoric. Gramick and Nugent recognize that most gays and lesbians experience their sexuality as a factor of identity, and labeling a person's identity as disordered is pastorally problematic. Couching it in the language of moral theology in order to assuage offense is a ruse. The commission reads this resistance to using exact terms as a lack of loyalty to the church's teachings: "They merely *present* the Church's teaching, but give no evidence of personal advocacy of it."[15] Nugent and Gramick are quick to point out in their response that the question of personal assent came up at the hearing, but Archbishop Maida decided it was not a fair question to ask. Yet the commission undoubtedly wanted Gramick and Nugent to be personally invested in the moral rhetoric. This issue would eventually come back to bite them.

At this point in the investigation, Nugent and Gramick had now submitted supportive letters from fifteen Roman Catholic bishops. Despite this (!), the Vatican commission was still not satisfied and even seemed to ignore them. Gramick and Nugent were asked to respond to three additional questions from the Congregation for the Institutes of Consecrated Life and Societies of Apostolic Faith. In their response, dated February 22, 1996, they clarify that while church teaching considers homosexual orientation "natural," it also describes it as "a pathological constitution judged to be incurable" and as "an objective disorder . . . ordered toward an intrinsic moral evil."[16] Yet Gramick and Nugent still maintain, "On a pastoral level, it is important to help people understand that this assessment of the homosexual orientation does not imply moral failing or sin and that fundamental respect is due to gay and lesbian persons as bearers of the image of God."[17] Talk about an impossible gap to bridge! I respect Nugent and Gramick for their persistence in the face of the commission's interrogation and their insistence on reconciling the two incompatible rhetorics; but most gays and lesbians will hear language such as "pathological," "incurable," "disorder," and "intrinsic moral evil" as attacks on their very souls.

The Vatican's emphasis on the moral rhetoric was ultimately symbolized by the transfer of the case to the Congregation for the Doctrine of the Faith (CDF), headed by Cardinal Joseph Ratzinger, in late 1995.[18] Clearly, the focus of the investigation was now officially centered around moral, doctrinal concerns. The CDF issued a "Contestatio" entitled "Erroneous and Dangerous Propositions in the Publications *Building Bridges* and *Voices of Hope* by Sister Jeannine Gramick, SSND, and Father Robert Nugent, SDS,"[19] which was approved by Pope John Paul II on October 24, 1997. This document deserves special attention because it represents the priorities of the Vatican at this point in time in relation to lesbian and gay Catholics: the moral condemnation of homosexual behavior and relationships must be defended at all costs and dissent from this teaching must be actively restrained. As disturbing as I find this document in terms of its notion of pastoral care and its lack of genuine respect of gays and lesbians, it does adhere closely to the logic of the moral rhetoric in church teaching. After all, it is Ratzinger's job to be the guardian of this rhetoric, and from that perspective, his document accurately names problems in Gramick and Nugent's ministry.

The document begins with a bow to the pastoral rhetoric and some remarks about the intrinsic dignity of all people. That being said, however, it then discusses the importance of "truth" in leading homosexuals to goodness and freedom. This truth is found in the *entirety* of church teaching:

> Clearly, every form of pastoral care must be undertaken in accord with the full truth of the Church's teaching on this problem. When pastoral initiatives are at variance with doctrinal truth, their inherent nature is compromised and they no longer constitute a true help[20]

I agree with this statement at face value, but it is problematic with regard to the issue of homosexuality on at least two levels: First, the bifurcation of church teaching into antagonistic rhetorics makes it virtually impossible to realistically communicate one "full truth." Indeed, Gramick and Nugent are perceived by the CDF to be in error precisely because they strive to convey the "full truth" of the church's teaching. Second, the "full truth" of the church's teaching does not adequately reflect reality as all gays and lesbians experience it.[21] The document is largely concerned with these issues of truth and experience, so it will be helpful to flesh out what I mean here by focusing on examples from the text.

The CDF cites passages from Gramick and Nugent's publications to address their methodology. It is flawed, they say, by "an appeal to a form of moral reasoning in which the category of 'experience' becomes the criterion through which the objective norms of morality are judged and set aside."[22] Several contemporary Christian sexual ethicists have suggested moral theological reflection should draw on more than one source. In general, these sources have been scripture, tradition, reason, *and* experience.[23] To their credit, Nugent and Gramick do utilize all of these categories in their work. The CDF's problem seems not to be that Nugent and Gramick overemphasize lesbian and gay experience as a source, but that they use such experience at all. Both the Maida commission and the CDF selectively cite passages in which lesbian and gay experience is articulated, without acknowledging Gramick and Nugent's use of the other categories. The CDF then accuses them of using experience as the sole criterion. Ratzinger is leery of allowing experience as a criterion because of its link with conscience. He is reacting to the use of obeying one's conscience as a defense for dissent from church teaching, a strategy often deployed by reform-minded Catholics.

This is no small matter. The very authority of the church's teaching is at stake. The primacy of one's conscience is enshrined in the documents of Vatican II (see the introduction), and lesbian and gay Catholics have long used this teaching to justify their life choices. In the passages selected by the CDF, Nugent and Gramick affirm such personal conscience decisions when they are made after a process of deep, prayerful discernment. Ratzinger calls this faulty moral reasoning. In a footnote, he quotes from John Paul II's Encyclical Letter *Veritatis Splendor* (The Splendor of the Truth):

> To the affirmation that one has a duty to follow one's conscience is unduly added the affirmation that one's moral judgement is true merely by the fact that it has its origin in the conscience. But in this way, the inescapable claims of truth disappear, yielding their place to criterion [*sic*] of sincerity, authenticity, and 'being at peace with oneself,' so much so that some have come to adopt a radically subjectivistic conception of moral judgment.[24]

Pope John Paul makes a valid point here. If personal moral decisions are to be taken seriously, at least within the framework of Catholic moral theology, then they must be rooted in something more substantial than an appeal to "what feels good to me." It is also not enough to speak solely of "gay and lesbian experience," when engaging in moral theology because that experience is too diverse to be captured in any single formulation. But I do not think John Paul's critique applies in this case. Nugent and Gramick are thorough in their use of sources other than experience, and gay and lesbian Catholics rarely make decisions to act on their sexuality solely from a position of "it feels good." Our "lived experience" in its multiplicity encompasses all that is involved in being fully alive and engaging with other human beings and the world. Indeed, we are (in)formed by and struggle with the tradition, as many of the autobiographies I discuss attest.

On the other side of the coin, if church teachings and moral doctrines are to be taken seriously, then they too must be rooted in something more substantial than an appeal to an "objective truth," which does not reflect the lived experience of those to whom the teachings are directed. For example, many lesbian and gay Catholics have chosen to express their sexuality by engaging in homosexual relationships, yet church teaching does not recognize any of these. All forms of homosexual expression are denied. Inasmuch as I agree with John Paul about the inadequacy of "radically subjectivistic" conceptions of moral reasoning, I would say church teaching on homosexuality is "radically nonsubjective." There are literally droves of faithful lesbian and gay Catholics acting on their sexuality; ignoring their life choices without even considering the possibility of learning from their experience is short-sighted. There is enough critical mass by now that it seems inadequate to conceive of all homosexual relationships as dissent from "the truth."[25] Church teachers must find a way to take this reality seriously. That is, in fact, what Gramick and Nugent are trying to do in their pastoral work: they know no ministry to gay and lesbian Catholics can succeed if it does not listen to their experience.

The CDF also accuses Nugent and Gramick of tendentiously using church documents to promote a reformist agenda. It is true enough that Nugent and Gramick selectively edit the church documents they cite, especially in *Voices of Hope*; but again, it is not so much to promote a radical agenda as it is to balance the moral and pastoral rhetorics. They even say as much in their book: "A change in the Church's teaching on homogenital expression is not the goal of the positive statements and documents found in this book. . . . We need to interpret, understand, and apply the tradition of the Church in an authentically *pastoral* way."[26] It should be remembered these documents are for the most part written by bishops and bishops' conferences. The CDF fails to address why so many church officials are themselves emphasizing the pastoral rhetoric and even calling for further development of the moral rhetoric. The CDF also brings up one of the passages the Maida commission considered in which Nugent and Gramick talk about having to choose between defending church teaching and proclaiming Jesus' message of love. To this, the CDF boldly responds: "There is, and in fact can be, no opposition between Jesus' message of love and the teaching of the Church."[27] Perhaps Ratzinger and his cohort are selectively forgetting the history of church teaching with regard to slavery, the crusades, the Jews, usury, and religious freedom, just to name a few.

After receiving the Contestatio from their Superiors in December 1997, Gramick and Nugent were given two months to respond independently. Sister Gramick's response is dated February 5, 1998, and Father Nugent's is dated February 6, 1998. Both are lengthy and deal with more of the same; the difference is each of them is much more conciliatory by this point. They concede the need to clarify the moral rhetoric in many ways more strongly in the future. I suspect they were advised to do so by their canon lawyers given the high level of the proceedings. The only thing they really contest is the language used to communicate the moral rhetoric. They are both careful to reiterate the condemnation of homogenital acts, but in language they feel is pastorally palatable and still theologically accurate.[28] Despite this and the positive assessment of their obedience by their Superiors General, the CDF was still not satisfied because neither of them unequivocally expressed *personal* agreement with the church's moral condemnation of homosexual behavior and relationships. It seems the debate over the orthodoxy of their ministry had reached an impasse and the crux of the investigation now hinged on Nugent and Gramick's private feelings. They each were asked to formulate a declaration of personal assent, using the formula "I firmly accept and hold that . . . ," and to ask for pardon for the errors contained in their publications. On July 29, 1998, Gramick submitted her declaration, stating she would not reveal her personal beliefs regarding the moral rhetoric of church teaching: "The approach I have taken in my pastoral ministry requires this reticence."[29] Nugent submitted his declaration on August 6, 1998, stating, in effect, he had never publicly denied church teaching regarding homosexual acts. In turn, the CDF drafted its own "Profession of Faith" for Nugent to sign, which he promptly modified and returned on January 25, 1999.[30] The CDF found both of their responses unacceptable and on July 10, 1999, informed their religious superiors of the order to cease all ministry to homosexuals.[31] Both of them accepted this order in the spirit of religious obedience, but by narrowly interpreting the edict, they continued to speak and write about the subject. Within a year, the order was expanded, forbidding them to speak or write about the case or anything having to do with lesbian and gay concerns.[32] The end result (for now, anyway) of the long investigation is thus an internal power struggle, while the bifurcation problem, which caused the whole unhappy situation in the first place, remains.

Notes

Preface

1. John J. McNeill, *The Church and the Homosexual* (Kansas City: Andrews & McMeel, 1976; 4th ed., Boston: Beacon, 1993); also *Taking a Chance on God: Liberating Theology for Gays, Lesbians, and Their Lovers, Families, and Friends* (Boston: Beacon, 1988); and *Freedom, Glorious Freedom: The Spiritual Journey to the Fullness of Life for Gays, Lesbians, and Everybody Else* (Boston: Beacon, 1995).

2. For example, Gareth Moore, *The Body in Context: Sex and Catholicism* (London: SCM, 1992); also *A Question of Truth: Christianity and Homosexuality* (London: Continuum, 2003). Also see Mark D. Jordan, *The Ethics of Sex* (Oxford: Blackwell, 2002); Other moral theologians of relevance include Charles Curran, Margaret Farley, Lisa Sowle Cahill, Daniel Maguire, Joan Timmerman, Rosemary Radford Ruether, and James P. Hanigan. A useful anthology is Robert Nugent, ed., *A Challenge to Love: Gay and Lesbian Catholics in the Church* (New York: Crossroad, 1983).

3. Some of the most significant of these include: Rebecca Alpert, *Like Bread on the Seder Plate: Jewish Lesbians and the Transformation of Tradition* (New York: Columbia University Press, 1997); Marilyn Bennett Alexander and James Preston, *We Were Baptized Too: Claiming God's Grace for Lesbians and Gays* (Louisville: Westminster John Knox, 1996); Christie Balka and Andy Rose, eds., *Twice Blessed: On Being Lesbian or Gay and Jewish* (Boston: Beacon, 1989); Gary David Comstock, *Gay Theology without Apology* (Cleveland: Pilgrim, 1993); Gary David Comstock and Susan E. Henking, eds., *Que(e)rying Religion: A Critical Anthology* (New York: Continuum, 1997); Comstock, *Unrepentant, Self-Affirming, Practicing: Lesbian/Bisexual/Gay People Within Organized Religion* (New York: Continuum, 1996); Marvin M. Ellison, *Erotic Justice: A Liberating Ethic of Sexuality* (Louisville: Westminster John Knox, 1996); Robert Goss, *Jesus Acted Up: A Gay and Lesbian Manifesto* (San Francisco: HarperSanFrancisco, 1993); Keith Hartman, *Congregations in Conflict: The Battle over Homosexuality* (New Brunswick, N.J.: Rutgers University Press, 1996); Carter Heyward, *Touching Our Strength: The Erotic as Power and the Love of God* (San Francisco: Harper & Row, 1989); James B. Nelson, *Embodiment: An Approach to Sexuality and Christian Theology* (Minneapolis: Augsburg, 1978); Jeffrey S. Siker, ed., *Homosexuality in the Church: Both Sides of the Debate* (Louisville: Westminster John Knox, 1994); Leanne McCall Tigert, *Coming Out While Staying In* (Cleveland: Pilgrim, 1997).

4. Needless to say, they reach a variety of conclusions. Some of the most notable are John Boswell *Christianity, Social Tolerance, and Homosexuality: Gay People in Western Europe from the Beginning of the Christian Era to the Fourteenth Century* (Chicago: University of Chicago Press, 1980); Bernadette J. Brooten, *Love Between Women: Early Christian Responses to Female Homoeroticism* (Chicago: University of Chicago Press, 1996). Robert L. Brawley, *Biblical Ethics and*

183

Homosexuality: Listening to Scripture (Louisville: Westminster John Knox, 1996);
L. William Countryman, *Dirt, Greed and Sex: Sexual Ethics in the New Testa-
ment and Their Implications for Today* (Philadelphia: Fortress, 1988); Daniel A.
Helminiak, *What the Bible Really Says about Homosexuality* (San Francisco:
Alamo Square, 1994); Marti Nissinen, *Homoeroticism in the Biblical World: A His-
torical Perspective*, trans. Kirsi Stjerna (Minneapolis: Fortress Press, 1998); Saul M.
Olyan, " 'And with a Male You Shall Not Lie the Lying Down of a Woman': On the
Meaning and Significance of Leviticus 18:22 and 20:13," *Journal of the History of
Sexuality* 5 (October 1994): 179–206; Robin Scroggs, *Homosexuality in the New
Testament: Contextual Background for Contemporary Debate* (Philadelphia: Fortress, 1983); Mark Smith, "Ancient Bisexuality and the Interpretation of Romans
1:26–27," *Journal of the American Academy of Religion* 64, no. 2 (Summer 1996):
223–56. For an interesting peek into the kinds of debates over homosexuality going
on among biblical scholars, see Robert Gagnon, *The Bible and Homosexual Practice: Texts and Hermeneutics* (Nashville: Abingdon, 2001), and the subsequent
review of and dialogue about it: Walter Wink, "To Hell with Gays?" *Christian
Century* 119 (June 5–12, 2002): 32–34; Gagnon, "Gays and the Bible" and Wink,
"A Reply by Walter Wink," *Christian Century* 119 (August 14–27, 2002): 40–44.

5. For example: Mary Hunt, *Fierce Tenderness: A Feminist Theology of
Friendship* (New York: Crossroad, 1991); Lisa Sowle Cahill, *Sex, Gender and Christian Ethics* (Cambridge: Cambridge University Press, 1996); Kelly Brown Douglas,
Sexuality and the Black Church: A Womanist Perspective (Maryknoll, N.Y.: Orbis,
1999); Christine E. Gudorf, *Body, Sex, and Pleasure: Reconstructing Christian
Sexual Ethics* (Cleveland: Pilgrim, 1994); Anne Bathurst Gilson, *Eros Breaking
Free: Interpreting Sexual Theo-Ethics* (Cleveland: Pilgrim, 1995); Rosemary Radford Ruether, *Sexism and God-Talk: Toward a Feminist Theology* (Boston: Beacon,
1983); and contributors to anthologies such as: Ruether, ed., *Religion and Sexism: Images of Woman in the Jewish and Christian Traditions* (New York: Simon
& Schuster, 1974); Catherine Mowry LaCugna, ed., *Freeing Theology: The Essentials of Theology in Feminist Perspective* (San Francisco: HarperSanFrancisco,
1993); Lois K. Daly, ed., *Feminist Theological Ethics: A Reader* (Louisville: Westminster John Knox, 1994); Charles E. Curran, Margaret A. Farley and Richard A.
McCormick, eds., *Feminist Ethics and the Catholic Moral Tradition* (New York:
Paulist, 1996); Rebecca S. Chopp and Sheila Greeve Davaney, eds., *Horizons in
Feminist Theology: Identity, Tradition, and Norms* (Minneapolis: Fortress, 1997).

6. I will discuss autobiography theory at some length in chapter 1. I should
note the turn to literary theory in religious studies has become more and more
"fashionable" as part of the postmodern movement. It offers a useful way of glean-
ing new insights about religious identity and expression. In Catholic studies, a
good example is found in many of the contributions to Thomas J. Ferraro, ed.,
Catholic Lives, Contemporary America (Durham: Duke University Press, 1997).
Also see Marian Ronan, "Tracing the Sign of the Cross" (Ph.D. diss., Temple
University, 2000).

7. Adrienne Rich, "Compulsory Heterosexuality and Lesbian Existence," in
The Lesbian and Gay Studies Reader ed. Henry Abelove, Michele Aina Barale, and
David M. Halperin (New York: Routledge, 1993), 239. The gay civil rights move-
ment still struggles to strike an appropriate balance between gender differences.
Some theorists also note masculine assumptions in the way autobiographical
selves are configured, e.g., Susan Henking, "The Personal Is the Theological: Auto-
biographical Acts in Contemporary Feminist Theology," *Journal of the American
Academy of Religion* 59, no. 3 (Fall 1991): 511–26; and Biddy Martin, "Lesbian

Identity and Autobiographical Difference[s]," in *Lesbian and Gay Studies Reader*, 274–93.

8. Michel Foucault, *The History of Sexuality, Volume 1: An Introduction*, trans. Robert Hurley (New York: Vintage, 1990; trans., 1978; Fr., 1976), 43.

9. Though the term "homosexual" was not coined until 1870, some scholars disagree with Foucault's marking of this as the birth of same-sex desire as an identity category. The histories by Boswell and Brooten, for example, which I mentioned earlier, describe a different reality. See also, Amy Richlin, "Not Before Homosexuality: The Materiality of the *Cinaedus* and the Roman Law against Love Between Men," *Journal of the History of Sexuality* 3, no. 4 (1993): 523–73.

10. Sadly, "gay" has also been reappropriated as negative slang by most kids in high school today.

11. Erving Goffman expounds on the difference between the terms in relation to the concept of deviance. See Erving Goffman, *Stigma: Notes on the Management of Spoiled Identity* (New York: Simon & Schuster, 1963), 143–44. John Cameron Mitchell's father recently declared his son is homosexual rather than gay because he "doesn't march in parades or festivals, . . . and he dresses very conservatively." This is despite the fact his son plays a flamboyant transsexual in a movie he also wrote and directed. A very revealing usage of the terms. Warren Epstein, "Parents Proud of 'Hedwig' Star . . . Sort Of," *Philadelphia Inquirer*, August 19, 2001, H6.

12. In mapping out these theoretical issues, I have drawn heavily on Annamarie Jagose, *Queer Theory: An Introduction* (New York: New York University Press, 1996). I strongly recommend this book to anyone seeking a concise articulation of the theoretical issues at stake in the study of sexual identity. As for sexual identity being essential or constructed, I think it is most useful to theorize it as both, rather than either/or.

13. Ibid., 3.

14. Ibid., 115. Civil unions and gay marriage, for example, rely on normative ideas of coupling and monogamy, rather than overturning such traditional ethical assumptions.

15. "Homosexuals engaged in religious communities are warring over a place at the table and so cannot devote much energy to anything beyond the polarizations and solidifications of identity that come in times of war." Laurel Schneider, "Homosexuality, Queer Theory, and Christian Theology," *Religious Studies Review* 26, no. 1 (January 2000): 11.

16. Interestingly, the use of "queer" predates the use of "gay" for homosexual men in this century. George Chauncey notes "queer" was a term of self-identification for homosexual men in the second and third decades of the twentieth century. George Chauncey, *Gay New York: Gender, Urban Culture, and the Making of the Gay Male World, 1890–1940* (New York: Basic Books, 1994), 101.

17. Even the editors of *The Lesbian and Gay Studies Reader*, queer theorists themselves, opted not to use the term "queer studies" in their title, as a way of acknowledging "the force of current usage" (Abelove et al., xvii). In my opinion, the institutionalization of "queer studies" as an academic discipline works against the ideals of the "queer agenda." Max Kirsch suggests queer theory paradoxically mirrors capitalist production rather than building resistance to it. See Max Kirsch, *Queer Theory and Social Change* (London: Routledge, 2000), 17–18.

18. I will explicate these categories more fully in chapter 2.

19. An important exclusion from my study I should mention is Henri Nouwen, whose spiritual journals have been so popular and influential in America. Although

his homosexuality was known by those close to him, he never publicly claimed a homosexual identity. By all accounts, he lived a celibate life; yet, he still experienced love and wrote eloquently of the devastation of a broken relationship. See Michael Ford, *Wounded Prophet: A Portrait of Henri J. M. Nouwen* (New York: Doubleday, 1999).

20. As the saying goes, "Once a Catholic, always a Catholic." Although this phrase is not literally precise, it suggests an important factor about religion. Religious identity is transmitted primarily through the context of everyday domestic life and when an adult "leaves" the religion, he/she is still likely to be influenced by that interpretive scheme. This is illustrated by the contributors to Peter Occhiogrosso, ed., *Once a Catholic: Prominent Catholics and Ex-Catholics Discuss the Influence of the Church on Their Lives and Work* (Boston: Houghton Mifflin, 1987). Peter Mullan, whose film *The Magdalene Sisters* is a scathing indictment of the now-closed Magdalene Asylums for "fallen" Catholic girls, still admires the material culture of Catholicism and says his religion is "in the bloodstream." See Steven Rea, "Mullan Proud of 'Prison Film' with Twist," *Philadelphia Inquirer,* August 17, 2003, H9.

21. By including ex-Catholics, but excluding "ex-gays" from my study, it may seem that I do not accept the former as a legitimate self-identification label. This is not my intention. In fact, I find the latter label to be much more questionable, hence my consistent usage of quotation marks to frame it. What I am doing is mapping out which identifications are pertinent for this particular study, which inevitably reflects my own biases and the way I formulate the issues involved. Because the problem I address in this book concerns religious teachings, I decided to cast a wider net in terms of religious identity, in order to account for a range of personal responses to the problem.

22. Ken Plummer, *Telling Sexual Stories: Power, Change and Social Worlds* (London: Routledge, 1995), 82.

Introduction: Whispers from the Housetop

1. For example, after coverage of a couple going to Canada to have their union blessed, the *Philadelphia Inquirer* received several letters criticizing the paper for running such a story and picture (in addition to several letters in support). One letter writer said the image of two men kissing was "the most revolting picture that I ever saw depicted in any newspaper." While this is incredible to me, it demonstrates the level of emotional response this issue engenders. *Philadelphia Inquirer,* August 21, 2003, A14.

2. In late June 1969, police raided the Stonewall Inn, a gay bar in New York's Greenwich Village. Although raids and arrests at gay establishments had been somewhat routine up to then, this time the patrons fought back and refused to back down for three days. Despite the fact that gay rights work was going on before this with groups like the Mattachine Society and the Daughters of Bilitis, especially in places like Los Angeles, New York, and Philadelphia, this event has taken on a mythic significance for the gay community — becoming a symbolic marker of a shift in gay visibility, definition, empowerment, and activism. A headline in the popular press a week after the event indicates how much things have changed: "Homo Nest Raided, Queen Bees Are Stinging Mad," story by Jerry Lisker, *New York Daily News,* July 6, 1969.

3. Hanna Rosin and Richard Morin, "As Tolerance Grows, Acceptance Remains Elusive," *Washington Post,* December 26, 1998, A1. The article suggests

gay rights would become the same kind of ideological litmus test for electoral candidates as abortion. I think this bore itself out in the 2000 presidential election when the candidates were repeatedly asked their views on gay marriage. Even more telling is the news that Randall Terry, former leader of Operation Rescue and a visible antiabortion activist, is now shifting his focus to the gay marriage issue. See Russ Bynum, "Activist Targets Gay Marriage," *Philadelphia Inquirer*, August 22, 2003, A2.

4. This is according to a Gallup Poll cited in Alfred Lubrano, "Supporting Gays, but Not Gay Marriage," *Philadelphia Inquirer*, October 12, 2003, A6. Unfortunately, the number finding it acceptable has dropped to 46 percent since the Supreme Court's overturning of state anti-sodomy laws in June 2003 — a reflection of the ever-changing context surrounding gay rights issues. These numbers should rebound and shift again with time.

5. Alan Wolfe, *One Nation, After All: What Middle-Class Americans Really Think about God, Country, Family, Racism, Welfare, Immigration, Homosexuality, Work, The Right, The Left, and Each Other* (New York: Viking, 1998), 77.

6. Ibid., 79.

7. As quoted in *Respect*, the news magazine of the Gay, Lesbian and Straight Education Network (GLSEN), Issue 12 (Summer 2003), 18.

8. Ibid., 18.

9. Quoted in Dick Polman, "Gays' Wins Met by Line in the Sand," *Philadelphia Inquirer*, August 10, 2003, A1, A14.

10. Quoted in ibid., A14.

11. Echoing Wolfe's findings, Richard Rodriguez observes that he is welcome to speak to religious groups about race and ethnicity, but he faces objections if he discusses same-sex love. These audiences have problems with his particular diversity. Richard Rodriguez, *Brown: The Last Discovery of America* (New York: Viking, 2002), 208.

12. Richard Morin and Alan Cooperman, "Poll: Many Americans Oppose Gay Unions," *Philadelphia Inquirer*, August 14, 2003, A4. Actually, the numbers immediately after the Supreme Court ruling were closer to four out of ten supporting the blessing of same-sex unions, but the numbers were almost 50–50 three months earlier before the Court's action. I suspect the numbers will shift back as people observe the world not coming to an end as a result of the removal of barriers to gay equality.

13. Quoted in ibid., A4.

14. From the *Lexicon on Ambiguous and Colloquial Terms about Family Life and Ethical Questions*, quoted in David O'Reilly, "New Church Glossary Angers Gay Community," *Philadelphia Inquirer*, April 2, 2003, C1.

15. Quoted in John L. Allen Jr., "Vatican Calls on All Catholics to Oppose Same-Sex Unions," *National Catholic Reporter*, August 15, 2003, 3. In a stunning bit of symbolism underscoring the document's defensive tone, it was signed on June 3, 2003, commemorating St. Charles Lwanga and his companions, who were martyred in Uganda in the nineteenth century for refusing a king's homosexual advances.

16. Quoted in *America* 189, no. 4 (August 18–25, 2003): 4.

17. The history of Christianity demonstrates dramatic shifts in attitudes toward marriage. Our modern glorification of marriage and family is a far cry from early Christianity and its apocalyptic call to sever all earthly ties. See Rosemary Radford Ruether, *Christianity and the Making of the Modern Family: Ruling Ideologies, Diverse Realities* (Boston: Beacon, 2000). Even in America's short history,

marriage has mirrored changes in society. See Nancy Cott, *Public Vows: A History of Marriage and the Nation* (Cambridge, Mass.: Harvard University Press, 2000).

18. Quoted in *America* 189, no. 4 (August 18–25, 2003): 4. Marianne Duddy, Executive Director of Dignity USA at the time, quickly condemned the document as "an absolute perversion of the Catholic social justice tradition." Media Release, July 29, 2003.

19. "Develop," in this case, is a euphemism for "change." Church leadership has always been reluctant to admit doctrine can change, opting instead to say doctrine develops over time as a result of historical circumstances and the concurrent maturation of human understanding. Nonetheless, church teaching has changed and will continue to change over time. See John T. Noonan Jr., "On the Development of Doctrine," *America* 180, no. 11 (April 3, 1999): 6–8; also, Maureen Fiedler and Linda Rabben, eds., *Rome Has Spoken: A Guide to Forgotten Papal Statements and How They Have Changed Through the Centuries* (New York: Crossroad, 1998).

20. For example, "Deep within his conscience, man discovers a law which he has not laid upon himself but which he must obey. . . . For man has in his heart a law inscribed by God. His dignity lies in observing this law, and by it he will be judged. His conscience is man's most secret core, and his sanctuary. There he is alone with God whose voice echoes in his depths." "Pastoral Constitution on the Church in the Modern World" (*Gaudium et Spes*), no. 16, from Austin P. Flannery, O.P., ed., *The Documents of Vatican II* (New York: Pillar Books, 1975), 916.

21. The 1960s were a time of volcanic changes for American Catholics in particular. With the election of John F. Kennedy in 1960, Catholics were symbolically seen as coming into their own as full-fledged Americans. This, combined with the Vatican II mandate to dialogue with the modern world and the new liturgy in the vernacular, caused a significant shift in consciousness and self-understanding among American Catholics. See Jay P. Dolan, *The American Catholic Experience: A History from Colonial Times to the Present* (Notre Dame, Ind.: University of Notre Dame Press, 1992), 421–54; and Robert S. Ellwood, *The Sixties Spiritual Awakening* (New Brunswick, N.J.: Rutgers University Press, 1994), 61–69, 210–19, 296–303.

22. This has been the primary teaching underlying the legacy of Christian sexual ethics. Our struggle today is to appropriately integrate contemporary understandings of sexuality into the tradition, so that we do not perpetuate faulty assumptions.

23. While some contemporary Catholic theologians have suggested alternative interpretations of the term "procreative," Pope Paul VI's encyclical *Humanae Vitae* (1968) was notoriously firm about all sexual acts being open to the possibility of pregnancy. It prohibited all so-called artificial means of birth control. Poll after poll reveals a solid majority of Catholics do not agree with or follow this particular teaching.

24. Andrew Sullivan, "Virtually Normal," in *Catholic Lives, Contemporary America*, ed. Thomas J. Ferraro (Durham: Duke University Press, 1997), 180.

25. CDF, "Letter to the Bishops of the Catholic Church on the Pastoral Care of Homosexual Persons," October 31, 1986: no. 3, in Jeannine Gramick and Pat Furey, eds., *The Vatican and Homosexuality* (New York: Crossroad, 1988), 2. The 1986 "Halloween" Letter was issued in response to what the CDF perceived was an "overly benign interpretation" being given to the homosexual condition itself since the 1975 document.

26. *Catechism of the Catholic Church*, nos. 2357, 2358 (Ligouri, Mo.: Ligouri Publications, 1994), 566. This phrase was echoed verbatim in the recent document against the recognition of gay unions, discussed above.

27. Robert Westerfelhaus, "A Significant Shift: A Pentadic Analysis of the Two Rhetorics of the Post–Vatican II Roman Catholic Church Regarding Homosexuality," *Journal of Gay, Lesbian, and Bisexual Identity* 3, no. 4 (October 1998): 269–94.

28. Ibid., 287.

29. Quoted in Michael Maher, *Being Gay and Lesbian in a Catholic High School: Beyond the Uniform* (New York: Harrington Park Press, 2001), 53.

30. From the 1991 USCC statement, "Human Sexuality: A Catholic Perspective for Education and Lifelong Learning," quoted in ibid., 119.

31. *Catechism*, no. 2358, p. 566.

32. CDF, "Some Considerations Concerning the Response to Legislative Proposals on the Non-Discrimination of Homosexual Persons," July 23, 1992 (personal copy).

33. From "Considerations Regarding Proposals to Give Legal Recognition to Unions Between Homosexual Persons," quoted in *America* 189, no. 4 (August 18–25, 2003): 4–5.

34. There are no exact numbers, but a report by the Urban Institute, based on the 2000 census, found more than 67,000 male couples and 167,000 female couples with children. This makes up about 32 percent of same-sex couples as reported in the census, so it does not even count gay single parents or those who did not report the relevant data. See Eils Lotozo, "Gay and Lesbian Parents Fueling a 'Gayby Boom'," *Philadelphia Inquirer*, June 29, 2003, A22; also, Lisa Leff, "Parents Change Face of Gay Pride," *Denver Post*, June 29, 2003, 11A.

35. This, of course, collides with the church's ban on artificial birth control in addition to the ban on homosexual acts. See Richard L. Smith, *AIDS, Gays, and the American Catholic Church* (Cleveland: Pilgrim, 1994). A growing number of moral theologians and bishops are calling for change in the doctrinal prohibition of condom usage in light of the global increase in HIV-infection. Bishop Kevin Dowling of South Africa notes that in sub-Saharan Africa, the infection rate in some countries is as high as 40 percent. One might justify condom usage as the lesser of two evils (protected sex or spreading a deadly virtus), but Bishop Dowling argues that condom usage need not be defined as an evil at all. Promoting good health and preventing death is a moral imperative. See Kevin Dowling, "Let's Not Condemn Condoms in the Fight against AIDS," *US Catholic* 68, no. 11 (November 2003): 20–22. Also see Catholics for a Free Choice, *Sex in the HIV/AIDS Era: A Guide for Catholics* (Washington, D.C.: Catholics for a Free Choice, 2003). Finally, for the most comprehensive treatment of numerous ethical issues related to AIDS, see *Catholic Ethicists on HIV/AIDS Prevention*, ed. James F. Keenan, with Jon D. Fuller, Lisa Sowle Cahill, and Kevin Kelly (New York: Continuum, 2000). This "landmark contribution to worldwide efforts to respond to HIV/AIDS," in Margaret Farley's words, includes presentations by thirty-six Roman Catholic moral theologians and AIDS workers from all over the world.

36. National Conference of Catholic Bishops, October 1, 1997.

37. In other words, people with same-sex desires do not simply "decide" to have such feelings, even when this orientation seemingly shifts over time. What one does with these desires and how one defines them is another matter.

38. This statement borrows directly from the *Catechism*. Teresa Malcolm, "Vatican Approves Changes to Message for Parents of Gays," *National Catholic Reporter*, July 17, 1998, 12.

39. Released on the Dignity listserv, July 1998.

40. Bishop William Newman, "Baltimore Bishop Asks Forgiveness of Gays/ Lesbians," *Bondings: A Publication of New Ways Ministry* (Spring 2001), 1.

41. Raymond P. Kempisty, "Reaffirming Teaching," *National Catholic Reporter*, May 4, 2001, 20.

42. Courage was founded in 1980 by Father John Harvey, and is based on the twelve-step model to encourage homosexuals to live chaste lives and ultimately reverse their orientation if possible.

43. Various bishops have attempted to "rein in" Dignity over the years by banning its members from meeting on church property or by forbidding priests to preside at Dignity liturgies. While such actions have been disheartening, they have also inspired Dignity to refine its mission and reassert its recognition of same-sex relationships.

44. Released by the National Conference of Catholic Bishops, November 11, 1976, "To Live in Christ Jesus" notes that homosexuals "have a right to respect, friendship and justice. They should have an active role in the Christian community." This "pastoral letter on moral values" reconfirms the separation between homosexual acts and persons. Jeannine Gramick and Robert Nugent, eds., *Voices of Hope: A Collection of Positive Writings on Gay and Lesbian Issues* (New York: Center for Homophobia Education, 1995), 10.

45. In 1971, Gramick met a young gay Catholic man who issued the challenge that the church was not doing enough for gay people. She began meeting with lesbian and gay Catholics and was soon joined by Nugent. Thus began their informal ministry.

46. This statement from the original order was quoted in a later letter (May 9, 1988) from Pio Laghi, the Apostolic Pro-Nuncio, to then-bishop of Green Bay, Wisconsin, Adam J. Maida, requesting that he chair the commission to investigate the orthodoxy of Gramick and Nugent's ministry. All documents related to the investigation and cited in this study, unless otherwise noted, were made publicly available in a nonpaginated format by Gramick and Nugent through the website of the *National Catholic Reporter*, www.natcath.com/NCR_Online/documents; accessed October 6, 1999.

47. Deeply related to this underlying issue is the matter of power and the fear that heterodoxy will undermine that power. I do not want to minimize this. In these kinds of controversies, church officials are often most concerned with maintaining the status quo and are reluctant to change moral teachings because it might upset the power structure which grants them their privileged position. For an excellent treatment of the way church proscriptions against homosexual acts reinforce the gendered hierarchy of power, see Kathy Rudy, *Sex and the Church: Gender, Homosexuality, and the Transformation of Christian Ethics* (Boston: Beacon, 1997). My concern in this book, however, is to focus specifically on the inadequacy of current moral doctrine and subsequent pastoral practice.

48. Dignity/USA, "Gay Catholics Dismayed and Angry at Vatican Authorities," July 13, 1999 (personal copy).

49. It would seem Gramick, after defying the order of complete silence, had one of her busiest years of speaking engagements ever. Her talks in the year following the last notification were about conscience and the use of silencing as a discipline

in the church. Nugent has addressed some groups on the topic of obedience in church history.

50. In fact, a year 2000 poll conducted by Belden, Russonello and Stewart, for Catholics for a Free Choice, revealed only 44 percent of "highly committed" Catholics look to church leaders for authoritative guidance on the issue of homosexuality. Patricia Miller, "Chasing Conservative Catholics," *Conscience* 22, no. 2 (Summer 2001): 14.

51. From an April 14, 2000, editorial in the *Southern Nebraska Register,* quoted in Tom Roberts, "Gramick on Conscience in Lincoln," *National Catholic Reporter,* May 5, 2000, 6. Bruskewitz is also the only American bishop to make the unprecedented move of excommunicating all Call to Action members in his diocese.

52. Thomas J. Billitteri, "Gay and Lesbian Catholics Beg to Differ," *U.S. Catholic* 62, no. 11 (November 1997), 11–12. Gumbleton has acknowledged his views have been shaped by the fact that he has a gay brother. He is the only bishop thus far to have spoken at a national Dignity convention (Denver, 1999).

53. Dignity was not permitted to be an official exhibitor and the president was disinvited from participating in a workshop because of Dignity's opposition to the moral rhetoric condemning homosexual expression.

54. Chuck Colbert, "Rifts, Questions Emerge at Meeting on Gays," *National Catholic Reporter,* October 2, 1998, 9.

55. The removal was in response to a letter from Cardinal Ratzinger of the CDF. It is widely believed the letter was instigated by Michael Macaluso, a member of the Rochester diocese who had complained for years about Bishop Clark's pastoral approach to gays and lesbians. See the A.P. news story of August 20, 1998. Also, Chris Schenk, "We Are the Body of Christ," *Focus on FutureChurch* 6 (Fall 1998), 1–2.

56. News brief in *National Catholic Reporter,* December 25, 1998, 7.

57. News brief in *National Catholic Reporter,* December 18, 1998, 8.

58. Ed Griffin-Nolan, "The Body of Christ Torn Asunder on 'Gray Day" in Rochester," *National Catholic Reporter,* March 12, 1999, 5.

59. Both ordinations were presided over by a bishop of the Old Catholic Church. The Old Catholic Churches are a group of national churches that broke away from Rome for reasons unrelated to the sixteenth-century Protestant reformation. Most were formed to protest the decree of papal infallibility during the First Vatican Council in 1870.

60. Quoted in Teresa Malcolm, "Letter Ends Parishioners' Two Decades of Service," *National Catholic Reporter,* November 5, 1999, 3.

61. Quoted in ibid.

62. Quoted in ibid.

63. See Gill Donovan, "Santorum's Remarks Draw Both Affirmation, Criticism from Catholics," *National Catholic Reporter,* May 9, 2003, 12.

64. Ibid., 12. Also see Lara Jakes Jordan, "Santorum Says Gays OK but Acts Aren't," *Philadelphia Inquirer,* April 23, 2003, A2.

65. "Response to the Report of the Findings of the Commission Studying the Writings and Ministry of Sister Jeannine Gramick, SSND, and Father Robert Nugent, SDS," January 12, 1995.

66. There are, of course, homosexual Catholics who experience their sexuality as a pathological condition, who would seek out ministries such as Courage to help them with their illness. They would eschew gayness as an identity category. My concern in this book is with those Catholics who self-identify as gay.

67. Another, more technical but helpful definition: "Subjectivity is the product of learning to think and handle the self in terms of the social practices and conceptualities of the culture in which a person lives." Ronald E. Long, "The Sacrality of Male Beauty and Homosex: A Neglected Factor in the Understanding of Contemporary Gay Reality," in *Que(e)rying Religion: A Critical Anthology*, ed. Gary David Comstock and Susan E. Henking (New York: Continuum, 1997), 268. When I speak of subjectivity, I am not here speaking of the concept of "agency," as in being the author of one's destiny. Postmodern theory has called the notion of an autonomous "subject" into question. I will take up the question of gay subjective moral agency in chapter 4.

68. James Nelson discusses a widely accepted quadrilateral combination of sources for moral reflection which includes scripture, tradition, reason, and experience. Most Catholic moral theologians since Vatican II have embraced this formula, though magisterial leaders are consistently leery of including experience, especially with regard to sexual ethics. James B. Nelson, "Sources for Body Theology," in *Sexuality and the Sacred: Sources for Theological Reflection*, ed. James B. Nelson and Sandra P. Longfellow (Louisville: Westminster John Knox: 1994), 374–86.

69. In a study of gay, lesbian, and bisexual Catholics in England, the vast majority of respondents ranked "personal experience" as the most important reference for their faith and sexual ethics. They then looked to "the Bible" and "human reason" as sources for theological inquiry. "Church authority" was consistently ranked the least important, which demonstrates the decreasing relevance church teaching holds for gay and lesbian Christians. See Andrew Yip, "The Persistence of Faith Among Nonheterosexual Christians: Evidence for the Neosecularization Thesis of Religious Transformation," *Journal for the Scientific Study of Religion* 41, no. 2 (2002), 199–212.

70. Robert Nugent and Jeannine Gramick, *Building Bridges: Gay and Lesbian Reality and the Catholic Church* (Mystic, Conn.: Twenty-Third Publications, 1992), 189.

71. At present, the magisterium is composed entirely of men due to the church's ban on women's ordination, so all church teaching is always already gendered.

72. Mark D. Jordan, *The Silence of Sodom: Homosexuality in Modern Catholicism* (Chicago: University of Chicago Press, 2000).

73. "Nugent Urges Homosexuals to Speak for Themselves," *National Catholic Reporter*, February 11, 2000, 9.

74. Pamela Schaeffer, "Seeking a 'Quantum Leap' on Homosexuality," *National Catholic Reporter*, June 30, 2000, 4.

75. It is not my goal to reify any one picture of gay Catholic identity or reality. The diversity of lives in these texts will speak for itself.

76. "Preliminary Draft of Responses to Questions Posed by the Commission," Submitted to Maida Commission, July 26, 1994.

77. From the Jerusalem Bible. My interpretation is part of a strategy in lesbian and gay studies to "queer" the reading of traditional texts. In this case, I am "queering" scripture.

78. James Olney, *Metaphors of Self: The Meaning of Autobiography* (Princeton: Princeton University Press, 1972), 49.

1. Surveying Autobiographical Acts

1. For an analysis of these kinds of stories, see Lucy Bregman and Sara Thiermann, *First Person Mortal: Personal Narratives of Illness, Dying and Grief* (New York: Paragon, 1995).

2. *Religion* usually relates to an organized belief system with formal rituals, moral codes and a community structure. *Spirituality* is more focused on the individual and his/her personal way of making meaning in life, which may or may not be associated with organized religion.

3. Raymond C. Holtz, *Listen to the Stories: Gay and Lesbian Catholics Talk about Their Lives and the Church* (New York: Garland Publishing, 1991): William G. Storey, James Abdo, Toby Johnson, Joe Izzo, Tom Cunningham, Malcolm MacDonald, Jim Bussen, Larry Sullivan, Paul Albergo, Tom McLaughlin, Lou Tesconi, John O'Leary, Jimmy Kennedy and Derrick A. Tynan-Connolly, Bill Knox and John Brady, Tom Kaun and Kevin Calegari, Jim Revak and Michael Conley, Gerald Allen, and Joe McGuire. (Gerald Allen represents the one African American autobiographer in my study.)

4. Brian Bouldrey, ed., *Wrestling with the Angel: Faith and Religion in the Lives of Gay Men* (New York: Riverhead, 1995).

5. Catherine Lake, ed., *ReCreations: Religion and Spirituality in the Lives of Queer People* (Toronto: Queer Press, 1999).

6. Andrew Sullivan, "Alone Again, Naturally," *The New Republic* 211, no. 22 (November 28, 1994): 47, 50, 52, 54–55.

7. Jeannine Gramick, ed., *Homosexuality in the Priesthood and the Religious Life* (New York: Crossroad, 1989): William Hart McNichols, S.J.; Brother Amos; Father Paul; Matthew Kelty, OCSO; Richard John Cardarelli, OFM Cap.; Brother Jonathan; and Father Aelred.

8. James Wolf, ed., *Gay Priests* (San Francisco: Harper & Row, 1989): Rev. T. Thompson; Rev. R. Roberts.

9. See my discussion of Mark Jordan's work above and in chapter 3.

10. I will give the full citation for each of these when they are specifically addressed in subsequent chapters.

11. Again, these will be fully acknowledged when they are cited in later chapters.

12. John J. McNeill, *Both Feet Firmly Planted in Midair: My Spiritual Journey* (Louisville: Westminster John Knox, 1998).

13. Fenton Johnson, *Keeping Faith: A Skeptic's Journey* (Boston: Houghton Mifflin, 2003).

14. Brian McNaught, *A Disturbed Peace: Selected Writings of an Irish Catholic Homosexual* (Washington, D.C.: Dignity, 1981); and *On Being Gay: Thoughts on Family, Faith, and Love* (New York: St. Martin's, 1988).

15. Andrew Sullivan, *Love Undetectable: Notes on Friendship, Sex, and Survival* (New York: Alfred A. Knopf, 1998).

16. James Morrison, *Broken Fever: Reflections of Gay Boyhood* (New York: St. Martin's, 2001).

17. Patrick E. Horrigan, *Widescreen Dreams: Growing Up Gay at the Movies* (Madison: University of Wisconsin Press, 1999).

18. Frank DeCaro, *A Boy Named Phyllis: A Suburban Memoir* (New York: Viking, 1996).

19. Will Fellows, *Farm Boys: Lives of Gay Men from the Rural Midwest* (Madison: University of Wisconsin Press, 1996, 1998): James Heckman, Larry Ebmeier, Rick Noss, Lon Mickelsen.

20. Richard Rodriguez, *Hunger of Memory: The Education of Richard Rodriguez* (New York: Bantam, 1982); and *Days of Obligation: An Argument with My Mexican Father* (New York: Penguin, 1992).

21. Richard Rodriguez, "Irish Catholic," in *Political Passages: Journeys of Change through Two Decades 1968–1988,* ed. John H. Bunzel (New York: Free Press, 1988).

22. Richard Rodriguez, *Brown: The Last Discovery of America* (New York: Viking, 2002). Rodriguez says *Brown* is "the most dynamically gay book that I've written." Quoted in Michael Depp, "An Angry Young Man Grows Older," *Chronicle of Higher Education* (August 2, 2002), accessed September 10, 2002, at www.chronicle.com.

23. Tommi Avicolli Mecca, Giovanna (Janet) Capone, and Denise Nico Leto, eds., *Hey Paesan! Writings by Lesbians and Gay Men of Italian Descent* (Oakland, Calif.: Three Guineas Press, 1999); Anthony Julian Tamburri, ed., *Fuori: Essays by Italian/American Lesbians and Gays* (West Lafayette, Ind.: Bordighera, 1996).

24. Rafael Campo, *The Desire to Heal: A Doctor's Education in Empathy, Identity, and Poetry* (New York: W. W. Norton, 1997); *The Other Man Was Me: A Voyage to the New World* (Houston: Arte Publico Press, 1994); *What the Body Told* (Durham, N.C.: Duke University Press, 1996); and *Diva* (Durham, N.C.: Duke University Press, 1999).

25. José Zuniga, *Soldier of the Year: The Story of a Gay American Patriot* (New York: Pocket Books, 1994).

26. David Kopay and Perry Dean Young, *The David Kopay Story: An Extraordinary Self-revelation* (New York: Donald I. Fine, 1988).

27. Dave Pallone with Alan Steinberg, *Behind the Mask: My Double Life in Baseball* (New York: Viking, 1990).

28. Fr. Robert L. Arpin, *Wonderfully, Fearfully Made: Letters on Living with Hope, Teaching Understanding, and Ministering with Love, from a Gay Catholic Priest with AIDS* (San Francisco: HarperSanFrancisco, 1993).

29. Fenton Johnson, *Geography of the Heart: A Memoir* (New York: Scribner, 1996).

30. Patrick Merla, ed., *Boys Like Us: Gay Writers Tell Their Coming Out Stories* (New York: Avon Books, 1996).

31. Andrew Holleran, *Nights in Aruba* (New York: William Morrow, 1983); and *The Beauty of Men* (New York: Plume, 1997); David Plante, *The Catholic* (New York: Atheneum, 1986); Daniel Curzon, *The World Can Break Your Heart* (Stamford, Conn.: Knight's Press, 1984).

32. Bregman and Thiermann suggest four different voices within the text separate from the human being who writes the text and stands outside of it: the author, the narrator, the protagonist, and the intended reader (18–19).

33. Olney, *Metaphors of Self,* 34.

34. James Olney, "Autobiography and the Cultural Moment," in *Autobiography: Essays Theoretical and Critical,* ed. James Olney (Princeton: Princeton University Press, 1980), 21.

35. Ibid., 22.

36. Some theorists contend the self in autobiography is never "discovered," but entirely created. Autobiographical discourse encourages an illusion of self-discovery that puts the self before language, even as it suggests the power of

language to reveal and sustain the self. Autobiographical acts would be disabled without this illusion. See Paul John Eakin, *Fictions in Autobiography: Studies in the Art of Self-Invention* (Princeton: Princeton University Press, 1985), 190–91.

37. "Indeed autobiography is fiction and fiction is autobiography: both are narrative arrangements of reality." Robert Elbaz, *The Changing Nature of the Self: A Critical Study of the Autobiographic discourse* (London: Croom Helm, 1988), 1. Paul de Man and Michael Sprinker also advocate this position.

38. Sidonie Smith, for example, borrows from Judith Butler's theory of gender performativity to insist that the unified self of an autobiography is strictly a performance, a repetition of convention. Sidonie Smith, "Performativity, Autobiographical Practice, Resistance," *a/b: Auto/Biography Studies* 10 (Spring 1995): 17–33.

39. Louis A Renza, "The Veto of the Imagination: A Theory of Autobiography," in Olney, ed., (1980), 268–95. For a similar position and an excellent overview of the range of theories and concerns, see Barry N. Olshen, "Subject, Persona, and Self in the Theory of Autobiography," *a/b: Auto/Biography Studies* 10 (Spring 1995): 5–16.

40. Plummer, 168. In Olney's most recent work, he borrows the term "peri-autography," from Vico, to express a similar idea: "writing about or around the self." James Olney, *Memory and Narrative: The Weave of Life-Writing* (Chicago: University of Chicago Press, 1998), xv.

41. Georges Gusdorf, "Conditions and Limits of Autobiography," trans. James Olney, in Olney, ed. (1980), 45.

42. Philip Lejeune calls this the autobiographical pact. See Philip E. Baruth, "Consensual Autobiography: Narrating 'Personal Sexual History' from Boswell's *London Journal* to AIDS Pamphlet Literature," in *Getting a Life: Everyday Uses of Autobiography,* ed. Sidonie Smith and Julia Watson (Minneapolis: University of Minnesota Press), 181–82.

43. More sophisticated contemporary authors may disrupt this understanding through rhetorical manipulations. See Albert Stone, "Modern American Autobiography: Texts and Transactions," in *American Autobiography: Retrospect and Prospect,* ed. Paul John Eakin (Madison: University of Wisconsin Press, 1991), 100.

44. Olney, *Memory and Narrative,* 343.

45. Ibid., 371. Diaries or journal entries may come closer to first perceptions of experience, but even these memories undergo a certain amount of editing and rethinking in the process of narrating them.

46. Gusdorf, 38.

47. Bregman and Thiermann, 53.

48. Plummer, 172.

49. See Goffman, 105.

50. Paul Ricoeur, "Narrative Identity," trans. Mark S. Muldoon, *Philosophy Today* 35 (Spring 1991): 73, 79.

51. Mark I. Wallace, ed., "Introduction" in Paul Ricoeur, *Figuring the Sacred: Religion, Narrative, and Imagination,* trans. David Pellauer (Minneapolis: Fortress, 1995), 13.

52. "The nature of the identity conflict often depends on the latent panic or, indeed, the intrinsic promise pervading a historical period." Erik Erikson, *Life History and the Historical Moment* (New York: W. W. Norton, 1966), 21.

53. Goffman, 100. Goffman describes this as moving from the position of being "discreditable," which requires vigilant secrecy to avoid stigma, to that of "discredited," which is managed without the ever-present fear of disclosure.

54. I have extended this argument in an unpublished paper, "The Coming Out Narrative in Gay and Lesbian Autobiographies," May 1996.

55. Goffman, 102.

56. Robert McRuer, "Boys' Own Stories and New Spellings of My Name: Coming Out and Other Myths of Queer Positionality," in *Genders 20: Eroticism and Containment*, ed. Carol Siegel and Ann Kibbey (New York: New York University Press, 1994), 263.

57. Karl J. Weintraub, "Autobiography and Historical Consciousness," *Critical Inquiry* (June 1975): 837.

58. Paul Robinson, *Gay Lives: Homosexual Autobiography from John Addington Symonds to Paul Monette* (Chicago: University of Chicago Press, 1999), xxii. The three contemporary autobiographers he profiles are Andrew Tobias, Martin Duberman, and Paul Monette, in a chapter entitled, "The Closet and Its Discontents."

59. Morrison, *Broken Fever*, 101 (emphasis mine).

60. See Goffman, 37.

61. Plummer, 87.

62. Olney, "Autobiography and the Cultural Moment," 13.

63. Ibid., 41.

64. This is Mark Wallace describing Ricoeur's theology of the narrative self. Wallace, in Ricoeur, *Figuring the Sacred*, 14.

65. Bregman and Thiermann, 56.

66. Wallace, in Ricoeur, 13.

2. Narrating Gay Identification

1. Holleran, *Beauty*, 69.

2. Ritch C. Savin-Williams, "*. . . And Then I Became Gay": Young Men's Stories* (New York: Routledge, 1998), 3. One could, of course, act sexually against one's sexual orientation, but this usually is distressing for the individual. This is the reason conversion therapists attempt to change not only the behavior but also the orientation of gay people. Some Catholic theologians like McNeill and Curran even suggest that acting against one's orientation is unnatural and thus morally problematic.

3. Ibid., 3.

4. C. Warren, *Identity and Community in the Gay World* (New York: Wiley, 1974), quoted in Barry D. Adam, "Love and Sex in Constructing Identity Among Men Who Have Sex with Men," *International Journal of Sexuality and Gender Studies* 5 (October 2000): 337.

5. Some studies of sexual orientation begin with an exploration of the "causes" of homosexuality, both psychological and physiological, and whether or not people are born this way. While the autobiographers I study may have their own ideas about such causes, it is not the focus of my project. My concern with self-identification and discourse renders debates about the biological origins of homosexuality irrelevant. For an interesting look at biology-based projects, see Simon LeVay and Dean H. Hamer, "Evidence for a Biological Influence in Male Homosexuality," and William Byne, "The Biological Evidence Challenged," in *Scientific American* 270 (May 1994), 44–55. Also, Bruce Bagemihl, *Biological Exuberance: Animal Homosexuality and Natural Diversity* (New York: St. Martin's Press, 1999).

6. Adam, 337.

7. See Foucault, *History of Sexuality*. The usefulness of identity as a tool for personal and political liberation is hotly debated among some gay/queer academics and activists. I have already highlighted some of these concerns in my prior discussion of gay communal identity and metanarratives. Bearing these in mind, I still find the concept useful in terms of self-definition and to overcome reductive notions of sexuality as desire and behavior completely isolated from personhood.

8. Michel Foucault, *Ethics: Subjectivity and Truth*, ed. P. Rabinow (New York: New Press, 1997), quoted in Jonathan Alexander, "Beyond Identity: Queer Values and Community," *Journal of Gay. Lesbian, and Bisexual Identity* 4 (October 1999): 306.

9. Schneider, 8.

10. From Tess Tessier, *Dancing after the Whirlwind: Feminist Reflections on Sex, Denial, and Spiritual Transformation* (Boston: Beacon, 1997), 10.

11. Alexander, 295.

12. Brian Utter, "Bisexuality and the Spiritual Continuum," in Lake, ed., 146.

13. A useful essay drawing on social scientific findings in order to critique the simplistic way sexuality is currently understood by both church and society is David T. Ozar, "Harming by Exclusion: On the Standard Concepts of Sexual Orientation, Sex, and Gender," in *Sexual Diversity and Catholicism: Toward the Development of Moral Theology*, ed. Patricia Beattie Jung, with Joseph Andrew Coray (Collegeville, Minn.: Liturgical Press, 2001), 252–66.

14. Brother Dave Berceli, M.M., quoted in Dan Grippo, "Why Lesbian and Gay Catholics Stay Catholic," *U.S. Catholic* 55 (September 1990), 23. It seems even the American bishops recognize a certain depth to the concept of sexuality: "Sexuality refers to a fundamental component of personality in and through which we, as male or female, experience our relatedness to self, others, the world, and even God." Quoted in Maher, 92.

15. See Patricia Beattie Jung and Ralph F. Smith, *Heterosexism: An Ethical Challenge* (Albany: SUNY, 1993). Jung and Smith offer an excellent analysis of the pervasiveness of heterosexism and shift the "problem" of homosexuality to straight people, whom they call to overcome bias and ignorance.

16. Rob Nixon, "Avondale: A Memoir of Identity," in Mecca et al., eds., 42.

17. As Lucy Bregman points out, this feeling of difference in childhood is common in autobiographies and may be the "spur toward cultivating the kind of interiority which makes autobiography possible." Part of the autobiographical project is fitting this sense of difference into a discernable category or pattern (private communication, January 31, 2002).

18. Philip Gambone, "Learning and Unlearning and Learning Again the Language of *Signori*," in Tamburri, ed., 63.

19. Tommi Avicolli Mecca, "Memoirs of a South Philly Sissy," in Tamburri, ed., 18.

20. Toby Johnson, in Holtz, ed., 38.

21. DeCaro, 15.

22. Horrigan, 60.

23. "Mark: A Spiritual Ancestry," interview in David Shallenberger, *Reclaiming the Spirit: Gay Men and Lesbians Come to Terms with Religion* (New Brunswick, N.J.: Rutgers University Press, 1998), 158.

24. I will discuss this more in the following chapter.

25. Johnson, *Keeping Faith*, 22.

26. Morrison, *Broken Fever*, 7.

27. DeCaro, 4.

28. Ibid., 109.

29. Campo, *Desire to Heal*, 109.

30. McNeill, *Both Feet*, 19.

31. Pallone, 12.

32. William Hart McNichols, "A Priest Forever," in Gramick, ed. (1989), 118.

33. Brother Jonathan, "You Are My People," in Gramick, ed. (1989), 160.

34. Rodriguez, *Brown*, 203.

35. Ibid., 206.

36. Ibid., 202, 205.

37. Ibid., 209–10.

38. Johnson, *Geography*, 55. This statement, with its blatant Catholic imagery, is an example of how intertwined sexual and religious identity can be. A nonreligious gay child would not have shared this feeling of being tested by God.

39. Ibid., 55–56.

40. Ibid., 56.

41. Fenton Johnson, "God, Gays, and the Geography of Desire," in Bouldrey, ed., 244.

42. Lon Mickelsen, in Fellows, 257.

43. Andrew Sullivan, "Virtually Normal," 172.

44. Allen Barnett, in Philip Gambone, ed., *Something Inside: Conversations with Gay Fiction Writers* (Madison: University of Wisconsin Press, 1999), 79.

45. In urban areas, there were gay bookstores for those gay boys with the self-confidence to enter them, and there was probably a richer collection of texts available in some public libraries by the late 1980s, though access could still be an issue. In any case, none of the autobiographers in my study are young enough to have come of age solidly in the "information age." For better or worse, the Internet has now become one of the primary sources for children and teens to learn about sex.

46. DeCaro, 100.

47. Ibid., 101–2.

48. Morrison, *Broken Fever*, 209.

49. Philip Gambone, "Searching for Real Words," in Bouldrey, ed., 229.

50. Campo, *Desire to Heal*, 86.

51. Ibid., 87.

52. Pallone, 17.

53. Matthew Bartosik, "A Winter Break," in *Equal Times* 7, no. 1 (Spring 2000), 7.

54. Morrison, *Broken Fever*, 213.

55. Kopay, 121.

56. Ibid., 129.

57. Campo, *Desire*, 68–69.

58. Sullivan, *Love Undetectable*, 141.

59. Zuniga, 48, 51.

60. Ibid., 108.

61. Ibid., 135.

62. Mickelsen, in Fellows, 254.

63. DeCaro, 136.

64. Johnson, *Geography*, 73.

65. Ibid., 79.

66. Johnson, *Keeping Faith*, 197.

67. Andrew Holleran, "Memories of Heidelberg," in Merla, ed., 93.

68. Ibid., 97.

69. Holleran, *Beauty*, 73.

70. Or something else. Some people are born with what doctors call "ambiguous genitalia," something other than the set of organs, chromosomes, and/or hormones considered to be standard for either male or female. The numbers are not insignificant, with over 2,000 such children born in the United States each year. It has become standard practice for doctors to assign a sex to these children and alter them accordingly. Over 90 percent are transformed into girls because it's "easier." This practice is being challenged by the visibility of intersexed people who are speaking out against such methods. Their existence and recognition should serve to further shake up the rigid binary economy of normative sex and gender expectations. We are obviously more than just male and female. See Cheryl Chase (Executive Director Intersex Society of North America), "What is Intersexuality?" in *PFLAGpole* (Fall 2001), 8–9; Also, Emily Nussbaum, "A Question of Gender," *Discover* 21, no. 1 (January 2000), 92–99. For thorough academic study and analysis, see Anne Fausto-Sterling, "The Five Sexes," *The Sciences* (March–April 1993): 20–25; "The Five Sexes, Revisited," *The Sciences* (July–August 2000): 18–23; and *Sexing the Body: Gender Politics and the Construction of Sexuality* (New York: Basic Books, 2000); Alice Dreger, *Hermaphrodites and the Medical Intervention of Sex* (Cambridge, Mass.: Harvard University Press, 1998); Bernice Hausman, *Changing Sex: Transexualism, Technology, and the Idea of Gender* (Durham: Duke University Press, 1998); and Suzanne Kessler, *Lessons from the Intersexed* (New Brunswick, N.J.: Rutgers University Press, 1998). For an excellent discussion of the religious ramifications of this knowledge, see Christine E. Gudorf, "The Erosion of Sexual Dimorphism: Challenges to Religion and Religious Ethics," in *Journal of the American Academy of Religion* 69, no. 4 (December 2001), 874–80.

71. In saying this, I want to emphasize the social relativity of gender roles and expectations over and against gender as something natural and inborn. This is not to dismiss the fact that many people experience gender factors as integral to their identity and selfhood, as transgendered people assert. I would liken this to my theoretical understanding of sexual identity, which I have already discussed. Here again, postmodern theorists following Foucault resist using identity language with gender because they want to destabilize subject categories like *man* and *woman*. Judith Butler sees these categories as "repetitions" rather than ontological truths, and uses the idea of gender "performance" as a way of subverting oppressive compulsory gender categories. See Judith Butler, *Gender Trouble: Feminism and the Subversion of Identity* (New York: Routledge, 1991). For a very insightful and articulate theological application of Butler's theory, see Mary McClintock Fulkerson, "Gender — Being It or Doing It? The Church, Homosexuality, and the Politics of Identity," in *Que(e)rying Religion: A Critical Anthology*, ed. Gary David Comstock and Susan E. Henking (New York: Continuum, 1997), 188–201.

72. Obviously, masculinity is more complicated than this explanation implies. It is not necessary for all men to fully live up to the ideal of hegemonic masculinity for it to be enforced, nor is it true that the bearers of the hegemonic ideal are the most powerful. Some correlation between the actual and the ideal is necessary, however, even if the imagery has to be forced by those in power. Most men do not in fact display all the qualities of hegemonic masculinity, but they may still benefit from its production and are thus complicit in sustaining it. See R. W. Connell, *Masculinities* (Berkeley: University of California Press, 1995); Stephen B. Boyd, W. Merle Longwood, and Mark W. Muesse, *Redeeming Men: Religion and Masculinities* (Louisville: Westminster John Knox, 1996); Krondorfer, Bjorn, ed.,

Men's Bodies, Men's Gods: Male Identities in a (Post-) Christian Culture (New York: New York University Press, 1996); Harry Brod and Michael Kaufman, eds., *Theorizing Masculinities* (Thousand Oaks, Calif.: SAGE, 1994); Michael Kimmel, *Manhood in America: A Cultural History* (New York: Free Press, 1996). For an interesting look at masculinities and the bible, see Howard Eilberg-Schwartz, *God's Phallus and Other Problems for Men and Monotheism* (Boston: Beacon, 1994). For a feminist analysis of the constrictions of current constructions of masculinity, see Susan Faludi, *Stiffed: The Betrayal of the American Man* (New York: William Morrow, 1999).

73. This too is not uncomplicated. Many gay men enjoy performing masculine gender identities, and attraction to masculinity is usually a primary component of gay sexual identity; so although gay men are victimized by hegemonic masculinity, they too can be complicit in its production. At the same time, the fact that these men engage in same-sex erotic behavior makes gay male gender identity a site where the scripts of normative masculinity are not exactly reproduced but rather interrogated and potentially rewritten. I like R. W. Connell's analysis of this, "A Very Straight Gay," in his book *Masculinities*, 143–63.

74. Horrigan, 80.

75. Ibid., 109–10.

76. In adulthood, these categories become somewhat less simplistic as masculinity becomes more associated with things like power and control (being figuratively on top). Still, the memory of these childhood and teenage categories remains as a point of reference in adult masculinity. The impressions are lasting, as the memories of these autobiographers attest.

77. Horrigan, 32.

78. Morrison, *Broken Fever*, 41.

79. Ibid., 164.

80. DeCaro, 97, also 106.

81. Arpin, 6.

82. McNaught, *On Being Gay*, 45.

83. Zuniga, 19–20, 35.

84. Rick Noss, in Fellows, 235–36.

85. Kopay, 50–51.

86. Ibid., 53–54.

87. Rodriguez, *Hunger*, 126.

88. McNeill, *Both Feet*, 14.

89. DeCaro, 158–65.

90. Ibid., 124.

91. Horrigan, 83.

92. Morrison, *Broken Fever*, 99–100.

93. Rodriguez, *Days*, 37, 32–33.

94. In his most recent book, Rodriguez deals openly with the fact that he never actually says he is gay in his memoirs. He uses the voice of a student interviewer to both raise the issue and speak the words: "He said it was cool with him that I was gay but he wanted to know how I measured the influence of homosexuality... *on your writing, since you never say.*" (Ellipsis and italics in original). See Rodriguez, *Brown*, 223.

95. Rodriguez differentiates American macho from Mexican machismo. He says in English, "the macho is publicly playful, boorish, counter-domestic. American macho is drag — the false type for the male — as Mae West is the false type

for the female." See Rodriguez, *Days*, 56–57. While his portrait of American macho is insightful, his usage of it to exalt Mexican machismo as something more about chivalry than power is perhaps a bit oversimplified. A number of studies of machismo have been published recently. See, for example, Matthew C. Guttman, *The Meanings of Macho: Being a Man in Mexico City* (Berkeley: University of California Press, 1996); also, Michael Hardin, "Altering Masculinities: The Spanish Conquest and the Evolution of the Latin American Machismo," *International Journal of Sexuality and Gender Studies* 7, no. 1 (January 2002), 1–22. For an insightful study of Chicano sexual identities, see Tomas Almaguer, "Chicano Men: A Cartography of Homosexual Identity and Behavior," in Abelove et al., eds., 255–73.

96. Rodriguez, *Hunger*, 128–30.
97. Rodriguez, *Days*, 46.
98. Ibid., 47.
99. James Heckman, in Fellows, 98.
100. Horrigan, 39; McNaught, *On Being Gay*, 45.
101. In addition to its relationship to masculine expectations, the drive to overachieve and appear "perfect" could also be interpreted as a response to internalized homophobia. This points out even more clearly the connection between gender expectations and sexual identity. The feared implication of falling short in terms of masculinity is that one is also a homosexual. It is no surprise then that reactions to falling short of the masculine ideal are also wrapped up in homophobia. Thanks to Rebecca Alpert for this insight.
102. Sullivan, *Love Undetectable,*138. Ironically, this ambition and scholarship while growing up has its own rewards later in life and can pay off in terms of career and intellectual success. Thanks to Lucy Bregman for this insight.
103. Gerald Allen, in Holtz, ed., 220.
104. "Dan: HIV Doubled My Spirituality," in Shallenberger, 41.
105. "Mark: A Gay Spiritual Ancestry," in Shallenberger, 142.
106. Campo, *Desire*, 105.
107. Philip Gambone, "Searching for Real Words," in Bouldrey, ed., 224.
108. James Abdo, in Holtz, ed., 22.
109. Toby Johnson, in ibid., 38; Tom Cunningham, in ibid., 75–76.
110. Joe Izzo, in ibid., 60.; Larry Sullivan, in ibid., 136.
111. McNaught, *On Being Gay*, 6.
112. Ibid., 29.
113. Ibid., 164.
114. Ibid.
115. Rodriguez, *Hunger,* 52.
116. Ibid., 48.
117. Joseph Kramer, "Body and Soul," in Mark Thompson, *Gay Soul: Finding the Heart of Gay Spirit and Nature with Sixteen Writers, Healers, Teachers, and Visionaries* (San Francisco, Harper San Francisco, 1994), 176. By the time a gay child *is* sexual, he has so internalized the feeling of being outside his parents' frame of reference that he is unlikely to share any concerns about his sexuality with them. He may not feel his parents are his allies because they do not know what it is like to grow up gay.
118. Andrew Sullivan discusses this in the context of Richard Isay's theories on homosexuality. Sullivan uses it to critique the idea that the alienation comes first and is a cause of homosexuality. Sullivan, *Love Undetectable*, 122–24.
119. J. D. McClatchy, "My Fountain Pen," in Merla, ed., 197.

120. Ibid., 198.
121. Stephen McCauley, "Let's Say," in Merla, ed., 189–90.
122. Brother Jonathan, "You Are My People," in Gramick, ed. (1989), 163.
123. Paul Albergo, in Holtz, ed., 146.
124. There is also no generalizable pattern of relationships to interpret as "causing" homosexuality, thus refuting antiquated Freudian stereotypes about absent fathers and overwhelming mothers. The autobiographers themselves seem entirely uninterested in the idea that their sexuality was "caused" by anything. It simply is part of who they are.
125. Noss, in Fellows, 241.
126. Zuniga, 12.
127. Ibid., 89.
128. Ibid., 272. (Joe is the English language equivalent for José.)
129. Arpin, 32. Sadly, sometimes even a diagnosis with a serious illness is not enough to reconcile parents and children who are alienated because of sexuality. The stigma associated with AIDS is just as difficult for some people to overcome.
130. Kopay, 169.
131. Ibid., 256.
132. Mecca, "Memoirs," 23.
133. Ibid., 28.
134. DeCaro, 207–12.
135. Ibid., 199.
136. Ibid., 203–4.
137. These would include Provincetown, Fire Island, and Key West. Like New York and San Francisco, they are at land's end, close to borders — metaphorically on the margins. This is the imagery Richard Rodriguez uses when he calls San Francisco the "farthest-flung possibility." Rodriguez, *Days*, 28. For another explicit use of this imagery, see Mark Doty, *Heaven's Coast* (New York: Harper Perennial, 1997).
138. DeCaro, 184.
139. Ibid., 88, 91.
140. Campo, *Desire*, 73.
141. Holleran, in Philip Gambone, ed., *Something Inside: Conversations with Gay Fiction Writers* (Madison: University of Wisconsin Press, 1999), 174.
142. DeCaro, 157.
143. Tom Cunningham, in Holtz, ed., 78.
144. Kramer, in Thompson, 177.
145. Nixon, "Avondale," 37.
146. Ibid., 37.
147. Johnson, *Geography*, 81, 83.
148. Heckman, in Fellows, 100–101.
149. Rodriguez, *Hunger*, 57.
150. Ibid., 189–90.
151. McNaught, *On Being Gay*, 20.
152. Ibid., 142.
153. Johnson, *Geography*, 83.
154. Campo, *Desire*, 177–78.
155. Philip Gambone, "Searching," 223.
156. Pallone, 88–89.
157. Peter M. Krask, "The Way the Stars Come Home," in Bouldrey, ed., 147.
158. Campo, *Desire*, 129–30.

159. Ibid., 119.

160. Ibid., 120.

161. Gambone, "Learning," 64.

162. Rev. R. Roberts, "The Fears of a Gay Priest," in Wolf, ed., 147.

163. Ebmeier, in Fellows, 158.

164. James Abdo, in Holtz, ed., 28.

165. Nixon, "Avondale," 32–33.

166. Gambone, "Learning," 79.

167. See Jonathan Ned Katz, *The Invention of Heterosexuality* (New York: Dutton Books, 1995). Also see his *Sex Between Men Before Homosexuality* (Chicago: University of Chicago Press, 2001), for a study of same-sex desire before gay identity was available.

168. William D. Glenn, "As God Intended: Reflections on Being a Gay Student at a Jesuit High School," *America* 184, no. 17 (May 21, 2001), 29.

169. As of 2002, legal protection from discrimination based on sexual orientation remains elusive in the majority of states. Where inclusion in protection ordinances is won, the victory is usually close. Many such protections face regular legal challenges.

170. Andrew Holleran, in *American Contradictions: Interviews with Nine American Writers*, ed. Wolfgang Binder and Helmbrecht Breinig (Hanover: Wesleyan University Press, 1995), 39.

3. Orbiting the Catholic Axis

1. Two volumes that use and explore these terms of identification are Mary Jo Weaver and R. Scott Appleby, eds., *Being Right: Conservative Catholics in America* (Indianapolis: Indiana University Press, 1995); and Mary Jo Weaver, ed., *What's Left? Liberal American Catholics* (Indianapolis: Indiana University Press, 1999). An approach that tries to steer the middle ground is Peter Steinfels, *A People Adrift: The Crisis of the Roman Catholic Church in America* (New York: Simon & Schuster, 2003). At the heart of the liberal/conservative dynamic is the question of authority as related to ideology. For an analysis of this issue with regard to the church hierarchy, see Gene Burns, *The Frontiers of Catholicism: The Politics of Ideology in a Liberal World* (Berkeley: University of California Press, 1992).

2. How political parties are positioned with respect to various issues also changes over time and in turn affects what is defined as liberal and conservative. In the late 1960s and 1970s, for example, positions on abortion were not easily linked with a particular party as they are today. Many democrats favored abortion restrictions and five of the seven Supreme Court justices joining in the Roe v. Wade opinion were Republican appointees. See Joe Feuerherd, "Politics and the Pro-Life Movement," *National Catholic Reporter*, January 17, 2003, 5.

3. Michele Dillon, *Catholic Identity: Balancing Reason, Faith, and Power* (Cambridge: Cambridge University Press, 1999).

4. (Lat., "from the chair"). This requirement must be met for a specific teaching to be considered infallible. The standard is so high that it is rarely met. It has only been employed with regard to the Immaculate Conception and the Assumption, both Marian dogmatic pronouncements. Scalia also emphasized the need for Catholic judges to follow American law on the death penalty. Interestingly, Scalia made his remarks about the same time the Pope urged American Catholic lawyers not to handle divorce cases because of the inherent conflict with church teachings. See David O'Reilly, "Pope's Words Unsettle Catholic Lawyers," *Philadelphia Inquirer*, February 3, 2002, B5.

5. Dillon, 4.

6. This is true for most religions practiced in the United States. While the American value of "separation of church and state" (however unevenly this ideal is actually realized) allows for the free practice of religion, it also insists upon a separation of sacred and secular that does not always make sense in the historical development of religions. This has a special resonance in American Catholic history, which demonstrates a tension between Catholic communal solidarity and American notions of individual autonomy. See John T. McGreevy, *Catholicism and American Freedom: A History* (New York: W. W. Norton, 2003).

7. See R. Laurence Moore, *Religious Outsiders and the Making of Americans* (New York: Oxford University Press, 1986). In addition to the texts discussed in the following paragraphs, other useful studies of American Catholicism include: James T. Fisher, *Communion of Immigrants: A History of Catholics in America* (New York: Oxford University Press, 2000); Bryan T. Froehle and Mary L. Gautier, *Catholicism USA: A Portrait of the Catholic Church in the United States* (Maryknoll, N.Y.: Orbis, 2000); Mark S. Massa, *Catholics and American Culture: Fulton Sheen, Dorothy Day, and the Notre Dame Football Team* (New York: Crossroad, 1999); Claire E. Wolfteich, *American Catholics Through the Twentieth Century: Spirituality, Lay Experience and Public Life* (New York: Crossroad, 2001). For excellent collections of original source documents, see Steven M. Avella and Elizabeth McKeown, eds., *Public Voices: Catholics in the American Context* (Maryknoll, N.Y.; Orbis, 1999); and Anne M. Butler, Michael E. Engh, and Thomas W. Spalding, eds., *The Frontiers and Catholic Identities* (Maryknoll, N.Y.: Orbis, 1999).

8. Jay P. Dolan, *The American Catholic Experience*, see especially his chapter on "The Catholic Ethos," 221–40.

9. Ann Taves, *The Household of Faith: Roman Catholic Devotions in Mid-Nineteenth-Century America* (Notre Dame: University of Notre Dame Press, 1986); Robert Orsi, *The Madonna of 115th Street: Faith and Community in Italian Harlem, 1880–1950* (New Haven: Yale University Press, 1985).

10. This dynamic can still be observed in more recent Catholic immigrant populations, as second and third generations become more assimilated.

11. Paula M. Kane, *Separatism and Subculture: Boston Catholicism, 1900–1920* (Chapel Hill: University of North Carolina Press, 1994).

12. William M. Halsey, *The Survival of American Innocence: Catholicism in an Era of Disillusionment, 1920–1940* (Notre Dame: University of Notre Dame Press, 1980).

13. James Terence Fisher, *The Catholic Counterculture in America, 1933–1962* (Chapel Hill: University of North Carolina Press, 1989).

14. For an excellent study of the impact of race on American Catholicism, see John T. McGreevy, *Parish Boundaries: The Catholic Encounter with Race in the Twentieth-Century Urban North* (Chicago: University of Chicago Press, 1996). In addition to attention given to gender concerns in Taves and Kane, mentioned above, also see Karen Kennelly, ed, *American Catholic Women: A Historical Exploration* (New York: Macmillan Publishing, 1989). For a collection of relevant documents dealing with gender issues throughout American Catholic history, see Paula Kane, James Kenneally, and Karen Kennelly, eds., *Gender Identities in American Catholicism* (Maryknoll, N.Y.: Orbis, 2001).

15. Rodriguez, "Irish Catholic," 336.

16. Ibid., 329.

17. It is interesting that Catholics were leaving their urban ghettos just as gay urban ghettos were becoming more visible and accessible. I am not implying a causal relationship here but rather noting how this opposite movement symbolizes the dilemma of holding gay identity and Catholic identity together.

18. See Arthur Jones, "Catholic Pioneers in the Suburban Landscape," *National Catholic Reporter*, November 2, 2001, 10.

19. Rodriguez, *Hunger*, 106. It is interesting that in the current movement to "reform the reform," which seeks to rid the new liturgy of problematic "American" innovations and influences, a return to "I believe" as the opening of the creed is being suggested. If we follow Rodriguez's analysis, this attempt to solidify a more distinctly Catholic approach by returning to a Tridentine formula would only further fragment Catholic identity in the current American context.

20. Given the context of the autobiographies I examine, it is worth noting that sexual identities, though increasingly multiple and complex, have become available and more defined at a time when Catholic identity seems especially contingent.

21. American Catholic identity is similarly implicated in Phillip Gambone's musings about the intersection of third-generation ethnicity and gay identity. See chapter 2, above.

22. Leslie Scanlon, "Here Come's Everybody's Church," *U.S. Catholic* 67 (May 2002), 28.

23. Carolyn Osiek and Laurie Brink, "Two Women, a Generation Apart, View Religious Life," *National Catholic Reporter*, February 18, 2000, 22.

24. These are also often the Catholics who want to apply an ideological litmus test for people to "prove" their Catholic identity. Unfortunately, such tests usually focus on one issue, such as abortion or homosexuality, at the expense of more central concerns.

25. Lucy Bregman aptly observes that the idealization of pre–Vatican II Catholicism — "nostalgia for a paradise now thoroughly lost" — is a response to the multileveled shifts and fragmentation that mark post–Vatican II Catholicism (personal communication, March 23, 2002).

26. Tom Beaudoin, "Our Catholic Watergate," *America* 186 (June 3–10, 2002), 19. Beaudoin believes this movement has been intensified by the clergy sexual abuse scandal made public in the first half of 2002. Andrew Sullivan also makes a generational argument in light of the scandal: "I think it's fair to say that very few people in my generation of 40-year-olds and younger can take the church's sexual teachings very seriously again." Andrew Sullivan, "Who Says the Church Can't Change?" *Time*, June 17, 2002, 63.

27. Dillon, 119.

28. Ibid., 203–16.

29. Published in detail in a series of articles and summaries in the *National Catholic Reporter*, October 29, 1999, 11–20.

30. Discussed in Dean R. Hoge, "What Is Most Central to Being a Catholic?" in *National Catholic Reporter*, October 29, 1999, 13.

31. "U.S. Catholics: Who Do We Think We Are? The Editors Interview James Davidson," *U.S. Catholic* 65, no. 2 (February 2000), 13.

32. I should note here a few important and useful texts that deal with negotiating an integrated Catholic identity that includes a conscious faith commitment: Daniel Donovan, *Distinctively Catholic: An Exploration of Catholic Identity* (New York: Paulist Press, 1997); Penelope Ryan, *Practicing Catholic: The Search for a*

Livable Catholicism (New York: Henry Holt, 1998); and Paul Wilkes, *The Seven Secrets of Successful Catholics* (New York: Paulist Press, 1998).

33. Lawrence S. Cunningham, *The Catholic Experience* (New York: Crossroad, 1985).

34. Andrew Greeley, *The Catholic Imagination* (Berkeley: University of California Press, 2000), 1. Also see Richard Blake, *Afterimage: The Indelible Catholic Imagination of Six American Filmmakers* (Chicago: Loyola Press, 2000).

35. Greeley, 1.

36. Ibid., 6. Here, Greeley draws on David Tracy's concept of "analogical" imagination in his discussion of metaphor.

37. Rosemary Haughton, *The Catholic Thing* (Springfield, Ill.: Templegate, 1979).

38. For many of these men, part of their Catholic identity was communicated to them in Catholic schools. Not surprisingly, it was not only from the educational content that these men learned about Catholicism but also through the whole atmosphere of the school system and from the brothers, nuns, and priests who ran it. I initially expected to find more stories resembling the darkly humorous stereotype of Catholic schools, in which cruel nuns exact unjust punishments on innocent students. There simply were not enough to warrant a special discussion. And for every mean nun mentioned in these autobiographies, there is another story of an encouraging teacher or positive experience.

39. McNaught, *Disturbed*, 94.

40. Kopay, 33–36.

41. Zuniga. 14.

42. Johnson, "God, Gays," 249.

43. Ibid., 249.

44. Johnson, *Geography*, 103.

45. Ibid., 139, 176.

46. Bouldrey, *Wrestling*, ix–x.

47. McNeill, *Both Feet*, 28.

48. Tony Laveccia, in Holtz, ed., 156.

49. Scott Trepania, "Prayer Life Provides a Focus as I cope with Dropping T-Cell Counts," *National Catholic Reporter*, September 2, 1994, 7.

50. Pallone, 176.

51. Ibid., 178.

52. Campo, *Desire*, 44, 45.

53. Ibid., 44–45.

54. Horrigan, 25, 28.

55. Ibid., 100.

56. Ibid., 85.

57. Rodriguez, *Hunger*, 77.

58. Ibid., 80.

59. Ibid., 78.

60. Sullivan, *Love Undetectable*, 58.

61. Rodriguez, *Hunger*, 84.

62. Johnson, *Keeping Faith*, 33. In another passage, he is even more descriptive: "Like all great theater, the mass transports the audience to a time outside of time, to the place where time is open to eternity, to the authentic experience of God...." Ibid., 283.

63. Horrigan, 162.

64. Nixon, "Avondale," 34.

65. Rodriguez, *Hunger*, 105.

66. I should mention here that the liturgical reform was instituted in varying degrees and with varying levels of expertise in different parts of the country (and the world, for that matter). By the mid-1980s, the pendulum of liturgical innovation was beginning to swing back so that some of the qualities of the old liturgy would be recovered. Some of this is due to Vatican interventions and their tightening grip of control, but some of it is also due to a greater attention to aesthetic detail and nostalgia for the Latin Mass.

67. Morrison, "Saved," in Bouldrey, ed., 64.

68. Johnson, *Geography*, 163.

69. Toby Johnson, in Holtz, ed., 39.

70. Rodriguez, *Days*, 29.

71. Ibid., 180.

72. Jim Bussen, in Holtz., ed., 132–33.

73. Tom Kaun and Kevin Calegari, in Holtz, ed., 208.

74. See Joe McGuire, in Holtz., ed., 232; and Father Paul, "We Shall Not Cease from Exploration," in Gramick, ed. (1989), 143.

75. Heckman, in Fellows, 98.

76. It would be interesting to do an analysis like this of heterosexual Catholic men's life writings. If "feeling different" is indeed part of what drives autobiographical writing in the first place, their life narratives may evidence more of them feeling drawn to the priesthood than I would initially expect.

77. Horrigan, 147.

78. Ibid., 15.

79. Zuniga, 15.

80. McNaught, *A Disturbed Peace*, 75.

81. Thanks to Lucy Bregman for this insight.

82. Donald B. Cozzens, *The Changing Face of the Priesthood: A Reflection on the Priest's Crisis of Soul* (Collegeville, Minn.: Liturgical Press, 2000).

83. See Garry Wills, *Papal Sin: Structures of Deceit* (New York: Doubleday, 2000), 194.

84. In a recent survey of 1,200 priests, 55 percent said a gay subculture exists in their dioceses or religious orders. "Survey: Half of Priests Detect Gay Subculture," *National Catholic Reporter*, September 6, 2002, 20.

85. James Martin, "The Church and the Homosexual Priest: Facing the Challenges and Accepting the Gifts Offered by Homosexual Priests in the Catholic Church," *America* 183, no. 14 (November 4, 2000), 14–15. Now, if only church leaders would recognize God is also calling women and married men as priests, then we could also acknowledge the special gifts these sets of people would bring to the priesthood.

86. Kevin Killian, "Chain of Fools," in Bouldrey, ed., 126.

87. Ibid., 128.

88. I will deal with the sexual abuse crisis more deeply in chapter 5.

89. Jordan, *Silence*, 107.

90. Johnson, *Geography*, 45.

91. Jordan, *Silence*, 159.

92. McNeill, *Both Feet*, 34.

93. Ibid., 42.

94. Ibid., 67.

95. McNichols, "A Priest Forever," 120.

96. Matthew Kelty, "The Land I Love In," in Gramick, ed., 145.

97. Richard John Cardarelli, "Lord, Make Me an Instrument of Your Peace," in Gramick, ed., 153, 155–56.

98. Brother Jonathan, "You Are My People," 166.

99. Rev. T. Thompson, "A Christian Spirituality," in Wolf, ed., 139.

100. Father Aelred, "Without Shame," in Gramick, ed., 177.

101. Arpin, 7.

102. Ibid., 153.

103. Ibid., 48.

104. Ibid., 150.

105. The legalities of the laicization process can be cumbersome and discouraging. Monetary compensation is also an issue, especially for priests who lived in community and have no savings of their own. Additionally, priests who have resigned are technically forbidden to be lay ministers or teachers of religious education.

106. This reflects the idea of the Catholic imagination as theorized by Greeley.

107. David Plante, "Images of the Body from My Religion," in Bouldrey, ed., 172.

108. Ibid., 172–73. This theme also appears in Plante's novel *The Catholic,* when the protagonist Dan imagines his night of love-making with Henry as a reenactment of Christ's love for the Mystical Body of the church. Dan concludes by saying, "In my Church, to deny your body was to deny your soul." Plante, *The Catholic,* 72.

109. Morrison, "Saved," 70.

110. Ibid., 80.

111. Ibid. Morrison echoes the traditional Catholic formula of "faith and works," over and against the "faith alone" or "grace alone" formula of the Protestant Reformation. Of course, Evangelical converts are expected to demonstrate the practical "fruits" of their conversion, which sometimes amounts to an even more severe moralism than that which is typically associated with Catholicism.

112. Kopay, 38.

113. Ibid., 39.

114. Johnson, *Keeping Faith,* 35.

115. Ibid.

116. Ebmeier, in Fellows, 157.

117. Zuniga, xii.

118. Ibid., 156.

119. Ibid., 28.

120. Mecca, "Memoirs," 18.

121. Gambone, "Beyond Words," in Merla, ed., 110.

122. Joseph Kramer, in Thompson, 171.

123. Richard John Cardarelli, "Lord, Make Me," 154.

124. Andrew Holleran, "The Sense of Sin," in Bouldrey, ed., 84.

125. Ibid., 85.

126. Ibid., 88.

127. Ibid., 92.

128. Ibid., 86–87. This story also shows up in his quasi-autobiographical novel *Nights in Aruba,* when the protagonist, Paul, says, "As I put my towel away I concluded that the Catholic Church was right: The body was the temple of the Holy Ghost — nothing more, nothing less." Holleran, *Nights,* 87–88.

129. Holleran, "Sense of Sin," 88. It is interesting that a remarkable number of these authors quote St. Augustine, whose autobiography is so influential and

whose views on sexuality are largely responsible for the sexual ethics we have inherited in the West.

130. Ibid., 95. Also see Holleran, *Nights*, 42–43.

131. David Plante, in Gambone, ed., *Something Inside*, 223.

132. Ibid., 224, 226.

133. Plante, *The Catholic*, 75.

134. In particular, he looks at autobiographies by Kathleen Norris, Terry Tempest Williams, China Galland, Patricia Hampl, and Mary Daly.

135. John D. Barbour, *Versions of Deconversion: Autobiography and the Loss of Faith* (The University Press of Virginia, 1994), 187.

136. Ibid., 200.

137. Campo, *Desire*, 40.

138. Ibid., 42.

139. Ibid., 47.

140. Ibid., 50.

141. Ibid., 40.

142. Gambone, "Searching," 227.

143. Ibid., 232.

144. Ibid., 239. (Ellipsis and format in original.)

145. Ibid., 238.

146. Johnson, *Keeping Faith*, 37.

147. Ibid., 31.

148. Ibid., 14.

149. See Ibid., 34–35.

150. Ibid., 92.

151. Ibid., 245.

152. Ibid., 198.

153. Ibid., 138 (italics in original).

154. Rodriguez, *Brown*, 224.

155. Ibid., 225.

156. Ibid., 230.

157. Ibid.

158. Krask, "The Way the Stars Come Home," 162.

159. Ibid., 164.

160. Kopay, 43–44.

161. Ibid., 244.

162. Killian is the only one of the autobiographers in my study who mentions being sexually abused by clergy. I will say more on this subject in chapter 5.

163. Kevin Killian, "Chain of Fools," 128.

164. Ibid., 128.

165. McNaught, *On Being Gay*, 32.

166. McNaught, *A Disturbed Peace*, 101.

167. McNaught, *On Being Gay*, 147.

168. Ibid., 126.

169. Johnson, *Keeping Faith*, 298.

170. Tony Laveccia, in Holtz, ed., 157.

171. Gerald Allen, in Holtz, ed., 223.

172. William G. Storey, in Holtz, ed., 11.

173. Rodriguez, *Brown*, 226.

174. Ibid., 226–27.

175. Jim Revak, in Holtz, ed., 211.

176. Tony Laveccia, in Holtz, ed., 156.
177. Tom McLaughlin, in Holtz, ed., 154.
178. This is supported in Dillon's study on Catholic identity. See Dillon, 119, 125.
179. Jon Soucy, "Speaking the Unspeakable," *The Hoya* (March 4, 2003), www.thehoya.com.

4. "Homosexual Acts"

1. Donna McKenzie calls this "the ethical importance of context," and notes, along with Charles Curran, how the church has refused to take this approach to sexual ethics. Donna M. McKenzie, "Is There a Moral Theologian in the House?" *Religion in the News* 5, no. 2 (Summer 2002): 19. It is disturbing that the church is usually more amenable to a range of opinion on war and killing than it is on sexual matters. This was abundantly clear with the 2003 U.S. military invasion of Iraq. Even though the pope said the action was not morally justified, many American Catholics voiced their dissent without fear of reprisal. The U.S. ambassador to the Vatican even invited a conservative American Catholic theologian to Rome to make a case for the war. Indeed, some conservative Catholics who insist there is no room for dissent on the church's sexual teachings found themselves on the other side of the "church teachings vs. sense of the faithful" debate. Why is this grayness and range of legitimate opinion not allowed when it comes to matters of gender and sexuality? It makes one wonder if the church's main problem with abortion is not so much about the sanctity of life but rather its aversion to sex.

2. Again, one of the best examples is the insistence that every sexual act must be so open to procreation that "artificial" contraception is forbidden. Yet a whopping 96 percent of all Catholic women who have ever had sex have used modern contraceptive methods at some point in their lives, and 73.5 percent of sexually active Catholic women who attend church once a week or more use a contraceptive method forbidden by the church. See the 1995 National Survey of Family Growth, quoted in "The Facts Tell the Story: Catholics and Contraception," brochure produced by Catholics for Contraception (undated).

3. Christine Gudorf, *Body, Sex, and Pleasure,* 29–32.
4. Kathy Rudy, *Sex and the Church,* 115.
5. Fulkerson, "Gender," 198–99. Fulkerson would advocate abandoning any reliance on the sexual identities which inform the heterosexual grid. I want to acknowledge the role these identities play in modern self-definition but also complicate how these identities are perceived and defined.
6. Sullivan, *Love Undetectable,* 45.
7. Margaret Farley, "A Feminist Version of Respect for Persons," in Curran, Farley, and McCormick, eds., 177.
8. Ibid., 178.
9. Andre Guindon, "Homosexual Acts or Gay Speech?" in Gramick and Furey, eds., 211.
10. Ibid.
11. Sullivan, *Love Undetectable,* 50.
12. From her remarks at "The Personal and the Political" panel, Second Sex Conference, New York, September 29, 1979. Reprinted in *Sister Outsider: Essays and Speeches by Audre Lorde* (Freedom, Calif.: Crossing Press, 1984), 110–13.
13. Lucy Bregman has pointed out how the majority of AIDS autobiographies reflect a pre-infection ethic of absolute sexual freedom that could almost be characterized as an absence of sexual ethics altogether. The focus is on sex acts, minus

any substantive attention to relationships. This might be a peculiarity of the genre, a reflection of persons whose identities are partially organized around a disease. The autobiographers in my study who are HIV-positive, like Andrew Sullivan and Robert Arpin, do not match that model. When they do allude to sexual "promiscuity," they do so with some regret, not primarily for themselves but for the stigma and marginalization that makes gay intimacy so hard to find and, in turn, exacerbates the need for casual or furtive encounters.

14. In general terms, one finds Eric Rofes, Michael Bronski, Urvashi Vaid, and Sarah Schulman on the left, rebutting Andrew Sullivan, Bruce Bawer, Gabriel Rotello, Larry Kramer, and Michelangelo Signorile, who have critiqued various aspects of gay activism as it has developed. Of course, the categories of right and left, or liberal and conservative, in no way capture their varied positions. Some relevant works include: Eric Rofes, *Dry Bones Breathe: Gay Men Creating Post-AIDS Identities and Cultures* (New York: Harrington Park Press, 1998); Michael Bronski: *The Pleasure Principle: Sex, Backlash, and the Struggle for Gay Freedom* (New York: St. Martin's Press, 1998); Andrew Sullivan, *Virtually Normal: An Argument about Homosexuality* (New York: Alfred A. Knopf, 1995); Bruce Bawer, *A Place at the Table: The Gay Individual in American Society* (New York: Poseidon Press, 1993). For an interesting treatment of sexual freedom by scholars of religion who are also queer activists, see Janet Jakobsen and Ann Pellegrini, *Love the Sin: Sexual Regulation and the Limits of Religious Tolerance* (New York: New York University Press, 2003).

15. James Morrison is the only one who calls explicitly for the abandonment of conventional norms in gay relationships. Others certainly problematize traditional norms and expectations, and they experiment with a variety of possibilities for their lives and relationships, but they are generally most concerned with how best to configure their desires and relationships within the ethical possibilities currently available to them. Even when they engage in casual or anonymous sex, they are conflicted in some way about it.

16. Remember that none of these life writers are explicitly engaged in an ethical project or writing especially to effect a change in church teachings. They are doing autobiography and I am interpreting their stories with these issues in mind. When I cite examples from their texts, I am lifting up the aspects most relevant to this project. That does not mean these are the most relevant issues for each of their projects.

17. Marilyn Gottschall, "The Ethical Implications of the Deconstruction of Gender," *Journal of the American Academy of Religion* 70, no. 2 (June 2002), 291–92.

18. Ibid., 296.

19. Diane Bjorklund, *Interpreting the Self: Two Hundred Years of American Autobiography* (Chicago: University of Chicago Press, 1998), 159.

20. Ibid.

21. Ibid., 160. Remember, it is always reality as the autobiographer sees it, not necessarily as the reader would. This is why Bjorklund says autobiographers "justify" their actions and choices. This is also the factor that makes these autobiographies so usable as examples of gay subjectivity.

22. See John Gettys, "Daniel Curzon (1938–)," in *Contemporary Gay American Novelists: A Bio-Bibliographical Critical Sourcebook*, ed. Emmanuel S. Nelson (Westport, Conn.: Greenwood Press, 1993), 93.

23. Daniel Curzon, *The World Can Break Your Heart*, 177.

24. As Gottschall says, quoting Judith Butler, "The ethico-political task that matters is neither revolution or critique — both of which inevitably take place 'immanent to the regime of power/discourse whose claims it seeks to adjudicate' — but, rather, subversion." Gottschall, 295.

25. Rev. R. Roberts, "Fears," 146.

26. Ibid., 146.

27. Campo, *Desire*, 93.

28. Ibid., 23.

29. Ibid., 23–24.

30. McNaught, *On Being Gay*, 65.

31. Ibid., 56–57.

32. Rodriguez, *Hunger*, 6.

33. Zuniga, 303.

34. See McNeill's book which takes this phrase as its title.

35. Johnson, *Keeping Faith*, 275.

36. Ibid., 204. This sentiment lies in stark contrast with what Johnson observes in church leaders. He says the church encourages men to become priests "who have so successfully repressed their experience of desire that they're able to speak with conviction about its evils." Ibid., 190.

37. Johnson, "God, Gays," 248.

38. Holleran, *Nights*, 156.

39. The hope at the time was for then-President Clinton to lift the ban. Instead, the ensuing debate resulted in the compromise that is the "don't ask, don't tell" policy, which has ironically resulted in more discharges of gay and lesbian soldiers each year. Gay activists have repeatedly denounced this policy for its simplistic assumptions about gay identity. Much like the bifurcation problem in church teaching, it assumes an easy separation between gay identity and its expression. It is a policy founded upon the use of facades masquerading as discretion. Consequently, it requires the same lack of personal integrity that is promoted by problematic church teaching. In Zuniga's words, "There is no on-off switch when dealing with human identity. This proposed policy affected gays at the core of who we are as a people. In essence, it forced us on an ongoing basis not to accept ourselves, to constantly live a lie." Zuniga, 254.

40. Zuniga, 44–45.

41. Ibid., 44.

42. Horrigan, 206.

43. Ibid., 205–6.

44. Pallone, 143.

45. Ibid., 266.

46. Ibid., 168.

47. Spousal health insurance is typically available for employees, even if they have only been married a short time. Gay and lesbian employees are typically not eligible for such benefits even if they have been with the same partner for a long time. While this unfairness seems fairly obvious, the majority of employers have yet to correct it. Only about 130 of the Fortune 500 firms offer domestic partner benefits (see Dianna Marder, "Gay, Lesbian Wedding Market Embraced," *Philadelphia Inquirer*, April 3, 2002, E1, E4). The reasons these companies offer such benefits are usually driven by the need to attract qualified employees. This makes these benefits vulnerable to the whims of the market. A more helpful and farsighted approach would be to disassociate benefits from marriage and find other foundations on which to provide fairly for basic human rights.

48. Mark Blasius, *Gay and Lesbian Politics: Sexuality and the Emergence of a New Ethic* (Philadelphia: Temple University Press, 1994), 134, 136–37. Other useful texts which explore the public/private issue and gay political strategies include: Timothy Murphy, ed., *Gay Ethics: Controversies in Outing, Civil Rights, and Sexual Science* (New York: Harrington Park Press, 1994); Steven Seidman, *Embattled Eros: Sexual Politics and Ethics in Contemporary America* (New York and London: Routledge, 1992); Ann Snitow, Christine Stansell, and Sharon Thompson, eds., *Powers of Desire: The Politics of Sexuality* (New York: Monthly Review Press, 1983). Another useful text, not specifically focused on gay and lesbian issues, is Iris Marion Young, *Justice and the Politics of Difference* (Princeton: Princeton University Press, 1990).

49. Sullivan, "Virtually Normal," 173.

50. Ibid., 185.

51. Sullivan, *Love Undetectable*, 43.

52. Derrick A. Tynan-Connolly, in Holtz, ed., 180.

53. Rodriguez, *Days*, 43.

54. Morrison, *Broken Fever*, 240.

55. Campo, *Desire*, 191.

56. Ibid., 192.

57. Ibid., 267.

58. Ibid., 192.

59. Ibid., 193.

60. Zuniga, 184. The report is called "Gay Male and Lesbian Youth Suicide, Report of the Secretary's Task Force on Youth Suicide." The document was never given full administrative support and it was not formally released, reputedly because of these "controversial" statistics and their implications.

61. Heckman, in Fellows, 99–100.

62. Cardarelli, "Lord, Make Me an Instrument," 156.

63. McNaught, *On Being Gay*, 12.

64. Ibid., 150–51.

65. Kopay, 279.

66. Fr. Raymond Calabrese, "One Gay Priest's Story," *U.S. Catholic* 68 (February 2003), 50.

67. McCauley, 192.

68. Rodriguez, *Brown*, 207.

69. Ibid., 208.

70. See, for example, *Catechism of the Catholic Church* no. 1644, which quotes *Familiaris consortio* about the love of spouses, who "are called to grow continually in their communion through day-to-day fidelity to their marriage promise of total mutual self-giving." *Catechism*, 410.

71. Johnson, *Geography*, 34.

72. Ibid., 70.

73. Ibid., 31.

74. Ibid., 92–93.

75. McNeill, *Both Feet*, 68.

76. Heckman, in Fellows, 100.

77. Kopay, 145.

78. Ibid., 179.

79. Ibid., 180.

80. Pallone, 76–77.

81. Ibid., 80–81.

82. Larry Sullivan, in Holtz, ed., 136.
83. William G. Storey, in Holtz, ed., 10.
84. James Abdo, in Holtz, ed., 26.
85. Ibid., 27.
86. Gerald Allen, in Holtz, ed., 223. Allen still identifies as gay rather than bisexual.
87. Morrison, *Broken Fever,* 148–49.
88. Zuniga, 171–72. Zuniga also identifies as gay rather than bisexual.
89. McNaught, *On Being Gay,* 118.
90. Ibid., 118.
91. Johnson, *Geography,* 129.
92. Ibid.
93. Morrison, *Broken Fever,* 214–15.
94. Ibid., 190.
95. Gambone, "Beyond Words," 112.
96. William G. Storey, in Holtz, ed., 10.
97. Campo, *Desire,* 155.
98. Eugene Kennedy, "Ministry, Homosexuality, and Psychological Wholeness" (plenary address made to the New Ways Ministry Symposium, "Out of Silence God Has Called Us: Lesbian/Gay Issues and the Vatican II Church," Louisville, Ky., March 8–10, 2002), Audio Recording #02094-0020, Chesapeake Audio/Video Communications, Inc., Elkridge, Md. Also see Kennedy's *The Unhealed Wound: The Church and Human Sexuality* (New York: St. Martin's Griffin, 2001), for an analysis of the way the church's teachings on sexuality uphold the institution at the cost of personal wholeness.
99. Johnson, "God, Gays," 255.
100. Johnson, *Geography,* 76–77.
101. Johnson, "God, Gays," 251.
102. This theme of authority over sexual lives by those who live them is further developed in Evelyn E. and James D. Whitehead, *Wisdom of the Body: Making Sense of our Sexuality* (New York: Crossroad, 2001).
103. A recent study indicates that as nonheterosexual Christians develop their sexual ethics based on lived experience, they do not wish this to mean one is simply free to do whatever one wants. Rather, they seek to locate sexual morality within a Christian framework. See Yip, 208.
104. Schneider, 4.
105. Ibid., 11.
106. Holleran, "Sense of Sin," 96.

5. Reconciliation

1. See, for example, *Catechism,* nos. 1749–61, in which we are told the morality of human acts depends on object, intention, and circumstances. It is interesting this formula in itself reflects the necessity of contextualizing human acts, yet church leaders avoid applying this formula to gay acts by branding all such acts *intrinsically* disordered.
2. Jordan, *Silence,* 4.
3. This principle "constitutes one of the central theological characteristics of Catholicism." Richard McBrien, ed., *The HarperCollins Encyclopedia of Catholicism* (San Francisco: Harper San Francisco, 1995), s.v. "Sacramentality," 1148.
4. Susan A. Ross, "God's Embodiment and Women: Sacraments," in Catherine Mowry LaCugna, ed., *Freeing Theology: The Essentials of Theology in*

Feminist Perspective (San Francisco: Harper San Francisco, 1993), 187. Eventually, the Latin *Sacramenta,* from the root *sacer* (sacred) was used as a translation for these moments of God's grace. Also see Mark Francis, "Sacrament," in McBrien, ed., 1146.

5. Doris Donnelly, "Reconciliation: The Continuing Challenge," in *Reconciliation: The Continuing Agenda,* ed. Robert J. Kennedy (Collegeville, Minn.: Liturgical Press, 1987), 284.

6. Bjorn Krondorfer, "The Confines of Male Confessions: On Religion, Bodies, and Mirrors," in Krondorfer, ed., 222.

7. Stephen Spender, "Confessions and Autobiography," in Olney, ed. (1980), 118.

8. Ron Hansen, "Hotly in Pursuit of the Real: The Role of the Catholic Writer," *America* 185, no. 15 (November 12, 2001): 8.

9. Johnson, *Keeping Faith,* 129.

10. Rodriguez, *Brown,* 203, 224.

11. Jordan, *Silence,* 258, 261.

12. Ibid., 258.

13. Kathleen Hughes, "Reconciliation: Cultural and Christian Perspectives," in Kennedy, ed. (1987), 119.

14. Toinette M. Eugene, "Reconciliation in the Pastoral Context of Today's Church and World: Does Reconciliation Have a Future?" in *Reconciling Embrace: Foundations for the Future of Sacramental Reconciliation,* ed. Robert J. Kennedy (Chicago: Liturgy Training Publications, 1998), 13–14.

15. Ibid., 13.

16. From the Jerusalem Bible.

17. Raymond-Jean Frontain, "A Professional Queer Remembers: Bibliography, Narrative, and the Saving Power of Memory," in *A Sea of Stories: The Shaping Power of Narrative in Gay and Lesbian Cultures,* ed. Sonya L. Jones (New York: Harrington Park Press, 2000), 227–28.

18. Walter Holland, "In the Body's Ghetto," in Jones, ed., 116.

19. Gusdorf, "Conditions and Limits," 47.

20. Jordan, *Silence,* 260.

21. Morrison, *Broken Fever,* 8.

22. Johnson, "God, Gays," 247.

23. Campo, *Desire,* 270.

24. Johnson, *Keeping Faith,* 15.

25. Warning bells about this crisis had been sounding for years from various corners of the church, and cases have been reported in previous years. See Thomas C. Fox, "What They Knew in 1985," *National Catholic Reporter,* May 17, 2002, 3, 6–7; and Thomas P. Doyle, "Reflections from the Eye of the Hurricane," *National Catholic Reporter,* June 21, 2002, 6–7. The difference this time around is the increased attention to this problem by the mainstream media and civil authorities.

26. In their defense, many bishops have noted how much more advanced our knowledge of pedophilia and ephebophilia is today than it was even two decades ago. Short-term treatment was thought to be an effective "cure." It was also normative in society as a whole to deal with such matters quietly and confidentially. Indeed, many of these cases predate our current tell-all culture. Even so, the evidence suggests the protection of priests was given a higher priority than the effective protection of children.

27. United States Conference of Catholic Bishops, "Charter for the Protection of Children and Young People," special supplement to the *Catholic Standard and Times*, June 27, 2002, not paginated. This document is far from perfect, primarily because it is a response to public pressure rather than a proactive response to the problem.

28. Kevin Clarke, "Whitewash or Renewal?" *U.S. Catholic* 68, no. 6 (June 2003): 14.

29. Gill Donovan, "Some See Big Reforms on the Horizon: Conservatives and Liberals Align in Call for Lay Involvement," *National Catholic Reporter*, July 19, 2002, 3–5.

30. See Fran Ferder and John Heagle, "Time for Bishops to Listen, Take Ordinary Catholics Seriously," *National Catholic Reporter*, July 19, 2002, 6.

31. Andrew Sullivan, "Who Says the Church Can't Change?" *Time*, June 17, 2002, 63.

32. Rachel Zoll, "Experts: Purging Gay Priests Isn't the Answer," *Philadelphia Inquirer*, March 23, 2002, A7.

33. Quoted in Jon Fuller, "On 'Straightening Out' Catholic Seminaries," *America* 187, no. 20 (December 16, 2002): 8.

34. James J. Gill, "Seminaries Await Vatican Visitation," *America* 187, no. 2 (July 15–22): 11. Fortunately, most bishops eschewed this line of thinking in addressing this crisis. Cardinal Bevilacqua even proudly announced there are no gay seminarians in Philadelphia. Apparently, he thinks he can see through closet doors.

35. A helpful article which unpacks some of these connections is Joseph J. Guido, "The Importance of Perspective: Understanding the Sexual Abuse of Children by Priests," *America* 186, no. 11 (April 1, 2002): 21–23.

36. Another dimension of this issue needing further analysis and exploration is the sexuality of teens and even children. We must always take very seriously all cases in which anyone reports being victimized, but other cases of adolescents seeking sexual "mentoring" from an adult may complicate our definitions of abuse and how we mark youth and adulthood. For a useful and challenging examination of these ideas, see Judith Levine, *Harmful to Minors: The Perils of Protecting Children from Sex* (Minneapolis: University of Minnesota Press, 2002).

37. Consider late night television ads for the phone sex line 1-800-WE-ARE-18.

38. Some abusive heterosexual priests have told therapists they believed having sex with teen boys did not technically break their vow of celibacy. As strange as this sounds to me, it reflects a societal confusion over what exactly "having sex" means, in addition to a sort of Clinton-esque tendency toward justification. See Sandra G. Boodman, "For Experts on Abuse, Priests' Orientation Isn't the Issue," *Washington Post*, June 24, 2002, B2.

39. According to Dr. Fred Berlin, associate professor of psychiatry at Johns Hopkins University: "Some of this has been about homosexual men giving in to temptation with adolescent males. At the same time, we should make it clear that homosexuals are no more risk to children than heterosexuals. In terms of the bigger picture, there are every bit as many heterosexual men giving into sexual temptation with female adolescents." Laurie Goodstein, "Homosexuality in Priesthood is Under Increasing Scrutiny," *The New York Times — on the Web*, www.nytimes.com (April 19, 2002).

40. See news brief, "Dismissing All Abusive Priests Is Ineffective Strategy, Vatican Told," *America* 188, no. 14 (April 21, 2003): 4–5.

41. In the words of A. W. Richard Sipe, an activist and writer on issues related to clergy sexual abuse, "So many of the priests are psychosexually immature, it makes them more vulnerable to taking advantage of, or falling in love with, if you will, age-inappropriate people." See Goodstein, "Homosexuality in Priesthood."

42. Linda Chavez, Michael Novak, and Richard John Neuhaus have all made assertions like this.

43. Sipe notes, "I found in my studies that homosexually oriented men are every bit as observant of their celibacy as heterosexual men." Quoted in Goodstein.

44. They were recognized as such in the early church. See Rosemary Radford Ruether, "Abuse a Consequence of Historic Wrong Turn," *National Catholic Reporter,* June 7, 2002, 19.

45. See the news brief cited earlier in *America* 188, no. 14 (April 21, 2003): 5.

46. As a result of the clergy sex abuse crisis, Bishop Wilton Gregory, current president of the U.S. Conference of Catholic Bishops, foresees "a greater collaborative approach [with the laity] to the issues that we have to face together." He says it's about "you respecting my office, my respecting your competence, realizing that together we can do an awful lot that neither of us can do apart." Amen to that! It's time for church leaders to demonstrate what "respecting our competence" can really mean. See David Van Biema, "Rebels in the Pews," *Time,* June 17, 2002, 58.

47. Maher, 15.

48. Maher, 115.

49. Hamilton College/MTV/Zogby International Gay Issues Poll, Press Release, August 27, 2001. Posted to the GLB-NEWS List, August 28, 2001.

50. Maryclaire Dale, "Cops Sued for Threat to Out Gay Teenager," *Philadelphia Daily News,* November 5, 2001, posted to the GLB-NEWS list, November 5, 2001.

51. Information based on a press release posted to the GLB-PRESS list by the Lambda Legal Defense and Education Fund, February 27, 2002.

52. This kind of problem is not peculiar to the American context. Fenton Johnson's partner Larry died in a hospital in France, and Johnson was not allowed to be at his bedside. He watched Larry die from the hall outside his door. Johnson, *Keeping Faith,* 201.

53. Quoted in Kathleen Hughes and Joseph Favazza, eds., *A Reconciliation Sourcebook* (Chicago: Liturgy Training Publications, 1997), 104.

54. Quoted in H. Kathleen Hughes, "Walking on the Edge of Two Great Abysses: Theological Perspectives on Reconciliation," in Kennedy, ed. (1998), 103.

55. Ahmar Mustikhan, "Catholic Church Fires Gay Choir Leader," a summary of an AP story, posted to the Gay.com/PlanetOut.com Network, July 1, 2003; posted to the Dignity News Service, DignityNews@yahoogroups.com, July 10, 2003.

56. Nicole Winfield, "Vatican Reaffirms Need for Penance," AP News Story, May 2, 2002, posted to GLB-NEWS list, May 3, 2002.

57. Rodriguez, quoted in Paul Crowley, S.J., "An Ancient Catholic: An Interview with Richard Rodriguez," in Ferraro, ed., 264.

58. Johnson, *Keeping Faith,* 305.

59. Quoted in Maher, 6.

Appendix: the Gramick and Nugent Investigation

1. "Cardinal Hickey's Letter to the Congregation for the Institutes of Consecrated Life and Apostolic Societies [formerly the Congregation for Religious and Secular Institutes]," October 10, 1989.

2. "Preliminary Draft of Responses to Questions Posed by the Commission," Submitted to Maida Commission, July 26, 1994.

3. Ibid.

4. Ibid.

5. Ibid.

6. Neither are these opinions *not* offered as viable alternatives, in my personal experience of their workshops. I would characterize their approach as presenting a range of Catholic opinion on the subject, all of which come across as valid because the teachings are not infallibly declared and are thus open to development. Gramick and Nugent never say church teaching should change, but they do insist that it be open to new data.

7. This highlights another difficulty for the church hierarchy: their inability to deal adequately and respectfully with dissenting voices within their own ranks. The Vatican II ideal of collegiality among all bishops seemingly has been abandoned; instead, we have a situation in which the bishops who agree with Rome are favored and others are vilified. This is especially irritating in a case such as this where the majority of American bishops are generally supportive of or at least neutral toward Nugent and Gramick's ministry.

8. "Preliminary Responses to selected passages from *Building Bridges*," Submitted to the Maida Commission, July 26, 1994 (emphasis mine). I often find all of this talk from church teachers and ministers of "confusing the faithful" annoying. I do not think we are all so easily confused; in fact, most Catholics can read between the lines of church teaching and see political biases in operation.

9. Ibid. (emphasis mine).

10. Quoted in ibid. Gramick and Nugent defend this as an example of hyperbole.

11. Quoted in ibid. In the book, they support this statement by noting two important things: (1) How thriving Dignity had been allowed to become in the United States; and (2) The fact that the 1986 (and then the 1992) letters from the CDF were both promulgated in English and likely meant for the American church. Today's situation is different. While there are still tensions between the U.S. hierarchy and Rome, many more bishops are appointees of Pope John Paul II and are more likely to agree with Rome on issues such as homosexuality. Even so, when tensions do arise between the two, it is always framed as a difference between Roman *doctrine* and American *pastoral* practice.

12. "Response to the Report of the Findings of the Commission Studying the Writings and Ministry of Sister Jeannine Gramick, SSND, and Father Robert Nugent, SDS," January 12, 1995.

13. "Report of the Findings of the Commission Studying the Writings and Ministry of Sister Jeannine Gramick, SSND, and Father Robert Nugent, SDS," October 4, 1994. Nugent and Gramick do state in their response, "We have never claimed that a moral judgment on sexual behavior is 'incidental' or that it is not 'a crucial issue,' but we believe the Commission has overemphasized this question by making it, in effect, the *only* crucial issue."

14. Ibid.

15. Ibid.

16. Quoted in "Response to Additional Questions from the Congregation for the Institutes of Consecrated Life and Societies of Apostolic Life," October 22, 1996.

17. Ibid.

18. Gramick and Nugent were not informed of the transfer until December 1997, when their Superior Generals were notified at a meeting with Cardinal Ratzinger. The two year lapse allowed time for the CDF to conduct its own internal investigation.

19. In 1995, Gramick and Nugent published *Voices of Hope: A Collection of Positive Catholic Writings on Gay and Lesbian Issues* (New York: Center for Homophobia Education). The CDF cites this book and *Building Bridges* for their evidence.

20. "Erroneous and Dangerous Propositions in the Publications *Building Bridges* and *Voices of Hope* by Sister Jeannine Gramick, SSND, and Father Robert Nugent, SDS," October 24, 1997.

21. In my project, I attempt to articulate a more realistic version of gay and lesbian reality by discussing how diverse that reality can be. Church teaching may indeed reflect some lesbian and gay reality, but it does not reflect the whole of it, as church officials might like to believe.

22. "Erroneous and Dangerous Propositions ... "

23. See Nelson, "Sources for Body Theology." While this "quadrilateral" interpretation of authority has its roots in Protestant theology, many Catholic ethicists have embraced this formula since Vatican II. Church officials would not dispute this equation, but they would not rate these sources equally, nor would they suggest it is valid to reach different conclusions than are already in place in church teaching.

24. Quoted in "Erroneous and Dangerous Propositions ... "

25. The same argument about critical mass could be made with regard to the church's absolute ban on "artificial" birth control. The tendency of late has been to dismiss dissenting Catholics as being caught up in modern, secular culture — what John Paul calls the "culture of death." I am struck by how this denigrates the education and moral agency of individual Catholics, not to mention how cynical this attitude is toward the world. How different this is from the optimism expressed at Vatican II!

26. Gramick and Nugent, eds., *Voices of Hope*, 67 (emphasis mine).

27. "Erroneous and Dangerous Propositions ... "

28. For example, Nugent builds a strong distinction, rooted deeply in the history of moral theology, between objective immorality and subjective culpability, to argue that using terminology like "objective disorder" in a pastoral setting is problematic. "Response of Father Robert Nugent, SDS, to the Congregation for the Doctrine of the Faith regarding 'Erroneous and Dangerous Propositions in the Publications *Building Bridges* and *Voices of Hope* by Sister Jeannine Gramick, SSND, and Father Robert Nugent, SDS.'" February 6, 1998.

29. "Response to the Congregation for the Doctrine of the Faith," July 7, 1998. She also notes her desire that her "personal views on contentious issues remain as far as possible in the background." While much of her writing would indicate her personal advocacy for a change in the church's moral rhetoric on homosexuality, she is indeed never clear *exactly* where she herself stands on this issue, especially in her workshops. Perhaps the no-win situation with the CDF and subsequent changes she has made in terms of her congregational affiliation will allow her the freedom to more openly clarify her own views and personal motivations.

30. An example of his emendations is his changing the phrase "homosexual acts are always objectively evil" to "homosexual [genital] acts are always, objectively speaking, morally wrong." He does this, he says, to be sure his public statements embody his commitment to treat homosexuals and their families with

respect, compassion, and sensitivity. Such are the linguistic gymnastics required to try to reconcile the moral and pastoral rhetorics. "Nugent: Response to CDF Profession of Faith," January 25, 1999.

31. Lisa Sowle Cahill describes this move as an ominous shift in the Vatican's method of dealing with theologians and ministers: "Now, people are being silenced *not* for contradicting any doctrine, and not even for contradicting any 'noninfallible teaching,' but for staying within church teaching while not equally emphasizing or including other points." Lisa Sowle Cahill, "Silencing of Nugent, Gramick Sets a Novel Standard of Orthodoxy," *America* 181, no. 4 (August 14–21, 1999): 10.

32. Nugent has thus far complied with the order of silence. Gramick has defied the order and transferred to the Sisters of Loretto. She hopes to continue her full ministry to gay people with the support of this community. Mary Hunt reads the Vatican's move to "silence them further" as a tacit admission that "the Vatican has lost on the substantive issue of homosexuality and can now only 'win' some credibility through brute force . . . to compel a person's conscience, and in doing so to shore itself up." Mary E. Hunt, "Rome's Not-So-Veiled Power Play," *National Catholic Reporter*, June 30, 2000, 20.

Select Bibliography

Primary Sources (Autobiographical Acts)

Aelred, Father. "Without Shame." In *Homosexuality in the Priesthood and the Religious Life*, ed. Jeannine Gramick, 170–77. New York: Crossroad, 1989.

Amos, Brother. "Inheritance for the Disinherited." In *Homosexuality in the Priesthood and the Religious Life*, ed. Jeannine Gramick, 126–33. New York: Crossroad, 1989.

Arpin, Fr. Robert L. *Wonderfully, Fearfully Made: Letters on Living with Hope, Teaching Understanding, and Ministering with Love, from a Gay Catholic Priest with AIDS*. San Francisco: HarperSanFrancisco, 1993.

Bartosik, Matthew. "A Winter Break." *Equal Times* 7, no. 1 (Spring 2000): 7.

Binder, Wolfgang, and Helmbrecht Breinig, eds. *American Contradictions: Interviews with Nine American Writers*. Hanover, N.H.: Wesleyan University Press, 1995.

Bouldrey, Brian, ed. *Wrestling with the Angel: Faith and Religion in the Lives of Gay Men*. New York: Riverhead Books, 1995.

Calabrese, Fr. Raymond (pseud.). "One Gay Priest's Story." *U.S. Catholic* 68 (February 2003): 50.

Campo, Rafael. *The Desire to Heal: A Doctor's Education in Empathy, Identity, and Poetry*. New York: W. W. Norton, 1997.

———. *Diva*. Durham, N.C.: Duke University Press, 1999.

———. *The Other Man Was Me: A Voyage to the New World*. Houston: Arte Publico Press, 1994.

———. *What the Body Told*. Durham, N.C.: Duke University Press, 1996.

Cardarelli, Richard John. "Lord, Make Me an Instrument of Your Peace." In *Homosexuality in the Priesthood and the Religious Life*, ed. Jeannine Gramick, 151–59. New York: Crossroad, 1989.

Crowley, Paul. "An Ancient Catholic: An Interview with Richard Rodriguez." In *Catholic Lives, Contemporary America*, ed. Thomas J. Ferraro, 259–65. Durham, N.C.: Duke University Press, 1997.

Curzon, Daniel. "Why I Am an Ex-Catholic." In *ReCreations: Religion and Spirituality in the Lives of Queer People*, ed. Catherine Lake, 103–5. Toronto: Queer Press, 1999.

———. *The World Can Break Your Heart*. Stamford, Conn.: Knight's Press, 1984.

"Dan: 'HIV Doubled My Spirituality.'" Interview by David Shallenberger, *Reclaiming the Spirit: Gay Men and Lesbians Come to Terms with Religion*. New Brunswick, N.J.: Rutgers University Press, 1998.

DeCaro, Frank. *A Boy Named Phyllis: A Suburban Memoir*. New York: Viking, 1996.

Fellows, Will. *Farm Boys: Lives of Gay Men from the Rural Midwest*. Madison: University of Wisconsin Press, 1996, 1998.

Gambone, Philip. "Beyond Words." In *Boys Like Us: Gay Writers Tell Their Coming Out Stories*, ed. Patrick Merla, 98–114. New York: Avon Books, 1996.

———. "Learning and Unlearning and Learning Again the Language of *Signori*." In *Fuori: Essays by Italian/American Lesbians and Gays*, ed. Anthony Julian Tamburri, 60–80. West Lafayette, Ind.: Bordighera, 1996.

———. "Searching for Real Words," In *Wrestling with the Angel: Faith and Religion in the Lives of Gay Men*, ed. Brian Bouldrey, 221–42. New York: Riverhead Books, 1995.

———, ed. *Something Inside: Conversations with Gay Fiction Writers*. Madison: University of Wisconsin Press, 1999.

Glenn, William D. "As God Intended: Reflections on Being a Gay Student at a Jesuit High School." *America* 184, no. 17 (May 21, 2001): 26–29.

Gramick, Jeannine, ed. *Homosexuality in the Priesthood and the Religious Life*. New York: Crossroad, 1989.

Holleran Andrew. *The Beauty of Men*. New York: Plume, 1997.

———. "Memories of Heidelberg." In *Boys Like Us: Gay Writers Tell Their Coming Out Stories*, ed. Patrick Merla, 88–97. New York: Avon Books, 1996.

———. *Nights in Aruba*. New York: William Morrow, 1983.

———. "The Sense of Sin." In *Wrestling with the Angel: Faith and Religion in the Lives of Gay Men*, ed. Brian Bouldrey, 83–96. New York: Riverhead Books, 1995.

Holtz, Raymond C. *Listen to the Stories: Gay and Lesbian Catholics Talk about Their Lives and the Church*. New York: Garland Publishing, 1991.

Horrigan, Patrick E. *Widescreen Dreams: Growing Up Gay at the Movies*. Madison: University of Wisconsin Press, 1999.

Johnson, Fenton. *Geography of the Heart: A Memoir*. New York: Scribner, 1996.

———. "God, Gays, and the Geography of Desire." In *Wrestling with the Angel: Faith and Religion in the Lives of Gay Men*, ed. Brian Bouldrey, 243–58. New York: Riverhead Books, 1995.

———. *Keeping Faith: A Skeptic's Journey*. Boston: Houghton Mifflin, 2003.

Jonathan, Brother. "You Are My People." In *Homosexuality in the Priesthood and the Religious Life*, ed. Jeannine Gramick, 160–69. New York: Crossroad, 1989.

Kelty, Matthew. "The Land I Love In." In *Homosexuality in the Priesthood and the Religious Life*, ed. Jeannine Gramick, 145–50. New York: Crossroad, 1989.

Killian, Kevin. "Chain of Fools." In *Wrestling with the Angel: Faith and Religion in the Lives of Gay Men*, ed. Brian Bouldrey, 117–29. New York: Riverhead Books, 1995.

Kopay, David, and Perry Dean Young. *The David Kopay Story: An Extraordinary Self-revelation*. New York: Donald I. Fine, 1988.

Kramer, Joseph. "Body and Soul." Interview by Mark Thompson, *Gay Soul: Finding the Heart of Gay Spirit and Nature with Sixteen Writers, Healers, Teachers, and Visionaries*. San Francisco: HarperSanFrancisco, 1994: 168–80.

Krask, Peter M. "The Way the Stars Come Home." In *Wrestling with the Angel: Faith and Religion in the Lives of Gay Men*, ed. Brian Bouldrey, 147–70. New York: Riverhead Books, 1995.

Lake, Catherine, ed. *ReCreations: Religion and Spirituality in the Lives of Queer People*. Toronto: Queer Press, 1999.

"Mark: A Gay Spiritual Ancestry." Interview by David Shallenberger, *Reclaiming the Spirit: Gay Men and Lesbians Come to Terms with Religion*. New Brunswick, N.J.: Rutgers University Press, 1998.

McCauley, Stephen. "Let's Say." In *Boys Like Us: Gay Writers Tell Their Coming Out Stories*, ed. Patrick Merla, 186–92. New York: Avon Books, 1996.

McClatchy, J. D. "My Fountain Pen." In *Boys Like Us: Gay Writers Tell Their Coming Out Stories*, ed. Patrick Merla, 193–203. New York: Avon Books, 1996.

McNaught, Brian. *A Disturbed Peace: Selected Writings of an Irish Catholic Homosexual.* Washington, D.C.: Dignity, 1981.

———. *On Being Gay: Thoughts on Family, Faith, and Love.* New York: St. Martin's, 1988.

McNeill, John J. "As My Body Grows Older, My Spirit Becomes Younger." *National Catholic Reporter*, April 14, 2000, 22–23.

———. *Both Feet Firmly Planted in Midair: My Spiritual Journey.* Louisville: Westminster John Knox, 1998.

McNichols, William Hart. "A Priest Forever." In *Homosexuality in the Priesthood and the Religious Life*, ed. Jeannine Gramick, 118–25. New York: Crossroad, 1989.

Mecca, Tommi Avicolli. "Memoirs of a South Philly Sissy." In *Fuori: Essays by Italian/American Lesbians and Gays*, ed. Anthony Julian Tamburri, 13–28. West Lafayette, Ind.: Bordighera, 1996.

Mecca, Tommi Avicolli, Giovanna (Janet) Capone, and Denise Nico Leto, eds. *Hey Paesan! Writings by Lesbians and Gay Men of Italian Descent.* Oakland, Calif.: Three Guineas Press, 1999.

Merla, Patrick, ed. *Boys Like Us: Gay Writers Tell Their Coming Out Stories.* New York: Avon Books, 1996.

Merrett, Jim. "My First Homosexual: Confessions of a Lapsed Catholic." *Advocate*, May 9, 1989, 48–49.

Minervini, Mark P. "Finding My Faith." *International Journal of Sexuality and Gender Studies* 5, no. 3 (July 2000): 279–82.

Morrison, James. *Broken Fever: Reflections of Gay Boyhood.* New York: St. Martin's, 2001.

———. "Saved." In *Wrestling with the Angel: Faith and Religion in the Lives of Gay Men*, ed. Brian Bouldrey, 59–82. New York: Riverhead Books, 1995.

Nixon, Rob. "Avondale: A Memoir of Identity." In *Hey Paesan! Writings by Lesbians and Gay Men of Italian Descent*, eds. Tommi Avicolli Mecca, Giovanna (Janet) Capone, and Denise Nico Leto. Oakland, Calif.: Three Guineas Press, 1999.

Pallone, Dave, with Alan Steinberg. *Behind the Mask: My Double Life in Baseball.* New York: Viking, 1990.

Paul, Father. "We Shall Not Cease from Exploration." In *Homosexuality in the Priesthood and the Religious Life*, ed. Jeannine Gramick, 134–44. New York: Crossroad, 1989.

Plante, David. *The Catholic.* New York: Atheneum, 1986.

———. "Images of the Body from My Religion." In *Wrestling with the Angel: Faith and Religion in the Lives of Gay Men*, ed. Brian Bouldrey, 171–74. New York: Riverhead Books, 1995.

Roberts, Rev. R. (pseud.). "The Fears of a Gay Priest." In *Gay Priests*, ed. James G. Wolf, 141–60. San Francisco: Harper & Row, 1989.

Rodriguez, Richard. *Brown: The Last Discovery of America.* New York: Viking, 2002.

———. *Days of Obligation: An Argument with My Mexican Father.* New York: Penguin, 1992.

———. *Hunger of Memory: The Education of Richard Rodriguez.* New York: Bantam, 1982.

———. "Irish Catholic." In *Political Passages: Journeys of Change through Two Decades 1968–1988,* ed. John H. Bunzel, 326–47. New York: Free Press, 1988.

Schimmel, David. "A Spiritual Self-Portrait: Using My Homosexuality to Develop an Honest Relationship with God." *National Catholic Reporter,* December 3, 1999, 34–36.

Shallenberger, David. *Reclaiming the Spirit: Gay Men and Lesbians Come to Terms with Religion.* New Brunswick, N.J.: Rutgers University Press, 1998.

Soucy, Jon. "Speaking the Unspeakable." *The Hoya,* March 4, 2003, online at www.thehoya.com.

Stahel, Thomas H. " 'I'm Here': An Interview With Andrew Sullivan." *America* 168, no. 116 (May 8, 1993): 5–11.

Stoltz, Eric. "Notes From a Community — Catholic and Gay." *America* 178, no. 10 (March 28, 1998): 10–13.

Sullivan, Andrew. "Alone Again, Naturally." *The New Republic* 211, no. 22 (November 28, 1994): 47, 50, 52, 54–55.

———. *Love Undetectable: Notes on Friendship, Sex, and Survival.* New York: Alfred A. Knopf, 1998.

———. "Virtually Normal." In *Catholic Lives, Contemporary America,* ed. Thomas J. Ferraro, 171–86. Durham, N.C.: Duke University Press, 1997.

Tamburri, Anthony Julian ed. *Fuori: Essays by Italian/American Lesbians and Gays.* West Lafayette, Ind.: Bordighera, 1996.

Thompson, Mark. *Gay Soul: Finding the Heart of Gay Spirit and Nature with Sixteen Writers, Healers, Teachers, and Visionaries.* San Francisco: Harper-SanFrancisco, 1994.

Thompson, Rev. T. (pseud.). "A Christian Spirituality." In *Gay Priests,* ed. James G. Wolf, 119–40. San Francisco: Harper & Row, 1989.

Trepania, Scott. "Prayer Life Provides a Focus as I cope with Dropping T-Cell Counts." *National Catholic Reporter,* September 2, 1994, 7–8.

Tucker, Scott. "Our Queer World: True Confessions." *The Humanist* 53, no. 5 (September–October, 1993): 45–46.

Utter, Brian. "Bisexuality and the Spiritual Continuum," In *ReCreations: Religion and Spirituality in the Lives of Queer People,* ed. Catherine Lake, 143–46. Toronto: Queer Press, 1999.

Wolf, James, ed. *Gay Priests.* San Francisco: Harper & Row, 1989.

Zuniga, José. *Soldier of the Year: The Story of a Gay American Patriot.* New York: Pocket Books, 1994.

Secondary Sources

Adam, Barry D. "Love and Sex in Constructing Identity Among Men Who Have Sex with Men." *International Journal of Sexuality and Gender Studies* 5, no. 4 (October 2000): 325–39.

Abelove, Henry, Michele Aina Barale, and David M. Halperin, eds. *The Lesbian and Gay Studies Reader.* New York: Routledge, 1993.

Alexander, Jonathan. "Beyond Identity: Queer Values and Community," *Journal of Gay, Lesbian, and Bisexual Identity* 4, no. 4 (October 1999): 293–314.

Alexander, Marilyn Bennett, and James Preston. *We Were Baptized Too: Claiming God's Grace for Lesbians and Gays.* Louisville: Westminster John Knox, 1996.

Almaguer, Tomas. "Chicano Men: A Cartography of Homosexual Identity and Behavior." In *The Lesbian and Gay Studies Reader,* ed. Henry Abelove, Michele Aina Barale, and David M. Halperin, 255–73. New York: Routledge, 1993.

Alpert, Rebecca. *Like Bread on the Seder Plate: Jewish Lesbians and the Transformation of Tradition.* New York: Columbia University Press, 1997.

Avella, Steven M., and Elizabeth McKeown, eds. *Public Voices: Catholics in the American Context.* Maryknoll, N.Y.: Orbis, 1999.

Bagemihl, Bruce. *Biological Exuberance: Animal Homosexuality and Natural Diversity.* New York: St. Martin's, 1999.

Balka, Christie, and Andy Rose, eds. *Twice Blessed: On Being Lesbian or Gay and Jewish.* Boston: Beacon, 1989.

Barbour, John D. *Versions of Deconversion: Autobiography and the Loss of Faith.* Charlottesville: The University Press of Virginia, 1994.

Baruth, Philip E. "Consensual Autobiography: Narrating 'Personal Sexual History' from Boswell's *London Journal* to AIDS Pamphlet Literature." In *Getting a Life: Everyday Uses of Autobiography,* ed. Sidonie Smith and Julia Watson, 177–97. Minneapolis: University of Minnesota Press, 1996.

Bawer, Bruce. *A Place at the Table: The Gay Individual in American Society.* New York: Poseidon, 1993.

Beaudoin, Tom. "Our Catholic Watergate." *America* 186, no. 19 (June 3–10, 2002): 18–20.

Billitteri, Thomas J. "Gay and Lesbian Catholics Beg to Differ." *U.S. Catholic* 62, no. 11 (November 1997): 10–15.

Bjorklund, Diane. *Interpreting the Self: Two Hundred Years of American Autobiography.* Chicago: University of Chicago Press, 1998.

Blake, Richard. *Afterimage: The Indelible Catholic Imagination of Six American Filmmakers.* Chicago: Loyola Press, 2000.

Blasius, Mark. *Gay and Lesbian Politics: Sexuality and the Emergence of a New Ethic.* Philadelphia: Temple University Press, 1994.

Boswell, John. *Christianity, Social Tolerance, and Homosexuality: Gay People in Western Europe from the Beginning of the Christian Era to the Fourteenth Century.* Chicago: University of Chicago Press, 1980.

———. *Same-Sex Unions in Premodern Europe.* New York: Villard Books, 1994.

Boyd, Stephen B., W. Merle Longwood, and Mark W. Muesse, eds. *Redeeming Men: Religion and Masculinities.* Louisville: Westminster John Knox, 1996.

Brawley, Robert L. *Biblical Ethics and Homosexuality: Listening to Scripture.* Louisville: Westminster John Knox, 1996.

Bredbeck, Gregory W. "Andrew Holleran (1943(?)–)." In *Contemporary Gay American Novelists: A Bio-Bibliographical Critical Sourcebook,* ed. Emmanuel S. Nelson, 197–204. Westport, Conn.: Greenwood Press, 1993.

Bregman, Lucy, and Sara Thiermann. *First Person Mortal: Personal Narratives of Illness, Dying and Grief.* New York: Paragon, 1995.

Brod, Harry, and Michael Kaufman, eds. *Theorizing Masculinities.* Thousand Oaks, Calif.: SAGE, 1994.

Bronski, Michael. *The Pleasure Principle: Sex, Backlash, and the Struggle for Gay Freedom.* New York: St. Martin's, 1998.

Brooten, Bernadette J. *Love Between Women: Early Christian Responses to Female Homoeroticism.* Chicago: University of Chicago Press, 1996.

Burns, Gene. *The Frontiers of Catholicism: The Politics of Ideology in a Liberal World.* Berkeley: University of California Press, 1992.

Butler, Anne M., Michael E. Engh, and Thomas W. Spalding, eds. *The Frontiers and Catholic Identities.* Maryknoll, N.Y.: Orbis, 1999.

Butler, Judith. *Gender Trouble: Feminism and the Subversion of Identity.* New York: Routledge, 1991.

Byne, William. "The Biological Evidence Challenged." *Scientific American* 270 (May 1994): 50–55.

Cahill, Lisa Sowle. *Sex, Gender and Christian Ethics.* Cambridge, Mass.: Cambridge University Press, 1996.

———. "Silencing of Nugent, Gramick Sets a Novel Standard of Orthodoxy." *America* 181, no. 4 (August 14–21, 1999): 6–10.

Catechism of the Catholic Church. Ligouri, Mo.: Ligouri Publications, 1994.

Chauncey, George. *Gay New York: Gender, Urban Culture, and the Making of the Gay Male World, 1890–1940.* New York: Basic Books, 1994.

Chopp, Rebecca S., and Sheila Greeve Davaney, eds. *Horizons in Feminist Theology: Identity, Tradition, and Norms.* Minneapolis: Fortress, 1997.

Clarke, Kevin. "Whitewash or Renewal?" *U.S. Catholic* 68, no. 6 (June 2003): 12–17.

Comstock, Gary David. *Gay Theology without Apology.* Cleveland: Pilgrim, 1993.

———. *Unrepentant, Self-Affirming, Practicing: Lesbian/Bisexual/Gay People within Organized Religion.* New York: Continuum, 1996.

Comstock, Gary David, and Susan E. Henking, eds. *Que(e)rying Religion: A Critical Anthology.* New York: Continuum, 1997.

Congregation for the Doctrine of the Faith. "Letter to the Bishops of the Catholic Church on the Pastoral Care of Homosexual Persons," October 31, 1986. In *The Vatican and Homosexuality,* ed. Jeannine Gramick and Pat Furey, 1–10. New York: Crossroad, 1988.

———. "Some Considerations Concerning the Response to Legislative Proposals on the Non-Discrimination of Homosexual Persons," July 23, 1992 (personal copy).

Connell, R. W. *Masculinities.* Berkeley: University of California Press, 1995.

Countryman, L. William. *Dirt, Greed and Sex: Sexual Ethics in the New Testament and Their Implications for Today.* Philadelphia: Fortress, 1988.

Cott, Nancy. *Public Vows: A History of Marriage and the Nation.* Cambridge, Mass.: Harvard University Press, 2000.

Cozzens, Donald B. *The Changing Face of the Priesthood: A Reflection on the Priest's Crisis of Soul.* Collegeville, Minn.: Liturgical Press, 2000.

Cunningham, Lawrence S. *The Catholic Experience.* New York: Crossroad, 1985.

Curran, Charles. "Is There Any Good News in the Recent Documents from the Vatican about Homosexuality?" In *Voices of Hope: A Collection of Positive Writings on Gay and Lesbian Issues,* ed. Jeannine Gramick and Robert Nugent, 159–72. New York: Center for Homophobia Education, 1995.

———. "Sexual Orientation and Human Rights in American Religious Discourse: A Roman Catholic Perspective," In *Sexual Orientation and Human Rights in American Religious Discourse,* ed. Saul Olyan and Martha Nussbaum. New York: Oxford University Press, 1998.

Curran, Charles E., Margaret A. Farley, and Richard A. McCormick, eds. *Feminist Ethics and the Catholic Moral Tradition.* New York: Paulist, 1996.

Daly, Lois K., ed. *Feminist Theological Ethics: A Reader.* Louisville: Westminster John Knox, 1994.

Dillon, Michele. *Catholic Identity: Balancing Reason, Faith, and Power.* Cambridge, Mass.: Cambridge University Press, 1999.

Dolan, Jay P. *The American Catholic Experience: A History from Colonial Times to the Present.* Notre Dame, Ind.: University of Notre Dame Press, 1992.

Donnelly, Doris. "Reconciliation: The Continuing Challenge." In *Reconciliation: The Continuing Agenda,* ed. Robert J. Kennedy. Collegeville, Minn.: Liturgical Press, 1987.

Donovan, Daniel. *Distinctively Catholic: An Exploration of Catholic Identity.* New York: Paulist, 1997.

Doty, Mark. *Heaven's Coast.* New York: Harper Perennial, 1997.

Douglas, Kelly Brown. *Sexuality and the Black Church: A Womanist Perspective.* Maryknoll, N.Y.: Orbis, 1999.

Dreger, Alice. *Hermaphrodites and the Medical Intervention of Sex.* Cambridge, Mass.: Harvard University Press, 1998.

Duberman, Martin B., Martha Vicinus, and George Chauncey Jr., eds. *Hidden From History: Reclaiming the Gay and Lesbian Past.* New York: New American Library, 1989.

Dukes, Thomas. "David Plante (1940–)." In *Contemporary Gay American Novelists: A Bio-Bibliographical Critical Sourcebook,* ed. Emmanuel S. Nelson, 309–15. Westport, Conn.: Greenwood Press, 1993.

Eakin, Paul John. *Fictions in Autobiography: Studies in the Art of Self-Invention.* Princeton: Princeton University Press, 1985.

———, ed. *American Autobiography: Retrospect and Prospect.* Madison: University of Wisconsin Press, 1991.

Eilberg-Schwartz, Howard. *God's Phallus and Other Problems for Men and Monotheism.* Boston: Beacon, 1994.

Elbaz, Robert. *The Changing Nature of the Self: A Critical Study of the Autobiographic Discourse.* London: Croom Helm, 1988.

Ellison, Marvin M. *Erotic Justice: A Liberating Ethic of Sexuality.* Louisville: Westminster John Knox, 1996.

Ellwood, Robert S. *The Sixties Spiritual Awakening.* New Brunswick, N.J.: Rutgers University Press, 1994.

Erikson, Erik. *Life History and the Historical Moment.* New York: W. W. Norton, 1966.

Eugene, Toinette M. "Reconciliation in the Pastoral Context of Today's Church and World: Does Reconciliation Have a Future?" In *Reconciling Embrace: Foundations for the Future of Sacramental Reconciliation,* ed. Robert J. Kennedy, 1–14. Chicago: Liturgy Training Publications, 1998.

Faludi, Susan. *Stiffed: The Betrayal of the American Man.* New York: William Morrow, 1999.

Fausto-Sterling, Anne. *Myths of Gender: Biological Theories about Men and Women* New York: Basic Books, 1985.

———. *Sexing the Body: Gender Politics and the Construction of Sexuality.* New York: Basic Books, 2000.

Farley, Margaret. "A Feminist Version of Respect for Persons." In *Feminist Ethics and the Catholic Moral Tradition,* ed. Charles E. Curran, Margaret A. Farley, and Richard A. McCormick, 164–83. New York: Paulist, 1996.

Fausto-Sterling, Anne. "The Five Sexes." *The Sciences* (March–April 1993): 20–25.

———. "The Five Sexes, Revisited." *The Sciences* (July–August 2000): 18–23.

Ferraro, Thomas J., ed. *Catholic Lives, Contemporary America.* Durham, N.C.: Duke University Press, 1997.

Fiedler, Maureen, and Linda Rabben, eds. *Rome Has Spoken: A Guide to Forgotten Papal Statements and How They Have Changed Through the Centuries.* New York: Crossroad, 1998.

Fisher, James Terence. *The Catholic Counterculture in America, 1933–1962.* Chapel Hill: University of North Carolina Press, 1989.

———. *Communion of Immigrants: A History of Catholics in America.* New York: Oxford University Press, 2000.

Flannery, Austin P., ed. *The Documents of Vatican II.* New York: Pillar Books, 1975.

Ford, Michael. *Wounded Prophet: A Portrait of Henri J. M. Nouwen.* New York: Doubleday, 1999.

Foucault, Michel. *Ethics: Subjectivity and Truth,* ed. P. Rabinow. New York: The New Press, 1997.

———. *The History of Sexuality, Volume 1: An Introduction.* Translated by Robert Hurley. New York: Vintage, 1990; trans., 1978; Fr., 1976.

Froehle, Bryan T., and Mary L. Gautier, *Catholicism USA: A Portrait of the Catholic Church in the United States.* Maryknoll, N.Y.: Orbis, 2000.

Frontain, Raymond-Jean. "A Professional Queer Remembers: Bibliography, Narrative, and the Saving Power of Memory." In *A Sea of Stories: The Shaping Power of Narrative in Gay and Lesbian Cultures,* ed. Sonya L. Jones, 217–38. New York: Harrington Park Press, 2000.

Fulkerson, Mary McClintock. "Gender — Being It or Doing It? The Church, Homosexuality, and the Politics of Identity." In *Que(e)rying Religion: A Critical Anthology,* ed. Gary David Comstock and Susan E. Henking, 188–201. New York: Continuum, 1997.

Fuller, Jon. "On 'Straightening Out' Catholic Seminaries." *America* 187, no. 20 (December 16, 2002): 7–9.

Gagnon, Robert. *The Bible and Homosexual Practice: Texts and Hermeneutics.* Nashville: Abingdon, 2001.

———. "Gays and the Bible: A Response to Walter Wink." *Christian Century* 119 (August 14–27, 2002): 40–43.

Gettys, John. "Daniel Curzon (1938–)." In *Contemporary Gay American Novelists: A Bio-Bibliographical Critical Sourcebook,* ed. Emmanuel S. Nelson, 89–95. Westport, Conn.: Greenwood Press, 1993.

Gill, James J. "Seminaries Await Vatican Visitation." *America* 187, no. 2 (July 15–22, 2002): 10–13.

Gilson, Anne Bathurst. *Eros Breaking Free: Interpreting Sexual Theo-Ethics.* Cleveland: Pilgrim, 1995.

Goffman, Erving. *Stigma: Notes on the Management of Spoiled Identity.* New York: Simon & Schuster, 1963.

Goss, Robert. *Jesus Acted Up: A Gay and Lesbian Manifesto.* San Francisco: HarperSanFrancisco, 1993.

Gottschall, Marilyn. "The Ethical Implications of the Deconstruction of Gender." *Journal of the American Academy of Religion* 70, no. 2 (June 2002): 279–99.

Gramick, Jeannine, and Pat Furey, eds. *The Vatican and Homosexuality.* New York: Crossroad, 1988.

Gramick, Jeannine, and Robert Nugent, eds. *Voices of Hope: A Collection of Positive Writings on Gay and Lesbian Issues.* New York: Center for Homophobia Education, 1995.

Greeley, Andrew. *The Catholic Imagination.* Berkeley: University of California Press, 2000.

Grippo, Dan. "Why Lesbian and Gay Catholics Stay Catholic." *U.S. Catholic* 55, no. 9 (September 1990): 18–25.

Gudorf, Christine E. *Body, Sex, and Pleasure: Reconstructing Christian Sexual Ethics.* Cleveland: Pilgrim, 1994.

———. "The Erosion of Sexual Dimorphism: Challenges to Religion and Religious Ethics." *Journal of the American Academy of Religion* 69, no. 4 (December 2001): 863–91.

Guido, Joseph J. "The Importance of Perspective: Understanding the Sexual Abuse of Children by Priests." *America* 186, no. 11 (April 1, 2002): 21–23.

Guindon, Andre. "Homosexual Acts or Gay Speech?" In *The Vatican and Homosexuality,* ed. Jeannine Gramick and Pat Furey, 208–15. New York: Crossroad, 1988.

Gusdorf, Georges. "Conditions and Limits of Autobiography." Translated by James Olney. In *Autobiography: Essays Theoretical and Critical,* ed. James Olney, 28–48. Princeton: Princeton University Press, 1980.

Guttman, Matthew C. *The Meanings of Macho: Being a Man in Mexico City.* Berkeley: University of California Press, 1996.

Halsey, William M. *The Survival of American Innocence: Catholicism in an Era of Disillusionment, 1920–1940.* Notre Dame, Ind.: University of Notre Dame Press, 1980.

Hanigan, James P. *Homosexuality: The Test Case for Christian Ethics.* New York: Paulist, 1988.

———. "Sexual Orientation and Human Rights: A Roman Catholic View." In *Sexual Orientation and Human Rights in American Religious Discourse,* ed. Saul Olyan and Martha Nussbaum. New York: Oxford University Press, 1998.

Hansen, Ron. "Hotly in Pursuit of the Real: The Role of the Catholic Writer." *America* 185, no. 15 (November 12, 2001): 6–10.

Hardin, Michael. "Altering Masculinities: The Spanish Conquest and the Evolution of the Latin American Machismo." *International Journal of Sexuality and Gender Studies* 7, no. 1 (January 2002): 1–22.

Hartman, Keith. *Congregations in Conflict: The Battle over Homosexuality.* New Brunswick, N.J.: Rutgers University Press, 1996.

Haughton, Rosemary. *The Catholic Thing.* Springfield, Ill.: Templegate, 1979.

Hausman, Bernice. *Changing Sex: Transexualism, Technology, and the Idea of Gender.* Durham, N.C.: Duke University Press, 1998.

Helminiak, Daniel A. *What the Bible Really Says about Homosexuality.* San Francisco: Alamo Square, 1994.

Henking, Susan. "The Personal Is the Theological: Autobiographical Acts in Contemporary Feminist Theology." *Journal of the American Academy of Religion* 59, no. 3 (Fall 1991): 511–26.

Herman, Didi. *The Antigay Agenda: Orthodox Vision and the Christian Right.* Chicago: University of Chicago Press, 1997.

Heyward, Carter. *Touching Our Strength: The Erotic as Power and the Love of God.* San Francisco: Harper & Row, 1989.

Holland, Walter. "In the Body's Ghetto." In *A Sea of Stories: The Shaping Power of Narrative in Gay and Lesbian Cultures,* ed. Sonya L. Jones, 109–38. New York: Harrington Park Press, 2000.

Hughes, Kathleen. "Reconciliation: Cultural and Christian Perspectives." In *Reconciliation: The Continuing Agenda*, ed. Robert J. Kennedy. Collegeville, Minn.: Liturgical Press, 1987.

———. "Walking on the Edge of Two Great Abysses: Theological Perspectives on Reconciliation." In *Reconciling Embrace: Foundations for the Future of Sacramental Reconciliation*, ed. Robert J. Kennedy, 95–107. Chicago: Liturgy Training Publications, 1998.

Hughes, Kathleen, and Joseph Favazza, eds. *A Reconciliation Sourcebook*. Chicago: Liturgy Training Publications, 1997.

Hunt, Mary. *Fierce Tenderness: A Feminist Theology of Friendship*. New York: Crossroad, 1991.

Jakobsen, Janet R., and Ann Pellegrini. *Love the Sin: Sexual Regulation and the Limits of Religious Tolerance*. New York: New York University Press, 2003.

Jagose, Annamarie. *Queer Theory: An Introduction*. New York: New York University Press, 1996.

Jones, Sonya L., ed. *A Sea of Stories: The Shaping Power of Narrative in Gay and Lesbian Cultures*. New York: Harrington Park Press, 2000.

Jordan, Mark D. *The Ethics of Sex*. Oxford: Blackwell, 2002.

———. *The Invention of Sodomy in Christian Theology*. Chicago: University of Chicago Press, 1997.

———. *The Silence of Sodom: Homosexuality in Modern Catholicism*. Chicago: University of Chicago Press, 2000.

———. *Telling Truths in Church: Scandal, Flesh, and Christian Speech*. Boston: Beacon, 2003.

Jung, Patricia Beattie, and Ralph F. Smith. *Heterosexism: An Ethical Challenge*. Albany: SUNY, 1993.

Jung, Patricia Beattie, with Joseph Andrew Coray, eds. *Sexual Diversity and Catholicism: Toward the Development of Moral Theology*. Collegeville, Minn.: Liturgical Press, 2001.

Kane, Paula M. *Separatism and Subculture: Boston Catholicism, 1900–1920*. Chapel Hill: University of North Carolina Press, 1994.

Kane, Paula, James Kenneally, and Karen Kennelly, eds. *Gender Identities in American Catholicism*. Maryknoll, N.Y.: Orbis, 2001.

Katz, Jonathan Ned. *The Invention of Heterosexuality*. New York: Dutton Books, 1995.

———. *Sex Between Men Before Homosexuality*. Chicago: University of Chicago Press, 2001.

Kennedy, Eugene. "Ministry, Homosexuality, and Psychological Wholeness." Plenary address made to the New Ways Ministry Symposium, "Out of Silence God Has Called Us: Lesbian/Gay Issues and the Vatican II Church," Louisville, Ky., March 8–10, 2002. Audio Recording #02094-0020, Chesapeake Audio/Video Communications, Inc., Elkridge, Md.

———. *The Unhealed Wound: The Church and Human Sexuality*. New York: St. Martin's Griffin, 2001.

Kennedy, Robert J., ed. *Reconciliation: The Continuing Agenda*. Collegeville, Minn.: Liturgical Press, 1987.

———, ed. *Reconciling Embrace: Foundations for the Future of Sacramental Reconciliation*. Chicago: Liturgy Training Publications, 1998.

Kennelly, Karen, ed. *American Catholic Women: A Historical Exploration*. New York: Macmillan Publishing, 1989.

Kessler, Suzanne. *Lessons from the Intersexed.* New Brunswick, N.J.: Rutgers University Press, 1998.

Kimmel, Michael. *Manhood in America: A Cultural History.* New York: Free Press, 1996.

Kirsch, Max. *Queer Theory and Social Change.* London: Routledge, 2000.

Krondorfer, Bjorn. "The Confines of Male Confessions: On Religion, Bodies, and Mirrors." In *Men's Bodies, Men's Gods: Male Identities in a (Post-) Christian Culture,* 205–34. New York: New York University Press, 1996.

Krondorfer, Bjorn, ed. *Men's Bodies, Men's Gods: Male Identities in a (Post-) Christian Culture.* New York: New York University Press, 1996.

LaCugna, Catherine Mowry, ed. *Freeing Theology: The Essentials of Theology in Feminist Perspective.* San Francisco: HarperSanFrancisco, 1993.

Laqueur, Thomas. *Making Sex: Body and Gender from the Greeks to Freud.* Cambridge, Mass.: Harvard University Press, 1990.

LeVay, Simon, and Dean H. Hamer. "Evidence for a Biological Influence in Male Homosexuality." *Scientific American* 270 (May 1994): 44–49.

Levine, Judith. *Harmful to Minors: The Perils of Protecting Children from Sex.* Minneapolis: University of Minnesota Press, 2002.

Long, Ronald E. "The Sacrality of Male Beauty and Homosex: A Neglected Factor in the Understanding of Contemporary Gay Reality." In *Que(e)rying Religion: A Critical Anthology,* ed. Gary David Comstock and Susan E. Henking, 266–81. New York: Continuum, 1997.

Lorde, Audre. *Sister Outsider: Essays and Speeches by Audre Lorde.* Freedom, Calif.: Crossing Press, 1984.

Maher, Michael. *Being Gay and Lesbian in a Catholic High School: Beyond the Uniform.* New York: Harrington Park Press, 2001.

Martin, Biddy. "Lesbian Identity and Autobiographical Difference[s]." In *The Lesbian and Gay Studies Reader,* ed. Henry Abelove, Michele Aina Barale, and David M. Halperin, 274–93. New York: Routledge, 1993.

Martin, James. "The Church and the Homosexual Priest: Facing the Challenges and Accepting the Gifts Offered by Homosexual Priests in the Catholic Church." *America* 183, no. 14 (November 4, 2000): 11–15.

Massa, Mark S. *Catholics and American Culture: Fulton Sheen, Dorothy Day, and the Notre Dame Football Team.* New York: Crossroad, 1999.

McBrien, Richard, ed. *The HarperCollins Encyclopedia of Catholicism.* San Francisco: HarperSanFrancisco, 1995.

McGreevy, John T. *Catholicism and American Freedom: A History.* New York: W. W. Norton, 2003.

——. *Parish Boundaries: The Catholic Encounter with Race in the Twentieth-Century Urban North.* Chicago: University of Chicago Press, 1996.

McKenzie, Donna M. "Is There a Moral Theologian in the House?" *Religion in the News* 5, no. 2 (Summer 2002): 18–19.

McNeill, John. *The Church and the Homosexual.* Kansas City: Andrews & McMeel, 1976; 4th edition, Boston: Beacon, 1993.

——. *Freedom, Glorious Freedom: The Spiritual Journey to the Fullness of Life for Gays, Lesbians, and Everybody Else.* Boston: Beacon, 1995.

——. *Taking A Chance on God: Liberating Theology for Gays, Lesbians, and Their Lovers, Families, and Friends.* Boston: Beacon, 1988.

McRuer, Robert. "Boys' Own Stories and New Spellings of My Name: Coming Out and Other Myths of Queer Positionality." In *Genders 20: Eroticism and*

Containment, ed. Carol Siegel and Ann Kibbey, 260–84. New York: New York University Press, 1994.

Miller, Patricia. "Chasing Conservative Catholics." *Conscience* 22, no. 2 (Summer 2001): 11–14.

Moore, Gareth. *The Body in Context: Sex and Catholicism.* London: SCM, 1992.

———. *A Question of Truth: Christianity and Homosexuality.* London: Continuum, 2003.

Moore, R. Laurence. *Religious Outsiders and the Making of Americans.* New York: Oxford University Press, 1986.

Murphy, Timothy, ed. *Gay Ethics: Controversies in Outing, Civil Rights, and Sexual Science.* New York: Harrington Park Press, 1994.

Nelson, James B. *Embodiment: An Approach to Sexuality and Christian Theology.* Minneapolis: Augsburg, 1978.

———. "Sources for Body Theology," In *Sexuality and the Sacred: Sources for Theological Reflection,* ed. James B. Nelson and Sandra P. Longfellow, 374–86. Louisville: Westminster John Knox, 1994.

Nelson, James B., and Sandra P. Longfellow. *Sexuality and the Sacred: Sources for Theological Reflection.* Louisville: Westminster John Knox, 1994.

Newman, Bishop William. "Baltimore Bishop Asks Forgiveness of Gays/Lesbians." *Bondings: A Publication of New Ways Ministry* (Spring 2001): 1.

Nissinen, Marti. *Homoeroticism in the Biblical World: A Historical Perspective.* Translated by Kirsi Stjerna. Minneapolis: Fortress Press, 1998.

Noonan, John T., Jr. "On the Development of Doctrine." *America* 180, no. 11 (April 3, 1999): 6–8.

Nugent, Robert, ed. *A Challenge to Love: Gay and Lesbian Catholics in the Church.* New York: Crossroad, 1983.

Nugent, Robert, and Jeannine Gramick. *Building Bridges: Gay and Lesbian Reality and the Catholic Church.* Mystic, Conn.: Twenty-Third Publications, 1992.

Nussbaum, Emily. "A Question of Gender." *Discover* 21, no. 1 (January 2000): 92–99.

Occhiogrosso, Peter, ed. *Once a Catholic: Prominent Catholics and Ex-Catholics Discuss the Influence of the Church on Their Lives and Work.* Boston: Houghton Mifflin, 1987.

Olney, James. "Autobiography and the Cultural Moment." In *Autobiography: Essays Theoretical and Critical,* 3–27. Princeton: Princeton University Press, 1980.

———. *Memory and Narrative: The Weave of Life-Writing.* Chicago: University of Chicago Press, 1998.

———. *Metaphors of Self: The Meaning of Autobiography.* Princeton: Princeton University Press, 1972.

———, ed. *Autobiography: Essays Theoretical and Critical.* Princeton: Princeton University Press, 1980.

Olshen, Barry N. "Subject, Persona, and Self in the Theory of Autobiography." *a/b: Auto/Biography Studies* 10 (Spring 1995): 5–16.

Olyan, Saul. " 'And with a Male You Shall Not Lie the Lying Down of a Woman': On the Meaning and Significance of Leviticus 18:22 and 20:13." *Journal of the History of Sexuality* 5 (October 1994): 179–206.

Olyan, Saul, and Martha Nussbaum, eds. *Sexual Orientation and Human Rights in American Religious Discourse.* New York: Oxford University Press, 1998.

Orsi, Robert. *The Madonna of 115th Street: Faith and Community in Italian Harlem, 1880–1950.* New Haven: Yale University Press, 1985.

Ozar, David T. "Harming by Exclusion: On the Standard Concepts of Sexual Orientation, Sex, and Gender." In *Sexual Diversity and Catholicism: Toward the Development of Moral Theology*, ed. Patricia Beattie Jung, with Joseph Andrew Coray, 252–66. Collegeville, Minn.: Liturgical Press, 2001.

Peiss, Kathy, and Christina Simmons, eds., with Robert A. Padgug. *Passion and Power: Sexuality in History*. Philadelphia: Temple University Press, 1989.

Plummer, Ken. *Telling Sexual Stories: Power, Change and Social Worlds*. London: Routledge, 1995.

Primiano, Leonard Norman. "Intrinsically Catholic: Vernacular Religion and Philadelphia's 'Dignity.'" Ph.D. diss., University of Pennsylvania, 1993.

Redmont, Jane. *Generous Lives: American Catholic Women Today*. Ligouri, Mo.: Triumph Books, 1992.

Renza, Louis A. "The Veto of the Imagination: A Theory of Autobiography." In *Autobiography: Essays Theoretical and Critical*, ed. James Olney, 268–95. Princeton: Princeton University Press, 1980.

Rich, Adrienne. "Compulsory Heterosexuality and Lesbian Existence." In *The Lesbian and Gay Studies Reader* ed. Henry Abelove, Michele Aina Barale, and David M. Halperin, 227–54. New York: Routledge, 1993.

Richlin, Amy. "Not Before Homosexuality: The Materiality of the *Cinaedus* and the Roman Law against Love Between Men." *Journal of the History of Sexuality* 3, no. 4 (1993): 523–73.

Ricoeur, Paul. *Figuring the Sacred: Religion, Narrative, and Imagination*. ed. Mark I. Wallace. Translated by David Pellauer. Minneapolis: Fortress, 1995.

———. "Narrative Identity." Translated by Mark S. Muldoon. *Philosophy Today* 35 (Spring 1991): 73–81.

Robinson, Paul. *Gay Lives: Homosexual Autobiography from John Addington Symonds to Paul Monette*. Chicago: University of Chicago Press, 1999.

Rofes, Eric. *Dry Bones Breathe: Gay Men Creating Post-AIDS Identities and Cultures*. New York: Harrington Park Press, 1998.

Ronan, Marian. "Tracing the Sign of the Cross." Ph.D. diss., Temple University, 2000.

Ross, Susan A. "God's Embodiment and Women: Sacraments." In *Freeing Theology: The Essentials of Theology in Feminist Perspective*, ed. Catherine Mowry LaCugna, 185–209. San Francisco: HarperSanFrancisco, 1993.

Rudy, Kathy. *Sex and the Church: Gender, Homosexuality, and the Transformation of Christian Ethics*. Boston: Beacon, 1997.

Ruether, Rosemary Radford. *Christianity and the Making of the Modern Family: Ruling Ideologies, Diverse Realities*. Boston: Beacon, 2000.

———. *Sexism and God-Talk: Toward a Feminist Theology*. Boston: Beacon, 1983.

———, ed. *Religion and Sexism: Images of Woman in the Jewish and Christian Traditions*. New York: Simon & Schuster, 1974.

Ryan, Penelope. *Practicing Catholic: The Search for a Livable Catholicism*. New York: Henry Holt, 1998.

Rynne, Xavier. *Vatican Council II*. With a New Introduction by the Author. Maryknoll, N.Y.: Orbis, 1999 (1968, Farrar, Straus & Giroux).

Savin-Williams, Ritch C. "... *And Then I Became Gay": Young Men's Stories*. New York: Routledge, 1998.

Scanlon, Leslie. "Here Come's Everybody's Church." *U.S. Catholic* 67, no. 5 (May 2002): 28–32.

Schneider, Laurel. "Homosexuality, Queer Theory, and Christian Theology." *Religious Studies Review* 26, no. 1 (January 2000): 3–12.

Scroggs, Robin. *Homosexuality in the New Testament: Contextual Background for Contemporary Debate.* Philadelphia: Fortress, 1983.

Seidman, Steven. *Embattled Eros: Sexual Politics and Ethics in Contemporary America.* New York: Routledge, 1992.

Siker, Jeffrey S., ed. *Homosexuality in the Church: Both Sides of the Debate.* Louisville: Westminster John Knox, 1994.

Smith, Richard L. *AIDS, Gays, and the American Catholic Church.* Cleveland: Pilgrim, 1994.

Smith, Mark. "Ancient Bisexuality and the Interpretation of Romans 1:26–27." *Journal of the American Academy of Religion* 64, no. 2 (Summer 1996): 223–56.

Smith, Sidonie. "Performativity, Autobiographical Practice, Resistance." *a/b: Auto/Biography Studies* 10 (Spring 1995): 17–33.

Smith, Sidonie, and Julia Watson, eds. *Getting a Life: Everyday Uses of Autobiography.* Minneapolis: University of Minnesota Press, 1996.

Snitow, Ann, Christine Stansell, and Sharon Thompson, eds. *Powers of Desire: The Politics of Sexuality.* New York: Monthly Review Press, 1983.

Spender, Stephen. "Confessions and Autobiography." In *Autobiography: Essays Theoretical and Critical,* ed. James Olney, 115–22. Princeton: Princeton University Press, 1980.

Steinfels, Peter. *A People Adrift: The Crisis of the Roman Catholic Church in America.* New York: Simon & Schuster, 2003.

Stone, Albert. "Modern American Autobiography: Texts and Transactions." In *American Autobiography: Retrospect and Prospect,* ed. Paul John Eakin, 95–119. Madison: University of Wisconsin Press, 1991.

Sullivan, Andrew. *Virtually Normal: An Argument about Homosexuality.* New York: Alfred A. Knopf, 1995.

Swidler, Leonard. *Toward a Catholic Constitution.* New York: Crossroad, 1996.

Taves, Ann. *The Household of Faith: Roman Catholic Devotions in Mid-Nineteenth-Century America.* Notre Dame, Ind.: University of Notre Dame Press, 1986.

Tessier, L. J. *Dancing after the Whirlwind: Feminist Reflections on Sex, Denial, and Spiritual Transformation.* Boston: Beacon, 1997.

Tigert, Leanne McCall. *Coming Out While Staying In.* Cleveland: Pilgrim, 1997.

Toman, James A. "Dual Identity: Being Catholic and Being Gay." Ph.D. diss., Cleveland State University, 1997.

United States Conference of Catholic Bishops. "Charter for the Protection of Children and Young People." A special supplement to the *Catholic Standard and Times,* June 27, 2002.

"U.S. Catholics: Who Do We Think We Are? The Editors Interview James Davidson," *U.S. Catholic* 65, no. 2 (February 2000): 12–17.

Wallace, Mark I. "Introduction." In Paul Ricoeur, *Figuring the Sacred: Religion, Narrative, and Imagination.* Translated by David Pellauer, 1–32. Minneapolis: Fortress, 1995.

Warren, C. *Identity and Community in the Gay World.* New York: Wiley, 1974.

Weaver, Mary Jo, ed. *What's Left? Liberal American Catholics.* Indianapolis: Indiana University Press, 1999.

Weaver, Mary Jo, and R. Scott Appleby, eds. *Being Right: Conservative Catholics in America.* Indianapolis: Indiana University Press, 1995.

Weintraub, Karl J. "Autobiography and Historical Consciousness." *Critical Inquiry* (June 1975): 821–48.

Westerfelhaus, Robert. "A Significant Shift: A Pentadic Analysis of the Two Rhetorics of the Post–Vatican II Roman Catholic Church Regarding Homosexuality." *Journal of Gay, Lesbian, and Bisexual Identity* 3, no. 4 (October 1998): 269–94.

Whitehead, Evelyn Eaton, and James D. Whitehead. *Wisdom of the Body: Making Sense of our Sexuality.* New York: Crossroad, 2001.

Wilkes, Paul. *The Seven Secrets of Successful Catholics.* New York: Paulist, 1998.

Wink, Walter. "To Hell with Gays?" *Christian Century* 119 (June 5–12, 2002): 32–34.

———. "A Reply by Walter Wink." *Christian Century* 119 (August 14–27, 2002): 43–44.

Wills, Garry. *Papal Sin: Structures of Deceit.* New York: Doubleday, 2000.

Wolfe, Alan. *One Nation, After All: What Middle-Class Americans Really Think about God, Country, Family, Racism, Welfare, Immigration, Homosexuality, Work, The Right, The Left, and Each Other.* New York: Viking. 1998.

Wolfteich, Claire E. *American Catholics Through the Twentieth Century: Spirituality, Lay Experience and Public Life.* New York: Crossroad, 2001.

Yip, Andrew. "The Persistence of Faith Among Nonheterosexual Christians: Evidence for the Neosecularization Thesis of Religious Transformation." *Journal for the Scientific Study of Religion* 41, no. 2 (2002): 199–212.

Young, Iris Marion. *Justice and the Politics of Difference.* Princeton: Princeton University Press, 1990.

Index